1981

TOUCHSTONE

A HISTORY
OF
AMERICAN LAW

Lawrence M. Friedman

A Touchstone Book
Published by Simon and Schuster

A Touchstone Book
Published by Simon and Schuster
A Division of Gulf & Western Corporation
Simon & Schuster Building, Rockefeller Center
1230 Avenue of the Americas
New York, New York 10020
TOUCHSTONE and colophon are trademarks
of Simon & Schuster
ISBN 0-671-21226-5
ISBN 0-671-21742-9 Pbk.
Library of Congress Catalog Card Number 72-83930
Designed by Irving Perkins
Manufactured in the United States of America

6   7   8   9   10   11   12   13   14   15

For my three girls

(CONTENTS)

(PREFACE)

American legal history, for a variety of reasons, has been a rather neglected field. It may come as a surprise to hear that this book, whatever its merits and demerits, is the first attempt to do anything remotely like a general history, a survey of the development of American law, including some treatment of substance, procedure, and legal institutions. The United States has four times the population of England; but it has nothing to compare with Sir William Holdsworth's *History of English Law,* a massive work in fifteen volumes; or with a number of solid one-volume histories of English law, good, bad, and indifferent. To be sure, there is a rich literature about certain American subsystems of law. This book could not have been written without them. There are dozens of articles and books about the Supreme Court, about great judges, great cases, about the legal profession, about this or that aspect of law. There are patches and pieces; but no fabric as a whole.

It is a serious thing, for a branch of history, to lack a general treatment. It means there is no tradition, no received learning, no conventional wisdom. But tradition is needed: to define what is important and what is not, to guide students, researchers, other historians—and the general public. Without tradition, there is no framework, no skeleton, nothing to hang one's ideas on, nothing to attack and revise.

The state of legal history is no mere accident. Part of the problem has been that in the United States, there was no place for legal history to come *from.* The conceptual blindness of legal education was not conducive to creative scholarship, at least not until recently. The dominant ideology of law schools was such that these were not centers of legal research. They taught legal method, legal reasoning, analytical skills, how to take cases apart, and how to put them together again. Legal scholars and lawyers were interested in precedents, but not in history; they twisted and used the past, but rarely treated it with the rigor that history demands. Historians, for their part, were not aware of the richness and importance of legal history; the lawyers, jealous of their area, showed them only a dreary battlefield of concepts; historians were unwelcome there; the landscape was technical and strewn with corpses and mines. Both of these attitudes are mellowing. Legal history is finally coming into its own. The literature is growing, and growing in quality. Lawyers and historians are making joint contributions.

This book is timely, then; and is offered up, not as a solution to the problems of legal history, but as a stage along the way: even, in a sense, as a whipping boy, a primer, something to react to; a shape for the field, even if others find it misshapen. The time is ripe; and the opportunity is here. Not that the obstacles are any the less—the embarrassment of primary sources, and the thinness of the secondary; the confounding factor of fifty separate state jurisdictions; the problems of definition of the field. These obstacles are balanced by opportunities. These include, first, the important work of scholars of first rank, men like Willard Hurst. Second, the development of modern social science, which, for all its deficiencies, gives us a way of looking at the world of law and legal history, a hope of cracking the code, a skeleton key to the horrendous mass of detail.

This key has been eagerly, even passionately grasped. This is a *social* history of American law. I have tried to fight free of jargon, legal and sociological; but I have surrendered myself wholeheartedly to some of the central insights of social science. This book treats American law, then, not as a kingdom unto itself, not as a set of rules and concepts, not as the province of lawyers alone, but as a mirror of society. It takes nothing as historical accident, nothing as autonomous, everything as relative and molded by economy and society. This is the theme of every chapter and verse.

A word or two about the scope and limitations of this book. The main narrative moves chronologically, from the beginnings in the 17th century, when a distinctive American law emerged, through the close of the 19th century. I have not attempted to trace the story past 1900 in any detail. But one final chapter tries to sum up main themes of the 20th century.

Historians of law have, quite understandably, paid more attention to national, federal developments, than to the separate histories of the law of the fifty states. In particular, constitutional law, and the Supreme Court, have inspired a rich literature, overshadowing most of the law. In this book, I try to redress the balance. State law occupies a central role in the narrative. I have deliberately kept to a minimum the story of constitutional law, partly because that story has been told, and told well; partly to try to bring forward the more mundane workings of the system, the pawns, foot soldiers, worker bees of law.

A person who writes a book runs up many debts. A glance at the footnotes shows how parasitic is such an enterprise as this. One major influence, not adequately reflected in citations, should be mentioned: the work, personality, and spirit of Willard Hurst, of the law school at the University of Wisconsin. American legal history stands enormously in his debt; and this work, whatever it merits, would be unthinkable without him. His influence, I think, is on every page.

During the years that I spent at the University of Wisconsin, I learned a great deal from my colleagues. There was an atmosphere of ferment that centered about studies in legal history and in law and the social sciences. A good deal of credit for this atmosphere must be ascribed to two private foundations, the Rockefeller Foundation, which supported legal-economic history at Wisconsin for many years, and the Russell Sage Foundation, which stimulated work in law and the social sciences. For the last few years, I have also benefited greatly from my colleagues at Stanford University.

Many colleagues and friends have also been helpful with substance and style. I thank them all, and particularly, Herbert L. Packer, Robert B. Stevens, Leah Friedman, Charles Rosenberg, Stanley Kutler, and Stanley Katz. The libraries and staffs of three university law schools, St. Louis, Wisconsin, and Stanford, were unfailingly helpful over the years. Generations (it seems) of typists labored over draft after draft of the text. I will not list them all, but I cannot ignore Mrs. Joy St. John, the last and most sorely burdened. Finally, I wish to acknowledge the special, subtle contributions of my family.

LAWRENCE M. FRIEDMAN

Stanford, California
1972

(PROLOGUE)

Modern communication and technology have made the world smaller. They have leveled many variations in world culture. Yet people still speak different languages, wear different clothes, follow different religions, and hold different values dear. They are also subject to very different laws. How different is not easy to sum up. Clearly, legal systems are not so different as different languages. The new world—urban, industrial—implies a certain kind of society; this society depends on and welcomes certain kinds of laws. An income tax, for example, is a common feature in the West. But the exact form that a tax law takes depends on the general legal culture. Americans are naturally used to American laws. Law is an integral part of their culture. They could adjust to *very* alien laws and procedures about as easily as they could adjust to a diet of roast ants or a costume of togas. Judge and jury, the familiar drama of a criminal trial, an elected assembly or council at work making laws, wills and deeds, licenses to get married, to keep dogs, to hunt deer—these are all part of a common experience and culture, peculiar to the United States. No other legal culture is quite like it. Presumably, no other culture fits the American system quite so aptly.

People commonly believe that history and tradition are very strong in American law. There is some basis for this belief. Some parts of the law can be traced back very far—the jury system, the mortgage, the trust, some aspects of land law. But other parts of the law are newborn babies. The living law in a broad social sense, including tax law, traffic codes, and social-welfare laws, contains some very recent accessions. While one lawyer is advising his client how to react to a ruling from Washington, issued that very day, another may be telling his client that some plausible course of action is blocked by a statute well known to the lawyers of Henry VIII or by a decision of some older judges whose names, language, and habits would be unfathomable mysteries to both attorney and client. As a spoken language, American English is an incredible mixture. Some of its words, its grammatical postures, sounds, and phrases are new; some are old; others are borrowed from Latin or

13

French; some (the most basic part) are derived from Old English or go back to even older strains. Part of the law is like that, too; layer on layer of geological formations, the new pressing down on the old, displacing, changing, altering, but not necessarily wiping out what has gone before. Law, by and large, evolves; it changes in piecemeal fashion. Revolutions in essential structure are few and far between. That at least is the Anglo-American experience. Some of the old is preserved among the mass of the new.

But what is kept of old law is highly selective. Society in change may be slow, but it is ruthless. Neither evolution nor revolution is sentimental. Old rules of law and old legal institutions stay alive when they still have a purpose—or, at least, when they do not interfere with the demands of current life. The trust, the mortgage, the jury, are of ancient stock; but they have the vigor of youth. They have come down from medieval times, but the needs they now serve are 20th-century needs. They have survived because they found a place in the vigorous, pushy society of today—a society that does not hesitate to pour old wine into new bottles and new wine into old bottles, or throw both bottles and wine away. At any rate, the theory of this book is that law moves with its times and is eternally new. From time to time, the theory may not fit the facts. But more light can be shed on legal history if one asks: why does this survive? than if one assumes that law, unlike the rest of social life, is a museum of accidents and the mummified past.

In one sense, law is always up-to-date. The legal system always "works"; it always functions. Every society governs itself and settles disputes. Every society, then, has a working system of law. If the courts, for example, are hidebound and ineffective, that merely means some other agency has taken over what courts might otherwise do. The system works like a blind, insensate machine. It does the bidding of those whose hands are on the controls. The laws of China, the United States, Nazi Germany, France, and the Union of South Africa reflect the goals and policies of those who call the tune in those societies. Often, when we call law "archaic," we mean that the power system of its society is morally out of tune. But change the power system, and the law too will change. The basic premise of this book is that, despite a strong dash of history and idiosyncrasy, the strongest ingredient in American law, at any given time, is the present: current emotions, real economic interests, concrete political groups. It may seem a curious beginning to a book of history to downgrade the historical element of law. But this is not really a paradox. The history of law has meaning only if we assume that at any given time the vital portion is new and changing, form following function, not function following form. History of law is not—or should not be—a search for fossils, but a study of social development, unfolding through time.

American social development and law have a long, elaborate history. Compared to some, the United States is a new country—but Boston and New York are more than three hundred years old, and the Constitution is one of the world's oldest *living* organic laws. In short, enough time has elapsed for American law to be essentially American—the product of American experience.

But American law has, and has had, close affinities to other legal cultures. The immediate ancestor is easy to identify. The basic substratum of American law, as of American speech, is English. Before the Europeans came, the country belonged to the Indians. Europeans came late, but they came in force. They settled first along the coast. The Spanish settled Florida; the French built New Orleans. Swedes settled briefly on the Delaware; the Dutch pushed them out. Then the Dutch were overwhelmed by the English. The Hudson and Delaware settlements were added to a chain of tiny colonies, all English-speaking, along the Atlantic coast. Their population grew. More Englishmen came. And English speakers, as Englishmen or Americans, ultimately threw out the Indians, the French, and the Spanish, and established an empire, stretching from sea to sea.

Each culture group had brought in its own law. Of Indian law and Swedish law, it is fair to say, not a trace remains.[1] Some scholars have claimed to find a speck or two of Dutch legal influence surviving to this day. The office of district attorney may be Dutch in origin. French law gained a more or less lasting foothold in Louisiana, and there (in translation) it stays. Spanish law sent down wider if not deeper roots; no state can call its law Spanish, but pieces of Spanish or Mexican law (for example, the community-property system), live on in California and in other parts of the West. Everything else, if not strictly native, is English, or comes by way of England, or is built on an English base.

It is not easy to say what part of English law was the immediate forebear of colonial law. For one thing, "colonial law" is an ab-

---

[1] Indian law, of course, still has some relevance to those Indian tribes which are more or less autonomous. Indian law, past and present, is a rich field of study in itself. See, for example, K. N. Llewellyn and E. A. Hoebel, *The Cheyenne Way* (1941); John P. Reid, *A Law of Blood, The Primitive Law of the Cherokee Nation* (1970).

straction; there was no "colonial law" any more than there is an "American law," common to all fifty states. There were as many colonial systems as there were colonies. The original union was made up of thirteen states; but this thirteen represents, if anything, only a head count at one arbitrary time. Some colonies—Plymouth and New Haven—were swallowed up by larger colonies. New Jersey was the product of a merger of two separate entities. Each entity once had its own legal system.

Each colony, moreover, was founded at a different time. At least a century separates the beginnings of Massachusetts from the beginnings of Georgia. During this time, English law did not stand still. This meant that the colonies began their careers at different points in the process of legal development. During the colonial period, the colonies were subordinate to England. The law of the mother country was theoretically superior. But the colonial condition was not like the relationship of a ward to a city, or a county to a state. Even as a matter of theory, it was not clear which acts of Parliament and which court decisions were binding on the colonies. Throughout the colonial period, the colonists borrowed as much English law as they wanted to take or were forced to take. Their appetite was determined by requirements of the moment, by ignorance or knowledge of what was happening abroad, and by general obstinacy. Mapping out how far colonial law fit English law is almost a hopeless job. Legal cultures differed in different colonies. New England deviated from standard English law more than the Southern colonies did. The connection between the two sides of the Atlantic was always strong but never harmonious. The colonies quarreled with the mother country over law as well as over politics and taxes. Even after the Revolution, the legal connection was not severed. A complex legal relationship survived after 1776. English law continued to be imported, in some quantity, when and as needed. Even today a thin, thin trickle remains, when and as needed.

The date when a colony was first settled gives some rough indication of the parts of English law likely to be transported. But what was English law? Two decades before the Revolution, Blackstone reduced to writing what he considered the essence of the royal common law. His *Commentaries on the Law of England* prints out to one very thick but manageable book. This book, in its sluggishly elegant style, became a great bestseller, both in England and America. Despite errors and failings, Blackstone did manage to put in brief order the rank weeds of English law. But even his picture was partial and defective, like a dictionary that omitted all slang, all dialect, all colloquial and technical words. And even this imperfect guide was not available to colonials before the 1750's. They lacked a handy key to English law. Yet a key was desperately needed. The English common law is one of the world's great legal systems—but one maddeningly hard to know.

English law stood apart and still stands apart from most European systems of law. It resisted the reception of that modified, modernized form of Roman law which swept over much of the Continent. Modern Continental law finds its highest expression in a code. "The law" in France and Germany is statutory. "Common law," on the other hand, was "unwritten law," as Blackstone called it. "Unwritten" was not meant literally; English and American law are, if anything, overwritten. But by "unwritten" Blackstone meant that the ultimate, highest source of law was not an enactment, but "general custom," as reflected in the decisions of the common-law judges. These judges were "the depositaries of the laws—the living oracles, who must decide in all cases of doubt, and who are bound by an oath to decide according to the law of the land." (1 Bl. Comm. *69). Common law was judge-made law— molded, refined, examined, and changed in the crucible of actual decision, and handed down from generation to generation in the form of reported cases. In theory, the judges drew their decisions from existing principles of law; ultimately these principles reflected the living values, attitudes, and ethical ideas of the English people. In practice, the judges relied on their own past actions, which they modified under the pressure of changing times and changing patterns of litigation. In other words, common law adhered to precedent as a general rule.

Precedent is commonly considered one of the basic concepts of the common law. It was never quite a straitjacket, as some laymen (and lawyers) have tended to think. American judges have always assumed power to overrule an earlier case, if they considered it egregiously wrong. The power was seldom exercised in the past. Still, it was there, along with the more important power to "distinguish" an embarrassing precedent. In any event, the common law was and is a system in which judges, whether following or distinguishing precedent, play a vital role in creating and expounding principles of law; in its prime, the decided case was one of the basic building blocks of law. For a long time, the proud judges looked at statutes with great suspicion. Statutes were unwelcome intrusions on the law, and were treated accordingly. In Continental law, all

law (in theory) is contained in the codes. In common law many
basic rules of law are found nowhere but in the recorded opinions
of the judges.

What Parliament can do in a month's intensive work, a court
can do only over the years—and never systematically, since the
common law does not look kindly on hypothetical or future cases.
It confines itself to actual disputes. If no one brings up a matter, it
is never decided. It is no answer to say that all important questions
will turn into disputes; "disputes" are not litigation, and only litigation—primarily, appellate litigation—makes new law. Nor is it
easy for judges to lay down quantitative rules, or rules that need
heavy public support (in the form of taxes) to carry out, or rules
that would have to be enforced by a new corps of civil servants.
Judges are supposed to decide on the basis of preexisting principle. This could hardly tell them what the speed limit ought to be,
or the butterfat content of ice cream. An English (or American)
court could not possibly "evolve" a Social Security law. The common law is therefore not only slow; it is impotent to effect certain
kinds of significant legal change.

Older English law was often as devious in making changes as it
was (sometimes) slow. Obsolete doctrines and institutions were
often not formally abolished, but merely superseded and ignored.
Trial by battle, a favorite of medieval romance and costume
movies, was not done away with in England until 1819. For centuries, it slept in its sarcophagus; but a chance mistake in court, in
1818, reminded the legal profession that battle was still a legal
possibility. An embarrassed Parliament quickly buried the corpse.
(59 Geo. III, c. 46, 1819).

Evolution sometimes took place through the use of shortcuts
called *legal fictions*. The rise of the action of ejectment is a famous
example. Suppose two men—we will call them Henry Black and
Richard Brown—are in dispute over title to a piece of land. Brown
is in possession, but Black has a claim to it. Each thinks he is the
rightful owner. The medieval common law had a form of trial that
could be used to resolve this dispute. As it happened, this form of
action was slow and heavy-handed. Ejectment developed as a way
around it. In ejectment, the pleadings—papers filed in court—told
an odd story. A man named John Doe, it seems, had leased the
land from Henry Black. Another man, named William Styles, held
a lease from Richard Brown. Styles (it was said) had "ejected"
John Doe. In fact, Doe, Styles, and the two leases were pure fig-
ments of legal imagination. Black and Brown were the only real

people in the case. This mummery (which everybody, the court included, knew to be false) served the purpose of bringing the issue of title before the court; but at the same time, because it was a *lease* case, the ancient land actions (which did not apply to leases) were avoided. In the course of time, ejectment itself came to be considered as too complicated, and a nuisance. But the action was not streamlined in England until past the middle of the 19th century.

The tortuous story of ejectment is not an isolated example of high technicality and fiction. What is the nonlegal mind to make of a social institution which treats corporations as "persons," which at times classified slaves as real estate, and which allowed a plaintiff to state that the city of Paris was located in England, refusing to let the defendant contradict him? One of these, the corporate fiction, is still alive (and useful); the others served their purpose and then died out. But though fictions were functional, they were dreadfully hard to manage.

Enough high technicality survives to make Anglo-American law a difficult system to master. But the common law was involute, overformalized, and fiction-ridden not because it was changeless, but precisely because it was constantly changing. Part of the problem lay in traditional theories, in which the common law lay tightly swaddled. In theory, the common law was not man-made in the ordinary sense; the judges uncovered the law (or "found" it); they did not make it, or tamper with it as it was found. The modern idea of law as essentially man-made, as essentially a tool or an instrument, was foreign to the classic common law. Change then had to be hidden, disguised. Blunt, overt reforms (by judges) were out of the question. Moreover, working doctrines of law, however quaint they may seem, must be acting as the servants of some economic or social interest. In a society with many rough, contentious holders of power, at war with each other, the court can effect power relations only slowly and subtly. Otherwise a delicate balance is upset.

Moreover, foolish traditions are tolerable as long as they are harmless. The abolition of trial by battle illustrates this point. If trial by battle had not been all *but* dead, it could not have survived to the 19th century. Powerful engines of change can and do exist *inside* the legal system but *outside* the courts. Some major changes take place in law by means of opening and shutting institutional valves. Subject matter moved from legal agency to agency. The courts gained work, lost work, then gained new work. Parliament's role got stronger; the king's waxed and waned. In the course of these changes, some ancient, specialized, essentially marginal business stayed with the courts. Because they are colorful and old, these fossils attract more attention than they deserve. They give an impression of the archaic, sometimes a false one.

Then, too, a good deal of the law is not addressed to the public directly. Lawyers stand between the laymen and the lawmaker. It is the business of the lawyer to tolerate and master artifice. After all, technical difficulty is the sole social excuse for the lawyer's monopoly, his stranglehold on court work, on the drafting of documents, on the counseling of clients. The English bar was, by the time our story opens, an important influence on the shape of English law. The evolution of the bar was complicated, full of riddles. But by 1600, English lawyers were plainly professionals—men educated in the law. They were not, however, trained at universities, at Oxford or Cambridge. Lawyers came out of the Inns of Court, in London. The Inns had no connection with the universities, hence no connection with Roman law and the general legal culture of Europe. Young men at the Inns, if they learned anything, learned English law, English pleading, English legal experience. Legal training was primarily practical, not jurisprudential. This peculiar bent in English legal education helped the common law to survive, while Continental law fell under the spell of a rejuvenated Roman law. In England, too, the bench was recruited from the bar. Lawyers and judges made up a single legal community, with a shared background and common experiences, as they do to this day. They were a cohesive group sharply set off from the public.

For a variety of reasons, then, the common law came down through the centuries with some of its past sticking to it, like a skin it never quite succeeded in molting. This skin was strongly colored by the feudal past. Medieval English practice left deep marks on the language and habits of common law. The common law was utterly obsessed by two central topics: formal legal process and the law of the land. A second's thought tells one, however, that these two topics could not have been *all* of the living law of England, any more than the life of great lords could have been the life of everyone in England. Common law was, essentially, the law of the royal central courts. It was this law, basically, that the great English jurists, up to and including Blackstone, described. But the royal central courts, by and large, handled the legal problems of a tiny group of people. Leaf through the pages of Lord Coke's reports, compiled in the late 16th and early 17th century; here one will find a colorful set of litigants, all drawn from the very top of British society—lords and ladies, landed gentry, high-ranking clergymen, wealthy merchants. Common law was an aristocratic law, for and of the gentry and nobility. The masses were hardly touched by this system and only indirectly under its rule. There was law on the manor—law that controlled the common people and bound them to their betters. This was largely subterranean law and made little impact on the treatises. Lawbooks were written at the seat of power: they dealt with the king's kind of law. Day-to-day law of the lower orders was barely chronicled.

Nor did common law, which was royal law, the law of the realm, in fact cover the whole kingdom. Authority was not so welded and compact. There was no single focus of law, no single legal culture. English law was pluralistic, comparable (at least roughly) to the loose aggregations of the later colonial empire, especially in Africa, where official law, derived from the mother country, ruled in the capital, among expatriates and businessmen, while in the country-side, customary law was left largely to fend for itself. In England, too, in the Middle Ages, many local customs, like local dialects, sur-vived alongside common law. Primogeniture, for example—inher-itance of land by the eldest son—was the common-law rule, but not the rule in the county of Kent. In Kent, under the system known as gavelkind tenure (abolished in 1925), land descended to all the sons equally. And local and customary law had an important bear-ing on the law of early America. Colonial practice derived in part from that law which the settlers knew best: the local laws and local customs of their communities back home.

Even for important affairs of important people, the reign of the common law was not undisputed; it had to contend with rival courts, institutions, and subsystems of law. Many of the rivals were eventually brought to heel. But the common law won only by granting deep concessions. Language once more is a useful analogy. The Anglo-Saxon language held out against onslaughts of Norse and French, and two culture tongues, Latin and Greek. But the surviving language—English—was drenched with foreign words, and heavily overlaid with foreign syntax. Modern common law is full of Roman-law words and ideas, and is also heavily indebted to equity, admiralty, and the law merchant.

Of the formal rivals of the common law, the most astounding was the peculiar system, administered by the chancellors, known as *equity*. Since early medieval times, the chancellor had been an im-portant royal official. The chancellor's office, the chancery, was re-

sponsible for issuing writs to the common-law courts. Through a
long and complex process, chancery itself became a court. But it
was a court with a difference. Chancery did not follow strict common-law rules. Looser principles governed, principles in accord
with prevailing ideas of "equity." The chancellor was said to be
"keeper of the king's conscience." As such, he had the power to
dispense with unjust rules. Actually, the chancellor, a literate
clergyman, with a staff of scribes, "commanded the machinery
which sooner or later would have to be set in motion to give redress
to petitioners." [2] This power gave him a strategic position in the
royal system of justice. Over the course of time, the chancellor, as
the king's delegate, loosened the rules of the common law in a
number of fields of law. The theory of "equity" developed to explain the chancellor's power, and reduce his work to some kind of
logical order. The *ad hoc* character of equity rules gradually disappeared. One could speak of rules, principles, and doctrines of
equity as well as of "law." Equity became, in short, almost a system
of antilaw.

In England, then, two contradictory systems of civil law coexisted—and not always peacefully. Yet in many ways law and equity
complemented each other. The common law could proclaim duties
and rights; but it could not compel any kind of performance, other
than the payment of money. Equity, on the other hand, had a
whole battery of other remedies. The injunction was one of these.
An injunction is an order commanding a person to do some specific
act or to forbear from something he had been or might be doing. It
is enforceable because, if a defendant disobeys, the chancellor can
declare him in contempt and put him in jail. Equity had power
over persons, not over things. It could not render judgments that
bound the title to land, for example; it could only act on the
parties. The chancellor could order B to give A's land back to him.
If B refused, the chancellor could send him to jail; but he could
not give A the land. Procedurally, the two systems were very different. Continental and ecclesiastical law heavily influenced the ideas
and processes of equity. This meant an infusion of Roman-law culture. The jury was a common-law institution; no jury sat in chancery. On the other hand, many familiar doctrines, and some whole
branches of law, such as the law of trusts, grew out of equity.

What was curious, perhaps unique, was the mutual isolation,
within one legal system and one country, of law and equity. It was

2 Theodore F. T. Plucknett, *A Concise History of the Common Law* (5th ed.,
1956), p. 180.

possible for a man to have a claim which equity would enforce but common law would not, and vice versa. For example, the common law tended to treat a deed of land as valid, if it was executed in proper form. In equity, however, the deed was good only if it was free from undue influence, fraud, or deceit. A claim based on a deed might win or lose, depending on which courtroom door the plaintiff went in. Courts of common law ignored doctrines of equity, and equity courts would dismiss a case if the plaintiff had an "adequate remedy at law."

Relations between the two systems were different, of course, at different times. In Tudor-Stuart days, open bitter conflict broke out between equity and law. The common lawyers did not succeed in crushing their rival, though they would have liked to. After a time, the two systems came to a rough and ready coexistence. In the 19th century, equity and law finally "merged." This meant, basically, that a single court administered both systems. Where rules of law and equity collided, equity usually prevailed. In the United States, the distinction between law and equity lingered on for a surprisingly long time. Some states—Massachusetts for one—never had a system of equity; New Jersey not only had separate courts, but did not abolish them until 1947. In Delaware, there is a separate chancery court to this very day. The historical distinction between equity and law still makes a difference in lawsuits. It may decide whether one has the right to a jury or not.

Chancery was not the only court which did not follow strict norms of common law. The court of star chamber was an efficient, somewhat arbitrary arm of royal power. It was at the height of its career in the days of the Tudor and Stuart kings. Star chamber stood for swiftness and power; it was not a competitor of the common law so much as a limitation on it—a reminder that high state policy could not safely be entrusted to a system so chancy as English law. The special commercial courts—also outside the common law—lasted longer than star chamber. The royal central courts, absorbed in the tangle of land titles, paid little attention to the Lombard merchants, and to the bankers and tradesmen, foreign and native, who came after them. The mercantile courts, however, were sensitive to the habits and customs of businessmen.

In these mercantile courts a body of law called the *law merchant* governed, rather than the ordinary law of England. The law merchant was international; its rules were derived from the general customs and law-sense of European traders. There were many types of merchant courts, including the colorful courts of piepow-

der, a court of the fairs where merchants gathered. Sir Edward
Coke spoke of it as a court of "speedy justice . . . for advancement of trade, and traffic," as fast "as the dust can fall from the
foot." [3]

Through fair courts and merchant courts English law and practice at last gave recognition to the merchant's basic ways of doing
business and dealing in money. From these sources, English law
learned to handle the documents from which modern checks, notes,
bills of exchange, and bills of lading are descended. The special
merchant courts decayed when the common law woke up to the
interests of business; the law merchant was gradually absorbed into
the bloodstream of the common law. By the 17th century the
process was well advanced. The final major figure in this development, by common consent, was the Scotsman Lord Mansfield, who
died in 1793. Mansfield, deeply versed in Roman and Continental
law, had a sure touch for commercial cases. His decisions were
sensitive and responsive to the merchant's needs and ways.

Admiralty, the law of the high seas and maritime commerce, was
another "rival." Admiralty had a long, involved international tradition, quite separate from the common law. As early as the 16th
century, the English court of admiralty came into conflict with
the common-law courts. The struggle for control over sea law
was not finally resolved for many years. It was not the romance of
the sea that was at stake, but power over naval policy and international transport. Family law—marriage and divorce—was also
largely outside the pale of common law. Marriage was a sacrament;
church courts, even after the Reformation, maintained jurisdiction. The law of succession to property (in modern law, wills and
estates) was curiously divided; the common law governed the descent of land; church courts governed distribution of personal
property. The two kinds of court used quite different rules. If a
man died intestate (without a will), his eldest son inherited his
land. But his personal property (money and goods) was equally
divided among his children. The ecclesiastical courts, like the
courts of equity, did not use common-law procedures; a jury, therefore, had no role in its decisions.

This prologue has laid heavy stress on courts. But the reader
must not assume that *all* English law was judge-made. A great deal
of law came, directly or indirectly, from King and Parliament. In
Renaissance England, there was nothing like the steady stream of

3 4 Co. Inst. 272. The name piepowder was said to be a corruption of two
French words meaning "dusty feet."

statutes one is familiar with today. But the State did not leave so important a matter as law to the sole care of judges. Some statutes fundamentally altered the structure and substance of law. Some were carried over into the colonies.

English law was never static. The law of Charles II was not the law of Edward I; it was light years from the law of King Alfred. Mostly, what has been described is the end-product of evolution and enactment, roughly at the time of the settlements. England, in 1600, stood on the brink of a period of the most profound changes, a period which has not yet ended. From the legal standpoint, the single most important aspect of this modern period is a revolutionary shift in the attitude of society toward law. In traditional cultures, law was a divine or time-honored body of rules, which defined people's place in the order of society. In modern times, law is an instrument; the people in power use it to push or pull toward some definite goal. The idea of law as a rational tool underlies all modern systems, whether capitalist, socialist, fascist, whether democratic or authoritarian. Law was a prime social mover in England, and then in America. By and large, the period covered by this book is a period of ceaseless and insatiable change.

⤙ PART I ⤚

The Beginnings: American Law in the Colonial Period

The colonial period is, for most lawyers and laymen, the dark ages of American law. The two sources of law an American lawyer first considers when he faces a legal problem are statutes and reports of high-court cases. The American lawyer has probably never seen, dealt with, or even heard of colonial cases and statutes. In the United States, reports did not become handy and accessible until well after Independence. Even now, only scattered collections of colonial cases have been published. Many colonial statutes survived only in ancient or rare editions; some have been altogether lost. The *Laws and Liberties of Massachusetts* (1648), one of the most important colonial codes, had utterly vanished, until a copy turned up in the 20th century.

That so much of the native tradition disappeared is not really surprising. Law constantly changes; and old law is useless, except for scholars. Only collectors and historians care about Massachusetts' laws of 1830. The laws of 1648 were already quaint and outdated when John Adams was alive. Conditions between the time of settlement and Independence were worlds apart; the legal needs of a small settlement, run by its clergymen, clinging precariously to the coast of an unknown continent, were fundamentally different from the needs of a bustling commercial state. Gross trends in the growth of the law followed gross trends in the larger society. In the 18th century, for example, colonial law noticeably swung back toward English models. Indeed, after the Revolution, American law became, in some ways, rather more than less English. This is no paradox. "English" is a misleading term. Economic growth and social division of labor called for tools of law the Puritan oligarch of 1630 had no need of and no use for. The law later needed was not to be found in the colonial past; so the country was forced to import it from abroad. Only England had a supply that American lawyers could use without translation and transformation. In the process, the native tradition was distorted, partly deliberately, partly inadvertently. Since colonial law was not widely studied or read, it easily slipped out of memory. As a general proposition, colonial law was dismissed as local, that is, as inferior law, lacking

29

in dignity and general authority, bearing the stigma of a dialect. Later colonial systems of law, from Australia to Zanzibar, suffered the same fate of indignity and obscurity. American jurists, who accepted the legal standards of England, and who were pressed by the needs of their times, sometimes stated as local custom what in fact was not custom at all. In this way, the true colonial tradition was buried in the rubble of indifference and myth. How much remained viable is difficult to say.

Colonial law has thus suffered from long-term neglect. Only in the last twenty years have large parts of it been worked over by scholars. It has been so slowly and so randomly excavated that scholars have tended to see, like the blind man first meeting an elephant, only a trunk, a tail, a leg, rarely the whole. The whole is very hard to describe. One hundred sixty-nine years went by between Jamestown and the Declaration of Independence. The same length of time separates 1776 and Hiroshima. No one would consider this last span of time as a single "period." Time comparisons *can* be misleading, since social (and hence legal) change does not proceed at an even rate. But even so, the colonial "period" was a grouping of periods rather than a single, recognizable age.

Some early theories of colonial law can by now be safely discarded. George L. Haskins, in a fine study of Massachusetts Bay, has summed up a number of prior misconceptions. One was "that the law of the colonies was essentially the common law of England, brought over to the extent applicable to colonial conditions." This theory denied "any native legal achievements in the colonial period" and is demonstrably false. A corollary assumption, that "because the law of the colonies was essentially that of England, colonial law was basically the same everywhere," is equally incorrect. Some scholars, too, saw more innovation than the facts warranted. They observed that colonial law (especially in early years) was very different from English law. Some took English common law as somehow the norm; colonial divergencies, then, were examples of "rudeness" or primitivity. Massachusetts Bay, to some, represented a more radical departure. Massachusetts law was not common law at all, but a new-made system of law, based on the Bible. These theories, too, if not wrong, are at least a dangerous overstatement.[1]

Professor Haskins proposes his own generalization: "The condi-

[1] George L. Haskins, *Law and Authority in Early Massachusetts* (1960), pp. 4ff.

tions of settlement and of development within each colony meant that each evolved its own individual legal system, just as each evolved its individual social and political system. Geographical isolation, the date and character of the several settlements, the degree of absence of outside supervision or control—all had their effect in ultimately developing thirteen separate legal systems." [2] At any particular time, then, the law of a certain colony was made up of a set of related traditions, some English, and some local—modified in the light of current conditions. This was equally true of post-Revolutionary law, except that the English element, after an initial outburst, became thinner with the passage of time. Both colonial law and the law of the United States were subject to centrifugal and centripetal forces: forces that pulled jurisdictions apart; forces that pushed them together. The mother country, its agents, its superior legal culture—these acted centripetally, before Independence; economic unity, guaranteed by the federal system, was a strong centripetal force after Independence. Geographical isolation, local politics, and the sovereignty, in law or fact, of different pieces of the country, provided an enormous amount of centrifugal legal force. One of the great, and constant, themes of American law is the pushing and pulling of these forces: uniformity and diversity in constant tension over time.

Professor Haskins mentioned thirteen separate legal systems. This number cannot be taken too literally. Throughout the colonial period, big colonies swallowed up littler ones. Moreover, if one stopped the clock at any particular moment in colonial times, one would find colonies in vastly different stages of economic and social maturity. Each colony suffered through a first, precarious period, before solid settlement and order was reached. In a way, it is more reasonable to compare early Georgia to early Massachusetts, than to compare an established Massachusetts, in the 1700's, to the infant colony of Georgia. Within each colony, too, old and new were mixed together—each a unique mix of established population centers and frontier toeholds. Early Massachusetts, middle Virginia, late New York: each was a specific adaptation of English law to local problems, experience, and habits. Each state had its commercial center and its hinterland. The year 1776 was not a sharp break in the facts of law and life. The country as a whole, throughout the 19th century, was similarly divisible. At any cross section of time, the country contained wilderness, isolated farms, boom towns,

2 Haskins, *op. cit.*, p. 6.

ports and railroad centers, capitals and outposts, seacoast and hinterland. Each type of community experience implied a different modality of law.

In this chapter, we can touch on only a few main themes of colonial law. Colonial legal experience was richly diverse from the outset, because conditions were different in the various colonies. Some differences were natural—climate, lay of the land; others were structural, depending upon whether the colony was a crown colony, a chartered colony, or a proprietorship. Others were ideological: Puritanism in New England, William Penn's "Holy Experiment" in Pennsylvania, the proprietary adventure in Maryland. Initial differences in land or form led to still further differentiation. A rich soil and a mild climate, to take one instance, may favor the growing of certain crops—tobacco, cotton, rice. A plantation economy rests on climate and soil, but it creates social conditions of its own.

Part of the chapter will document how these differences in condition were reflected in legal mutations. But the theme of unity will be equally strong. There were also underlying similarities in the colonial experience: the texture of social and economic life was open; the home government worked toward uniformity of colonial law. The English tradition slowly became uniquely American, moving in the various colonies in generally parallel directions.

THE SKELETON OF COLONIAL LAW:
THE COURTS

Generally speaking, court organization in the colonies followed one fundamental social law. The colonies began with simple, undifferentiated structures, and developed more complex ones, with more division of labor. England boasted an amazing, cumbersome collection of courts, at the same time highly specialized and wildly overlapping. Sir Edward Coke spent a whole volume, the fourth part of his *Institutes,* describing them. He listed about one hundred courts, ranging from the royal courts, with general jurisdiction, to such special local bodies as the courts of the stanneries, concerned with tin mines and tin workers, in Cornwall and Devon. That a hundred settlers huddled on an island near what is now the city of Newport, or freezing in the Plymouth winter, should have reproduced this system exactly, would have been both miraculous and insane. And indeed no such thing happened.

Life in these colonies was precarious. The factors that made for a judicial hierarchy simply did not exist at the time. Necessity was the supreme lawmaker; the niceties came later. The "laws" laid down in the early settlements, such as Virginia, were much like military orders. In the beginning, judicial business in the colonies was not separated from public business in general. The same people made laws, enforced them, decided cases, and ran the colony. The court system grew and subdivided only when there were people, problems and territory to warrant.

Massachusetts Bay Colony went through many convolutions of government and law between 1630 and 1639, when a more permanent scheme of courts was established. The charter of Massachusetts Bay (1629) was typical of charters modeled after those of trading companies. It granted a tract of land, and recognized that the land had to be governed. But in other respects it was much like the charter of a business corporation. The "Governour and Companye, and their Successors," were to have "forever one comon Seale, to be used in all Causes and Occasions of the said Companye." There was to be "one Governour, one Deputy Governour, and eighteene Assistants of the same Companye, to be from tyme to tyme constituted, elected and chosen out of the Freemen of the said Companye." The general court, equivalent to the meeting of stockholders of a corporation, was made up of the officers and all the freemen. The court of assistants (governor, deputy governor, and a number of assistants) constituted a smaller in-group, comparable perhaps to a board of directors. The ruling bodies of the company had power to make "Lawes and Ordinances for the Good and Welfare of the saide Companye, and for the Government and orderings of the saide Landes and Plantation, and the People inhabiting and to inhabite the same." These laws and ordinances, however, were to be "not contrarie or repugnant to the Lawes and Statutes of this our Realme of England." No one knew or knows exactly what "contrarie or repugnant" was intended to mean. The phrase was a significant one, however; it appeared in many other charters, including proprietary ones. The Maryland charter of 1632, granted by the king to "his well beloved and right trusty Subject Caecilius Calvert, Baron of Baltimore," used a similar phrase: laws "consonant to Reason, and . . . not repugnant or contrary, but (so far as conveniently may be) agreeable to the Laws, Statutes, Customs, and Rights of this Our Kingdom of England."

The phrase was certainly not based on a clear-cut theory that the common law was automatically transplanted. The king and his

ministers had no idea what problems would arise in the new plantations; they hardly even knew what shape the new ventures would
take. The Virginia colony was managed, initially at least, from a
London home office; the charter of Massachusetts Bay envisioned
management at the seat of the colony, probably from the very
start; the proprietary colonies looked toward still another kind of
formal structure.

The original charter of Massachusetts Bay gave power to two
bodies, a general court and a court of assistants. Neither was primarily a court in the modern sense. They handled all the affairs of
the infant enterprise. So, we read that a "Court holden at Boston
June 14th, 1631," in Massachusetts Bay, ordered "that noe man
within the limitts of this Jurisdiction shall hire any person for a
servant for lesse time than a yeare, unles hee be a setled house-
keeper." The court also noted that "Mr. John Maisters hath undertaken to make a passage from Charles Ryver to the newe Towne
12 foote broad and 7 foote deepe for which the Court promiseth
him satisfaction according as the charges thereof shall amount
unto." Also, William Almy was fined "for takeing away Mr.
Glovers cannoe without leave"; and Mr. Pelham was ordered to
pay over to Thomas Goilthayt a sum of money "which the Court
hath awarded him to pay to make good a covenant betwixte
them." At a court held "att Boston," on July 26, Lucy Smith was
"bound as an apprentice" to Roger Ludlow for seven years; it was
ordered "that there shal be a watch of sixe and an officer kept every
night att Boston"; and Francis Perry was ordered "whipped for his
ill speeches and misbehavior towards his maister." [3]

As the colony grew, it had to break through the bounds of this
simple, undifferentiated structure. The general court was a body of
all "freemen" and though the ruling magistrates defined "free-
man" to include only men of the right religious sort, membership
in the general court increased. The court very quickly demanded
the right to govern, as the charter had promised. Later, it was
turned into a representative body—a body of the elect, rather than
of all those with a share in the enterprise.

In 1639, Massachusetts Bay had a system of courts of a type more
familiar to the modern reader. The general court, acting both as
legislature and as the highest court, was the crown of the system. As
a court, it confined itself largely to appeals, though its exact jurisdic-

[3] *Records of the Court of Assistants of the Colony of the Massachusetts Bay
1630–1692*, Vol. II (1904), pp. 15–16, 17–18.

tion remained somewhat vague.[4] The court of assistants, composed of the governor, deputy governor, and magistrates, heard appeals from lower courts, and took original jurisdiction in certain cases— for example, cases of divorce. Below it were the county courts.[5] They had the same power in civil and criminal causes as the courts of assistants, but "tryalls for life, lims or banishment" were "wholly reserved unto the courts of Assistants." [6] The county courts were a vital part of the colony's system of social control. They were never merely courts. From time to time, laws gave them important administrative functions. They dealt with "probate and adminis-tration, apportionment of charges for the repair of bridges, pro-vision for the maintenance of the ministry, punishment of inter-ference with. church elections, punishment of heretics, ordering highways laid out, licensing of ordinaries, violations of town orders regulating wages, settlement of the poor, settlement of houses of correction, licensing of new meeting houses, and punishment of vendors charging excessive prices." [7]

Even the county courts had both appellate and original jurisdic-tion. They were not the absolute base of the system. Other courts (some *ad hoc*) were beneath them, to handle small cases or special matters. Single magistrates had judicial and administrative power in the towns where they lived, similar to that of an English justice of the peace. By an order of 1638, magistrates could hear and de-cide cases where the amount at issue was less than 20 shillings. Later laws gave more powers to the magistrates—to deal, for exam-ple, with people who broke the laws against drunkenness. Single magistrates also had power to give oaths to inspectors of pipe staves, to perform marriages, to impress laborers for repair of bridges and highways, to deal with vagabonds and drunken Indians, and to whip wandering Quakers.[8] In 1677, the general court form-alized the status of the magistrates; each one was to have a com-mission from the court, under the seal of the colony. In 1692, upon the fall of the Andros regime, the official who inherited the role of the magistrate bore the name "justice of the peace." Local govern-

---

[4] Joseph H. Smith, *Colonial Justice in Western Massachusetts (1639–1702); The Pynchon Court Record* (1961), p. 66.

[5] These were originally called particular courts or inferior quarterly courts. The first counties were established in 1642.

[6] *Laws and Liberties of Massachusetts, 1648* (1929 ed.), p. 15.

[7] Smith, *op. cit.*, p. 69.

[8] Smith, *op. cit.*, pp. 72–74.

ment had become thoroughly secularized; and, from then on, a good deal more English.[9]

One habit—creating special courts outside the regular pyramid of courts, to handle particular sorts of business—had appeared early in Massachusetts. A law in 1639 established strangers' courts, for the "more speedy dispatch of all causes which shall concern Strangers, who cannot stay to attend the ordinary Courts of justice." These courts had the same jurisdiction as the county courts, but their sessions were not confined to the regular terms of court.[10] Rather than loosen the jurisdiction of the county courts, the colony chose to set up a separate agency. This kind of choice had been frequently made in England.

The Massachusetts pattern has been described in detail, because it illustrates long-term characteristics of colonial court structure. As in England, separation of powers was notably absent. Functions were assigned to institutions without regard to the idea that courts ought to be independent bodies, distinct from the legislature and the executive. All but the lowest and the highest levels had mixed jurisdiction; they heard original cases and appeals. New Hampshire, Connecticut, and Rhode Island had, roughly, the same model of organization.

Some of the names of the courts were different in Virginia, but the general development ran parallel. Dale's code—the "Lawes Divine, Morall and Martiall" of 1611—set up a stern, undifferentiated system of authority; a single ruling group held tight control of the colony; there was little division of governmental labor. The "Martiall" part of the code dealt with the duties of soldiers. The "Divine" and "Morall" parts consisted of general criminal provisions and special regulations for the colony. The code was clearly neither lawyer's law nor English law in the usual sense. But neither was it foreign. It reflected the crudities of life in Virginia: the Indians, the "starving time," real or imagined problems of discipline. On paper, the code seemed very severe; it threatened death even for trivial crimes. But the harsh "penalties for embezzlement of public stores or the stealing of boats, speak not so loudly of severity as they do of the importance of the stores and of the

9 John M. Murrin, *Anglicizing an American Colony: The Transformation of Provincial Massachusetts* (unpublished Ph.D. thesis, Yale University, 1966), pp. 156–58.

10 *Laws and Liberties of Massachusetts*, p. 15. The governor or deputy governor, "with any two other Magistrates," was empowered to form a strangers' court.

boat." [11] Once the colony had a firmer footing, Dale's code was no longer needed. It was gone by 1620. The colony needed men; and a certain amount of mildness and self-government was essential to attract them to a new world. In the 1620's the forerunner of the Virginia legislative assembly was already in operation. By the late 1630's, Virginians were making laws for themselves in an organization where local people had a share of the power.

As in Massachusetts, the highest court was much more than a court. The governor and council (and the house of burgesses) decided cases and also made rules. Governor and council functioned as a "Quarter Court"; in 1658, sittings were reduced to three a year, in 1661, to two; the body was then called a "General Court." The general court handled the trial of serious crimes. It also reviewed cases initially decided in the county courts. The county courts began as "Monthly Courts" in 1623; the name was changed in 1642; by then, county government had become fully established. The county courts were manned at first by "commissioners"; after 1661, these men were called justices of the peace. The county courts, as in Massachusetts, were more than courts; they handled a wide range of what would now be considered administrative matters—tax collecting, road building, regulation of taverns and ferries. They also handled probate affairs. This feature of county courts was quite typical in colonial America. It was replicated in other colonies too.[12]

The county courts were at the heart of colonial government. As more and more of their records are published, a picture of colonial justice vividly unfolds. For example, one can now look in on the county court of Prince Georges County, Maryland, meeting "att Charles Towne the twenty fourth day of November in the Eight yeare of the Reigne of our Sovereigne Lord William the third" (1696). Five commissioners were present. The weather was hard, however, so the court "did Immediately Adjourne to Mr. David Smalls Store house by reason the new house Intended for a Church is Soe open that they Cannot Sitt." At Small's, the court discharged its business—judicial, administrative, quasi-legislative. James Paine, a seven-year-old boy, was bound over "by his Fathers Consent" to serve Samuel Westley "untill he arrives to twenty one

[11] Wesley Frank Craven, *The Southern Colonies in the Seventeenth Century, 1607–1689* (1949), p. 106; see also W. F. Prince, "The First Criminal Code of Virginia," *Ann. Rpt. Am. Hist. Ass'n.* (1899), Vol. 1, p. 311.

[12] See, for example, Paul M. McCain, *The County Court in North Carolina before 1750* (1954).

years of Age." Benjamin Berry and Robert Gordon were found to
have been drunk at an inn, "profanely Cursing and Swareing";
they were ordered to be put in the stocks. A number of citizens
recorded marks for their animals; William Bailey recorded "an
over halve and an under bitt on the Right Eare and a Swallow
forke on the Left Eare." George Hutcheson humbly petitioned
that "by Gods providence" he had "been Grievously Afflicted with
an ulcerated Legg for these many years" without a cure, and "being thus . . . disenabled from getting my Livelyhood by any hard
Labour I gett a poore maintenance in teaching of Childred to
reade but being growne in years and my Ability or Capasity being
but Small I only gett my Accomedations and a few old Cloaths to
Cover my nakedness"; he begged to be "Excused . . . from paying
his Leavye"; this the court allowed. Estate matters were handled,
constables chosen. A grand jury met and made presentments;
"Elizabeth Pole Servant woman . . . for haveing a bastard." [13] At
another session, the court licensed Jonathan Wilson to "keepe Ordinary [an inn] in the Saide towne Called Charles Towne dureing
pleasure," complying with "the Act of Assembly Conserning Ordinary keepers." At another, it was ordered "that the Sherife receive
of every Taxable person Ninety three pounds of Tobacco." At another, they appointed overseers of highways, and heard a complaint that a bridge was "so much out of repair that wee cannot
goe over there without the Danger of horse and man." [14]

Some 17th-century colonies organized their systems differently
from the Virginia and Massachusetts models. But the divergences
were in fact often less than the names of the courts suggested. The
grand council of South Carolina, in the 17th century, was the basic,
undifferentiated court of that colony; it sat sometimes as a court of
probate, or a court of chancery, or a court of admiralty, or a common law court.[15] It dealt with the defense and safety of the colony,
allocated lands, and laid down rules and regulations. In the province of East New Jersey, a court of common right was established
in 1683 "to hear, try and determine all matters, causes and cases,
capital, criminal or civil causes of equity, and causes tryable at
common law." The name of the court was unique, but its broad
jurisdiction was not unusual in the English-speaking colonies. The

13 Joseph H. Smith and Philip A. Crowl, eds., *Court Records of Prince
Georges County, Maryland 1696–1699* (1964), pp. 59 ff.

14 Smith and Crowl, *op. cit.*, pp. 168, 375–76, 615.

15 Anne K. Gregorie, ed., *Records of the Court of Chancery of South Carolina
1671–1779* (1950), pp. 22–25.

fate of the grand council was portentous. The council became identified as the outlet for the proprietors' interests. This made it unpopular with those leaders of the colony who opposed the proprietors. The court was, in short, associated with one class, one party, one economic interest. To defeat that interest meant to overthrow the court. When proprietary government collapsed, the court, "devoid of any litigants save the Proprietors themselves, inconspicuously, perhaps unknowingly, adjourned for ever." [16] This was in 1702.

In New York, legal institutions began work, quite literally, in a different language. Its *schouts* and *schepens* were Dutch. When the colony passed into English hands, in the middle of the 17th century, the cultural victory took longer to perfect than the political victory. In New York City, the old court of burgomasters and schepens changed its name to the "Mayor's Court," in 1665. English procedure was supposedly introduced at this time. But Dutch speech, personnel, and procedures lingered on. As late as 1675, when a plaintiff "declared in action of the Case," the defendant "read his answer and Soe replickt and duplickt, upon which, a Jury was empanneled," a "curious melange," in the words of Professor Morris, "of Dutch terminology and English remedy and procedure." By the early 1680's, however, "English verbiage culled from the standard folios on writs and entries published in the mother country supplanted the informal language of the previous [Dutch] record." [17] This was the first American success of common-law imperialism; the process would be later repeated, with varying results, in Louisiana, Florida, Illinois, Texas, and California.

There were exceptional courts in some of the colonies. In Pennsylvania, William Penn had the Quaker distaste for formal law and litigation. His laws (1682) called for the appointment of three persons in each precinct as "Common peacemakers." "Arbitrations" of these peacemakers were to stand as "valid as the judgments of the Courts of Justice." [18] These peacemakers were an early example of

[16] Preston W. Edsall, ed., *Journal of the Courts of Common Right and Chancery of East New Jersey 1683–1702* (1937), p. 34.

[17] Richard B. Morris, ed., *Select Cases of the Mayor's Court of New York City 1674–1784* (1935), p. 43. In Westchester County, however, which was settled by English-speaking people, common-law terminology was used from the beginning. In court records of March 22, 1659, there is a plaintive remark of the clerk that "the coppi of the sentence of the high corte being ritten in Duch we could not understand it." Dixon R. Fox, ed., *Minutes of the Court of Session, Westchester County, 1657–1696* (1924), pp. 12–13.

[18] Edwin B. Bronner, *William Penn's "Holy Experiment"* (1962), p. 36.

the Utopian strain in American law. This strain manifested itself, from time to time, in the noble experiment of prohibiting lawyers, or reducing or abolishing formal law. Early court organization in Maryland was unrealistic, but not Utopian; and in rather a different direction from Pennsylvania. On paper, the proprietors established a whole battery of courts after English models: hundred courts and manorial courts, courts of hustings and piepowder in St. Mary's and Annapolis, county courts, courts of oyer and terminer, a chancery court, a court of vice-admiralty, and a prerogative court, among others. Some of these apparently never came to life at all. There are records of one manorial court that actually sat between 1659 and 1672—as feeble and transient as later attempts to plant ostriches and camels in the West.

In short, despite experiments in diversity, colonial conditions shaped court organization in all, or almost all, colonies along similar lines in the 17th century. Court structures moved from the simple to the more complex, from the undifferentiated to the hierarchical. English models, English terms, and English customs were a more or less powerful influence everywhere. Executive, legislative, and judicial power were not clearly fenced off from each other. But as time went on, differentiation became more marked. Legislatures still heard appeals, but they conducted few or no trials.

The colonies had another trait in common. For all their geographic and political isolation, they owed some sort of allegiance to the crown. Their charters spoke explicitly of the duty to conform their laws to English laws. The distant king held at least some nominal authority, particularly in chartered colonies. Settlements of the trading-company type were beholden, at least in theory, to the company's home office, located usually in London. In proprietary colonies, the proprietor had some kind of appellate power.

Many colonies actively resisted English influence. The Child Remonstrance, in Massachusetts Bay (1646), is a well-known incident. Dr. Child attacked the ruling circles of the colony, in writing. He called for a return to the "Fundamentall and wholesome Lawes" of England. Dr. Child pointed out the large gap between England's laws and those of Massachusetts Bay. Implicitly, he appealed to the English to close the gap in some way. The colony tried to suppress news of the remonstrance. John Cotton supposedly warned a shipmaster not to "carry any Writings" that were "complaints against the people of God"; it would be "as *Jonas* in the ship," he said. If "storms did arise," the master should "search

if they had not in any chest or trunk any such Jonas aboard";
Jonahlike writings should be thrown to the boiling sea.[19]

The colony did not rely on the storm gods alone; it also insisted,
in England, that its charter preclude appeals from the colony to
London. As early as the Child Remonstrance, it was clear that the
distribution of power between center and periphery would have to
be resolved. It was also clear that the outlying lands would resist
encroachments from the center. While London worked out its
colonial policy, slowly and haltingly, the tiny settlements along the
coast assumed as much autonomy as they could. The colonies were
small, of marginal importance, and a long way from London: these
facts insulated them from king and council. Any convergence of
colonial and English law, substance and procedure, in the 17th
century was not so much a matter of imperial force as of convenience and free will. Massachusetts Bay was the most independent of
the colonies, the one most often said to have rejected common law.
But when the colonists compiled their code of 1648, they sent to
England for six legal texts, including *Coke on Littleton*.[20]

Moreover, especially in proprietary and crown colonies, there
were many absentee landlords and overlords. They assumed, naturally enough, that the law of England ruled in their property.
Then, too, Englishmen were constantly emigrating to America;
doctrines, documents, and devices came with them. There was constant tension between their dialect of law and the mother tongue.
A controversy in East New Jersey, in 1695, illustrates this point. In
1676, Governor Carteret had granted, by patent, to Simon Rouse,
certain land, including "58 acres of arable land & six acres of
meadow" situated "upon Raway River in the County of Essex." The
grant read: "to Have and to Hold to him the said Simon Rouse his
Heires or assigns for ever." Rouse left the land by will to Frances
Moore. Litigation arose over whether Moore had a valid title to
the land. One side referred to the doctrine in "My Lord Cooks
Institutes," that a valid grant of fee simple (that is, full ownership), could only be consummated by using the words "to A and
his heirs and assigns." The word *and* was essential; use of *or*
would not make a fee simple, but "only an Estate for life," leaving
A "no power to devise the same." This meant that Rouse's title
ended at his death. This mumbo-jumbo was indeed the law of England, according to the gospel of Sir Edward Coke; and a jury ver-

[19] Robert Child, *New Englands Jonas Cast up at London* (1869), p. 26.
[20] Haskins, *op. cit.,* p. 135.

dict so decided. The verbal misstep had been made, it seems, "through the ignorance of those infant times." But this decision cast in doubt the rights of many landholders, who claimed through Moore. The province was thrown into uproar. Remedial legislation was proposed, but the governor blocked it, hoping to exact payment of unpaid quitrents as the price of quieting the disputed titles. Ultimately, the proprietary party conceded the point, and an act was passed declaring that all of Governor Carteret's "grants, charters, or patents" bearing the "particle or . . . in the habendum" should be "taken, deemed and esteemed as effectual in law" as if the word *and* had appeared in place of the *or*. The complexity of law was perilous, in a land with too few technicians; but it was also unavoidable that men should return to English sources in legal disputes where English interests, using English legal documents and techniques, and applying English criteria, clashed with colonial habits and desires.[21] In short, the strings that bound colonial law to England were less political than social and cultural ties. Colonial law was more a child of English law than its subordinate.

THE COLONIAL JUDICIAL SYSTEM IN THE 18TH CENTURY

The colonial courts in the 18th century were noticeably more English—partly by choice, partly as a result of natural development, and partly because England was more serious about governing its children. At the end of the 17th century

> a new policy of constructive imperialism was introduced which proposed the supplanting of chartered colonies by royal governments, the combination of smaller self-governing or proprietary units into large units of administration, and the strengthening of the executive power at the expense of representative assemblies.[22]

These policies failed in the long run. But the British government at least managed to make the colonies pay more attention to England's demands. It was "necessary," said the Massachusetts charter of 1691, "that all our Subjects should have liberty to Appeale to us

[21] Preston W. Edsall, ed., *Journal of the Courts of Common Right and Chancery of East New Jersey 1683–1702* (1937), pp. 105–8, 273.

[22] Richard B. Morris, *Studies in the History of American Law* (2nd ed., 1959), p. 62.

our heires and Successors in Cases that may deserve the same." A right of appeal inhered in cases where "the matter in difference" was worth more than three hundred pounds sterling. As for legislation, copies of all "Orders Laws Statutes and Ordinances" were to be sent to England "by the first opportunity," for "approbation or Disallowance." Any laws disallowed in London, within three years after passage, "shall thenceforth cease and determine and become utterly void and of none effect."

It might have been possible to give the royal courts, in London, appellate jurisdiction over colonial courts. The royal courts, then, could have forced the colonial courts to conform some of their doctrines to the English common law. But this was not the system chosen. Appeals ran, not to the law courts, but to a special committee, formed within the Privy Council. The committee cared little for the purity and conformity of ordinary rules of law. It cared far more about how colonial law fit English politics and policy.

The Privy Council was never, then, an efficient overseer of the routine work of the courts. The volume of "appeals" was always small. Distance, expense, and political recalcitrance discouraged appeals. Rhode Island was the most appeal-prone colony; yet it sent, on the average, less than a case a year—76 between 1696 and 1783.[23] The council's working habits also limited its influence. Few council orders

> were embodied in the printed reports; few attained currency in manuscript form—most probable was verbal circulation in garbled form. For this reason the jurisdiction of the Privy Council was largely exercised in *ad hoc* fashion, from appeal to appeal with little lasting effect.[24]

A few privy council decisions were great cases, that is, they touched on issues of major political significance. One such case was *Winthrop* v. *Lechmere* (1727–28), a rare, controversial example of judicial review.[25] This case threw out, as void, Connecticut's intestacy laws. In general, the Privy Council was rather permissive and incompetent. Legislation, too, was reviewed in a haphazard way. Delays were frequent. The council found it hard to decide on a method of review. Practically all colonial statutes were in some way

---

[23] These figures are from Joseph H. Smith, *Appeals to the Privy Council from the American Plantations* (1950), p. 668. Smith's study is the source for much of the text on the work of the Privy Council.

[24] Smith, *op. cit.,* p. 660.

[25] On this famous case, see Smith, *op. cit.,* pp. 537–60.

repugnant to the laws of England. In theory, the council could have thrown them all out. In fact, most deviations were tolerated.

The results of the council's work are hard to assess. Quantitatively, it was not unimportant. According to one authority, 469 colonial laws were disallowed by orders in council—about 5.5 per cent of 8,563 laws submitted for approval.[26] The council struck down some laws because they crossed the invisible, shifting boundary between acceptable and unacceptable repugnance. The council voided other laws because they were carelessly written or so garbled as to be absurd. Still other laws fell because they contradicted English policy or English interests, as the council conceived them. When South Carolina placed a ten per cent duty on goods imported from England, an Order in Council of 1718 declared the law "null and void." [27]

Council orders were not always obeyed. But, in ways difficult to measure, the council may have had an important effect on legal behavior. Legislatures debating a bill, litigants pursuing lawsuits, may have been aware of the council's distant shadow; this awareness may have modified their action in real but unknowable ways.

Judicial organization as such was not fundamentally different in the 18th century. As before, each colony had a pyramid of courts. The court at the top was almost always more than a court—the governor and council, either as such, or sitting as a special high court. Below the high court were various intermediate courts, and at the base a single judge, justice of the peace, or the equivalent. In most colonies, the intermediate courts heard appeals and at the same time enjoyed some original jurisdiction. As in England, jurisdictional lines were fuzzy, and courts overlapped; to "appeal" often meant to retry the whole case at a higher level, not merely to send upstairs a few difficult issues for review.

As in the 17th century, the basic local court, usually called a county court, was very versatile, very influential in its neighborhood. These courts handled a huge volume of workaday administrative tasks. In Connecticut in the 18th century, the towns chose a group of men, called the *grand jury*, to help the county court in its work. As of 1747, these jurors

> were required to oversee workmen in clearing the commons, to present idle persons . . . to take care that the Sabbath be observed, to present persons for selling drink [and] . . . for not

26 Richard B. Morris, *Studies in the History of American Law* (2nd ed., 1959), p. 63.
27 Smith, *op. cit.*, p. 535.

attending public worship . . . to inform against killing deer,
to meet with selectmen and constables in nominating tavern
keepers, to present servants for being out unseasonable hours,
to see that Indian children learned to read, to present persons for
setting up lotteries, to inspect taverns, and to pull down secular
notifications posted on the Sabbath or a Day of Fast.[28]

The Connecticut variant was unique; the general idea was not.
The basic lower court was a *governing* court, as well as a court to
settle disputes. The business of government was not separated
neatly according to institution. Local rule was rule by the local
powers. In a colony like Virginia, then, the county court represented the planters and their interests. The judges were almost
universally laymen. But lay judges were not ignorant men by any
means. They knew a good deal of the relevant law. This was a
familiar state of affairs. In England, too, a country gentleman
knew the working law of his community. Law was the raw material
of government, and he was the governor. There is no reason to
doubt that the lay judges in America knew enough to govern their
men.

Functional specialization of courts was more prevalent in the
18th than the 17th century. Two specialized systems, vice-
admiralty and chancery, call for some special comment. Courts of
admiralty handled violations of trade and navigation laws, and
traditional admiralty questions of prize law, seamen's wages, salvage, and maritime commerce. These courts as such did not exist in
the 17th century. In crown colonies, the governor was *ex officio*
vice admiral; beginning in 1696, he had the power to "erect one or
more Court or Courts Admirall" in his jurisdiction. By 1763 nine
separate vice-admiralty courts had been established in the area of
the thirteen colonies.[29] They were mostly staffed by native judges.
The courts followed traditional English admiralty procedure,
which meant, among other things, that their cases were tried without juries.

The vice-admiralty courts, then, show how colonial practice and
English practice grew closer. The colonies needed these courts, too,
because they did so much overseas trade. But vice-admiralty courts
were not popular with independent-minded men. The crown took
a strong interest in the courts and their staffs; the courts were a

---

[28] John T. Farrell, ed., *The Superior Court Diary of William Samuel Johnson 1772–3* (1942), xlii.

[29] See, in general, Carl Ubbelohde, *The Vice Admiralty Courts and the American Revolution* (1960).

natural forum to disseminate and enforce the home country's policies on trade. The precious right of trial by jury was missing in vice-
admiralty courts. The jury meant, first, impartial justice; second
(and somewhat inconsistently), partiality to American interests.
Resistance to British colonial policy, therefore, spilled over naturally into resistance to vice-admiralty courts.

To make doubly sure of subservience, England established an all-
colonial vice-admiralty court in 1763, and gave it concurrent jurisdiction over vice-admiralty matters. The court sat, rather incon-
veniently, at Halifax, Nova Scotia. William Spry, an Englishman
trained in civil law, was named its judge. Unfortunately, no one
came to use the court; Spry sat in his cold little town, waiting
vainly for cases. Later, London assigned to Spry, and to the existing vice-admiralty courts, jurisdiction to decide cases under the
Stamp Act. The Stamp Act had nothing to do with the sea. But in
England the Exchequer court specialized in matters of crown revenue; there was no such court in the colonies; and in the colonies
the vice-admiralty courts were the only colonial courts sympathetic
enough to the king to be trusted with this and similar matters.

Spry's court was abolished in 1768. The British next tried a network of four regional courts, sitting at Halifax, Boston, Philadelphia, and Charleston. The regional courts were to share jurisdiction
with existing vice-admiralty courts. But in practice the regional
courts merely replaced the courts in the towns where they sat.[30]
Then came the Revolution. Curiously, the courts did not vanish
from the scene. Militants had objected to the courts on two
grounds: that their modes of procedure were abominable, and that
they enforced abominable laws. Since the regular courts also heard
some maritime matters, the real issue was who controlled which
courts. When war broke out, the new state governments found it
useful to create their own vice-admiralty courts—for cases of prize
law, for example. Massachusetts, among other states, created a system of these courts in 1775—though, true to ideology, issues of fact
were to be decided by "twelve good and lawful men." [31] But soon
the jury was abandoned, ostensibly because sea law was too intricate for the "good and lawful men." Admiralty law returned to the
"wisdom of all civilized nations" with "one judge to try, facts as
well as law." [32] Dispute over procedure in admiralty, then, was a
screen for the conflict of interests. A centralized network of admi-

30 Ubbelohde, op. cit., p. 158.
31 Ubbelohde, op. cit., p. 196.
32 Ubbelohde, op. cit., p. 200.

ralty courts had been a dismal failure in colonial America. Yet in 1787 the Constitution put admiralty law in the federal, central courts; and there it stays.

The history of chancery in the 18th century has points of similarity with the history of admiralty. The immediate background was rather complicated. Some colonies—Massachusetts and (except for one brief episode) Pennsylvania—lacked separate courts of equity. In these colonies other courts handled, piecemeal, those equitable matters felt essential. Another group of colonies—the Carolinas, Maryland, New York, New Jersey, and Delaware—had courts of equity. But even in these colonies, equity did not always have an institution of its own. In Delaware, for example, the court of common pleas, a common-law court, simply sat four times a year as an equity court.[33] In some colonies, the governor bore the title of chancellor. In 17th-century New Hampshire, the governor and council made up the "high Courte of Chancery"; and the governor had the right to "depute, nominate and appointe in his Stead a Chancellor" and staff. In 1699, when the Earl of Bellomont was acting as governor, a new judiciary act eliminated the court of chancery. Instead, the act gave courts of general jurisdiction the power to "moderate the Rigor of the Law" in certain cases.[34] The Southern colonies quite generally had courts of chancery. In New York, a supplement to the Duke's laws in 1665 provided that when the original complaint was a "matter of equity" the action should proceed "by way of Bill and delivering in Answers upon Oath and by the Examination of witnesses, in like manner as is used in the Court of Chancery in England." By 1684 a master of the rolls, a register, and clerks of chancery had been appointed. A separate court of chancery survived New York's many court convolutions, and was embodied in the Judiciary Act of 1691.[35]

Hostility to the chancery courts was quite widespread in the 18th century. Governor William Burnet of New York (1720–8) used the chancery court as a court of exchequer, to collect the colony's unpaid quitrents. This added nothing to the court's popularity.[36] Chancery was closely associated with executive power, in turn with the English overlords. Equity worked without a jury; thus public

[33] Roscoe Pound, *Organization of Courts* (1940), p. 76.

[34] *Laws of New Hampshire, Province Period 1679–1702* (1904), p. 665; Elwin L. Page, *Judicial Beginnings in New Hampshire 1640–1700* (1959), p. 42.

[35] Paul M. Hamlin and Charles E. Baker, *Supreme Court of Judicature of the Province of New York, 1691–1704*, Vol. 1 (1959), pp. 16, 53.

[36] Beverley W. Bond, Jr., *The Quit-Rent System in the American Colonies* (1919), pp. 268–69.

opinion could not effectively control the use of the court as a tool
of imperial policy. Besides, equity courts sat, as a rule, only in the
capital; unlike the common law, it was not brought to every man's
doorstep. Litigants complained, too, that chancery procedures were
clumsy, inefficient, interminable. An essay in a New York newspaper, written in 1752, reported rumors of equity suits "at Issue these
Thirty Years Past." Chancery was a "Gulf, that will in the End
swallow up the Estates of its Suitors." [37] This was a century before
Dickens' *Bleak House*. In South Carolina, when the proprietary
government was overthrown in 1720, the short-lived revolutionary
party stripped the governor and council of their chancery powers.
Instead, they were to appoint a chancellor, who would be remov-
able only by the king.[38] Yet, despite these uproars and complaints,
the American Revolution did not abolish courts of chancery.
Chancery merely passed to new masters. The procedural abuses,
once wrenched from political context, lost their power to stir revolt.

In England, ecclesiastical courts handled matters of probate.
These courts had no counterpart in the colonies. Massachusetts, by
acts of 1685 and 1686, simply made probate courts out of its county
courts, with "full power and authority as the ordinary in England." (The *ordinary* was an ecclesiastical official.) In Maryland,
up to 1673, the provincial court managed probate matters, or appointed a justice specially to do so; in 1673, "the English organization, with a prerogative court and a commissary general, was reproduced." [39] In New York, the Duke's laws gave probate matters to
the courts of sessions. A constable and two "overseers" took inven-
tory and reported to the court. All wills were registered in New
York City, where the probate process was gradually centralized. Ultimately, the governor delegated his probate powers to a subordinate, who presided over a "prerogative court."

Some colonies borrowed from the English the idea of roving
courts—courts of oyer and terminer and general gaol delivery.
These courts "heard and determined" criminal cases, held over in
the local community to await the coming of the court. New York
established these courts in 1683; local justices of the peace staffed
them, joined by an itinerant judge, who represented the central

37 Milton M. Klein, ed., *The Independent Reflector* (1963), p. 253.
38 Gregorie, *op. cit.*, p. 7. In 1721, the old structure was restored.
39 Carroll T. Bond, ed., *Proceedings of the Maryland Court of Appeals 1695–1729* (1933), xvii.

authorities, and who rode on circuit from county to county. Some cities, too, had borough courts. Georgia instituted a latter-day version of the old Bay Colony strangers' court. The Southern colonies, too, created special summary courts for slaves.

CIVIL PROCEDURE

Common-law pleading and procedure were exceptionally intricate. Colonial process never attained the heights, or depths, of English common law. There were wide differences between colonies—between the loose, informal justice of early Massachusetts and the more conservative, more formal process in the Middle Atlantic and Southern colonies. But everywhere, the general, long-run trend was the same: from simplicity and innovation to more complexity, and ever greater doses of secondhand English form.

Certainly, as compared to the 18th century or to royal English courts, 17th-century procedure was exceptionally lax. But it is easy to exaggerate this trait. When judges are laymen, and not fussy about separation of powers, a court is bound to be run informally. County court government was government at the point where the rules were applied to ordinary life. Justice there usually has a loose, unstructured look; but if one compares colonial process, not with England's high courts but with English local courts, the differences are not quite so striking.

Seventeenth-century procedure was certainly direct and pragmatic. But it did not ignore its English heritage. The basic institutions—jury, grand jury, writ, summons, written pleadings, and oral testimony—were in use in the colonies, as they were in England, though never exactly the same. In detail, colonial procedure was a curious mixture. In 1656, in the "Court of Trials of the Colony of Providence Plantations," in an "action . . . of detenew for detaining certaine . . . horsis and mares," the court "fownd in the plaintifs declaration a Verball oversight"; the word plaintiff "should have beine writ defendant." Never mind: the court ordered "that it may be Rectified according to the Answer put in by the defendant whoe clearly understood & Answers according to the scope of it." The court brushed aside technicality here, although almost in the next breath it used an ancient English term for a form of action ("detinue"). The same Rhode Island court, in a criminal matter, fussed over the "want of A Tittle" in one word in the indictment.[40] Many colonial records illustrate that courts liked the idea of conciliation and arbitration, avoiding the rigors of courtroom procedure. In the records of Kent County, Delaware, in 1680, Peter Groendyk and William Winsmore, by "Joynt Consent," referred their differences to the court's determination. It was a matter of "account of debt and Credit." The court "thought fi[t to] appoint" two arbitrators to decide the case; these two would, in case of a "non agreement . . . chuse a third person as an Umpire [to] make a final End thereof." [41]

Early procedure was simple by reason of convenience and necessity. Simplicity was also a matter of choice. Professor Haskins carefully examined the Massachusetts Bay colony's civil process and found little that was truly haphazard. The Puritan "zeal to reform every aspect of human activity," led to many legal innovations, including reforms of civil procedure. Procedure "was simplified so as to render justice inexpensive and easily accessible, and yet formal enough to provide adequate safeguards for litigants." [42] Process was speedy and cheap compared to English process; costs were measured in pennies, not pounds, and judgment was generally given on the day of the trial. The Massachusetts summons, unlike the English writ, was stripped of jargon, translated from Latin to English, and greatly streamlined in form. Forms of action were reduced to a few simple headings. The worst excesses of English law never were adopted; but there was considerable backsliding in the 18th century. The move toward English standards can be plainly traced in surviving records—even those of the lowest courts. In New Hampshire, where pleadings had always been simple, clear, and direct, the lawyers introduced more sophistication and complexity during the years 1692 to 1700; the action of ejectment, the writs of *scire facias* and *supersedeas,* the action of *trespass de bonis asportatis,* entered New Hampshire as immigrants at this time.[43] Students of Massachusetts law on the eve of the Revolution have found it to be quite conservative, judged both by later and earlier standards. The doctrine of precedent was in high fashion among

---

[40] *Records of the Court of Trials of the Colony of Providence Plantations, 1647–1662* (1920), Vol. 1, pp. 19, 32.

[41] Leon de Valinger, Jr., ed., *Court Records of Kent County, Delaware, 1680–1705* (1959), pp. 4–5.

[42] George L. Haskins, "The First American Reform of Civil Procedure," in Roscoe Pound, ed., *Perspectives of Law; Essays for Austin Wakeman Scott* (1964), pp. 173, 178.

[43] Elwin L. Page, *Judicial Beginnings in New Hampshire, 1640–1700* (1959), p. 96.

lawyers and judges. English law was held up as a model. In civil procedure, the common-law system of writs was "in full vigor." Courts were quite sticky about the niceties of pleading. Both civil and criminal actions could be, and sometimes were, turned out of court if there was a failure to state the full and absolutely correct name of a party; if the name was misspelled; if the defendant's occupation was incorrectly described.[44]

But the movement to adapt to English law was always a matter of more or less. Early colonial government had been oligarchic, paternal. In the 18th century, merchants and landowners gained greater influence in government. The merchant's idea of a good legal system was one that was rational and efficient, conforming to his values and expectations—traits that neither lay justice nor the baroque extravagances of English procedure supplied. Eighteenth-century civil process, on the whole, was an uneasy mixture of three basic strands: lawyer's law, merchant's ideals, and the ruler's will.

LAND LAW

In theory, the principle of tenure governed both the land law of the colonies and the land law of England. No one could own land absolutely. One could speak accurately, not of ownership of land, but of rights *to* land or *in* land. These rights might be arranged in layers of space and time; three, six, ten or more persons could have different sorts of interest in one tract of land—a right to receive rent, or a right to the land when and if someone else died childless, all while still other people actually lived on the land and grew crops. Imagine an apartment building, rented out to tenants, with a mortgage held by the bank, but administered on behalf of a widow who enjoys the rents until she dies, when her children (if they live so long) succeed to her interest. The bank collects the rents, and pays itself a fee. The state collects property taxes. Who "owns" the building? One can see many "estates" or interests in the building, but no single, individual owner. All these interests or

---

[44] See the excellent thesis of William E. Nelson, *The Americanization of the Common Law during the Revolutionary Era: A Study of Legal Change in Massachusetts, 1760–1830* (unpublished Ph.D. thesis, Harvard University, 1971), pp. 31 ff. See also John Adams' Pleading Book, in L. Kinvin Wroth and Hiller B. Zobel, *Legal Papers of John Adams* (Vol. I, 1965), p. 26 ff. For a glimpse of New York process during this period, see Herbert A. Johnson, "Civil Procedure in John Jay's New York," 11 Am. J. Leg. Hist. 69 (1967).

estates have names and all have had a solid wall of law built up around them.

In England, land was the basis of wealth and social standing, and land law was the heart of the royal common law. Land was a scarce commodity in England. It was parceled out in the Middle Ages in tiers of estates, with the king at the apex, and various vassals and subvassals underneath. Much of this feudal apparatus was gone by 1650. But rights to land still paralleled the way in which social and economic power was distributed. The colonies, on the other hand, though they were short of people, cattle, and hard money, had land to burn. The social system was not fixed along the lines of estates of land. What happened to land law, then, was the result of a collision between the past—and its supporters— and the colonial present. Three elements—tradition, state policy, and the market—jostled for influence on colonial land law. The traditional elements of land law remained quite strong. Land law was essentially English, though simplified, varied, adapted, and somewhat obscured, since parts of the land law derived from vulgar English law rather than from classic common law. The early New England towns, with their common fields, common herding of cattle, scattering land in allotments of a few acres each, rather than in compact grants, reconstructed "the community life . . . known in England insofar as consonant with local conditions and with the objectives of [the settlers'] migration." [45]

The ultimate overlord of all colonial land was, in theory, the king. He had granted the land to others: to proprietors, like Lord Baltimore, or by way of charter to the settlers in Massachusetts. These grants were not, theoretically, absolute; the crown retained an interest. Throughout the colonial period, most of the land, outside of New England, was liable in law to pay an annual rent forever to the overlord. These rents, called quitrents, were payable in some colonies to the proprietor, in others to the crown.

In England, the quitrent system had come about after a long process, which liberalized the position of a tenant of land. A small perpetual rent was much to be preferred over older, more onerous obligations. But in America quitrents had no such quality of liberalization. They were out of place in the land-abundant country. Crown and proprietors were drawn to the quitrents by their desire for cold cash. But attempts to collect the quitrents led to constant bickering and strife. They probably yielded less revenue than they

45 George L. Haskins, Law and Authority in Early Massachusetts (1960), pp. 69–70.

cost in disaffection. At the outbreak of the American Revolution, the system vanished forever.[46]

In New England, the quitrent system never took root. Here there was no attempt to use land rights as a way to squeeze money from the holders of land. But this did not mean that the magistrates and leaders in New England had any more use than the crown and the proprietors for the idea of a nation of freeholders, freely trading in land. The New England villages used land tenure and land allocation as a means of social control. How this was done has been carefully documented in Sumner Powell's study of Sudbury. In Sudbury, Massachusetts, a person's proper station in life determined whether his allotment was large or small. Strangers were not lightly given land in this community. In the 1640's, if a man left town without permission, he apparently forfeited his land.[47] But in New England, too, the swelling population and the abundance of land doomed this form of tenure and social control.

In Plymouth, the first settlers wanted land to be owned in common. Under their plan, settlers would work seven years for the general good; at the end of that period, they would divide profits and improved land among themselves. More than a century later, the new colony of Georgia adopted a strange land system of indivisible grants in *tail male*. If a grantee died without sons, his land reverted to the trustees of Georgia. Leases were forbidden, and restrictions placed on the maximum size of holdings.[48] Land communism was moribund in Plymouth by 1623; by 1738, the Georgia plan had to be modified. Plymouth had been planned as a business venture. Other colonial schemes were abortive Utopias. A grandiose plan for the Carolinas was drawn up, perhaps by John Locke. Carolina society would be elaborately stratified with a nobility of landgraves and "caciques," hereditary, indivisible domains, baronies, manors, and seignories. None of the Utopias, or planned economies—or any other *a priori* social system—really ever took hold.

Elsewhere, conditions proved just as hostile to the opposite urge: the attempt to reproduce too closely English land law and tenure. "Lords of the Manor" actually held brief court in Maryland.

---

[46] See, in general, Beverley W. Bond, Jr., *The Quit-Rent System in the American Colonies* (1919).

[47] Sumner C. Powell, *Puritan Village: The Formation of a New England Town* (1965), p. 122.

[48] Milton S. Heath, *Constructive Liberalism; The Role of the State in Economic Development in Georgia to 1860* (1954), p. 35.

There are records of manor-court proceedings for St. Clements
Manor in St. Mary's County, between 1659 and 1672. In 1660,
jurors presented Luke Gardiner "for not doeing his Fealty to the
Lord of the Mannor," and fined him 1,000 pounds of tobacco.[49]
The Maryland manors apparently died quickly. There were other
feudal forays. One at least had long-range consequences. In the
Dutch patroonships on the Hudson, settlers owed perpetual fealty
to the patroon, and, more importantly, perpetual rent. In 1685, the
patroonship of Van Rensselaer was transformed into an English
manor. Other baronial grants, overlapping and vague, were made
to English aristocrats in upstate New York. They were paid for in
pittances (or bribes). Within these vast domains, great families
like the Livingstons and the Philipses held land in an almost feudal form of tenure. They granted land to settlers, but on condition
that a nagging rent be paid to the grantor forever. Some lords of
the manor required a fee each time a piece of land changed hands.
Other tenants held land on lease for life; they owed rent and had
no formal guaranty that their heirs would have the right to renew.
This archaic land-tenure system bore bitter fruit; unrest plagued
New York until the middle of the 19th century, when the anti-rent
movement finally broke the power of the landlords.

All in all, it was easier to use land as a cheap, convenient subsidy
than as a means of fettering a restless population. Hence, in general, land policy tended to shake off its past, and grow prodigal.
The king gave empires to his friends. In early New England, simple servants, after serving out their term, gained their own acres of
land. William Penn's "Concessions" of 1681 offered fifty acres for
each servant that a master brought over, and fifty acres to the servant when his term expired. In Virginia, too, anyone who brought
over one body, to add to the population stock, earned a "head
right" of fifty acres.

By and large, it was a country without skilled conveyancers, particularly in the 17th century. Simplified land forms were thus a
necessity, the more so because of the turnover of land. Colonial
deed forms were bastard but effective documents. They were
roughly based on the English deed form called bargain and sale.
Land was not always transferred by written document. Sometimes
livery of seisin, an old English form of symbolic delivery, was used,
particularly in the 17th century. The grantor gave the land sym-
bolically to his grantee, investing him through "turf and twig."

49 *Archives of Maryland,* Vol. 53 (1936), p. 629.

The custom seems to have been most common in the conservative South. But there are references from the North as well. In Maine (then part of Massachusetts), according to a deposition of 1685, Thomas Withers used a "turf and twig" to give possession of half of an island to his daughter Elizabeth.[50]

This archaic survival is striking; but there was striking innovation in land transfer too. In some colonies, land passed from person to person in a free and easy way. Conveyancing habits developed that were unheard of in old England. These new, informal modes of conveyance flourished alongside of classic forms. In early Maryland, conveyances of land were often made by written assignment on the back of the original patent, like the endorsement on a check. The patent thus "passed from hand to hand," until some purchaser, to be on the safe side, would decide to record his ownership by enrollment in court.[51] This practice shows one important aspect of the land law—how land transactions were converted from status to contract, from a matter of family and birth, to the subject of a free and open market. This was a slow, but definite process. It was not to be completed until the 19th century, and in a sense not even then. But one of the first American inventions, legally speaking, was the registration and recording of land titles. Recording acts and a recording system were invented in New England, in the early days of 17th-century settlement, though perhaps there was some past experience in some English towns. The essence of the system was that the record itself guaranteed title to the land. An unrecorded deed could not stand up against a recorded deed, even though the recorded deed was *issued* later than the unrecorded deed. The recording system began as a tool of state policy; it made governance of the settlements much simpler. But in time it turned into a tool of the market.

The complicated, protean system of equitable estates, from which the modern trust is descended, also crossed the Atlantic. In 1664, Dr. Luke Barber, a Maryland physician, who faced a heavy suit for damages, transferred all of his property to two men "in trust to the only use and behoofe" of his "most deare . . . Wife Elizabeth . . . and her heyres for ever." [52] But it was not the form of this branch of English law so much as its substance and function that first found its way into colonial life. The forms appeared

50 *Province and Court Records of Maine,* Vol. 4 (1958), p. 127.
51 *Archives of Maryland,* Vol. 53 (1936), xxxvi.
52 *Archives of Maryland,* Vol. 49 (1932), p. 120.

somewhat later. In 1641, in western Massachusetts, the "widdow Horton" made an arrangement with Robert Ashly, her intended husband, in the presence of a magistrate. The widow

> doth assigne and set over her house and house lott . . . and all her hogges litle and greate . . . into the hands of Robert Ashly for the use and behafe of her two sonns one sucking and the other about Three years ould caled Jermy to be paid to them . . . when they shall come to the age of Twenty and one yeares: and the said Robert is to have the use and profits of the said land and hogges for the educatinge of her said Two sonns: and when they shall come to the age of 13 or 14 yeares to put them out as apprentises to some usefull trade.[53]

In classic English law, land law could hardly be extricated from the tangle of actions and writs relating to land. In the colonies, land was hardly of less importance than in England. But land ownership was more widespread; as we have seen, even servants became landlords on a modest scale. Land actions in the colonies followed the general rule, that growth in population, wealth, and English control brought greater approximation to English law. Even at the peak of this development, however, in the mid-18th century, American land actions were simpler, freer, and more innovative than in England. As in England, the legal system had to have some device to test title, that is, some method whereby Mr. A, who claimed to own a piece of land, could challenge Mr. B, who claimed the same land, and obtain an authoritative answer from the court as to who was right. The ancient mode, the so-called *real actions,* had died out by the time of Queen Elizabeth I. The action of ejectment replaced them; but even ejectment was cumbersome, riddled with fiction. In the Southern colonies (except, apparently, 17th-century Virginia), in New York, and in East New Jersey, ejectment was the principle method of trying title to land. In 17th-century New Jersey, fictional parties did not usually appear in the pleadings by name, though at least one instance—Robert Summer against James Winter—was recorded in 1695.[54] In 18th-century ejectment the shadow men were the familiar John Doe and Richard Roe. New England was more innovative. There is not a single mention of ejectment in the Pynchon court record (Massachusetts,

[53] Joseph H. Smith, ed., *Colonial Justice in Western Massachusetts, 1639–1702* (1961), p. 210.

[54] Preston W. Edsall, ed., *Journal of the Courts of Common Right and Chancery of East New Jersey 1683–1702* (1937), pp. 84–85.

1639–1702).[55] The New England colonies used simpler forms of testing title—for example, an action of trespass to land. In 18th-century Connecticut, the favorite device was an action "for Surrendry of Seizin and Possession," which essentially corresponded to the action of ejectment, with a new name, and stripped bare of fictions.[56] In Massachusetts, in the 18th century, all the ancient English actions had been swept away, and replaced, by a single, all-embracing form of action called by a number of names: a plea of ejectment, a plea of entry, or, most simply, a plea of land, which avoided the inherited technicalities and led to a trial similar to other civil suits.[57]

SUCCESSION AT DEATH

When a man died in England, his property was divided according to two quite different rules. Common-law rules and courts controlled his land; church law and courts his personal property. If he left no will, the common law gave his eldest son the land; the church courts divided his goods in equal shares among his children. The colonies either had no church courts; or fused, as in early Massachusetts, the laws of Caesar and God. Probate power was given to regular courts or to special (but secular) branches of these courts. The probate process, including the filing of inventories, carried over almost automatically into the colonies. But the substantive law of succession was in some respects quite different from that of England.

The colonies greatly modified the law of descent of lands. In English law, primogeniture was the rule; lands descended to the eldest son. Primogeniture fulfilled a definite function in the days of military tenure. It retained some residual utility in England well into modern times. In some parts of England, the rule was displaced by local customs. One of these was the so-called gavelkind tenure of Kent; land in Kent descended to all sons in equal shares. The New England colonies, remote from upper-class English law and upper-class English society, had little use for primogeniture. Except for Rhode Island, all of New England rejected

[55] Joseph H. Smith, ed., *Colonial Justice in Western Massachusetts, 1639–1702* (1961), p. 160.

[56] John T. Farrell, ed., *The Superior Court Diary of William Samuel Johnson 1772–1773* (1942), xxxiii–xxxv.

[57] William E. Nelson, *op. cit.*, p. 73.

the rule. The 17th-century Massachusetts codes gave the eldest son "a double portion" of the "whole estate reall, and personall." [58] This special birthright was apparently a gesture to the Bible, not to English law. Of the Middle Atlantic colonies, New York accepted primogeniture; Pennsylvania rejected it in favor of a double portion for the eldest son, as in Massachusetts. Primogeniture was a feature of the law in the Southern colonies, Maryland, Virginia, and the Carolinas, until Revolutionary times.[59]

Scholars do not agree on where New England's partible descent (that is, division of land among children) came from. Some have suspected direct borrowing from local English custom. Many colonial charters granted lands to be held of the king "as of his manor of East Greenwich." East Greenwich was located in Kent. Was it the purpose or effect of these charters to introduce gavelkind tenure to the colonies? The evidence is confusing, inconclusive, and probably irrelevant. Partible descent was the practice in New England, in the earliest stages of colonial life, no doubt long before anyone thought of arguments based on the charters. Primogeniture and the fee tail survived in the South, partly because these were relatively conservative colonies, partly because of their system of land use. Southern planters used slave labor, and grew sugar, rice, and tobacco on large estates. English institutions and an English style of landed gentry better suited this social order than they suited the North.

On the other hand, the basic document for gifts at death—the last will and testament—came over as part of the colonists' cultural heritage. The English middle class used wills widely. The English law of wills came to be embodied in great statutes, such as the Statute of Wills (1540). But these statutes presupposed, and modified, customs already in existence. English will forms appeared early in the colonies. The formal written will, signed by the decedent and attested by witnesses, was common. So was the oral (nuncupative) will. The Provincial Court of Maryland, for example, heard oral testimony of two witnesses that John Smithson, in 1638, "lying then very sick," had promised, "in case God should call him," to leave his estate to his wife; upon "these depositions . . . the Judge did approve the said last will and testament." [60]

58 Laws and Liberties of Massachusetts, 1648 (1929 ed.), p. 53.

59 On the subject of colonial land law, especially primogeniture and fee tail, see Richard B. Morris, Studies in the History of American Law (2nd ed., 1959), pp. 69–125.

60 Archives of Maryland, Vol. 4, (1887), pp. 45–46.

At first, memory alone must have preserved the essential pattern of the will. Wills from Maine to Georgia strikingly resembled English wills and each other, particularly in their use of singsong, almost balladlike phrases. Shakespeare's will begins with the words: "In the name of God Amen . . . I commend my soul into the hands of God my Creator . . . and my body to the earth whereof it is made." [61] The will of Henry Simpson, executed in Maine in 1648, begins as follows: "In the name of God Amen. I, Henry Simpson . . . Doe make this my last will and testament. . . . First commending my soule to God that gave it . . . And my body to Christian buriall." [62]

Thousands of colonial wills have survived. They shed a great deal of light on colonial society. Some were drawn up by important people and disposed of substantial estates. Slaves, servants, and the very poor stood outside the property system and left no wills to speak of. Yet wills were not only for the rich. Many wills merely disposed of household goods and odds and ends. Bethia Cartwright of Salem, Massachusetts, died in 1640, disposing by will of her bedding and bed, pewter platters, a "double saltseller . . . half a dozen spoones and a porrenger," and a "box of linning, with a payre of shetes." [63]

In the early days, probate administration was quite loose by English or later American standards. In classic English law, the widow's share of her husband's land—called dower—was a life interest in one third of her husband's lands. Colonial law, particularly in New England, was much less rigid. In Massachusetts, magistrates had discretion to modify the wife's share, according to her needs and the colony's social and ethical standards. Rules were not hard and fast: even the eldest son's double portion was not an absolute right; the general court "upon just cause alledged" could "judge otherwise." The rules hardened when the sheer volume of probate affairs became the prime fact; by this time the small face-to-face communities had given way to a society of strangers. At this point, economic rationality and predictability came to the fore. This meant more formality; but English formalism never completely returned. In the law of succession the gulf between rules about land and rules about goods was never so great as in England.

[61] Quoted in Virgil M. Harris, *Ancient, Curious, and Famous Wills* (1911), pp. 305–6.
[62] *Province and Court Records of Maine*, Vol. 1 (1928), p. 126.
[63] *Records and Files of the Quarterly Courts of Essex County, Massachusetts* Vol. I, *1636–1656* (1911), p. 18.

And the colonial innovations in intestacy law—particularly partible inheritance—survived every attack.

CRIMINAL LAW

The earliest criminal codes mirrored the nasty, precarious life of pioneer settlements. Dale's laws in Virginia (1611) were severe, almost martial, suitable only for a small, imperiled community. They were only a phase. Once the colony became more secure, Virginia's criminal procedure "fundamentally resembled that of England, though it was on the whole less formal and more direct; as time went on it developed in the direction of greater conformity to the English practice." [64]

In Massachusetts, early political struggles weakened the power of the oligarchy; the colony then embarked on an extraordinary course of drafting codes. Behind this creative urge was the philosophy that no one should be punished for crimes not clearly and openly labeled. This meant that the criminal law had to be embodied in a code. *The Laws and Liberties of Massachusetts* (1648) was one of the early, major products of this movement; and much of its content was criminal. It named and proscribed most of the standard crimes—murder, arson, theft—as well as more exotic ones. The code showed considerable ingenuity in sanctions. Its aim was to correct and teach the weak, and to expel from society those who were incorrigibly harmful. If a man forged legal documents, so as to "pervert equities and justice," he was to "stand in the *Pillory* three several lecture days and render double damages to the party wronged." Anabaptists were liable to be "sentenced to Banishment." Burglars, for the first offense, were to be "branded on the forehead with the letter (B)," for the second offense, whipped, for the third, "put to death, as being incorrigible." A burglar who committed his crime on the "Lords day" lost an ear as additional penalty. If he did it again, he lost his other ear. The crime of "fornication with any single woman" was punishable by fine, by corporal punishment, or "by enjoyning to marriage." "In-humane, barbarous or cruel" punishments were forbidden; and though the *Body of Liberties* (1641) and later codes had accepted torture as a legitimate device, its use was, on paper at least, severely limited:

64 Arthur P. Scott, *Criminal Law in Colonial Virginia* (1930), p. 136.

No man shall be forced by Torture to confesse any Crime against himselfe nor any other unlesse it be in some Capitall case where he is first fullie convicted by cleare and suffitient evidence to be guilty. After which if the cause be of that nature, That it is very apparent there be other conspiratours, or confederates with him, Then he may be tortured, yet not with such Tortures as be Barbarous and inhumane.[65]

Particularly interesting was a small subcode of "Capital Lawes," imbedded in the early Massachusetts lawbooks, and later copied by other New England and Middle Atlantic colonies. Those scholars who felt the basic stuff of Bay law to be Bible law, not common law, have used this subcode as prime evidence. The capital laws did have a strong Mosaic flavor; in print, the laws were buttressed with Biblical citations: "If any man or woman be a WITCH, that is, hath or consulteth with a familiar spirit, they shall be put to death. *Exod.* 22.18 *Levit.* 20.27 *Deut.* 18.10.11." But not all Biblical crimes were Massachusetts crimes, or vice versa. The Puritan mind filtered out of the Bible what was usable and appropriate for his wishes and his days. For many of these crimes, English law could have been cited as easily as Exodus. And the capital laws were only part of the criminal law, and an even smaller part of the whole of the law.

Neither in theory nor in practice was colonial law a bloodthirsty law. There were fewer capital crimes on the books than in England. In England, death was a possible punishment for any thief; in early Massachusetts, only for a repeated thief. The Quaker laws of West New Jersey substituted restitution of property or hard labor for hanging. The death penalty was not frequently carried out in the colonies. The colonies generally recognized the English doctrine of benefit of clergy, which released a condemned man from the death penalty if he could read (or at least memorize) one verse of the Bible. Edward Reddish of Virginia, convicted of manslaughter in 1671, "did read and by the Governor's clemency and mercy was acquitted from burning." [66] The doctrine, as its name suggests, had originally been a privilege of the clergy. Later laws extended it to anyone who could read. The ability to read was liberally construed; and finally abolished. In 1732, Virginia passed

[65] *Colonial Laws of Massachusetts 1660–1672* (1889), pp. 43, 187. *General Laws and Liberties of Massachusetts, 1672,* p. 129.

[66] George W. Dalzell, *Benefit of Clergy in America and Related Matters* (1955), p. 98.

an "Act for settling some doubts and differences of opinion in relation to the benefit of Clergy; for allowing the same to Women; and
taking away of Reading." This law abolished the reading test; and
thereafter, even illiterates (and women) could claim benefit of
clergy, in an appropriate case.[67] As an alternate punishment, those
who invoked the benefit of clergy were often branded on the
thumb. Sometimes, however, the colonies reimposed the death
penalty for crimes that seemed particularly heinous. In Maryland,
where tobacco was king, a statute of 1737 decreed "Death as a
Felon . . . without Benefit of Clergy" for anyone who broke into
and robbed a tobacco house.

Famous periods of hysteria, such as the notorious Salem episode,
beginning in 1692, have unduly blackened the colonial reputation.
In this "terrible assize" nineteen persons were put to death; fifty or
so were tortured or terrified into confessions. On September 22,
1692, eight persons were led to the gallows. Bloodletting also followed slave or servant riots and insurrections. County courts in
18th-century Virginia sometimes used castration as a punishment
for slaves convicted of rape.[68] In Massachusetts, the death penalty
was imposed on those who particularly outraged the morals of society. In 1673, Benjamin Goad, "being instigated by the Divill,"
committed the "unnatural & horrid act of Bestiallitie on a mare in
the highway or field," in the "Afternoone the sun being two
howers high." He was sentenced by the Court of Assistants to hang
until dead; it was ordered, too, "that the mare you abused before
your execution in your sight shall be knockt on the head." [69] The
colonial laws punishing gaming, idleness, drunkenness, lying, and
disobedient children are famous. A New Hampshire law of 1693—
of a common type—punished those who "on the Lords day" were
found to "doe any unnecessary Servall Labour, Travell, Sports," or
to frequent taverns, or "Idly Stragle abroad." [70] In colonial times,
these laws of morality were taken quite seriously. They were by no
means empty words. The laws of morality were by no means dead
letters; quite the opposite. Regulations of conduct and sexual moral-

[67] Dalzell, op. cit., pp. 103–4.

[68] Hugh F. Rankin, Criminal Trial Proceedings in the General Court of
Colonial Virginia (1965), p. 221.

[69] Records of the Court of Assistants of the Colony of the Massachusetts Bay
1630–1692, Vol. 1 (1901), pp. 10–11. Punishing or forfeiting the thing or animal
that had done wrong was an old English institution, called deodand. In Maryland in 1637, a tree that caused the death of one John Bryant was "forfeited
to the Lord Proprietor," Archives of Maryland, Vol. 4 (1887), p. 10.

[70] Laws of New Hampshire, Province Period 1679–1702 (1904), p. 564.

ity, by the evidence of county court records, fell most heavily on the lower social orders—on servants, on the poor, and on slaves. Early colonial law was strongly paternal. Trials were, in Garfinkel's striking phrase, status degradation ceremonies.[71] Punishment was frequently open and corporal; its goal was to reteach and retouch the erring soul, and it used, as means to this end, confession, public humiliation, and infamy. A Pennsylvania law of 1700 (disallowed by the British five years later), aimed at persons "clamorous with their tongues," gave the magistrate discretion to sentence the offender to be "gagged and stand in some public place." [72] The stocks and pillory were in common use. Crime and punishment meant shame, and beyond that, reform. The codes and their enforcers basically never abandoned this aim.

Fornication and drunkenness were the most commonly punished crimes in 17th-century Massachusetts.[73] The situation continued in Massachusetts right up to the Revolution. William E. Nelson has analyzed all the prosecutions in seven Massachusetts counties between 1760 and 1774. There were 2,784 in all; 1,074 of these—38 per cent—were for sexual offenses. Almost all of these were for fornication; almost all fornication actions were directed against mothers of illegitimate children; and often (but not always) there was an economic point to the proceedings, the burden of the bastard on the tax rolls. Thirteen per cent of the cases, 359 in all, were for religious offenses: blasphemy, profanity, nonattendance at church. Even at this late period, Nelson feels, "all crime was looked upon as synonymous with sin, . . . The typical criminal was not . . . an outcast from society, but only an ordinary member who had sinned." [74]

Servant codes and slave law were aimed at sin, too; but these also had the job of keeping social lines distinct, maintaining order in the lower ranks. If an indentured servant refused to serve his term, he was punished with extra years of service. This, too, was the usual fate of servant girls who gave birth to bastards. Fines were useless against the poor; and imprisonment would have punished the master as well as the servant. Extra service was the most effective sanction; it was freely used. In a typical example, in Kent

[71] Harold Garfinkel, "Conditions of Successful Degradation Ceremonies," 61 Am. J. Sociol. 420 (1956).

[72] *Statutes at Large of Pennsylvania, 1682–1801*, Vol. II (1896), p. 85.

[73] Edwin Powers, *Crime and Punishment in Early Massachusetts, 1620–1692, A Documentary History* (1966), pp. 404–7.

[74] Nelson, *op. cit.*, pp. 126–7.

County, Delaware, in 1704, John Mahon brought a mulatto servant, Charles, to court. Charles had been a runaway for twenty-six
days; it had cost his master three pounds, three shillings, and sixpence to bring him back. The court ordered the boy to serve "for
his Runaway time . . . One Hundred and thirty days and for the
said sume of three Pounds three Shillings and Six pence soe Expended . . . he shall Serve the said John Mahon or his Assigns the
time and terme of six Monts," all after his regular term of service
would have expired.[75]

To label behavior as criminal means, among other things, that
government will punish that behavior at its own initiative and expense. A crime is a wrong whose remedy falls to the cost of the
state. Criminal law, then, in any period, expresses more than current standards of morality. It is a vehicle for economic and social
planning, and an index to the community's division of power. Economic crimes are as much part of the criminal law as the classic
crimes of murder, rape, theft, and other crimes against morality. Of
course, the line between economic control and control of morality
and status is artificial; the laws governing servants and slaves had
both objectives. Many peculiarities of the criminal codes related
directly to the organization of economic life. In Virginia, hogs were
more vital than sheep; the stealing of hogs, then, was a more serious crime than the stealing of sheep.[76] In 1715, New York made it
unlawful "from & after the first day of May, until the first day of
September Annually to gather, Rake, take up, or bring to the
Market, any Oysters whatsoever, under the penalty of Twenty
shillings for every Offence"; or for "any Negro, Indian, or Maletto
[sic] Slave to Sell any Oysters in the City of New York at any time
whatsoever." [77] Criminal laws were a natural way of expressing economic policies, in societies with a sense of strong government and
with few special agencies of economic control. In Puritan New
England, civil obedience and respect for authority were the essence
of the social order; proprietary and crown colonies had a somewhat
different definition of authority, but the same sense of command.

It follows, then, that though the criminal codes were suffused
with notions of sin, there was a heavy dose of politics and economic
policy in them as well. Hence civil disobedience was not always
deviance or sin. Often, in colonial history, part of the population

---

[75] Leon de Valinger, Jr., ed., *Court Records of Kent County, Delaware, 1680–
1705* (1959), pp. 283–84.
[76] Arthur P. Scott, *Criminal Law in Colonial Virginia* (1930), pp. 225–27.
[77] *Colonial Laws of New York*, Vol. 1 (1894), p. 845 (Law of May 19, 1715).

opposed this or that part of the criminal code as tyrannical. What was tyrannical was not so much in the form of regulation as in the substance; or, at times, in the allocation of power—not how but who governed. The most obvious examples were laws against smuggling, violations of the Stamp Act, and the Acts of Trade, in the middle of the 18th century. The war of 1776 was a war of independence. But independence did not mean only the right to be free of the *general* controls of the law; it meant also a freedom from controls that were in the wrong hands.

GOVERNMENT, LAW AND THE ECONOMY

Colonial regulation of business was primitive by modern standards. It was fairly pervasive, however. Government regulated those businesses which were what would now be called public utilities and common carriers. The colonial world depended on roads, ferries, bridges and gristmills for transport, communication, and the basic food supply. These enterprises were therefore the public's concern, though private enterprise built and ran them. In a typical grant, East Haven, Connecticut, gave to a certain Heminway in 1681 an old dam, some land, timber, and stone, and exempted him from tax; in exchange, Heminway agreed to erect and maintain a gristmill to attend to the mill one day a fortnight, to grind all the corn brought that day, and to limit his toll to the legal rate.[78] Most colonies regulated the miller's rate of toll throughout the colonial period. In New Hampshire, for example, an act of 1718 set up "the Toll for grinding all Sorts of Grain" at "one Sixteenth part, and no more," except for "Indian Corn, for which the Mill shall take One Twelfth." [79] Government also regulated markets, road building, and the quality of essential commodities. As in England, the inns and taverns along the roads were controlled by colonial authorities.

Inevitably there were taxes to be raised. Money was scarce in the colonies. A labor tax was commonly used for building roads. Every adult man was liable to pay the tax in money, produce, or sweat, whichever he could best afford. So, a New York law of 1713, "for Mending and keeping in Repair the Post-Road from New York to Kings-Bridge," after deploring the "ruinous" and "very danger-

[78] Henry Farnam, *Chapters in the History of Social Legislation in the United States to 1860* (1938), p. 96.

[79] *Laws of New Hampshire, Province Period 1702–1745,* Vol. 2 (1913), p. 265.

ous" condition of the road, and providing for the appointment of surveyors, to chart out the necessary repairs, directed the inhabitants of the affected wards to "meet and convene with Carts and Carriages, Shovels, Spades, Pick-axes, Mattocks, and other Tools" to do the work, either themselves or by "a sufficient working hand."[80]

A century before Adam Smith, the proprietors, squires, and magistrates of America certainly did not believe that that government was best that governed least. But the desire to rule, and rule broadly, was tempered by the modest means, in taxes and men, that rulers had at their command. Regulation tended to be local, and as cheap in money and men as possible. When a government wished, therefore, to control the output of bread, it made bakers brand their bread. Under a Pennsylvania law of 1700, every baker had to have "a distinct mark to be set on all the bread he shall bake"; the better to facilitate control over size, taste, and price.[81] For many commodities, the laws provided for "viewers," "searchers," and "inspectors." These men were generally paid through users' fees, not out of tax funds. Fees supported public officials in general. Other social ends were to be achieved by forcing private persons to do public work. To light its dark streets, the town fathers of New York ordered private householders to hang lights on a pole, from the upper windows of houses, "in the Darke time of the moon." Philadelphia ordered citizens in 1700 to plant shade trees in front of their doors, "pines, unbearing mulberries, water poplars, lime or other shady and wholesome trees," so that the town might be "well shaded from the violence of the sun in the heat of the summer and thereby be rendered more healthy."[82]

From England, the colonies copied laws about public markets. These laws told where and when important products could be sold. A scattered market is difficult to administer. When all sellers of wood, or hay, or grain meet at one place and time, regulation can be cheap and effective. As in England, too, local—county and city —courts held much of the power to run the economy. This worked well enough, except for those important commercial laws which were imposed by distant England. The legal structure meant that local gentry, and local magistrates, could make or break im-

80 Colonial Laws of New York, Vol. 1 (1894), pp. 792–95 (Act of Oct. 23, 1713). The Act provided that "no person shall be compellable to work above Eight Days in the year, nor at any time in seed-time, Hay or Corn-Harvest."
81 Statutes at Large, Pennsylvania, Vol. II (1896), p. 61 (Act of Nov. 27, 1700).
82 Carl Bridenbaugh, Cities in the Wilderness (1968), p. 169.

perial rule. Local rule is efficient, from the standpoint of the center, only if local people can be trusted. American squires and American merchants had fallen out with their English overlords long before 1776—over the Stamp Act, the Acts of Trade, and other aspects of British rule.[83]

Colonial government made a constant effort, not always effective, to keep its staple crops under some kind of quality control. In Virginia and Maryland, tobacco was the major crop. A long series of laws governed the growth and sale of this commodity.[84] Very early, Virginia tried to reduce the dependence of the colony on a single cash-crop, and to improve quality and price of tobacco. In 1619, the Virginia House of Burgesses set up a system of tobacco inspection. Any tobacco which might "not proove vendible" was liable to be burned. In 1621, settlers were restricted to one hundred plants per person, and nine leaves to a stalk; the purpose of this act was to draw people away "from excessive plantinge of Tobacco." Maryland enacted its first inspection law in 1640. In 1657, second crops were outlawed, to prevent a glut on the market; and to cut down the flow of substandard tobacco, which depressed prices and ruined the reputation of Maryland tobacco.

Many New Deal and post-New Deal farm schemes were foreshadowed in old Maryland and Virginia: quality control, inspection laws, regulation of the size of containers, subsidies for planting preferred kinds of crop, public warehousing, export controls. In the 1660's, the tobacco colonies felt they were faced with a radical oversupply. Maryland in 1666 ordered a complete stop to tobacco cultivation, between February 1667 and 1668, if Virginia and Carolina followed suit (they did). (Lord Baltimore voided this act, which he felt was harmful to Great Britain.) Tobacco regulation was, if anything, more pervasive in the 18th century. Maryland, in 1747, enacted its most comprehensive statute, modeled on an equally elaborate Virginia law of 1730. The law required all tobacco to be brought to public warehouses and forbade the export of bulk tobacco. Inspectors at each warehouse would inspect, weigh, and repack the tobacco, branding each cask with the name of the warehouse, the tare, and the net amount of leaf. There were to be some eighty warehouses in all. Unacceptable tobacco was to be burned or repacked by the owners. Inspectors were to give out

---

[83] See, for example, on the Stamp Act resistance, Edmund S. Morgan and Helen M. Morgan, *The Stamp Act Crisis* (1953).

[84] See, in general, Vertrees J. Wyckoff, *Tobacco Regulation in Colonial Maryland* (1936).

tobacco notes, transferrable and redeemable, for all tobacco brought to the warehouse for payment of debts. These notes were legal tender—a kind of money. A later form of the act, passed in 1773, was in force when the Revolution came.

Virginia and Maryland were not the only colonies that regulated their staple crop. Connecticut grew tobacco too, and passed an inspection law in 1753. A Pennsylvania law of 1724 forbade the export of any flour not submitted to an inspecting officer, "who shall search and try the same in order to judge of its goodness." Merchantable export flour had to be branded with the "provincial brand-mark, . . . sufficient and capable to impress in a fair and distinguishable manner the arms of the province of Pennsylvania with the letter P on each side"; for his trouble, the officer was to have from the shipper "one penny per cask and no more." [85] Flour for domestic consumption was also to be inspected and branded, though with less stringent controls. A statute of the same session continued in effect a bounty of a penny a pound for hemp "to the end that the people of this province may be further encouraged in the raising of good and merchantable hemp." Georgia began colonial life as a planned economy, with public sawmills, farms, and herds of livestock. Even after Georgia became a crown colony (1752), lumber inspection laws were passed (1760), followed by laws setting up grades and specifications for beef, pork, pitch, tar, and turpentine. Later, special legislation dealt with leather and tobacco.[86] Massachusetts Bay had had a leather statute more than a century earlier. Under the *Laws and Liberties* of 1648, the towns were empowered to "choose one or two persons of the most honest and skilfull" to act as "Searchers" of leather. Searchers had power to seize all leather made contrary to the dictates of the law, which limited the tanning trade, and gave directions for the proper manufacture of leather:

> Nor shall any person or persons using or occupying the mysterie of tanning, set any their Fats [vats] in tan-hills or other places, where the woozes or leather put to tan in the same shall or may take any unkinde heats; nor shall put any leather into any hot or warm woozes whatsoever on pain of twenty pounds for everie such offence.[87]

85 Act of Mar. 20, 1724/5, *Statutes at Large, Pennsylvania, 1682–1801*, Vol. IV (1897), p. 5.

86 Milton S. Heath, *Constructive Liberalism* (1954), pp. 55–56.

87 *Laws and Liberties of Massachusetts, 1648* (1929 ed.), p. 33. "Wooze" is a variant of "ooze," and refers to the liquid in the tanning vats.

COMMERCE AND LABOR

When the colonies were first settled, the *law merchant*—the rules and practices of commercial law—had not been fully "received" into common law, that is, by the royal courts of England. Throughout the colonial period, merchants on both sides of the Atlantic followed much the same customs and practices. This was only natural. The law merchant was, in theory, international. More to the point, colonial merchants did business with English merchants; their ties with each other became even tighter in the 18th century. Negotiable instruments were known and used in all the colonies. In the 18th century, many colonies experimented with paper currency. In some, chattel notes were common; tobacco notes were ubiquitous in Maryland and Virginia.

An important point of mercantile custom was that commercial paper must be able to circulate freely, from hand to hand, and that a holder in due course—one who came into possession in the ordinary way—should have full rights to use, sue, and collect on the note or the bill. The common law, however, was quite stiff about honoring the rights of a person to whom intangibles had been transferred. Colonial law ran far ahead of English law. As early as 1647, Massachusetts provided by statute that "any debt, or debts due upon bill, or other specialtie assigned to another; shall be as good a debt & estate to the Assignee as it was to the Assigner at the time of its assignation . . . provided the said assignment be made upon the backside of the bill or specialtie." This statute appeared also in Connecticut (1650), Pennsylvania (1676), New York (1684); and also in Delaware, New Jersey, and the colonies to the South.[88] The colonies depended upon ocean commerce. They were free from—indeed, often ignorant of—the rigid institutions and doctrines that held back the union of common law and commerce law in England. Hard currency was in short supply in America. This meant that merchants were even more dependent on commercial paper to carry on trade. In the 18th century, commercial law, like other branches of law, crept closer to English standards. But the native variety was more functional than the law of the mother country, and survived the period of imitation.

Labor was as essential and problematic a factor of production as

[88] Frederick Beutel, "Colonial Sources of the Negotiable Instruments Law of the United States," 34 Ill. L. Rev. 137, 141–42 (1939).

money. The American colonies drew up major codes of labor law, and carefully and continuously elaborated upon them. These codes were not totally indigenous; they owed a good deal to mercantilist theory, and to Elizabethan labor policy and practices. But, in general, colonial labor law had rather fewer points of contact with English law than most other fields of law. Its special character unfolded in response to specific colonial needs and conditions. England had no law of slavery; its law of apprenticeship was the nearest thing to the law of indentured service. The colonies, by grim necessity, had to attract and hold a population, organize a work force, and keep it in place. The choices made were of course not predetermined. Mistakes were made that left permanent scars on the country. On the one hand, the law of indentured servitude, for all its abuses and inequities, held open to some servants the road to freedom and a decent living. It evolved quietly and with a minimum of friction into a system of free labor.[89] But the other new branch of labor law, the law of slavery, led downward into lasting trouble.

In the early days of colonial life, it was a common rule, both North and South, that every able-bodied man had a duty to work. Idleness was a punishable offense. No person, said the *Laws and Liberties of Massachusetts* (1648) shall "spend his time idlely or unprofittably under pain of such punishment as the Court of Assistants or County Court shall think meet to inflict." This principle was never formally abandoned. But in time, it became a matter of caste and class. The magistrates of early New England had to work hard with their hands, just as servants did. In the 18th century a leisure class formed out of the rich merchants and planters and their families. Only the poor were impressed into work gangs; only the poor paid their road taxes in sweat.

Early colonies also tried to control the cost of labor. Scarcity pushed up the workingman's price. John Winthrop reported that, in Massachusetts in 1633, "the scarcity of workmen had caused them to raise their wages to an excessive rate, so as a carpenter would have three shillings the day, a laborer two shillings and sixpence." As a result, commodity prices were "sometimes double to that they cost in England." The general court took action; they "made an order, that carpenters, masons, etc. should take but two shillings the day, and laborers but eighteen pence, and that no

89 On indentured servitude and labor conditions in general, see Richard B. Morris, *Government and Labor in Early America* (1946), which has been extensively followed in the text.

commodity should be sold at above four pence in the shilling more than it cost for ready money in England." Oil, wine, and cheese were excepted, "in regard of the hazard of bringing." [90] Massachusetts Bay later provided that "the freemen of every Town may from time to time as occasion shall require, agree amongst themselves about the prizes and rates of all workmens Labour and servants wages." [91] Particularly vital occupations, like draymen and ferrymen, were the most prone to be regulated. Price regulation, in turn, fell on suppliers of vital commodities, such as bakers. Wage-price regulation was virtually abandoned by 1700. It was briefly and ineffectively revived during the Revolutionary War, strictly as an emergency measure. Scarcity of labor probably frustrated most attempts to regulate wages and prices.

The colonies were anxious to attract skilled workmen. South Carolina, in 1741, prohibited artisans from keeping taverns, a less essential occupation. Skilled laborers tried, in some instances, to control entry into their trades and keep their prices up. These attempts were no more successful than wage controls. New York and other colonial cities at one time restricted crafts to men who enjoyed the "freedom" of the city. But by the middle of the 18th century this system too was dead; the "freedom of the city" was available to anyone, practically for the asking.

Up and down the coast, indentured servants acted as farm and household workers, hewers of wood, drawers of water—the laboring hands and feet of the colonies. Indentured servants were in essence temporary slaves, the personal property of their masters. The "indentures" were the written documents, somewhat similar to English articles of apprenticeship, under which so many of them served. In the early 17th century, many servants, with or without indentures, were Indians or blacks. Many white immigrants (probably more than one-half) either arrived as "redemptioners" or became redemptioners on arrival. This meant that they sold their labor, for a definite period of time, to pay for the price of passage. Some signed indentures in England, before sailing. They signed themselves over to the master of the ship; when ship and passenger landed, a New World broker would sell the indenture in the market, to raise the price of passage. Indentured servitude usually lasted from four to seven years. Those who came without indenture and without money to pay the captain had to serve "according to the custom of the country." "Custom" depended on the age and

[90] John Winthrop, *History of New England* (1908) Vol. 1, p. 116.
[91] *Colonial Laws of Massachusetts, 1660–1672,* Vol. 1 (1889), p. 174.

condition of the servant. Frequently, young immigrants and orphans were brought into court for a decision (or guess) about their age. Court records are full of these proceedings. In Kent County, Delaware, in 1699,

> Mr. John Walker brought into Court a Servant boy named Richard Cundon, to be Judged, he cominge in without Indentures, which being Considered, The Court doe deeme him the said Richard Cundon to be about Twelve years of age, and doe order that he shall serve the said John Walker or his Assignes, Untill he shall arrive to one and twenty years of age, and that at the Expiration thereof, the said John Walker or his assignes shall pay him his Corne, Cloaths and Tolls, accordinge to Law.[92]

At the end of his term, the servant went free, and in addition, recovered by right certain "freedom dues." In early Maryland, servants, whether indentured or not, had the right upon severance to an outfit of clothes, a hat, ax, hoe, three barrels of corn, and (until 1663) fifty acres of land.[93] In later times, clothing, food, and a sum of money were more typical dues (the "Corne, Cloaths and Tolls" of the example).

By no means all indentured servants were "free-willers." England dumped a certain number of convicts onto the colonies as indentured servants, to the distaste of the residents, who attempted (futilely) to legislate against "jail birds." Some unfortunates were kidnapped in England and sold into servitude. Others were cast into servitude as a punishment for crime. But most of those punished by a term of labor were already servants; they had no goods or lands to satisfy debts or pay fines. They paid, then, in additional servitude.

Even more than England, colonial society used indentures of apprenticeship to handle the poor orphan and the abandoned child. This social problem was thus shifted to private masters. The master gained an extra hand; in exchange, he was supposed to teach his charge to read and write, and to earn his living at a useful trade. The indenture system thus fulfilled a great many functions. It was a method of organizing labor, of financing immigration, a penal sanction, a way of training the young, a kind of welfare institution, and a crude instrument of credit. Court records show surprising uses of this protean device. In 1703, in Delaware, a "poor Aged

[92] Leon de Valinger, Jr., ed., *Court Records of Kent County, Delaware 1680–1705* (1959), p. 152.
[93] *Archives of Maryland,* Vol. 53 (1936), xxxii.

lame Man," Leviticus John Wassell, "did bind himselfe a Servant to One Edward Starkie . . . for the time and terme of foure years In Consideration that the said Starkies Wife Would cure the said Leviticus John Wassell his sore leg." And Joseph Groves "bound himselfe to serve Thomas Bedwell" for two years "In consideration Whereof the said Thomas Bedwell being here present in Court did Promise to learn the said Joseph to write and Cypher soe far as the said Joseph should be capable of receaving during the said time." [94]

Some men of wealth or position began their careers as servants or apprentices. Roger Sherman, for example, was apprenticed as a boy to a shoemaker. Daniel Dulany came to Maryland in 1703 as an indentured servant; he had the good fortune to be sold to Colonel George Plater, who needed a clerk in his law office. Ten years later, Dulany was a lawyer and a landowner.[95] These success stories were not rare; but neither were they typical. More commonly, former servants continued to work at their trades, only now as free men. So, Abraham Daphne, a carpenter, advertised in 1753 that he was "now acquitted and discharged" from servitude, and ready "to undertake any work in his business." [96] Many more no doubt never made it far up the ladder. Many Englishmen and Germans, enticed into servitude by glittering propaganda, found they had chosen a life of hardship and tyranny. The servant, by law, had the right of redress against a cruel or incompetent master. Court records are full of complaints by servants, about beatings, bad food, nakedness, cold, and general misery. No doubt the vast majority of ill-used servants were too ignorant or frightened ever to go to court. Thousands of servants ran away. And servants were subject to many legal disabilities. They could not marry without their master's consent. They could not vote or engage in trade. Masters could buy and sell their labor. They were, in short, temporary slaves.[97]

Indentured servants were a vital part of the labor system in the North, in Southern towns, and in frontier regions. But in the tobacco, rice, and sugar colonies, black slavery more and more replaced white servitude. The first blacks were servants, not slaves; their status was hardly different from that of white servants or In-

[94] Leon de Valinger, Jr., ed., *Court Records of Kent County, Delaware 1680–1705* (1959), pp. 274–76.

[95] Louis B. Wright, *The Cultural Life of the American Colonies 1607–1763* (1957), p. 14.

[96] Warren B. Smith, *White Servitude in Colonial South Carolina* (1961), p. 88.

[97] See, in general, Abbott E. Smith, *Colonists in Bondage, White Servitude and Convict Labor in America 1607–1776* (1947).

dian captives. But the Negro was pagan, and a different race. A special sentiment gradually crystallized about the status of the growing numbers of blacks. The American style of black-white relations, a peculiar mixture of bigotry, dread, sexual envy, and economic oppression, can be traced far back into the colonial past. The exact origins of the *legal* meaning of slavery are obscure, though, clearly, developing custom guided the lawmaker's hand. Before the end of the 17th century, slavery had become a definite legal status in both North and South; it was peculiarly associated with the Negro; it had become a terrible, timeless condition, inherited by children from their mothers. The legal status of the slave, as it took shape in the statute books, reflected and ratified social discrimination and the sense of race.[98] In Virginia, insofar as these developments can be dated, evidence points to the period between 1660 and 1680 as the period in which the status was formalized. In 1662, it became law in Virginia that children of slave mothers would themselves be slaves, regardless of the status of the father.[99] Originally, only pagans could be lawfully enslaved; but as early as a Maryland law of 1671, baptism no longer brought escape from slavery.[100] From that time on, converted slaves had to wait for their freedom in another world.

Once the fundamental lines of the law had been set, the colonies, particularly in the South, carried the logic of slavery to grim limits. The slave was property, a capital asset of his master. He passed by will, was bought and sold, stood attachable for debts, and was the subject of taxation. Virginia, in 1705, in fact declared him to be real estate, the same as houses, trees, or land. This law was meant to insure that uniform rules of inheritance, and liability for debt, would govern the law of an estate—the land and its slaves. Slaves themselves had few legal rights. Slaves could not testify in court against white men. They could not vote, own property, or marry. The master was bound by law to treat the slave with a certain minimal fairness, to feed him and clothe him, and to punish him no more severely than the situation demanded. These rights were occasionally enforced in court. But no one believes that these legal restraints had much effect on the way that masters behaved. Considerations of dollars and cents probably prevented

[98] Carl N. Degler, *Out of Our Past, The Forces that Shaped Modern America* (1959), p. 30; Winthrop D. Jordan, *White Over Black, American Attitudes Toward the Negro, 1550–1812* (1968), pp. 91–98.

[99] John H. Russell, *The Free Negro in Virginia, 1619–1865* (1913), p. 37.

[100] James M. Wright, *The Free Negro in Maryland, 1634–1860* (1921), p. 22.

more gross cruelty than fear of the law. Slaves were valuable assets; the rational owner would want to keep his property alive and in good health. But the system could not guarantee against mistakes and irrationality, and it took no account of the feelings, hopes, desires and humanity of slaves.

Slaveholders, North and South, had many fantasies about black men—about their intelligence, strength, and sensibilities. They were capable of believing, and saying, that the slave was best off as a slave. Yet white men never quite convinced themselves that slaves were happy with their lot. On the contrary, the white man had an almost paranoid fear of slave revolt. There was some concrete evidence of unrest, and a number of actual disturbances—all futile, all put down with barbarous severity.[101] Even so, fear of uprising verged at times on hysteria. The slave codes grew steadily more repressive. In North Carolina, for example, the Fundamental Constitutions codified the custom that slaveowners had "absolute power and authority over negro slaves." [102] A statutory revision of 1715 restricted trading with slaves, and outlawed intermarriage of blacks and whites. Any master who permitted blacks to build a "house under pretence of a meeting house upon account of worship" was liable to fine, presumably because of the risk of paganism and conspiracy. Emancipated slaves had to leave the colony within six months. Those who did not were liable to be sold into temporary slavery, to a person who would undertake to remove them from the state. An act of 1729 prohibited slaves from hunting with dog or gun on any but his master's land. In 1741, even the right to carry a gun and hunt on the master's land was limited to slaves who carried a certificate, signed by the master and countersigned by the chairman of the county court. Emancipation was restricted to slaves who had performed "meritorious services," as certified by the local courts. In 1753, courts were authorized to divide their counties into districts, and appoint "viewers" to search slave quarters and seize any weapons found. A ghastly fog of fear hovered about the plantation world.

The master himself was law, judge, and jury over most aspects of slave life: this was inherent in the system. But in North Carolina, at least as early as 1715, there were special courts for slaves who disobeyed the law. Whipping was the common mode of punishment. Serious crimes called for the death penalty; but a dead slave

101Edward Franklin Frazier, *The Negro in the United States* (1957), pp. 86–87.
102 For the following discussion, see John Spencer Bassett, *Slavery and Servitude in the Colony of North Carolina* (1896).

injured his owner's pocketbook; hence owners were repaid out of public funds. Castration was an alternative punishment for serious crimes. Happily, this punishment was eliminated in 1764. But in 1773 a Negro was burned alive for murdering a white man.

Few of the North Carolina provisions were original or unique. They were typical at least of the American South. Other colonies added or subtracted a detail here or there. A Georgia statute of 1770, fearful that Negroes might wish to "plot and confederate together," forbade slaves to "buy, sell, trade, traffic, deal, or barter for any goods or commodities," except under special circumstances. Slaves could not own or keep "any boat, perriagua, or canoe"; or breed cattle. To avoid "ill consequences," groups of seven or more slaves were forbidden to go on the highway, unless accompanied by a white man; violators were liable to be whipped. Since "inconveniences" might arise from book learning, anyone who taught a slave to read or write might be fined. Under a Virginia act of 1748, slaves who, "under pretense of practising physic, have prepared and exhibited poisonous medicines" were to suffer "death without benefit of clergy."

New England slave codes were milder than those of the South. Massachusetts alone had a statute against intermarriage; and Northern blacks were allowed to testify in court. But where blacks lived in sizable numbers (in Rhode Island, for example), or during times of panic over possible black unrest, Northern communities might react with great severity. Boston in 1723, in fear of black arson, enacted emergency regulations to punish all Negroes caught near a fire. A 1718 ordinance of South Kingston, Rhode Island, provided that, if a slave was found in the house of a free Negro, both slave and host would be whipped. In the 1750's no black in South Kingston might own a pig or a cow, or livestock of any kind. No cider could be sold to a slave. Indians and blacks could not hold outdoor gatherings. In New York, after 1705, a slave found traveling alone forty miles from Albany could, on conviction, be put to death.[103]

There were many free Negroes in the colonies in the 18th century. Some were emancipated slaves, some the descendants of the early class of free blacks. As the racist element in the slave codes increased, the legal position of the free Negro deteriorated. The great fear that blacks as a group might conspire against whites cost the free Negroes dearly. Free Negroes were discriminated against

[103] Lorenzo J. Greene, *The Negro in Colonial New England, 1620–1776* (1942), pp. 142, 161.

by law, and hounded from colony to colony. Law and society debased this class and used their low status as an excuse for further debasement. By 1776, the free Negro was a kind of half slave in many parts of the country.

THE POOR LAWS

In 1647, a Rhode Island statute enjoined the towns to "provide carefully for the reliefe of the poore, to maintayne the impotent . . . and [to] appoint an overseer for the same purpose. See 43 Eliz. c. 2." [104] The reference was to the Elizabethan poor laws, passed in the 43rd year of the reign of Queen Elizabeth I (1601). These laws were part of the colonies' legal background. New England colonies copied this law, at least in its general features. Local rule was one of its main characteristics. Each town maintained its own poor—those who were "settled" in the town. The concept of settlement was tricky, however. It grew luxuriantly through litigation. Since towns were most eager to dodge the problems and costs of their paupers, the records are full of cases in which one town sued another town, to palm a pauper off. By the Plymouth laws of 1671, any person who had been "received and entertained" in a town for three months became the responsibility of that town, if he later turned pauper. But the town escaped its responsibility if the new settler was "warned by the Constable, or some one or more of the Select men of that Town, not there to abide without leave first obtained of the Town." [105] Out of this kind of law grew the custom of "warning out." Between 1737 and 1788, 6,764 persons were "warned out" in Worcester County alone.[106] "Warning out" was not a sentence of banishment, but a disclaimer of responsibility; some towns "warned out" practically every new arrival. "Warning out" threw the burden of support back upon the former place of settlement. It points up that the system discriminated against the deviant and the stranger. Whatever kindness warmed the heart of the poor laws was expended on old friends and neighbors in town, who happened to fall upon evil days. There the sympathy stopped.

The poor laws were only part of the welfare system of the colonies. Orphans became apprentices. Those adults who were poor

104 Quoted in Margaret Creech, *Three Centuries of Poor Law Administration* (1936), p. 8.
105 Josiah H. Benton, *Warning Out in New England* (1911), p. 54.
106 Benton, *loc. cit.*, p. 59.

but could work became servants; the indenture was their ticket to relief. The poor laws were used, then, for a helpless residue of society. For all others, poverty and want meant an adjustment of status, not a draft on the public purse.

STATUTE AND COMMON LAW IN THE COLONIAL PERIOD

Colonial law, to a striking extent, was codified law. Yet these were common-law jurisdictions, after all; and common law was essentially uncodified. There was certainly no English precedent for general codification. Why then were there American codes, beginning with the earliest days and the earliest colonies?

One answer is that codification is a natural growth in a colony. A new settlement cannot sit back and wait for evolution. England could make do with an unwritten constitution; the United States could not. Any fresh start requires codification. Such countries as Japan, when they wanted to adopt a "modern" legal system, have turned to the European codes. The common law seems too shapeless, too complex. There are too many books. The law is too unknowable. It can never be restated authoritatively. A code may be a behavioral mirage; it may not mean what it says; it may be "interpreted" totally out of shape. But at least it has an authoritative text. It can be copied in letter if nothing else. The first codes of the colonies were fresh-start codes. Later ones were borrowed from these earlier codes.

Each code had, of course, a unique history of its own. The first Massachusetts codes rose out of political struggle in the colony. The desire for a code was, among other things, a desire to limit autocracy. The power and discretion of the magistrates in Massachusetts Bay was at first virtually unlimited. Out of an urge by some to control this power came the *Body of Liberties,* drafted by Nathaniel Ward, and adopted by the Massachusetts General Court in 1641. In 1648, a far more important and comprehensive code was adopted, the *Laws and Liberties of Massachusetts.* This was not a code in the sense of a logical, systematic arrangement of the law. Rather, it was a collection of important legal rules, arranged alphabetically by subject. The code began with a noble paragraph: "no mans life shall be taken away," or his "honour or good name . . . stayned," or his person arrested, or his goods taken, except by the vertue or equity of some expresse law of the Country," or in "defect of a law in any particular case by the word of God." Then came a provision on "Abilitie" (persons over 21 may make out wills and dispose of property), then "Actions," "Age," and "Ana-Baptists," ending (except for some "Presidents and Forms of things frequently used") with "Wrecks of the Sea." The code covered the general framework of government and the court system, and also included many items of substance. Once these laws were printed, the colonists could proudly assert that their laws were "now to be seen by all men, to the end that none may plead ignorance, and that all who intend to transport themselves hither may know that this is no place of licentious liberty." [107] The code also, as Professor Haskins has said, reflected the "traditional Puritan belief in the importance of the written word," evidenced by "literal use of the Bible as authority and by Puritan demand for explicit church canons which would leave no doubt as to what the law was." [108] Knowable and precise law is law that a citizen can easily follow—law that the rulers too must follow, or be clearly seen in default.

Case law did not easily pass from colony to colony. There were no printed reports to make transfer easy, though some 18th-century case materials in manuscript circulated among lawyers. These could hardly have been very influential. No doubt custom and case law slowly seeped from colony to colony. Travelers and word of mouth spread knowledge of living law. The extent is difficult to measure; consequently, it is hard to tell to what precise degree there was a common legal culture.

The borrowing of statutes (sometimes whole codes at a time) was more obvious and striking. Like the codes of modern Europe, colonial codes were easily taken by one jurisdiction from another. Due in part to the codes, some colonies had great influence on the others, almost as great as the influence of England on any one of them. Since legal skill was a rare commodity, newer settlements found it convenient to borrow laws from older neighbors with similar outlooks, goals, experiences, and problems. Virginia, in the South, and Massachusetts Bay, in the North, were major exporters of laws. The Massachusetts example is the most striking. The *Laws and Liberties* of 1648 were widely emulated.[109] Of 78 provisions in

107 Edward Johnson, *Wonder-Working Providence* (Jameson, ed., 1910), p. 244.

108 George L. Haskins, "Codification of the Law in Colonial Massachusetts: A Study in Comparative Law," 30 Ind. L. J. 1, 7 (1954).

109 Stefan A. Riesenfeld, "Law-Making and Legislative Precedent in American Legal History," 33 Minnesota L. Rev. 103, 132 (1949).

Robert Ludlow's Connecticut code of 1650, 22 were copied, almost verbatim, from the Massachusetts code, 36 were adopted with certain deletions or amendments, 6 came from other Massachusetts sources; only 14 (chiefly on local matters) were "original." [110] The New Haven code of 1656 was also much indebted to Massachusetts. Before the code was drafted, the general court charged the governor to "send for one of the new booke of lawes in the Massachusetts colony, and to view over a small booke of lawes newly come from England, which is said to be Mr. Cottons, and to add to what is already done as he shall thinke fitt." [111] New Hampshire drew most of its code of 1680 (the so-called Cutt code) from laws of Massachusetts and Plymouth. The famous Duke's laws of 1664, which were in force in the areas of New York, Pennsylvania, and Delaware, were "Collected out of the Severall Laws now in force in his Majesties American Colonyes and Plantations." [112] Massachusetts Bay was the original source of many of these laws, although Virginia also made a contribution. Like the *Laws and Liberties,* the Duke of York's laws were arranged alphabetically by subject headings and contained organic law, matters of procedure, and matters of substance. The criminal code of East New Jersey (1668–1675) was influenced both by the Duke's laws and the laws of the Northern colonies.

By the 18th century, the period of wholesale borrowing of codes had largely ended. In developing bodies of statutory law, the colonies worked within three distinct traditions: their own, that of their neighbors, and that of the mother country. Incipient nationalism operated to sustain, deepen, and enhance the special local element in these laws; English rule and commercial dependence pulled the laws together toward their common legal source. Statutes of the 18th century were more skillfully drafted than their predecessors. The privy council, as we have seen, reviewed colonial statutes, and had a certain influence both on substance and style. New codes in New Jersey and Pennsylvania were closer to English models, and in other respects more original, than the Duke's laws. The influence of Massachusetts faded. Trott's laws, compiled by Nicholas Trott and formally adopted by South Carolina in 1712,

[110] George L. Haskins and Samuel E. Ewing, "The Spread of Massachusetts Law in the Seventeenth Century," 106 U. of Pennsylvania L. Rev. 413, 414–15, (1958).

[111] Quoted in Haskins and Ewing, *op. cit.,* p. 416. The Cotton code had never been adopted in the Bay colony.

[112] *Charter to William Penn and Laws of the Province of Pennsylvania* (1879), p. 3.

merely declared which English statutes were in force in the colony. Many of the laws of England, Trott conceded, were "altogether useless" in South Carolina, "by reason of the different way of agriculture and the differing productions of the earth of this Province from that of England"; others were "impracticable" because of differences in institutions.[113] That left about 150 statutes which were relevant; the code reprinted these and declared them to be law.

THE LEGAL PROFESSION

The first years of the colonial experience were not friendly years for lawyers. Few of the earliest settlers were lawyers. In some colonies, no lawyers were welcome. In Massachusetts Bay, the *Body of Liberties* (1641) prohibited pleading for hire. The "attorneys" of early Virginia records were not trained lawyers, but attorneys-in-fact, laymen helping their friends in court. In 1645, Virginia excluded lawyers from its courts; Connecticut also prohibited them. The Fundamental Constitutions of the Carolinas (1669) was equally hostile; the draftsmen felt it was "a base and vile thing to plead for money or reward." Apparently, no professional practiced law in South Carolina until Nicholas Trott arrived in 1699.[114] The Quaker colony at Burlington, West New Jersey, managed "till the end of the seventeenth century with but one local professional lawyer." [115] In Pennsylvania, it was said, "They have no lawyers. Everyone is to tell his own case, or some friend for him . . . 'Tis a happy country." [116]

There is evidence, then, to back Daniel Boorstin's comment that "ancient English prejudice against lawyers secured new strength in America . . . [D]istrust of lawyers became an institution." [117] Thomas Morton, who arrived in Plymouth about 1624 or 1625, has been called the first Massachusetts lawyer. He was jailed and expelled for scandalous behavior. Thomas Lechford, who had

---

113 *Statutes at Large of South Carolina,* Vol. II (1837), p. 401.

114 Anton-Hermann Chroust, *The Rise of the Legal Profession in America,* Vol. I (1965), p. 297.

115 H. Clay Reed and George J. Miller, eds., *The Burlington Court Book of West New Jersey* (1944), xlii.

116 Quoted in Francis R. Aumann, *The Changing American Legal System* (1940), p. 13.

117 Daniel J. Boorstin, *The Americans; The Colonial Experience* (1958), p. 197.

some legal training, arrived in Boston in 1638. He practiced law in the colony as a courtroom attorney and draftsman of documents. Lechford had unorthodox religious views, and his attempts to practice law won him no friends among the magistrates, nor did the fact that he meddled with a jury by "pleading with them out of Court." He was made quite uncomfortable in the colony, and eventually went back to England.[118]

Distrust of lawyers arose from various sources. The Puritan leaders of Massachusetts Bay wished to govern an ideal state. Revolutionary or Utopian regimes are generally hostile to lawyers, at least in their first generation. The lawyers of the old regime must be banished, since a new (and ideal) commonwealth needs to start with new law and new habits. Some colonists, who had been oppressed in England, carried with them a strong dislike for all servants of government. Merchants and planters wished to govern without intermediaries. The more theocratic colonies were committed to a social order closely directed from the top. The legal profession, with its special privileges and principles, its private, esoteric language, seemed nothing so much as an obstacle to efficient government. The Quakers of the Middle Atlantic were opposed to the adversary system in principle. They wanted harmony and peace. Their ideal was the "Common Peacemaker," and simple, nontechnical justice. They looked on lawyers as sharp, contentious—and unnecessary—people. For all these reasons, the lawyer was unloved in the 17th century.

In the 18th century, too, there was sentiment against lawyers. Now the lower classes came to identify lawyers with the upper class. The governors and the royal parties, on the other hand, were not sure of the loyalty of the lawyers; and sometimes were afraid of their influence and power. In 1765, Cadwallader Colden, lieutenant governor of New York, told the Board of Trade in England that the "Gentlemen of the Law" had grown overmighty. They ranked just below the large landowners, and just above the merchants, in society. Lawyers and judges, said Colden, had such power that "every Man is affraid of offending them"; their "domination" was "carried on by the same wicked artifices that the Domination of Priests formerly was in the times of ignorance." [119] Lay

---

118 In England, he published *Plaine Dealing, or Newes from New England,* and warned, "Take heede my brethren, despise not learning nor the worthy lawyers . . . lest you repent too late." (1867 ed., p. 68).

119 *Colden Letter Books 1765–1775,* Vol. II (Collections of the New York Historical Society, 1877), pp. 68, 70, 71.

judges, too, may have resented the lawyers' threats to their competence and prestige. And as law became more "rational" and "professional," it became more confusing and remote to merchants and businessmen.

How strong the resentment against lawyers was, how deep it went, is hard to say. The evidence is partly literary; pamphlets and speeches are notoriously unreliable as measures of actual feeling among a diverse population. Some hatred was surely there; there is hard evidence of riots and disorders against lawyers and judges. Lawyers, like shopkeepers, moneylenders, and lower bureaucrats, are social middlemen; they are lightning rods that draw rage during storms in the polity. In 18th-century New Jersey, the "table of the Assembly groaned beneath the weight of petitions . . . invoking vengeance on the heads of the attorneys." The regulators, in late colonial North Carolina, rose up to smash corrupt and incompetent government. Lawyers were in the camp of the enemy. They perverted justice; they were "cursed hungry Caterpillars," whose fees "will eat out the very Bowels of our Common-wealth." [120] In Monmouth and Essex counties (New Jersey), in 1769 and 1770, mobs rioted against the lawyers.[121]

If lawyers were an evil, they were, however, a necessary evil. Only in the very beginning could the colonies even try to make do without lawyers. Partly, this was because there were makeshift alternatives. Practical texts of English law, which circulated in the colonies, provided information for layman or lay judge, enough to run a local court, or to plead in it. In Maryland in 1663, a layman, Dr. Luke Barber, accused of slandering a woman by calling her a whore ("taken . . . with her coates up," and with a "rogue" with "his Breeches downe") argued his own case and cited, in his own behalf, a recent English lawbook "Shephard, and his authorities." [122] The same magistrates of Massachusetts Bay, who struggled to keep the lawyers out, made use of their own legal knowledge in drafting legislation and in governing. John Winthrop was one of these. Nathaniel Ward, who drafted the *Body of Liberties* (1641), had had some legal training in England. Richard Bellingham, former town recorder of Boston, England, was governor of the Bay colony

120 H. T. Lefler, ed., *North Carolina History as told by Contemporaries* (1956), p. 87.
121 Richard S. Field, *The Provincial Courts of New Jersey* (1849), pp. 164 ff.
122 *Archives of Maryland*, Vol. 49 (1932), p. 116. The reference is to William Sheppard, *The Faithful Councellor, or the Marrow of the Law in English*; a second edition was published in 1653.

in 1641; according to a contemporary, this "much honored" man did much to "further civill Government of this wandering people, he being learned in the Lawes of England, and experimentally fitted for the worke." [123]

But as soon as a settled society posed problems for which lawyers had an answer or at least a skill, the lawyers appeared in force, and flourished despite animosity. Courts were in session; merchants were drawn into litigation; land documents had to be written, and the more skill the better. So, men trained in law who came from England found a ready market for their services; so did laymen with a smattering of law; and the semiprofessionals who had experience for sale. In the late 17th century, justices of the peace, sheriffs, and clerks, acted as attorneys in New Jersey.[124] In the literature, there are constant complaints against unauthorized lawyers, pettifoggers, shysters, and low-lifes—unprincipled men stirring up unprincipled litigation. These complaints, like the outcry against ambulance chasers more than a century later, often had a curiously inconsistent quality. Lawyers were criticized both for incompetence and for wrongful competence. As for the unauthorized or underground bar, it has been common in many societies; it signifies that the need for legal services has outstripped the legitimate supply of lawyers. At any rate, a competent, professional bar, dominated by brilliant and successful lawyers—Daniel Dulany of Maryland, Benjamin Chew of Philadelphia, and many others—existed in all major communities by 1750 despite opposition and adversity.

There were no law schools in the colonies to train these men. Many lawyers, particularly in the South, where there were no colleges at all, went to England for their training, and attended the Inns of Court, in London. The Inns were not law schools as such; they had "ceased to perform educational functions of a serious nature"; and had become little more than living and eating clubs. Theoretically, a man could become a counselor-at-law in England without reading "a single page of any law book." [125] But the Inns were part of English legal culture; the American travelers no doubt absorbed some of the ideas of English law; and they read law and observed English practice.

All other aspiring lawyers had to learn their trade through apprenticeship. Apprenticeship was a control device as well as a

---

[123] Edward Johnson, *Wonder-Working Providence* (Jameson, ed., 1910), p. 97.
[124] Anton-Hermann Chroust, *The Rise of the Legal Profession in America,* Vol. I (1965), p. 198.
[125] Paul M. Hamlin, *Legal Education in Colonial New York* (1939), pp. 16–17.

method of training. It kept the bar small and under the regulation of the older lawyers. How much the apprentice learned depended greatly on his master. At worst, an apprentice went through a haphazard course of drudgery and copywork, with a few glances, catch-as-catch-can, at the law books. William Livingston (a clerk at that time in the office of a New York lawyer) denounced the clerkship system in a letter to the *New-York Weekly Post-Boy* (Aug. 19, 1745). The system was an "Outrage upon common Honesty . . . scandalous, horrid, base, and infamous to the last degree!" No one could "attain to a competent Knowledge in the Law . . . by gazing on a Number of Books, which he has neither Time nor Opportunity to read; or . . . be metamorphos'd into an Attorney by virtue of a *Hocus Pocus.*" A young clerk "trifle[d] away the Bloom of his Age . . . in a servile Drudgery nothing to the Purpose, and fit only for a Slave." [126] For other young men, clerkship was a happy time and a valuable experience. Some senior lawyers were both good teachers and good men. Many famous lawyers trained or attracted clerks who later themselves became famous. Thomas Jefferson was a student of George Wythe. James Wilson studied with John Dickinson, paying Dickinson a fee raised from the sale of a farm.[127] The first law schools later grew out of law offices, which were so good at teaching that they gave up practice and did nothing else but teach.

Beginning in the 17th century, the British imported some lawyers to help them to govern. This was another fountainhead of the American bar. Nicholas Trott, an English lawyer, arrived in Charleston in 1699 as attorney general. He came to dominate the judicial life of South Carolina. In 1703, he was chief justice; he was also a member of the court of chancery, judge of the vice-admiralty court, the court of common pleas, and of the king's bench; he compiled the *Laws of the Province of South Carolina.* Contemporaries complained that "the sole Judicial Power [was] lodg'd" in his hands, "a Trust never repos'd in any one Man before in the World." [128] Only in 1719, when proprietary government was overthrown, did he lose his power. Some lawyers emigrated from England, and later held office in the colonies. Mathias Nicolls came to New York in 1664. He had been a barrister of Lincoln's Inn and

126 Reprinted in Paul M. Hamlin, *Legal Education in Colonial New York* (1939), pp. 167–68.

127 Charles P. Smith, *James Wilson, Founding Father* (1956), p. 24.

128 Anne K. Gregorie, ed., *Records of the Court of Chancery of South Carolina 1661–1779* (1950), pp. 6, 53.

Inner Temple; he had fifteen years' practice in London. In 1683, Governor Dongan appointed him a judge of the court of oyer and terminer.[129] In Massachusetts, too, most of the good lawyers in the generation after 1690 at one time or another held an appointive office.[130] The crown imported, hired, and thereby influenced the growth and sophistication of the bar.

Each colony had its own standards for admission to the bar. New Jersey even attempted to set up a graded profession on the English model. By a rule of 1755, the colony's supreme court established the order of *serjeants-at-law*, a higher rank than the ordinary counselor. Only the court could appoint to this rank; the court later restricted the number of serjeants to twelve. The serjeants had the power and duty to conduct examinations for admission to the bar.[131] In Virginia, a law of 1748 vested control over licensing and admission to the bar in the highest court of the colony. In Massachusetts, in the 18th century, each court admitted its own lawyers. The rank of barrister was established in 1762, and twenty-five lawyers were thereupon called to this rank.[132] In Rhode Island, any court could admit; but admission to one was admission to all. In many colonies, the requirements for admission included a long period of apprenticeship, though in some colonies, college graduates had to serve a lesser time.

The legal profession was one road to wealth and success in the 18th century. Wealthy lawyers tried to keep up their prices and prestige, by keeping down the supply of practitioners. They never quite succeeded. The lower ranks of the bar remained open and fluid. Lawyers, like actors and painters, were often part-timers and amateurs. In 17th century Maryland, most lawyers were planters, who spent part of their time on the practice. Up to the time of the Revolution, part-time lawyers formed a sizable portion of the Connecticut bar. Joseph Adams of New Haven "combined the duties of attorney and innkeeper"; but "did not do very well at either, for his estate proved insolvent when he died in 1782." Another Connecticut lawyer of 1750, Peletiah Mills of Windsor, doubled as

129 Paul M. Hamlin and Charles E. Baker, *Supreme Court of Judicature of the Province of New York 1691–1706,* Vol. I (1959), p. 19.

130 Murrin, *op. cit.,* p. 209.

131 Anton-Hermann Chroust, *The Rise of the Legal Profession in America,* Vol. I (1965), p. 200.

132 Gerard W. Gawalt, *Massachusetts Lawyers: A Historical Analysis of the Process of Professionalization, 1760–1840* (unpublished Ph.D. thesis, Clark University, 1969), p. 16.

"principal taverner of his home town." Other Connecticut lawyers
were cloth merchants, clergymen, and soldiers.[133]

Yet in some colonies, the bar was extremely, and artificially,
small. So few trained lawyers were qualified to practice before the
New York Supreme Court, that an act of 1695 told litigants not to
hire more than two "Attorneys at Law" to handle a case "in any of
the Courts of Record Within this Province." Apparently, it was
possible to "fee" all the attorneys, that is, hire the whole New York
bar, leaving one's opponent high and dry.[134] As of 1700, only about
a dozen men practiced before the New York high court. Between
1700 and 1720, six attorneys had the lion's share of the practice in
New York's mayor's court. In 1731, the New York City charter gave
seven attorneys (mentioned by name) a monopoly of this practice.
Two years before, a group of New York lawyers had formed an
"association," to supervise legal education, regulate practice, and
control admission to the bar. In 1756 these "gentlemen of the law"
agreed to take on no clerks, except their own sons, for the next
fourteen years.[135]

The New York lawyers were not the only ones with guildlike aspirations. In Rhode Island, eight lawyers signed a "Compact" in
1745, to ensure that fees would always be "sufficient for our support and subsistence." No case might be "pleaded at any Superior
Court under a three pound fee"; only a "standing client" was "to
be trusted without his note." Attorneys were not to sign "blank writs
and disperse them about the colony, which practice . . . would
make the law cheap." They agreed not to defend any client whose
lawyer was suing for his fee, unless three or more "brethren" determined that the lawyer's demand was "unreasonable." [136]

Wealth and a striving for status mingled here with some smattering of genuine concern for the public. These motives lay behind
John Adams' complaint, in 1759, that the "practice of law [was]
grasped into the hands of deputy sheriffs, pettifoggers and even
constables who filled all the writs upon bonds, promissory notes,
and accounts, received the fees established for lawyers, and stirred
up many unnecessary suits." Many inconsistencies in contemporary

133 John T. Farrell, ed., *The Superior Court Diary of William Samuel Johnson 1772-3* (1942), l-li.

134 Paul M. Hamlin and Charles E. Baker, *op. cit.,* pp. 99-101.

135 Richard B. Morris, *Select Cases of the Mayor's Court of New York City*
(1935), pp. 52 ff.

136 Quoted in Wilkins Updike, *Memoirs of the Rhode Island Bar* (1842),
pp. 294-95.

reports about lawyers vanish in the face of a single simple fact: that there were upper and lower lawyers, rich and poor, exclusive lawyers and lawyers hungry for clients, just as there are today. Many lawyers had to struggle for bread and paper. Others were rich or got rich. Many aristocrats, of mind and money, were lawyers. Politically, most lawyers were conservatives. But many founders of the Republic called themselves lawyers. John Marshall, John Adams, Thomas Jefferson, James Wilson; John Jay of New York, George Wythe of Virginia, Francis Hopkinson of Pennsylvania—all these were lawyers. Some leading lawyers—Anthony Stokes of Georgia and William Smith of New York—chose the losing side in the Revolution and left the country. Smith later became chief justice of the province of Quebec. Many lawyers, if not most, were of the loyalist persuasion; yet twenty-five of the fifty-six signers of the Declaration of Independence were lawyers, and thirty-one of the fifty-five delegates to the Constitutional Convention were lawyers. What these facts show, according to Professor Boorstin, is "the pervasiveness of legal competence among American men of affairs and the vagueness of the boundary between legal and all other knowledge in a fluid America." [137] Yet these men identified themselves as lawyers, not as doctors, politicians, or historians. There was a pride of profession among them, and a common fund of experience and training, whether or not they had ever replevied a cow or drawn up a chancery bill.

THE LITERATURE OF THE LAW

In one sense, colonial legal literature is quickly disposed of: there was no such thing worthy of the name before 1776. Law libraries were scarce, small, and scattered. What they contained was English law, with perhaps a collection of local statutes. Native lawbooks were few and utterly insignificant. No substantial body of case law was in print until after the Revolution. When Blackstone's *Commentaries* were published (1765–69), Americans were his most avid customers. Here at last was an up-to-date shortcut to basic English

---

[137] Daniel J. Boorstin, *The Americans; The Colonial Experience* (1958), p. 205. John M. Murrin, commenting on the "signs of creeping respectability" in the 18th-century bar in Massachusetts, remarks that "Before 1730, many gentlemen felt qualified to practice law on the side without bothering to study it. A generation later, gentlemen were beginning to study it with no intention of practising it." Murrin, *op. cit.*, p. 225.

law. An American edition was printed in 1771–72, on a subscription basis, for sixteen dollars a set; 840 American subscribers ordered 1,557 sets—an astounding response. Not all of the subscribers were lawyers and judges; but many were, and Blackstone's influence on American legal practice was at least potentially immense.[138]

Literature is conscious creation; but it is also recorded life. In this sense, the toiling scribes of colonial courts made literature. A few of their records were printed in the 19th century. Slowly, more have been unearthed; some have been edited and published. Much of the material is useful, but dreary, as formal legal prose tends to be. Yet among the reports are flashes of extraordinary vividness and color. These records, like no others, lift the veil that hides the face of daily life. They paint a marvelous picture, distorted to be sure by the fact that social disorders, large and small, were the subject of these chronicles. No one reading these records can cling to the view that Puritan life, for example, was uniformly solemn, dour and high-minded gray. Joseph Warrinar and Peter Swinck swore, in the Pynchon Court Record, for June 20, 1661,

> that in the forenoone last Sabbath in sermon tyme they saw Samuell Harmon thrust and tickle Jonathan Morgan and Pluckt him of [off] his seate .3. tymes and squeased him and made him cry.[139]

The cruelty of life is recorded, along with lust and sin. William Myers, testifying in West New Jersey in 1686, shows us slavery bare and unadorned:

> Hee heard at, a Considerable distance many blowes or stripes . . . hee thought hee heard a Negro Cry out many tymes . . . he supposed it to be James Wills beating his Negro woman, and heard still many Lashes more and Crying out, until hee was greevd and went into his owne house and shut the dore, and said to his wife oh! yond cruell man.[140]

The voice of truth sounds, too, in pleadings and formal speech. Legal phrases and popular speech mingled, for example, in the papers of South Carolina's chancery court (1721), where Mrs. Elizabeth Weekley, the "Relict" and "Executrix" of Richard

---

[138] Paul M. Hamlin, *Legal Education in Colonial New York* (1939), pp. 64–65.

[139] Joseph Smith, ed., *Colonial Justice in Western Massachusetts, 1639–1702; The Pynchon Court Record* (1961), p. 253.

[140] H. Clay Reed and George J. Miller, eds., *The Burlington Court Book of West New Jersey 1680–1709* (1944), p. 57.

Weekley, "Planter," told how she was induced to intrust her share of the estate to Mrs. Sarah Rhett:

> the said Mrs. Sarah Rhett did advise your Oratrix That it was not safe for your Oratrix being a Widow and an Ancient Woman and living on the Broad Path to keep soe much moneys in her own House least she should be robbed thereof by her Negroes or otherwise and offered to take charge thereof. . . . Your Oratrix . . . delivered over to the said Mrs. Sarah Rhett the said four hundred and Eighty pounds in Bills of Credit who took the same out of a paper Wrapper . . . and the said Mrs. Sarah Rhett then counted the said Bills into her lap . . . and cryed Lord Bless me Woman here's five hundred pounds wanting twenty pounds I did not think you had soe much money . . . then taking your Oratrix by the hand put her other hand upon her own Breast and told your Oratrix That the said moneys should be as safe as if it were in her . . . own hands and that as she was a Christian she would never wrong Your Oratrix of a Farthing.[141]

These and similar happenings were carefully preserved in court records, leading to the paradox that the living law is in some ways more knowable for this most forgotten period of American law than for later, more systematically documented times. An avalanche of papers and forms covered the minds and the mouths of ordinary litigants in the 19th and 20th centuries. The clear sound of American law, in its lusty youth, speaks from the pages of colonial county courts.

141 Anne K. Gregorie, ed., *Records of the Court of Chancery of South Carolina 1671–1779* (1950), p. 272.

◅ PART II ▻

From the Revolution to the
Death of Chancellor Kent—
1776-1847

(CHAPTER I)

THE REPUBLIC OF BEES

REVOLUTIONARY ARDOR

In 1776, the colonies declared themselves independent. The bitter war that followed ended in an American victory. Peace, of course, raised as many questions of government as it answered. A plan of government is a plan for distribution of the power and wealth of a society. The choice of system, then, is no idle exercise in political theory. How to plan the new American government was the major policy issue of the late 18th century. The first grand scheme was embodied in the Articles of Confederation. It proved unsatisfactory to powerful circles in the country. After the failure of the Articles, a federal Constitution was drawn up, and ratified in 1787.

Each colony, too, underwent its own revolution. Colonies became states, and embarked on a new course, with new problems. First, they had to fight a war, and patch up domestic disruptions. All this called for a major outburst of lawmaking. In Pennsylvania, for example, a constitutional convention, in 1776, declared a general amnesty and established a new form of government. Old officials were replaced by men loyal to the Revolution. The ordinary business of government was to continue, where possible; and the emergencies of war had to be coped with. In October 1777, British troops "penetrated into [the] state, and after much devastation and great cruelty in their progress," seized Philadelphia; the state government then created a "council of safety," with vast and summary powers "to promote and provide for the preservation of the Commonwealth." It had power to seize goods "for the army and for the inhabitants," punish traitors, and "regulate the prices of such articles as they may think necessary." But the "ordinary course of justice" was to continue as far as was feasible. In the same year, the legislature passed a bill of attainder against a number of men who had "traitorously and wickedly" gone over to the king. The state redefined and punished treason, declared bills of credit of the Continental Congress and the state to be legal tender; [1] and, inevitably, legislated about the militia, army supplies, taxes, and the policy of war.

When the war ended, debates over law continued. The king of England and his government had been successfully overthrown. Should the king's law be also overthrown? Should ordinary private law be radically altered? The first generation seriously argued the question. The common law was badly tarnished; so was the reputation of the lawyers, many of whom had been Tories. It seemed to some men that new democratic states needed new democratic institutions, from top to bottom, including fresh, nonmonarchical law. A pamphleteer, who called himself Honestus, asked, in 1786: "Can the monarchical and aristocratical institutions of England, be consistent with . . . republican principles?" It was "melancholy" to see the "numerous volumes" of English law, "brought into our Courts, arranged in formidable order, as the grand artillery to batter down every plain, rational principle of law." [2] Thomas Paine, an old firebrand, spoke for at least some zealots when he denounced, in 1805, the "chicanery of law and lawyers." He complained that Pennsylvania courts, even at that late date, had "not yet arrived at the dignity of independence." The courts, he said, still "hobble along by the stilts and crutches of English and antiquated precedents," which were often not democratic at all, but "tyrannical." [3] During Shay's Rebellion, in Massachusetts (1786), mobs stopped the courts from sitting, and forcibly staved off execution of judgments against debtors. It was easy to attribute class bias to the courts, and attribute this class bias in turn to the antiquated, oppressive, inappropriate common law.

There were two apparent alternatives to the stilts and crutches. The common law could be replaced by some rival system. Or all systems could be abandoned in favor of natural principles of justice. The first alternative had some slight basis, in hope if not in fact. There *were* other systems of law. After the French revolution, American liberals were particularly attracted to the French civil law. In the early 19th century, the Napoleonic Code served as a symbol and model of clarity and order. Some civil-law jurists were

---

[1] *Statutes at Large, Pa., 1682–1801,* Vol. IX (1903), p. 149 (Act of Oct. 13, 1777); p. 201 (Act of Mar. 6, 1778); p. 34 (Act of Jan. 29, 1777).

[2] The strictures of Honestus were ultimately published in Boston, in 1819, under the title *Observations on the Pernicious Practice of the Law;* and have been reprinted in 13 Am. J. Leg. Hist. 244, 257 (1969).

[3] Philip S. Foner, ed., *Complete Writings of Thomas Paine* (1945), Vol. II, p. 1003.

translated into English during this period: *A Treatise on Obligations, Considered in a Moral and Legal View,* "translated from the French of [Robert] Pothier," appeared in New Bern, North Carolina, in 1802. To some small extent, French scholars influenced American legal thought. Compared to civil law, common law seemed, to some, to be feudal, barbaric, uncouth.

In hindsight, the common law had little to fear. It was as little threatened as the English language. The courts continued to operate, continued to do business; they used the only law that they knew. Few lawyers had any knowledge of French. French lawbooks were rare and inaccessible; English authorities flooded the country. To be sure, some American jurists were equipped to deal with Continental law—James Kent of New York; and the Supreme Court's Joseph Story. They cited and used bits of foreign law in their writings and opinions. But these men were not revolutionaries. They believed in purifying and improving the law, not in overthrowing it. They were willing to snatch doctrines and ideas from Continental Europe; but even English law did that. One of the culture heroes of the American legal elite was England's Lord Mansfield, who died in 1793. Mansfield was Scotch by birth and an ardent admirer of Roman-flavored civil law.

And of course the common law had many defenders. Not everybody saw the common law as old and despotic. It was also the birthright of free men, a precious inheritance, perverted by the British under George III, but still a vital reality. One rhetorical pillar of the men of 1776 was that the common law embodied fundamental norms of natural law. The first Continental Congress, in 1776, adopted a Declaration of Rights; it declared that the colonies were "entitled to the common law of England," in particular the right of trial by jury. Americans were also entitled to the benefit of those English statutes, which "existed at the time of colonization; and which they have, by experience, respectively found to be applicable to their several local and other circumstances." [4]

Common-law lawyers were among the heroes of the Republic. John Adams was one; Thomas Jefferson, for all his ambivalence toward common law and its judges, another. Lawyers mostly drafted the state and federal constitutions. Courts were increasingly manned by lawyers, who listened to the arguments of other lawyers. Lawyers moved west with the line of settlement; they swarmed into state capitals and county seats. Wherever one looked

[4] Quoted in Elizabeth Gaspar Brown, *British Statutes in American Law, 1776–1836* (1964), p. 21.

in political life—in town, city, county, state, and national government—the lawyers were there. Unlike some later revolutions, and some earlier colonial Utopias, the new republic did not try to do business without lawyers. Old lawyers continued to function, training new lawyers in their image, who, like their teachers, turned almost instinctively to common law. The common law was also a weapon of integration. The Northwest Ordinance imposed its doctrines on the American frontier. In the prairies and forests, where French settlers lived and worked in the path of the American onrush, the common law was an agent of American imperialism.

The common law would have to be Americanized, of course. Now that the states had freedom to choose, what parts of English law would remain in force? This was a tortuous question, not easily solved. States passed statutes to define the limits of the law in force. A Virginia law of 1776 declared that the "common law of England, all statutes or acts of Parliament made in aid of the common law prior to the fourth year of the reign of King James the first, and which are of a general nature, not local to that kingdom . . . shall be considered as in full force." [5] The Delaware constitution of 1776 (art. 25) provided that "The common law of England as well as so much of the statute law as has been heretofore adopted in practice in this State, shall remain in force," except for those parts which were "repugnant to the rights and privileges" expressed in the constitution and in the "declaration of rights." The New York experience was particularly complex. A law of 1786 declared the common law in force, and such English statutes as were in effect in the colony on April 19, 1775. Later, New York specifically re-enacted some British laws—the Statute of Frauds, for example, first passed in 1677 and considered virtually part of the common law. In 1788, "An Act for the Amendment of the Law, and the better Advancement of Justice," declared that "after the *first* day of *May* next," no British statutes "shall operate or be considered as Laws" in New York.[6] The New York Constitution of 1821 (art. VII, sec. 13) stated that "Such parts of the common law, and of the acts of the legislature of the colony of New York, as together did form the law of the said colony" on April 19, 1775, and the resolutions of the colonial Congress, "and of the convention of the State of New York," in force on April 20, 1777, would continue to be law, unless altered or repealed, and unless they were

5 William Waller Henning, *Statutes at Large . . . of Virginia* (Vol. 9, 1821), p. 127.

6 On the New York reception laws, see E. G. Brown, *op. cit.*, pp. 69–75.

"repugnant" to the constitution. No mention was made of British statutes; for good measure, an act of 1828 specifically pronounced the British statutes dead.

Yet even this flock of statutes fell short of solving the problem. A New York court later held that some English statutes had become part of the "common law" of the colony.[7] This meant that an undefinable, unknowable group of old laws somehow maintained a ghostly presence. They lived on, of course, only insofar as they were not "repugnant" to the constitution or unsuitable to conditions. One could never, then, be sure if an old law were dead or alive. New York was not the only state whose judges sentenced the public to uncertainty. To this day, an occasional case still turns on whether some statute or doctrine had been "received" as common law in this or that state. "Reception" had been a colonial dilemma too. Independence merely altered the form of the question. And in a broader sense, the question is an abiding one in all common-law jurisdictions. Judges must constantly re-examine the law, to see which parts still suit society's need, which parts must be finally discarded.

The reception statutes dealt with the *older* English law. What of the newer? There was, as expected, a strong burst of national pride. Jesse Root of Connecticut, writing in 1798, felt it was "unnecessary, and derogatory" for courts of an independent nation to be governed by foreign law. He referred to "the republic of bees," whose members "resist all foreign influence with their lives," and whose honey, "though extracted from innumerable flowers," [8] was indisputably their own. In pursuit of the republic of bees, New Jersey passed a law, in 1799, that

> no adjudication, decision or opinion, made, had or given, in any court of law or equity in Great-Britain [after July 4, 1776] . . . nor any printed or written report or statement thereof, nor any compilation, commentary, digest, lecture, treatise, or other explanation or exposition of the common law, . . . shall be received or read in any court of law or equity in this state, as law or evidence of the law, or elucidation or explanation thereof.[9]

Kentucky prohibited the mere mention of recent British law. Its statute, passed in 1807, declared that "reports and books contain-

[7] *Bogardus* v. *Trinity Church,* 4 Paige 178, 198–99 (1833), discussed in Brown, *op. cit.,* pp. 72–73.

[8] 1 Root's Reports (Connecticut), xlii, xliii (1798).

[9] Quoted in E. G. Brown, *op. cit.,* p. 82.

ing adjudged cases in . . . Great Britain . . . since the 4th day of
July, 1776, shall not be read or considered as authority in . . . the
courts of this Commonwealth." [10] During Spring Term, 1808,
Henry Clay "offered to read" a "part of Lord Ellenborough's opinion" in Volume 3 of East's reports, before the court of appeals of
Kentucky; the "chief justice stopped him." Clay's co-counsel argued
that the legislature "had no more power to pass" such a law than
to "prohibit a judge the use of his spectacles." The court decided,
however, that "the book must not be used at all in court." [11]

But Lord Ellenborough was not so easily banished, in New Jersey, or Kentucky, or elsewhere. The New Jersey statute was repealed in 1819. As a practical matter, English law continued to
come in, throughout the period, throughout the country. England
remained the basic source of all law that was not strictly new or
strictly American. The habits of a lifetime were not easily thrown
over, despite ideology. Indigenous legal literature was weak and
derivative. American cases were not commonly reported until a
generation or more after Independence. To common law lawyers, a
shortage of cases was crippling. To fill the gap, English materials
were used, English reports cited, English judges quoted as authority. In the first generation, more English than American cases were
cited in American reports. Blackstone was widely used by ordinary
lawyers as a shortcut to the law; and Blackstone was English to the
core. Some curiously old-fashioned law that turned up on the frontier can be blamed on the ubiquity of Blackstone.

American law continued, in short, to borrow. The English over-
lay was obvious, pervasive—but selective. The English doctrines
that were invited to this country were those which were needed and
wanted—and only those. Sweeping changes took place in American
law, in the sixty-one years between 1776 and the death of James
Kent. In that time, there developed a true republic of bees, whose
flowers were the social and economic institutions that developed in
their own way in the country. They, not Lord Ellenborough and
Lord Kenyon, were the lawmakers who made American law a distinctive system: a separate language of law within the family
founded in England.

The second apparent alternative to the common law was also a
mirage. To abolish the tyranny of rules, to reduce law to the level

10 Quoted in E. G. Brown, *op. cit.*, p. 132.
11 *Hickman* v. *Boffman*, Hardin 356, 372–73 (Kentucky, 1808). Vol. 3 of East's
Reports contains cases from the court of king's bench for the years 1802 and
1803.

of the common man: this is an age-old yearning, but it flared up with special vigor after 1776. Partly, the antilaw movement was a sign of radical politics. One current of thought distrusted the common law as remote from the needs of ordinary people, and as biased toward the rich. Another current of thought distrusted law because it lacked relevance to the wants of businessmen. Both groups could make common cause against lawyers' law, which suited nobody's interest but the lawyers. There was a general interest, then, in a reform of legal institutions, in which rich and poor, radical and conservative could share. In a complex society, however, lawyers' law could not be overthrown and replaced by natural justice, whatever that might mean. On the contrary, more and more rules, of more and more definite shape, were needed as time went on. The reform urge, as we shall see, did not abate; but it came to mean, not artlessness, but adaptation to the needs of a market economy.

One basic, critical fact of 19th-century law was that the official legal system began to penetrate deeper into society. Medieval law was not law everywhere in England; nor was it everybody's law. American law was more popular, in a profound sense. It had no archaic or provincial rivals. It had no competitive substratum. Paradoxically, American law, divided into as many subsystems as there were states, was less disjointed than the one "common law" of older England.

Of course, millions were beyond the reach of formal law and indifferent to it. But comparatively speaking, American law had an enormous range. It drew its strength from the work and wealth of millions, and it affected the work and wealth of millions more. In 16th- or 18th-century England, few people owned or dealt in land. Only a small percentage were inside the market economy. Only a few were potential customers for family law, the law of torts, the law of corporations. There was surely less oligarchy in the United States than in the old kingdoms of Europe. A law for the millions, for the middle class, had to develop. And this law, to survive, had to be more pliant and accessible than a law for the wealthy few.

Complicated or not, law had to be relevant to consumer demand, or at least usable by the legal profession, as brokers of legal information. What happened to American law in the 19th century, basically, was that it changed to conform to the vast increase in number of consumers. It is dangerous to sum up long periods and great movements in a sentence. But if colonial law had been, in the first place, colonial, and in the second place, paternal, emphasizing order and the struggle against sin, then, gradually, a new set of attitudes developed, in which the primary function of law was not suppression but service. In this period, law was seen more and more as a utilitarian tool: to protect property and the established order, of course, but beyond that, to further the interests of the middle-class *mass*, to foster growth, to release and harness the energy latent in the commonwealth: "Dynamic rather than static property, property in motion or at risk rather than property secure and at rest." [12]

It was not only property that was more and more seen as dynamic rather than static. These two polar words aptly describe a fundamental change in the concept of law. The source of the change lay not so much in the Revolution as in the revolution of society and economy. A dynamic law is a man-made law. The Constitution talked about natural rights, and meant what it said; but these rights were a framework for the fulfillment of people's wishes and desires, not a definition of their duties and their status. Gradually, an instrumental, relativistic theory of law made its mark on the system. It meant a more creative view of precedent. It meant asking for the functions of the past, and measuring these against the demands of the present and future. Once, change in law was looked on as rare, and treated almost apologetically. In the 19th century, Americans made law wholesale, without any sense of shame. Basically, this was legislative law, and relatively less law made by the judges—though the boldness and opportunity of the judges gave them a mighty, even if secondary, role in the making of law.

CONSTITUTIONS: FEDERAL AND STATE

The Revolutionary period was, by necessity, an age of innovation in fundamental law. The old ties with England had been snapped. The states and the general government decided to put their basic political decisions in the form of written constitutions. Some states had begun as chartered colonies; they had gotten the habit of revering their charters, as guarantees of liberty. Many of the political leaders of the United States looked on a written constitution as a kind of social compact—a basic agreement among citizens, and

12 J. Willard Hurst, *Law and the Conditions of Freedom in the Nineteenth Century United States* (1964), p. 24.

between citizens and state, setting out mutual rights and duties, in permanent form.

The Articles of Confederation (1777) envisioned a loose, low-key grouping of states. It did not provide for a strong executive. It had no provision for a federal judiciary. Congress, however, was given some judicial power; it was "the last resort on appeal in all disputes and differences . . . between two or more states concerning boundary jurisdiction or any other cause whatever." Congress also had power over matters of admiralty law, with "sole and exclusive right" to establish "rules for deciding, in all cases, what captures on land or water shall be legal," and how prizes might be "divided or appropriated." Congress also had sole right to set up "courts for the trial of piracies and felonies committed on the high seas," and courts "for receiving and determining, finally, appeals in all cases of captures" (art. 9).

The Articles of Confederation failed to satisfy; the Constitution of 1787 was a stronger, more centralizing document. The Northwest Ordinance (1787), on the government of the Western lands, enacted shortly before the Constitution, took it for granted that all future states would have a "permanent constitution." Any new states carved out of the Northwest Territory would have a "republican" constitution, consistent with federal law (Northwest Ordinance, 1787, art. V).

The original states had in theory the option to write or not write a constitution. But most of them quickly chose the way of the new-written word. Within a short time after the war broke out, eleven states had drafted and adopted new constitutions. To some, a constitution was a rallying point, a symbol of unity during war. The New Jersey Constitution (1776) put it this way:

> in the present deplorable situation of these colonies, exposed to the fury of a cruel and relentless enemy, some form of government is absolutely necessary, not only for the preservation of good order, but also the more effectually to unite the people, and enable them to exert their whole force in their own necessary defense.

A few states chose to rest upon their original charters. But these, too, were eventually replaced by new drafts. Connecticut discarded its charter and adopted a constitution in 1818. Every state in the union came to have a constitution in the strict sense of the word. All, in short, embarked on careers of making, unmaking, and remaking constitutions.

Constitutionalism answered to a deep-seated need, among members of the articulate public, for formal, outward signs of political legitimacy. This urge had driven tiny, isolated colonies in what is now Rhode Island or Massachusetts to express the structure and principles of government in the form of an agreement—a visible, legible bulwark against the lonely disorder of life outside the reach of the mother country. Much later, but by something of the same instinct, the remote Oregon pioneers, in a no-man's land disputed among nations, drew up a frame of government and called it a constitution. So did the residents of the "lost state of Franklin" in the 1780's, in what is now part of eastern Tennessee. So did the handful of citizens of the "Indian Stream Republic," in disputed territory near the border of New Hampshire and Canada. And so did the Mormons of the "State of Deseret." These "constitutions," to be sure, lacked originality; they borrowed provisions from existing constitutions, taking a phrase here, a clause there, and making what changes were considered appropriate. They were short-lived and of dubious legality. But they illustrate how strong the *idea* of a constitution had become in American life.

The substance of the constitutions varied. Some of the earliest, written before the 1780's, were bold and forward-looking. The first Pennsylvania Constitution (1776) represented a sharp victory for the liberals of the state. Virginia pioneered a Declaration of Rights (1776). The idea and content of the Bill of Rights came from sources in the states. The federal Constitution could not have been ratified, without the promise of a bill of rights, which took the form of ten amendments.[13] After 1787, the language and organization of the federal Constitution became in turn a powerful model for state constitutions. One feature, however, was not easily transferred to the states: durability. There has been only one federal Constitution. It has been amended from time to time—but never overthrown. A few states (for example, Wisconsin) have also had only one constitution. Other states have had a far more colorful constitutional career. Louisiana has had nine constitutions, perhaps ten, depending on how one counts. Georgia has had at least six.

The federal Constitution was marvelously supple, put together with great political skill. The stability of the country—Civil War crisis aside—has been the main source of its amazing survival. But the Constitution itself deserves a share of the credit. It turned out

13 See, in general, Robert Allen Rutland, *The Birth of the Bill of Rights 1776–1791* (1962).

to be neither too tight nor too loose. It was in essence a frame, a skeleton, an outline of the form of government; it mostly held its tongue on specifics. The earlier state constitutions, before 1787 and for some decades after, also guarded against saying too much. There were, of course, some idiosyncratic features, even before 1787, in state constitutions. New Hampshire (1784), in the spirit of Yankee thrift, solemnly declared that "economy" was a "most essential virtue in all states, especially in a young one; no pension shall be granted, but in consideration of actual services, and . . . with great caution, . . . and never for more than one year at a time." [14] But most state constitutions began with a bill of rights, described the general frame of government, and left it at that.

A constitution, if at all different from ordinary law, has two functions. First, it provides a terse exposition of the permanent shape of the government, what its parts are, their boundaries and limits. Second, it may contain a list of essential rights, essential limitations on government, essential rules—all those propositions of high or highest law, which society means to secure against the winds of temporary change. But this second function has no natural boundary. Opinions differ from generation to generation on what rights and duties are most fundamental. Even the federal Constitution was more than mere framework. Imbedded in it were fragments of a code of law. Trial by jury, for example, was guaranteed (art. III, sec. 2, par. 3). The Constitution defined the crime of treason (art. III, sec. 3), and set out minimum requirements for convicting any man of this crime. The Bill of Rights contained a miniature code of criminal procedure.

What existed in embryo, and in reasonable proportions in the federal Constitution, was carried to much greater lengths in the states. The inflation of constitutions reached its high point (or low point) after the Civil War. But the process began long before that. Even the state bills of rights became bloated. The federal Bill of Rights had ten sections; Kentucky, in 1792, had 28. Some of these were quite vague: "elections shall be free and equal" (art. XII, sec. 5); others seemed hardly to warrant their exalted position—for example, the provision that estates of "such persons as shall destroy their own lives shall descend or vest as in case of natural death." [15]

The Delaware constitution of 1792 was another offender. It in-

14 N.H. const., 1784, art. XXXVI.

15 Art. XII, sec. 21. This was not by any means a unique clause. See Alabama const., 1819, art. 1, sec. 21; Mississippi const., 1817, art. 1, sec. 21; Tennessee const., 1796, art. XI, sec. 12; Delaware const., 1792, art. 1, sec. 15.

cluded many details of court organization and procedure: for example, "No writ of error shall be brought upon any judgment . . . confessed, entered, or rendered, but within five years after the confessing, entering or rendering thereof." [16] This constitution also specified minutely how courts should handle accounts of executors, administrators, and guardians. The Alabama constitution of 1819 provided that "A competent number of justices of the peace shall be appointed in and for each county, in such mode and for such term of office, as the general assembly may direct." Their civil jurisdiction, however, "shall be limited to causes in which the amount in controversy shall not exceed fifty dollars." [17] Clearly, the fifty-dollar limit was no immutable right of man. The Tennessee constitution of 1796 set a ceiling on the governor's salary ($750 a year) and forbade any change before 1804.[18] No one could deduce these numbers from natural law.

There was a point to every clause in these inflated constitutions. Each one reflected the wishes of some faction or interest group, which tried to make its policies permanent by freezing them into the charter. Constitutions, like treaties, preserved the terms of compromise between warring groups. These sometimes took the form of a clause that postponed the power of the state to enact a given kind of law. The federal Constitution left the slave trade untouchable until 1808; until that year "the Migration or Importation of such Persons as any of the States now existing shall think proper to admit, shall not be prohibited by the Congress" (art. I, sec. 9, par. 1). Ohio (1802) made Chillicothe the "seat of government" until 1808; the legislature was not to build itself any buildings until 1809.[19] For very delicate issues, the tactics of constitutionalism appeared essential. Otherwise, slight changes in political power could upset the compromise. One legislature can swiftly repeal the work of another; a constitution is harder to change.

Between 1790 and 1847, state constitutions became more diverse and diffuse. Some developments, like some problems, were peculiar to one state, or to one group of states; some were common to the country as a whole. The most general problems were apportionment and suffrage. Any change in the electoral map or in the right to vote meant a reallocation of political power. The suffrage was a bottleneck of law; who voted determined who ruled. Hence, con-

16 Del. const., 1792, art. VI, sec. 13; const., 1831, art. VI, sec. 20.
17 Alabama const., 1819, art. V., sec. 10.
18 Tennessee const., 1796, art. 1, sec. 20.
19 Ohio const., 1802, art. VII, sec. 4.

stitutional disputes over suffrage and apportionment were widespread and sometimes bitter. In Rhode Island, the franchise was narrow, and the apportionment scheme outdated. Conservatives stubbornly resisted any change. The so-called "rebellion" of Thomas Dorr (1842) was an unsuccessful, mildly violent attempt to force a change. Later, in 1842, a new constitution finally reformed the structure of government.[20] In other states, bloodless revolutions overthrew constitutions and reformed the suffrage. The search for permanence was constant, but permanence escaped men's grasp. The Pennsylvania constitution of 1776, a product of advanced 18th-century liberalism, was replaced in 1790 by a much more conservative constitution; and in 1838 by a moderate one. Statute books were supple; new governments changed them as they wished. Constitutions were brittle. They could be patched up at times; but when they were too deeply impregnated with the policies and interests of an old or lost cause, they had to be completely redone. Inflexibility was the vice of constitutions as well as the virtue.

An observer with nothing in front of him but the texts of these state constitutions could infer a great deal about state politics, state laws, and about social life in America. The protection of slavery, and repression of free Negroes garnered more and more attention in Southern constitutions. Legislatures were forbidden to emancipate slaves, unless the master agreed and was compensated. In Pennsylvania (1838) any person who fought a duel, or sent a challenge, or aided or abetted in fighting a duel, was "deprived of the right of holding any office of honor or profit in this State." [21] The Connecticut constitution of 1818, though it paid lip service to freedom of worship, froze every resident into his "congregation, church, or religious association." A man might withdraw only by leaving a "written notice thereof with the clerk of such [religious] society." [22] Constitutions often dealt with the state militia, a matter of much importance in the Revolutionary generation. In Ohio (1802) brigadiers-general were to be "elected by the commissioned officers of their respective brigades." [23] Some states barred practicing clergymen from public office. The Tennessee constitution of

[20] Peter J. Coleman, *The Transformation of Rhode Island 1790–1860* (1963), pp. 254–94. Rich material on suffrage questions is contained in Merrill D. Peterson, ed., *Democracy, Liberty and Property, The State Constitutional Conventions of the 1820's* (1966).

[21] Pennsylvania const., 1838, art. VI, sec. 10. Many states had similar clauses.

[22] Conn. const., 1818, art. VII, sec. 2.

[23] Ohio const., 1802, art. VIII, sec. 4.

1796 testily remarked that "ministers of the gospel are, by their professions, dedicated to God and the care of souls, and ought not to be diverted from the great duties of their functions." [24] The draft constitution of "Franklin," in 1784, would have extended this ban to lawyers and "doctors of physic." The Georgia constitution of 1777 declared that "Estates shall not be entailed; and when a person dies intestate, his or her estate shall be divided equally among their children; the widow shall have a child's share, or her dower, at her option." [25] As early as 1776, North Carolina provided that "the person of a debtor, where there is not a strong presumption of fraud, shall not be confined in prison, after delivering up, *bona fide,* all his estate real and personal, for the use of his creditors, in such manner as shall be hereafter regulated by law." [26] Many 19th-century constitutions contained similar provisions on imprisonment for debt.

State constitutions reflected the theories of the day on separation of powers, and on checks and balances. The earlier the constitution, however, the weaker the executive branch. For example, 18th-century constitutions gave only feeble powers to the chief executive (called a governor, like his colonial antecedent). His term of official life was brief. The Maryland constitution of 1776 solemnly asserted that "a long continuance" in "executive departments" was "dangerous to liberty"; and "rotation" was "one of the best securities of permanent freedom." This constitution practiced what it preached. The governor—a "person of wisdom, experience, and virtue"—was to be chosen each year, on the second Monday of November, for a one-year term, by joint ballot of the two houses of the legislature. But he could not continue his wisdom in office "longer than three years successively, nor be eligible as Governor, until expiration of four years after he shall have been out of that office." [27]

Early constitutions preferred to give the lion's share of power to the legislature. In the light of American political history, this was only natural. The colonial governor—and the judiciary, to a cer-

[24] Tenn. const., 1796, art. 8, sec. 1.

[25] Ga. const., 1777, art. LI.

[26] N. Car. const., 1776, art. XXXIX. This was also a feature of the Pennsylvania constitution of 1776.

[27] Maryland const., 1776, declaration of rights, art. XXXI, const., arts. XXV, XXXI. The governor had to be rich as well as wise. Only residents above twenty-five years of age, "and having in the State real and personal property above the value of five thousand pounds, current money (one thousand pounds whereof, at least, to be freehold estate) shall be eligible as governor" (art. XXX).

tain extent—represented foreign domination. The assemblies, on the other hand, were the voice of local influentials. The Pennsylvania constitution of 1776 gave "supreme legislative power" to a single house of representatives. No upper house or governor's veto checked its power.[28] Over the course of the years, however, the states became somewhat disillusioned with legislative supremacy. The governor was one beneficiary of this movement. Typically, he gained a longer term of office and the veto power (which the federal President had from the start). Judicial power, too, increased at the legislature's expense. Judicial power took the form called judicial review—review, through private litigation, of acts of other branches of government; with the right to declare these acts void, if, in the judges' opinion, they were unauthorized by the constitution. Judicial review fed on constitutional detail; the more clauses a constitution contained, especially clauses that did something more than merely set out the basic frame of government, the more potential occasions for the exercise of the power of review. In the landmark decision of *Marbury* v. *Madison* (1803), John Marshall and the Supreme Court, for the first time, declared an act of Congress unconstitutional. The Court did not use the power again in this period. They used this weapon more frequently against *state* statutes. State supreme courts, too, began to make use of the power. It was still a rare weapon, rarely used; it was hated by Jeffersonians; some judges resisted it; it made little impact on the ordinary working of government. But when its occasion arose, it was an instrument of unparalleled power.

Legislative supremacy declined because influential Americans were more afraid of too much law than of not enough. In a number of states, scandals tarnished the reputation of the legislatures. Blocs of voters became afraid that landlords, "moneyed corporations," and others of the wealthy and powerful were too strong in the lobbies of these assemblies. A movement arose to limit the power of the legislatures, thus protecting the public from harm. Rules to control legislation were written into one constitution after another. The process began modestly enough. Georgia's constitution (1798) outlawed the practice of legislative divorce, except if the parties had gone to "fair trial before the superior court," and obtained a verdict upon "legal principles." Even then, it took a "two-thirds vote of each branch of the legislature" [29] to grant a divorce. Indiana, in 1816, forbade the establishment by statute of

28 J. Paul Selsam, *The Pennsylvania Constitution of 1776* (1936), pp. 183–84.
29 Ga. const., 1798, art. III, sec. 9.

any "bank or banking company, or monied institution for the purpose of issuing bills of credit, or bills payable to order or bearer." [30]

The Louisiana constitution of 1845 was something of a turning
point. More than those that came before, this constitution was a
charter of economic rights and obligations, and a code of legislative procedure, as well as a plain frame of government whose economic import was implicit. The constitution sharply restricted the
state's power to pledge its credit or to lend its money. The state was
not to "become subscriber to the stock of any corporation or joint-
stock company." Lotteries, legislative divorces, and special corporate charters were forbidden. Every law was to "embrace but one
subject, and that shall be expressed in the title." No new corporation was to last more than twenty-five years. No exclusive privileges
or monopolies were to be granted for more than twenty years. No
banks of any sort were to be chartered.[31] These were not chance
notions. They were not, in the eyes of contemporaries, extreme.
What was new (and ominous) was that Louisiana was trying here to
reach legitimate legislative goals through anti-legislation: by foreclosing whole areas of life to statutory change. Other states enthu-
siastically followed Louisiana's lead. But as the conditions of society changed, these overblown constitutions became embarrassments.
They were therefore evaded, or amended, or totally abandoned.

No two state constitutions were ever exactly alike. But no constitution was pure innovation. Among the states, there was a great
deal of copying, of constitutional *stare decisis*.[32] A clause or provision tended to spread far and wide when it caught the fancy of
lawmakers and constituents. New states embarked on political careers by borrowing great numbers of clauses and sections from
older states. Some new states favored the latest, most recent model;
others looked to their neighboring states; others to the old home of
most of their settlers. The New York constitution of 1846 left a
deep mark on Michigan and later on Wisconsin. The first constitution of California was heavily indebted to Iowa; Oregon was indebted to Indiana.

Borrowing and influence are not, of course, the same. The states
shared a common political culture. Michigan was not a legal satellite of New York; the people in the two states were Americans of
their period, and, for the most part, thought alike on political,
legal issues. Since the New York constitution came first, people in

---

30 Indiana const., 1816, art. X, sec. 1. But a state bank was allowed.
31 Louisiana const., 1845, arts. 113, 114, 116, 117, 118, 121, 122, 123, 124, 125.
32 J. Willard Hurst, *The Growth of American Law* (1950), p. 224.

Michigan used it. When sound models were readily at hand, it was inefficient to start drafting from scratch. Borrowing was always selective. No constitution was swallowed whole. On matters of great importance, conscious choice was never absent. No state was *bound* to adopt the constitution of another state, or any part of it. They adopted out of expedience and fashion.

THE JUDGES

In a common-law system, judges make at least some of the law, even if their theory denies this fact. American statesmen were not naïve; they knew that it mattered what the judges believed and who they were. How judges were to be chosen and how they were to act was a political issue in the Revolutionary generation, at a pitch of intensity rarely reached before or since. State after state— and the federal government—fought political battles on issues of selection and control of the bench.

The bench was not homogeneous. Judges varied in quality and qualification, in level and place, from local justices of the peace to the Supreme Court Chief Justice. English and colonial tradition had room for lay judges, as well as for judges learned in law. Lay judges flourished both at the top and the bottom of the pyramid. In the colonies, the governor frequently served, *ex officio,* as chancellor. New Jersey continued this system, in its constitution of 1776. This constitution also made the governor and council "the Court of Appeals in the last resort, of all causes of law, as heretofore." [33] Since governor and council were or might be laymen, this meant that nonlawyers had final control of the conduct of trials and the administration of justice. In the New York system, too, laymen shared power at the apex of the hierarchy of courts. The constitution of 1777 set up a court "for the trial of impeachments, and the correction of errors," consisting of senators as well as judges.[34] This system lasted well into the 19th century.

The lay judges were not necessarily politicians, though this was ordinarily the case. But they were invariably prominent local men. William E. Nelson has studied the background and careers of the eleven men who served as justices of the superior court of Massachusetts between 1760 and 1774, on the eve, that is, of the Revolu-

[33] New Jersey const., 1776, art. ix.
[34] New York const., 1777, art. 32. In England, too, the highest court, the House of Lords, included laymen as well as judges.

tion. Nine had never practiced law; six had never even studied law. All, however, of these lay judges had "either been born into prominent families or become men of substance." Stephen Sewall, chief justice in 1760, was the nephew of a former chief justice; he had served thirteen years as a tutor at Harvard College.[35]

The base of the pyramid was even more dominated by laymen. Lay justice did not necessarily mean popular or unlettered justice at the trial-court level. The English squires were laymen, but hardly men of the people. Lay justice in America had something of the character of rule by the squires. Nor was lay justice necessarily informal. Laymen, after years on the bench, often soaked up the lawyer's jargon and tone. After all, lawyers frequently came to the bar after the briefest of clerkships and with little more than a smattering of Blackstone. Lay judges, then, did not absorb their law much differently than the average trained lawyer.

There are many anecdotes in print about the coarseness and stupidity of lay judges. Later lawyers, and historians of bench and bar, dragged the reputation of these judges through the mud. It was in the sentimental and material interests of these lawyers and lawyer-historians to romanticize the crudeness of the past, and to emphasize that laymen who wore lawyers' clothes were incompetent. The actual facts are harder to unearth. The anti-court movements of the late 18th century depended very little on whether laymen or lawyers ran the courts. The suggestion is that courts were run, not crudely, but in a biased and class-oriented fashion.

In any event, the lay judge was in slow retreat throughout the period. Eventually, he disappeared entirely from upper courts. The first lawyer on Vermont's supreme court was Nathaniel Chipman (1752–1843). He took office, in 1787, as an assistant judge of the court. Not one of the other four judges was an attorney.[36] On such a court, the lawyer could easily take the lead. Chipman later became chief justice, and edited law reports for Vermont. In other states, professionalization came earlier. All five of the judges of the Virginia Court of Appeals, established in 1788, were lawyers; Edmund Pendleton headed the court.[37]

Historically, judges were appointed from above. But democracy

---

35 William E. Nelson, *The Americanization of the Common Law During the Revolutionary Era: A Study of Legal Change in Massachusetts, 1760–1830*, pp. 23–24.

36 Daniel Chipman, *Life of Nathaniel Chipman* (1846), p. 69.

37 See S. S. P. Patteson, "The Supreme Court of Appeals of Virginia," 5 *Green Bag* 310, 313 ff. (1893).

meant public control over government and law; this clearly implied some popular way to choose the judges. The Vermont constitution of 1777 gave to the "freemen in each county" the "liberty of choosing the judges of inferior court of common pleas, sheriff, justices of the peace, and judges of probate." [38] Under the Ohio constitution of 1802, "judges of the supreme court, the presidents, and the associate judges of the courts of common pleas" were to be "appointed by a joint ballot of both houses of the general assembly, and shall hold their offices for the term of seven years, if so long they behave well." [39] This gave the electorate at least an indirect voice in judicial selection. Georgia in 1812, and Indiana in 1816, provided for popular election of some judges; [40] Mississippi in 1832 adopted popular election for all. New York followed in 1846, and the rush was on.

The movement, according to Willard Hurst, was "one phase of the general swing toward broadened suffrage and broader popular control of public office which Jacksonian Democracy built on the foundations laid by Jefferson." It was a movement, however, "based on emotion rather than on a deliberate evaluation of experience under the appointive system." [41] The hard facts about judicial behavior were never easy to come by. There is no simple way to compare elected and appointed judges. Still, it was felt, if judges were not elected, how could the public be sure that judges would respond to the public will?

There was plenty of evidence from which a jaundiced mind could conclude that judges were political men, and had to be kept in check. The followers of Jefferson were sure of this fact. Federal judges were appointed for life. Before Jefferson came to power,

38 Vermont const., 1777, art. II, sec. XXVII. See, in general, Evan Haynes, *The Selection and Tenure of Judges* (1944).

39 Ohio const., 1802, art. III, sec. 8.

40 In Georgia, the "justices of the inferior courts" were to be elected for four-year terms, Georgia const., 1798, art. III, sec. 4 (amendment, ratified 1812); in Indiana, the supreme court was appointed by the governor, the president of the circuit court by "joint ballot of both branches of the General Assembly"; associate judges of the circuit courts were to be "elected by the qualified electors in the respective counties." Indiana const., 1816, art. V, sec. 7.

41 J. Willard Hurst, *The Growth of American Law: The Law Makers* (1950), p. 140. Jacksonian democracy did not mean, necessarily, that every man could or should be a judge. Jackson himself, for example, did not appoint the common man to the bench. His appointments were men of high status, by background or achievement, just as Adams' were. But the Jacksonian *attitude* differed from the earlier one; this may have led to change in the long run. See Sidney H. Aronson, *Status and Kinship in the Higher Civil Service* (1964), p. 170.

they were naturally Federalists. Their behavior was quite controversial. To Jefferson's men, the judges seemed "partial, vindictive,
and cruel," men who "obeyed the President rather than the law,
and made their reason subservient to their passion." [42] As John
Adams was leaving office, in 1801, Congress passed a new Judiciary
Act.[43] The act created new judgeships, among other things. Adams
nominated judges to fill the new jobs; they were confirmed by the
Senate in the last moment of the Adams regime. Jefferson's party
raged at these "midnight judges." It was a final attempt, Jefferson
thought, to stock the bench forever with his political enemies.

The law that created the "midnight judges" was repealed; the
judges lost their jobs; but the other Federalist judges stayed on
serenely in office. These holdover judges threatened Jefferson's program, he felt; there was no easy way to be rid of them: "Few die and
none resign." He wanted to limit their power; he wanted them more
responsive to national policy—as embodied, of course, in Jefferson
and in his party. John Marshall, the Chief Justice of the Supreme
Court, was particularly obnoxious to Jefferson. He was a man of
enormous talents, and (as luck would have it), enjoyed good
health and longevity. He outlived a score of would-be heirs to the
office, including Spencer Roane of Virginia, and cheated a whole
line of Presidents of the pleasure of replacement. Equally annoying
to Jefferson and his successors was the fact that later justices, who
were not Federalists, seemed to fall under Marshall's spell, once
they were safely on the bench. Madison appointed Joseph Story,
who was at least a lukewarm Democrat. On the bench, he became a
rabid fan of his Chief Justice. Roger Brooke Taney, who finally
replaced John Marshall, had been a favorite of Andrew Jackson,
and a member of his cabinet. But Taney, too, turned out to prove
the perils of lifetime tenure. He outlived his popularity with dominant opinion, at least in the North. The author of the *Dred Scott*
decision tottered on in office until 1864, when the Civil War was
almost over.

The prestige of the federal courts stands high today with liberals
and intellectuals. The independence of the courts seems a tower of
strength for the poor, for the downtrodden, for the average man
against the power of big government. Hence Jefferson's famous

---

[42] Quoted in Charles Warren, *The Supreme Court in United States History*,
Vol. I (1922), p. 191.

[43] 2 Stats. 89 (Act of Feb. 13, 1801); repealed, 2 Stats. 132 (Act of March 8,
1802). See Erwin C. Surrency, "The Judiciary Act of 1801," 2 Am. J. Leg. Hist.
53 (1958).

fight against Federalist judges is one policy of his party that has badly stood the test of time. Undeniably, some federal judges behaved in ways that would be considered disgraceful today. In the early Republican period, federal judges did not run for reelection; but they played a more active political role than is standard for appellate judges today. Some Federalists made what were in effect election speeches from the bench. They harangued grand juries in a most partisan way. This gave some point to the attacks. Other judges were more discreet, but (in Jefferson's view) equally partisan. One of the sources of Marshall's strength was his tremendous solemnity. His opinions, mellifluous, grandly styled, even pompous, purported to be timeless and nonpolitical. They appealed to principle, to the sacred words of the Constitution. Their tone implied that their true author was the law itself in all its majesty; the judge was a detached, impartial vessel. This attitude annoyed Jefferson inordinately, who saw in it nothing but a subtle, maddening hypocrisy. Either way, it was an effective piece of political theater.

Jefferson's attacks on the judges did not totally fail. Like Roosevelt's plan to pack the court in 1937, Jefferson and his successors may have lost the battle but won the war. In both cases, an extreme tactic—the threat of impeachment, a court-packing plan—failed; but perhaps it served its real role as a bogeyman, not without impact.

The Constitution gave federal judges tenure for life. It left open only one way to tame the judges: the terrible sword of impeachment. Federal judges could be impeached for "Treason, Bribery, or other high Crimes and Misdemeanors" (art. II, sec. 4). The South Carolina constitution of 1790 permitted impeachment for "misdemeanor in office" (art. V, sec. 3). Literally interpreted, then, the law permitted impeachment only in rare and extreme situations.[44] But there were a few notable cases, in the early 19th century, in which impeachment was used to drive enemies of party and state out of office. In 1803, Alexander Addison, presiding judge of the fifth judicial district in Pennsylvania, was impeached and removed from his office. He was a bitter-end Federalist; as a lower-court judge, he harangued grand juries on political subjects. On one oc-

[44] In some states, the wording of the constitution was much less emphatic. So, in New Hampshire, under the constitution of 1792, the governor, with the consent of the council, might "remove" judges "upon the address of both houses of the legislature" (Part II, Sec. 73).

casion, he refused to let an associate judge speak to the grand jury in rebuttal; impeachment was grounded on this incident. A straight party vote removed Addison from the bench. Eighteen Republicans in the Pennsylvania senate voted him guilty; four Federalists voted for acquittal.[45]

On the federal level, the purge drew first blood in 1804. It was a rather shabby victory. The Senate impeached John Pickering, a Federalist judge. He had committed no "high crimes and misdemeanors"; but he was an old man, a drunk, and seriously deranged. It was understandable to want him off the bench; but it was far from clear that the Constitution provided for this kind of case. Pickering's removal was, in fact, a stroke of politics, a dress rehearsal for a far more important assault, the impeachment of Samuel Chase.[46]

This celebrated affair took place soon after Pickering's trial. Chase was a Justice of the United States Supreme Court. He had had a long and distinguished career, but he was an uncompromising partisan, and a man with a terrible temper. He too was notorious for grand-jury charges that were savage attacks on the party in power. President Jefferson stayed in the background; but his close associates moved articles of impeachment against Chase. The articles of impeachment made a number of specific charges of misconduct against Chase; among them, that at a circuit court, in Baltimore, in May 1803, he did "pervert his official right and duty to address the grand jury" by delivering "an intemperate and inflammatory political harangue," behavior which was "highly indecent, extra-judicial and tending to prostitute the high judicial character with which he was invested to the low purpose of an electioneering partisan." [47]

The anti-Chase faction overplayed its hand, however. In a frank private conversation, Senator Giles of Virginia admitted what was really at stake:

[45] S. W. Higginbotham, *The Keystone in the Democratic Arch: Pennsylvania Politics 1800–1816* (1952), pp. 53–55.

[46] Lynn W. Turner, "The Impeachment of John Pickering," 54 Am. Hist. Rev. 485 (1949). It is not certain that the constitutional provision on impeachment was as restricted in meaning as has been commonly supposed. For background, see Raoul Berger, "Impeachment of Judges and 'Good Behavior' Tenure," 79 Yale L. J. 1475 (1970).

[47] *Report of the Trial of the Hon. Samuel Chase* (1805); Appendix, pp. 5–6; see also Richard B. Lillich, "The Chase Impeachment," 4 Am. J. Leg. Hist. 49 (1960).

a removal by impeachment [is] nothing more than a declaration by Congress to this effect: You hold dangerous opinions, and if you are suffered to carry them into effect you will work the destruction of the nation. *We want your offices,* for the purpose of giving them to men who will fill them better.[48]

The trial was long, bitter, sensational. Republicans defected in enough numbers so that Chase was acquitted, by the slimmest of margins. John Marshall and his court were thenceforward "secure." Albert Beveridge claimed that "One of the few really great crises in American history had passed." [49] In January 1805, an attempt was made to impeach all but one of the judges on Pennsylvania's highest court; it failed by a narrow vote.[50] Impeachment was not a serious threat after these years.

Another radical plan to get rid of bad judges was to abolish their offices. Jefferson could not have abolished the Supreme Court, even if he had wanted to, without changing the Constitution. But his administration repealed the Judiciary Act of 1801; that put the midnight judges out of business. An ingenious method for removing unpopular judges was tried in Kentucky. In 1823, the Kentucky court of appeals struck down certain laws for relief of debtors; this act aroused a storm of protest. Under the law, the legislature could remove judges by a two-thirds vote; the "relief party" could not muster that percentage. Instead, the legislature abolished the court of appeals; and created a new court of four judges, to be appointed by the governor. The old court did not quietly give up its power. For a time, two courts of appeal tried to function in the state, and state politics was dominated by the dispute between "old court" and "new court" factions. Most lower courts obeyed the old court; a few followed the new court; a few tried to recognize both. Ultimately, the "old court" party won control of the legislature, and abolished the new court (over the governor's veto). The old court was awarded back pay; the new court was treated as if it had never existed at all.[51]

48 Quoted in J. Willard Hurst, *The Growth of American Law* (1950), p. 136.
49 Albert Beveridge, *The Life of John Marshall,* Vol. III (1919), p. 220.
50 S. W. Higginbotham, *The Keystone in the Democratic Arch,* p. 79.
51 On this controversy, see George DuRelle, "John Boyle," in *Great American Lawyers,* Vol. II (1907), pp. 223–259. There were cleaner ways than impeachment or abolition of courts to get rid of old and inconvenient judges. Under the New York constitution of 1821 (art. V, sec. 3), the chancellor and justices of the supreme court had to retire at the age of sixty. Among others, this cost James Kent his office, in 1823.

As these crises died down, the forces of light seemed to have triumphed over darkness—a free, independent judiciary over a servile mouthpiece of state. That the impeachment of Chase failed is said to show that both parties believed in a strong, independent judiciary, in the ideal of separation of powers. Many politicians did have qualms about impeachment; it smacked of overkill. Some of Jefferson's own men shared these qualms. They did not feel that a sitting judge should be replaced on political grounds. But the failure of impeachment was not a clear-cut victory for either side. It was rather a kind of social compromise. The judges won independence, but at a price. Their openly political role was reduced; and ultimately, most states turned to the elective principle. There would be no more impeachments, but also no more Chases. What carried the day, in a sense, was the John Marshall solution. The judges would take refuge in professional decorum. The essence of their job would always be to make and interpret policy; but policy would be divorced from overt, partisan politics. Principles and policy would flow, at least ostensibly, from the logic of law; they would not follow the naked give and take of the courthouse square. Justice would be blind; and it would wear a poker face. This picture of the behavior of judges had enough truth, and enough hypnotic force, to influence the role-playing of judges; and to bring some peace and consensus to issues of tenure, selection, behavior, and removal of judges.

Courts could not totally avoid stepping into dangerous places. Some issues, of course, were so charged with emotion that the veil of objectivity fell or was torn from the judges' faces. *Dred Scott*, in 1857, was an example of the court overreaching itself. There were many minor *Dred Scotts* at lower levels of decision. Prejudice and arrogance in court did not die out in 1810, or 1820, or ever, but it became less blatant; in any event, it became harder to document. Long after Chase, there were political trials in the United States, and judges who persecuted unpopular or dissenting men. In 1845, Circuit Judge Amasa J. Parker presided at the trial of the antirent rioters of upstate New York; his behavior was as partisan and prejudiced as any Federalist judge of the early 1800's.[52] But more and more, the judges were forced into an outward posture of propriety.

Meanwhile the actual power of judges, as makers of doctrine and framers of rules, may have actually grown somewhat after 1800. The courts had to hammer out legal propositions to govern the country, to sift what was viable from what was not in the common-

[52] Described in Henry Christman, *Tin Horns and Calico* (1945), ch. 18.

law tradition. Once case reports began to be published, judges had rich opportunities to mold law as their logic and social sense directed and as the docket, responsive to outside pressure and the demands of the litigants, required. They did not let the opportunity slide. The legal generation of 1776 had been a generation of political thinkers and statesmen. The Constitution of the United States is their greatest legal monument. In the next generation, there were no greater state papers than such judicial opinions as *Marbury* v. *Madison,* or the *Dartmouth College Case.* The best of the early 19th century judges had a subtle, accurate political sense; and a strong set of economic and social beliefs. They turned their attention to law in one of its prosaic meanings: the workaday rules of American life. They built and molded doctrine—scaffolding (as they saw it) to support the architecture of human affairs.

Perhaps the greatest of the judges was John Marshall, Chief Justice of the United States Supreme Court. He, more than anyone else, gave federal judgeship its meaning. The judges, all conceded, formed a co-ordinate branch of government. They were separate, but were they equal? In *Marbury* v. *Madison* (1803), John Marshall invented or affirmed the power of judicial review over acts of Congress. But the Marbury decision was only one dramatic instance of Marshall's work. His doctrines *made* constitutional law. He personally transformed the function and meaning of the Supreme Court. When he came on the bench, in 1801, the Supreme Court was a frail and fledgling institution. In 1789, Robert Hanson Harrison turned down a position on the court to become chancellor of Maryland. John Jay resigned in 1795 to run for governor of New York.[53] In the first years, the court heard very few cases. By the time Marshall died, the court was fateful and great.

Marshall had a sure touch for institutional solidity. Before he became Chief Justice, the judges delivered *seriatim* (separate) opinions, one after another, in the English style. Marshall, however, put an end to this practice. The habit of "caucusing opinions," and delivering up one unanimous opinion only, as the "opinion of *the Court*" had been tried by Lord Mansfield in England. It was abandoned there; but Marshall revived it. Unanimity was the rule on the Court; for a while, until William Johnson (1777–1834) was appointed by Jefferson, in 1804, the unanimity

<hr/>

53 The election for governor of New York was held in April 1795; and Jay's opponent happened to be Abraham Yates, chief justice of the New York supreme court; in short, a chief justice was deserting the bench for a governorship—no matter who was victorious.

was absolute, with not a single dissenting opinion. Johnson broke this surface consensus.[54] Yet neither Johnson nor any later justices could or would undo Marshall's work. Doctrines changed; personalities and blocs clashed on the court; power contended with power; but these struggles all took place within the fortress that Marshall had built. The court remained strong and surprisingly independent. Jefferson hoped that Johnson would enter the lists against Marshall. Yet Johnson more than once sided with Marshall, in opposition to Jefferson, his leader and friend. The nature and environment of the court—life tenure, the influence of colleagues—loosened his other allegiances. It was to be a story often told. Joseph Story betrayed Madison; Oliver Wendell Holmes bitterly disappointed Theodore Roosevelt; the first decision of the Warren Burger court was a slap in the face to Richard Nixon.

There were strong leaders and builders in the state courts, too. James Kent dominated his court in New York, in the early 19th century. As he remembered it, "The first practice was for each judge to give his portion of opinions, when we all agreed, but that gradually fell off, and, for the last two or three years before I left the bench, I gave the most of them. I remember that in eighth Johnson[55] all the opinions for one term are 'per curiam.' The fact is I wrote them all." [56] Kent's pride in his work was justified. But admittedly the opportunity to be creative was there. The judges were independent in two senses: free from England, but also free, for the moment, from stifling partisan control. Also, they were published. The colonial judges, who left no monuments behind, are forgotten men. From 1800 on, strong-minded American judges, whose work was recorded, influenced their courts and the law. In New York there was Chancellor Kent (1776–1847); in Massachusetts, Theophilus Parsons (1750–1813) and Lemuel Shaw (1781–1861); in Pennsylvania, John B. Gibson (1780–1853); in North Carolina, Thomas Ruffin (1752–1819); in Ohio, Peter Hitchcock (1781–1853); in Louisiana, Francis Xavier Martin (1762–1846).

54 Donald G. Morgan, *Justice William Johnson: The First Dissenter* (1954), pp. 168–189; the phrase about "caucusing opinions" is from a letter written by Jefferson. See also Karl M. ZoBell, "Division of Opinion in the Supreme Court: A History of Judicial Disintegration," 44 Cornell L. Q. 186 (1959).

55 That is, the eighth volume of Johnson's *Reports* of New York cases. Kent is referring to the October term, 1811, of the New York Supreme Court. 8 Johns. 361–493. *Per curiam* means "by the court," that is, not attributed to any specific judge.

56 Quoted in William Kent, *Memoirs and Letters of James Kent* (1898), p. 118.

Their spheres were less floodlit, of course, than the great federal courts; their work had less national significance. Some were excellent stylists; all wrote in what Karl Llewellyn has called the Grand Style: [57] their opinions were often little treatises, moving from elegant premise to elaborate conclusion, ranging far and wide over subject matter boldly defined. They were, at their best, farsighted men, impatient with narrow legal logic. Marshall, Gibson, and Shaw could write for pages without citing a shred of authority. They did not choose to base their decisions on precedent alone; law had to be chiseled out of basic principle; the traditions of the past were merely evidence of principle, and rebuttable. Their grasp of the spirit of the law was tempered by what they understood to be needs of a living society. Many were conservative men, passionately attached to tradition; but they honored tradition, not for its own sake, but for the values that inhered in it. They became famous not for adherence to the past, but as reinterpreters of living law. Most of the great judges were scholarly men; a few were very erudite, like Joseph Story, who studded his opinions, unlike Marshall, with acres of citation. The great judges were creative, self-aware, and willing to make changes. James Kent described his work as chancellor as follows:

> I took the court as if it had been a new institution, and never before known in the United States. I had nothing to guide me, and was left at liberty to assume all such English Chancery powers and jurisdiction as I thought applicable. . . . This gave me grand scope, and I was checked only by the revision of the Senate, or Court of Errors.

> My practice was, first, to make myself perfectly and accurately . . . master of the facts. . . . I saw where justice lay, and the moral sense decided the court half the time; and I then sat down to search the authorities until I had examined my books. I might once in a while be embarrassed by a technical rule, but I most always found principles suited to my view of the case.[58]

Kent noticed that no one ever cited the work of his predecessors. Their opinions, unpublished, were gone with the wind. He made sure he would not share that fate. He worked closely with William Johnson (1769–1848), who reported his cases. Other judges did this

[57] Karl N. Llewellyn, "Remarks on the Theory of Appellate Decision and the Rules or Canons About How Statutes Are to Be Construed," 3 Vanderbilt L. R. 395, 396 (1950). See below, part III, ch. 11, p. 540.

[58] Quoted in William Kent, *Memoirs and Letters of James Kent* (1898), pp. 158–59.

job themselves. F. X. Martin compiled Louisiana decisions from 1811 to 1830; during much of this time, he was himself on the bench. Many judges were active in collecting, revising, or digesting the statutes of their states, and in writing or rewriting treatises. Joseph Story wrote a series of definitive treatises on various branches of law. James Kent, after retiring from the bench, wrote his monumental *Commentaries*. John F. Grimke (1753–1819) published the laws of South Carolina, wrote a treatise on the "Duty of Executors and Administrators," and the inevitable "South Carolina Justice of the Peace" (1788). Harry Toulmin (1766–1823) edited the statutes of Kentucky; then, as judge of Mississippi Territory, he edited the territorial statutes. Still later, in Alabama Territory, he edited the statutes there too.

Many appellate judges were versatile and highly educated. George Wythe of Virginia (1726–1806), chancellor of the state from 1788 to 1801, was perhaps the foremost classical scholar in the state; as "professor of law and policy" at William and Mary (1779–1780), he occupied the first chair of law in an American college. Augustus B. Woodward (1774–1827), judge of Michigan Territory from 1805, prepared a plan for the city of Detroit, wrote on political subjects, and published a book called *A System of Universal Science*.[59] Some judges were classicists, had gifts for science or language, or, like Story, wrote bad poetry. Theophilus Parsons of Massachusetts published a paper on astronomy, and dabbled in mathematics. His "Formula for Extracting the Roots of Adjected Equations" appears as an appendix to the memoir of his life, which his son published in 1859. Parsons was also a Greek scholar and wrote a Greek grammar, which was never published. John Gibson of Pennsylvania was a devotee of French and Italian literature, a student of Shakespeare and an excellent violinist. He was probably the only major judge who designed his own false teeth. William Johnson, while a Supreme Court justice, wrote and published a life of Nathanael Greene, in two volumes and nearly 1,000 pages.[60] He was also an active member of the Charleston, South Carolina, Horticultural Society, and wrote a "Memoire on the Strawberry" in 1832.[61] John Marshall himself wrote a life of George Washington.

59 On Woodward, see Frank B. Woodford, *Mr. Jefferson's Disciple, A Life of Justice Woodward* (1953).

60 Donald G. Morgan, *Justice William Johnson: The First Dissenter* (1954) pp. 148–49.

61 Irwin F. Greenberg, "Justice William Johnson: South Carolina Unionist, 1823–1830," 36 Pa. Hist. 307, 331n (1969).

Most frequently, judges had political careers before they reached the bench. Although most of them willingly "put aside ambition" when they "donned the ermine," their prior lives probably included elective or appointive office. On the frontier, judging was only one aspect of a politician's busy life. Harry Toulmin, in the Old Southwest, was "also postmaster, preached and officiated at funerals and marriages, made Fourth of July orations, practiced medicine gratuitously, and in general was the head of the settlements." [62] Before his arrival in the territory, he had been secretary of state in Kentucky. John Boyle (1774–1835), chief justice of Kentucky, was a member of Congress before he became a judge. Joseph Story was speaker of the Massachusetts House when he was appointed to the court. For some judges—John Jay, for example—judgeship was an interlude between other political posts.

Judgeship, then, was not a lifetime career for all judges. It was a stepping-stone, or a refuge from politics, or a political reward. It was not a distinctive career, with its own distinctive pattern of training and background, as in many Continental countries. Judgeship was a matter of luck and opportunity, not special skill, background, or aspiration. It was and is an offshoot of the bar—of that part of the bar active in political affairs.

A prominent lawyer usually took a cut in income if he became a judge. The salaries of judges, as of public officials in general, were not generous. Judges continually complained that they were pinched for money. By statute in 1827, New Jersey fixed the salary of the justices of the state supreme court at $1,000. The chief justice earned $1,200. The governor earned $2,000.[63] Lemuel Shaw became chief justice of Massachusetts in 1830 at a salary of $3,000. The salary was the source of his only reluctance. For trial judges, the fee system was common. A New York law of 1786 awarded fees to the "judge of the court of probates, . . . to wit: For filing every petition, one shilling; for making and entering every order, six shillings; for every citation, under seal, to witnesses, or for any other purposes, six shillings . . . for copies of all records and proceedings, when required, for each sheet consisting of one hundred and twenty-eight words, one shilling and six pence." [64] Under the fee system, lower-court judges sometimes got rich. But higher levels of the bench paid off in the coin of high status.

[62] Dunbar Rowland, Courts, Judges and Lawyers of Mississippi 1798–1935 (1935), p. 21.

[63] Acts N.J. 1827, p. 9.

[64] Laws N.Y. 1778–1792, Vol. 1 (1792), p. 240.

THE ORGANIZATION OF COURTS

The Constitution of 1787 created a new system, the federal courts. Like the privy council before 1776, the federal courts had power to review the work of state courts. The extent of that power was and still is a matter of constant redefinition. It was limited severely in scope by the Constitution; yet, in its sphere, it was more potent than colonial review by the British government. Federal courts were close at hand; no ocean intervened; they were familiar with local problems and how to handle them. The Constitution gave the federal courts jurisdiction in admiralty; and, on matters of federal law, litigants could appeal from state to federal courts. In non-federal matters, however, the states and their courts were supreme. Of course, the judicial clauses of the Constitution merely set an evolution in process and marked off some of its obvious limits. No one even dreamt of the vast powers that would grow from these 18th-century seeds.

The federal Constitution was a document of its time, bearing the mark of contemporary theory. In particular, it embodied concepts of separation of powers, and the idea of checks and balances in government. These theories also influenced judicial organization in the states. But the states did not immediately choose to separate judicial from other powers completely. It was a deep-seated tradition to mix branches of government at the highest level. In Connecticut, the governor, lieutenant governor, and council constituted a "Supreme Court of Errors." Formerly the legislature itself had acted as the court of last resort.[65] In New Jersey, under the constitution of 1776, the governor held the office of chancellor; and together with his council, constituted "the Court of Appeals, in the last resort." In New York, the "court for the trial of impeachments, and the correction of errors," the highest court, under the constitutions of 1777 and 1821, consisted of the president of the senate, the senators, the chancellor, and the justices of the supreme court.[66]

One by one, however, states began to give their highest court final judicial authority. In New Jersey, the constitution of 1844, in

[65] Roscoe Pound, *Organization of Courts* (1940), p. 95.
[66] New Jersey const., 1776, art. IX; New York const., 1777, art. XXXII; New York const., 1821, art. V, sec. 1.

New York, the constitution of 1846, put the seal on this change. Rhode Island was the last state to join the movement. As late as the 1850's, the legislature passed an act, which in effect granted a new trial in a pending case. The Rhode Island court, in 1856, interposed itself, labeled the practice intolerable, and appealed to the concept of separation of powers.[67] By that time, political opinion, almost universally, considered this kind of legislative pretension out-of-date. Yet throughout the period legislatures passed private acts that filled functions now thought purely judicial or executive. They granted divorces to end marriage, and charters to begin corporations. They quieted title to property, declared heirships, and legalized changes of name.

As in colonial days, in most states there was no clear-cut division between trial and appellate courts. High-court judges often doubled as trial or circuit judges. Appellate terms of court were held in the capital at fixed times of the year. In between, judges spent part of the year on coach or horseback, traveling circuit. Circuit duty was a considerable hardship. The country was large and sparsely settled, the interior a wilderness. Roads were muddy or dusty torture, depending on the season. Often, the judges rode circuit in their home districts, which somewhat lightened the burden. Still, many judges complained ceaselessly of their gypsy life. The system did have some virtues. It brought justice close to home; it conserved judicial manpower. Circuit duty gave the appellate judge actual trial experience. This brought him closer to real litigants, and (some felt) was good for his soul. Trial work also cemented relations between bench and bar. Around 1800, in York County, in what later became the state of Maine, judges and lawyers traveled together, argued together, joked together, drank and lived together; this traveling "collection of lawyers, jurors, suitors, and witnesses filled up the small villages in which the courts were held." Often there was literally no room at the inn. "It was quite a privilege, enjoyed by few, to obtain a separate bed." The members of the bar "were no ascetics. The gravity and dignity of the bar . . . were very apt to be left in the courtroom—they were seldom seen in the bar room." [68] On the frontier, the circuit system bred a rugged type of judge. In Missouri, around 1840, Charles H. Allen, appointed to one of the Missouri circuits, traveled "on horseback from Palmyra," his home, about two hundred miles; then "around

[67] *Taylor & Co.* v. *Place,* 4 R.I. 324 (1856).
[68] William Willis, *A History of the Law, the Courts, and the Lawyers of Maine* (1863), p. 278.

the circuit, about eight hundred more. This he did three times a year, spending nearly his whole time in the saddle. He was, however, a strong, robust man, and capable of the greatest endurance. He always traveled with a holster of large pistols in front of his saddle, and a knife with a blade at least a foot long. But for his dress, a stranger might have readily taken him for a cavalry officer." [69]

But as the states grew in wealth and population, they tended to sharpen the distinction between trial courts and courts of appeal. Some states established tiers of intermediate courts, called circuit courts, superior courts, or courts of common pleas. These middle courts were typically trial courts of quite general jurisdiction. They also heard appeals, or retried matters begun in the lowest courts. The supreme court tended to become more and more an appeal court, even if the judges, on occasion, still rode circuit.

Only the highest courts, chiefly the Supreme Court of the United States, have been the subject of any sizeable amount of historical research. The judges of the Supreme Court wore robes, stood heir to a great tradition, and heard cases of far-reaching importance. Very little work has been done on the personnel of lower courts, and their impact on society. Who served as justices of the peace? What was their background and influence? The justice of the peace was "arch symbol of our emphasis on local autonomy in the organization of courts," reflecting the "practical need, in a time of poor and costly communications, to bring justice close to each man's door." [70] But what was the quality of that justice? How much of the justice's work was social control of the English type—autocratic guidance through democratic forms? The role and function of lower-court judges probably changed greatly between 1790 and 1840; and there were probably great differences between East, West, and South. But little about form, function, and staff is definitely known.

State courts were more highly specialized than the federal courts. Some states, for example, used separate courts for wills and probate matters. Others, as is the practice today, gave these problems over to courts of general jurisdiction. In New Jersey, the "ordinary" probated wills, and granted letters of administration and guardianship in his "prerogative court." Other estate matters were han-

69 W. V. N. Bay, *Reminiscences of the Bench and Bar of Missouri* (1878), p. 211.

70 J. Willard Hurst, *The Growth of American Law* (1950), p. 148.

dled in New Jersey by the oddly named orphans' court.[71] This tribunal was composed of judges who also served on the court of common pleas in the New Jersey counties.[72] Some states kept separate courts for equity. Georgia's constitution of 1789 (art. III, sec. 3) declared that "Courts-merchant shall be held as heretofore"; but the constitution of 1798 deleted the clause. In Delaware, there were courts of oyer and terminer, and courts of general sessions and jail delivery. Memphis, Cairo, and Chattanooga had their own municipal courts, New York its mayor's court; Richmond's hustings court preserved an ancient, honorable name. The St. Louis Land Court (1855) was an unusual example of specialization.

Unlike the state constitutions, which often discussed the structure of courts in some detail, the federal Constitution was quite laconic on the subject. Judicial power was to be vested in a "Supreme Court" and such "inferior courts" as "the Congress may from time to time ordain and establish." The Supreme Court was given original jurisdiction in a few types of cases: cases involving ambassadors, and those to which a state was party. Congress was to decide how much appellate jurisdiction the court would have. The President had power to appoint justices, subject to Senate confirmation. The Senate proved to be no rubber stamp. George Washington appointed John Rutledge of South Carolina to succeed Chief Justice Jay. A bloc of Federalists, annoyed that Rutledge had opposed Jay's treaty, punished him by refusing confirmation, though Rutledge had already served a few months on an interim basis, and had even written a few opinions.[73]

Under the Constitution, Congress could have dispensed with any lower federal courts. State courts would then have had original jurisdiction over all but a few federal issues. The famous Judiciary Act of 1789 provided otherwise.[74] It divided the country into districts, each district generally coextensive with a state, each with a Federal District Court, and District Judge. The districts, in turn, were grouped into three circuits. In each circuit, a circuit court, made up of two Supreme Court justices and one district judge, sat twice a year. In general, the circuit courts handled cases of diversity

[71] Pennsylvania too had a court with this name. An "ordinary," in England, had been an official in the church courts.

[72] Stats. N.J. 1847, p. 205.

[73] Charles Warren, op. cit., Vol. 1, pp. 128–139.

[74] For the early history of federal jurisdiction, see Felix Frankfurter and James Landis, The Business of the Supreme Court (1928), pp. 4–52.

of citizenship; the district courts, cases of admiralty. In certain limited cases, the circuit courts heard appeals.

One defect of the system was that it forced the justices to climb into carriages and travel to their circuits. At first, the justices were on circuit twice a year, later lightened to once a year. Additional judges were added to the court, and new circuits were created as the country grew. But these changes helped only a little. In 1838, Justice McKinley traveled 10,000 miles in and to his circuit (Alabama, Louisiana, Mississippi, Arkansas). Five other justices traveled between 2,000 and 3,500 miles each.[75] As with state courts, some argued that circuit duty was beneficial. It brought the judges closer to the people; it retaught them the legal problems of trial work. But, as Gouverneur Morris pointed out, no one could argue that

> riding rapidly from one end of this country to another is the best way to study law. . . . Knowledge may be more conveniently acquired in the closet than in the high road.[76]

Reform proved politically impossible. In Congress, a strong states-right bloc was hostile to the federal courts. This bloc saw no reason to cater to the judges' convenience. The Judiciary Act of 1801 abolished circuit riding for Supreme Court justices. Unhappily, this was the famous act of the midnight judges. It was an admirable law in the technical sense, but doomed by its political implications. The Jefferson administration promptly repealed it. Again and again, reform proposals became entangled in sectional battles or battles between Congress and the President, and went down to defeat. As was so often true, notions of technical efficiency were sacrificed to more powerful values and interests.

CIVIL PROCEDURE

Left to themselves, the colonies might have developed modes of procedure more rational and streamlined than anything in England. The process was retarded in the 18th century by the trend toward Anglicization. Many lawyers and judges were English-trained; English legal texts were in use. Imperial rule, English prestige, and the growth of a professional bar led to a reaction against the "crudities" of colonial procedure. The colonial systems became compromises between English law and native experiment.

[75] Frankfurter and Landis, *op. cit.,* pp. 49–50.
[76] Quoted, *ibid.,* p. 17.

THE REPUBLIC OF BEES

By the time of the Revolution, colonial procedure was bewilderingly diverse.

There was no chance that classical English pleading would be established after Independence. The American bar was not equipped to handle this dismal lore. Nor could the business community tolerate the complexity of English pleading. It was one matter to evolve such a system, as the English had; to bring it in from outside was quite another. But since English lawbooks were easily available, English procedure had great influence. This was particularly true of the first generation after 1776, and for the upper reaches of the profession. Some pleading and practice manuals were written in America, stressing local forms and procedures. When Joseph Story published *A Selection of Pleadings in Civil Actions* (1805), he took some of his forms from Massachusetts lawyers; and he justified his book on the basis of differences in "customs, statutes, and common law between England and Massachusetts." But basically the book was English, some of it culled from fairly ancient sources, merely adapted for Americans, thereby, in that process, avoiding "the high price of foreign books." James Gould's *Treatise on the Principles of Pleading in Civil Actions,* published in Boston in 1832, had the grandiose aim of setting out principles of pleading as a "science." It paid scant attention to American law as such:

> As the *English* system of pleading is, in general, the basis of that of our country; the former has, in the following treatise, been followed exclusively, without regard to any peculiarities in the latter; excepting a very few references to those, which exist in the law of my native State.[77]

Popular English manuals were actually used in this country. In addition, special American editions of English treatises were prepared. Joseph Chitty's treatise on pleading was so well received that an eighth American edition was published in 1840. Chapter 9 of this dreary book bore the following title: "Of Rejoinders and the Subsequent Pleadings; of Issues, Repleaders, Judgments non Obstante Veredicto, and Pleas Puis Darrein Continuance, or now Pending Action; and of Demurrers and Joinders in Demurrer." In this book, the American lawyer could drink in such strictures as the following:

> A traverse may be *too extensive,* and therefore defective, by being taken in the *conjunctive* instead of the *disjunctive,* where

[77] Preface, ix.

proof of the allegation in the conjunctive is not essential. Thus, in an action on a policy on ship and tackle, the defendant should not deny that the ship and tackle were lost, but that *neither* was lost.[78]

Clearly, English common-law pleading was no model to follow slavishly. Pleading was an elaborate contest of lawyerly arts, and winning a case did not always depend on substantive merits. There were too many rules, and they were too tricky and inconsistent. The idea behind English pleading was not itself absurd. Pleading was supposed to distill, out of the amorphousness of fact and fancy, one precious, narrow issue on which trial could be joined. Principles of pleading were, in theory, principles of economy and order. Pleading demanded great technical skill. Those who had the skill —highly trained lawyers and judges—saw no reason to abandon the system. But the country was not run by lawyers. Merchants, bankers, and landowners were more important in American life. To these, the "science of pleading" could not appear otherwise than obfuscation, a lawyer's plot to kill justice, or to frustrate the expectations of an ordinary man of affairs. It is a question, what Chitty's ship-merchant would have thought of disjunctive and conjunctive traverses.

English procedure, then, was too medieval for the modern world. (One wonders why it was not too medieval for the Middle Ages.) Reform of civil procedure, at any rate, found fertile soil in the United States. Pleading reform was one of the changes made necessary by the explosion in legal consumers. Legal skill was a resource; and it was scarce. It had to be husbanded. Shrewdness in pleading was not cheap enough and universal enough to pay its way in American society. Popular democracy, the colonial tradition, business demands for rationality and predictability: these too joined to oppose the strict "science of pleading." Against them were arrayed a few troops of bench and bar. But this was a raggle-taggle army, halfhearted in defense of its position. Francophile judges had contempt for the common law. Rank-and-file lawyers were too untrained for Chitty. English procedure had become like a drafty old house. Those born to it and raised in it loved it; but no outsider could tolerate its secret panels, broken windows, and on-again, off-again plumbing.

Reform did not come in one great burst. The actual practice of courts, particularly trial courts, was freer and easier than one might assume from reading manuals of procedure. As more re-

[78] Joseph Chitty, *Treatise on Pleading*, 645.*

search is done, more variance between book learning and reality comes to light. Alexander Hamilton prepared a manuscript manual of practice in 1782, probably for his own use in cramming for the bar. In it, he noted a decline in "nice Learning" about pleas of abatement. These pleas, he said,

> are seldom used; and are always discountenanced by the Court, which having lately acquired a more liberal Cast begin to have some faint Idea that the end of Suits at Law is to Investigate the Merits of the Cause, and not to entangle in the Nets of technical Terms.[79]

New York was, relatively speaking, quite conservative in legal affairs. Hamilton's manual of New York pleading, if it can be trusted, shows deep dependence on English formalities and forms. Yet even here many cracks in the armor appear; many defections in favor of "the Merits of the Cause." Other jurisdictions departed much further from English propriety. Georgia, in the 18th century, passed a series of laws that went a long way toward rationalizing civil procedure. The climax was the Judiciary Act of 1799. Under Georgia's laws, a plaintiff might begin civil actions simply by filing a *petition,* setting out the case "plainly, fully and substantially"; the defendant would file his *answer,* stating whatever was necessary to constitute "the cause of his defense." [80] Georgia's law was, among other things, a courageous attempt to unite equity and common-law pleading. It also got rid of the forms of action, pigeonholes (or straitjackets) of procedure into which pleaders were forced to fit their plea. Conservative Georgia courts, outraged by the reforms, supposedly undermined the Georgia scheme and led to its downfall. But the evidence for this charge rests on nothing more than scraps of talk from appellate courts. Quite possibly, the reform had lasting effects on trial court behavior in Georgia.

By the 1830's, reform of procedure was in the air. In England itself, native lair of the common law, reform was a definite force. Jeremy Bentham cast a long shadow. Lord Brougham, in Parliament in 1828, had begged for reform. These men and their supporters set off a process with enormous internal significance. After all, England too was a modernizing society, years ahead of America in industrial development, if not in class structure. During the

[79] Quoted in Julius Goebel Jr., ed., *The Law Practice of Alexander Hamilton,* Vol. 1 (1964), p. 81.

[80] Robert W. Millar, *Civil Procedure of the Trial Court in Historical Perspective* (1952), p. 40.

19th century the two nations were mutually influential—their experiences meshed neatly together in parallel currents of change. But the key developments occurred toward the middle of the century, and later.[81]

In the Middle Ages, equity courts had been a source of law reform. Equity boasted a flexible collection of remedies; hence it had often prodded and pushed the more lethargic common law toward rationality. But equity had itself become hidebound; by 1800, it needed procedural reform as desperately as the common law. The very existence of equity was an anomaly—a separate and contradictory jurisprudence, living uneasily beside the "law." In the United States, many states gave equity jurisdiction to the same court that handled suits at law; the judges simply alternated roles. North Carolina, for example, in an act of 1782 empowered "each superior court of law" to "be and act as a court of equity for the same district." [82] In a few states (Mississippi, Delaware, New Jersey), the courts were distinct, with different judges for law and equity. This was true of New York until the 1820's, when the circuit judges were made "vice-chancellors," and given full equity powers within their circuits. But one did not appeal from these "vice-chancellors" to ordinary appellate courts; instead, one appealed to the chancellor.[83] Finally, some states had no developed system of equity at all (as distinct from "law"). Louisiana was one of these, because of its civil-law heritage. Massachusetts and Pennsylvania were outstanding common-law examples. Before 1848, however, only Georgia (and Texas, whose history was deviant) had actually *abolished* the distinction.

States that lacked "equity" had developed a rough union of their own. Statutes made equitable defenses available in cases at "law." In Massachusetts, the supreme judicial court had "power to hear and determine in equity all cases . . . when the parties have not a plain, adequate and complete remedy at the common law." The statute listed what these "cases" were; for example, "All suits for the specific performance of any written contract." [84] In Pennsylvania, "Common law actions were used to enforce purely equitable claims; purely equitable defenses were permitted in common law actions; and, at rare times, purely equitable reliefs were obtained

81 See below, Part III, ch. 3.
82 Laws N. Car. 1782, ch. 11.
83 Rev. Stats. N.Y. 1829, Vol. II, Part III, ch. 1, Title II, Sections 2, 59.
84 Rev. St. Mass. 1836, ch. 81, sec. 8.

by means of actions at law." [85] Throughout the period, Pennsylvania legislatures, by private laws, gave permission to individuals to do acts, which, in other states, were within the scope of equity power. For example, they sometimes permitted executors to sell parcels of land to pay the debts of a deceased.[86] In 1836, on the advice of a law-revision commission, Pennsylvania gave broad equity powers to some state courts. Thus, Pennsylvania (and Massachusetts), by a piecemeal process, attained "a curious anticipation of future general reforms." [87] In essence, "law" was bent to suit "equity"; but movement was not wholly in this one direction. Equity was addicted to written evidence, and classically tolerated nothing else. But the Judiciary Act of 1789 provided for oral testimony in federal equity cases. Georgia allowed trial by jury in some causes which by tradition belonged to the equity side of the bench. North Carolina, in a statute of 1782, did the same. And a North Carolina law of 1801 provided a simple way to continue equity actions after the death of a party on either side. This replaced the "bill of revivor," one of the prime procedural culprits, and one that by its sloth and technicality had given rise to the suspicion that a chancery bill, once begun, would never come to an end.[88]

In English law there were countless kinds of "appeal," calling for different pleadings and forms, full of dark mysteries, tripping and trapping the unwary. The word *appeal*, strictly speaking, applied only to review by higher equity courts. The states, continuing a trend that began in the colonial period, fixed on and emphasized two kinds of review by higher courts: the equity *appeal* and, for common-law actions, proceedings by writ of *error* or the equivalent. Local variations were frequent. In North Carolina, instead of writs of error, writs of certiorari were used—a form of review which in England was confined to review of noncommon-law courts.[89] In Connecticut the writ of error reviewed decisions in equity, usurping the place of the appeal.

The basic problem of review or appeal is how to avoid doing

[85] Spencer R. Liverant and Walter H. Hitchler, "A History of Equity in Pennsylvania," 37 Dickinson Law Rev. 156, 166 (1933).

[86] Thomas A. Cowan, "Legislative Equity in Pennsylvania" 4 Univ. of Pittsburgh Law Rev. 1, 12 (1937).

[87] Millar, *op. cit.*, p. 40. The Pennsylvania law of 1836, incidentally, did not put an end to private acts of "legislative equity"; these lasted for almost forty more years.

[88] Laws N. Car. 1782, ch. 11; 1801, ch. 10.

[89] Roscoe Pound, *Appellate Procedure in Civil Cases* (1941), p. 288.

everything over again—which would be a tremendous waste—but at the same time make sure that lower-court mistakes are corrected. In essence, writs of error corrected only some kinds of errors, those that appeared on the face of the formal record. These were pleading errors mostly, except insofar as a party, in a bill of exceptions, preserved complaints that the judge had let in illegitimate evidence. These errors rarely went to the heart of the matter. The appeal system suffered from what Roscoe Pound has called "record worship"—"an excessive regard for the formal record at the expense of the case, a strict scrutiny of that record for 'errors of law' at the expense of scrutiny of the case to insure the consonance of the result to the demands of the substantive law." [90] The system might be defended as a reasonable way to allocate power between high and low courts. High courts expounded the law, low courts decided cases. By correcting errors of record, high courts were able to adjust any kinks in formal doctrine. But at the same time, they left the day-to-day work of the trial courts alone. Still, record worship meant that injustices went unreviewed, and fresh injustice was done by the reversal of just cases on technical grounds. But the actual control of lower courts by upper courts—and the actual impact of record worship on the life cycle of a typical trial—is exceedingly hard to measure.

Record worship was a disease that probably did not randomly infect every type of case. Courts are stickier, for example, about small errors in cases where life or liberty is at stake. It is no surprise, then, that the law of criminal procedure outdid civil procedure in record worship and technical artifice. This branch of law had a special place in American jurisprudence. The Bill of Rights contained what amounted to a miniature code of criminal procedure. Warrants were not to be issued "but upon probable cause, supported by Oath or affirmation, and particularly describing the place to be searched, and the persons or things to be seized" (art. IV). No person "shall be held to answer for a capital, or otherwise infamous crime" without presentment or indictment by grand jury (art. V). No one "shall be compelled in any Criminal Case to be a witness against himself" or be "deprived of life, liberty or property, without due process of law" (art. V). The accused "shall enjoy" the right to a "speedy and public trial," by an "impartial" jury of the vicinage; he must be told the nature of his crime; must be able to confront the witnesses; must "have compulsory process for obtaining witnesses in his favor" and the "Assistance of Counsel for

90 Roscoe Pound, *Criminal Justice in America* (1930), p. 161.

his defense" (art. VI). "Excessive bail" was not to be required (art. VIII).

Many states adopted their own bill of rights even before the federal government. Other states copied federal law. No other field of law garnered as much constitutional attention as criminal procedure. The basic rights of man turned out, in large part, to be rights to fair criminal trial. These rights guarded against the tyranny of autocrats and kings. Abuse of power by Federalist judges only strengthened the ideas that underlay the Bill of Rights. Criminal procedure, on paper, gave a whole battery of protections to persons accused of crime. The defendant had the right to appeal a conviction; the state had no right to appeal an acquittal.[91] The reviewing court often seemed to be searching the record with a fine-tooth comb, looking for faulty instructions, improper evidence, error in formal pleadings, or prejudicial actions by the judge. Sometimes the upper court went rather far in quashing an indictment, for a tiny slip of the pen; or setting aside a verdict for some microscopic error at the trial. In *State* v. *Owen,* a North Carolina case of 1810, the grand jurors of Wake County had presented John Owen, a cabinet-maker, for murder. According to the indictment, Owen, in Raleigh, on April 21, 1809,

> not having the fear of God before his eyes, but being moved and seduced by the instigations of the Devil . . . with force and arms, at the city of Raleigh . . . in and upon one Patrick Conway . . . feloniously, wilfully, and of his malice aforethought, did make an assault . . . with a certain stick, of no value, which he the said John Owen in both his hands then and there had and held . . . in and upon the head and face of him the said Patrick Conway . . . did strike and beat . . . giving to the said Patrick Conway, *then and there* with the pine stick aforesaid, in and upon the head and face of him the said Patrick Conway, several *mortal wounds,* of which said mortal wounds, the said Patrick Conway then and there instantly died.

Owen was found guilty, and appealed. His attorney argued that the indictment was defective, in that it did not "set forth the *length and depth* of the mortal wounds." A majority of the supreme court of North Carolina regretfully agreed: "It appears from the books, that wounds capable of description must be described, that the Court may judge whether it be probable, that death might have been produced by them." Hence, since the in-

91 *State* v. *Jones,* 5 N. Car. 257 (1809).

dictment did not allege that the wounds were two inches long and four inches deep, or the like, Owen won a new trial.[92]

Roscoe Pound has called this kind of case the "hypertrophy of procedure." [93] This hypertrophy, he felt, stemmed from 19th-century individualism run riot. The criminal law tolerated "hypertrophy" because it served the needs of the dominant American type—the self-reliant man, who lived in a small town or on the frontier. This was a man confident of his own judgment, but jealous of the power of the state. Better to let the guilty free on a technicality, than allow courts and prosecutors real power or discretion.

There is a serious question, how far Pound's description fits the working law, and how much *State* v. *Owen* describes an important phenomenon. Pound's picture of criminal procedure best describes a tiny group of instances, preserved in appellate records like a fly in amber. Recorded appellate cases have always been a small minority of litigated cases. Who was it that took advantage of procedural rights, and the record worship of the appellate courts? Certainly not the slaves, the dependent poor, the urban masses. It is hard to tell how fair the *average* trial was. American law had its dark underside—vigilantism, lynching, mob rule. These show that in some communities, for some cases, public opinion did not tolerate the niceties of fair trial. Some *formal* rights, recognized today, were not recognized in the 19th century. Thousands were arrested, tried, and sentenced without lawyers. Yet only a good lawyer could make effective use of the full guarantees of the Bill of Rights, let alone take advantage of record worship and "hypertrophy." Probably the average criminal trial fell far short of the ideal of procedural due process. And even some major trials—trials with political overtones—were by any standards unfair.

THE LAW OF EVIDENCE

There is good reason to believe that the law of evidence tightened considerably between 1776 and the 1830's. Judging from surviving transcripts of criminal trials, courts had rather loose attitudes toward evidence around 1800. In the trial of the so-called Manhattan

Well Mystery—the transcript was found among Alexander Hamilton's papers—hearsay was freely admitted; and "some of the most important testimony was not elicited by questions" from the attorney, but rather "by allowing the witness to give a consecutive and uninterrupted account." [94] Opposing counsel did not meekly wait their turn to cross-examine. Rather, they broke in with questions whenever they wished.

When a field of law becomes cancerously intricate, some fundamental conflict of interest, some fundamental tension between opposing values, must lie at the root of the problem. The American political public has always resisted strong, central authority. Rather, power is fragmented, balkanized, dispersed. This attitude, which found expression in the theory of checks and balances, affected the law of evidence. The modern European law of evidence is fairly simple and rational; the law lets most everything in and trusts the judge to separate good evidence from bad. But American law distrusts the judge; it gives the jury full fact-finding power, and in criminal cases, the final word on innocence or guilt. Yet the law has distrusted the jury almost as much as it has distrusted the judge, and the rules of evidence grew up as a countervailing force. The jury only hears part of the story; that part which the law of evidence allows. The judge is bound too. If he lets in improper testimony, the case may be reversed on appeal. Hence the rules control both judge and jury.

It was during this period that many rules of evidence received classic formulation. The rules were heavily influenced by the jury system, and the attitude of the law toward the jury. In medieval times, the jury had been a panel of neighbors—knowing busybodies, who perhaps had personal knowledge of the case. When the function of the jury changed to that of an impartial panel of listeners, the law of evidence underwent explosive growth. The rules began to exclude all shaky, secondhand, or improper evidence from the eyes and ears of the jury. Only the most tested, predigested matter was fit for the jury's consumption. Consequently, in the 19th century, the so-called *hearsay rule* became one of the dominant rules of the law of evidence. This was a bizarre kind of rule—one simple, if Utopian, idea, along with a puzzle box of exceptions. The general rule was that juries should not hear secondhand evidence: they should hear Smith tell his story, not Jones' account of what Smith had said. But in many situations, the rule

[94] Julius Goebel, Jr., ed., *The Law Practice of Alexander Hamilton: Documents and Commentary*, Vol. 1 (1964), p. 701.

was deemed too strict, and exceptions were recognized—from involuntary utterances ("ouch!"), to shopbooks, to the dying words of a murder victim, naming his killer.

Hearsay rules grew luxuriantly, on both sides of the Atlantic. Most of the doctrines appeared first in England; but not all. The business-entry rule admits records made in the ordinary course of business, even though these are, strictly speaking, hearsay. The rule seems to have started in America around 1820.[95] In general, the American law of evidence outstripped English law in complexity, probably because of a deeper American fear of concentration of power.

The rules relating to witnesses were as complicated as rules about the kind of evidence that could be heard, and for similar reasons. In 1800, husbands and wives could testify neither for nor against each other. No person could testify as a witness if he had a financial interest in the outcome of the case. Parties to the lawsuit were therefore not competent to testify on their own behalf. New rules about witnesses were invented, too. The doctor-patient privilege, for example, prevents a doctor from giving medical testimony without his patient's consent. It seems to have first appeared in a New York law of 1828. Missouri passed a similar law in 1835.[96]

In theory, the rules of evidence were supposed to be rational rules of legal proof. Trials were to be orderly, businesslike, and fair. Each rule had its reason. But the rules as a whole, their sheer complexity, tended to defeat the rationale. They seemed bewildering and irrational, as liable to cheat justice as to fulfill it. Exclusionary rules, said Jeremy Bentham, had "the effect of shutting the door against . . . true . . . evidence." They gave "license to oppression by all imaginable wrongs." Quakers would not take an oath on religious grounds; the rule excluding their testimony,

> in a case of rape . . . includes a licence to the whole army to storm every quakers' meeting-house, and violate the persons of all the female part of the congregation, in the presence of fathers, husbands, and brothers.[97]

95 *Two Centuries Growth of American Law* (1901), pp. 324–5.

96 John H. Wigmore, *A Treatise on the System of Evidence*, Vol. IV (1905), sec. 2380, pp. 3347–8.

97 Jeremy Bentham, *Rationale of Judicial Evidence*, Vol. IV (1827), pp. 491–92. This particular horrible example could not occur in the United States. Quakers were, in general, competent witnesses in the United States. They were allowed to make "affirmations" instead of taking oaths.

It was unlikely that this gang rape ever took place. But there was plenty of real and possible abuse, to feed the appetite for reform. At the very time that courts were putting the final building blocks in place, the law of evidence began to be purged. But major changes were achieved only later in the century.

At the close of a trial, the judge instructs the jury—tells them of the applicable law. In the 20th century, the lawyers write these instructions; they tend to be stereotyped, antiseptic statements of abstract rules. Often juries may not understand them at all. They seem to matter only to lawyers, who argue about the wording, and base appeals on "errors" in instructions. In 1776 or 1800, judges tended to talk more freely to the jury. They summarized and commented on the trial; they explained the law in simple, nontechnical language. Instructions were clear, informative summaries of the state of the law. Chief Justice Richard Bassett, of Delaware, explaining adverse possession to a jury, in 1794, remarked: "If you are in possession of a corner of my land for twenty years by adverse possession, you may snap your fingers at me." [98] All this changed in the 19th century; the finger snapping ended. As early as 1796, a statute in North Carolina made it unlawful, "in delivering a charge to the petit-jury, to give an opinion whether a fact is fully or sufficiently proved," since that was "the true office and province of the jury." [99] Statutes took away the judge's right to comment on evidence, in many states in the 19th century. This made the jury less liable to domination by the judge. The stereotyped instructions may have confused the jury, but they helped maintain its autonomy. The judge was more rule-bound than before—hamstrung, one might even say. In 1800, the roles of judge and jury were relatively free. The trend thereafter was toward tighter definition of these roles. Gradually, what took shape was the distinction that became firmly embedded in the law: that the judge was master of "law," the jury of "fact." [100] The result, in theory at least, was a better balance of power. Checks and balances were more than constitutional concepts; they pervaded the whole of the law.

[98] Daniel J. Boorstin, ed., *Delaware Cases, 1792–1830*, Vol. I (1943), p. 39.

[99] Laws N. Car. 1796, ch. 4. See the comments on this statute by Ruffin, in *State* v. *Moses*, 13 N. Car. 452 (1830).

[100] See Note, "The Changing Role of the Jury in the Nineteenth Century," 74 Yale L. J. 170 (1964).

CHAPTER II

OUTPOSTS OF THE LAW: THE FRONTIER
AND THE CIVIL LAW FRINGE

THE FRONTIER

Colonial America was a seacoast country. But even before Independence, the line of settlement crept far inland. The colonies claimed vast tracts of inner wilderness. The Louisiana Purchase added another immense and largely unsettled area. Throughout the period, population flowed into the West and Southwest. These lands of forest and plain, great gushing rivers, fertile soil, and sweeping distances captured and held the American imagination. In 1800, the American frontier represented an empire of the future. By 1900, the frontier was an empire of the past, whose death was widely mourned in scholarship and myth. In literature, the frontier was a land of heroes. Life on the edge was lawless but vital; here the democratic spirit flourished, without the defects and troubles of the older East. The withering eye of modern scholarship has reduced the frontier myth to more human scale. The law of the frontier, too, has been gradually stripped of its legend.

At Independence, the states faced the problem of what to do with the western lands. The new republic, a collection of former colonies, itself became a kind of colonial power—once the decision was made to treat the western lands as common property of the nation. The Ordinance of 1787 prescribed basic law for that part of the West which later became Ohio, Indiana, Illinois, Michigan, and Wisconsin. The Ordinance of 1798 extended the influence of the 1787 ordinance into the Southwestern territories—to Alabama and Mississippi.

The Ordinance of 1787 adopted a bold policy of decolonization. Everyone expected that the territories would gradually fill with settlers. When adequately populated, they were to take their place in the Union as full, free, sovereign states. First, however, came a period of tutelage. Until such time as "five thousand free male inhabitants, of full age," lived in the territory, a governor and three judges were to hold the lawmaking power. The three judges had to reside in the district; any two could "form a court." They were to exercise "a common-law jurisdiction." [1] They had to be men of means, each of whom owned in the district "a freehold estate, in five hundred acres of land, while in the exercise of their offices." The governor and a majority of the judges had power to "adopt and publish in the district such laws of the original States, criminal and civil, as may be necessary, and best suited to the circumstances of the district." [2] Congress had veto power over these laws. This power formed a striking—and by no means accidental—parallel to the British power of review over the colonial statutes.

The phrase "adopt and publish" was troublesome, and confusing, from the start. It seemed to mean that territories had no right to make law on their own. They might only select, for their use, among prior alternatives in the statutes of the older states. The provision could not be literally carried out. At the very least, dates and place names had to be changed in borrowed statutes. In practice, the "adopt and publish" rule was avoided and evaded. Some territories adopted laws from states like Kentucky, which was not an "original" state. Some statutes were patched together from more than one statute in the older states. One critic charged that

> They parade the laws of the original states before them, on the table, and cull letters from the laws of Maryland, syllables from the laws of Virginia, words from the laws of New York, sentences from the laws of Pennsylvania, verses from the laws of Kentucky, and chapters from the laws of Connecticut—jumble the whole into such form as they conceive the most suitable to facilitate their schemes . . . and then call it a law.[3]

This was, of course, exaggeration; still, many territorial statutes were the product of scissors and paste.

However odd the "adopt and publish" rule may seem today, in a small sense it merely expressed, in extreme form, and as a norm, a procedure that new states in the West followed in making up their

[1] The term "common law" was ambiguous. Probably—but by no means certainly—the term was meant to exclude equity jurisdiction.
[2] This provision was not applicable to Louisiana and Arkansas territories. On territorial government in general, see Jack E. Eblen, *The First and Second United States Empires, Governors and Territorial Government, 1784–1912* (1968).
[3] Quoted in William W. Blume, ed., *Transactions of the Supreme Court of the Territory of Michigan*, Vol. 1 (1935), p. xxiii.

laws, even *without* compulsion. They took texts from their parent states, adding a patch of novelty here and there. Policy choices were made by choosing among old models, not by drafting fresh law. It was to be expected that settlers would borrow most from states whose law they knew best. From 1795 on, the governor and judges of Northwest Territory listed the source of each law they adopted for the territory. From 1795 to 1798, twenty-seven out of forty-nine came from Pennsylvania, the home state of the governor, Arthur St. Clair. Michigan Territory, between 1814 and 1823, adopted 268 laws from thirteen states; 134 of these were from Ohio, while Tennessee supplied only one.[4] In 1795, Michigan adopted from Virginia its general statute receiving the common law. In theory at least, this brought the entire body of the common law, and an unascertained number of statutes of Parliament, into force in the forests of Michigan.

When "five thousand free male inhabitants, of full age" lived in the district, the second stage of territorial life was to be reached. This stage, too, had a certain family resemblance to the British colonial practice. In this stage, the governor and judges shared lawmaking power with an elected body. Property owners were to choose one representative "for every five hundred free male inhabitants," up to twenty-five; beyond this "the number and proportion of representatives shall be regulated by the legislature." The elected assembly was to nominate ten persons to serve on the governor's council. Every nominee had to be a resident; and each had to be "possessed of a freehold in five hundred acres of land." Congress was to select five councilmen from these ten nominees. The governor, council, and house had authority "to make laws," so long as the laws were "not repugnant" to the Ordinance. The third stage, statehood, became possible when sixty thousand free inhabitants lived in the territory.

The pattern set by the Ordinance was both durable and workable. It guided the old Northwest and Southwest smoothly into statehood.[5] Colonial unrest was avoided. The Wisconsin territorial act of 1836 was the next major model. The first stage of territorial life was eliminated. Property qualifications were discarded; the population elected its legislature directly. The new model also paid more attention to details of court organization. Wisconsin's law, for example, specified "a supreme court, district courts, pro-

[4] William W. Blume, "Legislation on the American Frontier," 60 Michigan L. Rev. 317, 334 (1962).

[5] Louisiana and Florida territories were differently handled.

bate courts, and . . . justices of the peace." [6] But even in this, and later territorial laws, there were strong echoes of the Northwest Ordinance. Residents of Wisconsin Territory were guaranteed "all the singular rights, privileges, and advantages granted and secured to the people of the territory of the United States northwest of the river Ohio, by the articles of the compact contained in the ordinance for the government of the said territory, passed on the thirteenth day of July, one thousand seven hundred and eighty-seven."

The working law of the frontier cannot, of course, be deduced from its outer skin. Patient research[7] has dispelled some mists and legends about frontier law, and added new knowledge. Civilization advanced in undulating waves, generally along river valleys. Law followed the ax. The land was not empty before the Americans came. There were Indians scattered throughout the area. In the Mississippi Valley, a cluster of Frenchmen lived by a half-remembered form of the law of France. The Americans, by sheer force of numbers, overwhelmed this alien system. Only in the very earliest days was frontier law as crude as its reputation. At the outset, rough men of the forest administered justice. What they did passed for government, until the opportunists came. If the tales of the pioneers are true, a drunken, corrupt form of personalized justice ruled in the earliest courts. At Green Bay, in 1816, two decades before Wisconsin Territory was established, an "old Frenchman" named Charles Reaume, who "could read and write a little," acted as justice of the peace. In his court, it was said, "a bottle of spirits was the best witness that could be introduced." Once, when the losing party scraped up some whiskey for the judge, Reaume ordered a new trial and reversed his prior decision, on the strength of this "witness." Reaume's "court" was a long, difficult journey from the county seat. His word, in effect, was final. He took care not to decide cases against those traders who were "able to bear the expense of an appeal"; hence his incompetence was not exposed to a wider public. At Prairie du Chien, at the same period, Nicholas Boilvin, a French-Canadian, was "clothed with the dignified office of . . . Justice of the Peace." Boilvin was as uneducated as Reaume. He owned a library of exactly three lawbooks: the statutes of Northwest, Missouri, and Illinois territories. But in deciding a case, "he paid no attention to the statute"; he merely "decided according to his own idea of right and wrong." [8]

6 Act Establishing the Terr. Govt. of Wisconsin (1836), sec. 9.
7 Notably by Francis Philbrick and William Wirt Blume.
8 James H. Lockwood, "Early Times and Events in Wisconsin," *Second An-*

Polish and legal skill were in short supply, too, in the Illinois country. A small group of amateur lawyers, merchants, and political adventurers ran the government. Litigation on land claims and grants was the staple business of the courts. The judges were speculators themselves, and judged their own claims. A federal board of land commissioners was appointed in 1804, to investigate land claims in the Illinois country. The board uncovered "incredible forgeries, fraud, subornation and perjuries," the "very mire and filth of corruption." [9] A certain Robert Reynolds had rushed to file claims with the commissioners, an act of great "effrontery," since Reynolds "forged the names of witnesses, deponents and grantors . . . gave depositions under an assumed name, and appeared before a magistrate with deponents who deposed under false names for his benefit. He forged a grant to himself from a slave woman." [10] Yet Reynolds had once been a judge. He had been appointed a county court judge in 1801 and "attended very regularly to his duties." Reynolds was not the only forging judge. He was, however, the only one ever indicted for fraud; and his indictment, it was said, was due more to his political enemies than to public outrage. Even after Illinois became a state, "a great rascal" named William P. Foster served on the state supreme court. According to Governor Thomas Ford, Foster was "no lawyer, never having either studied or practised law; but . . . a man of winning, polished manners, and . . . withal a very gentlemanly swindler." Foster was assigned to hold courts "in the circuit on the Wabash; but being fearful of exposing his utter incompetency, he never went near any of them." After a year he resigned, pocketed his salary, and left the state to become a "noted swindler, moving from city to city, and living by swindling strangers, and prostituting his daughters, who were very beautiful." [11]

Life was undeniably violent and crude in parts of the frontier. Henry Marie Brackenridge visited Missouri in 1810–11. He saw lawyers and judges who went about armed with pistols and knives. Duels were an everyday affair.[12] Governor Ford of Illinois has given

nual Report and Collections of the State Historical Society of Wisconsin (1856), Vol. II, 98, 105, 106, 126.

9 Francis S. Philbrick, ed., The Laws of Indiana Territory 1801–9 (1930), lxxxvii.

10 Ibid., lxxxix, xc.

11 Governor Thomas Ford, A History of Illinois From Its Commencement as a State in 1818 to 1847 (1854), p. 29.

12 William F. Keller, The Nation's Advocate, Henry Marie Brackenridge and

us a graphic, convincing picture of a trial court in Illinois, around 1818:

> The judges . . . held their courts mostly in log-houses, or in the barrooms of taverns, fitted up with a temporary bench for the judge, and chairs or benches for the lawyers and jurors. At the first circuit court in Washington county, held by Judge John Reynolds, the sheriff, on opening the court, went out into the court-yard and said to the people: "Boys, come in, our John is going to hold court." This was the proclamation for opening the court. In general, the judges were averse to deciding questions of law if they could possibly avoid doing so. They did not like the responsibility of offending one or the other of the parties, and preferred to submit everything they could to be decided by the jury. They never gave instructions to a jury unless expressly called for; and then only upon the points of law raised by counsel in asking for them. They never commented upon the evidence, or undertook to show the jury what inferences and presumptions might be drawn from it; for which reason they delivered their instructions hypothetically, stating them thus: "If the jury believe from the evidence that such a matter is proved, then the law is so and so." This was a clear departure from the practice of the judges in England and most of the United States; but the new practice suited the circumstances of the country. It undoubtedly requires the highest order of talent in a judge to "sum up" the evidence rightly to a jury, so as to do justice to the case, and injustice to neither party. Such talent did not exist to be put on the bench in these early times; or at least the judges must have modestly believed that they did not possess it.[13]

Still, Ford felt that the judges were "gentlemen of considerable learning and much good sense." The power of the judge to comment on evidence was declining in Eastern trial courts as well as on the frontier, for reasons already explored. The modesty of the judges, then, like other phenomena lovingly remembered as typically "frontier," was actually part of the general development of American law. The laxity and informality of Reynolds' court had parallels elsewhere, including some 20th-century traffic courts.

Young America (1956), pp. 101, 104. It may be worth mentioning, however, that the most famous duel among lawyers was the duel in which Aaron Burr killed Alexander Hamilton, who was (among other things) a successful commercial lawyer at New York. The duel took place, not on the frontier, but in Weehawken, New Jersey.

13 Ford, *op. cit.*, pp. 82–83.

Trained legal talent existed on the frontier, alongside fraud and animal cunning. The level of legal sophistication in a community depended on its size, on its economic base, and on whether it was close to the centers of government. The tales about men like Reaume and Foster may represent distortions or exceptions. After territorial government was organized, the worst of frontier justice usually ended for good. Samuel Holden Parsons and James Mitchell Varnum, solid lawyers with good reputations, were among the first judges of Northwest Territory. In Michigan Territory, Augustus Brevoort Woodward, a versatile, cultured lawyer with a college education, compiled the Woodward Code, a collection of thirty-four laws adopted in 1805. The governor of Michigan was also a lawyer, and another Michigan judge had studied law, though he had never practiced.[14]

In time a mobile, vigorous bar flourished in the West: a bar made up of quick-witted, adventurous young operators. Law practice required their full cunning. Joseph G. Baldwin (1815–1864) described them, with frontier hyperbole, as they were during the "flush times" of Alabama and Mississippi. In those days

> many land titles were defective; property was brought from other States clogged with trusts, limitations, and uses . . . universal indebtedness . . . made it impossible for many men to pay, and desirable for all to escape paying . . . a general looseness, ignorance and carelessness in the public officers . . . new statutes to be construed . . . an elegant assortment of frauds constructive and actual . . . in short, all the flood-gates of litigation were opened, and the pent-up tide let loose upon the country. And such a criminal docket! What country could boast more largely of its crimes? What more splendid role of felonies! What more terrific murders! What more gorgeous bank robberies! What more magnificent operations in the land offices! . . . Such superb forays on the treasuries, State and National! . . . And in INDIAN affairs! . . . the romance of a wild and weird larceny! . . . Swindling Indians by the nation! . . . Stealing their land by the township! . . . Many members of the bar, of standing and character, from the other States, flocked in to put their sickles into this abundant harvest.[15]

---

[14] William W. Blume, "Legislation on the American Frontier," 60 Mich. L. Rev. 317 (1962).

[15] Joseph G. Baldwin, *The Flush Times of Alabama and Mississippi* (1957), pp. 173–4. See also Elizabeth G. Brown, "The Bar on a Frontier: Wayne County, 1796–1836," 14 Am. J. Legal Hist. 136 (1970).

There were fortunes to be made. The new states and territories were ripe for the plucking, ripe with careers for ambitious young men. The economic base was land: town land and country land. Who, if not a lawyer, could decipher titles to land? Who could master the maze of rules on land grants, on the sale and transfer of land? Government jobs were another rich plum. The territories at first were net importers of the taxpayer's money. Washington distributed judgeships and clerkships with a lavish hand. Local jobs became available by the thousands—in courts, in legislatures, and in the executive branch, in territory, state, county, and town. The lawyer, again, was peculiarly suited for these jobs. He scrambled for public office. He also collected debts for Eastern creditors; he dabbled in land speculation and townsite booming. He scrounged around for any niche that required his generalist's skill. He did whatever his nose sniffed out as promising and lucrative. In the process, many young lawyers failed, and moved on to other jobs or places. But many others stayed with it, and some became rich.

Of the lawyers, some had gone West after college and clerkship. Others had to learn their law as they went along. In any case, frontier law was not book law in the usual sense. There were no libraries, and books were expensive. The practice put no premium on erudition. The best trial lawyers used and enjoyed good tricks, jokes, a neat technicality or two. The poverty of source materials left a vacuum, filled in by Blackstone, local statutes, and native wit. Few lawyers could know how to distinguish the fossils in Blackstone from the living law back East. For this reason, court law was, simultaneously, freewheeling and curiously archaic. The papers of Thomas Rodney, judge in the Old Southwest (1803–1811), preserve such museum pieces as the writ of account and *de homine replegiando*.[16] Rodney wrote that "Special Pleading is adhered to in our Courts with as much Strictness Elegance and propriety as in any of the States, so that Even the young Lawyers are obliged to read their books and be very attentive to their business or want bread." [17] In one equity proceeding, when a litigant objected that "the practice in G.[reat] B.[ritain] does not apply here," the judges replied:

> We Shall be guided by The practice in England So far as it is admissible here because there is no Other Safe and Regular

16 The writ, literally "for replevying a man," was a means of procuring the release of a prisoner—an earlier equivalent of the writ of *habeas corpus*.

17 William Baskerville Hamilton, *Anglo-American Law on the Frontier: Thomas Rodney and His Territorial Cases* (1953), pp. 137–38.

guide, for there it has been brought to perfection by long Experience and the practice of the ablest Judges, and being Contained in their books of practice They can always be resorted to —without which the practice here would be always irregular and Uncertain.[18]

Professor William W. Blume studied the work of the court of common pleas of Wayne County, Michigan (1796–1805). He saw

almost no evidence of the informality often supposed to be a characteristic of frontier justice. Instead, we find a strict compliance with applicable statutes, and, where the procedure was not governed by statute, with the English common law.[19]

Though most of the territorial statutes were pragmatic and natural, a few of these, too, had the musty air of museum pieces. The laws of Michigan spoke of essoins and wager of law, no doubt needlessly, and no doubt to the utter bewilderment of the public. The first Illinois legislature "imported [laws] . . . for the inspection of hemp and tobacco, when there was neither hemp nor tobacco raised in the country." [20]

Blume and Elizabeth Brown found in frontier law "two general attitudes and resultant influences attributable to frontier life." The first was a "strong desire to have all statute law published locally so that reliance on laws not available on the frontier would be unnecessary—codes were welcome." The second was a "lack of 'superstitious respect' for old laws and legal institutions; in other words, a readiness to make changes to suit new conditions." [21] These attributes of frontier law—archaism and hypertechnicality on the one hand, crudity, rough-hewn justice, and frontier impatience with form on the other—were not as inconsistent as they might seem. They flowed from the need to make law work in a transplanted setting. Old law was accepted, not out of love for tradition, but because it was, under the circumstances, quite unavoidable. The use of old law was merely an attempt to make use of materials at hand.

Frontier legal history echoed some aspects of colonial legal history. Territories, when they reached statehood, had complete

18 Hamilton, *op. cit.*, p. 197.

19 William W. Blume, "Civil Procedure on the American Frontier," 56 Mich. L. Rev. 161, 209 (1957).

20 Ford, *op. cit.*, p. 34.

21 William W. Blume and Elizabeth G. Brown, "Territorial Courts and Law: Unifying Factors in the Development of American Legal Institutions." Part II, 61 Mich. L. Rev. 467, 535 (1963).

power to make their own law. But they did so slowly, like the colonies when they broke their English ties. Governor Ford thought that Western legislatures passed too many laws, that they overturned too much too soon: "A session of the legislature was like a great fire in the boundless prairies of the State; it consumed everything. And again, it was like the genial breath of spring, making all things new." [22] But this is surely an exaggeration. The statute books of the Northwest states were, by modern standards, skimpy and undernourished. New states and territories were thankful for legacies of law. Ohio kept the statutes of Northwest Territory, even after statehood. The territorial laws were handed on to Indiana Territory (1800); Indiana passed them to Michigan and Illinois territories (1809); Michigan Territory was the source of the earliest laws of Wisconsin Territory (1836), which in turn gave them to Iowa (1838) and Minnesota (1849). In the Southwest the line went from Louisiana to Missouri Territory (1812), from there to Arkansas (1819), and from Mississippi to Alabama (1817). In most cases the basic process was simple: the old territory divided, like an amoeba, into two, and the laws of the original territory now governed in both parts.[23] Without particular thought or debate, traditional statutes were handed on to new jurisdictions. The statute of frauds and the statute of limitations traveled cross-country without major change. In 1799, Northwest Territory enacted a statute "making Promissory Notes and Inland Bills of Exchange negotiable"—another standard American law. These statutes became part of the basic legal framework. Town laws, election laws, laws about the militia, tax laws, laws on court process: all were freely borrowed and passed along.

In time, some of the new states repaid their legal debt. They trained new legal and political leaders. Henry Clay (born and educated in Virginia), Thomas Hart Benton, and Abraham Lincoln were all Western lawyers. The West was mobile, fluid; like the colonies in comparison to Britain, it was freer from the dead hand of the past, freer from the friction and inertia of tradition. Out of the West, then, came legal innovations that became enduring features of the law. The homestead exemption began in Texas; from there, it spread to the North and the East. A number of institutions began life in this experimental milieu, on the outskirts of American society.

22 Ford, *op. cit.*, p. 32.
23 William W. Blume and Elizabeth G. Brown, "Territorial Courts and Law," Part II, 61 Mich. L. Rev. 467, 474–75 (1963).

THE CIVIL LAW FRINGE

In the first generation of independence, the civil-law domain, vast but sparsely settled, encircled the domain of the common law. Civil law—French and Spanish—governed along the Mississippi and the river bottoms of its tributaries; in Kaskaskia, St. Louis, New Madrid, and St. Charles; in the bustling port of New Orleans; in the Floridas, and in Texas. When this empire became American property, it fell subject to American government and law.

A massive invasion of settlers doomed the civil law everywhere, except in Louisiana. The new judges and lawyers were trained in the common-law tradition. They supplanted judges of French and Spanish background. The United States did not disturb rights of property that had vested under civil law. American courts wrestled for years with civil-law problems of land and family, laws of descent and inheritance. Among Thomas Rodney's papers, from the Natchez district, are case records in which points at issue were resolved by reference to Spanish law or jurisprudence, translated for the benefit of jury and court.[24] The Northwest Ordinance, after prescribing its own rules about wills and inheritance, promised "the French and Canadian inhabitants, and other settlers of the Kaskaskies, Saint Vincents, and the neighboring villages" the benefit of "their laws and customs now in force among them, relative to the descent and conveyance of property."

But American policy insisted, for the long haul, that the law must be thoroughly Americanized. Around the old river town of St. Louis, Spanish law was technically in force, supplemented by French customs. From the very first, however, American officials aimed "to assimilate by insensible means, the habits and customs of the American and French inhabitants; by interweaving some of the regulations of the latter into our Laws, we procure a ready obedience, without violence or complaint." [25] As the American population increased, more direct action was used in addition to these gentle and "insensible means." A statute of 1807, applicable to what later became Missouri Territory, repealed the civil law on wills and inheritance, and introduced American intestacy laws and laws about wills. American lawyers lobbied successfully for a law

[24] E.g., Hamilton, *op. cit.*, p. 176.
[25] Judge John Coburn to Secretary of State James Madison, 1807, quoted in William F. English, *The Pioneer Lawyer and Jurist in Missouri* (1947), p. 56.

which made the common law of England the basis of law in Missouri Territory (1815–16). When it entered the Union, Missouri had little left of its civil-law past, except some tangled land titles, and a passion for procedural simplicity.

The French in Illinois were similarly doomed. The guaranty of the Ordinance applied only to laws of succession. The French were immediately subjected to an elaborate county and township organization, on the model developed in the British colonies, despite the fact that they had "retained in their isolation . . . the political and economic traditions of the France of Louis XIV, of common fields and manorial organization." [26] American officials were unsympathetic to the culture of the French. Judge John C. Symmes, who came to Vincennes in 1790, reacted to the French with chauvinistic disgust. They "will not relish a free government," he wrote. "They say our laws are too complex, not to be understood, and tedious in their operation—the command or order of the Military commandant is better law and speedier justice for them and what they prefer to all the legal systems found in Littleton and Blackstone. It is a language which they say they can understand, it is cheap and expeditious and they wish for no other." [27] It was natural for these settlers to resent the coming of Americans. The French lost their influence, and with it, their law. Traces of French *coutumes* lingered on briefly in family law. Gradually, French law and language disappeared.

An indigenous law, without prestige, and in a minority status, can hardly survive. The sheer mass of American settlers easily conquered Spanish law in Florida, where the original population was sparse. In 1821 Andrew Jackson imposed, by proclamation, common-law procedure in criminal cases, including the right to trial by jury. But Spanish law had gained only a temporary reprieve for civil cases. In 1829, a statute established the common law, and English statutes passed before 1776, as norms of decision in the territory. The Spanish period left behind, in the end, only a few archeological traces in Florida's law.

Spanish-Mexican law left a much greater imprint on Texas. Partly this was because Texas was rather fully formed, as a polity, before it passed into American hands. Here, too, however, trial by jury was a very early import. The constitution of Coahuila and Texas (1827), during the Mexican period, exhorted the legislature,

26 Francis S. Philbrick, *The Laws of Indiana Territory 1801–1809* (1930), p. ccxviii.
27 Quoted in Philbrick, *op. cit.*, ccxvi–ccxvii.

as one of its "principal subjects," to enact legislation "to establish, in criminal cases, the trial by jury, extending it gradually, and even adopting it in civil cases, in proportion as the advantages of this precious institution may be practically developed." [28] American settlers probably pressed for this enactment. The Texas government later enacted a form of trial by jury, but not exactly in the American mold.[29] The constitution of the republic of Texas (1836), in its declaration of rights, affirmed the right of an accused "to a speedy and public trial, by an impartial jury. . . . And the right of trial by jury shall remain inviolate."

"Congress," said this constitution, "shall, as early as practicable, introduce, by statute, the common law of England, with such modifications as our circumstances, in their judgment, may require" (art. IV, sec. 13). But Texas never really "received" English law, in its classical purity. Rather, the republic adopted a Texas subdialect of the American dialect of law. There was thoroughgoing acceptance of trial by jury, "that ever-to-be-prized system of jurisprudence," as the supreme court of Texas called it in 1840.[30] But law and equity were never distinguished in court organization and procedure in Texas. The constitution of 1845 specifically gave to the district courts jurisdiction "of all suits . . . without regard to any distinction between law and equity." [31] In 1840, the civil law was formally abolished; but even then Texas did not introduce the full rigors of common-law pleading. Rather, it preferred to retain "as heretofore" the civil-law system of "petition and answer." Procedure, then, conformed neither to common-law nor civil-law norms. It was a hybrid system. Judges and lawyers, in the early years, seemed genuinely ambivalent toward common law and civil law. On the one hand, civil law was alien, and few lawmen could cope with it. The law of 1840, by keeping some parts of civil-law pleading, forced courts (as one judge said) to look for "principles and criteria in a language generally unknown to us. . . . Constant perplexities . . . annoy and delay us at each step." [32] But in a later case, another Texas judge condemned aspects of common-law plead-

[28] Coahuila and Texas const., 1827, sec. 192.

[29] Edward L. Markham, Jr., "The Reception of the Common Law of England in Texas and the Judicial Attitude toward that Reception, 1840–1859," 29 Texas Law Review 904 (1951).

[30] *Edwards* v. *Peoples,* Dallam 359, 360 (Tex., 1840).

[31] Texas const., 1845, art. IV, sec. 10. On Texas procedure, see Joseph W. McKnight, "The Spanish Legacy to Texas Law," 3 Am. J. Leg. Hist. 222, 299 (1959).

[32] *Whiting* v. *Turley,* Dallam 453, 454 (Tex., 1842).

ing as "Bold, crafty, and unscrupulous." [33] Still a third judge took a middle view:

> The object of our statutes on the subject of pleading is to simplify as much as possible that branch of the proceedings in courts, which by the ingenuity and learning of both common and civil law lawyers and judges had become so refined in its subtleties as to substitute in many instances the shadow for the substance.[34]

The civil-law tradition, though too alien and inaccessible to survive, did undermine the inevitability—and therefore the legitimacy—of strict common-law pleading. What resulted was a procedure that used common-law terms and some common-law attitudes, but was considerably more streamlined and rational. Peripheral Texas was, in short, free to do what other states could do only by breaking with habit and tradition. But in Texas, divergences from the common law did not *look* like reforms; they looked like civil-law survivals. In a sense they were; what survived, however, survived because it suited the needs and wants of Texas jurists.

Chunks of civil law also remained imbedded in the substantive law of Texas. Texas recognizes the holographic will—an unwitnessed will in the dead man's handwriting. Texas has also kept the community-property system; indeed, Texas gave the system constitutional recognition.[35] Texas shares these survivals with Louisiana, and with the states carved out of Mexican territory, notably California. That these persisted, despite the tremendous surge toward common law, indicates either that they were toughly sewn into the social fabric, or that they fulfilled some unique social function. The holographic will invited ordinary people to make wills by themselves, without consulting a lawyer. The community-property system suited the facts of family life as well as or better than the common-law rules of marital property; besides, the common-law rules were themselves in process of change.

Louisiana was the only solid, durable enclave of civil law. Here American expansion collided with an entrenched civil-law population. Louisiana's brand of civil law had no particular intrinsic merits. At the time of the Louisiana Purchase it was an arcane, bewildering hodgepodge of French and Spanish law, a mélange of codes, customs, and doctrines of various ages. The French had set-

33 *Long* v. *Anderson,* 4 Tex. 422, 424 (1849).
34 *Hamilton* v. *Black,* Dallam 586, 587 (Tex., 1844).
35 Texas const., 1845, art. VII, sec. 19.

tled Louisiana, but the Spanish had governed it from 1766 to 1803. Louisiana law was as baffling as the common law at its worst. Its "babel" of legislation, according to Edward Livingston, was only equaled by "the Dissonances of our Court of Pleas where American shop-keepers, French planters and Spanish clerks sit on the same bench." [36]

In Louisiana, too, the usual conflict developed between the native population and incoming lawyers and judges.[37] Jefferson was anxious to Americanize the government and law. He controlled the governorship and the territorial judges. But the Creole population was a continuing problem. The territorial legislature, in 1806, under some pressure to move toward common law, did accept trial by jury and the writ of *habeas corpus,* but otherwise declared the civil law in force, that is, the "Roman Civil code . . . which is composed of the institutes, digest and code of the emperor Justinian, aided by the authority of the commentators of the civil law. . . . The Spanish law, consisting of the books of the *recopilation de Castilla* and *autos acordados* . . . the seven parts or *partidas* of the King Don Alphonse the learned [and others] . . . the ordinances and royal orders and decrees [applicable to] . . . the colony of Louisiana"; and "in matters of commerce," the "ordinance of Bilbao," supplemented by "Roman laws," a number of named English and civil-law treatises, "the commentaries of Valin," and "the respectable authors consulted in the United States." Governor William Charles Claiborne vetoed the law. The legislature was under the control of the Creole population; and Claiborne looked on the law of 1806 as particularly dangerous.[38]

The matter, of course, did not end there. The leading Creole residents of Louisiana clamored for a code, to clarify the law, and to insure them against sudden, disruptive change in their social and economic status. They wanted familiar law in a workable form. The code of 1808, designed to bring order out of chaos, was influenced by drafts of the new French code, the Code Napoleon. The Louisiana code, then, was a civil-law code to the core; but in new-French not old-Spanish style. Its political meaning was great. A careful student of codification in Louisiana feels that, from a long-

---

[36] Quoted in George Dargo, *Legal Codification and the Politics of Territorial Government in Jefferson's Louisiana, 1803–1808* (unpublished Ph.D. thesis, 1970, Columbia University), p. 228.

[37] See, in general, Elizabeth G. Brown, "Legal Systems in Conflict: Orleans Territory 1804–1812," 1 Am. J. Leg. Hist. 35 (1957).

[38] Dargo, *op. cit.,* pp. 70–72, 280–82.

term historical perspective, the civil code of 1808 "was the political compromise on the basis of which the so-called 'ancient Louisianans' finally accepted permanent American rule." Essentially, the Jefferson administration accepted the code, and thereby gave up the possibility of total Americanization, in return for a speedier and less bumpy absorption of "what was essentially a colonial possession." [39] This compromise worked, and outlasted the fate of the code itself.

The supreme court of Louisiana later held (in 1817) that the Code of 1808 had not driven out all of the old Spanish law. "Our civil code," said the court, "is a digest of the civil laws, which were in force in this country, when it was adopted"; those laws "must be considered as untouched," wherever the "alterations and amendments, introduced in the digest, do not reach them." [40] This unfortunate decision brought back the confusion of the days before the code, when the civil law of Louisiana was "an indigested mass of ancient edicts and Statutes . . . the whole rendered more obscure by the heavy attempts of commentators to explain them." [41] At legislative request, Louis Moreau Lislet and Henry Carleton translated and published "The Laws of Las Siete Partidas which are still in force in the State of Louisiana," in 1820. The legislature also moved to recodify the basic law of Louisiana. They appointed three commissioners for this purpose. These commissioners drafted what became the famous Civil Code of 1825.

The leading figure in drafting this code was Edward Livingston. He was a New Yorker, devoted to law reform, who found fertile soil for his talents in Louisiana. About eighty per cent of the code's provisions were drawn directly from the Code Napoleon. French legal commentary was another important source. The common law had some influence, particularly on the law of obligations. The special needs of Louisiana were only one factor in the minds of the commissioners. They also wanted to prove that a pure, rational system of law was attainable in America. They rejected

> the undefined and undefinable common law. . . . [In England] the Judge drew his own rule, sometimes with Lord Mansfield, from the pure fountain of the Civil Code, sometimes from the

[39] George Dargo, *op. cit.*, p. 6. Recent scholarship has suggested that the code of 1808 owed more to Spanish law than has been usually conceded. But see Dargo, *op. cit.*, pp. 359–64.

[40] *Cottin* v. *Cottin,* 5 Mart. (O.S.), 93, 94 (1817).

[41] Quoted in William B. Hatcher, *Edward Livingston* (1940), p. 247. For Livingston's role in the making of the civil code of 1825, see Chapter XI, "The Codifier," pp. 245–88.

> turbid stream of doubtful usage, often from no better source
> than his own caprice. . . . [In Louisiana] our Code . . . will
> be progressing toward perfection. . . . The Legislature will not
> judge, nor the Judiciary make laws. . . . [W]e may hope to
> have the rare and inestimable blessing of written Codes, con-
> taining intelligible and certain rules to govern the ordinary re-
> lations and occurrences of life, the operations of commerce and
> the pursuit of remedies by action.[42]

As the quotation shows, the commissioners expected that the
civil code would be only the first of a series. A code of practice was
adopted in 1825. It was one of the most original of the codes. It
blended French, Spanish, and common-law forms into a skillful,
efficient whole. The common-law writs which were retained, did
not have to "pursue the forms, and be conducted according to the
rules and regulations prescribed by the common law," as the code
of 1805 had asserted. Louisiana came, then, to use a tripartite system of procedure, vaguely comparable to the compromise of Texas.
The court structure was American. Some aspects of the common
law were preserved, notably trial by jury in criminal cases. The rest
of the system was a joining of two civil-law streams. In Texas common law dominated, in Louisiana civil law. In both cases, the
blend was more streamlined and efficient than the common law, as
the 19th century conceived it. Other states, less free to innovate,
reached this state of development more gradually.

Once it had enacted a civil code and a code of procedure, the
Louisiana legislature lost its zeal for novelties. A proposed code of
commerce was never adopted.[43] Livingston's codes of evidence and
criminal law were too advanced for the legislature to swallow. The
age of innovation passed. French language and French customs
also slowly lost their grip. The civil-law substrate remained solid,
in translation. The constitution of 1812 expressly provided that
the legislature "shall never adopt any system or code of laws, by a
general reference to the said system or code, but in all cases, shall
specify the several provisions of the laws it may enact" (art. IV, sec.
11). This was meant to rule out passage of a general statute purporting to "receive" the common law. The gesture was probably
not necessary. The civil law, like the right to trial by "an impartial
jury of the vicinage" [44] (also preserved by the constitution), was too
important to the people who mattered in New Orleans. They were

[42] Louisiana Legal Archives, Vol. 1 (1937), p. xcii.
[43] The civil code already covered some aspects of commercial law.
[44] Louisiana const., 1812, art. VI, sec. 18.

used to it; they did business by it. The codes survived the destruction of a distinctive French culture; they became an element of Louisiana's *legal* culture—part of the learning and lore of lawyers, part of the life and experience of consumers of law. Once this had occurred, the social and educational costs of changing the system became far greater than the possible benefits of matching local law to the law of the neighboring states. The "reform" elements of Louisiana's codes were based on civil law; but their goal was clear, concise, and useful law, law that a man could count on and make business predictions by; law, which, as Edward Livingston boasted, could be mastered any evening before dinner.[45] These were, as we shall see, also goals of common-law reform. In the main, then, Louisiana's codes were not survivals, no more than Texas pleading was. The codes were rather a reworking of an inherited legal culture, along paths that ran parallel to those the common law would follow.[46]

It remains a matter of some pride in Louisiana that its legal tradition is different from its neighbors. Louisiana is proud to belong to the great civil-law family. Hence, it is natural, and easy, to overstate differences between Louisiana's legal culture and that of (say) Arkansas or Texas. Louisiana is part of a federal system, and is subject to federal law. That was significant even in the early 19th century; it has grown more so with the passage of time. It shares a common economic system with its neighbors. The political system is not much different from Mississippi or Alabama. American settlers streamed in and out across the border, neither noticing nor caring, by and large, that they were crossing the frontier between civil and common law. Attitudes toward law and expectations about law, one guesses, are more or less the same in Shreveport as in Little Rock or Natchez. The cultural elements of Louisiana law were and are closer to Mississippi and Texas than to Ecuador or France. Whole raw pieces of common law—such as the trust—were eventually absorbed by Louisiana. Much new law that was added during the 19th century was not noticeably "civil law" in its con-

---

[45] Dargo, *op. cit.*, p. 228. Livingston was actually speaking of the Practice Act of 1805.

[46] The same 1812 constitution, which forbade a change to the common-law system, declared that all laws and public records had to be in "the language in which the constitution of the United States is written" and the same for "judicial and legislative . . . proceedings." Louisiana const., 1812, art. VI, sec. 15. For those who did not speak French, French was a nuisance. This callous attitude toward the historic tongue of the settlers suggests obliquely that the preservation of the civil law in Louisiana owed precious little to sentiment.

tent: business law, railroad law, the law of slaves. The civil law lives on in Louisiana, but mostly as lawyers' law and lawyers' process. In most other essential regards, Louisiana law has long since joined the Union.

CHAPTER III

LAW AND THE ECONOMY: 1776–1847

By reputation, the 19th century was the high noon of *laissez-faire*. Government, by habit and design, kept its heavy hand off the economy. But recent historical research and explication have shown 19th-century developments in a different light. Certainly, during much of the century, there was a great deal of public sympathy for business, productivity, growth. Particularly, the first half of the century was a period of promotion of enterprise, of the release of creative energy; government, reflecting its powerful constituencies, wanted business and the economy to grow; where this required subsidy or intervention, no overriding theory held government back.

It has been easy to accept a distorted picture of government regulation of business in 1800 or 1830. Most of it was undertaken by the states, not the federal government. The literature of the law never gave it its due. Then, as now, jurists concentrated on what was most general about the law, those features which could be most easily summed up in textbooks, and which most concerned lawyers in their courtroom work. This left little room for (say) a Vermont statute on the licensing of peddlers. Historians, for their part, were concerned with dramatic and striking events, acted out on a national stage. Quite naturally, they emphasized the public law of slavery and the slave trade, and the delicate relationship between state and federal governments. In the economic sphere, they watched the debates over tariff policy, a national banking system, and internal improvements. But an accurate picture of law and the economy requires close study of local law.

The federal government was not totally passive. Its urge to construct major works of internal improvement actually bore some fruit in the National Road. The federal effort was not frustrated by a *laissez-faire* philosophy; the "real issue," rather, was "between national and state action." [1] The state action view prevailed.

[1] Carter Goodrich, *Government Promotion of American Canals and Railroads, 1800–1890* (1960), p. 44.

Thus, it was true that the federal government owned no railroads, and that acts of Congress showed little awareness of railroads, before the Civil War. But this did not mean that the railroad effort was essentially, as in England, private. The states were feverishly legislating about railroads. The Pennsylvania Railroad was once quite literally the railroad of the state of Pennsylvania. State governments, furthermore, turned to railroad building after years of involvement with turnpikes, plank roads, ferries, and bridges. In this half of the century, to be sure, the major theme of legal concern was not, in the main, regulatory, in the sense of hostile control. Overall, the thrust of the law was promotional, though from time to time, there were serious moves to cut down the overpowerful to size. The men who held political power meant to create a sound basis for economic growth. This itself was partly a matter of ideology; partly it was a response to rampant pressure groups within each state. Indeed, Professor Harry Scheiber, in his study of the Ohio canal era, has demonstrated that strong political forces not only demanded state intervention to provide a general basis for economic growth, but demanded "equal distribution of costs and benefits among all members of the polity as well." This meant, in essence, giving every identifiable interest group (geographical ones included), its cut of the pie, its canal, railroad, turnpike, bank, bridge, patronage, county seat, or whatever.[2] If there was an age of *laissez-faire* philosophy at all, it came later in the century; and government promotion of railroads besmirches that era's purity as well, not to mention a constant undercurrent of state legislation.

In the first half of the century, *franchise* was a key legal concept. The franchise was a grant to the private sector, out of the inexhaustible reservoir of state power. Historically, it meant a freedom, a release from restraint. To be sure, there was a great deal of controversy over franchises, in general and particular. But much of the controversy, particularly before 1850, centered on how to unlock the door of enterprise, without destroying fundamental values, or upsetting the balance of power.

There was a public right—a public duty—to lend a hand to productivity. This meant that government must provide public goods, especially transport, but also currency and credit. The monetary

---

[2] Harry N. Scheiber, *Ohio Canal Era: A Case Study of Government and the Economy, 1820–1861* (1969). See also the seminal works of J. Willard Hurst, *Law and the Conditions of Freedom in the Nineteenth Century United States* (1956); *Law and Economic Growth: The Legal History of the Lumber Industry in Wisconsin 1836–1915* (1964).

system was one of the irritants that led to Shay's Rebellion; a bitter struggle between debtors and creditors raged in the background as the Constitution of 1787 was debated; and the background noise profoundly affected the debate. The Constitution federalized the coinage of money; the states could not "emit Bills of Credit"; they could not "make any Thing but gold and silver Coin a Tender in Payment of Debts." [3] Twice, the federal government chartered a national bank. The second Bank of the United States fell during the presidency of Andrew Jackson. But both before and after this event states tried to ensure a sound supply of money and credit by creating their own banks or by encouraging private banking.[4] Pennsylvania owned one-third of the capital of the Bank of Pennsylvania, chartered in 1793. The Bank of the State of South Carolina, chartered in 1812, acted as the state's depository and fiscal agent; it was in effect the banking arm of the state itself.[5] Later on, states did not, typically, participate directly in ownership of banks. Instead, they enacted programs of regulation, heavy at least on paper. In either case, the banks, public and private, were deeply enmeshed in politics. The currency and credit problem seemed central to the life of the community. An unsound bank—and there were many—threatened its community with financial ruin.

States chartered their banks one by one. The chartering process was therefore a *rite de passage* in the life of every bank; at this crucial point, the state could (in theory) exert critical control by forcing clauses into the charter. In practice, this was not a convenient or effective rein on behavior. Later, states adopted general banking laws, applicable to any and every bank. In 1829, New York passed a safety-fund law. Under this law, banks had to contribute a portion of their capital to a general fund, which would be used to insure payment of the notes of insolvent banks.[6] In 1837, Michigan passed the first free banking law, which dispensed with the need for a special charter, and authorized any group of individuals to set up a bank by following the statutory formula. New York passed a similar law in 1838. As we shall see, corporation law went through the same cycle of development, from special charter to general laws.

Transport, like money, was part of the economic infrastructure,

3 U.S. Const., Art. I, sec. 10.

4 The subject is exhaustively treated in Bray Hammond, *Banks and Politics in America, from the Revolution to the Civil War* (1957).

5 Hammond, *op. cit.,* p. 168.

6 Hammond, *op. cit.,* pp. 556–63.

the skeletal frame of economic life. As the chance of a major federal role faded, the states and cities moved into the vacuum. After 1820, a tremendous amount of statutory law dealt with bridges, roads, ferries, and canals. Much of the work of the legislatures, in the first half of the 19th century, consisted of chartering transport companies, and amending these charters. Taking the Maryland laws of 1835–36 as a sample, we find in the first pages an amendment to "an act for building a bridge over the Little North-East, in Cecil County, near McCauley's mill" (ch. 12), three more bridge laws, and an amendment to "the act incorporating the Annapolis and Potomac Canal Company" (ch. 37), all in January 1836; many other laws in the same session incorporated or amended the charters of road or turnpike companies, or authorized road building— for example, "An Act to lay out and open a road through a part of Frederick and Baltimore Counties," passed Mar. 2, 1836 (ch. 121).

Chartering, however, was only a small aspect of government participation. The states and cities played a more critical role: they supported, by money and credit, internal improvements; and some they constructed themselves. New York built the great Erie Canal between 1817 and 1825—363 miles long—at a cost of a little more than $7,000,000. It was a tremendous financial success. The tolls surpassed all expectations. Even more important, the canal stimulated commerce, and served as a "great channel of westward migration." Its opening "may be regarded as the most decisive single event in the history of American transportation." [7] The Erie Canal naturally invited emulation. In the peak year of 1840, an estimated 14.19 million dollars was invested in canals in the United States.[8]

By this time, the railroad was already moving into the center of the stage. The full flowering of the railroad era came later. But both the Pennsylvania Railroad and the Baltimore and Ohio were founded in this period; and both were supported if not controlled by government. It was the city of Baltimore which supplied the money for the B & O. Other states chose one or the other path of support for their railroads during the early, flush period of enthusiasm. In Ohio, in 1837, the state passed a general law—the "Loan Law"—promising support in the form of matching funds, to *any*

[7] Carter Goodrich, *Government Promotion of American Canals and Railroads 1800–1890*, pp. 52–55.

[8] Carter Goodrich *et al.*, *Canals and American Economic Development* (1961), p. 209; see also the excellent study by Harry N. Scheiber, *Ohio Canal Era: A Case Study of Government and the Economy, 1820–1861* (1969).

internal improvement company (railroad, canal, or turnpike) that met certain standards. The law was repealed in 1842; but more than a hundred special laws, between 1836 and 1850, authorized local aid to the promoters of railroads.[9]

Outside of the basic areas of transport and finance, state regulation was rather random and planless. Not that a massive ideology dictated boundaries. The country was underdeveloped; most Americans no doubt felt that the state should encourage development, though perhaps they also felt that the state, like the Lord, helped those who helped themselves. Economic law was practical and promotional. Trade laws were tailored to specific needs. The states continued colonial programs of quality control over export commodities. Georgia law (1791) required tobacco to be "packed in hogsheads or casks" and "stamped by some inspector legally thereunto appointed";[10] unstamped tobacco could not be legally exported. In Connecticut, by a law of 1794, bar iron could not be sold, unless "stamped with the name of the manufacturer thereof, and of the town where such iron is manufactured." [11] In New York, salt was to be packed "in barrels, casks or boxes" and inspected to make sure that the salt was "free from dirt, filth and stones, and from admixtures of lime . . . and fully drained from pickle." [12] The New York revised statutes of 1827–28 included laws to regulate sales by auctioneers, hawkers, and peddlers; and provisions for the inspection of flour, meal, beef, pork, "pot and pearl ashes," fish, "fish or liver oil," lumber, staves, flaxseed, sole leather, leaf tobacco, butter, and pressed hay. Not all of these were export commodities. Some were merely staple goods.

It was an ancient task of government to regulate weights and measures, and to provide standard measures for commodities. Massachusetts, for example, prescribed standard measures for potatoes, onions, salt, and wood. Statutes also tried to protect consumers against false labeling and adulteration. In Massachusetts (1833), only "pure spermaceti oil" could be "sold under the names of sperm, spermaceti, lamp, summer, fall, winter and second winter oils." A seller who sold "adulterated" oils under these names had

[9] Carter Goodrich, *Government Promotion of American Canals and Railroads,* pp. 136–37; Harry Scheiber, *Ohio Canal Era,* pp. 110–11, 152.

[10] Oliver H. Prince, comp., *Digest of the Laws of the State of Georgia* (2nd ed., 1837), p. 817 (act of Dec. 23, 1791).

[11] Stats. Conn. (1808), pp. 421–22 (act of May, 1794).

[12] Rev. Stats. N. Y. (1829), Vol. I, Part I, Title 10, ch. 9, sec. 103.

to pay double the difference between the value of pure and adulterated spermaceti oil.[13] But no statutory machinery was set up to enforce this law. Hopefully, the crude penalties would be attractive enough to the aggrieved consumer or merchant, that he would enforce the law on his own initiative.

Some preliminary attempts were made to safeguard natural resources. Massachusetts in 1819 made it unlawful to take pickerel "with spears, in the night time," or to shoot these fish, "at any time." This act attached a money penalty of fifty cents per unlawful fish, payable "to and for the use of the person who shall sue for the same." [14] The usual motive was economic, rather than a love of nature. Massachusetts (1818) prohibited indiscriminate killing of birds which were "useful and profitable to the citizens, either as articles of food or as instruments in the hands of Providence to destroy various noxious insects, grubs, and caterpillars." [15] New Jersey, in 1789, restricted the picking of cranberries between June 1 and October 10, because "cranberries, if suffered to remain on the vines until sufficiently ripened, would be a valuable article of exportation." [16] By a protectionist act of 1822, Massachusetts forbade nonresidents to "take any lobsters, tautog, bass or other fish, within the harbors, streams, or waters of the towns of Fairhaven, New Bedford, Dartmouth, and Westport," and transport the catch "in smacks or vessels" of over fifteen tons, or in those of any size owned outside the Commonwealth.[17]

Public health was also a matter of some state concern, though the tools were primitive and the scope of regulation rather narrow. Quarantine laws were common, however. New York had an elaborate law in the 1820's, directing ships to anchor near "the marine hospital on Staten-Island," dividing ships into classes depending on the perceived danger, and prescribing rules for clearing quarantine, including whitewashing and fumigation "with mineral acid gas," and the washing and airing of clothing and bedding. The rules were especially strict for ships coming from places where "yellow, bilious, malignant, or other pestilential or infectious fever" had existed, or when disease had broken out on board.[18] "Nuisances" could be "abated," when they were a danger to health.

---

13 Laws Mass. 1833, ch. 215.
14 Laws Mass. 1819, ch. 45. A later act subjected the operation of this law to local option.
15 Laws Mass. 1818, ch. 103.
16 N.J. Rev. Stats. 1821, p. 89 (act of Nov. 10, 1789).
17 Laws Mass. 1822, ch. 97.
18 Rev. Stats. N.Y. (1829), Vol. I, p. 425 ff.

Land-use controls were in their infancy; but Michigan, for example, in the 1830's authorized township boards, village government, and the mayors and aldermen of cities to "assign certain places for the exercising of any trade or employment offensive to the inhabitants, or dangerous to the public health." Any such "assignment" could be revoked if the place or building became a "nuisance" because of "offensive smells or exhalations," or was "otherwise hurtful or dangerous." [19] When food products were regulated, economic health was usually the primary goal; but consumer protection was sometimes at least a secondary aim.[20] Some states gave local medical societies the power to examine and license prospective doctors. Unlicensed doctors could not collect fees through court process. Other laws made unauthorized practice subject to fines.[21] Lastly, laws on gaming, drinking, and gambling aimed to protect public morality. In New York, no "puppet-show . . . wire or rope-dance, or . . . other idle shows" could be exhibited for profit.[22] Regulations of morality were also economic regulations, in that they defined the permissible limits of earning a living. From this point of view, too, much of the penal code was concerned with economic control: laws against theft, to take the simplest example.

Despite all these examples of economic regulation, 19th-century government was no leviathan. Even in the large Eastern states, its hold over the economy was weak. Many programs must have existed only on paper. Many of the inspection laws, licensing laws, and laws about weights and measures were feeble and vapidly enforced. Two pillars of the modern state were missing: a strong tax base and a trained civil service. Without these two, and perhaps without more economic knowledge, the state could not hope to make the economy its servant.

State government depended chiefly on the property tax. This tax was locally assessed and locally collected. It was supplemented by excise taxes—on slaves, on carriages, or on personal property in general. Hard money was scarce, and the voting public was not accustomed to the idea that they should pay a substantial share of income or wealth to the state. John Marshall, in one of his most

[19] Rev. Stats. Michigan, 1838, p. 171.

[20] Oscar and Mary Handlin, *Commonwealth, A Study of the Role of Government in the American Economy: Massachusetts 1744–1861* (rev. ed., 1969), p. 206.

[21] Laws N.Y. 1806, ch. 138; Laws Mass. 1819, ch. 113; Laws N.Y. 1830, ch. 126; unauthorized doctors were liable to forfeit "a sum not exceeding twenty-five dollars." See, in general, Richard H. Shryock, *Medical Licensing in America, 1650–1965* (1967).

[22] Rev. Stats. N.Y. 1829, Vol. 1, p. 660.

famous dicta, equated the power to tax with the power to destroy what was taxed.[23] Power to destroy was not lightly conceded in the 19th century. In some statutes, constitutions, and case-law decision, the notion appears that taxes should be limited to a few categories; and those as general as possible.[24] The level of taxation and expenditure was low. The state of Massachusetts spent $215,200, all told, in 1794. More than half of this was interest on debt.[25] The puniest sewer district today could better that mark.

State action, then, was pinched for pennies. It had to substitute artifice for cash; hence heavy use of the fee system. Wherever possible, users bore the costs of state services. Litigants paid judges for their lawsuits; bride and groom paid for their marriage licenses. Local users had to pay by assessment for local roads—or, if they were cash-poor, use their bodies to pay off this tax. Under a Virginia act of 1818, staves could not be exported before an inspector general and "cullers" had inspected them. The inspector general was "entitled to demand and receive" a fee of ten cents "on every thousand merchantable staves"; cullers too had to be paid their fee.[26] An elaborate Pennsylvania act of 1835 set up a similar system for meat. For "inspecting, examining and branding each tierce, barrel and half barrel of salted beef or pork," the inspectors could demand eight cents.[27]

There was no trained civil service in the modern sense. Government was not run by experts, except experts in running a government. Politics was a way to make money or use power. It was sometimes an occupation, less frequently a calling. Many politicians were amateurs or lawyers, who were amateurs except at law. That every man could aspire to high office was part of the democratic faith. Jefferson and Jackson considered high turnover a virtue in government, not an evil. Jackson, especially, felt that government

23 The case was *McCulloch* v. *Maryland,* 4 Wheat. 316 (1819).

24 A clause in the Arkansas constitution of 1836 declared that "no one species of property . . . shall be taxed higher than another species of property, of equal value," excepting taxes on "merchants, hawkers, peddlers, and privileges" (art. VII, Revenue, sec. 2). Citing this clause, the state supreme court declared void a special tax on billiard tables, and a tax on "the privilege of keeping each stallion or jack." The right to own a billiard table or to keep a stallion was a "property right" not a "privilege"; it was unlawful, therefore, to tax these rights specially. *Stevens* v. *State,* 2 Ark. 291 (1840); *Gibson* v. *County of Pulaski,* 2 Ark. 309 (1840).

25 Handlin and Handlin, *op. cit.,* p. 62.

26 Va. Rev. Code 1819, Vol. II, pp. 197, 200.

27 Laws Pa. 1834–5, sec. 82, p. 405.

jobs called for basic, fungible skills; any man of intelligence and
honor could hold office. In fact, Jefferson and Jackson tended to
appoint men of elite background and standing to higher offices,
despite their words. These men were not experts, but they were
educated and skillful. If there was any lack of trained men in government, the lawyers filled it. Lawyers had some education, some
grasp of the machinery of government, some insight into state-
ways.[28]

In general, however, both the scope and administrative strength
of regulation were limited. Regulation tended to be local, self-
sustaining—as in the fee system—and conservative in the use of
staff. Typically, administrative tasks were given to existing officeholders. When a state created an insurance commission, it might
appoint the state treasurer commissioner. For simplicity of regulation, laws frequently required private citizens to stamp, mark,
label, or post. Every ferry keeper in Illinois had to maintain "a
post or board, on which shall be written the rates of ferriage . . .
by law allowed." [29] Basically, the law left it to private persons, to
enforce what regulation there was. If no one brought a lawsuit, or
complained to the district attorney about some violation, nothing
was done. The state did not seriously try to administer, or carry
through independently, what the statutes decreed.

Some types of social control, which may have worked well
enough in tight, narrow seabound colonies, were strained to the
breaking point after 1800. They did not suit a country of great
distances, scattered population, diverse social conditions. Statutes
in the Western states and territories, borrowed from the East,
spoke of public markets and commodity inspection. Probably these
programs never lived except on paper. In the rest of the country,
the gap between book law and living law was perhaps only slightly
less real. In part, the private sector blossomed when culture and
technology made social demands that government was too poor
and too weak to respond to. Historically, government controlled
money and credit, and government built and ran highways, ferries,
bridges, and canals. In the 19th century, the commercial and land-
owning public wanted more and more of these improvements. The
economy had an unquenchable thirst for infrastructure; but at the
critical time, the power of government fell short of the demand;

28 See, in general, Sidney H. Aronson, *Status and Kinship in the Higher Civil
Service* (1964).
29 Francis S. Philbrick, ed., Pope's Ill. Digest 1815, Vol. I (1938), p. 264.

and control of the infrastructure passed into private hands. *Laissez-faire,* it may turn out, was more powerful as practice than as theory, even in the 19th century.

THE BUSINESS CORPORATION

A corporation, in the jargon of lawbooks, is an artificial person. This means that it is a legal entity, which, like a person, can sue and be sued, own property, and transact business. Unlike natural persons, the corporation can survive the death of any particular member or members. Its life begins with a charter; and it dissolves when its charter expires. An unlimited, or perpetual, charter is a definite possibility; and in fact is the normal case for 20th-century corporations.

The charter is a grant of authority from the sovereign, which specifies the powers, rights, and duties, of the entity. In an American state in the 1970's, those who fill out a simple form, and pay a small fee, may receive articles of incorporation and begin corporate life. In the early 19th century, however, the legislature granted charters by statute, one by one. Every charter was in theory tailor-made to the case at hand.

In the colonial period, this system was not at all inappropriate. Corporations were uncommon before 1800. And few of those which existed were business corporations. Almost all of the colonial corporations were churches, charities, or cities or boroughs.[30] In all of the 18th century, charters were issued to only 335 businesses. Only seven of these were during the colonial period; 181 were issued between 1796 and 1800.[31] Banks, insurance companies, water companies, and companies organized to build or run canals, turn-

[30] In England, only the crown had the right to incorporate. In the colonies, royal governors, proprietors, and in some cases legislative bodies issued charters. Actually, not many colonial cities and towns were technically corporations at all. This seems to have made little difference in the way these municipalities behaved.

In 1778, Governor Livingston of New Jersey tried to issue a charter himself without legislative approval; but that was an isolated incident. It was generally recognized after the Revolution that the legislature was the branch of government that made corporations. John W. Cadman, Jr., *The Corporation in New Jersey: Business and Politics 1791–1875* (1949), p. 4.

On the colonial corporation in general, see Joseph S. Davis, *Essays in the Earlier History of American Corporations* (1917).

[31] Joseph S. Davis, *Essays in the Earlier History of American Corporations,* (1917), Vol. II, p. 24.

pikes, and bridges made up the overwhelming majority of these early corporations. A mere handful, notably the New Jersey Society for Establishing Useful Manufactures (1791), were established for manufacturing purposes. In the 19th century, more charters were issued each year. And while most charters in the first half of the century were still connected with finance and transport, a small but growing minority had more general commercial or industrial aims. In Pennsylvania, 2,333 special charters were granted to business corporations between 1790 and 1860. Of these about 1,500 were transportation companies; less than two hundred were for manufacturing.[32] Joseph S. Davis has pointed out that

> The English tradition that corporate powers were to be granted only in rare instances, never deeply intrenched here, was opposed by a strong and growing prejudice in favor of equality—a prejudice which led almost at once to the enactment of general incorporation acts for ecclesiastical, educational, and literary corporations. Partiality in according such powers was to be expected of the English crown, but it was a serious charge to lay at the door of democratic legislatures. . . . Not least important, the physical ease of securing charters was far greater in the new states than in England. . . . Legislatures were not overworked and did business free of charge and with reasonable promptness. . . . Finally, the practice in creating corporations for non-business purposes, though it did not lead promptly to granting freedom of incorporation to business corporations, undoubtedly smoothed the way for special acts incorporating business associations.[33]

But as the economy developed, entrepreneurs demanded access to the corporate form, as an efficient way to structure and finance their business ventures. If each charter had to be scrutinized, its clauses cut to order for the particular case, legislatures would have been simply unable to handle the demand. Except for projects of special importance, charters became stylized, standardized, matters of rote. They were finally replaced, as we shall see, by general incorporation laws.

Early charters had many features which, from the standpoint of 20th-century corporation law, appear odd and idiosyncratic. In the early 19th century, charter terms of five, twenty, or thirty years' life were quite common. In New Jersey, every manufacturing company (except one) had a limited term of life before 1823; perpetual du-

32 Louis Hartz, *Economic Policy and Democratic Thought, Pennsylvania 1776–1860* (1948), p. 38.
33 Davis, *op. cit.*, Vol. II, pp. 7–8.

ration remained rare before the Civil War.[34] In Maryland, a general law of 1839 limited corporate life (for mining and manufacturing companies) to a maximum of thirty years.[35] Early charters did not necessarily adhere to the principle that one share of stock was entitled to only one vote. It was not the rule in Maryland, for example, until after 1819. In New Hampshire, under the charter of the Souhegan Nail and Cotton Factory (1812), each of the fifty shares of capital stock was entitled to a vote, but no member was entitled to more than ten votes, regardless of the number of his shares.[36] The 1836 charter of a Maryland company, incorporated to build a turnpike from Hagerstown to the Pennsylvania border, allocated votes as follows: "for every share . . . not exceeding three, one vote each; for any number of shares greater than three, and not exceeding ten, five votes; for any number of shares greater than ten, and not exceeding fifty, seven votes; for any number of shares greater than fifty, and not exceeding one hundred, ten votes; and for every additional hundred shares above one hundred, ten votes"; thirty votes was the maximum for any shareholder.[37] Some charters restricted the number of shares any individual might hold in any one corporation. In Pennsylvania, after 1810, bank charters usually prohibited the transfer of bank stock to "foreigners." [38] In 1822, a bank charter in New Jersey required the new corporation to use some of its capital to aid the fisheries at Amboy.[39] Limited liability—now considered one of the main objects of incorporation—was not universal in the 19th century. Bank stock did not possess this great boon in New York, for example. In Connecticut, limited liability was common for manufacturing companies before the 1830's; but in some charters—for example, that of the Mystic Manufacturing Company of 1814—the stockholders were to be "responsible in their private capacity," if the corporation became insolvent.[40]

But the main line of development was clear. Gradually, oddities were leveled out in the direction of a kind of common law of corporations, whose basic contours were given by business practice and the needs of entrepreneurs. Between 1800 and 1850, the essential nature of the corporation changed. No longer was the business

34 John W. Cadman, *The Corporation in New Jersey 1791–1875* (1949), p. 366.
35 Joseph G. Blandi, *Maryland Business Corporations 1783–1852* (1934), p. 56.
36 Laws N.H., Vol. 8, 1811–1820 (1920), p. 149.
37 Laws Md. 1835–6, ch. 321, sec. 4.
38 Hartz, *op. cit.*, p. 255.
39 Cadman, *op. cit.*, p. 68.
40 *Resolves and Private Laws, Conn. 1789–1836,* Vol. II (1837), p. 851.

corporation a unique, *ad hoc* creation, vesting exclusive control over a public asset or natural resource in one group of favorites or investors. Rather, it was becoming a general form in which to cast the organization of one's business—legally open to all, and with few real restrictions on entry, duration, and management. Business practice led the way. The living law on proxy voting, general and special meetings, inspection of books, and the transfer of stock, gradually created demands (which were granted) for standard clauses of corporate charters; and ultimately these norms were embodied in the statute and case law of corporations.

There were many detours along the way, before the law reached a stage in which there was simple access to the corporate form, open to all. Something must be said about state partnership in corporate affairs; about the anticorporation movement; and about rival forms of business organization.

State partnership in corporate enterprise seemed natural in the early 19th century. In the first place, many corporations were chartered to do work traditionally part of the function of the state. These jobs included road building, banking and the digging of canals. Secondly, since each franchise was a privilege and favor, the state had the right to exact a price,[41] which might include strict control or even profit sharing. Thirdly, state participation was a good way to help out an enterprise. It was a way of priming the pump, a way of supporting vital enterprise that would in turn enliven the economy. Fourth, public participation enhanced public control: if the state owned stock, and its men sat on the board, they could make sure the company acted in the public interest. Fifth, state investment might enrich the state. If the dreams of the enterprise came true, big dividends would flow to the public coffers. Pennsylvania, for example, not only owned stock in its banks, but, after 1806, invested in turnpikes, bridge companies, canal companies, and finally in railroads. States and cities both engaged in railroad boosting. Between 1827 and 1878, New York state lent, leased, or donated $10,308,844.77 for construction of sixteen railroads.[42] Some of these loans turned very sour in the aftermath of the panic of 1837. The New York constitution of 1846 severely restricted state aid to private corporations. The railroads then turned to the cities

[41] Sometimes quite literally. The charter of the Bank of Philadelphia (1803) required the bank to pay a bonus of $135,000 to the state. The bonus practice was not abolished in Pennsylvania until 1842. Hartz, *op. cit.*, pp. 54–56.

[42] Harry H. Pierce, *Railroads of New York, A Study of Government Aid* (1953), p. 15.

170 FROM THE REVOLUTION TO DEATH OF CHANCELLOR KENT

and towns with "astonishing success." Cities and towns were passionately eager to induce the lines to build routes that went
through their communities; a railroad line, they felt, meant access
to markets, rising land values, and general prosperity. Most commonly, the cities bought stock in the railroads. The city of Buffalo,
for example, subscribed $1,000,000 for stock in the Buffalo &
Jamestown Railroad. A few towns bought bonds; a few donated
money outright; and in 1842, the city of Albany guaranteed, by
endorsement, $100,000 worth of bonds of the Mohawk & Hudson.[43]

Pennsylvania experimented with mixed public and private enterprises. At one stage in the state's marriage with its railroads, in
the 1830's, Pennsylvania furnished locomotives; private companies
supplied the other cars. Before 1842, the state of Maryland chose
ten of the thirty directors of the Baltimore & Ohio; the city of
Baltimore chose eight. In New Jersey, the "monopoly bill" of 1832
granted exclusive transport franchises in exchange for gifts of
stock to the state. The state's shares carried a higher priority for
dividends than other shares—one of the earliest instances of preferred stock. For years, New Jersey profited nicely from railroad
investments; the income helped the state hold down and even reduce the taxes it levied on its residents.

State participation in enterprise was only a phase. Periodic out-
cry was heard that the state had no business meddling in what was
the proper sphere of private capital. These voices were weak at
first. The business cycle strengthened them; during periods of depression, state investments often went bad. This led to disillusion-
ment with the whole idea of state participation. States and cities,
nearly bankrupted in the years after 1837, were tempted to sell off
their assets for cash. In 1844, a referendum in Pennsylvania approved sale of the Main Line to private interests. As it happened,
the sale was not consummated until 1857. The Pennsylvania Railroad then bought the line for cash and railroad bonds. In exchange,
the state gave the railroad all tracks and equipment of the line, and
exempted it "forever, from the payment of taxes upon tonnage or
freight carried over the said railroads; and . . . on its capital
stock, bonds, dividends or property, except for city, borough,
county, township, and school purposes." This extraordinary boon
was declared unconstitutional one year later, in the great case of
Mott v. *Pennsylvania Railroad*.[44] Pennsylvania's Chief Justice Ellis
Lewis wrote a strong opinion, denying that the state had any right

[43] Pierce, *op. cit.*, pp. 18–19.
[44] 30 Penn. State 9 (1858).

to commit "political suicide" by giving up the power to tax. Legislative authority was not for sale. It was necessary, too, that the public exert some control over the legislature, to keep it from pawning its sovereignty. The public could not rest on its faith in the "fidelity of the legislature":

> Limitations of power, established by written constitutions, have their origin in a distrust of the infirmity of man. That distrust is fully justified by the history of the rise and fall of nations.[45]

This typical, American fear was the source out of which the system of checks and balances had grown. It was a fear of unbridled power, as possessed by large landholders and dynastic wealth, as well as by government. An influential segment of the public was willing to try many techniques to prevent concentration of authority and to offset the corrosive effect of money and power. The triumph of the corporation as a form of business association was therefore neither painless nor noiseless. The corporation was an object of great controversy in the first half of the 19th century. Partly because of its past, people in 1800 were likely to think that the monopoly aspect of a franchise was the essence of a corporation. Corporations were creatures of state, endowed with breath for the sole purpose of holding franchise or privilege, that is, some power or right that no one else could lay claim to. Most corporations were transportation monopolies, banks, insurance companies —aggregations of "capital," representing the "few" against the "many." Unlike farm and industrial enterprise, they did not *produce* any product (so people thought). They were in a sense parasitic; and yet unduly powerful. Hence, multiplicity of corporations seemed to present grave dangers to the health of the body politic. James Sullivan, attorney general of Massachusetts, warned in 1802 that "The creation of a great variety of corporate interests . . . must have a direct tendency to weaken the power of government." [46]

The word "soulless" constantly recurs in the debates on corporations. Everyone knew that corporations were really run by human beings. Yet the metaphor was not entirely pointless. Corporations did not die and had no ultimate size. There were no natural limits to their life or to their greed. Corporations, it was feared, could concentrate the worst urges of whole groups of men; the economic power of a corporation would not be tempered by the mentality of

45 *Ibid.*, p. 28.
46 Quoted in Handlin and Handlin, *op. cit.*, p. 260.

any one man, or by considerations of family or morality. People hated and distrusted corporations, the way some fear the computer today, which is also soulless, also capable of joining the wit, skill, and malevolence of many men.

In theory, the special charter system was a strong method of control. But the demand for charters was so great by the 1840's and 1850's that legislatures would have been swamped unless the job were made more routine. Even so, state session laws bulged with special charters. Valuable time was spent in the drudgery of issuing, amending, and extending hundreds of charters. In the rush, there was little time to supervise even those charters which needed supervision. Since even a radical routinization was not the answer, the legislatures turned to the next logical step, delegation: that is, the passage of general acts. The legislature could save itself time; could make effective law for all corporations, in one carefully considered law; and could make of the corporate form a freely available right, rather than a privilege of the few.

Even in the late 18th century a few general laws were passed, which applied to churches, academies, and library societies. A New York law of 1811, "relative to incorporations for Manufacturing purposes," is considered the first general law specifically for business corporations. Under this law, "any five or more persons who shall be desirous to form a company for the purpose of manufacturing woollen, cotton, or linen goods, or for the purpose of making glass, or for the purpose of making from ore bar-iron, anchors, mill-irons, steel, nail-rods, hoop-iron and ironmongery, sheet copper, sheet lead, shot, white lead and red lead," who filed a certificate with some standard information in the office of the secretary of state, became, for "the term of twenty years next after the day of filing such certificate," a "body corporate and politic, in fact and in name." [47]

Other corporation acts picked up the New York plan. These laws were general in the sense that they applied to all corporations in a particular field—manufacturing, banking, or insurance. Typically, too, the laws were not exclusive. They left the door open for private charters, if the incorporators preferred. For this reason, the early general laws were not effective. If they imposed rules of any bite at all, the business community ignored them and took the private-charter route. At most, entrepreneurs would incorporate temporarily under a general law, until they could extract a private charter from the legislature. To put teeth into the general laws, the

[47] Law N.Y., 1811, ch. 47.

New York constitution of 1846 took a somewhat more drastic step. It restricted special charters to "cases where in the judgment of the Legislature, the objects of the corporation cannot be attained under general laws." [48] As it turned out, the legislature was quite accommodating in making such a judgment. At the close of the period, then, the special charter was still dominant. But the handwriting was on the wall. The Louisiana constitution of 1845, a bellwether in many ways, contained a much stronger clause: "Corporations shall not be created in this State by special laws except for political or municipal purposes." [49]

It was no accident to find clauses about charters in state constitutions. When Chief Justice Lewis spoke of the infirmity of man, he meant man in government as well as private man. Officeholders were bound to be tempted by rich and unscrupulous corporations. In many states, actual scandals underscored this fear, and weakened public confidence in elected officials. To win the war against the great agglomerations, it was felt necessary to put restraints on the legislatures too. Under the New York constitution of 1821, the "assent of two-thirds of the members elected to each branch of the legislature" was needed for passage of any bill "creating, continuing, altering, or renewing any body politic or corporate." [50] A similar provision appeared in Delaware's constitution of 1831. Delaware little dreamed it would some day be a snug harbor for foreign corporations; its constitution added sternly that no act of incorporation "shall continue in force for a longer period than twenty years, without the re-enactment of the Legislature, unless it be an incorporation for public improvement." [51]

Despite controversy, corporations never lacked for defenders. When a two-thirds provision, like New York's, was proposed in the New Jersey convention of 1844, one delegate remarked he was "a friend to corporations. They have done more to increase the prosperity of our State than anything else. Let the legislature grant all that may apply, if the object is to benefit the community." Proponents of the two-thirds rule had "ventured to show their teeth at these little monsters, but if they believe them to be such dangerous creatures as they have represented them to be, they had better come manfully up to the work and strangle them at once, than to

48 N.Y. const., 1846, art. 8, sec. 1.
49 La. const., 1845, art. 123. This provision was copied in Iowa the following year. Iowa const., 1846, art. 8, sec. 2.
50 N.Y. const., 1821, art. 7, sec. 9.
51 Del. const., 1831, art. 2, sec. 17.

keep up this continued snapping at their heels." [52] The proposal was defeated.

The movement against corporations could never muster the strength or consensus to strangle them, as opposed to snapping at their heels. Yet no issue was more persistent, perhaps, in the period between 1815 and 1850, than the issue of public control over corporations. In the famous case of *Dartmouth College* v. *Woodward* (1819),[53] the United States Supreme Court faced the issue squarely. By the terms of the federal Constitution, no state could impair the obligation of a contract. But what was a "contract"? In *Dartmouth College,* the court decided that a corporate charter was "a contract made on a valuable consideration," a "contract for the security and disposition of property." Consequently, no legislature could change the terms of any charter which a previous legislature had granted; to do so would "impair" the charter. Dartmouth College was no business corporation; but the court, and the newspaper-reading public, well understood that the decision went beyond any question of the charters of colleges. News of the decision evoked a great howl of protest. Many contemporaries (and their intellectual descendants) felt that the *Dartmouth College* case was a blow to popular sovereignty; it took away from "the people and their elected representatives" a "large part of the control over social and economic affairs." [54] That was one way of looking at the case. The court and its defenders saw it differently. The purpose of the decision was to secure property interests, and to protect ownership and management rights from shifting, temporary winds of public opinion. A climate of legal stability promoted economic growth, while doing simple justice.

Dartmouth College had a far less sweeping effect on the law of corporations than one might have guessed. In the case itself, Joseph Story's concurring opinion suggested, perhaps offhandedly, a simple way to avoid the impact of the rule. If the legislature, Story said, really wanted to alter corporate charters, it ought to reserve

---

[52] *Proceedings of the New Jersey State Constitutional Convention of 1844* (1942), pp. 537–38, 539.

[53] 4 Wheat. 518 (1819). In *Fletcher* v. *Peck,* 6 Cranch 87 (1810), which arose out of the Yazoo land scandals in Georgia, the Marshall court had held that a legislative land grant was a "contract"; what one legislature gave, the next could not take back. See C. Peter Magrath, *Yazoo, Law and Politics in the New Republic* (1966).

[54] Charles Grove Haines, *The Role of the Supreme Court in American Government and Politics, 1789–1835* (1944), p. 419.

the right to do so when it issued them. If it did, then the right to alter the charter would, legally speaking, be part of the "contract" between the state and the corporation; and when the legislature passed a law changing the terms of the charter, that would be no "impairment." In later years, charters did contain a standard clause (at the insistence of legislatures), reserving to the state the right to alter, amend, and repeal. This right was also a common feature of general incorporation laws. Finally, the right was inserted in state constitutions. The New York constitution of 1846 provided that "all general laws and special acts" about corporations "may be altered from time to time or repealed" (art. 8, sec. 1).

Corporations were rare before 1800; hence the *case law* on corporations was thin. As corporations multiplied, so did their litigation. The prior law was not germane to these new situations. The rights and duties of stockholders, in a factory or bank, were hardly comparable to those of an academy or church; and the powers of management posed different questions in these two polar types of corporation. The law of corporations was, therefore, thoroughly revamped, so much that for all practical purposes, it was created new out of nothing.

At first, the courts treated corporate powers rather gingerly. They adhered to the "general and well settled principle, that a corporation had no other powers than such as are specifically granted; or, such as are necessary for the purpose of carrying into effect the powers expressly granted." [55] This "principle" followed logically from the concept of a corporation as an occasion for aggregating capital toward a single venture or purpose—a bridge, a factory, a bank. Chief Justice Roger Taney built on this concept in the famous case of the *Charles River Bridge* (1837).[56] This case stood for the proposition that charters were to be strictly construed; like government itself, charters had to be narrowly confined within written borders. Courts recognized, of course, that a certain latitude in interpretation might be necessary. "Public prosperity" required some "facility" for corporations in "acting and contracting." [57] Hence, like the federal government, corporations could

[55] Joseph K. Angell and Samuel Ames, *A Treatise on the Law of Private Corporations Aggregate* (2nd ed., 1843) p. 66.

[56] *Proprietors of the Charles River Bridge* v. *Proprietors of the Warren Bridge*, 11 Pet. 420 (1837).

[57] Angell and Ames, *op. cit.*, p. 162.

enjoy some powers that were "implied" by their functions, even though not literally spelled out in their charters. In the long run, the creative draftsmanship of the men who wrote the charters helped bury strict construction. Business practice led the way; the charters reflected what was fact: the growing scope and flexibility of enterprise. The logic of economic growth, invisible to most contemporaries, was drawing up law for itself. What the draftsmen devised, the courts accepted, and legislatures only weakly resisted. The old controls on corporations, meant to reduce their power or their economic role, either disappeared or became innocuous.

But while one kind of restriction faded, another was in process of birth. The business corporation, unlike its predecessors, was an economic venture. Law had to be devised to govern the relationship of officers, directors, shareholders, and creditors. Some of this law was hammered out in the cases. Joseph Story, for example, is credited with inventing the so-called trust-fund doctrine. It stemmed from *Wood* v. *Drummer* (1824).[58] Stockholders of the Hallowell and Augusta Bank, of Maine, which was winding up its corporate existence, declared dividends amounting to seventy-five per cent of the capital stock of $200,000. The bank thus became a hollow shell, especially since not all of the capital stock had been actually paid in. The plaintiffs held bank notes that became worthless. Story held that it was wrong for the stockholders to distribute the capital to themselves, in such a way as to defraud the bank's creditors, that is, the holders of the bank notes. The capital stock of banks was "to be deemed a pledge or trust fund for the payment of the debts contracted by the bank." Creditors could "follow" the funds "into the hands of any persons, who are not innocent purchasers," and recover it from them. This gave the plaintiffs a right to recover from the stockholders, who had lined their pockets with the money from the bank. Later cases repeated the rule, and extended it to analogous situations. Meanwhile, the courts slowly built up a body of rules about the internal life of corporations and their relations to the outside world.

The triumph of enterprise was probably inevitable; but the *corporate form* was not the only possibility. A New York statute of 1822, later widely copied, introduced the limited partnership into American law, in part based on a French business form, the *société en commandite*. In a limited partnership, some members ("general partners") stood fully responsible for partnership debts. Limited (or "special") partners, however, were liable "no further than the

[58] 3 Mason C.C. Rpts. 308, Fed. Cas. No. 17,944 (1824).

fund which he or they have furnished to the partnership stock." [59]
A limited partnership (with its "one or more sleeping partners")
was "supposed to be well calculated to bring dormant capital into
active and useful employment." [60] (The words are Chancellor
Kent's.) Another form of enterprise was the Massachusetts or business trust; this was an unincorporated association that carried on
business in the form of the trust. Managers (trustees) held title to
the property of the trust. Instead of stockholders, there were "beneficiaries"; instead of capital stock, they held certificates of beneficial interest. A "trust government," something like a charter,
spelled out the powers and duties of the managers. The joint-stock
company was another business form in common use. It resembled a
partnership, but its capital, unlike that of a partnership, was divided into transferable shares.

It was by no means certain that a corporation, as that term was
understood in 1800 or 1820, was the best way to raise and manage
money for enterprise. Early American land companies, studied by
Shaw Livermore, made use of a great variety of business forms.
Speculative land companies, even before 1800, showed "all the
various states of complexity in modern business organization beyond the partnership"; yet they were not incorporated. Livermore
has argued that these associations were the "true progenitors of the
modern business corporation." [61] In other words, the general corporation did not evolve from the special charter system; rather, it
reflected the richness of business practice in private associations,
operating without charters. These associations were similar to later
full-blown business corporations because they were functionally so
much alike. The argument is that the old law of corporations provided nothing but words and forms, like rubble from which a new
bridge is built; the architecture and the plans derived from current
business practice and economic drive. That the triumphant business form, as it ultimately emerged, was a "corporation," not some
mutation of the partnership or Massachusetts trust was due to almost random factors, which tipped an unimportant balance. Similarly, in the 20th century, before the Uniform Commercial Code,
the dominant form of installment sale was different in different
states. In some places, it was called a conditional sale; in some, a

59 See Edward H. Warren, *Corporate Advantages Without Incorporation*
(1929), pp. 302 ff.
60 James Kent, *Commentaries on American Law* [cited hereafter as Kent,
Commentaries], Vol. III (2nd ed., 1832), p. 35.
61 Shaw Livermore, *Early American Land Companies* (1939), p. 216.

chattel mortgage; in Pennsylvania, a bailment lease; in England, a hire-purchase contract. Where one form was dammed up by an unfavorable doctrine or statute, practice flowed freely into another channel. The triumph of the corporation over its rivals was the same phenomenon a century before. The overriding need was for an efficient, trouble-free device, to aggregate capital and manage it in business, with limited liability and transferable shares. But in a sense, the argument over origins is merely an argument over words. French law was not the "progenitor" of the limited partnership; charters of towns, colleges, and hospitals were not the "progenitors" of railroad charters; land syndicates were not the "progenitors" of general corporation laws. All these were merely models and occasions. The theory of legal history is that the architect of contemporary law is always contemporary fact. History does not supply decisions; only raw materials and plans.

(CHAPTER IV)

THE LAW OF PERSONAL STATUS:
WIVES, PAUPERS, AND SLAVES

MARRIAGE AND DIVORCE

In England, ecclesiastical courts had jurisdiction over marriage and divorce, and family law was strongly influenced by religious law. The United States had no such courts, and, after the early 19th century, no established churches. Family law was secular in the United States. Marriage was a civil contract in theory. Religious ceremonies were neither forbidden nor discouraged; and moral and religious ideas remained powerful influences in the law of marriage and divorce. But two secular forms of marriage were legitimated in the United States: the civil ceremony, which had colonial antecedents, and the so-called common-law marriage, which was probably an American innovation.

The concept of a "common-law marriage" is often misunderstood. People sometimes use the term to mean a liaison, without any pretense of marriage. Legally, however, a common-law marriage was as valid as any other kind of marriage, though highly informal. Its essence was a "verbal contract," that is, an agreement by man and woman to consider themselves husband and wife, followed by cohabitation. Its origins are in dispute. Probably there was no such institution in England. Chancellor Kent and others were of the opinion that under the common law no "peculiar ceremonies" were "requisite . . . to the valid celebration of the marriage." The presence of a clergyman, though a "very becoming practice," was unnecessary; the "consent of the parties is all that is required." [1]

Kent and other judges of the early 19th century probably misread the English authorities. But the common-law marriage did not blossom out of mistakes in reading cases. It had a more solid basis in the intellectual and social climate of America. Joel Bishop,

[1] Kent, *Commentaries*, Vol. II (2nd ed., 1832), pp. 86–87.

writing in 1852, advanced this explanation. In England, only Episcopalian clergymen were authorized to perform marriages. The Puritan dissenters had "fled to these western wilds for the single purpose of escaping from what they regarded as oppression and moral contagion flowing from those churches." They would not have tolerated any requirement that they import an "Episcopal ecclesiastic . . . paying him tithes, simply that he might become an invited guest at their weddings. Though the American colonies were not all settled by puritans, the spirit of this suggestion will apply to most of them." [2] This factor, Bishop felt, explained why some states came to accept the idea of a common-law, informal marriage.

In any event, there was a shortage of clergymen of every faith. Most of the population lived outside the cities; some parts of the country were thinly populated, and large numbers of half-educated people were owners of property and took part in the economy. Many American couples lived together after makeshift ceremonies, or none. The law tended to recognize these "marriages" as holy and valid. Bishop, who was a shrewd observer of law and morals, sensed that the character of the early settlers was one inclined to make a virtue of necessity, or at least come to terms with it. Despite their "pure morals and stern habits," the settlers could not tolerate a strict adherence to the English marriage laws (or their American imitations), which did not suit American conditions. The stringent marriage laws of Pennsylvania, for example, were "ill adapted to the habits and customs of society"; a "rigid execution of them," remarked Chief Justice John Bannister Gibson in 1833, "would bastardize a vast majority of the children which have been born within the state for half a century." [3] Hence the recognition of the common-law marriage.

The laxity of its form did not escape opposition. There were those who denounced it as a "strange and monstrous crossbreed between a concubinage and a marriage." There were other problems, too. An informal marriage might be a secret marriage; it might lead to disputes over property rights, to public scandal, and to the peril of bigamy. In *Grisham* v. *State* (1831),[4] the highest court of Tennessee refused to validate the concept of common-law

2 Joel Bishop, *Commentaries on the Law of Marriage and Divorce* (1852), p. 130.
3 C. J. Gibson, in *Rodebaugh* v. *Sanks,* 2 Watts 9, 11 (Pa., 1833).
4 10 Tenn. 588 (1831).

marriage. John Grisham, a widower, and Jane Ligan, a widow, had agreed to cohabit as man and wife; they swore an oath, before witnesses, to that effect. They were indicted and convicted of "lewd acts of fornication and adultery . . . to the great scandal of the . . . good and worthy citizens." The law, said the court, was the "guardian of the morals of the people"; so saying, the court upheld this conviction. But in most states, the guardian bowed to the inevitable, and accepted informal marriage, overcoming any doubts and ignoring the costs.

England had been a "divorceless society," and remained that way until 1857. There was no way to get a judicial divorce. The very wealthy might squeeze a rare private bill of divorce out of Parliament. Between 1800 and 1836 there were, on the average, three of these a year. For the rest, unhappy husbands and wives had to be satisfied with annulment (no easy matter), or divorce from bed and board (*a mensa et thoro*), a form of legal separation, which did not entitle either spouse to marry again. The most common solutions, of course, when a marriage broke down, were adultery and desertion.[5]

In the colonial period, the South was generally faithful to English tradition. Absolute divorce was unknown, divorce from bed and board very rare. In New England, however, courts and legislatures occasionally granted divorce. In Pennsylvania, Penn's laws of 1682 gave spouses the right to a "Bill of Divorcement," if their marriage partner was convicted of adultery. Later, the governor or lieutenant governor was empowered to dissolve marriages, on grounds of incest, adultery, bigamy, or homosexuality. There is no evidence that the governor ever used this power. Still later, the general assembly took divorce into its own hands. The English privy council disapproved of this practice, and, in the 1770's disallowed legislative divorces in Pennsylvania, New Jersey, and New Hampshire. The Revolution, of course, put an end to the privy council's power.[6]

After Independence, divorce remained uncommon, but the law was quite different in different parts of the country. In the South, divorce was rare or absent. Henry William Desaussure, writing in

[5] See Gerhard O. W. Mueller, "Inquiry into the State of a Divorceless Society, Domestic Relations Law and Morals in England from 1660 to 1857," 18 U. Pittsburgh L. Rev. 545 (1957).

[6] Nelson M. Blake, *The Road to Reno, A History of Divorce in the United States* (1962), pp. 34–47.

1817, stated flatly that South Carolina had never granted a single divorce.[7] In other states there was an occasional legislative divorce. The Georgia constitution of 1798 allowed the legislature to grant divorces, on a two-thirds vote of each branch of the legislature—and after a "fair trial" and a divorce decree in the superior court. The judges were unsure of their role in granting divorces.[8] The legislature later resolved these doubts, by passing a law reserving full and exclusive rights to grant divorces. Between 1798 and 1835, there were only 291 legislative divorces in Georgia. The frequency curve was rising toward the end of the period. Twenty-seven couples were divorced legislatively in 1833—for example, Green Fuller and Susannah Fuller, whose "matrimonial connection, or civil contract of marriage" was "completely annulled, set aside, and dissolved"; so that the two would "in future be held as distinct and separate persons, altogether unconnected by any mystical union or civil contract whatever." [9]

North of the Mason-Dixon line, courtroom divorce was more normal than legislative divorce. Pennsylvania passed a general divorce law in 1785, Massachusetts one year later. Every New England state had a divorce law before 1800, along with New York, New Jersey, and Tennessee. Grounds for divorce varied somewhat from state to state. New York's law of 1787 permitted absolute divorce only for adultery. Vermont, on the other hand, in 1798 allowed divorce for impotence, adultery, intolerable severity, three years' willful desertion, and long absence with presumption of death. Rhode Island allowed divorce for "gross misbehaviour and wickedness in either of the parties, repugnant to and in violation of the marriage convenant." [10] In New Hampshire, it was grounds for divorce if a spouse joined the Shaker sect—not an unreasonable rule, since the Shakers did not believe in sexual intercourse.[11]

This efflorescence of divorce laws must have stemmed from a real increase in demand for legal divorces. The size of the demand doomed the practice of divorce by statute. Like corporate charters, private divorce bills became a nuisance, a pointless drain on the legislature's time. At the end of the period, some states still granted them; but Pennsylvania had abolished legislative divorce, and

---

[7] Henry W. Desaussure, *South Carolina Eq. Rpts.*, Vol. I, p. liv; Vol. II, p. 644.
[8] See Oliver H. Prince, comp., *A Digest of the Laws of the State of Georgia*, Vol. II (2nd ed., 1837), p. 187.
[9] Laws Ga., 1833, pp. 82–83.
[10] Blake, *op. cit.*, p. 50.
[11] See *Dyer* v. *Dyer*, 5 N.H. 271 (1830).

later in the century, the private divorce law became fully extinct.

So much was structural. But what was the source of this sudden desire for a simple legitimate way to divorce? The divorce rate, of course, was the merest trickle in comparison to the rate in more recent times. But it was noticeable; and to some self-appointed guardians of national morals, it was an alarming fire bell in the night, a symptom of moral dry rot, and a cause in itself of still further moral decay. President Timothy Dwight of Yale, in 1816, called the rise in divorces "dreadful beyond conception." He sensed "stalking, barefaced pollution" in Connecticut; he foresaw that the state would become "one vast Brothel; one great province of the World of Perdition." The "whole community," he warned, could be thrown "into a general prostitution." [12]

In hindsight, the rise of divorce does not appear quite so obviously as a sign of the breakdown of the family. It was precisely at this time, rather than earlier, that the modern concept of the family reached fruition. According to William O'Neill, "when families are large and loose, arouse few expectations, and make few demands, there is no need for divorce." The need arises when "families become the center of social organization." At this point, "their intimacy can become suffocating, their demands unbearable, and their expectations too high to be easily realizable. Divorce then becomes the safety valve that makes the system workable." [13] Moreover, a divorceless state is not a state without adultery, prostitution, fornication. It is, more likely than not, a place sharply divided between official law and unofficial behavior. A country with rare or expensive divorce is a country with two sets of divorce laws, one for the rich, and one for the poor. The United States was two nations, too: yet enormous numbers of people owned property and had some stake in society. Easy divorce laws grew out of popular desire: desire to stabilize and legitimize relationships, to settle doubts about ownership of family property. Divorce was simplest to obtain and divorce laws most advanced in those parts of the country—the West especially—least stratified by class.

Even in Timothy Dwight's day, many people did not agree with his fire-eating words. Zephaniah Swift, who wrote at the end of the 18th century, thought it morally wholesome that Connecticut's laws should recognize absolute divorce. The alternative was divorce from bed and board—legal separation. This, he felt, was an "irresistible temptation to the commission of adultery," suitable

12 Quoted in Blake, *op. cit.*, p. 59.
13 William L. O'Neill, *Divorce in the Progressive Era* (1967), pp. 6–7.

only to those with "more frigidity or more virtue than usually falls to the share of human beings." Liberal divorce laws, on the other hand, were "favourable . . . to the virtue, and the happiness of mankind." [14]

Since there was strong opinion on both sides, it was only natural that the law should embody compromise. It never tolerated full, free consensual divorce. Divorce became simpler than in prior generations, but never automatic. In form, divorce was an adversary proceeding. A divorce decree was a reward for the virtuous spouse, dissolving a marriage when the other partner was grievously at fault. The collusive or friendly divorce eventually became the normal case, since both partners usually wanted the divorce, or considered their marriage not worth fighting for, by the time it reached the court. The collusive divorce did not dominate the dockets until later in the century. But it was not unknown, say, in 1840. Collusion was probably most common in strict states, like New York, where adultery was the only practical grounds for divorce. Chancellor Kent observed, from his experience as a trial judge, that the sin of adultery "was sometimes committed on the part of the husband, for the very purpose of the divorce." [15] This must have been extreme behavior; since perjury is a somewhat lesser sin, collusion probably flourished in the New York courts.

FAMILY PROPERTY

At common law, elaborate rules governed the property rights (and duties) of married women. These rules, however, were mainly deducible from one grand "principle of the common law, by which the husband and wife are regarded as one person, and her legal existence and authority in a degree lost or suspended, during the continuance of the matrimonial union." [16] Essentially, husband and wife were one flesh; but the man was the owner of that flesh:

> The husband, by marriage, acquires a right to the use of the real estate of his wife, during her life; and if they have a child born

[14] Zephaniah Swift, *A System of the Laws of the State of Connecticut* (1795) Vol. I, pp. 192–193. Bishop called the divorce *a mensa et thoro* a "carbuncle on the face of civilized society," a "demoralizing mock-remedy for matrimonial ills." Bishop, *op. cit.*, pp. 217–18.

[15] Kent, *Commentaries,* Vol. II (2nd ed., 1832), p. 106.

[16] Kent, *Commentaries,* Vol. II (2nd ed., 1832), p. 129.

alive, then, if he survives, during his life, as tenant by the curtesey. He acquires an absolute right to her chattels real, and may dispose of them. . . . He acquires an absolute property in her chattels personal in possession. . . . As to the property of the wife accruing during coverture, the same rule is applicable.[17]

Actually, common-law doctrine was more complex than appears from this quotation. The law distinguished between types of property; and courts of equity had for a long time softened the husband's dictatorial control, by allowing a father or other relative to establish a separate estate for the woman, through a premarital settlement or by way of a trust. In England, such settlements were common. Marriage settlements were accepted as valid by the courts, and a rich body of law grew up about them. They were, of course, practically speaking, confined to the wealthy, landed classes.

In the United States, these English doctrines and practice had been recognized and, to some extent, followed. Chancery courts were absent or atrophied in some jurisdictions; this was a complication. Colonial law treated married women much more as free souls than the law of England did; this American legal tradition never completely died out. In 1787, Massachusetts, recognizing that "sometimes . . . husbands absent themselves from this Commonwealth, and abandon their wives . . . who may be thereby reduced to great distress," by statute gave the deserted wife authority to petition the court for the right to sell land, "as if she was sole and unmarried." [18] Essentially, the English system was tolerable, in England, only for upper-class landowners, and even then only because of the institutions mitigating its impact. Plantation owners of the South were also able to adapt to the law of settlements and trusts. But these devices were far too intricate for the average person to handle, even the average landowner, and even when aided by the average lawyer. Major reforms came in the married women's property acts. The first of these, a crude and somewhat tentative version, was enacted in 1839, in Mississippi (another example of reform that began on the legal periphery). The early statutes on married women's property did not give married women full legal equality; they attacked the problem piecemeal. Four of the five

---

[17] Chief Justice Zephaniah Swift, in *Griswold* v. *Penniman*, 2 Conn. 564 (1818). A lease is an example of a "chattel real." The term "coverture" means marriage.

[18] *The Perpetual Laws of the Commonwealth of Massachusetts* (1788), p. 362 (act of Nov. 21, 1787).

sections of the Mississippi act regulated the rights of married women to own and dispose of slaves (the husband retained "control and management of all such slaves, the direction of their labor, and the receipt of the productions thereof").[19] In Michigan, for example, a statute of 1844 merely exempted the wife's earned or inherited property from liability for her husband's "debts and engagements." Still, by 1850, about seventeen states had granted to married women some legal capacity to deal with their property.

Real changes had occurred in the social and economic position of women between 1800 and 1845. More important was the *number* of women with a stake in society—and the slow breakdown, in the United States, of the kind of legal pluralism so characteristic of England, where the classic common law was primarily geared toward the needs of the landed gentry. In the United States, the middle-class family was part of and participant in the working legal system. English land-law practices were too cumbersome, technical, and expensive for this class to bear. Moreover (and this was critical), the tangle of rules and practices was potentially an impediment to the speed and efficiency of the land market. The statutes spoke of rights of husband and wife, as if the issue was the intimate relations between the sexes. But the real point of the statutes was to rationalize more cold-blooded matters, such as the rights of a creditor to collect debts out of land owned by husbands, wives, or both. Most litigation over married women's property was not litigation between the spouses, or in the family at all. In almost no case did a husband sue his wife or vice versa. The typical cases, both before and after the married women's property acts, were cases of creditor's rights. The married women's property acts, therefore, did not signal a revolution in the status of women; rather, they *ratified* and adjusted a silent revolution. A curious fact provides striking, though indirect confirmation of this point: passage of these laws seemed to effect an enormous, radical change, in that most basic of institutions, the family; yet the laws were hardly debated, or discussed at the time. Newspapers made almost no mention of them. Little agitation preceded them; great silence followed them. It was the silence of a *fait accompli*.[20]

19 Laws Miss., 1839, ch. 46.
20 On this point, the text has drawn upon the research of Kay Ellen Thurman, in *The Married Women's Property Acts* (unpublished LL.M. thesis, University of Wisconsin Law School, 1966).

POOR LAWS AND SOCIAL WELFARE

In every period, society makes some attempt to care for its weaker members; its institutions insure at least some of its people against some social risks. Law and order are themselves devices of social insurance. They guard property owners against physical attacks on their wealth. Debtor protection laws keep merchants and landowners from falling too far in the social scale too fast. The family takes care of small children until they can care for themselves. Church groups, the extended family, and the web of personal friendships provide relief for many more of the helpless. All this was true in the 19th century, perhaps to a greater degree than today. The poor laws were residual. Paupers were those at the absolute bottom of the social ladder, those who had nowhere and no one but government to turn to. Even so, the poor laws probably worked best in small towns and rural areas. The failures of the welfare system became glaring when its creaking institutions faced a large class of the urban landless poor.

Few have had a kind word to say about 19th-century poor laws. But their weaknesses must be understood in context. To contemporaries, there were no real alternatives to the poor laws, except complete abolition and recourse to private charity. For want of better solutions, the colonial poor laws continued after 1776, at first with little change. The basic principle was local rule. The poor were to be supported by and in their own community. They were a charge on that political subdivision in which they were "settled." As expressed in the New York law of 1788: "Every city and town shall support and maintain their own poor." [21] The administrative unit was local; the city, town, township, or county, or some combination of these.[22] Centralized state administration was a century away.

A fortiori, the federal government had nothing to do with the poor laws. It played a minute role in social welfare. The exceptions were few and revealing. On Feb. 17, 1815, after the great earthquake in New Madrid, Missouri, Congress passed an act to help those whose lands had "been materially injured by earthquakes."

[21] Quoted in David M. Schneider, *The History of Public Welfare in New York State, 1609–1866* (1938), p. 112.
[22] Fern Boan, *A History of Poor Relief Legislation and Administration in Missouri* (1941), pp. 22–23.

These sufferers were allowed to locate "the like quantity of land" in other parts of the public domain in Missouri Territory.[23] This act, one notes, did not extract a cent of hard cash from the treasury. The federal government was short of money, but long on land. It gave away geese, not golden eggs. Even at that, land grants for welfare purposes were rare. Only after long and bitter debate did the federal government assign land to the Kentucky Deaf and Dumb Asylum (1826). Dorothea Dix lobbied vigorously for land grants to aid the insane. Yet President Franklin Pierce vetoed her bill in 1854, partly because he felt it was inappropriate for the federal government to act as "the great almoner of public charity, throughout the United States."

In some instances, the federal government was more lavish, and its authority was not questioned by states' righters. A law of 1798 imposed a payroll tax on the wages of sailors. The money was to be used to support hospitals for sick and disabled seamen.[24] Veterans of national wars received pensions and bonuses of land. Neither veterans nor sailors, of course, were pariahs. They were in the same category as the victims of the New Madrid earthquake: their deprivations were in no way their own doing. They were respectable people, voters, the man who lived next door.

The public was relatively generous to others who were also clearly not to be blamed—the sick, the old, the deaf and dumb, the insane. Kentucky had established a state home in the 1820's for those "who, by the mysterious dispensation of Providence, are born deaf and of course dumb." The law called on all "philanthropic citizens" to "promote an object so benevolent and humane," and backed up its words with a cash appropriation. Kentucky also established a public asylum for the insane. Massachusetts set up a State Reform School in 1847, for young offenders.[25]

The township pauper, on the other hand, particularly if he was a stranger in town, was considered an idler, a profligate, a weak-

23 3 Stats. 211 (act of Feb. 17, 1815).

24 Henry W. Farnam, *Chapters in the History of Social Legislation in the United States to 1860* (1938), pp. 232–4.

25 Sophonisba P. Breckinridge, *Public Welfare Administration in the United States* (2nd ed., 1938), pp. 98, 99, 101, 113. The treatment of dependent children, however, seems by modern standards barbaric. Orphans were liable to be sold as apprentices. But there was little else to be done with homeless boys and girls. A master was at least supposed to teach his apprentice to read and write. Girls learned to cook and sew. Boys worked, and learned a trade, in exchange for meals and a home. In 1794, for example, ten New York boys from the almshouse were "bound to Andrew Stockholm & Co. at the Cotton Manufactury." Schneider, *op. cit.*, p. 181.

ling. Communities resented him and the money they had to pay for his support. Consequently, the poor laws were punitive. They were meant to deter, to make poverty unpalatable, to make relief come bitter and dear.

How the poor laws actually worked has not been so carefully researched as one would like. Perhaps they were not so bad as pictured. History does not record routine acts of kindness. The abuses, however, scream from the record. Indeed, the surfaces are alarming. A substantial body of law bore on the question whether a pauper was "settled" in this or that county or town. "Settlement" fixed responsibility for the pauper's upkeep. Under a New Hampshire law of 1809, which was not atypical, a town might support a pauper even if he was not technically "settled" there. The creditor town then sued the town of settlement to recover its costs.[26] Towns and counties often fought out the question of "settlement" in court, to fix the burden of these costs on the receiving or the shipping jurisdiction.

A legal concept begins its career as smooth and as perfect as an egg; if the concept has important economic or social consequences, and leads to contention among interest groups, litigation may batter and bruise it out of shape. Dozens of reported cases turned on the concept of settlement. In one volume alone of the Connecticut Reports (volume 7, for 1828–1829), four cases on poor relief were reported. The town of Litchfield sued the town of Farmington over support of a pauper named Asabel Moss and his family. The town of Reading sued the town of Weston "for supplies furnished to *Harriet,* the wife, and *Sally* and *Lucinda,* the minor children, of Samuel Darling." The keeper of the county jail in Norwich sued the town of Norwich "to recover for support furnished by the plaintiff, to *James Hazard* and *John Blake,* prisoners in such gaol." In the same volume, the town of Plainfield sued a putative father, one Hopkins, "for the maintenance of a bastard child." And these were appellate cases only—the visible tip of the iceberg. After decades of litigation, the whole settlement concept became one of the most intricate known to the law.

The right of one township to recover from another was supposed to remove the bite from the concept of settlement; a person without settlement would not necessarily starve. But lawsuits have always been expensive. Since the concept and facts of settlement were in constant dispute, no town could predict the precise outcome of a difficult case. An action for reimbursement, then, must

26 Laws N.H., 1809, ch. 36.

have been a town's last, desperate resort to get its money back. Far better to have no paupers to begin with. Moreover, a pauper, if he stayed long enough, might gain a valid settlement in town. In many states, it was a crime to bring a pauper into a new county. Paupers, as in colonial days, were "warned out" to prevent them from gaining a settlement. Sometimes, they were escorted to the county or township line, and dumped over the border. In extreme cases, paupers were passed on from place to place, "sent backwards and forwards . . . like a shuttlecock, without end." [27]

Local authorities were constantly at pains to keep down the costs of relief. Under a law of Indiana Territory (1807), by no means unique, overseers of the poor in each township had the duty "to cause all poor persons, who have, or shall become a public charge to be farmed out at public vendue, or out-cry, to wit; On the first Monday in May, yearly and every year, at some public place . . . to the person or persons, who shall appear to be the lowest bidder or bidders." [28] In 1845, Emaley Wiley bought all of the paupers of Fulton County, Illinois, for $594.[29] Obviously, the system of farming out the poor could drive down the standard of care to the lowest conceivable level or maximize exploitation of the labor of the poor.

There were plenty of contemporary critics who saw the inhumanity of the system, and its failure to get poverty at its roots. The medicine was not working; paupers seemed to be multiplying in the land. Josiah Quincy's report of 1821, on the pauper laws of Massachusetts, issued blunt words of warning. The "pernicious consequences of the existing system" were "palpable" and increasing.[30] The report called for a radical restructuring. It rejected *outdoor* relief (support for the pauper in his own home), and the auction system, and strongly urged adoption of what came to be called *indoor* (that is, institutional) relief. A New York report on the welfare laws, published in 1824, agreed with Quincy; indoor relief was the preferable course. The almshouse or poor house would be a more efficient place to give moral education, and to put the poor to work. Best of all, the government would save money:

27 Quoted in Martha Branscombe, *The Courts and the Poor Laws in New York State 1784–1929* (1943), p. 102.

28 Francis S. Philbrick, ed., *The Laws of Indiana Territory 1801–1809* (1930), pp. 308–309.

29 Sophonisba P. Breckinridge, *The Illinois Poor Law and Its Administration* (1939), p. 63.

30 Quoted in Sophonisba P. Breckinridge, *Public Welfare Administration in the United States* (2nd ed., 1938), p. 32.

It is believed that with proper care and attention, and under favorable circumstances, the average annual expense *in* an almshouse, having a convenient farm attached to it, will not exceed from 20 to 35 dollars for the support of each pauper, exclusive of the amount of labour he may perform; while *out* of an almshouse, it will not be less than from 33 to 65 dollars, and in many instances where the pauper is old and infirm, or diseased, from 80 to 100 dollars, and even more.[31]

The poor farm was not a new invention; but these two reports helped give the idea new popularity. In 1824, New York passed a comprehensive act "to provide for the establishment of county poorhouses." This act, a "historic step," established the "principle of indoor relief"; it made the county poor house "the center of the public relief system." It also introduced some wholesome reforms; it "advanced the principle of county responsibility for all poor persons lacking settlement," and prohibited "removals of indigent persons across county lines." [32] Of course, this law could not and did not guarantee that poor farms would be efficient or humane, despite the hopes of its sponsors. As was true of prison reform, well-meant changes sometimes merely centralized the horror. By 1838, some county homes were reported to be in a state of inhuman squalor.[33]

The root of the problem was not structural. It lay in society's indifference. The mass of the public feared and distrusted vagrants. Even men of good will were blinded by the fantasy of the able-bodied poor, unwilling to earn an honest living. Reform movements fed on a few noisome scandals, emphasized the failures of the old system, and called for fresh approaches. But reformers lacked the will to follow through, and no concrete interest group stood to gain from a thorough reform of public welfare. Thus, even when reform succeeded in changing formal law, the actual operation of the programs soon lapsed into their former evil habits. From poor laws to poor farms to AFDC is a continuous lesson, on the consequences of powerlessness in America.

31 *Ibid.*, p. 43.
32 Schneider, *op. cit.*, p. 236.
33 *Ibid.*, pp. 244–45.

SLAVERY AND THE NEGRO

The most visible American pariah, before the Civil War, was the Negro slave. As we have seen, an indigenous system of law grew up to govern the "peculiar institution" of slavery.[34] What was at first a law for the servant class developed deeper and deeper overtones of color. The slave laws then became laws about the fate of a race.

No feature of American life has been so marked with blood and failure as the confrontation of white and black. Yet in 1776, liberals could well be optimistic. The air rang with hopeful speeches on the inherent rights of man—rights which seemed to apply to the black man as well as the white. There was wide agreement too, that the slave trade was an abomination and should be destroyed. A society was formed in Pennsylvania in 1784 "for promoting the abolition of slavery, and the relief of free Negroes, unlawfully held in Bondage, and for Improving the Condition of the African Race." In New York in 1785, John Jay and Alexander Hamilton helped organize a "Society for the Promotion of the Manumission of Slaves and Protecting such of them that have been or may be Liberated." [35] Before the end of that century, Northern states took definite steps to rid themselves of slavery. A Pennsylvania law of 1780, "for the gradual abolition of slavery," recited its belief that all "inhabitants of the . . . earth," were "the work of an Almighty Hand," even though different "in feature or complexion." To "add one more step to universal civilization by removing as much as possible the sorrows of those who have lived in undeserved bondage, and from which by the assumed authority of the Kings of Britain, no effectual legal relief could be obtained," [36] the statute provided that all slaves held in the state had to be registered, and that no more slaves could be created; it also took steps to assimilate the legal condition of Negro servants to that of indentured whites.

Even the South felt some of this moral fervor. Quaker and Methodist leaders were dead set against slavery. A distinguished

---

34 See, in general, Kenneth M. Stampp, *The Peculiar Institution, Slavery in the Ante-Bellum South* (1956).

35 Merrill Jensen, *The New Nation* (1950), pp. 135, 136.

36 *Statutes at Large of Pennsylvania 1682–1801*, Vol. X, 1779–1781 (1904), pp. 67–68; see, in general, Arthur Zilversmit, *The First Emancipation, the Abolition of Slavery in the North* (1967).

and respected minority in the South, including such political leaders as Jefferson, Washington, and Madison, opposed the "peculiar institution." St. George Tucker, one of the most eminent of Virginia lawyers, wrote a *Dissertation on Slavery; with a Proposal for the Gradual Abolition of it, in the State of Virginia* (1796). The word "abolition" was not yet a curse. Some slaveowners actually set their slaves free. Southern legislatures had for some time indulged in passage of private acts of manumission. In 1782, Virginia passed a general, and permissive, law. Maryland in 1790 authorized owners to set slaves free by their last will and testament.

It was, for the blacks, a false dawn only. The Constitution compromised on many slavery issues. On the question of fugitive slaves it was firm. Such slaves "shall be delivered upon Claim of the Party to whom [his] Service or Labour may be due" (Art. IV, sec. 2). A similar provision appeared in the Ordinance of 1787, though slavery itself was outlawed in Northwest Territory. As the years went on, it became clear that the legal rights of man stopped at the color line. The cleavage between North and South did not dissolve; on the slavery question, it deepened and darkened.

In some ways, economic motives seem too flaccid to explain the Southern passion about race. The South was a kingdom of fear—a puzzling sexual fear of the black man, fear of the influence of free Negroes, fear of the North, fear of abolitionists. But above all, race war was the fear. Race war, said De Tocqueville, "is a nightmare constantly haunting the American imagination," both in the North and the South.[37] In the South, laws were passed to crush any possible slave revolt, and to punish disobedience and rebellion with brute force. Slaves could not legally own guns. Penalties for actual insurrection were particularly harsh—in many states, death. Free persons who incited rebellion were not spared. Incitement to insurrection by free persons became a capital crime in Alabama in 1812; in 1832, the state authorized the death penalty for those who published or distributed literature which might tend to arouse slave rebellion.[38]

The days of easy manumission also came to an end. Even in the 1780's manumission was more common in progressive Virginia than in South Carolina. After 1805, any slave who tarried in Virginia for more than a year after manumission, might legally be

[37] Alexis de Tocqueville, *Democracy in America* (ed. J. P. Mayer and Max Lerner, 1966), p. 329.
[38] Farnam, *op. cit.*, p. 187.

"apprehended and sold by the overseers of the poor of any county . . . in which he or she shall be found." [39] This cruel law was sometimes softened by acts of the legislature. In 1814, for example, a special act in Virginia allowed an old black, George Butler, to remain in Virginia with his family, who were still slaves. By the 1830's petitions for this sort of private act were common enough to warrant a general law on the subject. In the new law (1837), the legislature washed its hands of the matter, and referred individual cases to the courts.[40]

It was fortunate that exile laws were not strictly enforced. Free blacks had nowhere to go. Northern states did not greet them with open arms, to put it mildly. By an Illinois statute of 1829, any "black or mulatto person" who wanted to settle in Illinois had to show the county court of his county "a certificate of his or her freedom"; and he had to post a thousand-dollar bond "conditioned that such person will not, at any time, become a charge to said county, or any other county of this state, as a poor person, and shall . . . demean himself, or herself, in strict conformity with the laws of this state, that now are or hereafter may be enacted." [41] A Tennessee law put it bluntly: "No free person of color shall remove from any other State or territory of the Union into this State to reside here and remain in the State twenty days." [42] The city of Cincinnati tried to enforce a law requiring blacks to post a five-hundred-dollar bond (1829). Blacks petitioned for relief; white mobs took to the streets; riots ensued; afterwards, more than a thousand blacks moved to Canada.[43]

There was, of course, another side to this picture: the growing abolition movement, and the stubbornness of the North toward the various fugitive-slave laws. A federal law supplementing the Constitutional mandate was passed in 1793. In the 1820's, resistance to its enforcement showed itself strong in the North. Fugitive slaves figured in some of the most celebrated cases of the decades after 1820; these cases generated enormous heat, exacerbated relationships in a federal union becoming more and more attenuated, and fed the appetite of a growing body of constitutional law. The 1850 fugitive-slave law added fuel to the fire; gave impetus to the

39 Laws Va. 1805, ch. 63, sec. 10.
40 Laws Va. 1836–7, ch. 70.
41 Rev. Code Ill. 1829, p. 109.
42 Tenn. Code 1858, sec. 2726.
43 Leon F. Litwack, *North of Slavery, the Negro in the Free States, 1790–1860* (1961), pp. 72–73.

so-called Underground Railway spiriting fugitives to Canada; and set off a course of legal wrangling that reached a climax in the *Dred Scott* case.[44]

The Southern states, for their part, defended their institution with great vigor. From an early date, the states began to limit manumission more and more. Strict laws made it impossible for slavery to wither away. Some control over manumission was, in context, understandable. Otherwise, when a slave became too old or too sick to be productive, the owners might be tempted to set him free, and shift the cost of food, medicine, and clothes to the state. Or an insolvent master might manumit his slaves to thwart his creditors. Still, it was probably the political sins of emancipation that stood uppermost in the minds of the legislatures. The South did not want an expanding population of free Negroes. As early as 1800, a law of South Carolina declared the emancipation of depraved or dependent slaves to be a social abuse. Emancipation could not take place unless and until "five indifferent freeholders living in the neighborhood" were satisfied that the slave had good character and could support himself. By 1820, South Carolina cut off all emancipations except by legislative act. In 1822, Mississippi outlawed manumission except by will, and only as a reward for meritorious service. The final step, outlawing all manumission by will or by deed, was taken reluctantly and late, in 1858 in Arkansas; in 1860 in Maryland and Alabama.[45] The issue of freedom was then decided by the war.

The "issue," however, was not full equality for blacks. That was nowhere conceded. There were many free Negroes who could testify to this proposition. All Northern blacks were free men; almost 60,000 free Negroes lived in Virginia, and 25,000 lived in the city of Baltimore alone. Only in the newer slave states, such as Mississippi, were the numbers of free Negroes negligible. But the law of the free Negro was a kind of modified law of Negro slavery. The free Negro (in John Hope Franklin's word) was "quasi-free." [46] As of 1830, only four states, all in New England, allowed free Negroes the same voting rights as free whites. Many northern states—for example, Illinois—did not allow intermarriage between Negro and

44 Russel B. Nye, *Fettered Freedom, Civil Liberties and the Slavery Controversy 1830–1860* (1963), pp. 257–78. Matching the enforcement problems of the fugitive-slave laws were the problems of enforcing the laws against the slave trade. For an account of this, see Warren S. Howard, *American Slavers and the Federal Law, 1837–1862* (1963).

45 Farnam, *op. cit.*, pp. 199–200.

46 John Hope Franklin, *From Slavery to Freedom* (2nd ed., 1956), ch. 14.

white. In slave states, there were extreme disabilities. In Maryland (1806), a free Negro could not own a dog. In Georgia, free Negroes could not own, use, or carry firearms, dispense medicine, set type, or make contracts for repairing buildings. They could not deal in agricultural commodities without permission. They could not acquire land or slaves in Savannah and Augusta; in some Georgia cities, they could not operate restaurants and inns. Under some criminal laws, free Negroes might suffer punishment more severe than whites who committed the same crime.[47] Free Negroes, as a Virginia legislator said, had "many *legal* rights but no constitutional ones." [48] They had formal rights, in other words, but no real protection from oppression.

The formal rights too were subject to constant attrition. The South saw the black man as black; whether he was slave or free was almost incidental. The free Negro was a danger to the state. As we have seen, newly freed slaves were usually required to leave their states. Immigration of free Negroes was also outlawed—in Virginia as early as 1793. Later, Virginia appropriated money to help send free Negroes to Africa. The status of free Negroes who stayed in the state was not too many steps above that of the slave. After 1830, law often frowned on giving an education to blacks, free or slave. The Georgia penal code made it a crime to "teach any slave, negro, or free person of color, to read or write, either written or printed characters." [49] In South Carolina, it was already unlawful in 1800 for "any number of slaves, free negroes, mulattoes, or mestizoes, even in company of white persons, to meet together for the purpose of mental instruction or religious worship, either before the rising of the sun or after the going down of the sun." White fraternizers were highly unwelcome. By an 1834 law in South Carolina, a white man who gambled with a black, slave or free, was liable to be whipped "not exceeding thirty-nine lashes." In New Orleans, in 1835, the city council adopted an ordinance which allocated the city's cemeteries one-half to whites, one-fourth to slaves, one-fourth to free Negroes. In 1841, an ordinance required separate burial registration lists for whites and blacks.[50]

William Goodell, an antislavery writer, stated wryly that Ameri-

47 W. McDowell Rogers, "Free Negro Legislation in Georgia before 1865," 16 Ga. Hist. Q. 27 (1932).

48 Quoted in John H. Russell, *The Free Negro in Virginia 1619–1865* (1913), p. 122.

49 Laws Ga. 1833, p. 202.

50 Roger A. Fischer, "Racial Segregation in Ante Bellum New Orleans," 74 Am. Hist. Rev. 926, 933 (1969).

can slavery might be added "to the list of the strict sciences. From a single fundamental axiom, all the parts of the system are logically and scientifically deduced." The axiom was that the slave was property; that he had "no rights." [51] To be sure, the slave was a "person," for purposes of the criminal law, and indeed, more answerable for crimes than free whites. But in other regards, he was a commodity. He could not vote or hold office, he could not contract or own property; he was bought and sold like a bale of cotton. The case reports of the slave states are full of wrangles about sales, gifts, mortgages, and bequests of slaves. In a case from Kentucky, one of the parties took "a negro boy" to the races at New Orleans, and bet him on the horse Lucy Dashwood.[52] The slave, moreover, could not marry, under white man's law, or in a way that white man's law would recognize as binding. The family could be, and often was, broken up by sale, gift, or transfer of a parent, spouse, or child. Some scholars have seen a deep contrast between the law and practice of slavery in the United States and Latin America. The Latin American slave was allowed to marry; to the Church, he was a soul, to be treated as a soul; he was, at worst, only more or less a chattel.[53] American law was more rigorous; it reflected a much harsher attitude toward slaves. Of course, the laws governing slavery—the slave codes of the South—were not responsible for this social attitude. Race feelings, whatever their psychic or economic background, helped write the codes.

The slave was a capital asset. He belonged to the land. A law of colonial Virginia (1705), as we have seen, had declared slaves to be real estate, not personal property. Kentucky in 1798, and Louisiana Territory in 1806, had similar laws.[54] In those jurisdictions, a single set of rules governed transfer and inheritance of the estate as a whole—that is, both the plantation or farm and the slaves who labored on the land. In these jurisdictions, for example, widows had dower rights in their husbands' slaves. Virginia repealed its law in 1792, perhaps because it was technically cumbersome. Nonetheless, law remained sensitive to the connection between slaves and the land. A Virginia statute of 1794, for example, prohibited the sale of slaves to satisfy the master's debts, unless all other per-

---

51 William Goodell, *The American Slave Code in Theory and Practice* (1853), p. 105.

52 *Thomas* v. *Davis,* 7 B. Mon. 227 (Ky., 1846). The horse won the race.

53 For this thesis, see Stanley M. Elkins, *Slavery, A Problem in American Institutional and Intellectual Life* (1959); Herbert S. Klein, *Slavery in the Americas, A Comparative Study of Virginia and Cuba* (1967).

54 Farnam, *op. cit.,* p. 183.

sonal property had been exhausted. This put slaves halfway between the legal position of land, which could not be levied on until *all* personalty had been sold, and that of ordinary chattels. After 1823, slaves owned by a child, who died before twenty-one, were treated as if real estate, for purposes of settling the dead child's estate.

Slaves themselves had little claim on the law for protection. A South Carolina judge, in 1847, put the case bluntly. A slave, he said "can invoke neither *magna charta* nor common law. . . . In the very nature of things, he is subject to despotism. Law as to him is only a compact between his rulers." [55] The Louisiana Black Code of 1806 (sec. 18) declared that a slave "owes to his master, and to all his family, a respect without bounds, and an absolute obedience, and . . . is . . . to execute all . . . orders." The Texas penal code of 1856 recognized the power of the master "to inflict any punishment upon the slave not affecting life or limb . . . which he may consider necessary for the purpose of keeping him in . . . submission." [56] On the other side, ten Southern codes made it a crime to mistreat a slave. The law of six states required the masters to provide suitable food and clothing for his slaves. The Black Code of Louisiana of 1806 made "cruel punishment" a crime (except "flogging, or striking with a whip, leather thong, switch or small stock, or putting in irons, or confining such slave"). Under the Louisiana Civil Code of 1825 (art. 192), if a master was "convicted of cruel treatment," the judge could order his mistreated slave to be sold, presumably to a better master.[57] A black who was held illegally in slavery had the right to sue for his freedom. Some Southern courts honestly enforced this and other rights of slaves, in cases that came before them. Cases are on record in which a master was punished for cruelty that passed beyond the boundaries of custom and law. The highest state court of Alabama, in 1843, upheld

[55] Wardlaw, J., in *Ex Parte Boylston,* 2 Strob. 41, 43 (S. Car., 1847).

[56] Quoted in Farnam, *op. cit.,* p. 184.

[57] But in an interesting case, *Markham* v. *Close,* 2 La. 581 (1831), the Louisiana court refused to allow a third party to bring a civil suit to compel the sale of a mistreated slave. A certain D. K. Markham, probably out of the kindness of his heart, alleged that defendant had acted cruelly toward his slave. The slave, Augustin, had run away and been recaptured. There was testimony that he was then lashed "severely," his "back and hips very much cut and skinned. The weather being warm, the wounds smelled badly"; the slave was so severely hurt that he could not sit or lie. But because the master had not been actually *convicted* of the cruelty, the court held it was powerless to order Augustin to be sold.

the conviction of William H. Jones, indicted for murdering a slave girl Isabel. Jones, it was charged, "did . . . feloniously, wilfully and of his malice aforethought, cruelly, barbarously and inhumanly beat and whip" the girl to death.[58] But only especially blatant cases, or cases where the black man was exceptionally tenacious, or had a champion, were at all likely to come to court. The rights of slaves were narrow, and not often invoked. These rights gave Southern law the appearance of justice, without upsetting the real social order. Had these rights been widely used, or used beyond the limits of Southern toleration, they would not have survived, even on paper.

As it was, a slave who wanted his day in court faced formidable barriers. No slave could testify against his master. In some states, no black could testify against a white man at all. In "free" Indiana Territory, for example, by a law of 1803:

> No negro, mulatto, or Indian shall be a witness except in the pleas of the United States [i.e., criminal cases] against negroes, mulattoes, or Indians, or in civil pleas where negroes, mulattoes or Indians alone shall be parties.[59]

Forty-three years later, in 1846, the law was still on the books. This fact drew caustic remarks from a select committee of the Indiana Assembly:

> The track of the foot, the nail of the shoe, the bark of the dog, or the bray of the donkey, may be given in evidence to ferret out villainies; but the negro . . . though acquainted with the villain, and cognizant to the villainy, for no reason than because he is a negro, is not even permitted to develope corroborating circumstances.[60]

On countless occasions, the rule must have frustrated justice. In 1806, the chancellor of Virginia, George Wythe, together with his black servant, died after drinking from a pot of coffee. The coffee had been poisoned with arsenic. Suspicion pointed toward Wythe's great-nephew; he was arrested for murder. A black cook could have

---

[58] *State* v. *Jones*, 5 Ala. 666 (1843). Between 1830 and 1860, there were thirteen reported appellate cases in which a master's conviction for homicide or attempted homicide of a slave was upheld. A. E. Keir Nash, "A More Equitable Past? Southern Supreme Courts and the Protection of the Antebellum Negro," 48 N. Car. L. Rev. 197, 215 (1970).

[59] Francis S. Philbrick, ed., *Laws of Indiana Territory 1801–1809* (1930), p. 40. Mulatto was defined as a person with "one fourth part or more of negro blood."

[60] Quoted in Emma Lou Thornbrough, *The Negro in Indiana* (1957), p. 122.

given evidence against him. But the court was unable to hear this testimony; and the nephew went free.[61]

On the other hand, the law dispensed with many niceties in exposing the slave to social control. The black criminal codes were clear and severe. Slaves were already prisoners, already penniless; fines and imprisonment meant nothing. Slave punishment was therefore largely corporal. Slaves who transgressed were whipped—thoroughly, soundly, and often. Under a Mississippi law of 1822, if any "Negro or mulatto" gave "false testimony," he was to be nailed by the ear to the pillory for one hour; then the ear was to be cut off; then "the other ear to be nailed in like manner," and after one hour cut off.[62] For serious crimes, slaves were liable to the death penalty. Burning grain or stealing goods were capital crimes for slaves in Georgia (1806). Under the codes, arson by slaves was frequently made a capital crime. Attempted rape of a white woman was punishable by death in Georgia and Louisiana in 1806, in Kentucky in 1811, in Mississippi in 1814 and 1822, Tennessee in 1833, Texas in 1837, South Carolina in 1843.[63] We have noted how severely the law looked on slave insurrection. Slaves were liable, too, for all the white man's crimes; and slaves were no doubt punished with special severity, even when the law did not specifically so provide.

A dead slave was a capital loss for his master. This put at least *some* natural check on the cruelty of master. But there was danger that a master might conceal his slaves' crimes, to keep them from the gallows. To avoid this collusion, states gave compensation to owners of slaves put to death. A law of Alabama of 1824 provided that the jury, trying a slave for a capital offense, should also "assess the value of the slave"; the owner was entitled to claim up to one-half this amount.[64] Virginia appropriated $12,000 in 1839, to pay owners "for slaves executed and transported." [65]

[61] See William Draper Lewis, ed., *Great American Lawyers* (1907), Vol. I, pp. 84–85.

[62] Laws Miss. Adj. Sess. 1822, p. 194 (Act of June 18, 1822, sec. 59). In addition, there would be thirty-nine lashes on the "bare back, well laid on." Note that the punishment applied to free Negroes as well as to slaves.

[63] Farnam, *op. cit.*, pp. 184–85.

[64] Laws Ala. 1824, p. 41. The law also levied a tax—"one cent on all negroes under ten years, and two cents on all negroes over ten and under sixty"—to provide a compensation fund. The slaveowner had to employ "good and sufficient counsel" to defend the slave; and was forbidden from concealing a slave "so that he or she cannot be brought to condign punishment."

[65] Laws Va. 1839, ch. 3.

Crime and punishment usually imply courtrooms, due process, some measure of fair play. Day-to-day government of slaves called for quicker, less formal procedures. Basically, the master's will, uncontrolled by formal rules, was law for the slave. For special problems, the South evolved special procedures. In some states there were "slave patrols," which roamed the countryside, looking for erring blacks. If a stray black in Georgia could not show a pass (or "free papers") the patrol might "correct" him on the spot, "by whipping with a switch, whip, or cowskin, not exceeding twenty lashes." [66]

Slave law, in short, had its own inner logic. Its object was repression and control. Everything tended toward this end. Every door was shut to Negro advancement. The South deprived and depraved the black man, and then despised him, and was afraid of his revenge. Apartheid was a trap for the white man too. The white, of course, had the upper hand; but even he paid a price. And hundreds of thousands died in the Civil War, which would probably never have been waged, except for the "peculiar institution."

[66] Prince, *Digest of the Laws of Georgia* (2nd ed., 1837), p. 775 (law of 1765).

CHAPTER V

AN AMERICAN LAW OF PROPERTY

THE LAND: A NATIONAL TREASURE

Land law was the kernel and core of common law. More exactly, real-property law was the core. Real property meant more than land; the term applied to that cluster of privileges and rights which centered on land, or on the exercise of power which had a geographical focus. In medieval England, rights to real property meant jurisdiction as well as ownership. The lord of the manor was a little sovereign as well as an owner of houses, land, and growing crops. Only people with land or land rights really mattered: the gentry, the nobles, the upper clergy; land was the source of their wealth and the source and seat of their power. Well into modern times, power and wealth were concentrated in the hands of great landlords. The social system turned on rights in land.

Clearly, American conditions were quite different. But in America, too, land was the basic form of wealth. This was especially true in the West, where land was abundant and fertile. After 1787, the vast stock of public land was at once a problem and a great opportunity. The federal government claimed title to millions and millions of acres. The Louisiana Purchase brought in millions more. As the frontier moved toward the West, the nation had to plan how to map, settle and distribute this almost limitless treasure of land.

How the federal government disposed of its land is a story of staggering detail.[1] The issue was as persistent as issues of war, slavery, and the tariff. The public-land question touched every other national issue—fiscal policy, veterans' benefits, the spread or containment of slavery, population diffusion, and the political

[1] See, in general, Benjamin H. Hibbard, *A History of the Public Land Policies* (1924); Paul W. Gates, *History of Public Land Law Development* (1968); Everett N. Dick, *The Lure of the Land* (1970).

strength of factions and regions. Federal law determined the very shape of the land. The act of May 18, 1796, "for the Sale of the Lands of the United States, in the territory northwest of the river Ohio, and above the mouth of [the] Kentucky river," [2] created the office of surveyor general. Public lands were to be surveyed "without delay," and divided into townships of six miles square. Half of the townships were to be further divided into sections; each section contained one square mile, that is, 640 acres. Under later acts, sections were further divided into half-sections, and tracts of 160, 80, and 40 acres. In any event, the land had to be surveyed before it was sold, and the units of sale were strict rectangular plots. No chain of title could escape federal land policy, any more than the lots and farms could ignore the merciless, invisible grids stretched over the land at government order.

Once land was surveyed, it was disposed of. Public-land law flowed from one basic choice. The government did not choose to manage its land as a capital asset, but to get rid of it in an orderly, fruitful way. A whole continent was sold or given away—to veterans, settlers, squatters, railroads, states, colleges, speculators, and land companies. On the surface, one sees in this policy the powerful influence of free enterprise and *laissez-faire*. The government possessed a resource of incalculable value; but it was determined to denationalize it as soon as possible. True, the land was sold for cash, but money was not to be used to aggrandize the government. Yet divestment was never the whole policy, nor ever the sole *reason* for policy. The professed social goal was not to make government weaker or smaller; but to create a country of free citizens, living independently on their land. Where strict market principles seemed to clash with this goal, these principles had to yield. Government was never merely a passive umpire of the market; it did more than chop the land into units and market it. It used land as a lever of policy. And this, too, was not a question of philosophy, but of the concrete interests, demands, and needs that pressed in politically upon Washington.

Nor was the federal government purely supine, disposing of its wealth like a spendthrift, without any checks and controls. The government fought stubbornly to keep mineral rights out of private hands, dreaming of the precious metals that might be hiding in the West. The Ordinance of 1785 reserved to the government "one-third part of all gold, silver, lead and copper mines."

2 1 Stats. 464 (Act of May 18, 1796).

The law of 1796 held back from sale "every . . . salt spring which may be discovered."[3] In 1807, Congress provided that lead-bearing lands should be leased, not sold.[4] Local administration of this law was peculiarly ineffective, but the government kept to its policy. Land grants in general were gifts on condition. They were used to advance national policy—to encourage colleges and railroads and to provide new states with a source of cash. Unfortunately, national land programs never worked as they were meant to work on paper. Field administration was the weak point: feeble, incompetent, corrupt.[5] Where national policy was congruent with the economic interests of the locals, that policy was carried out more or less well. But when the two conflicted, Washington's arm was never long enough or steady enough to carry through.

In general, for most of the 19th century, there was little deviation from the basic theme of land disposal. All along, however, subsidiary decisions had to be made. Would land be sold, in great blocks, to wholesalers, or in small bits to actual settlers? Should the land be sold in such a way as to raise some money for the treasury? Should farmers or veterans be given some preference, or should the man with cash on hand call the tune? On these points, federal government was pushed now in this, now in that direction, by the interplay of pressure groups and regional interests.

To begin with, the act of 1796 clearly called for sales of large tracts of land. This policy, however, was politically dangerous. It raised the bogeyman of land monopoly, and seemed to favor dealers and speculators over farmers. In any event, the land sold badly. To encourage sales, the government sharply reduced the minimum unit of sale to half-sections, quarter-sections, eighty-acre tracts, and then finally (in 1832) to forty-acre tracts.[6] The price of public land weakened, too. The act of 1796 had fixed a minimum price of two dollars an acre—much higher than the price at which huge blocks had earlier been sold. For a while, the price held firm. Between 1800 and 1820, public land sold at or near the two dollar price; during sieges of speculative fever, the price went even higher. Yet the Western states and territories insisted strenuously that the price must come down.

An important law of 1820 tried to meet these Western demands,

[3] 1 Stats. 464, 466, sec. 3 (act of May 18, 1796).
[4] 2 Stats. 445, 446, sec. 2 (act of March 3, 1807).
[5] See, in general, Malcolm J. Rohrbough, *The Land Office Business: the Settlement and Administration of American Public Lands 1789–1837* (1968).
[6] Hibbard, *op. cit.*, p. 75.

while reforming the methods of sale. Under earlier acts, the government had sold its land on credit. By 1820, settlers owed the federal government about $21,000,000. Periodically, Congress passed laws giving its debtors some relief; an act of 1816, for example, gave land claimants in Mississippi Territory two years and eight months more to pay what they owed.[7] Still, many settlers forfeited their lands. The act of 1820 reduced the minimum price to $1.25. At the same time, it put an end to sales on credit. Every buyer had to make "complete payment" at the time he bought his land.[8]

The act meant to vest land and power in the hands of smallholders, without giving up the hope of making some money off public land. But votes and voices of settlers, real and potential, outshouted the greed of the government. These votes and voices also molded national policy toward squatters on public land. Settlers (and speculators) streamed into the West far in advance of the formal date of sale, even in advance of the official survey. Theoretically, no one could gain a good title without survey and sale. But a series of laws gave piecemeal preference (pre-emption rights) to actual settlers, even illegal settlers, or recognized and ratified state policies on pre-emption.[9] Finally, in 1841, Congress passed a general pre-emption law. The head of a family, who had settled "in person" on land and "improved" it, had first choice or claim to buy his land, up to 160 acres, at the minimum government price.[10] Somewhat naïve safeguards against abuse were written into the act. Big landowners were excluded from participation. No one was allowed to squat in the same state or territory as his former residence. But the most important feature of the law was embodied in its general concept; it removed the last shred of pretense, that squatters on government land were in violation of either legal or ethical norms.

THE LAW OF PRIVATE LAND

Land-law reform was well under way even before the Revolution. After the Revolution, legislatures carried on the work of dismantling the feudal past. The new economics saw no reason why land

7 3 Stats. 300 (act of April 24, 1816).
8 3 Stats. 566 (act of April 24, 1820).
9 E.g., 5 Stats. 412 (act of February 18, 1841) (Tennessee).
10 5 Stats. 453, 455 (act of September 4, 1841, sec. 10).

should be treated differently from any other commodity; and the holders of political and social power—big and small landowners, and speculators—stood to gain, in general, from a free, mobile market in land. Primogeniture, dead in most of New England, vanished from the South by 1800. The rules of inheritance of land were brought closer to the rules of inheritance of money and goods. Feudal tenures, most of which had lived only paper lives, were swept off the statute books. "The title of our lands," wrote Jesse Root proudly in 1798, "is free, clear and absolute, and every proprietor of land is a prince in his own domains, and lord paramount of the fee." [11]

In the first generation, statutes and court cases brushed aside many obnoxious or ill-fitting English doctrines. One casualty, for example, was a common-law rule that when two or more persons held interests in land, their cointerests were presumed to be joint tenancies, not tenancies in common. The difference between the two forms of co-ownership was technical, but not unimportant. If two persons owned land in common, each had a separate, distinct, undivided share. Each could sell, give away, or divide his interest. A joint tenancy carried with it the right of survivorship; if one tenant died, the other automatically succeeded to the property. A joint tenancy, then, was a sort of last-man club in land. It was suitable for family lands; less so, for lands of men dealing at arm's length with each other in the market. The change in presumption was defended in terms of the probable intention of the parties: "In ninety-nine cases out of a hundred, of persons purchasing land together, they would prefer not to be joint tenants, but tenants in common. The law ought therefore to follow what is the common wish of parties." [12] If this presumption was in fact correct, the reason was that land purchasers meant to treat land as a market good.

Changes in land law were generally of this quality. They were in the first place empirical. They strove, to a marked degree, to follow the "common wish of the parties." But the common wish of parties reflected the rapid, volatile quality of dealings in land.

[11] Jesse Root, *Reports* (Conn., 1798), Intro., xxxix.

[12] 1 Am. Jurist 77 (1829). Another doomed doctrine was the doctrine of "tacking," in the law of mortgages. In English law, a third mortgagee might get the jump on a second mortgagee by buying the interest of a first mortgagee and "tacking" that interest to his own. This doctrine was "very generally exploded" in the United States. Chancellor Kent reported hearing Alexander Hamilton himself, in 1804, "make a masterly attack upon the doctrine, which he insisted was founded on a system of artificial reasoning, and encouraged fraud." Kent, *Commentaries,* Vol. IV (2nd ed., 1832), p. 178.

Land not only could be traded on the market; it *was* traded, openly and often. In land lay the hope of national wealth, and the hope of countless individuals for private fortune. As soon as land could be cleared of Indians, and properly surveyed, it was traded with speed and fury. Speculation in raw land was almost a national lottery. Even when genuine settlers arrived, built houses, and planted crops, land continued to be rapidly transferred. Farmers themselves were speculators, who gambled on the rising price of land. Many farmers worked their land for a while, then were eager to sell out (at a profit) and move on to a newer frontier.

In such a climate, the law of conveyancing had to undergo a sea change. In the United States, every man was or might be a conveyancer. The elaborate forms of English law were clearly unsuitable. Legal sophistication was a scarce resource. What was acceptable or tolerable to a small upper class of landlords was intolerable in the great American mass market. Vestigial modes of tenure and conveyancing survived in some parts of the country, particularly the plantation South. But even in South Carolina, a court of equity showed genuine surprise that Alicia H. Middleton and Sarah Dehon of Charlestown had executed "deeds of feoffment, with livery of seisin," in 1836, instead of using more streamlined forms.[13] In the rest of the country, the enormous demand meant that land documents had to become simple and standard. They had to be mass-produced at minimal cost for mass use. At exactly that point of time when conveyancing skills had become so rare, draftsmanship in fantastic quantity was needed. There were, of course, plenty of lawyers. But there were not half enough *if* every land transfer needed careful counseling and delicate architecture. And the lawyers who practiced in small towns or on the frontier could not cope with the jigsaw puzzles of English land law.

In many ways, reform was clean and swift. The old conveyance by feoffment, with livery of seizin—the turf and twig—was unnecessary and unsuitable. Little used, the New York revised statutes of 1827–28 expressly abolished it.[14] Deeds had to be in writing, but were valid if they followed simple, rational form. Out of the welter of available models, lawyers in the republic worked out two basic types of deed. The *warranty deed* grew out of the old deed of bargain and sale, with covenants of warranty. The *quit-claim deed* developed from the common-law release.[15] A warranty deed was

13 See *Dehon* v. *Redfern,* Dudley's Eq. Rpts. (S. Car., 1838), 115.
14 Kent, *Commentaries,* Vol. IV (2nd ed., 1832), pp. 489–90.
15 A. James Casner, ed., *American Law of Property* (1952), Vol. III, p. 223.

used to make a full transfer of land from one owner to another. The seller guaranteed that he had and could transfer good title. The quit-claim deed made no such promises. It simply transferred whatever rights the transferror had, good or bad; and was so understood. People used quit-claim deeds to give up or pass on cloudy or contingent rights to land. The historical origin of both kinds of deed was clearly visible in wording and form; but drastically shortened and streamlined. It would be too much to say that their use was within the grasp of an average layman. But they were accessible to lawyers of some training and experience, and to shrewd land dealers as well. They were available in popular form books, and in various versions of books called *Every Man His Own Lawyer*, or some similar title, which sold thousands of copies in America. Using these books, a businessman or lawyer could easily make his own deeds. All that was needed was to copy down the forms and fill in the blanks.

Statute and practice worked hand in hand to simplify land remedies. Joseph Story grew almost ecstatic at the efficiencies of the action of ejectment, which tested title to land, "on the picturesque banks of the Hudson, the broad expanse of the Delaware and Chesapeak, the sunny regions of the South, and the fertile vales and majestic rivers of the West." [16] Reform often began at the periphery. In 1821, when Story wrote, Massachusetts, Maine, and New Hampshire still did not share the national passion for ejectment. These states, instead, used "writs of entry for the trial of land titles." The writs had been "disembarrassed . . . of some troublesome appendages and some artificial niceties," but were still, by comparison, archaic.[17]

In a federal system, solving problems is highly decentralized. Local diversity is therefore hard to root out of the law. Massachusetts could keep, and even cherish, its traditions, so long as these were not lethal to the land market. The states had different economic needs, different quantities of legal skill, different geographical features. They shared many innovations. But the land law of no two states was identical. There was no central authority to make codes, and no central codes of law; so, despite all the labor of simplification, there were bound to be great amounts of complexity left in the land law.

Some English land law was retained because it was useful; some

[16] Joseph Story, "An Address delivered Before the Members of the Suffolk Bar," Sept. 4, 1821, in 1 Amer. Jurist 1, 17 (1829).
[17] *Ibid.*, p. 17.

precisely because it was too irrelevant to be worth abolition. Much of the English law of tenures and estates was nominally in effect. American lawyers spoke of fee simple and life estates, terms of years, easements, covenants, and profits. This much was part of the marrow of American law. But the strange wonderland of executory devises, powers of appointment, contingent remainders, shifting and springing uses, though not formally abolished, lay asleep, like Rip Van Winkle. This ancient body of learning had little to do with the general land market. When, in the 1820's, a reform movement arose that was thoughtful as well as pragmatic, it eliminated three elements of the land law: first, doctrines and institutions that seemed to do positive harm; second, those which, whatever their impact, appeared to be "tyrannical" or "feudal"; third, those purged as part of a general codification. These three prongs were especially visible in New York's revisions of its property laws in 1827–28. But this was a summing up rather than a beginning.

The rules of *capacity* were among those most thoroughly revamped. Ideally, every adult was to be made capable of owning and dealing in land. The property rights of married women, as we have seen, were modernized. At common law, aliens could not, for reasons of policy, inherit land. The rule, and the bias against aliens, seemed somewhat out of place in America. The provisions against aliens "originated in ages of barbarism, out of the hatred and jealousy with which foreigners were regarded . . . [To] those [aliens] who are actually resident amongst us, the best policy" would be "to encourage their industry by giving them all reasonable facilities in the acquisition of property." [18] There was, on occasion, plenty of xenophobia in America; one need only cite the Alien and Sedition Laws, of the late 18th century. But too many people played the land market, as their descendants played the stock market; an expanding population meant rising prices of land; this implied an open-door policy for aliens, and alien investment. The absolute disability of aliens faded into local compromises. As early as 1704, a South Carolina act, praising resident aliens for "their industry, frugality and sobriety," for their "loyal and peaceable" behavior, pointed out that they had acquired "such plentiful estates as hath given this Colony no small reputation abroad, tending to the encouragement of others to come and plant among us," and granted them full rights to acquire property by gift, inheritance, or purchase.[19] An Ohio law (1804) made it "lawful" for aliens

18 1 Am. Jurist 87–8 (1829).
19 *Statutes at Large of South Carolina*, Vol. II (1837), pp. 251–52 (act of Nov.

who became "entitled to have" any "lands, tenements or heredita-
ments" by "purchase, gift, devise or descent," to "hold, possess, and
enjoy" their lands, "as fully and completely as any citizen of the
United States or this state can do, subject to the same laws and
regulations, and not otherwise." [20] Federal pre-emption and homestead laws also gave rights to resident aliens.

Against the "tyrannical" and "feudal," legislators slashed away
with might and main. Primogeniture, as we noted, fell by the way-
side. The fee tail was another casualty. When a man held land in
fee tail, possession was forever vested in the heirs of his body, that
is, in his lineal descendants. No one could sell such a "fettered
inheritance," as Kent called it,[21] because the land belonged to the
tenant's children, and his children's children thereafter. As a matter of fact, as far back as the 15th century, tenants in tail had been
able to sell their land, free of the claims of unborn generations,
through tricks of conveyancing which "barred" the entail. But this
was no job for an amateur. In a nation of amateurs, the fee tail was
offensive; since it did not work even in England, there was no point
in preserving it. It was abolished in Virginia in 1776, in New York
in 1782. Not every state carried abolition through to a neat and logical conclusion. In some places, the fee tail survived in a weak and
fossilized form; any attempt to create a fee tail was treated automatically as a life estate followed by a plain fee simple. But even in
those states the fee tail was never of any significance.

In general, fear of land monopoly and land dynasties haunted
the lawmakers. New York state was particularly sensitive on this
score, perhaps because of the long shadow cast by the estates on the
Hudson. Even Chancellor Kent, certainly no radical, saw a clear
connection between republican government and free transfer of
land:

> Entailments are recommended in monarchical governments, as
> a protection to the power and influence of the landed aristoc-
> racy; but such a policy has no application to republican estab-
> lishments, where wealth does not form a permanent distinction,
> and under which every individual of every family has his equal
> rights, and is equally invited, by the genius of the institutions, to
> depend upon his own merit and exertions. Every family, stripped

---

4, 1704). To qualify, however, an alien had to take an oath to the crown "on the
Holy Evangelists, or otherwise according to the form of his profession."

[20] Laws Ohio 1803–4, ch. 19 (Act of Feb. 3, 1804).

[21] Kent, *Commentaries*, Vol. IV (2nd ed., 1832), p. 12.

of artificial supports, is obliged, in this country, to repose upon
the virtue of its descendants for the perpetuity of its fame.[22]

This attitude, and those like it, underlay the New York revision
of property laws of 1827–28. This famous enactment could be
properly called a code. It arranged, changed, and simplified great
parts of the law of property. The English law of perpetuities was
tightened. A more severe limit was placed on the time that land
could be tied up within a family. Under the English rule, future
interests in property were void for "remoteness of vesting." The
New York rule made future interests invalid if they unduly "suspended" the "power of alienation." The difference between the
two concepts was technical, and, in most cases, inconsequential.
But the New York version of the rule expressed one dominant aim
of land law reform: to keep the land market open and mobile. For
the same reason, the code frowned on the creation of trusts of land.
Trusts were only allowed for a few, specific purposes—for example,
for the benefit of a minor. Here the dangers seemed slight, the
utility obvious, and the trust would come to a predictable natural
end.

The legislature watered down the more radical New York innovations in later years. Others were misconstrued or mishandled by
the courts. The judges' hostility was not just blind reaction. There
were flaws in the draftsmanship of the code. The novelty of its
schemes bred confusion and encouraged litigation. Also, some of its
provisions mistook the direction in which economy and society
would go. Chancellor Kent had been skeptical from the start; the
trust provisions of the code, he felt, could not work. The desire to
"preserve and perpetuate family influence and property," he
noted, was "very prevalent with mankind," and was "deeply seated
in the affections." [23] Trusts would probably not wither away. "We
cannot hope," he wrote, to "check the enterprising spirit of gain,
the pride of families, the anxieties of parents, the importunities of
luxury, the fixedness of habits, the subtleties of intellect." The law,
he predicted, would bring wholesale evasion: the "fairest and
proudest models of legislation that can be matured in the closet"
could not prevail against the "usages of a civilized people." [24]
Time has proved Kent to be correct, on the whole, and a far better
sociologist than his cohorts. As the country grew wealthy, the dynastic urge reared its ugly head once more among the moneyed

22 Kent, *Commentaries*, Vol. IV (2nd ed., 1832), p. 20.
23 Kent, *Commentaries*, Vol. IV (2nd ed., 1832), p. 19.
24 *Ibid.*, p. 313.

elite. No political force withstood the aristocracy of money, at least in its minor aspirations. Land baronies were dead for good; but the long-term trust later blossomed forth, as a dynastic device not tied to land, to an extent even Kent would have found astounding; it is still growing today.

Land-law reform had, on the whole, made the law of real property more serviceable. But as old problems were solved, new ones emerged. There were chronic difficulties in determining title. Government surveys, for all their defects, made it possible to identify the physical aspects of the land. But title is a concept more elusive than longitude, more nebulous than a tree stump or a stream. Title became as vexatious and intractable a subject as the abolished law of tenure. Sometimes title depended upon the terms of some vast, ambiguous grant—from the federal government, or the King of Spain, or a dead proprietor. Or it had to take into account the patents (grants) of American state governments, possibly equivocal, possibly corrupt. There were rights to land unknown to England. Georgia continued its headright system until past 1800.[25] Raucous squabbles, arising under state and federal pre-emption laws, and the law and practice of local land offices, were meat and bread to Western lawyers. The very marketability of land added to the general confusion. Federal and state governments floated land scrip and bounty warrants, to veterans, for example. Some issues were freely transferable; some fluctuated on the market, like modern stocks and bonds. These land certificates, passing from hand to hand, gave rise to a whole new body of law, a whole new body of controversies.

Especially in the West, local officials were weak and corrupt. The effect on land titles was devastating. Forgery and fraud, if we can believe the stories, were epidemic. Since land was the soul of trade, ths meant that there was weakness in the quality control of a staple commodity. Public weakness and private greed were a formidable combination. Joseph Story was struck by the land law of Kentucky, its "subtle and refined distinctions," its labyrinth of titles. "Ages will probably elapse," he wrote in 1829, "before the litigations founded on it will be closed." To outside lawyers, "it will forever remain an unknown code with a peculiar dialect, to be explored and studied, like the jurisprudence of some foreign nation." [26] And Kentucky was not a conservative state, but a new state

[25] Milton S. Heath, *Constructive Liberalism, The Role of the State in Economic Development in Georgia to 1860* (1954), pp. 84–92.
[26] Joseph Story, in 1 Am. Jurist 20 (1829).

at the periphery. Its problem was not archaic law, but the unrestrained clash of interests. The same tangle of titles occurred time and time again: in Missouri, in Illinois, in California. With one hand, government labored to create a rational land system. It provided for survey and recording of land interests. It did all it could to further orderly exploration and settlement. But at the same time, government would not and could not resist political pressures; would not and could not correct its weakness in the field. The result was constant tension between chaos and order. Kentucky wanted orderly settlement and land registration as much as other states. But it also attempted to do justice to—or coddle—the "actual settler" (and voter). The courts heard endless disputes over questions of priority and validity of claims. Had A or B raised a crop of corn on the land or built a cabin? And which had done it first? Where were the boundaries between vague, overlapping claims, claims impossible to rationalize, even without human error and barefaced lies? In one case, reported in 1799, a Kentucky court heard a witness say that a certain Berry "blazed a white ash or hickory" to mark his claim, "but which of them he can not be certain, and cut the two first letters of his name and blacked them with powder, and . . . sat down at the foot of a small sugar tree and chopped a hole with his tomahawk in the root of it. . . . [At] the place where Berry made his improvement the branch [of a river] made a bend like a horse shoe." Where was the ash or hickory now? "Cut down, but the stump remained," in a "very decayed state." The sugar tree was still standing, and identifiable; the tomahawk mark was "still perceivable"; presumably the horseshoe bend could still be found. None of these was exactly an unambiguous sign.[27] This kind of evidence could be easily invented, or contradicted. Sometimes a man's livelihood was at stake; when the land was of baronial size, or a mighty city had grown up on top of it, vast fortunes hung in the balance. Some of the greatest American trials, in terms of cost, time, and acrimony, have been trials over title to land.

Free alienability of land was always an aim of the land law; but never an end in itself. The goal of public policy was economic growth, a rising, spreading population, a healthy, aggressive middle class. At times this goal seemed to require that the market principle had to give way. Devices and doctrines to protect smallholders (a politically potent class) came to permeate the law. One such device was the mechanics' lien, though on the surface it seemed to

27 *McClanahan* v. *Berry*, Hughes' Ky. Rpts., Vol. 1, pp. 323, 327–28 (1799).

have a different thrust. Essentially the mechanics' lien gave special remedies and preferences to "mechanics," artisans who labored on buildings or made improvements to land. If the landowner failed to pay the "mechanic," the "mechanic" could enforce his claim directly against land and improvements.[28]

The mechanics' lien was a purely American invention. It can be traced back to 1791. In that year, commissioners, in charge of building the new capital city of Washington, D.C., suggested a lien to "encourage master builders to contract for the erecting and finishing of houses." Maryland, the relevant state, passed necessary legislation. Pennsylvania was the next state to enact a form of the lien. Its first law (1803) applied only to certain kinds of "mechanic," and only to certain sections of the city of Philadelphia. Gradually more and more states adopted broader and broader versions of the lien. By the end of the period, the mechanics' lien was a sweeping security device. In Illinois, in 1845,

> Any person who shall . . . furnish labor or materials for erect-ing or repairing any building, or the appurtenances of any build-ing . . . shall have a lien upon the whole tract of land or town lot . . . for the amount due to him for such labor or materials.[29]

The mechanics' lien was a pro-labor statute, but not in the New Deal sense. The "mechanics" of the lien law were not poor urban workers; they were suppliers and artisans. The law protected labor, in the early 19th-century sense of the word: those who added tangible value to real assets. The law preferred their claims over those of general creditors. Not least of all, the lien was intended to *help* the landowner, in an age when cash, hard money, liquid capital was short. The law promised a safe and immovable form of collateral to those who supplied materials and labor. The lien was a kind of bootstrap finance (the phrase is Willard Hurst's), almost a subsidy, almost a kind of government credit to encourage building and improvement of land.

The ideal of the small freeholder, backbone of the nation, lay at the root of another American innovation, the homestead exemption. The exemption defined certain kinds of property (the "homestead"), and immunized this property from the fangs and claws of creditors. The homestead exemption first appeared in Texas, before Texas was admitted to the Union. The legislature expanded the doctrine steadily until, in 1839, up to 50 acres of

28 See Farnam, *op. cit.*, pp. 152–56.
29 Rev. Stats. Ill. 1845, p. 345.

land or one town lot—when these constituted a family's "homestead"—tools, books, livestock, feed, and some household furniture were immune from seizure for debt. The idea was attractive, and spread from the periphery toward the center. The first adoption was in Mississippi (1841). By 1848, Connecticut, Wisconsin, and Michigan, along with some of the Southern states, had enacted one form or other of the homestead exemption. By the time of the Civil War, all but a few states had done the same.[30]

On the surface, the homestead exemption and the mechanics' lien seem contradictory. One law made home and farm a sanctuary against creditors; the other gave creditors a sharp new legal tool, to use against home and farm. In practice, there was little conflict. The small farmer did not use hired workmen on a scale that exposed him to the lien laws. Economic interests protected by the two acts did not usually collide. And both acts were in a sense developmental. The homestead law, in Texas, was specifically meant to encourage immigration. It sought, indirectly, through the office of security, to mobilize labor and capital toward the prime job of the times: building population, and enriching the land—precisely the aims of the mechanics' lien. To new settlers, the homestead exemption promised a haven of safety in a boom-and-bust world. The mechanics' lien got their homes built; and, if a crisis came, preferred productive laborers against mere lenders of money—middlemen, who, in 19th-century thought, did not produce or add to the nation's stock of wealth.

BOOM AND BUST: THE LAW OF MORTGAGES

Lien and exemption laws were enormously important because of the pervasive, ruinous force of the business cycle. Crisis struck the economy with shock waves at regular and irregular intervals. Volcanic eruptions and disruptions in prices caused deep insecurity among debtors, creditors, and merchants. The money system was disastrously weak; credit information was primitive. No man was safe unless he held silver and gold, rare metals indeed. The law reflected a desperate search for security—how to protect one's own

30 Farnam, *op. cit.*, pp. 148–52. The Texas constitution of 1845 specifically mentioned the right of the legislature to pass a homestead act. The Wisconsin constitution of 1848 specifically instructed the legislature to pass a "wholesome" exemption law.

assets and how to get recourse against the other man's. Since land was so large a part of the national wealth, land law was very sensitive to the business cycle. Legislatures, courts, and the business community shaped security devices in land with one eye to the volatile nature of land values.

The prime instrument of land security, then as now, was the mortgage. Mortgage means, literally, "dead pledge." A mortgage is "dead" to the creditors, since the borrower stays in possession of the land and keeps whatever it produces, over and above the debt; by contrast, a pawnbroker takes his pledges "live." The mortgage was an old, old legal device, in constant adjustment to fresh reality.[31] Its development in modern times bears the scars of the neverending struggle between debtor and creditor. In 19th-century America, there was a definite debtor or borrower class; this class exerted its influence to gain law reform (abolition of imprisonment for debt), political reform (widening of the suffrage), and economic reform (inflation and easy money). There was an equally definite creditor class. But it was not always clear what policy benefited debtors or creditors. A strong mortgage law, giving creditors strong rights, was as necessary for debtors as for creditors, if there was no other way to make capital flow into real-estate investment. In many states (Wisconsin, for example), the homestead exemption did not cover a purchase-money mortgage. This was a large hole in the law, but apparently vital for farmers and homeowners. Most men had no capital security except the land itself; yet, only a fool would lend money to a man to buy land, without this security.

Debtors were, on the whole, inconsistent men, but for understandable reasons. They took one attitude during good times and another during bad. In good times they needed money to buy land, and to build and raise crops; they were willing to promise the moon, hoping that land values would go up and lighten their debts. During bad times the promises turned sour, the debts became mountainous, and debtors looked about for avenues of escape.

Legislatures, particularly in the West, found debtor relief politically irresistible. On the other hand, businessmen and creditors

[31] Much of mortgage law was developed in or through courts of equity. This required technical adjustments in those jurisdictions which had no chancery courts. Pennsylvania, for example, substituted, through the action of *scire facias sur mortgage* (1705), a common-law mode of foreclosure for the usual procedures in equity. *Scire facias sur mortgage* was a writ, used when the mortgagor lapsed into default, requiring him to "show cause" why the mills of the law should not begin to grind, foreclosing the mortgage.

were not without resources. They appealed, sometimes successfully, to the law for protection. Quite early, they found that the courts, free from the pressures of frequent election, were willing to take a longer view of economic policy than the legislatures. Creditors too were expert at evasion. Where there was an economic demand for their product, formal law was almost helpless against this demand. Law, at least in the United States, has often lacked both the means and the will to impose strong economic regulation. Men in the market have been clever at inventing small-scale, half-visible ways of getting around some obnoxious rule. Legal history has demonstrated time and again that there is more than one way to skin a cat. There is no mystery in the process. The clash of interests naturally produces inconsistent, half-enforced, largely symbolic rules and doctrines. Particularly does this happen in a decentralized system, where the losers in one forum merely proceed to the next.

The outline history of mortgage law is instructive.[32] Over the years a costly and complicated system of *equitable foreclosure* had evolved, partly to give the debtor some protection. Its essential feature was the debtor's "equity" or right to redeem his lost land. Draftsmen then invented a clause to undo this "equity." The debtor agreed, in advance, that if he defaulted, his creditor could sell the land without going to court. As early as 1774, a New York statute specifically ratified this practice, though with some procedural safeguards. In some Southern states, however, courts held that one could not legally give the mortgagee such a power of sale. Mortgages then began to name third persons ("trustees") to exercise this power of sale, in case of default. The "deed of trust," then, acted as the functional equivalent of the Northern mortgage with power of sale.

A mortgage armored with a power of sale was an effective instrument of credit. But while the courts accepted the power of sale, and the deed of trust (undercutting the old equity of redemption), new laws were passed that had the opposite effect. 1819 was a year of panic. A New York statute of 1820 gave a year of grace to hard-pressed land debtors. It was not clear whether this type of law applied to mortgages at all. The question was decided one way by a court in New York, another way by Tennessee, which had adopted a similar law. The panic of 1837 produced a fresh crop of redemption statutes. Illinois' law (1841) specifically applied to "mort-

32 See Robert H. Skilton, "Developments in Mortgage Law and Practice," 17 Temple L. Q., 315 (1943). This excellent article is the source of much of the discussion of mortgage law in this chapter.

gaged lands." It gave the mortgagor, in essence, one year to redeem his property. It further provided that no mortgaged land could be sold at foreclosure sale, to any bidder, for less than two-thirds the appraised value of the land. This too was an attempt to salvage something from the land-debtor's equity. The *New York Journal of Commerce* spoke in disgust of this kind of law as "dishonest and knavish." "More than all the defalcations of individual swindlers," it "attests the almost hopeless depravity and corruption of the age." [33] The law applied to existing, as well as to future, mortgages. Indeed, that was the point of it: to relieve the debtors of Illinois who were crushed by the fall in prices and values. In the famous case of *Bronson* v. *Kinzie*,[34] the United States Supreme Court struck down the Illinois statute as an impairment of the obligation of contracts. A storm of protest arose in Illinois, but the burden of inertia had now shifted; the creditors were once more in the saddle. *Bronson* precipitated a second crisis: a confrontation between the legislature, responsive to the debtors, and the courts, defending stability and creditors' rights. Ultimately, it was conceded that the legislature could validly impose a redemption right on future mortgages, regardless of what creditors wished. The courts' impact, though great, was not decisive: but courts were able to force a delay, to exact a compromise from the legislatures that were too "ultra" on the debtors' side.

SUCCESSION: WILLS AND TRUSTS

In a market economy, property is freely bought and sold, and freely transferred by way of gift. Most gift transactions take place within the family. Few property owners make major gifts during their lifetime; but when they die, all must be given away. Almost the entire stock of private wealth turns over each generation, by last will and testament, or through the intestacy laws, or by a gift in the light of death. Only public, corporate, and dynastic property is immune from this law of mortality.

There had been some colonial adventures in probate law and practice. There were early attempts to administer the estates of the dead rather flexibly, treating each case as the family situation re-

[33] Quoted in Charles Warren, *The Supreme Court in United States History*, Vol. II, p. 102.

[34] 1 How. 311 (1843).

quired. These tendencies were abandoned and replaced by a network of tighter rules. This made up in efficiency and certainty of result what was lost in flexibility. But flexibility and individualized handling of estates was a luxury that a mass society, with mass ownership of wealth, could not afford.

American probate laws were not by any means slavish imitations of English models.[35] The law of wills, however, owed a great deal to English statutes and practices. The statute of frauds (1677) had required a written, witnessed will for real estate. The Wills Act (1837) covered both realty and personality. The two statutes differed, slightly, in other details. After 1837, American states tended to follow one or the other of these models, or a mixture of both. Statutory rules for the formal execution of a will distinctly hardened. With few exceptions, American states imposed the same formal requirements on wills of land and on testaments of personal property.[36]

A formal, standard, precise law of wills was vital to the property system. The Ordinance of 1787 authorized wills of land, "provided such wills be duly proved." This was one of the few substantive provisions in the Ordinance of 1787, and a clear departure from English law. In England, a man could introduce a will of land into court, as evidence of his title, even though the will had never gone through probate. Even if it had, that fact did not bind the court trying title to land. The Ordinance of 1787, and the practice that grew up under it, gave much more weight to the probate *process*.[37] There was colonial precedent for this practice.[38] But it is best understood in the context of post-Revolutionary land law. Land instruments had to be rational, simple, and standard; land procedures had to be objective, and routine. The will, like the deed, was a fundamental instrument of transfer. Probate was to the will what recording was to the deed. Transitions were smoother, records were more exact, and title was less clouded, if all wills were funneled through probate.

Because of their importance to land titles, the wills themselves

35 The Massachusetts double share for the eldest child was given up in 1789.

36 In a group of Southern and Western states, and states where civil law influence was strong (Texas, Louisiana), holographic wills were also valid. These wills, if entirely handwritten by the testator, required no witnesses.

37 Willard Wirt Blume, "Probate and Administration on the American Frontier," 58 Mich. L. Rev. 209, 233 (1959).

38 See Thomas E. Atkinson, "The Development of the Massachusetts Probate System," 42 Mich. L. Rev. 425, 448 (1943).

have been carefully preserved in many counties. They exist in an unbroken line from the beginnings of county history to the present. An occasional title searcher disturbs their dust. An occasional genealogist tunnels into the caves, in search of a lost forefather. Historians have generally neglected them; but from these old wills, stiff and stereotyped as they are, the voice of social history speaks out. One finds in them an occasional fact of rare beauty, some aspect or insight of the era, trapped in county archives as if in amber. John Randolph of Roanoke freed his slaves by will, "heartily regretting" that he ever owned slaves. He bequeathed to his "old and faithful servants, Essex and his wife Hetty . . . three-and-a-half barrels of corn, two hundred weight of pork, a pair of strong shoes, a suit of clothes, and a blanket each, to be paid them annually; also, an annual hat to Essex, and ten pounds of coffee and twenty of brown sugar." Benjamin Franklin left to his daughter "The King of France's picture, set with four hundred and eight diamonds." It was his wish that "she would not form any of those diamonds into ornaments, either for herself or daughters, and thereby introduce or countenance the expensive, vain and useless pastime of wearing jewels in this country." [39]

Wills are ambulatory, that is, they can be revoked or replaced by the testator up to the moment of his death. In the 19th century, the deathbed will was more common than in later, more calculating times.[40] For this reason, some 19th-century wills were more poignant and direct than the wills of the 20th century. The typical will, however, did little preaching and betrayed little sentiment. Only the wealthy, by and large, made out wills. Even at the very end of the period, probably less than five per cent of the persons who died in the typical county in any one year left wills that passed through probate.[41] Even fewer intestate estates were formally administered. All in all, more than ninety per cent of the population passed on without benefit of probate. Willmakers tended to be landowners, men of some substance. Their estate plans (to use a modern term) nearly always disposed of their land within their family. They took particular care to protect the interests of their wives, sisters, and

[39] Virgil M. Harris, *Ancient, Curious and Famous Wills* (1911), pp. 370, 414.

[40] In earlier times and in England, wills were even more likely to be deathbed documents; see Wilbur K. Jordan, *Philanthropy in England 1480–1660* (1959), p. 16, on 16th-century wills.

[41] Some probably wrote out a will, but left so small an estate that probating the will made no sense.

daughters. But women were not usually granted actual control over land. Before the Married Women's Property Acts, property left to a woman might pass out of the testator's bloodline, might even fall prey to creditors of the woman's husband. Among the wealthy, then, there was a definite tendency not to make major gifts in fee simple to a woman. Rather, property was *settled* on women; or left in trust; or given to women in the form of lesser "estates": life interests for daughters, estates during widowhood for a surviving wife. Almost forty per cent of a group of New Jersey wills, in the period 1810–1813, which contained gifts to a widow, gave her an estate measured by the duration of her widowhood.[42] In New York City, seven out of twelve wills probated, in the summer of 1843, contained some sort of nonfee disposition.[43]

One has the impression that more of the population stood outside the formal system of succession in New York in 1840 than in Massachusetts Bay two centuries before. In the early colonial period, probate was cheap, accessible, and relatively informal. In the 18th century, probate was more elaborate and costly; only the well-to-do made use of it. At some point, perhaps about 1800, the curve reached a peak and slowly changed direction. From then on participation in the probate process gradually increased, along with national literacy and wealth. In absolute terms, the number of nonfee dispositions (trusts, settlements, chains of future interests) certainly increased, in the 19th century—at least as fast as the population and probably much faster.

Trust litigation was fairly sparse in the early 19th century. Except for marriage settlements, living trusts were probably not common. Most trusts were short-term, "caretaker" trusts, created to protect some weaker member of the family: married women, minors, incompetents. Frequently, too, a man would set up a trust to avoid passing property on to a bankrupt son or son-in-law. Thomas Jefferson left the residue of his estate to his grandson, Thomas J. Randolph, and two friends, in trust for Jefferson's daughter. Her husband, Thomas M. Randolph, was insolvent. The trustees were to hold the estate "in base fee, determinable on the death of my said son-in-law"; at that time, the estate would vest in the daughter and her heirs. This arrangement would "preclude the rights, powers and authorities" that would otherwise devolve

42 N.J. Archives, 1st series, Vol. XLI (Vol. 12 [1949], Calendar of Wills, 1810–13).

43 New York, Surr. N.Y. Cnty., Will Bk. No. 88, pp. 2–65 (July–Sept. 1843).

on the son-in-law "by operation of law." In this way, the estate was guarded against the creditors of Jefferson's son-in-law.[44] In a Pennsylvania case, *Ashhurst* v. *Given* (1843),[45] the deceased left to his son Samuel Given, a kind of trusteeship over the estate, consisting of an "undivided half part of the Kidderminster estate, including the factory buildings, dwelling-house, water-powers . . . machinery and fixtures." Samuel was to manage the estate for the benefit of his children, paying himself a "reasonable support out of the trust fund." Through this circuitous scheme, the testator hoped to provide for the family, without exposing the estate to "those debts which he [Samuel] contracted in an unfortunate business."

A second, rarer, use of the trust device might be called dynastic. Through trusts and settlements, a testator who wished could bind an estate within his family for as long as the law would permit. The rule against perpetuities was the limiting doctrine. The rule, which had reached full flower in England by 1800, was at least nominally in force in the United States. The New York revision of 1827–28 modified the rule, but in the direction of even greater stringency. The New York statutes on trusts were, as we have seen, antidynastic. Only caretaker trusts were intended to survive the onslaught of reform, although the point was blunted by later amendments. Neither in New York, nor in Michigan, Wisconsin, and Minnesota, which borrowed the code, were the rules to stamp out the dynastic trust ever fully carried out.

The draftsmen of the New York code had a specific picture of a dynasty in mind. They were thinking of the great English landed estates. Under a settlement or long-term trust, such an estate was "tied up" in a family in two senses: no current member of the family had the right to sell his interest, nor could anybody, including the trustee, treat land and improvements as market commodities; land and family were tied together. New York had some estates of this type; they were also known in the plantation South. But a new type of trust was developing, which was dynastic in a different sense. Some great merchant families were wealthy in capital assets other than land—factories, banking houses, ships, and stocks and bonds. Particularly in Boston, rich men in the early 19th century began planning dynastic trusts that were fundamentally different from the baronial land trusts. These long-term trusts needed flexible management; it was taken for granted that their portfolio would be frequently changed.

[44] Harris, *op. cit.,* p. 398.
[45] 5 Watts & Serg. 323 (Pa., 1843).

Massachusetts law proved quite permissive to these paper dynasties. In the famous *Harvard College* case (1830),[46] the court enunciated a standard of investment for trustees, which has come to be known as the "prudent investor" rule. It freed the trustee from rigid restrictions on trust investment, recognized in other jurisdictions—rules that stated that a trustee could invest only in government bonds or first mortgages on land. From 1830 on, the trustee in Massachusetts could manage and invest assets, as a prudent investor would; he could, for example, buy sound corporate stocks. The rule was the Magna Charta for a Boston phenomenon, the private, professional trustee. This shrewd Yankee figure, manager of other people's fortunes, first appeared in Boston around 1820. For several decades, until the rise of trust companies, he managed the wealth of the Brahmins. The *Harvard College* case freed him from restraints suitable only for caretaker trusts managed by non-professionals. Some old firms of private trustees, grown rich and indispensable, still survive on Boston's State Street, with a century or more of prudence in their files. They are still able to compete for a corner of the business which, in general, the trust companies captured after the Civil War.[47]

There is also a kind of dynastic trust that is not based on family: the long-term charitable trust. It has had a curiously checkered career in this country.[48] Charities, so goes the maxim, are favorites of the law. The favor was not always very obvious. In the early 19th century, charity was associated with privilege, with the dead hand, with established churches, with massive wealth held in perpetuity.

In New York, the Elizabethan statute of charitable uses was not in effect; and the revisions of 1827–28 did not restore it. Virginia and Maryland did not recognize the charitable trust at all. Some states enacted "mortmain" laws. These, based on an English statute, cut down deathbed gifts to charity by voiding any such gifts in a will made less than thirty days before death. Charity, the law felt, began at home. A faint odor of anti-Catholicism also hangs over these laws—the fantasy of the evil priest, extorting ransom for the Church as the price of absolution.

Attitudes of hostility toward charity weakened, but slowly. A charitable trust was the subject of the *Harvard College* case. John

---

46 *Harvard College* v. *Amory*, 26 Mass. (9 Pick.) 446 (1830).
47 See Lawrence M. Friedman, "The Dynastic Trust," 73 Yale L. J. 547 (1964).
48 See, in general, Howard S. Miller, *The Legal Foundations of American Philanthropy 1776–1844* (1961).

McLean, the deceased, had left $50,000 to trustees; after the death of his wife, one-half of the trust would be paid to the Massachusetts General Hospital, the other half to Harvard College, to be "exclusively and forever appropriated to the support of a professor of ancient and modern history." A college endowment, whose corpus was made up of stocks and bonds, and which supported a professor of history, was not as frightening as a barony or church. A favorable attitude toward charity emerged in the great case of *Vidal* v. *Girard's Executors* (1844).[49] The banker Stephen Girard had died childless, leaving an enormous estate. His will established Girard College, and provided American legal history with more than a century of litigation. The question in *Vidal* was whether charitable trusts were valid at all. Specifically, did courts of chancery have inherent powers to administer charitable trusts, without a special authorizing statute? (The English statute was missing in most states.) To uphold the charitable trust, which it did, the Supreme Court reversed a prior line of cases. New York, Virginia, Maryland, and some followers, continued to constrict the charitable trust. In other states, *Vidal* encouraged a fresh look at the social utility of nonprofit dynasties.

INTELLECTUAL PROPERTY: PATENTS AND COPYRIGHTS

The Constitution (Art. 1, sec. 8) gave Congress power "To promote the progress of science and useful arts, by securing for limited times to authors and inventors the exclusive right to their respective writings and discoveries." This was the formal source of federal power over patents and copyrights.

In English law, a patent was a monopoly grant, an exclusive right to make and deal in some item of trade. Patents had been occasionally and individually granted by the colonies. For example, South Carolina passed an "Act for the due Encouragement of Dr. William Crook," who had devised a "Composition" of "Oyl or Spirit of Tar, which with other Ingredients will preserve the Bottoms of Vessels from the River-Worm, and also the Plank from rotting" (1716).[50] Monopoly was in bad odor by 1776, except for

49 2 How. 127 (1844).
50 Bruce W. Bugbee, *Genesis of American Patent and Copyright Law* (1967), p. 76.

the special case of the patent, felt to serve as incentive for technical innovation. The first patent act (1790) gave patent power to the secretary of state, the attorney general, and the secretary of war, "or any two of them." They were to issue a patent if they felt "the invention or discovery [was] sufficiently useful and important." [51] The first American patent was for a process of "making Pot and Pearl Ashes." Only sixty-seven patents were granted under this first patent act, which was replaced in 1793.[52] In the new act, the secretary of state, with the approval of the attorney general, had power to issue patents valid for fourteen years. The federal government did not independently investigate patents under this law.[53]

By 1836, 9,957 patents had been issued, and the rate was accelerating. An important handful of these were inventions of immense importance to business. A major patent act was passed in 1836. It established a Patent Office, headed by a commissioner of patents, within the Department of State. The commissioner was to grant patents only when the subject of the patent had not been previously "invented or discovered," when the applicant was the actual inventor of the device, and when the article was "sufficiently useful and important" to deserve a patent. In case of doubt, a board of "three disinterested persons," appointed by the secretary of state, would decide the issue of patentability. One of the three was to be an expert in "the particular art, manufacture, or branch of science to which the alleged invention appertains." [54]

A fundamental question haunted patent law. A liberal policy encouraged innovation, but it also created monopoly power. The liberal policy won early victories in court. In *Earle* v. *Sawyer* (1825),[55] the question was whether a certain "new and useful improvement in the machinery for manufacturing shingles," could be patented. The "improvement" consisted mostly of using a circular instead of a perpendicular saw. It was objected that "the combination itself is so simple, that, though new, it deserves not the name of an invention." Joseph Story, on circuit, brushed this objection aside. To be patentable, an object must simply be "new." That was the heart of the matter; a "flash of mind" or "genius" was not

[51] 1 Stats. 109–110 (act of April 10, 1790).

[52] Floyd L. Vaughan, *The United States Patent System* (1956), pp. 18–19; *Two Centuries Growth of American Law* (1901), p. 392.

[53] *Two Centuries Growth of American Law* (1901), p. 393; 1 Stats. 318 (act of Feb. 21, 1793).

[54] 5 Stats. 117, 119, 120 (act of July 4, 1836).

[55] Fed. Cas. No. 4247 (C.C. Mass., 1825).

necessary.[56] The act of 1836, which tightened the requirements for a patent grant, represented a definite turn of the wheel of opinion. Here was a judgment that the disincentive costs of monopoly could well outweigh the incentive benefits of patents.

Between 1783 and 1786, every state but Vermont passed a copyright law, at the urging of Congress. The first federal Copyright Act became law in 1790. An author might gain "sole right and liberty of printing, reprinting, publishing and vending" his "map, chart, book or books," for fourteen years, renewable for one additional term of fourteen years. The author had to deposit a printed copy of his work with the clerk of his federal district court, before publication. Another copy had to be delivered within six months to the secretary of state as well.[57] In 1831, the original term was extended to 28 years. By this time, the act covered musical compositions, designs, engravings, and etchings as well as maps, charts, and books.[58]

In the case law of copyright, *Wheaton* v. *Peters* (1834) was a landmark decision.[59] Curiously, this was a lawsuit by one Supreme Court reporter, Henry Wheaton, against another, Richard Peters. The Supreme Court here ruled on copyright aspects of its own decisions. Richard Peters had reprinted the decisions reported by his predecessors, without offering to pay. Wheaton did not have a statutory copyright, and he lost the case. The Supreme Court held that no common-law right of literary property existed. An author's sole source of protection was the federal copyright statute. There was therefore only one source of copyright law, relatively uniform and simple. As in the law of patents, there was a tension between the (monopoly) rights of creators and the free-market interests of the business public. In *Wheaton* v. *Peters,* the Supreme Court leaned away from the monopoly aspects of copyright, by restricting copyright to its statutory place.

An allied field—trademark law—was relatively undeveloped in this period. No trademark infringement case was decided in the United States before 1825.[60] Joseph Story granted the first injunction for trademark infringement, in 1844, to protect the makers of

56 The "flash of mind" requirement did not stay permanently buried; it was resurrected later on in patent law. See below, Part III, Ch. IV, p. 381.

57 1 Stats. 124 (act of May 31, 1790).

58 Richard Rogers Bowker, *Copyright, Its History and Its Law* (1912), pp. 36–37; a more modern treatment of the subject is Lyman R. Patterson, *Copyright in Historical Perspective* (1968), pp. 180–212.

59 8 Pet. 591 (1834).

60 *Two Centuries Growth of American Law* (1901), p. 435.

"Taylor's Persian Thread." Congress provided neither guidance nor any machinery of registration. Legal protection for designers of trademarks had to be forged in the rough mills of the courts. The economy was still deeply rooted in land and its produce. Intellectual property, despite the name, was not valued for intellectual reasons at all; but because of mercantile and industrial applications. As such, this property was not a central concern of the law, until the full-blown factory age.

CHAPTER VI

THE LAW OF COMMERCE AND TRADE

A FEDERAL QUESTION: ADMIRALTY
AND GENERAL COMMERCE

By all contemporary accounts, American commercial law was deeply and persistently in debt to England. New developments in English case law traveled across the Atlantic, almost with the speed of the clipper ships. Nationalism was not even a theoretical barrier. Admiralty, marine insurance, commercial paper, and sale of goods were not, in theory, English law, but international. "The marine law of the United States," wrote Chancellor Kent, "is the same as the marine law of Europe. It is not the law of a particular country, but the general law of nations." [1]

The statement has to be taken with a grain of salt. It contains some truth; and, what is more important, it reflects the opinion of leading American lawyers. Trade was in fact international. American settlement in 1776 was strung out narrowly along the coast. Commerce was, in large measure, ocean commerce; the customs and documents of trade were also those of ocean commerce. The received law of admiralty and ocean trade was part of the stock in trade of a developing country with its door to the sea. Law was a vital segment of the infrastructure. But American commercial law soon developed its own substance and style.

The Constitution federalized admiralty jurisdiction; it put an end to state admiralty courts, and to Congress' own creature, the "Court of Appeals in cases of capture," which was proposed in the Articles of Confederation. Under the Constitution, the judicial power of the United States extended to all "Cases of admiralty and maritime Jurisdiction" (Art. III, sec. 2). But how far did that jurisdiction extend? What did the clause mean? What situations did it cover, and what areas of law?

English precedent was not entirely unequivocal. Some judges

[1] Kent, *Commentaries*, Vol. III, (2nd ed., 1832) p. 1.

and statesmen read the English tradition to mean that admiralty power reached only those waters within the "ebb and flow of the tide." [2] The "ebb and flow of the tide" was perhaps a good enough criterion in England, an island nation. England had no Great Lakes and no Mississippi River. To use the same test in the United States was not, however, merely a case of blind imitation of the past. Those who defended the tidewater concept, in America, were those who took a narrow view of admiralty power; they wanted to keep federal power within limits, and expand the power of the states. Chancellor Kent warned that a broad admiralty power would injure the right of trial by jury (admiralty courts used no jury). Expansion would also divest the state courts "at one stroke, of a vast field of commercial jurisdiction." Justice Story consistently defended the tidewater concept as "the prescribed limit," which courts were not "at liberty to transcend." Justice William Johnson spoke in 1827 of the "silent and stealing progress of the admiralty in acquiring jurisdiction to which it has no pretensions."

But as population moved toward the interior, lakes and rivers became arteries of commerce as important as turnpikes and roads. The tidewater concept now came in for serious re-examination. In 1833, in *Peyroux* v. *Howard*,[3] the Supreme Court discovered what one judge later called an "occult tide," invisible to the naked eye, but strong enough to bring the Mississippi at New Orleans into the nets of federal admiralty power. In 1845, Congress passed an act that gave district courts jurisdiction over "matters of contract and tort" concerning "steamboats and other vessels of twenty tons burden and upwards, enrolled and licensed for the coasting trade," and operating on "lakes and navigable waters." The act was vague, the wording clumsy. But this act, and a collision on Lake Ontario between the schooner *Cuba* and the propeller *Genesee Chief*, provided the occasion for the great case of the *Genesee Chief* (1851).[4] The Supreme Court, through Chief Justice Taney, at last swept away the tidewater limitation. Federal power unequivocally reached all public navigable waters.

Admiralty cases were staples of the docket of all the federal courts. The federal judges became adept at handling matters of

2 On admiralty power, see Milton Conover, "The Abandonment of the 'Tidewater' Concept of Admiralty Jurisdiction in the United States," 38 Oregon L. Rev. 34 (1958); Note, "From Judicial Grant to Legislative Power: The Admiralty Clause in the Nineteenth Century," 67 Harv. L. Rev. 1214 (1954).
3 7 Pet. 324 (1833).
4 *The Propeller Genesee Chief* v. *Fitzhugh*, 53 U.S. 443 (1851).

admiralty law, and Joseph Story, characteristically, was a master. His opinions swarmed with erudition (quotations from Latin sources, references to Richard Zouch, the laws of Oléron, and other mysteries of the maritime past.) But admiralty law was not a game; it was, among other things, a branch of foreign policy. Decisions on prize law, neutrality, and the embargo were its meat and drink. The docket cast up cases like *Brig Short Staple and Cargo* v. *U.S.*, decided by the Supreme Court in February term, 1815; the brig had been seized "for having violated the embargo laws of the United States, by sailing to a foreign port." [5] In an 1814 case, a vessel, the *Cordelia,* on its way to Surabaya, was boarded by a British officer, who warned the ship not to put in at any port in Java. The shipmaster obeyed, and sailed for Philadelphia. The ship was insured; its policy covered, among other risks, "unlawful arrests, restraints, and detainments." But the Supreme Court held that the policy did not reach the *Cordelia*'s situation. "The right to blockade an enemy's port . . . is a right secured to every belligerent by the law of nations." The restraint therefore was not "unlawful." [6]

The federal courts also decided many cases of maritime commerce. In *De Lovio* v. *Boit* (1815), Joseph Story, on circuit, held that a policy of marine insurance was a "maritime contract." [7] This gave federal courts jurisdiction over the matter. But the jurisdiction was concurrent, not exclusive, that is, it was shared with state courts. New York state reports of the period bristled with cases on marine insurance.[8] But in this partnership, federal power was growing, a process that led to the *Genesee Chief.* One clear goal of the trend was centralization of foreign policy. But there was also a strong domestic motive. The Supreme Court, with other important political factions, believed that the country should be governed as a single large free-trade area. Commerce should flow smoothly across state borders; no robber barons should extract toll on the way. The issue came to the fore in the mighty case of *Gibbons* v. *Ogden,* decided by Marshall's court in 1824.[9] New York had given to Robert R. Livingston and Robert Fulton the exclusive right to navigate "all the waters within the jurisdiction of that

[5] *Brig Short Staple and Cargo* v. *U.S.*, 9 Cranch 55 (1815). The shipowners admitted the fact, but claimed, in justification, that an armed British vessel had captured her and forced her into port.

[6] *M'Call* v. *Marine Insurance Co.*, 8 Cranch 59 (1814).

[7] Fed. Cas. No. 3776 (C. C. Mass., 1815).

[8] On the law and practice of marine insurance, see Julius Goebel, ed., *The Law Practice of Alexander Hamilton,* Vol. II (1969), pp. 391–778.

[9] 9 Wheat. 1 (1824).

State, with boats moved by fire or steam." Ogden operated a steamboat line between New York and New Jersey, under license from Livingston. Gibbons owned two steamboats, which he ran between New York and Elizabethtown, New Jersey. Ogden got an injunction against Gibbons. On appeal, the Marshall court voided the New York act and struck down the monopoly. The decision rested on two bases. There were acts of Congress, licensing ships that plied the coasting trade; arguably these laws "pre-empted" or shoved aside the state's overlapping legislation. The second basis was the clause of the Constitution that gave Congress power to regulate interstate commerce. *Gibbons* v. *Ogden* did not flatly hold that the commerce power was exclusive, that the states had no residuum of power over commerce across state lines. Because of the presence of the federal licensing law, the thrust of the case was ambiguous; and its full potential was veiled. Perhaps the court wished it that way. Still, to some unplumbed extent, federal power over commerce—a dormant giant in regard to domestic trade—cut down, by its very existence, the power of the states to pursue independent policies on trade.

The Supreme Court also moved to unify the commercial law of the country. It hoped that a single body of law would emerge under federal hegemony. *Swift* v. *Tyson* (1842)[10] decided that federal courts, in ordinary commercial cases, had the right to apply the "general" law of commerce, even if this was different from the law of the state in which the court was sitting, and even if no "federal question" was presented, and the case came to a federal court solely because plaintiff and defendant were residents of different states. The actual question in the case came from the law of negotiable instruments—specifically, the rights of a person to whom a bill of exchange was endorsed. If he did not buy the bill with fresh money or goods, but took it to satisfy an old debt owed him by the endorser, was he a holder in due course? The law of New York, where the bill was accepted, at least arguably said no; the majority view was yes. But the law of commerce, Story said, speaking for the court, was and ought to be international—not the "law of a single country only, but of the commercial world."

10 16 Pet. 1 (1842). The precise question was whether the Judiciary Act of 1789 required the court to follow state law. Section 34 of the Act directed federal trial courts to follow "the laws of the several states" except where the case presented a federal question. Did "laws" mean only statutes or did it include common-law doctrines? Not the latter, said the court, at least in cases of "contracts and other instruments of a commercial nature."

SALE OF GOODS

The law of sales of goods developed rapidly in the first half of the 19th century. Many, if not most, of the leading cases were English. They were adopted in the United States with some rapidity. Two strains of law, contract and the law merchant, each with a somewhat different emphasis, acted as parents of the law of sales. The law merchant was suffused with what one might call the psychology of market overt. In market overt ("open market"), goods were as freely transferable as bills, notes, and paper money. A buyer of goods in market overt acquired full rights to the goods. If he bought in good faith and for value, his claims were superior to those of any prior owner, even if the goods had been stolen. At one time, every shop in London was considered a market overt; but by the 18th century, the doctrine in the literal sense had gone into decline. Chancellor Kent condemned it as a barbarous survival; in any event, it never took root in the United States.[11]

In common-law countries, the law merchant was subtly altered in the direction of principles of contract. This meant that rules at least *appeared* to be less rigid and objective, and that the "intention of the parties" was emphasized. The law of sales grew up about the concept of *property* or *title* to goods. Title was an invisible rope which tied a chattel to its original owner, until title legally "passed" to a buyer. Title was a concept of intention: in broad theory, it passed when it was intended to pass. But the rules of title were subtly skewed in the direction of favoring sellers' rights. English and American cases agreed that title could pass without either payment or delivery, if so intended. This meant that the buyer bore risk of loss at an early stage of the bargain. In a well-known English case, *Tarling* v. *Baxter* (1827),[12] the parties bought and sold a haystack. The buyer agreed not to remove the hay until he paid for it. The seller drew a bill of exchange on the buyer, payable in one month; the buyer accepted the bill. The bill was then negotiated to a good-faith purchaser. Meanwhile, the haystack was completely consumed by fire. The buyer was held liable to make good on payment. Title to the haystack had passed; therefore, it was the *buyer's* haystack that had burned. On the other hand, if the buyer went bankrupt or failed to pay, so that

11 *Wheelwright* v. *Depeyster,* 1 Johns. R. 471, 480 (N.Y. 1806).
12 6 Barn. & C. 360 (1827).

right to repossess, rather than risk of accidental loss was at issue, the courts invented a shadowy security interest that did not "pass" so quickly.

These and other doctrines were gradually woven into a tight, logical fabric of rules. In operation, in the actual reported cases, these rules were more flexibly applied than one might deduce from their abstract formulation. As a total package, they were rather too elegant (and too unknown except to lawyers) to have had much effect on the actual working of the market. But whatever their practical import, one may ask why commercial law should have moved away from the classic "mercantile" principles, even on paper, in the heyday of the market economy. The answer may lie in the difference between a market economy and a merchant's economy. Commercial law was once the province of a small in-group of merchants; in a typical transaction, both buyer and seller were middlemen, who understood the business background and were familiar with documents and customs. In the early 19th century, the law concerned itself more with the needs and activities of ultimate buyers and sellers. It shifted its emphasis to favor manufacturers and producers, a class vaguely correlated with sellers rather than buyers.

Even so, American commercial law, on paper, had a certain Adam Smith severity, a certain flavor of the rugged individual. American lawyers liked to contrast the stern simplicity (real or imagined) of the common law with the paternalism (real or imagined) of civil law. In California, just after statehood, a minority group of San Francisco lawyers petitioned the legislature, asking that "the Legislature . . . retain, in its substantial elements, the system of the Civil Law." The judiciary committee of the California Senate denied their request; the committee extolled the virtues of the common law, specifically in the commercial field. The common-law doctrine, said the report, "is *caveat emptor*. . . . In other words, the Common Law allows parties to make their own bargains, and when they are made, holds them to a strict compliance"; the civil law, on the contrary, with its dangerous doctrine of implied warranty, "looks upon man as incapable of judging for himself, assumes the guardianship over him, and interpolates into a contract that which the parties never agreed to. The one is protective of trade, and a free and rapid interchange of commodities— the other is restrictive of both." The committee ascribed almost magical qualities to the common law. English and American commerce "whitens every sea, woos every breeze. . . . Its merchants

234 FROM THE REVOLUTION TO DEATH OF CHANCELLOR KENT

are princes—its ships palaces. . . . The Commerce of Civil Law
countries . . . creeps timidly along a few familiar shores . . .
sluggish in its progress, and unprofitable in its results. It is not
fostered by the quickening influence of English and American law
. . . the spirit of life is not in it—it is dead." [13]

The actual facts are not so clear-cut. It is doubtful that majestic
capitalism would have smothered in its crib without the rule of
caveat emptor.[14] It is doubtful whether specific doctrines of commercial law were cause, effect, or condition of American capitalism;
or all or none of these. *Caveat emptor* was loudly proclaimed in
some American cases. In *McFarland* v. *Newman* (1839),[15] a Pennsylvania case, one Newman bought a horse from McFarland. The horse
"had a defluxion from the nose at the time of the bargain," but
McFarland "assured Newman it was no more than the ordinary
distemper to which colts are subject." In fact, the horse had glan-
ders. In a crisp, biting opinion, Pennsylvania's John Gibson reversed a lower-court decision for the buyer. "He who is so simple as
to contract without a specification of the terms, is not a fit subject
of judicial guardianship." The civil-law rule would have made the
seller liable; but this rule was obnoxious to the health of the economy. It "would put a stop to commerce itself in driving everyone
out of it by the terror of endless litigation."

Caveat emptor had not always been so highly favored.[16] In South
Carolina, at least one judge called *caveat emptor* a "disgrace to the
law." In the case in question, decided in 1818, barrels of blubber
were sold as "oil." The judge adopted the civil-law rule: "A sound
price requires a sound commodity." [17] But the case was regarded as
exceptional. Most decisions in most states in the first half of the
19th century agreed with Gibson's formulation of the rule. But although common-law courts refused to *imply* warranties, they
showed a marked tendency to read *express* warranties into a seller's
words, at the slightest provocation.

In the 20th century, warranty means a promise of quality enforceable regardless of intention or fault. A supermarket is liable to
its customer if he takes sick from adulterated soup, even though
the soup company sealed the soup can before it ever reached the

13 Report of Feb. 27, 1850, reprinted in appendix to 1 Cal. Rpts. 588, pp.
595, 597.

14 See Walton Hamilton, "The Ancient Maxim Caveat Emptor," 40 Yale L.
Journal 1133, 1178–1182 (1931).

15 9 Watts 55 (Pa., 1839).

16 See *Baker* v. *Frobisher,* Quincy 4 (Mass., 1762).

17 *Barnard* v. *Yates,* 1 Nott & M'Cord 142 (S. Car. 1818).

supermarket shelf. In Gibson's day, warranty was still strongly colored with its historical meaning, which restricted recovery to open, blatant deceit. The civil-law rule—that a sound price requires a sound commodity—*seems* more consonant with market principles, because it carries out the reasonable intention of honest parties. Gibson's language hid a paradox. *Caveat emptor,* though individualistic, defeated contractual intent. It is best seen as another attempt to accommodate law to the conditions of a broadly based market. The Gibson rule on warranties favored sellers, to be sure. But more significantly, it enhanced the finality of bargains. It made it harder for parties to drag into court their harangues over warranty and quality. This is what Gibson had in mind when he spoke of the "terror of endless litigation." A clear, harsh rule, he felt, was necessary. Otherwise, the courts might be overburdened with cases, the canals of commerce clogged.

Rules about bills, money and notes made up the law of negotiable instruments, a somewhat different mix of law merchant and common law. The key concept in this field was negotiability. Paper money has this quality in the highest degree. Money is "bearer paper"; it can be transferred from hand to hand. A check is also negotiable, though by endorsement. A negotiable instrument, when validly transferred, cuts off "equities" between the original parties. In other fields of law, a buyer of rights or goods steps into his seller's shoes. A buyer of land rises no higher in right than his seller; any charges, claims, liens, or doubts about title follow and haunt him. But a good-faith buyer of a check takes fresh, unobstructed title.

The colonies, as we have seen, had enacted liberal assignment statutes, so that the law of negotiable instruments was in some ways more advanced than in England. This liberality continued. A Georgia statute of 1799 declared that "All bonds, and other specialties, and promissory notes, and other liquidated demands . . . whether for money or other things . . . shall be . . . negotiable by endorsement in such manner and under such restrictions as are prescribed in the case of promissory notes." [18]

The reference to "other things" was significant. Today, only instruments payable in money can claim to be negotiable. But the chattel note was widely used and recognized in colonial times. In

[18] Prince, *Digest of the Laws of Georgia* (2nd ed., 1837) p. 426. (act of Feb. 16, 1799, sec. 25); Frederick Beutel, "The Development of State Statutes on Negotiable Paper Prior to the Negotiable Instruments Law," 40 Col. L. Rev. 836, 848 (1940).

the tobacco colonies and states, notes were commonly made payable in tobacco. After Independence, and well into the 19th century, chattel notes were common in the West, where hard money was in chronically short supply. In a Wisconsin case (1844), a note had been made payable in "five thousand three hundred and seventy-five lbs. of lead." [19] An Ohio case (1827) refused to treat as negotiable a note payable in "good merchantable whiskey." [20] The chattel note had the defect that it was not very easy to standardize. Negotiable instruments do their job best when they are as simple and formal as possible. A check is a bare, unvarying document of stereotyped appearance and wording. Chattel notes were tolerated only because money was so scarce; or where (as in the tobacco states) a certain chattel, like wampum or cowrie shells in other cultures, was a recognized medium of exchange. These were transient conditions, however. By the end of the period, courts were regularly holding that no chattel note could be truly negotiable; only money instruments had that quality.

Throughout the period, there was no satisfactory national currency. Gold and silver were rare. Private bank notes constituted the circulating medium of exchange. Credit depended on these bank notes and on personal promissory notes. The law of bills and notes was a vital part of the economic system for this reason; as the pale of settlement moved west, the law of negotiable instruments went with it. Law reports were thick with cases on bills and notes. The bill of exchange was a commercial instrument; it produced most of its case law in the East. The promissory note, on the other hand, was ubiquitous. Case law confirms the guess that basic aspects of the law of bills and notes were part of the living law. People were as familiar with basic rules about notes, and endorsements of notes, as they are familiar with checks today.

In the 19th, as in the 20th century, the economy sailed on a sea of credit. Credit, however, was a high-risk matter in an age of radical business cycles, an age without Dun and Bradstreet,[21] an age without public insurance of money and deposits. It was a life-and-death matter to know your debtor, and whether he was solvent. The law saw to it that a creditor could rely on the *validity* of a circulating note, provided it conformed on its face to the simple requirements of negotiability. The solvency of the maker was another matter. The more endorsements of solid, solvent citizens a

---

19 *Garrison* v. *Owens,* 1 Pin. 471 (1844).

20 *Rhodes* v. *Lindly,* 3 Ohio St. 51 (1827).

21 By the 1840's, there was some rudimentary credit rating.

note might bear, the more the note could be counted on. Endorsements were a form of credit guarantee. But when a signer signed a note as an "accommodation"—that is, for nothing—he deeply resented being called to account, if the true maker of the note failed to pay. These failures were all too frequent. The country was large, the possibilities for escape from debt were rich. In a great, young, runaway economy, subject to violent outbursts of boom and bust, fortunes were easily made and unmade. During the downswings, banks drowned in a sea of debt, leaving behind heaps of worthless paper. Makers and endorsers failed or dodged their obligation; the sureties sometimes tried to wriggle out through tiny holes in law or practice. Many cases, then, turned on the rights and obligations of sureties who signed for another. In general, the case law was lenient to them; unless the creditor swiftly and sternly pursued his rights, courts had a tendency to let the surety go. And if the creditor took any action that might be harmful to the surety —for example, if the creditor gave his debtor extra time to pay, without consulting the surety—then the surety was considered released.[22]

The *note* was paper of a thousand uses. It was a "courier without luggage": one scratch of the pen, and it moved swiftly and easily into the stream of commerce. Simplicity and ease of travel meant a great deal in a nation of continental size, whose population moved restlessly from place to place. New types of negotiable instrument developed, borrowing the virtues of the old. Municipal and corporate bonds were drawn into the orbit of negotiability. Before 1850, the negotiable certificate of deposit had been launched by the banks. The bank check had been in use for at least a century; but had never been of much consequence. Ultimately, it became the people's instrument of payment, just as the note was the people's instrument of credit. In Story's treatise on promissory notes and other commercial paper (1845), the check was important enough to merit a chapter of its own.[23] Some of these new developments came by way of England. Some changed radically in the United States. The bill of lading, in England, was a document of ocean freight. In the United States, name and doctrine came to be used for railroad documents too.

Much of this law was, and had always been, judge-made. Practice governed, and the courts slowly ratified what business did. The

22 See, for example, *Clippinger* v. *Creps*, 2 Watts 45 (Pa., 1833).
23 Joseph Story, *Commentaries on the Law of Promissory Notes* (1845), ch. xi, pp. 614–645.

statute book played an important but secondary role in developing the law. But on other aspects of the law of commercial paper, on questions of currency and banking, public policy spoke with a louder voice. The rise and fall of the two Banks of the United States has already been mentioned. There was always tremendous pressure for policies that would stimulate lending. Cash was always in desperately short supply. Entrepreneur, industrialist and small-holder alike needed credit. Public debates over monetary policy, as usual, invoked political and economic principle; but, regardless of principle, that policy usually won out which seemed to promise the highest payoff to those with political and economic power.

BANKRUPTCY AND INSOLVENCY

Bankruptcy law was another branch of commercial law with intense economic significance. The Constitution gave Congress the power "to establish uniform laws on the Subject of Bankruptcy throughout the United States." But Congress did not accept this clear invitation to establish a national system. Before the Civil War, only two federal bankruptcy acts were passed. The first, in 1800, lasted two and a half years.[24] The second, in 1841, was repealed with even more indecent haste.[25]

Charles Warren has said that "desire for bankruptcy legislation and depression have always been coupled in our history." [26] Panic and commercial failure were the backdrop for the first act, the law of 1800. It followed closely the scheme of the contemporary English statute. Only creditors could initiate bankruptcy proceedings, and only "traders" (merchants) were liable to be put through bankruptcy. (Actually, some merchants used the law to get rid of their debts by inducing friendly creditors to push them into bankruptcy.) The law was bitterly criticized in Congress. Thomas Newton, Jr., of Virginia, denounced it as "partial, immoral . . . impolitic . . . anti-Republican." [27] The law was administratively inconvenient. In some parts of the country, it was awkward to travel long distances to reach the federal court. Some rich debtors abused the law; they canceled their old debts and contracted new ones, in such a

[24] Act of Apr. 4, 1800, 2 Stats. 19, repealed Dec. 19, 1803, 2 Stats. 248.
[25] Act of Aug. 19, 1841, 5 Stats. 440, repealed Mar. 3, 1843, 5 Stats. 614.
[26] Charles Warren, *Bankruptcy in United States History* (1935), pp. 21–22.
[27] Quoted in Charles Warren, *Bankruptcy in United States History* (1935), p. 21.

way as to offend public opinion. But these scandals were not causes of the downfall of the law; they were merely used as fuel for the fires of repeal. The main opposition came from those congressmen who spoke for agriculture and the debtor class.

In the second bankruptcy act, too, a creditor could force into bankruptcy only members of the commercial class: "all persons, being merchants, or using the trade of merchandise, all retailers of merchandise, and all bankers, factors, brokers, underwriters, or marine insurers, owing debts to the amount of not less than two thousand dollars." But the act, significantly, opened the door to "all persons whatsoever," to file a petition for voluntary bankruptcy. The act was passed, somewhat belatedly, in the wake of the shattering economic crisis of 1837. The act marked something of a shift in emphasis, as the debate over passage made clear. Earlier bankruptcy laws had been drafted primarily to protect the creditors of an insolvent man; the point was to make sure that everyone with cargo in a sinking ship was fairly and equitably treated. The act of 1841 was at least equally interested in the other goal of a bankruptcy law: to wipe clean a debtor's slate. During debate, the proposed law was frequently denounced as not truly a bankruptcy law, but rather an "insolvency law." The term referred to state laws, which emphasized debtor relief rather than fair treatment of creditors. Debtor relief was certainly a major result of the act. Charles Warren, who had studied its operation, reported that 33,739 persons took advantage of the law; $440,934,000 in debt was canceled; a mere $43,697, 357 was surrendered by the debtors.[28] One of the factors that doomed the law was in a sense its very success. Economic revival, and the rapid discharge of hundreds of debtors, removed some of the sense of urgency; soon a bankruptcy law did not seem quite so necessary.[29]

The collapse of the federal law was in many ways a misfortune. Such a law could have ensured fair, uniform division of assets among creditors. But it was too much to hope for a long-lasting federal law, if only because of the "cankering jealousy of the general government with which some of the states are so deeply affected." [30] In between federal laws, the states did not leave the subject untouched. In the broadest sense, few legal relationships led to more ceaseless agitation and enactment than the relation-

[28] Warren, *op. cit.*, p. 81.
[29] Peter Coleman, *The Insolvent Debtor in American History* (unpublished ms., 1970, p. 37).
[30] 1 Am. Jurist 49 (1829).

ship between debtor and creditor. In the process, the law of debt gained in political passion, but lost moral affect. Bankruptcy had originally a punitive ring. It was at one time a crime, later a disgrace. In the mercantile era, the triumph of the merchant meant the triumph of a cool neutrality toward debt.

One symptom of changing attitudes was the abolition of imprisonment for debt. This was a humanitarian gesture, of course; but it was particularly appealing in a new age. As William E. Nelson has pointed out, bankruptcy and insolvency laws are "sensible arrangements in an industrialized society"; a man does not lose his productive capacity when bankrupt, but he does when in jail. Land, on the other hand, can remain productive while a man is in prison; but when a man goes through bankruptcy he is stripped of his land or most of it. The end of imprisonment for debt, therefore, and the rise of bankruptcy and insolvency, reflected economic change, bringing change in modes of social control over debtors.[31]

Imprisonment for debt was not only cruel; it was also inefficient. Like the death penalty, imprisonment for debt had decayed considerably before it was done away with formally. By the end of the 18th century, in New England, few debtors actually spent much time in prison—less than two per cent spent a year or more; many were released after one day. The concept of a "prison" was also rather loose. Many debtors were only nominally in jail. Often they were allowed to roam about the city, or to work by day, and return to the prison by night. This situation was expressly authorized by statutes, some of colonial age—for example, a New Hampshire law of 1771, "for the Ease and Relief of Prisoners for Debt," which gave imprisoned debtors the "liberty" of the prison yard, and established these limits at "within one hundred feet of the walls of the Prison"—on posting of bond.[32] This and similar ameliorations did not mean that imprisonment for debt was totally dead; there were pathetic cases of people who did in fact lie in jail for trivial debts, well into the 19th century. In Rhode Island, in 1830, a widow from Providence was put in jail for a debt of sixty-eight cents; in 1827 and 1828, a sick, 67-year-old laborer named Freeborn Hazard was kept in prison for four months, and later recommitted for a debt of one dollar and costs of $3.22. Nonetheless, the abolition was, in part, a ratification of pre-existing social change. The very idea of imprisonment for debt became quite intolerable.

31 Nelson, *The Americanization of the Common Law*, p. 218.
32 *Laws N.H. Province Period 1745–1774* (1915), pp. 548, 549–50 (act of Jan. 17, 1771).

The mass basis of American law meant that imprisonment was a risk for the many, rather than the miscreant few. Hundreds of thousands played the land market; the business cycle, when it crashed, shook the economy with the primitive force of an earthquake, and brought down many small, not undeserving men. For these, even one day, and even in an expansive prison, was too much. The risk was at least sporadically real. In Boston, 1,442 debtors went to jail in 1820.[33]

Many state constitutions specifically restricted imprisonment for debt. The Pennsylvania constitution of 1776 provided that "the person of a debtor . . . shall not be continued in prison after delivering up his Estate, for the benefit of his creditors, in such manner as shall be prescribed by law" (art. 9, sec. 16). This type of provision, of course, did not prevent debtors from going to prison in the first place. That was a later step, often achieved in stages. In New Hampshire, for example, a law passed before 1820 restricted imprisonment to those who owed more than $13.33. In 1831, imprisonment of women debtors was ended. Finally, in 1840, the last, most general step was taken.[34] In other states, however, final, complete abolition did not become law until much deeper in the century.

For most states, if not all, to ameliorate or abolish imprisonment for debt was only one aspect of debtor relief. There were insolvency laws, stay laws, mortgage moratoria. The colonies had experimented constantly with debtor-relief laws, and the Revolution was no interruption; indeed, the dislocations of the war provided a positive impetus to attack the problems of debtor and creditor once more. A South Carolina law of 1787, reciting that "many inhabitants of this country before the revolution owed considerable sums of money," but could not pay because of the "embarrassment of the war," and because of "very considerable importations of merchandise since the peace, and the loss of several crops," passed an "installment" act. Debts contracted before Jan. 1, 1787, might be paid in three installments, on Mar. 1, 1788, 1789, and 1790. Ominously, a special section of the act imposed heavy penalties on "any person or persons [who] shall assault, beat, wound, or oppose" those who tried to carry the act into effect.[35]

The South Carolina law was a planters' relief law, on the face of

33 Coleman, op. cit., p. 73. The widow and Freeborn Hazard are discussed in Coleman, p. 133A.

34 Coleman, op. cit., pp. 94–95.

35 Statutes at Large, So. Car., Vol. V (1839), p. 36 (act of Mar. 28, 1787).

it. Other states also tailored relief laws for groups of dominant debtors—farmers and landowners, typically. But the state laws were neither complete, nor uniform, nor fair. Insolvency laws and debtor-relief laws naturally followed the business cycle. Lawmaking was most shrill and frenetic in the lean years following a crash. In some states (for example, Connecticut), insolvent debtors petitioned for private acts of relief, and these were frequently granted. The volume of these added point to the demand for insolvency laws. The Rhode Island legislature received more than 2,300 petitions between 1758 and 1828.[36] Peter Coleman's research suggests that as many as one householder out of five in the early 19th century became insolvent during his working lifetime.[37] The panic of 1819 stimulated a fresh burst of activity; everywhere there was agitation for stay laws and other forms of debtor relief; in some states, creditor interests blocked the legislation, but in others, particularly in the West, the agitation bore fruit.[38]

The typical state insolvency law gave the *debtor* the right to set the process of insolvency in motion. Some laws did, and some did not, provide for ratable division of assets among all creditors. Under some of these laws, creditors complained long and loud of unfair preferences, fraud, and great inconveniences. So much smoke suggests at least a little fire. The laws were probably poorly administered, in most cases. They badly needed workable rules about what claims had first rights to be paid, and rules about how the rules should work. Without these, the laws were picked clean by the elemental greed of creditors and debtors. A contemporary witness (in 1829)judged state insolvency laws very harshly:

> Instead of one uniform, unbending rule for dividing the estate of an insolvent among his creditors, it is left to be disposed of by accident or caprice. One man prefers his father, brothers, and uncles, because they are his relations; another prefers his endorsers and custom-house sureties, because that is the general practice; and the business of a third is often settled by the sheriff's seizing his stock, before he has time to complete his arrangements.[39]

Moreover, there were simply too many of these laws. Businessmen did business across state lines; but insolvency law stopped at the borders. "There should not be one law at New York and another

36 Coleman, *op. cit.,* p. 242.
37 *Ibid.,* p. 506.
38 See Murray N. Rothbard, *The Panic of 1819* (1962), pp. 24–56.
39 1 Am. Jurist 45 (1829).

at Philadelphia, one law at Charleston and another at New Orleans." [40] And yet there was.

Insolvency laws were under an almost continual legal cloud.
They were politically and economically important. Even before
the Civil War, it had become quite usual that laws of great heat or
conflict were drawn into court and their constitutional pedigree
questioned. As a rule, state courts upheld their own insolvency
laws. The judges generally were similar in background to the legislators who enacted these laws, and understood the reasons why.
But insolvency laws raised a ticklish federal question. Did the
bankruptcy clause of the Constitution pre-empt the field? In 1819,
in *Sturges* v. *Crowninshield*,[41] John Marshall's court held otherwise.
The case, however, embodied a deft and typical Marshall compromise. A New York insolvency law of 1811 was the subject of the
case. The court threw it out, as an impairment of the obligation of
contracts, insofar as it discharged contracts and debts entered into
before the act had been passed. State insolvency laws were not held
illegal *per se*. But they would have to meet the court's exacting
standards; they must not impair legitimate business expectations
retroactively; they must not strangle the instruments of credit.

State insolvency laws heavily favored debtors. Yet the same legislatures who passed these laws passed lien laws; and were attentive
to certain forms of creditors' rights, in lean years as well as in fat.
State governments were poor; they could make only limited use of
subsidy and tax. But they did have power to bind and to loose, to
create legal rights and impose legal duties. Sometimes this power
could serve in place of direct intervention with money. To attract
the capital that debtors so desperately desired, some aids to creditors were essential, but not too much. Debtors had to be relieved in
times of crisis—but again, not so as to murder the economy forever.
At any moment, the state of the law reflected the results of this
ambivalence, of this crude push-and-pull of interests for control of
the law of insolvency and creditors' rights.

40 *Ibid.*, p. 36.
41 4 Wheat. 122 (1819).

CONTRACT

The 19th century was the golden age of the law of contract.[42] As late as Blackstone, contract occupied only a tiny corner of the temple of common law. Blackstone devoted a whole volume to land law, but a few pages at most to informal, freely negotiated bargains.[43] In the 19th century, contract law, both in England and America, made up for lost time. This was a natural development. The law of contract was a body of law well suited to a market economy. It was the general branch of law that made and applied rules for arm's-length bargains, in a free, impersonal market. The decay of feudalism and the rise of capitalist economy made the law of contract possible; and the age of Adam Smith made it indispensable. After 1800, contract greedily swallowed up other parts of the law. Land law remained vitally important, of course. But land dealings were more and more treated contractually. Special rules still governed deeds, leases, and other kinds of conveyance; but these documents were now called "contracts" and were subjected to many general doctrines of contract law.

The amazing expansion of the contract clause also illustrates the voracious appetite of the concept of contract. The Constitution forbade states from impairing the obligation of a contract. But what was a contract? The Supreme Court gave broad and unexpected answers. A legislative land grant, a college charter, even a legislative exemption from tax: all these constituted contracts.[44] In part, these cases used the concept as a metaphor, as a tool of the constitutional trade. The root notion was no metaphor, however. The state was duty-bound to support a broad, free market; to do so, business needed the right to rely on the stability of arrangements legally made, at least in the short and middle run. The contract clause guaranteed precisely that kind of stability. The root notion of the growing law of contract was basically the same. Freely made bargains would be honored and, if necessary, en-

[42] On the meaning and role of contract law in the 19th century, see in general, Lawrence M. Friedman, *Contract Law in America* (1965).

[43] He did devote somewhat more space to doctrines of commercial law, which were also concerned with economic exchange.

[44] Respectively, *Fletcher* v. *Peck*, 6 Cranch 87 (1810); *Dartmouth College* v. *Woodward*, 4 Wheat. 518 (1819); *Piqua Branch of the State Bank of Ohio* v. *Knoop*, 16 How. 369 (1853).

forced. There would be no *ex-post-facto* tampering with bargains, for whatever reason.

Contract as a branch of law can best be called residual; it dealt with those areas of business life not otherwise regulated. Its cardinal principle was to give to agreements whatever full effect parties meant them to have. But the search for "assent" was a search for objective reality, not merely for subjective intention. A contract was defined as a "meeting of the minds," but this phrase must not be taken too literally. The law emphasized the document itself, if there was one, and the plain meaning of its words, just as it did in land law or the law of negotiable instruments, and probably for similar reasons. For example, a rule, which came to be called the parol-evidence rule, shut off any evidence that might contradict the terms of a written document, if it had been drawn up in final form. As Theophilus Parsons explained, "the parties write the contract when they are ready to do so, for the very purpose of including all that they have finally agreed upon, and excluding everything else." If evidence of "previous intention" or earlier conversations were allowed, "it would obviously be of no use to reduce a contract to writing, or to attempt to give it certainty and fixedness in any way." [45] In *Mumford* v. *M'Pherson* (New York, 1806), the buyer of a ship complained that he had been orally promised that "the ship was completely copper-fastened." The bill of sale contained no such promise. The parol-evidence rule prevented the buyer from winning his case; where a contract "is reduced to writing," said the court, "everything resting in parol becomes thereby extinguished." [46]

Another major principle of contract law was its insistence on a true bargain between the parties. One party must have made an offer, which the other must have literally accepted. And offer and acceptance had to be glued together with a mysterious substance called *consideration*. Consideration was a term of many meanings; it signified, among other things, the *quid pro quo,* the exchange element of the contract. "The common law . . . gives effect only to contracts that are founded on the mutual exigencies of men, and does not compel the performance of any merely gratuitous engagements." [47] But it was an element whose presence and "adequacy" were not to be measured by the court. If one man ex-

45 Theophilus Parsons, *The Law of Contracts* (3rd ed., 1857), Vol. II, p. 57.
46 *Mumford* v. *M'Pherson,* 1 Johns. R. 414 (N.Y., 1806).
47 Theron Metcalf, *Principles of the Law of Contracts* (1874), p. 161.

changed ten dollars in consideration for a tract of land worth (apparently) vastly more, the law was not to interfere. For purposes of the law of contract, price as fixed by the parties was conclusive proof of objective market value. As in sales law, where courts believed themselves bound by *caveat emptor,* contract courts insisted that no inquiry could be made into the price and the terms of the bargain. On the other hand, mere "moral" obligations, with no element of exchange, could not be enforced. When one part owner of a brig, the *Sea Nymph,* promised to buy insurance for the brig, and forgot, and the ship was lost, he was not liable to the other owner. When a father gave a note to one son who was "not so wealthy as his brothers," and "had met with losses," that note too could not be enforced.[48] But some cases showed results much less unyielding on both scores. For one thing, in a broad market, not everyone who made a contract was a hard, shrewd businessman. In some cases, the unsophisticated, the amateurs, the weak—widows and orphans—sued on or defended claims in contract. Judges were only human. In particular cases, the rigor of the rules was bent. In the long run, the rules of consideration, which had seemed to be made of the toughest stone, were worn away.

In general, the law of contract was not as technical as land law or civil procedure. It had little jargon of its own. Its rules were few, and departed less from common sense than the rules of other fields of law. Contract law asked for very little; agreements, to be enforced, had to have a definite shape, but the law of contract was itself relatively passive and amorphous. There was therefore little need for trans-Atlantic differences. Of all the staple fields, contract was perhaps the most similar on both sides of the water. It was also one of the most rigorously common law. Few statutes intruded upon it. Of these few, the old statute of frauds (1677) was perhaps the most notable. The statute listed certain classes of contracts which could not be enforced, unless they were in writing and signed by the party "to be charged therewith," or his agent. The classes included land contracts, contracts "to answer for the debt, default, or miscarriage" of another person; contracts for the sale of goods above a minimum value (fifty dollars in New York). The states adopted the statute almost verbatim.[49] In one sense, the stat-

---

48 *Thorne* v. *Deas,* 4 Johns. R. 84 (N.Y., 1809); *Fink* v. *Cox,* 18 Johns. R. 145 (N.Y., 1820).

49 There were some local variations. In New York, contracts that offended the statute were "void" rather than (as in England) merely unenforceable. Rev. Stats. N.Y. 1836, Vol. II, p. 70. This difference was not of much moment.

ute of frauds was hardly a statute at all. It was so heavily warped by "interpretation" that it had become little more than a set of common-law rules, worked out in great detail by the common-law courts.

The statute of frauds has been criticized as an anachronism. This venerable law is now just short of its three-hundredth birthday, still under attack as empty formality. Formality it was, but not quite empty. To require land contracts, in 1800 or 1850, to be in writing, was not unreasonable; nor was it out of tune with the way land law was developing. An orderly land market (people thought) required orderly form: simple, standard deeds, duly recorded. In the state of the market, oral land deals were an abomination. What was valued was not form for form's sake, but useful form. The statute of frauds survived; other formalities, which had no purpose or place, disappeared from the law of contract. Among them was that ancient device, the seal. Early contract law paid great homage to the seal. Sealed documents were specially treated and favored in the law; the seal, for example, "imported" consideration, which meant that no further proof of consideration was needed when a document was sealed. In the United States, few people actually owned and used a seal; and literacy was high enough to undercut the need for this device. Strictly speaking, a seal meant an impression in wax; but in some states, any scrawl or scroll on paper was good enough. In New York, Chancellor Kent was insistent on the traditional method, wax and all.[50] But this was probably because he was an enemy of the seal, and wanted to kill it with strictness.[51] Later, state statutes were passed that undercut considerably the meaning of the seal. In New York, by the close of the period, a seal was "only . . . presumptive evidence of a sufficient consideration"; its effect could be "rebutted in the same manner, and to the same extent, as if [the] instrument were not sealed." [52] Sentiment and tradition had little place in commercial law; only the fittest and most functional survived.

[50] *Warren* v. *Lynch,* 5 Johns. R. 239 (1810).
[51] Joseph Dorfman, "Chancellor Kent and the Developing American Economy," 61 Columbia L. Rev. 1290, 1305 (1961).
[52] Rev. Stats. N.Y. 1836, Vol. II, p. 328.

(CHAPTER VII)

CRIME AND PUNISHMENT:
AND A FOOTNOTE ON TORT

The American Revolution, whatever else was at issue, fed on resentment against English oppression. Like all revolutions, it was a
struggle for control of the reins of power. The criminal law is one
of the levers through which governments bring power to bear on
the individual citizen. The Revolutionary leaders, quite naturally,
identified oppression with abuse of criminal law, and identified the
rights of man with basic rights to fair criminal trial. The Bill of
Rights, as we have seen, contained a minicode of criminal procedure. The late 18th century, moreover, was a period in which intellectuals began to rethink the premises on which criminal law
rested. Great reformers—men like Cesare Beccaria, whose *Treatise
on Crime and Punishment* was written in Italy in 1764—suggested
that the premises were wrong, and argued for a more enlightened
criminal law.[1]

Reform ideas left an imprint on the early state constitutions.
Section 38, of the liberal Pennsylvania constitution of 1776, stated
that "the future legislature" had the duty to "reform" the "penal
laws." Punishment must be made "in some cases less sanguinary,
and in general more proportionate to the crimes." Enlightened
opinion was revolted by the severity of criminal codes. The Bill of
Rights outlawed cruel and unusual punishment. "No wise legislature," said the New Hampshire constitution of 1784, "will affix the
same punishment to the crimes of theft, forgery and the like, which
they do to those of murder and treason. . . . [A] multitude of
sanguinary laws is both impolitic and unjust. The true design of
all punishments being to reform, not to exterminate, mankind"
(art. 1, sec. 18).

Of course, these were mere exhortations. Real penal reform was

[1] Marcello T. Maestro, *Voltaire and Beccaria as Reformers of Criminal Law*
(1942), pp. 51–72.

not easy to achieve. Pennsylvania's 1776 constitution was not implemented for ten years. In 1786, the death penalty was abolished for robbery, burglary, and sodomy. In 1790, a new, more conservative constitution omitted the clause on penal reform, and the act of 1786 was repealed. But in 1794, Pennsylvania enacted an important, innovative law about murder. The statute stated that the "several offenses, which are included under the general denomination of murder, differ . . . greatly from each other in the degree of their atrociousness." The statute then proceeded to distinguish between two different "degrees" of murder. Murder "in the first degree" was murder "perpetrated by means of poison, or by lying in wait, or by any other kind of wilful, deliberate, or premeditated killing, or which shall be committed in the perpetration, or attempt to perpetrate, any arson, rape, robbery, or burglary." All other murder was murder in the second degree. Only murder in the first degree was punishable by death.[2] This idea of degrees was borrowed, first in Virginia, then in Ohio (1824), New York (1827), and Missouri (1835). Some states (for example, Missouri), also divided manslaughter into degrees.

The agitation in Pennsylvania was part of a wider movement, which wanted to do away with the death penalty altogether.[3] In the new penology, the proper goal of criminal law was deterrence of crime and rehabilitation of the criminal. Death was dubious as a general deterrent, and as an agent of rehabilitation, impossible. It had no place, then, in a rational system of law. These propositions were put forward with great vigor, but they probably never commanded a majority of articulate people. Many, then as now, put the case strongly on the other side—people like the "citizens of Albany," who, by petition in 1842, asked the New York legislature not to do away with the death penalty for murder:

> The Penalties inflicted by human law, having their foundation in the intrinsic ill-desert of crime, are in their nature vindictive as well as corrective. . . . Beyond all question the murderer deserves to die. . . . Death is the fitting penalty for murder; fitting because, in addition to its correspondence with the enormity of the crime, it must needs be more efficacious than any other, in preventing its repetition . . . God has revealed to us His will,

[2] On the statute in general, see Edwin R. Keedy, "History of the Pennsylvania Statute Creating Degrees of Murder," 97 Univ. Pa. L. Rev. 759 (1949).

[3] See, in general, David B. Davis, "The Movement to Abolish Capital Punishment in America, 1787–1861," 63 Am. Hist. Rev. 23 (1957).

both through the laws of reason and conscience, and in his written word, that the murderer should be put to death.[4]

Judging by the results, neither side carried the day. The penal codes changed (quite dramatically in some instances), but the death penalty was not fully abolished in the majority of the states. In 1800, Kentucky restricted it to murder. Edward Livingston had no provision for capital punishment in the penal code he wrote for Louisiana; but the code was never enacted. In 1837, Maine passed a statute which *almost* went the whole distance. A man under sentence of death would be placed in the state prison, in "solitary imprisonment and hard labor." He could not be executed for one year. The whole record of his case had to be certified to the governor; and the death sentence would be carried out only if the governor issued a warrant, under the great seal of the state, "directed to the Sheriff of the County wherein the State Prison shall or may be situated, commanding the said Sheriff to cause execution to be done." [5] In 1845, Michigan became the first state to abolish capital punishment completely, followed by Wisconsin. All other states kept the death penalty; but they drastically shortened their list of capital crimes. In South Carolina, 165 crimes carried the death penalty in 1813. By 1825, only fifty-one, by 1838, only thirty-two, and by 1850, only twenty-two crimes remained in this group.[6]

In these states, the death penalty was not an everyday matter; yet men and women continued to be hanged—and hanged publicly, before morbid or festive crowds. A hanging was an occasion, a spectacle. People eagerly watched the trip to the gallows, eagerly listened to the last speech of the condemned man, when, as sometimes occurred, he spoke from the shadow of the gallows.

Liberal reformers and humanitarians had led the movement to abolish the death penalty; but a strong practical argument could be made for taking the blood out of criminal law. Severe penalties were not terribly effective, because they were not consistently applied. And their very severity distorted the working of criminal justice. A jury, squeezed between two distasteful choices, death or acquittal, often acquitted the guilty. The New Hampshire consti-

4 *Memorial to the Legislature,* N.Y. Senate Documents, Vol. 4, 1842, Doc. No. 97, pp. 21–39.

5 Laws Maine 1837, ch. 292.

6 Jack K. Williams, *Vogues in Villainy: Crime and Retribution in Ante-Bellum South Carolina* (1959), p. 100. In general, there were more capital crimes in the South than in the North. Some of the difference is accounted for by the special, severe laws relating to slaves and free Negroes.

tution of 1784, criticizing "sanguinary laws," voiced a fear that "where the same undistinguishing severity is exerted against all offences; the people are led to forget the real distinction in the crimes themselves, and to commit the most flagrant with as little compunction as they do those of the lightest dye" (part 1, art. 18). In South Carolina, the typical defendant in a homicide case was either acquitted or found guilty only of manslaughter. In one district, thirty-three men were tried on murder indictments between 1844 and 1858. Eighteen were acquitted, ten found guilty of manslaughter; only five were convicted of murder.[7]

This gap between indictment and conviction probably prevailed in other parts of the country. The problem was not harsh punishments in themselves, but formal harshness compared to what the moral sense of the community allowed. Severe penal codes are often instruments of repressive policy, imposed by the rulers on the ruled. In the United States, however, there was a greater degree of overlap between the rulers and the ruled than in England. This led to much looseness in the actual use of penal measures. Moreover, a group may be less severe on its own forms of deviance than on the deviance of outsiders, particularly outsiders whom the group regards as inferior. Juries in America were more tolerant of violations of game laws than the king and his servants would have been; on the other hand, the slave codes, which dealt with a class outside of power, were more bloody in theory and deed than the ordinary law of crimes.

A system of criminal justice is more than rules on paper. It is also a plan for distribution of power among judges, jurors, legislators, and others. In American legal theory, jury power was enormous, and subject to few controls. There was a maxim of law that the jury was judge both of law and of fact in criminal cases. This idea was particularly strong in the first, Revolutionary generation, when memories of royal justice were fresh. In some states the rule lasted a long time, and in Maryland, the slogan was actually imbedded in the constitution.[8] But the rule came under savage attack from some judges and other authorities. There was fear that the rule, if taken seriously, would destroy the "chances of uniformity of adjudication." It also threatened the *power* of judges. By the end of the period, many states, by statute or decision, had repudiated the

[7] Williams, *op. cit.*, p. 38.

[8] Md. const. 1851, art. 10, sec. 5. It was a common provision that juries were judges of fact and law in "prosecutions or indictments for libel," for example, N.J. const. 1844, art. 1, sec. 5.

doctrine.[9] In any event, the maxim probably meant very little in practice. Juries did not divide their verdicts into separate bundles of fact and of law. The maxim did recognize explicitly that the jury held ultimate power to make decisions about crime and criminal law. Juries were not afraid to exercise this power. In South Carolina, according to Jack K. Williams, "the same jury which would change a murderer's indictment to manslaughter would condemn a common thief to the gallows without hesitation," if so inclined.[10] On the other hand, the jury could be quite cavalier about the letter of the law, not to mention the facts of the world. In *State* v. *Bennet* (1815), a South Carolina jury found as fact that the goods John Bennet had stolen were worth "less . . . than twelve pence," even though all the witnesses had sworn they were "of much greater value." This "pious perjury" let the jury find Bennet guilty of petty larceny, rather than grand larceny, which would have sent him to the gallows. The appeal court affirmed the jury's right to do as it pleased.[11] This same process had made England's long list of capital crimes random and toothless in operation. This type of behavior has been called jury lawlessness; but there is something strange in calling lawless a power so carefully built into law. Jury power meant that a measure of penal "reform" could take place without formal change in legal institutions. Jerome Hall has suggested that, as social attitudes toward criminals and crime begin to change, the changes first appear in the administration of criminal justice; penal "reform"—enacted laws and new rules—follows as a "ratification of practices" already developed.[12]

The South Carolina experience, studied by Jack Williams, shows that few people were convicted in the 19th century, compared to the number indicted. Even fewer men were actually punished, because the governor used his pardoning power lavishly. Today, indictment usually leads to conviction, and pardons are relatively rare. Police and prosecutors filter out the weakest cases; most of these never get to court. Most of those accused plead guilty to the charge brought against them, or to some lesser crime. Judge and jury played *more* of a role in the screening process in the 19th century, partly because police and prosecutor staffs were weak. They were at best on the brink of professionalism. Cities did not

9 See Francis Wharton, *A Treatise on the Criminal Law of the United States* (4th ed., 1857), pp. 1115–25.

10 Williams, *op. cit.*, p. 39.

11 *State* v. *Bennet*, 3 Brevard (S. Car.) 515 (1815).

12 Jerome Hall, *Theft, Law, and Society* (2nd ed., 1952), p. 140.

even have police forces until late in the period, if at all—in Boston
not until 1838, under Mayor Samuel Eliot; before that, the watch-
men and constables of Boston did not and could not hope to cope
with "the incendiary, burglar, and the lawlessly violent." [13] In
rural areas, there was no professional enforcement at all.

The jury system had its faults. Outcomes were unprofessional
and unpredictable. The rules of evidence were one way the law attempted to keep the jury under control. We have described how a
system of checks and balances, in the trial process, grew almost cancerously. It was in criminal justice that the system of checks and
balances worked, *par excellence*. Judge was played off against jury,
state against citizen, county against state; state against federal government. Every master had to submit to another master. Whatever
its benefits, such a system, from the standpoint of any particular
group, had the defect that one could never be sure that policies,
however well formulated, would be actually carried out. This was
one reason for the periodic outbursts of lynching and vigilantes.
These cracks in law and order were no accidents. The degeneracy
(or overvigor) of judge, jury, state, or national authority sometimes reached the point where justice (as defined by the vigilantes)
demanded that "the public" take the law into its hands. Vigilantes
and lynch mobs, in other words, were pathologies of a system with
too many checks and balances for public opinion. Vigilantes flourished in the South. Here the legal culture nurtured them. Lawlessness was a way of life; violent crime was common; men habitually
walked the streets carrying guns. Vigilantes were the logical negative of the governor's power to pardon. The pardoning power was
itself one kind of check and balance; the mob was another. In
Montgomery, Alabama, for example, a vigilante group called the
Regulating Horn sprang up in the 1820's. The men blew horns to
summon the rest of the group. They gave suspects a hearing on the
spot. If they found a man "guilty," they tarred and feathered him,
and rode him out of town on a rail. Violence can be an addictive
habit; with success came excess: the Regulating Horn lost legitimacy, and community tolerance evaporated. After that, they were
doomed to fail.[14]

In South Carolina, the abolitionists were the prime target of
vigilantes in the 1840's. Here mob rule luxuriated in the cleft between official, national doctrine, and opinion in the local commu-

[13] Roger Lane, *Policing the City: Boston, 1822–1885* (1967), p. 34.
[14] Jack Williams, "Crime and Punishment in Alabama 1819–1840," 6 Ala. R.
1427 (1953).

nity. The abolitionists were guilty of no crime, except that they offended Southern opinion. The Southern slave patrols, on the other hand, were legitimized lynch law. There was no precise Northern equivalent. But the South was not the only region of bloodshed. Riots, mock law, and mob violence were a dark stain on the whole country, crossing every border, entering every state. Between 1830 and 1860 "at least 35 major riots occurred in the four cities of Baltimore, Philadelphia, New York, and Boston." [15]

The strength of the idea of checks and balances was also one of the factors that impelled penal law toward codification. To build up the power of citizen against state, rules of criminal law had to be open and knowable. The criminal law therefore tended to become highly codified. Codification, as the Puritan magistrates found, can be looked at as a means of controlling authorities. The same theory was behind codification of penal law in Europe, after the shock waves of the French Revolution.

The common law was supposed to rest on the community's moral consensus, refined by the collective mind of the judges. Courts had invented and elaborated doctrines of crime at common law, just as they had elaborated other sorts of doctrine. But the common-law crime was potentially an instrument of oppression. Common-law decisions were in a sense retroactive; and judges were less subject to public control than legislators. Statutory rules, on the other hand, were prospective only; and they were enacted by the people's representatives. The way the king's judges had behaved, in England and in the colonies, made it easy to disapprove of the power of judges to invent and define new crimes. There were instances on record where the concept was used in this country, too. In *Kanavan's case* (Maine, 1821), the defendant dropped the dead body of a child into the Kennebec River.[16] No statute covered the case explicitly; but the highest court of Maine affirmed the man's conviction. An appeal court in Tennessee sustained an indictment for "eavesdropping" in 1808.[17] But the concept of the common-law crime was in retreat during the whole of the 19th century.

There were special reasons to object to the idea of a *federal* common-law crime. The concept was completely and early exploded.

[15] Richard Maxwell Brown, "Historical Patterns of Violence in America," in Hugh D. Graham and Ted R. Gurr, eds., *Violence in America: Historical and Comparative Perspectives* (1969), pp. 45, 54.

[16] 1 Greenl. (Me.) 226 (1821).

[17] *State* v. *Williams,* 2 Overton (Tenn.) 108 (1808).

The case was *United States* v. *Hudson and Goodwin* (1812);[18] defendants were indicted for "a libel on the President and Congress of the United States, contained in the Connecticut Courant of the 7th of May, 1806, charging them with having in secret voted $2,000,000 as a present to Bonaparte, for leave to make a treaty with Spain." No statute covered such an "offense" against the federal government. The Supreme Court held that no federal court was "vested with jurisdiction over any particular act done by an individual in supposed violation of the peace and dignity of the sovereign power. The legislative authority of the Union must first make an act a crime, affix a punishment to it, and declare the court that shall have jurisdiction of the offense." If federal prosecutors and judges could define crimes for themselves and punish them, enormous (and in this instance, unwelcome) power would accrue to the central government.

Codification was only a partial curb on the power of the judges. Judges lost power to invent new crimes; but the common law still *defined* the precise meaning and application of old crimes, like rape or theft. The strong, sometimes freewheeling power of judges to interpret the laws remained. The judges developed and used *canons of construction*—rules of interpretation—that maximized their discretion and authority. One such canon declared that penal statutes had to be narrowly construed, that is, limited to the smallest possible compass their language would bear. The canon made some sense; otherwise, retroactive, judge-made criminal law could be brought in through the back door, so to speak. Only those acts ought to be crimes which were plainly so labeled. Courts should not widen the coverage of a penal law beyond the unvarnished meaning of its words. Criminal law had to be known and knowable, without subtlety and artifice:

> The law to bind (the prisoner) should first be *prescribed;* that is, not only willed by the legislature, but should also be announced, and clearly and plainly published, that every citizen, if he would, could learn its meaning and know the measure of its punishment.

This was said by counsel at the trial of one Timothy Heely of New York, charged with stealing a lottery ticket. The statute made it a crime to steal a "public security." The court agreed with counsel that a state lottery ticket was not a public security, and let

18 7 Cranch 32 (1812).

Heely go.[19] The canon of strict construction, in theory, expressed the humble role of judges, subordinate to the people and their elected representatives. But there was no short-run control over whether courts used the canon or avoided it. Hence its application was in fact if not theory a matter of discretion. And what was or was not a strict or narrow construction was itself a difficult question, which gave still more discretion to the courts.

THE SUBSTANTIVE LAW OF CRIMES

In English law, treason had been a complex, protean concept, used to suppress all sorts of persons or groups defined as enemies of state. It was treason to levy war on the kingdom; it was treason, too, to violate the king's (unmarried) eldest daughter. It was treason to alter or clip coins; or to color "any silver current coin . . . to make it resemble a gold one." [20] When war broke out, the colonists seized this terrible weapon for themselves. New York, for example, passed a fire-breathing law in 1781: anyone who preached, taught, spoke, wrote, or printed that the king had or ought to have dominion over New York thereby committed a "Felony without Benefit of Clergy," punishable by death or by banishment.[21] When the war ended, passions cooled. Maryland, Massachusetts, New York, Pennsylvania and Vermont all provided, in their early constitutions, that the legislatures had no power to attaint any person of treason.[22] The federal Constitution radically restricted this king of crimes: it defined its content, once and for all, and hedged treason trials about with procedural safeguards. Treason against the United States "shall consist only in levying War against them, or in adhering to their Enemies, giving them Aid and Comfort. No Person shall be convicted of Treason unless on the testimony of two Witnesses to the same overt Act, or on Confession in open Court." [23]

Treason was a special crime, with unusual political significance. The shrinking law of treason mirrored a prevailing theory of criminal law. A total state, even a semitotal state, has trouble distinguishing between treason and ordinary crime. In the Soviet Union,

[19] *People* v. *Heely,* New York Judicial Repository, 277 (1819).

[20] 4 Blackstone, *Commentaries,* 90.

[21] J. Willard Hurst, "Treason in the United States," 58 Harv. L. Rev. 226 (1944); see also Bradley Chapin, *The American Law of Treason, Revolutionary and Early National Origins* (1964).

[22] Hurst, *op. cit.,* p. 256.

[23] U.S. Const., Art. 3, sec. 3.

for example, it is a crime against the state, severely punished, to deal in currency, or to steal factory property (which is all state-owned). The United States took a strikingly different path. It shrank the concept of state crime to an almost irreducible minimum. The men who drafted penal codes were willing to accept a lot of slippage in enforcement, to protect the innocent, and (even more) to keep the government in check. No doubt much of this liberality was only on paper. The Sedition Law of 1798, passed by a nervous, partisan federal government, showed that historical fears were not groundless.[24] But the theory helped determine how government was structured, and what resources government was given to do its job.

Not that the criminal law was not important in the United States. By any measure, the *number* of acts defined as criminal grew steadily from 1776 to 1847, despite the decline in the use of the common-law crime. The classic crimes (theft, murder, rape, arson) remained on the books. There were great numbers of economic crimes, and laws defining public morality; and new ones were constantly added. The revised statutes of Indiana of 1831—a fair sample—made it a crime to allow epsom salts "to remain unenclosed and exposed to the stock, cattle or horses of the neighborhood." It was a crime in Indiana to "alter the mark or brand" of domestic animals; to sell retail liquor without a license; to ferry a person across a creek or river for money, within two miles of any licensed ferry. It was a crime, too, to keep "either of the gaming tables called A.B.C., or E.O. Tables, billiard table, roulette, spanish needle, shuffle board, [and] faro bank." It was an offense, punishable by fine, to "vend any merchandize which may not be the product of the United States, without having a license." Profane swearing was a crime; so was "open and notorious adultery or fornication." Major statutes often included, as a final clause, a provision punishing violation or frustration of the policy expressed.

One usually thinks of a crime as an act which offends some deep-seated moral sense. But crime can also be neutrally defined, as any behavior punished at public expense and through criminal process. An unpaid seller, or a person who slips on the ice, sues the buyer or landowner at his own expense, and on his own initiative. The costs of punishing a murderer are socialized, partly because violence is thought to be a danger to everyone, not only the victim's little circle of family and friends. Murder was once privately en-

[24] See, in general, James Morton Smith, *Freedom's Fetters: the Alien and Sedition Laws and American Civil Liberties* (1956).

forced. But private justice was not always effective, and when it was, it escalated the letting of blood. Regulatory and economic crimes are enforced at public expense and initiative, but for rather different reasons. If a man sells ten baskets of defective strawberries to ten different people, it would not pay any one buyer to sue the seller. The lawsuit would eat up far more money than could possibly be recovered. If the sheriff and district attorney—public servants, paid by the state—had the power to enforce the rules, they might deter the seller's behavior far more effectively. This is quite apart from whether or not selling spoiled strawberries is considered especially immoral or not. Criminal process, then, can act as a kind of crude, undifferentiated administrative agency. This (largely inarticulate) conception was one of the reasons for the flowering of the regulatory crime. Economic crimes never gave trial courts much work. They never captured the imagination of the public. Criminal provisions of regulatory laws were not always even *meant* to be rigorously enforced. They were meant more as a last resort, as a threat to persistent and flagrant violators. When administrative justice developed in later generations, some of these "crimes" actually disappeared from the books.

The *relative* rise of the economic crime, on the statute books, was probably an external sign of a real change in the center of gravity of the criminal law. If crime was sin—fornication, blasphemy—before the Revolution, it gradually shifted to concern for protection of private property and furtherance of the community's economic business. William E. Nelson's research, in Massachusetts, supports this notion. Nelson found that prosecutions for fornication, Sunday violation, and the like declined after 1780; prosecutions for theft, on the other hand, rose. By 1800, more than forty per cent of all prosecutions in seven counties studied were for theft; only seven per cent for offenses against morality. The criminal "was no longer envisioned as a sinner against God, but rather as one who preyed upon the property of his fellow citizens." [25] From this attitude, however, it was a short step to the instrumental use of criminal law, the use of criminal law, in other words, as a means of fostering economic growth.

[25] William E. Nelson, *The Americanization of the Common Law during the Revolutionary Era: A Study of Legal Change in Massachusetts, 1760–1830*, pp. 344–57.

THE CRIME OF PUNISHMENT: THE AMERICAN PRISON

The typical jail of 1776 was a corrupt, inefficient institution—a warehouse for the dregs of society. Men and women were thrown into common cell rooms. Administration was totally unprofessional. Dirt and ordure were everywhere. Discipline was lax; yet brutality went unchecked. The new wave of theory about crime included new theories of punishment. Prison, it was agreed by penologists, should act to reform the criminal. As prisons were constituted, they could hardly be expected to improve the inmate in any way. To do the job, radical new structures were needed. In 1790, the Walnut Street prison, in Philadelphia, was remodeled as a showplace for an enlightened policy. Its chief novelty was a "penitentiary House" (the name is significant) containing sixteen solitary or separate cells:

> Each cell was 8 feet long, 6 feet wide, and 10 feet high, had two doors, an outer wooden one, and an inside iron door. . . . Each cell had a large leaden pipe that led to the sewer, and thus formed a very primitive kind of a closet. The window of the cell was secured by blinds and wire, to prevent anything being passed in or out.[26]

Some convicts in the prison worked in shops during the day; but the convicts in the solitary cells did no work at all. This lonely asceticism would presumably lead the prisoners of Walnut Street to rethink their lives, and meditate on self-improvement.

In New York, the north wing of Auburn prison was remodeled in 1821 to conform to advanced principles of penology. In the Auburn system, the prisoners worked together during the daytime, and slept in solitary cells at night. The Cherry Hill prison in Philadelphia (1829) was another innovation in prison styles.[27] Cherry Hill was built in the form of a grim fortress, surrounded by walls of medieval strength. Great stone arms radiated out of a central core. Each arm contained a number of individual cells connected

[26] Orlando F. Lewis, *The Development of American Prisons and Prison Customs, 1776–1845* (1922), p. 27.

[27] See in general, Negley K. Teeters and John D. Shearer, *The Prison at Philadelphia: Cherry Hill* (1957); for New York, W. David Lewis, *From Newgate to Dannemora, The Rise of the Penitentiary in New York, 1796–1848* (1965).

to tiny walled courtyards, one to a cell. The prisoners lived in cell and courtyard, utterly alone, night and day. Sometimes they wore masks. Through peepholes, the prisoners could listen to religious services. In both Auburn and Cherry Hill, absolute silence was imposed on the prisoners—a punishment more inhumane than the flogging and branding that the penitentiary supposedly supplanted.

Charles Dickens visited Cherry Hill on his American tour, and was horrified. "Those who devised this system of Prison Discipline," he remarked, "and those benevolent gentlemen who carry it into execution, do not know what it is that they are doing." This "dreadful punishment" inflicts "immense . . . torture and agony" on the prisoners. It was a "slow and daily tampering with the mysteries of the brain . . . immeasurably worse than any torture of the body." The silence, Dickens felt, was "awful. . . . Over the head and face of every prisoner who comes into this melancholy house, a black hood is drawn; and in this dark shroud . . . he is led to the cell. . . . He is a man buried alive." [28] Many prisoners were indeed reclaimed from a life of crime; they went insane in their cells. Administration also quickly degenerated. In a few years, strait jackets, iron gags, and savage beatings were a way of life at Cherry Hill.

What went wrong? There was no lack of theory; there was no lack of detail in inventing plans. The laws were models of specificity. When Massachusetts converted its state prison to the Auburn system in 1828, its statute carefully provided that

> each convict shall be allowed, for his yearly clothing, one pair of thick pantaloons, one thick jacket, one pair of thin pantaloons, one thin jacket, two pairs of shoes, two pair of socks, three shirts, and two blankets, all of a coarse kind.

The daily ration was part of the law, down to an allowance of "two ounces of black pepper" per hundred rations.[29] The pepper ration could not guarantee good government behind stone walls. Society in the 19th century, fearful of moral failure, committed to a dour theory of deterrence, intensely suspicious of power, yet governed by interest blocs, factions, markets and political smallholders, could not devise a humane prison system, let alone carry one out. What little vigor and talent was available expended itself on theory, on legislation and, occasionally, on administration at the apex of the

28 Charles Dickens, *American Notes* (1842), pp. 118, 121.
29 Mass. Laws 1828, ch. 118, secs. 14, 15.

system. The central problem was administrative failure: not enough talent, and money, and care, to make the ideal real. This was the vice from top to bottom. Local jails—county and city— were scandals; and what is more, archaic scandals. The great new prisons were wrecked in the war between the aims of reformers and the anarchic indifference of everybody else. The real power in the country did not belong to reformers. It belonged to the rest of the public: people who wanted criminals safely behind bars, out of sight. It was, indeed, this interest that explains why prison reform was possible at all. Before the Walnut Street reforms in Philadelphia in 1790, the good citizens of the city had to suffer the sight of shaven-headed men working the streets, heavily guarded, in "infamous dress . . . begging and insulting the inhabitants, collecting crowds of idle boys, and holding with them the most indecent and improper conversations." [30] Reform at least got convicts off the streets. The men of Walnut Street lived like monks, out of sight and out of mind.

Once prisoners were removed from their midst, the public lost interest, in both senses of that word. Prisons, like poorhouses and insane asylums, continued to serve primarily as storage bins for deviants. Beatings and strait jackets, like the well-meant cruelty of solitary confinement, were visited on a class of men who had no reason to expect good treatment from the world, no hope of changing that world, and no power to do so. Their interests were represented by proxies in the outside world, and their fate was determined by the strength and persistence—never great—of those proxies who stood for reform.

A FOOTNOTE ON TORT

A tort is a civil, that is, noncriminal wrong; any one of a miscellaneous collection of misdeeds that lay one open to a lawsuit. One type of action, for negligence, has come to outweigh all the others in importance. The lesser torts include assault and battery, trespass to land, and libel and slander.

All in all, tort law was not a highly developed field in 1776, or for a good many years thereafter. Not a single treatise on the law of torts was published before 1850, on either side of the Atlantic. Negligence was the merest dot on the law. Blackstone's *Commentaries* had almost nothing to say about the concept. Nathan Dane's

[30] Orlando F. Lewis, *op. cit.,* p. 18.

Abridgment, in the 1820's, treated the subject quite casually. Negligence was a kind of residual category—those torts which could not "be brought conveniently under more particular heads." Only one or two of his examples of negligence had much empirical significance: "If the owner of a ship, in the care of a pilot, through *negligence* and want of skill, sinks the ship of another, this owner is liable." [31] Indeed, well into the 19th century, Morton Horwitz has argued, the negligence concept was quite different from its later form. It referred, by and large, to failures to perform a specific duty —often a contractual one.[32] It was not defined as a failure to measure up to a general standard of care, the behavior of the reasonable man.

The explosion of tort law, and negligence in particular, must be entirely attributed to the age of engines and machines. In preindustrial society, there are few personal injuries, except for assault and battery. The machines and tools of modern man, however, blindly cripple and maim their servants. From about 1840 on, one specific machine, the railroad locomotive, generated, on its own steam (so to speak), more tort law than any other in the 19th century. The railroad engine swept like a great roaring bull through the countryside, carrying out an economic and social revolution; but it exacted a toll of thousands, injured and dead.

The existing law of tort was not prepared to bear the burden of these accidents. It had been devised with other situations in mind. American law had to work out some fresh scheme to distribute the burden of railroad accidents, among workers, citizens, companies and state. Because the job was new, the resulting law was also new, except for some continuity in phrasing.

The law developed in a way which the power-holders of the day considered socially desirable. This way, in brief, was to frame rules friendly to the growth of young businesses; or at least rules the judges thought would foster such growth. The rules put limits on enterprise liability. This was the thrust of the developing law of negligence; and there were parallel developments in other branches of law—compensation for public taking of property, and nuisance law, for example.[33] The most famous (or infamous) new doctrine was the fellow-servant rule. This was the rule that one

---

[31] Nathan Dane, *A General Abridgment and Digest of American Law,* Vol. III (1824), pp. 31, 35.

[32] Morton J. Horwitz, *Damage Judgments, Legal Liability and Economic Development Before the Civil War* (unpublished ms., 1970).

[33] This thesis is brilliantly expounded in the Horwitz essay just cited.

servant (employee) could not sue his master (employer), for injuries caused by the negligence of another employee. In the law of agency, the principal is generally liable for negligent acts of his agent:

> If an inn-keeper's servants rob his guests, the master is bound to restitution. . . . So likewise if the drawer at a tavern sells a man bad wine, whereby his health is injured, he may bring an action against the master.[34]

But this general rule was never extended to the factory and to railroad yard workers. The reason was most notably expressed in the leading American case, *Farwell* v. *Boston & Worcester Railroad Corporation* (1842).[35] Farwell was a railroad engineer. A switchman carelessly allowed a train to run off the track. Farwell lost his hand in the accident and sued the railroad, pointing out the switchman's negligence. Chief Justice Lemuel Shaw of Massachusetts wrote a brilliant opinion, denying recovery. Shaw argued that the workman who takes on a dangerous job must be held to have assumed the ordinary risks of that job. In theory, the wage rate included an adjustment for the added danger. Since that was so, the risk must be left on the person who had, for a price, voluntarily assumed it. The injured workman was thus thrown back on his own resources, or, if he had none, left to the tender mercies of the poor laws. The economic impact of railroad accidents was thereby socialized (or ignored), relieving the lines of one possible heavy cost; or so an enterprise-minded judge might have thought.

The fellow-servant rule had far-reaching consequences. An employee could not sue his employer for negligence, unless his injuries were caused by the employer's own personal misconduct, not those of the fellow servants.[36] But in factories, mines, and on railroads, any negligent conduct was likely to be conduct of a fellow servant. Factory and railroad owners and managers were not usually at the work site at all; and every year, corporate masters em-

---

[34] 1 Blackstone, *Commentaries,* p. 430. On the rise of the fellow-servant rule, see Lawrence M. Friedman and Jack Ladinsky, "Social Change and the Law of Industrial Accidents," 67 Columbia L. Rev. 50, 51–58 (1967).

[35] 45 Mass. (4 Metc.) 49 (1842). The rule was foreshadowed in *Priestley* v. *Fowler,* 3 M. & W. 1 (Ex. 1837), an English case, which did not, however, arise out of an industrial setting. *Murray* v. *South Carolina R.R.,* 26 So. Car. L. (1 McMul.) 385 (1841) was decided one year before *Farwell* but was never so influential.

[36] The injured worker could also sue the negligent worker, of course; but this was a hollow right, because the fellow servant almost certainly had no money.

ployed a higher percentage of the work force. In the years after *Farwell*, state after state adopted the fellow-servant rule. The doctrine of contributory negligence, which grew up in the first half of the 19th century, added another barrier to plaintiffs who sued in tort. If an injured party was negligent himself, even slightly, he could not rest his claim on the negligence of another. Contributory negligence applied to passenger injuries as well as to injuries to workers. This made it doubly useful to the railroads.[37]

[37] The law of torts was never quite so harsh and unyielding as its rules may have made it appear. Almost from the very first, juries, judges, and legislatures took away with their left hand what had been built up with their right. The full sweep of this countertrend appeared most clearly only after 1850. See below, Part III, Ch. VI.

(CHAPTER VIII)

THE BAR AND ITS WORKS

THE BAR

It is said that lawyers became even more unpopular during the Revolution than they had been before. If so, it was not for lack of heroes. Many lawyers were loyalists, to be sure; more than two hundred of these, perhaps, eventually left the country.[1] But, on the other side, almost half of the signers of the Declaration of Independence, and more than half of the members of the Federal Constitutional Convention were lawyers. Jefferson, Hamilton and John Adams, patriots without blemish, were lawyers.

The two groups might have canceled each other out in the public mind. If they did not, one must search deeper for causes of unpopularity. Some lawyers, not Tories themselves, defended the Tories against state confiscation laws between 1780 and 1800. Alexander Hamilton built a career by working for these unpopular clients. Yet even this fact does not carry one very far. One must look for broader social forces. Economic depression followed the end of the war. Clamor against lawyers seemed a tide that rose and fell with the business cycle. In Massachusetts, during Shay's Rebellion, there were uprisings against courts and lawyers; they seemed to be too zealous in the oppression of debtors. It was a common lay opinion that the law was all tricks and technicalities, run by unscrupulous men who built legal careers "upon the ruins of the distressed."[2] "Lawyers," wrote St. John Crèvecoeur in 1782, "are plants that will grow in any soil that is cultivated by the hands of others; and when once they have taken root they will extinguish every other vegetable that grows around them. The fortunes they daily acquire in every province, from the misfortunes of their fellow

[1] Charles Warren, *A History of the American Bar* (1912), p. 213 ff.
[2] Quoted in Oscar Handlin and Mary Handlin, *Commonwealth: A Study of the Role of Government in the American Economy, Massachusetts, 1774–1861* (rev. ed., 1969), p. 43.

citizens, are surprising! . . . They are here what the clergy were in past centuries. . . . A reformation equally useful is now wanted." [3]

At various points in history, the lawyer has been labeled a Tory, parasite, usurer, land speculator, corrupter of the legislature, note shaver, panderer to corporations, tool of the trusts, shyster, ambulance chaser, and loan shark. Some of his bad odor is due to his role as hired hand. The upper class needs lawyers and has the money to hire them. Also, lawyers were upwardly mobile men, seizers of opportunities. The American lawyer was never primarily a learned doctor of laws; he was a man of action and cunning, not a scholar. He has played a useful role, sometimes admired, but rarely loved. The role, of course, was shaped by concrete circumstances. A revolution is an attack upon a specific government; and the government in turn means specific men, in this case the local agents of the tyrant king, many of them lawyers. Later, with the rise of Jeffersonian and Jacksonian democracy, the leading political party opposed the idea of government by experts. This was a point of view that meant either limitation of the power of the bar, or opening the bar to all or more comers.

Under the pressure of American practical politics, it would have been surprising if a narrow, elitist profession grew up—a small, exclusive guild. No such profession developed. The doors to the profession were at all times relatively open. Control over admission to the bar was loose. Legal education was not very stringent. The bar became a great avenue of social advancement. Young men entered the profession for reasons not very different from those which attract them today. "Law," wrote young James Kent, "is a field which is uninteresting and boundless." It was "so encumbered with voluminous rubbish and the baggage of folios that it requires uncommon assiduity and patience to manage." Yet he pushed ahead, because law, despite its faults, "leads forward to the first stations in the State." [4]

Maxwell Bloomfield sampled death notices of lawyers, carried in the *Monthly Law Magazine,* around the end of the period. He found a rich diversity of family backgrounds. There were forty-eight in his sample. In their backgrounds were three doctors, five merchants, eleven ministers, ten farmers, two mechanics, two soldiers, eleven lawyers, and four judges. [5] Careers in law were the

3 *Letters from an American Farmer* (ed. 1904), pp. 196–7.
4 Quoted in William Kent, *Memoirs and Letters of James Kent* (1898), p. 16.
5 Maxwell Bloomfield, "Law vs. Politics: The Self-Image of the American Bar (1830–1860)," 12 Am. J. Leg. Hist. 306, 313–14 (1968).

vehicle through which poor men's sons sometimes reached wealth and position. Others, of course, tried and failed. The American myth was not that everyone succeeds, but that everyone had a chance to succeed. Some of the openness of the bar, moreover, was more formal than real, just as the Jackson ideology need not necessarily be taken at face value. Mobility at the bar did not mean, for one thing, that the bar was not stratified. In the 20th century, there is tremendous social distance between a Wall Street partner and the bottom of the bar. Studies have shown that lawyers from wealthy backgrounds are far more likely to reach the heights than lawyers from working-class homes. In 1800 or 1847, one could not measure success by the size of a lawyer's firm. But there were rich lawyers and poor lawyers in those years; there were lawyers who represented well-to-do clients and rich merchants; and there were those who squeezed out a living handling petty claims in petty courts. Some of the best, most famous lawyers came up the hard way; but all in all, good social background seemed to have been important then too. A person of Jefferson's background found it easier to get the right education and contacts than a poor man's son. He was more likely to *become* a lawyer; and more likely to become an elite of the bar. Of 2,618 trained lawyers who practiced in Massachusetts and Maine between 1760 and 1840, 71.4 per cent, or 1,859, were college-trained. There is evidence, indeed, that the bar, after the first Revolutionary generation, drew upon the children of professionals rather than farmers or laborers. Between 1810 and 1840, more than half the lawyers, who were college graduates, admitted to the bar in Massachusetts, seem to have been the sons of lawyers and judges; before 1810, the figure was about 38 per cent. The percentages with farmers or laborers in their background declined slightly at the same time.[6]

It hardly needs to be documented that some lawyers were rich and others poor. Gerard Gawalt's figures for Massachusetts show great variations in the income and property holdings of lawyers. A typical income seemed to be something less than $1,000 a year, in 1810 or 1820. But Lemuel Shaw probably grossed more than $15,000 in private practice in the late 1820's.[7]

There were many styles and types, then, of law practice. We have

[6] Gerard W. Gawalt, *Massachusetts Lawyers: A Historical Analysis of the Process of Professionalization, 1760–1840* (unpublished Ph.D. thesis, Clark University, 1969), pp. 140, 189–98.

[7] Leonard Levy, *The Law of the Commonwealth and Chief Justice Shaw* (1957), p. 17; Gawalt, *op. cit.*, pp. 214–21.

already mentioned that colorful subspecies, the frontier or Western lawyer. No frontier town was too raw and muddy for the lawyers. They were out to seek their fortune in land and litigation, sometimes even in genteel larceny. Politics had an irresistible appeal for Western lawyers, as one road to fame or to fortune, or both. Many began their careers in the West as politicians, who wangled a job in the territories. Some took up one public office after another. Lewis Cass, born in New Hampshire in 1782, received a "classical education of a high order"; taught briefly in Wilmington, Delaware; and crossed the Alleghenies in 1799, at the age of seventeen, "on foot, carrying his knapsack and seeking, unaided, and without the help of wealth or power, a new home in the wilderness of Ohio." [8] In Marietta, Ohio, he learned law in a law office. Then he became a general, a politician, and governor of Michigan.

Some lawyers wandered from town to town, almost like itinerant peddlers, until they found the right opening for their talents. David Davis, Lincoln's friend, later a justice of the United States Supreme Court, was born in Maryland. He attended Yale, studied law in a Massachusetts office, and arrived in Pekin, Illinois, in 1835. A little while later he moved to Bloomington. George Grover Wright (1820–96), who became president of the American Bar Association in 1887, was born in Indiana, in 1820, the "son of a poor man." He settled in Keosauqua, Iowa, in 1840, where, it is said, his stagecoach from Keokuk broke down.[9] Joseph G. Baldwin (1815–64), whose word pictures of frontier justice have earned him a small but honorable place in American literature, was born in Virginia, read Blackstone, settled in Dekalb, Mississippi, moved to Gainesville, Alabama, stayed put for eighteen years, then moved on to a newer frontier—San Francisco. Before he died, he was appointed to the supreme court of California.[10]

A taste for the frontier was not limited to sons of the poor. Almost all of the thirty-six members of Harvard's law class of 1835 were natives of New England and the Middle Atlantic States, mostly middle class and above. One-third of them (twelve) ended their careers in another part of the country: Michigan, California (two), Ohio (two), Louisiana (two), South Carolina, Tennessee,

[8] William T. Young, *Sketch of Life and Public Services of General Lewis Cass* (1853), pp. 18–19.

[9] James G. Rogers, *American Bar Leaders* (1932), p. 47.

[10] William A. Owens, Introduction to Joseph G. Baldwin, *The Flush Times of Alabama and Mississippi* (1957).

Georgia, Illinois, and Missouri.[11] No doubt the idea of seeking a
fortune in the West was romantically appealing; but the main reason for this shifting about was not wanderlust but ambition. It was
not easy to scratch out a living in new soil. Some lawyers, however, found a quick niche, stayed put, watched their rude villages
grow to cities, and became rich and respectable. If they lived long
enough, they wrote colorful "recollections" of bench and bar for
local historical journals and lawyers' magazines. Their practice
took patience, luck, and skill. They did not bother asking what was
or was not fit work for an attorney's pride. Whatever was lucrative
was fair game. Some, indeed, had to leave the practice for a while
or for good, to make ends meet. John Dean Caton, later chief justice of Illinois, arrived in Chicago in 1833 with fourteen dollars in
his pocket. He found a few lawyers there but little business. A
"very good lawyer," Russell E. Heacock, who had practiced down-
state, found the going so rough in Chicago that he "built a log
carpenter's shop at the corner of State and South Water Street,
where he worked at the trade which he had learned before he
studied law. He also held the office of justice of the peace." [12]

Some lawyers came West as agents for Eastern land speculators,
then later struck out on their own. Their main legal business was
the land—buying it and selling it for others, searching titles, making deeds. Land was the backbone of everyone's practice. It was
also a medium of payment. Michael Stoner hired young Henry
Clay, in 1801, to "prosecute a claim . . . to five hundred acres of
land." Clay would pay all the costs; if he won, he was to receive one
fourth of the winnings.[13] Another staple of the lawyer's practice was
collection work. Lawyers dunned and sued, both for local people
and for Easterners who held debts in the form of promissory notes.
The lawyer usually paid himself from the proceeds—if he collected. Indiana attorney Rowland, collecting two notes in 1820 for
E. Pollard, one "for 100 dollars in land-office money," the other for
$100.37, "payable in leather to be delivered four miles from
Bloomington," was to "receive the customary fees when the money
is collected, and if it is never collected then a reasonable fee for [his]
trouble." [14] As this example shows, hard money was at all times

11 Charles Warren, *History of the Harvard Law School*, Vol. III (1908), pp.
11–12.
12 John Caton, *Early Bench and Bar of Illinois* (1893), p. 2.
13 James F. Hopkins, ed., *The Papers of Henry Clay*, Vol. I (1959), pp. 59–60.
14 *Pollard* v. *Rowland*, 2 Blackf. 22 (Ind., 1826); see, for a general picture of
Western practice, William F. English, *The Pioneer Lawyer and Jurist in Missouri* (1947), pp. 65–80, 94–119.

scarce; a lawyer who got his hands on some cash would cast around for the most profitable investment. So, some frontier lawyers added to collections and land speculation the high-risk venture of lending out money at interest. For nonresidents, the Western lawyer searched titles, paid taxes, and in general looked after the absentee's affairs. He might also scramble for a share of petty criminal work.

Courtroom clients were a shifting if not shiftless lot. House counsel was unknown, though in time, successful lawyers and affluent clients did enter into an occasional retainer agreement. Almost all lawyers, then, were constantly seeking new business and were in constant need of advertisements for themselves. There was then no prohibition against advertising in the literal sense, and lawyers reached out for the public through notices in the newspaper. Word of mouth was probably a more effective way to attract good clients. The flamboyance, tricks, and courtroom antics of 19th-century lawyers were more than a matter of personality; this behavior created reputation; and a courtroom lawyer who did not impress the public and gain a reputation would be hard pressed to survive.

Since many lawyers had no settled relations with definite clients, and since so much of practice was litigation, their lives were spent in close contact with other lawyers, as colleagues, friends, and friendly enemies. Riding on circuit was a hard but rewarding school of experience, a school whose most famous alumnus was Abraham Lincoln. As John Dean Caton described it, in its Illinois version, lawyers traveled

> with the judge . . . on horseback in a cavalcade across the prairies from one county seat to another, over stretches from fifty to one hundred miles, swimming the streams when necessary. At night they would put up at log cabins in the borders of the groves, where they frequently made a jolly night of it. . . . This circuit practice required a quickness of thought and a rapidity of action nowhere else requisite in professional practice. The lawyer would perhaps scarcely light from his horse when he would be surrounded by two or three clients requiring his services. . . . It is surprising how rapidly such practice qualifies one to meet . . . emergencies.[15]

Typically, the lawyer traveled light; he took with him a few personal effects, a change of linen, a handful of lawbooks. In some

15 Caton, op. cit., p. 51.

cases, a young lawyer, too poor to buy a horse, trudged along the circuit on foot.[16]

It was not only country lawyers who went on circuit. The Supreme Court bar, mainly recruited from Pennsylvania, Maryland, and Virginia, was also an itinerant group. Peter S. DuPonceau, of Pennsylvania, described the life of these lawyers:

> counsel . . . were in the habit of going together to Washington to argue their cases . . . We hired a stage to ourselves in which we proceeded by easy journies . . . We had to travel in the depth of winter through bad roads in no very comfortable way. Nevertheless, as soon as we were out of the city, and felt the flush of air, we were like school boys in the playground on a holiday . . . Our appearance at the Bar of the Supreme Court was always a scene of triumph.[17]

But any kind of settled practice—even debt collection—was an enemy of the personal, itinerant style. The circuit-riding era slowly passed on, and its importance may have been exaggerated, thanks to its romance and color.[18]

In any event, the Eastern and Southern statesman-lawyer was a far cry from the dusty rider of the plains. Some, like Jefferson, were great squires who studied law as a gentleman's pursuit. In the North, too, there were lawyers from elite backgrounds. They formed a small but sophisticated bar of commerce, together with some upwardly mobile colleagues. These lawyers advised the great mercantile houses on matters of marine insurance and international trade. Yet, they too were basically courtroom lawyers, in practice on their own, like their poor Western cousins. Alexander Hamilton had a general practice in the late 18th century, and frequently appeared in court. He was "a very great favorite with the merchants of New York." There were many questions of marine insurance that went to court and Hamilton had an "overwhelming share" of this business.[19] According to one estimate, about five hundred lawyers practiced in New York City in 1830, when the city had a population of about 200,000.[20] Almost all of

16 John W. McNulty, "Sidney Breese, the Illinois Circuit Judge, 1835–1841," 62 J. Ill. State Historical Society 170 (1969).

17 Charles Warren, *History of the American Bar,* p. 256.

18 Daniel H. Calhoun, *Professional Lives in America* (1965), pp. 59–87.

19 The quotations are from Chancellor Kent, in William Kent, *Memoirs and Letters of James Kent* (1898), p. 317. On Hamilton's career, see the two volumes of Julius Goebel, ed., *The Law Practice of Alexander Hamilton* (Vol. I, 1964; Vol. II, 1969).

20 Henry W. Taft, *A Century and a Half at the New York Bar* (1938), p. 7.

these men were solo practitioners. There were a handful of two-man partnerships, but no firms of any size. In a few of these partnerships, the partners began to specialize. George Washington Strong and John Wells formed a partnership in 1818; the two partners soon agreed on a rough division of labor. One was a better advocate in court; the other preferred to stay in the office and prepare necessary papers and briefs.[21]

At least three embryo partnerships of old New York were ancestor firms of large "factories" of law on Wall Street. One of these, forefather of the Cravath firm of New York, has been carefully traced by Robert T. Swaine.[22] To Swaine we owe a valuable picture of the practice of R. M. Blatchford, one of the founding fathers, in the years 1826–32, when he was still practicing alone. Blatchford's practice was exceptional but probably not unique. It was, in a way, far more like its Wall Street descendants than like the work of Blatchford's contemporaries in small towns, or out West, or at the petty criminal courts of New York. Blatchford in 1826 had become American financial agent and counsel for the Bank of England; this connection brought him "a great deal of business from English solicitors whose clients had American investments." He became counsel, too, to the second Bank of the United States. Blatchford went to court once in a while; but most of his work was as an adviser. When he formed a partnership with his brother, in 1832, he again dropped out of litigation. The early years of this brotherly firm were spent in large measure on "office practice—advising on legal problems and drafting legal documents affecting industry, trade and finance. . . . There were many loan transactions, commercial and on real estate mortgages, much of the latter business coming from English clients, who also sent occasional marine insurance and other admiralty matters. There was also much collection business for City merchants and for English exporters."

Blatchford was active as a professional trustee, and probated estates of wealthy clients. Later, as industry grew, there were cases where businesses needed loans "too large for a single lender." Here "the practice developed of pledging or conveying the security to a trustee for the joint benefit of a group of lenders. Blatchford developed a business as trustee in such transactions—the forerunner of the modern corporate trust. In the '30s there also appeared a form

21 Taft, *op. cit.*, p. 22.
22 Robert T. Swaine, *The Cravath Firm and Its Predecessors, 1819–1947* (Vol. I, 1946).

of investment security as a means of attracting British capital to America of the same general nature as the modern investment trust. In this field, too, Blatchford was active, both as a trustee and as a lawyer. Out of that activity grew the North American Trust & Banking Company litigation which was in the New York courts from 1841 to 1858 and was one of the Blatchford firm's principal matters after . . . 1854." [23]

Blatchford was one kind of wave of the future. Few lawyers could afford to stray so far from litigation. Courtroom advocacy, both East and West, was the main road to prestige, to recognition as a leader of the bar. It was surely the only way for a lawyer, as a lawyer, to become famous. Daniel Webster was a celebrity; Blatchford was not. Webster, the courtroom lawyer, lives on in literature and in folklore. Chancellor Kent, who was learned and influential, but whose courtroom delivery was "most shocking," [24] is remembered only by specialists and scholars.

Eloquence in court gained attention, and attention gained clients. There was a ready audience too. In the days before radio and television, the public appreciated a good trial and a good courtroom speech. In the provinces, when the court arrived at the county seat, law broke up the monotony of life. In the rather dull society of Washington, ambassadors, congressmen, and the wives of politicians crowded into the Supreme Court galleries to hear the giants of the bar hold forth. "Scarcely a day passes in Court," Story wrote in 1812, "in which parties of ladies do not occasionally come in and hear, for a while, the arguments of learned counsel. On two occasions, our room has been crowded with ladies to hear Mr. [William] Pinkney, the present Attorney General." [25] Speeches at the bar went on for hours, sometimes for days. Alexander Hamilton supposedly spoke for six hours before the New York supreme court in Albany, in a case of criminal libel in 1804.[26] The federal Supreme Court was described in 1824 as "not only one of the most dignified and enlightened tribunals in the world, but one of the most patient. Counsel are heard in silence for hours, without being stopped or interrupted." [27]

[23] Swaine, *op. cit.*, pp. 14–15.
[24] Diary of George T. Strong, quoted in Taft, *op. cit.*, p. 102.
[25] Quoted in Charles Warren, *The Supreme Court in United States History*, Vol. I (1922), p. 473.
[26] Julius Goebel, ed., *The Law Practice of Alexander Hamilton*, Vol. I (1964), p. 793.
[27] Quoted in Charles Warren, *The Supreme Court in United States History*, Vol. I, p. 467.

Some of these marathon speeches became famous. Daniel Webster argued for four hours in *Dartmouth College* v. *Woodward* (1818),

> with a statement so luminous, and a chain of reasoning so easy to be understood, and yet approaching so nearly to absolute demonstration, that he seemed to carry with him every man of his audience. . . . Now and then, for a sentence or two, his eye flashed and his voice swelled into a bolder note . . . but he instantly fell back into [a] tone of earnest conversation.

The judges listened, we are told, with rapt attention. At the end of his formal argument, Webster added his famous peroration: "Sir, you may destroy this little institution; it is weak; it is in your hands . . ." At the words: "It is, sir, as I have said, a small college. And yet there are those who love it—"

> the feelings which he had thus far succeeded in keeping down, broke forth. His lips quivered; his firm cheeks trembled with emotion; his eyes were filled with tears, his voice choked . . . he seemed struggling to . . . gain . . . mastery over himself.

At that point, according to Webster's biographer, John Marshall's eyes were "suffused with tears"; when Webster sat down, there was "a deathlike stillness" in the room; it lasted for "some moments; every one seemed to be slowly recovering." [28] These tears may be purely a legend; but the oratorical athletics were not. Old Horace Binney, looking back at the bar of his youth from the Civil War period, saw the great lawyers in this light: flamboyant, oratorical, anything but businesslike and gray. There was Theophilus Parsons, before the turn of the century: "Socratic in his subtlety," but "careless" of dress: "his purple Bandana handkerchief curled loosely over his neckcloth." William Lewis, born in 1745, appeared in court with a "full suit of black" and a "powdered head."

> His first attitude was always as erect as he could make it, with one hand insinuated between his waistcoat and his shirt, and the other lying loose upon his loin; and in this position, without any action but that movement of his head, he would utter two or three of his first sentences. . . . Then, with a quick movement, and sometimes with a little jerk of his body, he would bring both his hands to his sides, and begin the action. And it was pretty vehement action from that time to the conclusion; his head dropping or rising, his body bending or straightening

[28] Quoted in George T. Curtis, *Life of Daniel Webster,* Vol. I (1872), pp. 169–71.

up, and his arms singly or together relieving his head. . . . His
voice . . . was deep, sonorous, and clear to the last . . . not
sweet, but . . . a fine working voice for a courtroom.[29]

Judges, too, were in a sense oratorical. Charges to the jury, in the
early part of the period, sometimes ran on at enormous length.
The judges expatiated on subjects far distant from the business at
hand. Inflammatory speeches to grand juries, as we noted, helped
bring on the crisis between Federalist judges and Republicans in
office. In time, the free-flown speeches of the judges were curbed;
and what one might call the oratorical style of law practice died
down, though it never died out. The style was essentially suited for
small elites and small communities, and for generalist, courtroom
lawyers. The rise of big business and the Wall Street style of practice spoiled the monopoly held by the oratorical style. Law-office
law meant a different relationship with clients, different ways of
getting and keeping business. Then, too, a growing economy
brought with it a swelling of dockets; this put an end to the leisurely pace of litigation. After the Webster days, hard-pressed
courts, even had they wanted to, could not listen to long speeches
and still get on with their work.

ORGANIZATION OF THE BAR

The English distinctions of grade—between attorneys, counselors,
barristers, and sergeants—exerted a certain fascination, but failed
to leave a permanent mark on the American bar. A few colonies
had recognized a graded bar; some—New Jersey and Massachusetts
—held on to a distinction between two classes of attorneys for a
number of years after Independence. The statutes of Northwest
Territory also briefly distinguished between attorneys and "counsellors." Only "counsellors," more exalted than ordinary attorneys,
could appear before the highest court. This gradation (1799) lasted
only a few years, even on paper.[30] New York distinguished between
attorneys and counselors between 1829 and 1846; Virginia distinguished between solicitors, who practiced in equity, and the ordinary attorneys of the common-law courts. The distinction had no
great significance; a common-law attorney could easily and
quickly, with a few additional formalities, get for himself the solic-

29 Horace Binney, *The Leaders of the Old Bar of Philadelphia* (1866), pp. 17,
38–40.
30 Francis S. Philbrick, ed., *Laws of Indiana Territory 1801–1809*, cxcii–cxciii.

itor's right to practice in equity court.[31] Soon Virginia did away with this small formal distinction too.

The graded bar was thus a rather transient phenomenon. The old established bar did struggle to keep their guild small and elite. They did not succeed. By the early 19th century, the bar was, formally speaking, an undifferentiated mass. There were rich and poor lawyers, high ones and low; but all were members of one vast sprawling profession. The few primitive bar clubs, associations, and "moots" [32] did nothing to provide real cohesion or self-control. The bar was very loose, very open. Nobody controlled it at the top, or from within. Requirements for admission to the bar were lax.[33] In New England and New York, during the late colonial period, the lawyers had had a great deal of power, formal or informal, over admissions. But then the courts took over; thereafter only they prescribed qualifications, and handled applications. This was a plain symptom of loss of professional cohesion. The courts' rein was bound to be looser than the practicing bar; courts had less interest in keeping fee schedules high and the supply of lawyers low.

At the time of the Revolution, there was no uniform mode of admission to the bar. In Massachusetts, each county court admitted its own attorneys; the high court theoretically controlled all admissions in South Carolina; in Rhode Island, Delaware, and Connecticut local courts admitted lawyers; but admission to one bar gave an attorney the right to practice in all. After the Revolution, New York (1777) and the federal courts (1789) switched to the Massachusetts system. This then became the "dominant system in the north-eastern, conservative section of the country." In the 1830's, the Delaware method became more popular. The lawyer who could get himself admitted, even by the most slipshod local court, was a fully licensed member of the bar of the state, and could practice before any court.

Requirements for admission were also not uniform. A few states were uncommonly strict. In New Hampshire, between 1805 and 1833, the federated county bars required five years of preparation

---

[31] Alfred Z. Reed, *Training for the Public Profession of the Law* (1921), p. 80.

[32] See Charles Warren, *A History of the American Bar* (1912), p. 203. In Massachusetts, the associations of the bar under rules of court of 1810, were given power they had long desired. Recommendation from the county bar association became a prerequisite for admission to the court of common pleas and the Supreme Court. These rules lasted about one generation. Gerard W. Gawalt, *Massachusetts Lawyers: A Historical Analysis of the Process of Professionalization, 1760–1840* (unpublished Ph.D. thesis, Clark University, 1969), pp. 87–88.

[33] The best treatment is Reed, *op. cit.,* pp. 67–103.

for admission to the lower courts, in the case of applicants qualified to enter Dartmouth (but they did not have to know Greek).
Three years was the term for college graduates. Two years further
practice was required for admission to the superior court. New
York, between 1829 and 1846, by rule of court, demanded seven
years of preparation for the right to practice as an "attorney" before the supreme court, "toward which there might be counted up
to four years of classical study pursued after the age of fourteen." [34]
It took three years more of practice to become a "counsellor." This
kind of rigorous timeserving was rapidly discarded in most other
states. In 1800, fourteen out of the nineteen states or organized
territories prescribed a definite period of preparation for the bar.
In 1840, only eleven out of thirty jurisdictions did so. In Massachusetts, a statute was passed in 1836 which obliged the courts to
admit anyone of good moral character who had studied law three
years in an attorney's office. A person who did not meet this requirement could take his chances on an examination. In the 1840's,
a few states eliminated all requirements for admission to the bar,
except good moral character. One was Maine (1843); another New
Hampshire (1842), reversing its former stringency. At this point,
then, there could be no pretense that law was a learned, exclusive
profession. Yet these rules must not be taken too literally. Laymen
did not practice law, even in New Hampshire and Maine. New
Hampshire and Maine were extreme only in frankness. Rules of
admission and preparation were probably nowhere rigorously administered. In other states—particularly in the West—"examination" of lawyers-to-be in court was almost a farce, if we can believe
a mass of anecdotes. Gustave Koerner, who had immigrated from
Germany, began to practice in the 1830's, in Illinois; he reported
that his examination was very informal, lasted about half an hour,
consisted of a few perfunctory questions; then everyone adjourned
for brandy toddies.[35] Salmon P. Chase had almost as perfunctory an
examination in Maryland, in 1829. The judge wanted him to
"study another year"; but when Chase begged for a favorable ruling, because he had "made all . . . arrangements to go to the Western country and practice law," the judge swore him in.[36]

34 Reed, op. cit., p. 83. The New Hampshire rule was continued by order of
court to 1838.
35 Jack Nortrup, "The Education of a Western Lawyer," 12 Am. J. Leg. Hist.
294, 301 (1968).
36 J. W. Schuckers, The Life and Public Services of Salmon Portland Chase
(1874), p. 30.

Theories of Jacksonian democracy have been used to explain why the bar let down its bars on admission. But basic social facts pushed the profession in the same direction. Government control of occupations was, in general, weak and diffuse. Geographical and social mobility were high. There were many jurisdictions; no one of them could really define standards for itself; and the weakness of one was the weakness of all, as was later true of divorce and corporation law. Besides, a factotum profession, within the grasp of ambitious men of all sorts, was socially useful. In many ways, loose standards enhanced the vigor of the bar. *Formal* restrictions disappeared; but the market for legal services remained, a harsh and efficient control. It pruned away deadwood; it rewarded the adaptive and the cunning. Jacksonian democracy did not make everyman a lawyer. It did encourage a scrambling bar of shrewd entrepreneurs.

LEGAL EDUCATION

A lawyer was a man with legal training, or some legal training and some legal skill. Even at the low point of professional self-government, no one practiced law without some pretense at qualification. Most lawyers gained their pretensions by spending some time, in training, in the office of a member of the bar. For a fee, they read Blackstone and Coke, and copied legal documents. If they were lucky, they benefited from watching the lawyer do his work, and do it well. Some lawyers were conscientious about their clerks, anxious to give them proper training. Some became popular teachers. Theophilus Parsons, in Massachusetts, was so much in demand, shortly after 1800, that a special rule of court, aimed at him, restricted law offices to a maximum of three students at any one time.[37] Lemuel Shaw, too, was a popular and diligent teacher. He drew up rules to govern the conduct and training of his students. The students were to report each Monday on their previous week's reading. They were also encouraged to "enter into free conversation" with Shaw "upon subjects connected with their studies, and especially in reference to those changes and alterations of the general law which may have been effected by the Statutes of the Commonwealth and by local usage, and in respect to which therefore

[37] Frederic Hathaway Chase, *Lemuel Shaw, Chief Justice of the Supreme Judicial Court of Massachusetts* (1918), p. 37.

little can be found in books." [38] Shaw's office became almost a small private school for lawyers. A few lawyers, with a flair for teaching, took the next logical step; they practiced less and less and spent more time with their clerks. In this category may be placed a certain Leonard Henderson of North Carolina, who advertised in 1826 in the *Raleigh Register* that he had "four offices for the reception of Law Students" and was on the verge of opening a fifth. "I shall not," he promised, "deliver formal lectures, but will give explanations whenever requested, examinations will be frequent, and conversations held on law topics," most usually "at table after meals." Henderson fixed the fee for "instruction and boarding, exclusive of washing and candles," at $225 a year. [39]

The first law schools grew out of these specialized law offices. They used much the same techniques as the offices. The earliest such school was founded in Litchfield, Connecticut, by Judge Tapping Reeve, probably in 1784. It proved successful, and grew rapidly in size. Eventually, it gained a national reputation, and attracted students from all over the country. [40] In 1813, fifty-five students were in attendance. In the late 1820's, the school felt the keen effects of competition; it went into decline and closed its doors in 1833. More than a thousand students had been "graduated" from Litchfield by that time.

The Litchfield school taught law by the lecture method. Its lectures were never published; to publish would have meant to perish, since students would have no reason to pay tuition and attend to class. The lecture plan was modeled on Blackstone's *Commentaries,* but the Litchfield lectures paid more attention to commercial law, and little or none to criminal law. Daily lectures lasted about an hour and a quarter or an hour and a half. The full course took fourteen months, including two vacations of four weeks each. Students were required to write their notes up carefully, and to do collateral reading. Every Saturday there was a "strict examination" on the week's work. During the later years of the school, "optional moot courts and debating societies" were in operation. [41]

The Litchfield school spawned a number of imitators. Most of

38 *Ibid.,* p. 123.
39 Quoted in Robert H. Wettach, ed., *A Century of Legal Education* (1947), p. 15.
40 Reed, *op. cit.,* p. 130.
41 Reed, *op. cit.,* p. 131.

them were ephemeral. Ultimately, university law schools replaced the Litchfield type as the major alternative to office training. But legal training at universities was rare. A few colleges taught law as part of their general curriculum. The first American chair of law was at William and Mary College, where, at the behest of Thomas Jefferson, George Wythe was appointed professor of "Law and Police." St. George Tucker, who later held this chair, published an American edition of Blackstone in 1803, with copious notes and additions, to be used as a kind of textbook for students. Professorships were also established, in the late 18th and early 19th century, at the University of Virginia, the University of Pennsylvania, and the University of Maryland. Some of these were not meant for lawyer training at all. James Wilson projected a series of lectures at Pennsylvania (1790) "to furnish a rational and useful entertainment to gentlemen of all professions." David Murray Hoffman's lectures at Maryland and James Kent's at Columbia produced works which enriched legal literature. But these early experiments did not produce lasting results, from the standpoint of legal education.

The Harvard Law School proved more permanent. Out of funds left to the college by Isaac Royall, Harvard set up a chair of law in 1816. The first professor was Isaac Parker, chief justice of Massachusetts. Parker, in his inaugural address, spoke of law as a "science," one "worthy of a place in the University," and "worthy to be taught, for it cannot be understood without instruction." [42] At Harvard, there were already separate faculties in theology and medicine. Parker expected, or hoped for, a professional, independent law school too. It would live with Harvard College but be clearly distinct from it. A major gift, from Nathan Dane, helped bring this hope to fulfillment. Dane had written a most successful lawbook, *A General Abridgment and Digest of American Law.* In England, in the 18th century, Charles Viner had written a popular abridgment of English law, and used the proceeds to endow a chair in law, which Sir William Blackstone filled. Dane followed the Vinerian precedent; he gave $10,000 to support a professorship. Dane specifically urged that the professor's "residence at Cambridge shall never be required as a condition of his holding the office; believing the best professors will generally be found among Judges and lawyers, eminent in practice in other places conveniently situated, and who, while professors, may continue their

[42] Quoted in Charles Warren, *History of the Harvard Law School,* Vol. I (1908), p. 301.

offices and practice generally; also thinking law lectures ought to increase no faster than there is a demand for them. Clearly, their great benefit will be in publishing them." [43] Dane himself suggested the name of the first Dane professor: Joseph Story. Story was indeed only a part-time professor, out of sheer necessity; when he accepted the post, in 1829, he was a justice of the United States Supreme Court.[44]

The Harvard Law School, at least during the Story period, was extremely successful; by 1844, 163 students were in attendance, an unheard-of number.[45] Those who completed their course earned an LL.B. The fame and skill of the professors undoubtedly acted as a drawing card. Students who could afford it must have preferred life at Cambridge to the typical sort of office apprenticeship, with its dreary routine. As the oldest and most successful law school, Harvard became the model for all newer schools. It was a pure and rigorous model, as Story wished it to be. It defined the province of law school and legal training severely. Politics and the study of government were put to one side;[46] common law, rather than the study of statutes, was stressed.

Within this narrow domain, the school bore copious fruit. The Harvard ethos was a soil out of which a rich academic literature came to flower. Ultimately, the law faculty turned into a veritable treatise-writing machine. Story wrote *Commentaries* on an amazing variety of subjects: promissory notes, equity jurisprudence, the conflict of laws, agency, bailments, bills of exchange, partnership. Simon Greenleaf wrote a popular basic treatise on evidence. The law school also began to amass a major law library. The catalogue for the academic year 1846–47 claimed that the law-school library owned 12,000 books.[47] The success of Harvard demonstrated that professional training at a university could satisfy the needs of budding lawyers as well as office training could. Yet Harvard did not succeed in raising the *period* of training for the bar above the statu-

[43] Quoted in Warren, *op. cit.*, p. 420.

[44] Isaac Parker resigned as Royall professor in 1827. The subsequent holders of this chair—first John Ashmun, then Simon Greenleaf—were in regular full-time attendance.

[45] Reed, *op. cit.*, p. 143. On the later vicissitudes of Harvard, see below, Part III, Ch. XI, pp. 528–34.

[46] By way of contrast, James Kent, in his *Introductory Lecture to a Course of Law Lectures* (1794), pp. 19–23, proposed to "begin with an Examination of the nature and duties of Government in general . . . The Political History of the United States . . . a summary review of the Law of Nations."

[47] *Centennial History of the Harvard Law School: 1817–1917* (1918), p. 94.

tory minimum. And the main path to practice still went through apprenticeship for the overwhelming majority of lawyers. Apprenticeship influenced Harvard, in this period, more than Harvard influenced general legal education.

THE LITERATURE OF THE LAW

The common law, as it developed over the years, was embodied in reported cases—opinions of high-court judges. What was not reported was barely law. In England, *reporters* (some skillful and accurate, others less so) privately prepared many volumes of cases. There were no American reports to speak of in the colonial period.[48] By and large, the practicing lawyer had to rely on English reports or on secondhand knowledge of English cases, gleaned out of English treatises. He knew the local statutes, to be sure, and the local practice of his court. Some lawyers prepared, for themselves, collections of local cases. Occasionally, manuscript volumes of cases circulated among lawyers. This practice was certainly followed in the Republican period. Eleven manuscript notebooks, covering the period 1792 to 1830, have been recovered and reprinted for the small state of Delaware alone.[49]

But manuscripts could not serve the hunger of lawyers for cases, in an expanding legal system. In 1789, Ephraim Kirby published a volume of *Connecticut Reports*. In the preface, Kirby voiced the hope that a "permanent system of common law," and an American one, would emerge in the country. This hope was soon realized. The lawyers wanted reports and were willing to pay for them. In 1790, Alexander Dallas published a volume of "Reports of Cases Ruled and Adjudged in the Courts of Pennsylvania, Before and Since the Revolution." The earlier cases, from 1754 on, were "kindly furnished by Mr. Rawle"; sitting judges helped Dallas, by giving him notes on their current cases. Dallas, like Kirby, professed a patriotic aim; he hoped that his reports would "tend to show the pure and uniform system of jurisprudence that prevails in PENNSYLVANIA." In the second volume, Dallas added cases from the United States Supreme Court, which was then sitting at Philadelphia. In this volume, quietly and unobtrusively, began

---

[48] Some colonial reports were printed later; Josiah Quincy's *Massachusetts Reports* (1761–1772), for example, published in 1865. Recently, volumes of colonial reports have been edited by scholars.

[49] Daniel J. Boorstin, ed., *Delaware Cases: 1792–1830* (3 vols., 1943).

that magnificent series of reports, extending in an unbroken line down to the present, that chronicles the work of the world's most powerful court.

William Cranch, chief justice of the circuit court of the District of Columbia, was the Supreme Court's next reporter. Cranch's first volume appeared in 1804, bright with the hope (as a newspaper put it) that a "code of Common Law" would grow "out of our own Constitutions, laws, customs and state of society, independent of that servile recourse to the decisions of foreign Judicatures to which, since our revolution, we have been too much accustomed." [50] In his preface, Cranch added another theme, quite characteristic of the times. Reports, he said, were essential to "a government of laws." The "least possible range ought to be left to the discretion of the Judge. Whatever tends to render the laws certain, equally tends to limit that discretion; and perhaps nothing conduces more to that object than the publication of reports. Every case decided is a check upon the Judge." Cranch was succeeded by another able reporter, Henry Wheaton, who later became famous as a diplomat and scholar of the law.[51]

More and more state reports were also issued. Nathaniel Chipman published *Reports and Dissertations* in Vermont, in 1793. By 1810, reports appeared in New York, Massachusetts, and New Jersey as well. Some of these had official status—for example, George Caines' reports of the supreme court of New York, beginning in 1804. Many early reporters were judges, who collected their own opinions and those of their colleagues. Other judges worked closely with their reporters, helping them bring out full, accurate work. Chancellor Kent had a close relationship with William Johnson, whose New York reports were very popular at the bar. Caines acknowledged his debt to "Their Honors on the bench [who] . . . have unreservedly given their written opinions . . . the whole bar has frankly and generously afforded their cases, and every other communication that was wished or desired. To these aids the clerk of the court has added an unlimited recurrence to the papers and pleadings his office contains." [52] Rhode Island was the last state to fall in line. Only in 1847 did the first volume of Rhode Island cases, reported by J. K. Angell, appear.

Some early reports were far more than slavish accounts of the

50 Quoted in Charles Warren, *The Supreme Court in United States History*, Vol. 1, p. 289n.

51 See, in general, Elizabeth F. Baker, *Henry Wheaton 1785–1848* (1937).

52 George Caines, preface, *Reports* (1804).

judges' words. Like the great English reports, they were guidebooks for the practitioner. Some reporters added little essays on the law to the oral and written courtroom materials they collected. Chipman filled out his book with "dissertations," including a "Dissertation on the Negotiability of Notes." The full title of Jesse Root's first volume of Connecticut Reports (1798) gives some indication of the contents:

> Reports of Cases adjudged in the Superior Court and Supreme Court of Errors. From July A.D. 1789 to June A.D. 1793; with a Variety of Cases anterior to that Period, Prefaced with Observations upon the Government and Laws of Connecticut. To Which is Subjoined, Sundry Law Points Adjudged, and Rules of Practice Adopted in the Superior Court.

But Root's "cases" were not full verbatim reports. Frequently they were little more than brief notes, recounting some point of interest in a trial or appellate case. The following is one "report," *Bacon* v. *Minor,* given in its entirety:

> Action of defamation; for saying that the plaintiff had forged a certain note. Issue to the jury.
> Daniel Minor was offered as a witness and objected to, on the ground that he was a joint promissor in said note, and is sued for speaking the same words.
> By the Court—Not admitted being interested in the question.[53]

Eventually, appointed officials replaced private entrepreneurs as law reporters. Official reports tended to be fuller and more accurate than unofficial reports, but they were also much more standardized. Caines remarked that his "exertions have been reduced to little more than arranging the materials received, and giving, in a summary manner, the arguments adduced." What was lost in style was gained in authenticity.

The ultimate influence of the reports can hardly be measured. They enabled the states to put together their own common law, independent of England, rival systems, and other states. At the same time, they enabled the states to borrow more freely from each other. Big states and famous judges were considered more authoritative, and were cited more frequently than small states and small judges. New York's reports carried high prestige, especially the opinions of Chancellor Kent. Lemuel Shaw in Massachusetts was another great name. At first, few state cases could be decided on

[53] That is, the testimony was not allowed on the grounds that Minor had a financial stake in the matter litigated. The case is 1 Root 258 (1791).

the basis of local precedents alone. And in practice, local decisions, even when they were available, were not exclusively relied upon. The sense of the judges was that the common law was a single great language of law; one did not move out of step unduly or without good cause. English decisions were still frequently cited. In the first volume of Saxton's chancery reports (New Jersey, 1830–32) well over half the citations were English—more than fifty years after Independence. State reports made English doctrines more digestible, giving them a local habitation and a name. Yet basically, the case reports were building blocks of an indigenous system of law—indeed, of a system of systems, each state on its own.

With few exceptions, only appellate cases were reported in official reports. Occasionally, newspapers covered important or lurid trials; a few trial transcripts appeared as pamphlets. A few especially succulent grand-jury charges, by noted judges, were privately printed.[54] The best courtroom oratory was also published. In 1844, an enterprising publisher brought forth the arguments by Horace Binney and Daniel Webster in the noted case of the will of Stephen Girard.[55]

A body of jurisprudential and practical literature also began to appear in the republic. Publishers brought out English works in "American editions"; often, the editor added footnotes to bring these books up to date, and to point out American innovations. A fourth American edition of Joseph Chitty's *Practical Treatise on the Law of Contracts* was published by J. C. Perkins in 1839, with "copious notes of American decisions to the present time." St. George Tucker, scholar and jurist, of Virginia, published a five-volume Blackstone, in 1803. This was an important work in its own right; its thoughtful "Appendices" discussed government, law, and Virginia jurisprudence. John Reed published a *Pennsylvania Blackstone* in 1831, in three volumes. Reed retained the general plan of Blackstone (that "invaluable treasure of correct information, clothed in the most pure and classical style"),[56] and large chunks of the original (in quotation marks); but Reed also rewrote extensively and added much new material, in order to form "in a connected view, an elementary exposition of the entire law of

54 For example, Alexander Addison, *Charges to Grand Juries of the Counties of the Fifth Circuit in the State of Pennsylvania* (1800); a 1806 grand-jury charge of Chief Justice Parsons of Massachusetts is reprinted in 14 Am. Jurist 26 (1835).

55 See Entries, Catalogue of the Law School of Harvard University (Vol. II, 1909), p. 1084.

56 Preface, p. iv.

Pennsylvania, common and statute." But gradually, more and more treatises were written that owed little or nothing to English models, except in the most general way.[57]

With some exceptions, American legal literature was (and is) rigorously practical. Books were written for the practicing lawyer. The object to be served was his search for the dollar, not his intellectual curiosity. Systematic legal theory was studiously ignored by most writers as well as by the bar. Legal theory has never been a strong suit in common-law countries. There was, of course, a notable literature of political theory, and the law can lay some claim, not wholly farfetched, to the writings of Thomas Jefferson, James Wilson, and the *Federalist Papers*. Some education in government was part of the general training of the better lawyers. Many general treatises on law devoted space to politics, natural law, and the sources and aims of the law.[58] James Sullivan, in his *History of Land Titles in Massachusetts*, published in 1801 in Boston, saw fit to add to his book some "General Observations on the Nature of Laws in General, and those of the United States in particular." [59] The rest of the book was a conventional treatment of the American law of real property.

Even before 1800, some American lawyers struck out on their own. Zephaniah Swift published his *System of the Laws of Connecticut* in 1795–96. In 1810, he wrote a *Digest of the Law of Evidence in Civil and Criminal Cases* and a *Treatise on Bills of Exchange and Promissory Notes*. His books were informative and as readable as their subjects would allow. He propounded no grand theories; but was content, as he said in the *Evidence*, "to arrange the subject in a plain but systematic manner." [60] Swift was not afraid to criticize as well as arrange. For example, he attacked the American rule, that the plaintiff (in discovery proceedings) was bound by the defendant's disclosures, and might not contradict them. "This practice," he said, "must have been adopted at an early period, without due consideration." [61] Characteristically, Swift's criticism did not

[57] See in general, ch. xiii, "Early American Law Books," and ch. xx, "American Law Books, 1815–1910," in Charles Warren, *A History of the American Bar* (1912).

[58] The first volume of Blackstone's *Commentaries* had also dealt with these general subjects.

[59] James Sullivan, *History of Land Titles in Massachusetts* (1801), pp. 337–56.

[60] Zephaniah Swift, *Digest of the Law of Evidence in Civil and Criminal Cases* (1810), preface, p. x.

[61] *Ibid.* p. 120.

flow from some systematic theory of justice or law, clearly articu-
lated. Criticism was always piecemeal and pragmatic. Later treatises had the same general features. Among the most popular or
durable were the *Treatise on the Law of Private Corporations
Aggregate* by Joseph K. Angell and Samuel Ames (1832); Simon
Greenleaf's treatise on *Evidence* (1842); Henry Wheaton's *Elements of International Law* (1836); and Theodore Sedgwick's *Treatise on the Measure of Damages* (1847). A more general work was
Timothy Walker's *Introduction to American Law* (1837). The book
was designed for students, was enormously successful, and went
through many editions. Nathan Dane's *General Abridgement and
Digest of American Law,* in eight volumes (1823–24) (a supple-
mental ninth volume was published in 1829) has already been
mentioned. The "abridgment" was a loosely organized work, arranged much like the earlier English "abridgements." As literature,
it had little to recommend it. In a contemporary's view, Dane "had
no graces of style, either native or borrowed; neither did he ever
seek for any." [62] But lawyers bought the abridgment for their
working libraries; and Dane made enough money to become a
patron at Harvard.

Even less pretentious were the works at the other end of the spec-
trum of generality—local practice manuals and helpful guides of
one sort or another for particular jurisdictions. William W. Hen-
ing's *The New Virginia Justice* (1795), a guide for justices of the
peace, represented a numerous genre, with many English and colonial ancestors. The book was vaguely designed for lay judges—
perhaps for fledgling lawyers too. It quoted statutes, set out simple
legal forms, and digested some relevant cases. Similar works appeared in other states. John F. Grimke (1752–1819) wrote *The
South Carolina Justice of the Peace* in 1788 and the *Duty of Executors and Administrators* in 1797. Esek Cowen wrote a *Treatise
on the Civil Jurisdiction of Justices of the Peace in the State of
New York* in 1821; this was a guide for the perplexed (lay) justice,
perhaps also (Cowen hoped) "useful to the man of business," and
even to Cowen's "brethren of the profession." Still lower on the
literary scale were simple formbooks and guides for the laymen,
works with the ubiquitous title *Every Man His Own Lawyer,* or
books with names like the *Western Clerks' Assistant,* or *The Business Man's Assistant.* This last was a compendium of "useful forms
of legal instruments," together with tables of interest, currency

[62] "Biographical Notice of the Honorable Nathan Dane," 14 Am. Jurist 62,
67–8 (1835).

information, "laws, instructions and forms necessary for obtaining a patent," and "agreements for constructing railroads." It claimed to have reached its 33rd thousand at the time it was reprinted in Boston in 1847, by one D. R. Butts, "assisted by an attorney." Richard Henry Dana (1815–82), best known as the author of *Two Years Before the Mast* (1840), wrote a manual on the law of the sea, called *The Seamen's Friend,* in 1841.

Legal periodicals were few, and even fewer had much of a life span.[63] Before 1830, twelve periodicals were founded. The *American Law Journal and Miscellaneous Repository* was one of these, published in Philadelphia in 1808, but it expired within a decade. Most of its pages were devoted to case reports and digests of statutes; but there was also some secondary writing on legal subjects. Periodicals of this type competed weakly with the reporters; they reprinted key decisions and other primary sources of law. Better reporting put most of them out of business. In 1810 only one periodical was actually in existence; this was also true of 1820. In 1830 there were five. *The American Jurist and Law Magazine* (1829–42), founded by Willard Phillips, was one of the five. More pretentious and successful than most, it contained scholarly essays on points of law, case notes, historical notes, and question-and-answer materials. Prominent members of the Boston bar, including Joseph Story, often contributed to the journal.

By common consent, the two most significant figures in American legal literature in the first half of the 19th century were James Kent and Joseph Story. Both were erudite teachers and judges. Both had enormous reputations in their day. Both have since suffered a decline in prestige, and an irretrievable decline in their readership. In their day, their reputations went further than any other legal scholars in America. No one on the Continent had ever heard of James Sullivan or Zephaniah Swift. But Joseph Story was a name that won respect, even from continental jurists. And when Kent's *Commentaries* were published, George Bancroft said: "Now we know what American Law is; we know it is a science." [64]

Joseph Story was born in 1779 and died in 1845.[65] In 1811, at the

[63] On the periodicals of this period, see Maxwell Bloomfield, "Law vs. Politics: The Self-Image of the American Bar (1830–1860)," 12 Am. J. Leg. Hist. 306, 309–10 (1968).

[64] Quoted in Warren, *op. cit.,* p. 543.

[65] See Mortimer D. Schwartz and John C. Hogan, eds., *Joseph Story* (1959); Gerald T. Dunne, "Joseph Story: The Germinal Years," 75 Harv. L. Rev. 707 (1962); Gerald T. Dunne, *Justice Joseph Story and the Rise of the Supreme Court* (1970).

age of thirty-two, he was appointed to the United States Supreme Court. Contrary to expectations, since he was nominally a follower of Jefferson, he became John Marshall's strong right arm on the court. In 1829, he was named Dane professor at Harvard. He did not resign from the Court. As Dane professor, however, he wrote his series of *Commentaries,* published between 1831 and 1845. He was a man of vast, almost ponderous erudition. According to his son,

> He was well versed in the classics of Greece and Rome. . . . He was a good historical scholar; and in the sciences and mechanic arts, he had attained to considerable proficiency. He was omnivorous of knowledge. . . . No legal work appeared, that he did not examine.[66]

Story was not one to wear his erudition lightly. In his seminal work on the conflict of laws (1834), which systematized a new field out of virtually nothing, one page (360) has three lines of French and six of Latin, and quotes from Louis Boullenois, Achille Rodemburg, P. Voet, J. Voet, C. d'Argentré, and U. Huberus, names that the American lawyer would find totally mysterious.

Story's erudition was not always so blatant; and this particular subject matter had hardly been treated by writers in English. Learning did not interfere with the main line of Story's argument, which proceeded clearly and stoutly, even gracefully at times. Story's erudition was organic; it involved his whole attitude toward law. He was a scholar and a traditionalist; he had reverence for the law and for the past. As he saw it, law was completely a product of history, of the historical dialectic of ideas. Only a fool would dare to interfere with its manner of operation, without deep and total understanding. Story fully agreed with Sir Edward Coke that the common law was reason personified; that it was not the parochial product of English or American experience, but a branch of the great, ancient tree of human wisdom. He was, in a sense, a legal pantheist. He saw divinity in Roman law as well as in common law. But for that very reason, he worshiped the law of his state and his nation; he saw them as connected with mighty currents of law that swept through human history; yet the precise development of one's own legal institutions was a specific adaptation of general principles. In his treatise on *Equity Jurisprudence* (1835), Story asked:

> Whether it would, or would not, be best to administer the whole of remedial justice in one Court, or in one class of Courts, with-

[66] Schwartz and Hogan, *op. cit.,* p. 202.

out any separation or distinctions of suits, or of the form or modes of proceeding and granting relief.

One might have guessed that a Massachusetts lawyer, with a profound knowledge of European law, would have no difficulty in seeing that law and equity should properly be joined.[67] But Story does not commit himself. He begins by quoting Francis Bacon: all nations have some equivalent of equity, at least in the broad sense of the word. Bacon thought it might be harmful to mix law and equity in one and the same institution. Six lines of Baconian Latin follow. Then Story refers to the civil law, where "the general, if not the universal, practice is the other way."

> But, whether the one opinion, or the other, be most correct in theory, it is most probable, that the practical system, adopted by every nation, has been mainly influenced by the peculiarities of its own institutions, habits, and circumstances; and especially by the nature of its own jurisprudence, and the forms of its own remedial justice. . . . The question . . . never can be susceptible of any universal solution.[68]

James Kent, the second major figure of American legal literature, was born in New York in 1763. He went to Yale, then read law, and became a member of the New York bar in 1785. Like Story, Kent had a distinguished career on the bench. He served as chancellor of New York from 1814 to 1823. He was forced into premature retirement, at the age of sixty; the New York constitution of 1821 made sixty the maximum age for a sitting judge (art. 5, sec. 3). In retirement, Kent wrote his masterpiece, *Commentaries on American Law,* in four volumes, published between 1826 and 1830. The work had an immediate and enthusiastic reception by the bar. Kent continued to bring out fresh editions until his death in 1847. The work was so popular that more editions continued to appear after Kent's death, with new editors. The 12th edition (1873) was edited by young Oliver Wendell Holmes, Jr.

Kent, like Joseph Story, and even Blackstone, is no longer read. Perry Miller found Kent a "bore"; he was repelled by Kent's "stiffly neoclassical rhetoric"; Kent's "treatment of almost all areas" he thought "platitudinous." [69] But it is possible to read Kent

---

[67] Massachusetts, it will be recalled, had no separate courts of equity; and such a thing was of course unknown to Continental law.

[68] Joseph Story, *Commentaries on Equity Jurisprudence* (1836) Vol. I, pp. 34–36.

[69] Perry Miller, *The Legal Mind in America* (1962), p. 92.

and find it enjoyable. Kent intended his huge work to be the national Blackstone. To a considerable degree, he succeeded in this aim. Like Story, he was cautious and erudite. But he had little of Blackstone's smugness and self-satisfaction, and little of Story's stultifying pedantry. The style is at all points clear, the exposition transparent. Occasionally, Kent even turns a decent phrase or two. He had a sure and impressive grasp of the whole fabric of American law. His jurisprudential thought was not original or profound; but his attitude toward the living law was pragmatic, hard-boiled, and often shrewd.

Too much emphasis has been placed on Kent's conservatism. His modern biographer subtitled his book "A Study in Conservatism." [70] To be sure, Kent was not on the left, even in his day. He fought doggedly in New York against repeal of the property qualification for voters; he lost this fight. History is cruel to losers. Kent was old-fashioned, in a sense, but he was never romantic or naïve. He had no use for the obsolete, no aversion to productive change. No American, except a dyed-in-the-wool Tory, could have been thoroughly committed to the legal *status quo*. This would have meant denouncing American law in general, and defiling the American revolution. Kent was no Tory of this stamp. His love for the American way emerges constantly in his discussions of the law. On dower, for example, he remarks that, "In this country, we are, happily, not very liable to be perplexed by such abstruse questions and artificial rules, which have encumbered the subject . . . in England to a grievous extent." [71]

Kent is often put in the camp of enemies of codification. But he had praise for the American law of "crimes and punishments. . . . The law . . . has become quite simple in its principles, and concise and uniform in its details. Our criminal codes bear no kind of comparison with the complex and appalling catalogue of crimes and punishments . . . in England." [72] He had a deep respect for property rights, but a tremendous concern for enterprise as well. He loved law as an instrument both of security and of mobility. He had no sentimental attachment to tradition, if it interfered with the "stability and energy" of property. He wanted law to serve the cause of economic growth; to protect institutions that worked. What was conservative, perhaps, was his pessimism. He was profoundly skeptical about human nature. This made him suspicious

[70] John T. Horton, *James Kent, A Study in Conservatism, 1763–1847* (1939).
[71] Kent, *Commentaries*, Vol. IV (2nd ed., 1832), p. 52.
[72] *Ibid.*, p. 544.

of some kinds of reform; he doubted that tinkering with statutes would alter fundamental behavior. Many lawyers shared his belief. Many drew different political conclusions from similar premises. But there was no disputing Kent's clarity, his common sense, his skill in expounding the law. The *Commentaries* deserved to be what they were, an American best seller of the law.

⤙ PART III ⤚

American Law to the Close of the 19th Century

BLOOD AND GOLD: SOME MAIN THEMES IN THE LAW IN THE LAST HALF OF THE 19TH CENTURY

The fifty-three years from the death of James Kent to the end of the 19th century were crowded with events and evolutions. The most dramatic outward happening was the Civil War, when the country tore apart along the jagged line between North and South. Hundreds of thousands died between 1861 and 1865. The century also ended with a war—a splendid little war, compared to the bloodletting of the Civil War; but this war, with Spain, gave the country an overseas empire.

In many ways, wars fundamentally disrupt the operation of the legal system. The Civil War was fought on American soil. It was an unusually violent episode, and it did unusual violence to the ordinary administration of justice. It was also a constitutional crisis. It was followed by a major episode of martial law and domestic upheaval in the South. The war called for dramatic escalation in the role of the national government, and this too was reflected in many ways in every part of the law.

Yet, in a sense, the major developments in American law between 1847 and 1900 were not revolutionary. These were years of rapid, unprecedented change; but the elements of change were a series of tiny events, gross only in their cumulative effect. The most important of these changes continued trends set earlier in the century.

Between 1847 and 1900, the population swelled; the cities grew enormously; the Far West was settled; the country became a major industrial power; transportation and communication vastly improved; overseas expansion began. New inventions and new techniques made life easier and healthier; at the same time, the social order became immeasurably more complex, and perhaps more difficult for the average man to grasp. New social cleavages devel-

oped. The North-South cleavage was bandaged over in the 1860's
and 1870's. The black man was put back in his subordinate place.
When the blood of the Civil War dried, the Gilded Age began.
This was the factory age, the age of money, the age of the robber
barons, of capital and labor at war. And the frontier died. The
pioneer, the frontier individualist, had been the American culture
hero, free, self-reliant, unencumbered by weakness that inhered
in the cities. The frontier had been a symbol of an open society;
opportunity was as unlimited as the sky. In 1893, Frederick Jackson Turner wrote his famous essay, "The Significance of the Frontier in American History." He traced the influence of the frontier
on American character and institutions; but when he wrote the essay, Turner also announced that the frontier was irrevocably dead.

What really passed was not the frontier, but the idea of the frontier. This inner sense of change was one of the most important
influences on American law. Between 1776 and the Civil War,
dominant public opinion exuberantly believed in growth, believed
that resources were virtually unlimited; that there would be room
and wealth for all. The theme of American law before 1850 was
the release of energy, in Willard Hurst's phrase. Develop the land;
grow rich; all segments will gain. By 1900, if one can speak about so
slippery a thing as dominant public opinion, that opinion saw a
narrowing sky, a dead frontier, life as a struggle for position, competition as a zero-sum game, the economy as a pie to be divided, not
a ladder stretching out beyond the horizon. By 1900 the theme was:
hold the line.[1] Many trends and movements give indirect evidence
of the basic cultural change already discussed. One such piece of evidence was the propensity of Americans to form groups. The United
States became a "nation of joiners." De Tocqueville had already
noted in his travels a magnificent flowering of clubs and societies in
America. "Americans," he wrote, "of all ages, all stations in life, and
all types of disposition are forever forming associations . . . religious, moral, serious, futile, very general and very limited, immensely large and very minute." [2] But organization in the last half
of the 19th century was more than a matter of clubs and societies.

[1] We are speaking only of the United States, and only relatively. It was probably also true *after* 1870 that, compared to other societies and other periods,
Americans were still a "people of plenty" and that the sense and reality of
abundance profoundly shaped the national experience. David M. Potter, *People
of Plenty* (1954).

[2] Arthur Schlesinger, "Biography of a Nation of Joiners," 50 Am. Hist. Rev. 1
(1944); Alexis de Tocqueville, *Democracy in America* (J. P. Mayer and M.
Lerner, eds., 1966), p. 485.

Noticeably, many strong interest groups developed—labor unions, industrial combines, farmers' organizations, occupational associations—to jockey for position and power in society. These groups molded, dominated, shaped American law.

A group or association has two aspects: it defines some persons in, and some persons out. People joined together in groups not simply for mutual help, but to exclude, to define an enemy, to make common cause against outsiders. Organization was a law of life, not merely because life was so complicated, but also because life seemed so much a zero-sum game.

The consequences were fundamental. Open-arms immigration laws were replaced by Chinese exclusion laws, demands for literacy tests, and (ultimately, in 1924) the quota system.[3] Resources, in 1800, looked inexhaustible; by 1900, it seemed clear that natural resources could be chopped, burned, and eroded past recovery; a conservation movement was already under way. Government, in 1840, was boosting railroads; in 1880, it was trying to control them, or pretending to try. In general, before the Civil War, leaders of opinion looked at government, and law, as ways to unleash the capacity of the nation. After the war, government's role began slowly to change to that of regulator and trustee. There was bitter opposition, of course, to this new-minted role. Much of the opposition was couched in ideological terms. But the fundamental issues were issues of economic and political strength. The Revolutionary generation had been suspicious of *any* governmental power. The generation of the Gilded Age was still suspicious of imbalance of power. But significant segments of the public saw danger, not merely from one but from various sides: not only from government, but from populists, or trusts, or farmers, or the urban proletariat. American optimism was balanced by a growing pessimism; that the charmed life of America might come to an end, unless people mounted a major battle against creeping decay.

In an important sense, the increasing formation of groups, in American life, merely carried on a major trend of prior generations. Classic English law was a law of and for an elite. In America, more and more people had a stake in the system. This meant that law was necessary, and accessible, to a broad and diverse middle class; that law could serve as a social instrument of great power. Hence the struggle to control the operations of law. Each session of an American legislature was a cockpit of contention between interests. In the Midwest, in the early 1870's, the organized

3 Maldwyn A. Jones, *American Immigration* (1960), pp. 247–77.

farmers had their day. Their legislation (the Granger laws) merely paid railroads and grain elevators back for what *they* had done to farmers when *they* were at the helm. Or so the farmers thought. Less dramatically, in the 1890's, there was a great rush to pass occupational licensing laws: for plumbers, barbers, horseshoers, lawyers, pharmacists, midwives, and nurses. These laws cemented the power of the group that lobbied for their passage: the organized profession. It is naïve to think of them as hostile regulation.

The struggle against industrial combines—the dreaded trusts— was part of the general struggle for a "fair share" of the economy, as the various interest groups viewed it. It was not a struggle to keep free enterprise pure. It would be a mistake to read much economic theory into the passage of the Sherman Anti-Trust Act (1890). Small business, farmers, independent professionals, all feared the *power* of the trusts; antitrust laws were an attempt to use law to cut that power down to size. Regulation, trust-busting, licensing, labor legislation: all these were part of the same general battle of all against all, a battle for security, wealth, prestige, authority, for all the social goods. The power of the state—the law, in short—was both a means and an end in the battle; a way to achieve social goods, and a charter of the dominance of one set of norms and values. Of course, the typical outcome of contention in the legislative chamber was some sort of compromise. No one group was ever absolute. Law was made by hammering out bargains, some explicit, some not.

Different legal institutions were valuable in different ways and to different groups. Because there were so many power centers, so many little fiefs and bailiwicks, so much checking and balancing, groups could pick and choose among parts of the system, for leverage and for veto power. Since labor was strong in some legislatures, management turned to the courts. In this period, judicial review reached its most bizarre excesses. Social Darwinism had some converts on the bench. It was also the period of the equity receivership, and the birth of the labor injunction. It was the period in which lawyers themselves felt the urge to organize, to cement their positions, to move ahead. It was therefore an age in which lawyers and judges invented fresh myths and disguises to protect their roles. Quite naturally, in this period, great changes took place in every significant field of law. Some changes were swift, and the rite of passage plain to see. Other changes took place obscurely, in the dull dishwater law of the dockets. But each hard little nugget of new doctrine had its point of origin in some concrete, living issue. However much judges liked to clothe doctrine in history and in the costume of timeless values, doctrine was still at bottom flesh and blood, the flesh and blood of current struggles over goods and positions.

ORGANIC LAW

The Civil War was a profound constitutional crisis. The Union broke apart in 1861; but the Constitution survived. In fact, the idea of the Constitution was never really attacked. The Confederate states adopted their own constitution, suspiciously like the federal Constitution in many details. It provided for a Supreme Court; but this court in fact never sat, or came into existence at all.[4] The end of the Civil War proved, not that American government was stable and permanent, but that crisis and change could be accommodated within the aging language of that one and only constitution, somewhat amended from time to time.

The Constitution did not look much different, on paper, in 1900 than it looked in 1800. The major novelties were the three Civil War amendments, the thirteenth through fifteenth. These were rammed down the throats of the Southern states. Ratification was so highhanded that a century later, the process still gives color to diehards, who argue that the process was illegal, and even dream that these clauses may somehow go away. These were crucial amendments in making the Civil War victory permanent. The thirteenth amendment abolished slavery. The fifteenth amendment guaranteed the right to vote to all citizens, regardless of "race, color, or previous condition of servitude." The fourteenth amendment has had the most marvelous career of the three. It was the longest of the amendments; most of its language was also tied to specific consequences of the Civil War. But some of its language was broad and sweeping. All persons born or naturalized in the United States were "citizens of the United States and of the State wherein they reside." No state could "abridge" their "privileges or immunities." No state could deprive any "person" of "life, liberty, or property, without due process of law"; nor could a state deny "to any person within its jurisdiction the equal protection of the laws."

4 William M. Robinson, Jr., *Justice in Grey, A History of the Judicial System of the Confederate States of America* (1941), pp. 437–57; see, in general, Charles R. Lee, Jr., *The Confederate Constitutions* (1963).

Did these clauses fundamentally change the power relationship between the states and the federal government? Were they intended to engraft some kind of *laissez-faire* theory onto organic law? Were they meant to give Congress, or the courts, some undefined power to supervise the social and economic activities of local governments? Were they nothing more than expanded guarantees of rights for the Negroes? Whatever the original intent, phrases in the amendment turned out to have marvelous powers of germination. The innocent words "due process" were part of one such phrase. "Equal protection of the laws" was another. In the last two decades of the century, the due-process clause was the hook on which state courts hung their authority to void offensive and unreasonable state laws. In some famous and infamous cases, the courts made the clause seem the very voice of economic reaction. A law which regulates or prohibits an activity can be said to take away "liberty," or "property," from the person who would otherwise want to pursue the activity. If the law is "unreasonable," the deprivation can be said to be without "due process of law."

This use of the clause was foreshadowed in Justice Joseph Bradley's dissent, in the famous *Slaughter-House* cases (1873).[5] Louisiana had passed a statute, in 1869, that gave to the Crescent City Live-Stock Landing and Slaughter-House Company the exclusive right to slaughter cattle in the city of New Orleans. The law threatened to drive all other butchers out of business; they went to court to fight off the law. A bare majority of the Supreme Court held what would have been self-evident two generations before: that the Constitution had nothing to say about the killing of intrastate pigs. Bradley, however, argued that the law was "onerous, unreasonable, arbitrary and unjust"; that a law which "prohibits a large class of citizens from . . . following a lawful employment previously adopted" deprives them of "liberty" and "property." In the course of time, Bradley's ideas won greater acceptance. In *Chicago, Milwaukee and St. Paul Railway Company* v. *Minnesota* (1890),[6] Minnesota had established a railroad and warehouse commission, and had given it power to fix freight rates. The commission ordered the railroad to reduce freight rates from three cents a gallon to not more than two and a half cents a gallon on milk transported from Owatonna, Faribault, Dundas, Northfield, and Farmington, to St. Paul and Minneapolis. This half-cent a gallon made legal history. The Supreme Court, speaking through Justice

[5] 16 Wall. 36 (1873).
[6] 134 U.S. 418 (1890).

Samuel Blatchford, struck down the Minnesota statute creating the commission:

> The question of the reasonableness of a rate of charge for transportation by a railroad company . . . is eminently a question for judicial investigation, requiring due process of law for its determination. If the company is deprived of the power of charging reasonable rates for the use of its property, and such deprivation takes place in the absence of an investigation by judicial machinery, it is deprived of the lawful use of its property, and thus, in substance and effect, of the property itself.[7]

Two aspects of the case are worth noting: first, the conservative tenor of the decision as far as the *economy* is concerned; second, its radical tenor as far as *judicial power* is concerned. Both aspects drew fire from the great American left of center, which was at war with the court off and on until the days of the New Deal court-packing plan. Undeniably, *some* major constitutional decisions, both state and federal, were both conservative in result and radical in method. The number of these cases can be easily exaggerated. On the whole, federal courts threw out only a minority of the state regulatory statutes that came before them, though they may have dampened the propensity of legislatures to pass laws on some social and economic subjects. Toward the federal government, the court was more deferential. After *Marbury* v. *Madison,* no federal law was declared void until the *Dred Scott* case in 1857,[8] which destroyed the Missouri Compromise. The Court's experience with this case and with the *Legal Tender* cases[9] was not calculated to encourage overuse of this powerful weapon. But the Melville W. Fuller court, between 1889 and 1899, did declare five federal acts unconstitutional, along with thirty-four state acts and four municipal ordinances.[10]

---

[7] *Id.,* p. 458. Interestingly enough, Justice Bradley dissented in this case. One effect of the case was to weaken the authority of *Munn* v. *Illinois,* 94 U.S. 113 (1877), which had upheld an Illinois statute fixing maximum charges for grain elevators.

[8] *Dred Scott* v. *Sandford,* 60 U.S. 393 (1857). There is a huge literature on this case. See Stanley I. Kutler, ed., *The Dred Scott Decision: Law or Politics?* (1967).

[9] *Hepburn* v. *Griswold,* 75 U.S. 603 (1870), which ruled that the Legal Tender Acts, passed during the Civil War, were invalid, was overruled in the *Legal Tender* cases, 79 U.S. 457 (1871).

[10] These figures are from William F. Swindler, *Court and Constitution in the 20th Century: The Old Legality, 1889–1932* (1969), p. 344. The worst was yet to come. The Edward D. White court invalidated twenty-two state statutes in a single year (1915); the William H. Taft court's finest hour was 1926, when twenty statutes fell. *Ibid.,* p. 345.

302 AMERICAN LAW TO THE CLOSE OF THE 19TH CENTURY

Heavy use of the fourteenth amendment occurred only at the very end of the 19th century. In the first decade of the amendment, the United States Supreme Court decided only three cases, in the next decade, forty-six. After 1896, "the flood burst. Between that date and the end of the 1905 term of court, two hundred and ninety-seven cases were passed upon under the amendment—substantially all under the 'due process' and 'equal protection' clauses." [11] These figures do not tell the whole story of the impact of the court on the legal and economic systems. The impact, unfortunately, cannot be measured. Whatever that impact, clearly the Supreme Court had developed a dangerous appetite for power. From then on, it was like a man-eating tiger; everyone in its shadow had to cope with its awesome and lethal tastes.

STATE CONSTITUTIONS

The United States Constitution was a steadfast rock compared to the much more brittle state constitutions. A few states did not discard any constitution (though perhaps with liberal use of the amending power). No state had a *coup d'état*. But almost every state convened a constitutional convention, at least once in the period, to draft a new constitution. Some conventions labored in vain. A convention was held in Springfield, Illinois, in 1862: it produced a constitution that was massively rejected at the polls.[12] But particularly in the South, there was a great deal of molting of constitutions. Each Southern state typically had a Reconstruction constitution.[13] This came to be denounced as a carpetbag charter, when the wheel of politics turned, and a new constitution was then adopted. The Arkansas constitution of 1868 restricted the right to vote or hold office of leaders of the "late rebellion." In 1874, when the older elites were restored to power, a new constitution was adopted. This constitution, among other things, dropped the elaborate franchise provisions of 1868. It provided that "no power, civil or military," should ever interfere "to prevent the free exercise of the right of suffrage"; and that no law would make the right to

11 Edward S. Corwin, *The Twilight of the Supreme Court* (1934), p. 77.

12 Emil J. Verlie, ed., *Illinois Constitutions* (1919), p. xxvii.

13 The Federal Reconstruction Acts—14 Stats. 428 (Act of March 2, 1867), 15 Stats. 2 (Act of March 23, 1867) and 15 Stats. 14 (Act of July 19, 1867)—made restoration of civil government dependent on approval of the fourteenth amendment, and on adoption of a constitution, with full suffrage for blacks, ratified by Congress and by an electorate from which Confederate leaders were excluded.

vote dependent on "previous registration of the elector's name" (Ark. const. 1874, art. III, sec. 2; Ark. const. 1868, art. VIII, secs. 3, 4, 5).

There was great diversity in state constitution-making. Region differed from region, state from state; but some clear patterns emerged. For one thing, state constitutions grew longer and bigger. Most of the states had come to feel that public order demanded more of a constitution than a bare frame of government; and particularly that a legislature could not be trusted to make proper laws. This trend had appeared before 1850; it now grew stronger. The constitution would control the problem of bad laws through its own, overriding superlaws, which took the form indeed of anti-laws—that is (constitutional) laws against (legislative) laws. Hence, the constant inflation of constitutions continued. Indeed, it was almost out of hand.

Louisiana takes some sort of prize for fickleness and inflation. By 1847, it had already gone through two constitutions; before 1900 it added five more, in 1852, 1864, 1868, 1879 and 1898 (six, if one counts as a separate charter the revised constitution of 1861, which carried Louisiana out of the Union). The constitution of 1879 was already obese; that of 1898 was grotesque. It ran to 326 articles. It fixed the yearly salary of the governor at $5,000 and the lieutenant governor's pay at $1,500 (art. 68, art. 70). It put a limit on the "clerical expenses" of state officials; the state treasurer, for example, was not to spend more than $2,000 a year. Twenty-eight separate articles dealt with the government of the city and parish of New Orleans. The jurisdiction of state courts was specified to the last jot and tittle. One article created a "Railroad, Express, Telephone, Telegraph, Steamboat and other Water Craft, and Sleeping Car Commission" (art. 283). The article went on to enumerate the commission's powers, in elaborate detail. Buried in the mass of specifics were provisions of sharper bite—cutting off, in effect, the black man's right to vote. But the detail was so gross, and so stultifying, that the constitution was bound to fail, or, if it survived, to need a constant bandaging with amendments. In fact, this constitution was amended twenty-six times before 1907. The twenty-fifth amendment (1906) authorized, among other things, an appropriation for the Southern University at New Orleans, but of no more than $10,000 a year.

As before, states freely borrowed constitutional clauses from each other, either from important recent constitutions, or (in the West) from the home state of the settlers. Major issues were, and had to be, thrashed out each time afresh. But settled matters, dead issues, and convenient ways of saying things were freely borrowed. Settled, of course, did not mean unimportant; for example, each new state copied the by-now established Bill of Rights, in a fairly stereotyped form. More than half of the Oregon constitution of 1859 can be traced to the Indiana constitution of 1851. Other bits were modeled on clauses from the Iowa, Maine, Massachusetts, Michigan, Ohio, Illinois, Connecticut, Wisconsin, and Texas constitutions. The Wisconsin constitution of 1848 borrowed, without much thought, provisions against long-term agricultural leases and feudal tenures. These came from New York and reflected the Hudson Valley problem and the antirent disorders—problems with no counterpart in frontier Wisconsin. The Nevada convention of 1864 was inspired by California models. This was no wonder; all but two of the delegates had moved to Nevada from California.[14] The Colorado constitution of 1876 was a model and a debating point for those Rocky Mountain states—Idaho, Wyoming, Montana— with similar problems of eminent domain, taxation of mining industries, and water rights.[15]

The trend toward curbing legislative power was strong in the 1850's. Rhode Island, by an amendment of 1854, took the pardoning power away from the legislature and gave it to the governor. State after state decided that their legislature could meet less often and still get its business done. State after state decided to limit the power of the legislature to make law and spend money. Maryland, in 1851, increased the governor's term from one to four years. At the same time, a biennial legislature was told not to establish lotteries, grant divorces, use the credit of the state for the special benefit of private persons or corporations, appropriate money for internal improvements, or contract debts for more than $100,000.[16] Small issues, such as the legislative divorce, were only symptoms. There was a general rejection of ideas of constitutional growth and elasticity. The real issue was fear of unbridled power.

Actually, most constitutional conventions were called to deal with major problems—railroad or bank regulation, or the suffrage problem. Reapportionment was another frequent issue—the at-

---

[14] *Official Report of the Debates and Proceedings in the Constitutional Convention of the State of Nevada, 1864* (1866), p. xvi.

[15] Gordon M. Bakken, "The Impact of the Colorado State Constitution on Rocky Mountain Constitution Making," 47 Colo. Magazine, No. 2, p. 152 (1970).

[16] Fletcher M. Green, *Constitutional Development in the South Atlantic States, 1776–1860* (1966), pp. 285–86.

tempt to shift political power from the east end of a state to the west, or from lowland to highland. The Iowa convention of 1857 was convened, after a referendum, partly because the "people of Iowa were anxious to repeal the restrictions upon banking." [17] The Southern constitutions of the postwar 1860's were called to accept the results of losing the war. The Southern constitutions of the 1870's were called to undo these constitutions, and to win the peace. At the Nevada convention of 1864, there were furious debates about taxation of mines and mining enterprise. Some issues turned out to be so divisive that the convention turned them over to popular referendum. This was done with a controversial banking provision, in Wisconsin in 1848, and with the women's-suffrage issue, thirty years later, in Colorado.

The constitutions of the 1870's, in general, went far in restricting legislative power. In the third Illinois constitution, adopted in 1870, the judiciary was revamped; the governor's power was increased; the legislature was put under restriction. The constitution outlawed many kinds of "local or special laws"; the legislature was not to use this vehicle to grant divorces, change rates of interest on money, provide for "the sale or mortgage of real estate belonging to minors or others under disability," make laws to protect fish or game, grant "to any corporation, association, or individual the right to lay down railroad tracks," or do many other things. There were twenty-three of these prohibitions in all. Moreover, "in all other cases where a general law can be made applicable, no special law shall be enacted." [18] Later states copied this list, or similar lists, and often added new restrictions. In the 1889 constitution of North Dakota, the twenty-three specific prohibitions had grown to thirty-five.[19]

Behind the Illinois constitution was fear of gross economic power, so gross it could buy and sell an upper and lower house. The constitution reflected the fears and interests of the farmers of the state. It was the first of the midwestern granger constitutions. These 1870's constitutions typically provided for tighter regulation of railroads and warehouses. They wanted to balance the great lobbies with countervailing force. A special article (art. XIII) of the Illinois constitution, seven sections long, dealt with regulation of grain elevators and warehouses. In another section, the general as-

[17] *Debates of the Constitutional Convention of the State of Iowa,* Vol. I (1857), p. ii.
[18] Ill. const. 1870, art. IV, sec. 22.
[19] N. Dak. const., 1889, art. II, sec. 69.

sembly was specifically told to "correct abuses and prevent unjust discrimination in the rates of freight and passenger tariffs on the different railroads in this State." [20] Nebraska, in 1875, was so bold as to empower its legislators to establish "maximum rates of charges" for railroads.[21] Legislatures were to work in the public interest; they were not to pass narrow, selfish laws, as tools of the railroads and banks. Constitutions in other parts of the country also mirrored this point of view. The Pennsylvania constitution of 1873 took many a leaf from Illinois' book. It outlawed free passes on railroads, and attempted to work out a fair and rational way to tax these companies.[22]

Control of railroads was also an issue in California, in the brawling, bitter convention of 1878–79.[23] A large and voluble bloc of radicals, called Kearneyites, after their leader Dennis Kearney, clashed repeatedly with more moderate delegates. But the end result was not notably different from, say, Illinois' or Nebraska's constitution. Agitation over Chinese labor and immigration was one special feature, however. The debates were rabidly racist in tone. The Chinese, said one delegate, were "unfit for assimilation with people of our race"; to mix with them would produce "a hybrid of the most despicable, a mongrel of the most detestable that has ever afflicted the earth." Behind the oratory was a real fear of the Chinese impact on wage scales. The Chinese

> have disorganized our labor system, brought thousands of our people to wretchedness and want, degraded labor to the standard of brute energy, poisoned the blood of our youth, and filled our streets with the rot of their decaying civilization. . . . [The Chinese] is a sinewy, shriveled human creature, whose muscles

20 Ill. const. 1870, art. XI, sec. 15.

21 Neb. const. 1875, art. XI, sec. 4.

22 Rosalind L. Branning, *Pennsylvania Constitutional Development* (1960), pp. 101–05. The specter of the mighty railroads lurked behind some apparently unrelated provisions of this constitution. One section, for example, denied to the legislature the power to authorize "investment of trust funds by executors, administrators, guardians, or other trustees in the bonds or stock of any private corporation." The clause was proposed by George W. Biddle, a Philadelphia lawyer and delegate. Biddle charged that the legislature had once passed, in indecent haste, a law which in effect made it legal for fiduciaries to buy fourth mortgage bonds of the Pennsylvania Railroad. It was his desire—and the convention agreed—that such things never be allowed to happen again to the money of widows and orphans. See Lawrence M. Friedman, "The Dynastic Trust," 73 Yale L. J. 547, 562 (1964).

23 Carl B. Swisher, *Motivation and Political Technique in the California Constitutional Convention 1878–9* (1930).

are as iron, whose sinews are like thongs, whose nerves are like
steel wires, with a stomach case lined with brass; a creature who
can toil sixteen hours of the twenty-four; who can live and grow
fat on the refuse of any American laborer's table.[24]

Fear of the foreigner, distrust, xenophobia, sexual paranoia were
thus added to the powerful, rotting sense of economic insecurity.
Only one or two delegates—spokesmen of industry—defended the
Chinese. The convention was strongly in favor of turning its invec-
tive into law. A proposed ban on "Asiatic coolieism" would have
made it illegal for any corporation, or the state, to hire a Chinese
to do any work. The convention was restrained partly by awareness
of the distant but powerful federal constitution.

New Western states, in the late 1880's and the 1890's, drew up
constitutions that reflected suspicion of big business. The Washington constitution (1889) outlawed free railroad passes, and ad-
jured the legislature to "pass laws establishing reasonable maximum rates of charge for the transportation of passengers and
freight, and to correct abuses." It prohibited corporations from
issuing watered stock. Another provision of this constitution declared that "monopolies and trusts shall never be allowed in this
state." Corporations were not to join together to fix prices, or limit
output, or regulate "the transportation of any product or commodity." [25] Particularly in the West, organized labor began to make an
impact on fundamental law. Colorado, in 1876, ordered the general assembly to "provide by law for the proper ventilation of
mines, the construction of escapement-shafts and other such appliances as may be necessary to protect the health and secure the
safety of the workmen therein"; law was also to "prohibit the employment in the mines of children under twelve years of age." [26]
Idaho, in 1889, prohibited the "employment of children under the
age of fourteen (14) years in underground mines." [27] Provisions on
labor relations were absent from the New York constitution of
1894. But this constitution was forward-looking in other respects
—in its emphasis on a professional, bureaucratic civil service (in
which appointments and promotions "shall be made according to

24 *Debates and Proceedings of the Constitutional Convention of the State of
California,* Vol. 1 (1880), pp. 632–33 (remarks of John F. Miller, December 9,
1878).
25 Wash. const. 1889, art. XII, secs. 18, 22. "The legislature shall pass laws,"
the text went on, "for the enforcement of this section," if necessary by declaring
forfeitures of corporate charters.
26 Colo. const. 1876, art. XVI, sec. 2.
27 Idaho const. 1889, art. XIII, sec. 4.

merit and fitness to be ascertained, as far as practicable by [competitive] examinations") and in its new interest in conservation (the "forest preserve as now fixed by law . . . shall be forever kept as wild forest lands").[28]

A different kind of conservation pervaded Southern constitutions in the last part of the century. They were concerned with keeping the black man in his social and legal place. The constitutions of the 1870's had taken away restraints on the right of "rebels" to vote. Later, when the North, the federal government, and the judiciary had evidently lost their Reconstruction passion, the South proceeded to make white supremacy a matter of fundamental law. As early as 1870, the Tennessee constitution provided that no school aided by the state "shall allow white and negro children to be received as scholars together" (art. XI, sec. 12). This constitution also prohibited the "marriage of white persons with negroes, mulattoes, or persons of mixed blood, descended from a negro to the third generation" (art. XI, sec. 14). The South Carolina constitution of 1895 had a similar clause. Ominously, this constitution contained a long paragraph on the penalties for lynching, including damages of "not less than two thousand dollars," assessed against the *county* in which the lynching took place (art. VI, sec. 6).[29] These constitutions also set out systematically to deprive the black man of his vote. The Mississippi constitution of 1890 set up a poll tax of two dollars. It also required (after January 1, 1892) that "every elector shall . . . be able to read any section of the constitution of this State; or . . . be able to understand the same when read to him, or give a reasonable interpretation thereof" (art. 12, secs. 243, 244). Local officials would know how to use these provisions. The Louisiana constitution of 1898 contained the famous grandfather clause: all males entitled to vote on January 1, 1867, their sons and grandsons, and naturalized persons and their sons and grandsons, were excused from the onerous "educational or property qualification" of the constitution (art. 197, sec. 5). This meant that only blacks faced the hurdles local registrars were only too eager to impose.

The Utah constitution of 1895 may be taken as a summary of the state of the constitutional art toward the close of the century. It balanced the old and the borrowed against the particular and the new. Bitter conflict between Mormon and Gentile left its traces on

---

28 N.Y. const. 1894, art. V, sec. 9; art. VII, sec. 7.

29 The amount could, of course, be recovered by the county from those actually at fault.

provisions outlawing polygamy and plural marriages, in the emphasis placed on religious freedom and separation of church and state, in the abolition of the probate system through which, it was thought, Mormon elders helped perpetuate their power. Western radicalism was reflected in other provisions. The legislature was ordered to prohibit women and children from working in the mines, to restrict convict labor, and to prevent "political and commercial control of employees" by their masters (art. XVI, sec. 3). The new conservation motif was present too: "The legislature shall enact laws to prevent the destruction of and to preserve the forests on the lands of the State" (art. XVIII, sec. 1). Most of the rest of the constitution (bill of rights and all) was boiler plate. The constitution as a whole was long, detailed, and diffuse. It set out the salaries of seven state officials, headed by the governor at $2,000 a year. It thus provided ample fodder for litigants and courts to feed upon.

There was all the more fodder in that many constitutions did *not* change, and all constitutions dragged along old matters from prior versions without re-examination. There *was* a high turnover in state constitutions; but many undramatic provisions were altered only at high cost and at a snail's pace. Some constitutions (for example, Delaware in 1897) went into great detail about the number and organization of courts, jurisdiction, civil procedure, and appeal practice. In such states, court reform proceeded very slowly. Many provisions, which seemed valuable when enacted, became nuisances later on. In Michigan, for example, no general revision of the statute laws was constitutionally possible after 1850. Before 1850, a single man had revised the Michigan statutes; this struck many politicians in Michigan as too much concentration of power. Their solution to the problem lasted long after the problem had ended, and became a problem in its own right.[30] Michigan also found itself in acute political and financial embarrassment in the 1950's, partly because the constitution did not allow the state to contract any sizable debts, a provision left over from the 19th century.

More often, fossil constitutional clauses led to elaborate circumlocution. Prohibition against "local" legislation gave rise to one of these. At the time, this ban seemed important. It struck at logrolling, venality, inefficiency. If local legislation were permitted, the legal system might fragment into something like the Holy Roman

30 See W. L. Jenks, "History of Michigan Constitutional Provision Prohibiting a General Revision of the Laws," 19 Mich. L. Rev. 615 (1921).

Empire, and every town and village would have its own rules. Yet different parts of the state—and different cities—might *need* special legislation. Legislatures were allowed to classify municipalities. A class might have only one member; in Wisconsin, a law of 1893 defined cities with more than 150,000 population as cities of the first class. Only Milwaukee was a member.[31] More blatantly, Ohio passed an act in 1891, to authorize village councils to float improvement bonds; but the act was restricted to villages which, according to the 1880 or "any subsequent federal census," had a "population of not less than three thousand three hundred and nine nor greater than three thousand three hundred and twenty." Another act, of the same year, purported to "provide a more efficient government for cities having a population of not less than 33,000 and not more than 34,000 inhabitants." This kind of pinpointing, however, ran considerable judicial risk.[32]

The cost of circumventing the ban on local laws was relatively small. To say "big cities" rather than "Chicago" (a forbidden word) was hardly a burden. But when, as in Wisconsin, it was a constitutional limit on debt that had to be evaded, the evasion was *not* so free of cost. The state could not float its own bonds; the constitution outlawed "public debts" except for "extra-ordinary expenditures," and even these could not exceed $100,000 (art. 8, sec. 6). Obviously, this limitation was hard to live with in the 20th century. To get around the law, the state used various devices. Ultimately, it hit on the device of the so-called "dummy corporation." Improvements, such as university dormitories, would be built by these corporations on state land; the corporation would lease the land from the state, then lease it right back to the state university. The university agreed to pay rent, including rent sufficient to retire the loan, which had been made from the bank to finance part of the construction. The device was upheld in 1955 as valid, and not a violation of the state constitution.[33] But the debt probably carried higher than normal interest, because it was not directly backed by the state's own credit. The fact that these nuisance clauses survived meant that they had *some* lingering political strength or attractiveness—enough to amount to a veto power,

31 Laws Wis. 1893, ch. 312. See *State ex rel. Risch* v. *Board of Trustees of Policemen's Pension Fund,* 121 Wis. 44, 98 N.W. 954 (1904).

32 Laws Ohio 1891, p. 74 (Act of Mar. 4, 1891); Laws Ohio 1891, p. 77 (Act of Mar. 5, 1891). A later version of this latter law, covering all cities with between 27,000 and 34,000 population, was upheld as sufficiently general in *State ex rel. Monnett* v. *Baker,* 55 Ohio St. 1, 44 N.E. 516 (1896).

33 *State ex rel. Thomson* v. *Giessel,* 271 Wis. 15, 72 N.W.2d 577 (1955).

enough force to block any change in so tough a structure as a state constitution. Moreover, legislators sometimes feel they cannot get *rid* of a useless prohibition, because the public will misinterpret what they have done. To repeal the constitutional limit on debts of state may be like repealing the adultery laws; it looks like a vote in favor of sin. It was not until 1969 that Wisconsin pulled the teeth of this archaic limitation.[34]

Judicial review of state statutes was a rare, extraordinary event in 1850; it was a common occurrence in 1900. What happened in the state courts paralleled what happened in the federal courts. The taste for power was even more intoxicating to state tribunals. The figures speak loud and clear. In Virginia, for example, up to the outbreak of the Civil War, the state's high court had decided only thirty-five cases in which the constitutionality of a law or practice was questioned. Of these, the court declared only four unconstitutional. Between 1861 and 1875, "a dozen or more laws or practices were declared unconstitutional." [35] The Alabama supreme court went so far as to declare the entire constitution of 1865 null and void. The real spurt, however, came at the end of the century. In Minnesota, the supreme court declared nineteen laws unconstitutional in the 1860's. Only thirteen statutes fell in the next fifteen years. But between 1885 and 1899, approximately seventy state statutes were struck down, with a decided bunching in the last few years of the century.[36] In Utah, between 1896 and 1899, twenty-two statutes were reviewed by the Utah supreme court. Exactly half of these were declared to be mere parchment and ink.[37]

It would be an exaggeration to call the state high court a third chamber of the legislature. But such a court was a force to be reckoned with. The explosion of judicial review did not rest on the due-process clause alone or on other clauses borrowed from federal law. Due-process cases grew voluptuously; but many dramatic cases of judicial review turned on clauses with no federal counterpart at

34 An amendment to art. 8, sec. 7, adopted in 1969, authorized the state to "contract public debt . . . to acquire, construct, develop . . . land, waters, property, highways, buildings . . . for public purposes," subject to certain limitations.

35 Margaret V. Nelson, *A Study of Judicial Review in Virginia, 1789–1928* (1947), p. 54.

36 These figures are from Oliver Field, "Unconstitutional Legislation in Minnesota," 35 Am. Pol. Science Rev. 898 (1941).

37 Martin B. Hickman, "Judicial Review of Legislation in Utah," 4 Utah L. Rev. 50, 51 (1954).

all. The wordy, excessive texts of the state constitutions were made to order for an aggressive judiciary. There were many technical controls over sloppy, corrupt, and selfish legislation; these too played into the hands of litigants and courts. In Indiana, for example, not a single statute in the 19th century failed because it violated the right of free speech. Eight statutes were void because they were ex post facto or because they were guilty of "impairing the obligation of contract." But eleven statutes could not meet the test that "No act shall ever be revised or amended by mere reference to its title, but the act revised, or section amended, shall be set forth and published at full length." [38]

Another fruitful example was the clause that provided that "Every act shall embrace but one subject . . . which subject shall be expressed in the title." The quoted version is from Indiana, and cost nine statutes their lives in the 19th century.[39] As early as 1798, as part of the backlash against the Yazoo shenanigans, the Georgia constitution provided that no law might contain "any matter different from what is expressed in the title." The New Jersey constitution of 1844 added to this a requirement that every law could "embrace but one object." [40] A year later the Louisiana constitution picked up the clause. It soon became quite common. It fit neatly into the general reform of legislative procedure which, along with restriction on the legislature's power, formed a striking aspect of constitution-making in the last half of the 19th century. The clause was by no means senseless. It was designed, as Thomas Cooley explained,

> first, to prevent hodge-podge, or "log-rolling" legislation; second, to prevent surprise or fraud upon the legislature by means of provisions in bills of which the titles gave no intimation, and which might therefore be overlooked and carelessly and unintentionally adopted; and third, to fairly apprise the people . . . of the subjects of legislation that are being considered, in order that they may have the opportunity of being heard thereon.[41]

Whether the clause actually had these effects is another question. It did give the judiciary another meat ax to butcher legislation. In most instances, statutes attacked under the clause were upheld by

[38] Ind. const. 1851, art. IV, sec. 21. Oliver P. Field "Unconstitutional Legislation in Indiana," 17 Indiana L. J. 101, 118, 121 (1941).

[39] Field, op. cit., p. 120.

[40] Ernst Freund, Standards of American Legislation (1917), pp. 154–55.

[41] Thomas M. Cooley, A Treatise on Constitutional Limitations (5th ed., 1883), p. 173.

the courts. But the power was there; it had to be reckoned with. Litigants could use the clause to delay, to thwart, sometimes to defeat legislation. Courts, too, could use the clause, in a number of ways, to get at real abuses in the legislative process, or as a mere device to further ends quite different from those which Cooley mentioned.

In *State v. Young*, an Indiana case of 1874, the legislature had passed an act entitled, "An act to regulate the sale of intoxicating liquors, to provide against evils resulting from any sale thereof, to furnish remedies for damages suffered by any person in consequence of such sale, prescribing penalties, to repeal all laws contravening the provisions of this act, and declaring an emergency." The ninth section of the act prescribed a five-dollar fine for any person "found in a state of intoxication." This section, the court ruled, was unconstitutional. The title "points to the sale of intoxicating liquors," not the "intemperate use of such liquors." Hence the punishment of drunks was a "matter not expressed in the title," and the act was void.[42]

How courts made use of constitutional technicality is strikingly illustrated by a bizarre West Virginia case, *Rachel Cutlip v. Sheriff of Calhoun County*.[43] The county seat of Calhoun County had once been located at Arnoldsburg, West Virginia. In 1867, the legislature passed "An Act locating the county seat of Calhoun County." The first section of the act put the county seat "at the farm of Simon P. Stump, on the Little Kanawha river." The third section of the act authorized the board of supervisors "to sell any county property at Arnoldsburg." The next legislature unceremoniously repealed this act. Later, Rachel Cutlip was indicted for murder in the circuit court of Calhoun County, sitting at Arnoldsburg. She argued that she had been "unlawfully detained," that all the proceedings were invalid, that there was in fact *no* county seat in Calhoun County, and that the circuit court, meeting in what it imagined to be the county seat, had no real power to indict her. It was not a frivolous argument. The act of 1867 eliminated Arnoldsburg as county seat. The next statute got rid of Simon Stump's farm as county seat. Through ignorance or inadvertence, it failed to put the county seat back at Arnoldsburg. The court had no wish to let Rachel Cutlip go free. Nor did they want to leave Calhoun County in a state of nature. They reached, in despair, for the West Virginia constitution. The title of the law of 1867 referred only to

[42] *State v. Young*, 47 Ind. 150 (1874).
[43] *Rachel Cutlip v. Sheriff of Calhoun County*, 3 W. Va. 588 (1869).

a change in the location of the county seat. Another section authorized sale of county property at Arnoldsburg. This was a different "object" altogether, not expressed in the title of the law. Hence, the statute of 1867 was never valid, and the county seat had never really moved away from Arnoldsburg.

This crabbed, misbegotten, petty technicality served, at least arguably, a useful purpose. It gave the court an excuse to intervene. The court patched up the job that the legislature had badly or corruptly done, and sternly reminded the other branch that the court took standards of performance, prescribed by the constitution, quite seriously.

This was a legitimate role. Far more controversial were cases that seemed to have a sinister goal: to "annex the principles of *laissez faire* capitalism to the Constitution and put them beyond reach of state legislative power." [44] An early and startling example, where judicial review seemed to run wild, was *Wynehamer* v. *People* (New York, 1856).[45] New York had passed a prohibition law; *Wynehamer* declared it unconstitutional. The road to this surprising conclusion led through the due-process clause. The court pointed out that stocks of liquor were undeniably "property" in the "most absolute and unqualified sense," before the law was enacted. Afterwards, "intoxicating liquors" were "laid under" the ban, "the right to sell them . . . denied, and their commercial value . . . thus annihilated." The law was a clear deprivation of property rights, then, and without due process of law.

The precise holding of *Wynehamer* never won much of a following. Free enterprise in liquor, lottery tickets, gambling, and sex never appealed much to 19th-century judges. The case would be only an historical curiosity, except that its daring use of the due-process clause later became so popular. Activist courts fed on this kind of food, particularly after constitutional theorists made the idea intellectually palatable.[46] In *Matter of Jacobs* (1885),[47] the New York Court of Appeals held unconstitutional "An act to improve the public health, by prohibiting the manufacture of cigars and preparation of tobacco in any form, in tenement-houses." The law, said the court, "interferes with the profitable and free use of

[44] Edward Corwin, *The Twilight of the Supreme Court* (1934), p. 78. The quote actually referred to the work of the United States Supreme Court.

[45] 13 N.Y. 378 (1856).

[46] See, in general, Clyde Jacobs, *Law Writers and the Court* (1954); Arnold M. Paul, *Conservative Crisis and the Rule of Law, Attitudes of Bar and Bench, 1887–1895* (1960).

[47] 98 N.Y. 98 (1885).

his property by the owner or lessee of a tenement-house who is a cigarmaker." It "trammels him in the application of his industry and the disposition of his labor, and thus, in a strictly legitimate sense, it arbitrarily deprives him of his property and of some portion of his personal liberty." Of course, the law claimed to "improve the public health." But the court, on its own, reviewed this claim skeptically, even though in theory the legislature, a coordinate branch of government, had aired this question thoroughly and come to a decision. The court concluded that the law really had "no relation whatever to the public health."

In *Godcharles* v. *Wigeman* (1886),[48] the Pennsylvania court passed on a statute, enacted in 1881, which required all businesses "engaged in mining coal, ore or other mineral . . . or manufacturing iron or steel . . . or any other kind of manufacturing," to pay their employees "at least once in each month," to pay in cash or legal tender, not in "other paper," and forbade the companies from overcharging in company stores.[49] Enraged, the court declared this act to be "utterly unconstitutional and void." It was an attempt "to do what, in this country, cannot be done, that is, prevent persons who are *sui juris* from making their own contracts." The law was "an insulting attempt to put the laborer under a legislative tutelage, which is not only degrading to his manhood, but subversive of his rights as a citizen of the United States." The court did not bother to cite any clause, either from state or federal constitution, in defense of its action. (Perhaps the "utterly void" was a self-evident category.) In *Ritchie* v. *People,* an emanation of the Illinois supreme court in 1895,[50] the law under attack had limited the labor of women in "any factory or workshop" to eight hours a day and forty-eight hours a week. The court denounced the statute as a "purely arbitrary restriction upon the fundamental rights of the citizen to control his or her own time and faculties."

Cases such as these provided occasion for liberal outrage. Labor groups and social reformers had struggled and lobbied for protective legislation. They learned soon enough that enactment was only a battle, not the war. Courts had the power to destroy their legislation, sometimes on the flimsiest legal basis, sometimes, as in *Godcharles,* with apparently no basis at all. Out of these cases arose

48 113 Pa. St. 431, 6 Atl. 354 (1886).

49 Laws Pa. 1881, No. 173, p. 147. One point of the law was to prevent companies from paying their workers in slips of paper redeemable only at the company store.

50 155 Ill. 98, 40 N.E. 454 (1895).

the reputation of courts as fortresses of dark and deep reaction. To conservatives, of course, the courts were bulwarks of traditional liberty. Only the courts seemed to understand that there were "un-foreseen dangers," hidden costs, that lurked in legislation which, though seemingly beneficial, actually ran "counter to the broad general basis of Anglo-Saxon civilization." [51] The court's reputation among conservatives was not decisively reversed until the days of the Warren court.

Neither praise nor blame were entirely deserved. The cases cited were famous, horrible examples. Basically, courts let the great wave of social legislation, of the last two decades of the century, pass undisturbed. Some courts were even outspokenly friendly to these laws. Constitutional madness was not distributed evenly across the country; the Illinois supreme court, for example, was exceptionally hostile to labor laws. What was nationwide was the *threat,* the *possibility* of a court contest. The test case became an accepted part of the life cycle of major legislation. This cloud, hanging over the fate of specific laws, may have been the major effect of judicial review.

What caused the outburst of judicial review? Limitations and controls over legislative acts had been written into state constitutions. Who would enforce them? Either no one or the courts. High courts had good reputations for integrity and craftsmanship. They had the technical skill to oversee legislative behavior. They could criticize and correct draftsmanship and parliamentary process when these were contradictory. It was tempting for the courts to cross over from procedure to substance. And the demand for the product was there. When a power bloc was thwarted in one branch of government, it naturally turned to another. If the legislatures were populist or Granger, there was always one last hope for a railroad or mining company: the courts.

Of course, courts might have resisted the temptation, and many of them did. But a significant proportion of the judges leaped to the bait. Judges, after all, were members of the same society as their litigants. They shared the general outlook that American life was a zero-sum game. Their business was the rule of law, legal tradition, adjudication. Legislation, whatever its subject, was a threat to their primordial function, molding and declaring the law. Statutes were brute intrusions, local in scope, often shortsighted in principle or effect. They interfered in a legal world that belonged, by right, to the judges. Particularly after 1870, judges may have seen themselves more and more as guardians of a precious and

51 Frederic J. Stimson, *Popular Law-Making* (1910), p. 238.

threatened tradition. The world about them seemed to be growing more turbulent and unsettled. The clash of interests, the warfare of classes brutally destroyed time-honored values. The judges read their constitutions as instruments of caution, delay, and honest doubt; they read them as instruments that preserved historic truths, about democratic society and right reason; they read them as middle-class texts, embodying middle-class values, striving toward middle-class goals. The power that the courts assumed was not used solely in the service of the powerful and rich. In some blatant cases, to be sure, judges used constitutional doctrine to strengthen the hand of big business at the expense of organized labor. They allowed themselves to be persuaded that organized labor was dangerous and un-American, that it threatened the balance of society. But the judges were, by and large, almost equally afraid of the sinister un-American trusts. The constitution, as they interpreted it, did not prevent the licensing of barbers, plumbers, doctors, and lawyers; did not prevent farmers, artisans, and professional men from uniting to form strong, solid middle-class groups; did not protect giant industrial combines from the righteous wrath of the people. Their taste for power was general, but the prejudices of the judges—predominantly old-American, conservative, middle-class—dictated where the effects of the power would fall.

The worst thing about this power was that it was randomly and irresponsibly exercised. It could be neither predicted nor controlled. Judges did not declare *all* social laws unconstitutional, only a small minority of them. Nor were *all* statutes challenged in court. The court had no way to pull cases onto its docket. A private litigant had to be willing to finance the case. Even then, the court might evade or avoid the constitutional issue. Judicial review was slow at best. One scholar studied 172 Indiana cases in which the court declared laws unconstitutional. On the average, the statutes were slightly under five years old when they fell. In fifty cases, the statutes had been on the books for more than five years. Seventeen statutes were struck down after ten years or more of apparent validity; in one case the elapsed time was 42 years.[52] On balance, over the whole range of American history, there is a strong argument that judicial review has been eminently worth while; but its benefits have been by no means without cost. The main effect may have

---

[52] Oliver P. Field, "Unconstitutional Legislation in Indiana," 17 Ind. L. J. 101, 108–09 (1941). The figures include cases up to 1935. But the conclusions hold reasonably well for the 19th century. Field cites a case in 1879, voiding a statute of 1861; a case in 1880 overturned a law of 1855. *Ibid.*, pp. 116–17.

been preventive, to keep down the rate of legislative change. All in all, in the 19th century, the costs, not the benefits of judicial review, may have weighed in the balance most heavily.

THE WEST

Westward expansion brought the United States face to face with a legal frontier. Before 1840, the United States had already absorbed millions of acres of land once subsumed under civil law—in Florida, Texas, and the Mississippi Valley. Now, after the Mexican War (1848), the United States squeezed out of Mexico another gigantic domain, sparsely settled, over which the civil law held at least nominal reign. In most of it, the struggle between the two legal systems was brief; the outcome was never much in doubt. American lawyers and judges poured in along with other American settlers. In Utah, for example, Spanish-Mexican law never really had any force. The immigrants were Americans, who "tacitly" brought common law with them, to an empty country.[53]

In California, however, and particularly in New Mexico, there lived substantial numbers of Spanish-speaking residents. In New Mexico, judges frequently cited civil law, sometimes approvingly.[54] California was not so close a case. The gold rush brought a cataclysmic inflow of population. The new residents were basically Americans, totally ignorant of civil law. Spanish-Mexican law had its spokesmen—members of the existing San Francisco bar vigorously defended it; but the more influential majority felt otherwise. The "Common Law of England" (insofar as not "repugnant" to the United States Constitution and the laws and constitution of California) was formally adopted in 1850 as the "rule of decision in all the Courts of this State." [55]

The civil law left some legacies behind. One was a muddled collection of land grants, which plagued the land law of California and New Mexico for decades. The civil-law tradition influenced many specific doctrines and institutions—the community property

[53] See the remarks of Emerson, J., in *First National Bank of Utah* v. *Kinner*, 1 Utah 100, 106–7 (1873).

[54] In *Chavez* v. *MacKnight*, 1 Gildersleeve (N.M.) 147, 150–1 (1857), the judge cited "Escriche" writing "under the head[ing] of Mujer Casada" (married woman), a reference to the work of Joaquin Escriche y Martin (1784–1847); the judge spoke of the "humane regard" and "wise and just policy" of the civil law toward married women.

[55] Laws Cal. 1850, ch. 95.

system, for example.[56] Civil law background may have inclined Western states to be hospitable toward codes and procedural reform, but other explanations are equally persuasive. Idaho was a code state, too, without the slightest shadow of civil-law influence.

Many frontier traits, familiar from earlier generations, were repeated in the far West: the mixture of old and new in the substantive law; the code-making habit; the bar composed of young hustlers. The shape of the land was itself sometimes determinative for legal change. Some states—Texas and California—were rich in climate and resources; most of the West was bleak, arid, mountainous. Landscape strikingly affected water and resource law. The common-law doctrine of riparian rights was altered. Prior appropriation, a kind of rule of first-come-first-served, became popular in the West, where there was never enough water to give every landowner who fronted on a river an equal share. Significantly, the new doctrine was completely in effect only in the wholly arid states; California and Texas, with their double climates, had mixed systems of water law too.[57]

Two famous Western institutions were the miners' codes and the vigilante movement. The miners' codes were little bodies of law, adopted as binding customs in Western mining camps. The miners' courts and codes had a certain similarity to the claim clubs of the Midwest. These had been organizations of squatters, who banded together to control the outcomes of public land auctions, and who also drew up rules and procedures for recording and judging their own land claims. These clubs flourished in Wisconsin in the late 1830's, in Iowa through the 1840's. There is some slight evidence of connection between the claim clubs, miners' groups in the Midwest (near Galena, Illinois, and in southwestern Wisconsin), and the miners' codes of the Far West. These last were at least as old as the California gold rush, and were also found in the West—in Gregory Diggings (Colorado), in 1859, in the Black Hills of Dakota Territory in the 1870's, and in Nevada. Many codes were reduced to written form. They set up rough but workable rules and processes, for recording claims, for deciding whose claim was first, for settling disputes among claimants, and for enforcing decisions of miners' "courts." The Gregory Diggings ruled itself through its little legal system, two years before Colorado Territory was formally organized. The mining code served the func-

[56] On the civil law legacy, see also pp. 148–56.
[57] See Walter P. Webb, *The Great Plains* (1931), pp. 431–52; Betty E. Dobkins, *The Spanish Element in Texas Water Law* (1959).

tion, well known in American legal history, of a makeshift judicial and political order, where settlement had run past borders of legitimate government. The Gregory code was copied by other mining districts. As business increased, "judges" handled a wide range of disputes. The Colorado territorial legislature in 1861 and 1862 ratified, with a broad sweep, the system of local claims and judgments rendered by these informal courts. A squatter, or his assignee, or any person whose title rested on a "decree or execution, of any of the so-called Provisional Government Courts, People's or Miners' Courts," could bring actions of trespass, ejectment, and forcible detainer (except against the United States government itself.) [58]

More flamboyant, and at the same time more sinister, was the vigilante movement. This was not exclusively a western phenomenon; but the West was its major locale. Two famous examples were the San Francisco Vigilance Committees, of 1851 and 1856. The Committees were "businessmen's revolutions," directed against corrupt, inept local government. Most favorably viewed, they were sincere attempts by "decent" citizens to curb violence and misrule in San Francisco by self-help. The city was turbulent; its population swelled with gold-hungry hordes. The first committee began its work by arresting and trying a "desperate character" named Jenkins. He was convicted and hanged from a heavy wooden beam, on a small adobe house left over from the Mexican period.[59] The Second Vigilance Committee was more powerful than the first. It even presumed to seize and try David Terry, a Justice of the California supreme court; it hanged some unsavory local characters; it defied local, state, and national governments; in general, it held San Francisco in the grip of a benevolent despotism. "The safety of the people," said the San Francisco Bulletin, which spoke for the vigilantes, "is above all law." [60] The trials of the Vigilance Committees were highly irregular; but they never quite descended to barbarism, and they would not have been totally unrecognizable to a lawyer. Best of all, the movement had the decency to die a natural death.

Vigilante justice was older than the gold rush; but San Francisco gave it new life, and inspired imitation. There were twenty-

58 Ovando J. Hollister, The Mines of Colorado (1867), p. 75 ff.; pp. 359–63; Laws Terr. Colo. 1861, p. 249; Laws Terr. Colo. 1862, p. 69.

59 Alan Valentine, Vigilante Justice (1956), pp. 54–58. On the American vigilante movements in general, see Richard Maxwell Brown, "The American Vigilante Tradition," in Hugh D. Graham and Ted R. Gurr, eds., Violence in America: Historical and Comparative Perspectives (1969), p. 154.

60 Quoted in A. Russell Buchanan, David S. Terry of California (1956), p. 43.

seven vigilance committees in California in the 1850's. In 1858, there was a vigilance committee in Carson Valley, Nevada. There were vigilantes in Denver, Colorado, from 1854 to 1861. In the 1860's the Vigilantes of Montana rode high. This was a rougher breed than the San Francisco boys. Their version of justice was quick and sure; they had little regard for the niceties of trial. Sometimes they avenged crimes never committed, or hanged the wrong man, by mistake. The vigilantes were quite willing to put up with these errors. Wyoming had vigilantes too—beginning with "two lethal movements in the wild railroad boomtowns of Cheyenne and Laramie," in 1868–69.[61]

For the vigilantes, formal justice clearly seemed too slow; or, in other cases, formal justice was an invited guest who had not yet arrived. Willard Hurst has suggested that vigilantism was not really a "pre-law phenomenon," a "groping towards the creation of legal institutions," but more accurately a "reaction against the corruption, weakness, or delays" of the established legal order.[62] From one point of view, vigilantes merely put together a makeshift criminal law, just as the miners put together a makeshift property code, in accordance with their customs and needs. In another view, they were reacting against a code which was not to their liking. In either case, it is clear that social control, like nature, abhors a vacuum. The population was not really lawless; quite to the contrary, people were accustomed to norms and institutions of law and order; they were unwilling to tolerate too sharp a break in social continuity; or the existence of formal law too slow or too corrupt for their purposes.

There may have been another, subtler factor at work. The men of the mob had the satisfaction, grim though it was, of a justice that lay literally in their hardened hands; they pulled on the ropes themselves, not through surrogates. The regular courts, even had they been as sure of result as the vigilantes (or the lynch mob of the South), would not have been quite so swift. To many people, punishment seems twice as rich when it is carried out with white-hot immediacy, and when the purity of emotion is not sullied by the arguments and doubts of a trial.

Just as some look on the vigilantes and the miners' law as blood-thirsty and antidemocratic, so others, quite the contrary, saw in these institutions the outcroppings of genuine popular justice, an

61 Brown, *op. cit.*, pp. 162–3.
62 Willard Hurst, "The Uses of Law in Four 'Colonial' States of the American Union," 1945 Wisconsin L. Rev. 577, 585.

Anglo-Saxon inheritance as old as Teutonic folkmoots, transplanted here to fresher soil. This was, by and large, a 19th-century
idea. The historian H. H. Bancroft advanced this point of view.
The frontier thesis of Frederick Jackson Turner also pictured the
man of the West as nature's democrat, a noble breed, dying along
with the buffalo, the Indian, the whooping crane.

Benjamin Shambaugh, writing in 1902, similarly idealized the
Midwestern claim clubs. He saw them as "fountains of that spirit
of Western Democracy which permeated the social and political
life of America during the 19th century." [63] Modern scholarship has
been more hard-headed, much less lyrical about the claim clubs.[64]
These tight little organizations were hardly fountains of Western
democracy; they were meant to protect early claimants from later,
more innocent arrivals; also to force the government to sell land at
the lowest legitimate price. The miners' groups, too, were less
democratic than guildlike and protectionist. What traveled west,
more important than form, was a notion quite the antithesis of
primitive democracy. The notion was: organize or die; and it was
the theme of American law, East and West, in the last half of the
19th century, in every area and arena of life.

[63] Benjamin F. Shambaugh, *History of the Constitutions of Iowa* (1902), p. 65.
He added that the members were men who "in the silent forest, in the broad
prairies, in the deep blue sky, in the sentinels of the night, in the sunshine and
in the storm, in the rosy dawn . . . must have seen and felt the Infinite," a rather florid way of saying that the pioneers rarely went to church. *Ibid.*, p. 24.

[64] See, for example, Allan G. Bogue, "The Iowa Claim Clubs: Symbol and
Substance," 45 Miss. Valley Hist. Rev. 231 (1958).

JUDGES AND COURTS: 1847–1900

After 1847, popular election of judges was more and more accepted as normal. Every state that entered the union after 1846 provided that the voters would elect some or all of their judges. The California constitution of 1849 made the whole system elective, from the supreme court down to justices of the peace. In the year 1850 alone, seven states changed laws to provide for more popular election of judges. In 1850, both the Michigan and Pennsylvania supreme courts turned elective.[1]

Only a few states still appointed their judges—Maine and Massachusetts, for example, and, of course, the federal government. In Connecticut the legislature chose judges; but, in 1856, the term of office was changed to eight years; before that, judges had served during "good behavior," which meant, in practice, for life. The traffic did not entirely go one way, that is, toward the elective principle. Some Southern states returned to the appointive system, during Reconstruction. Texas, between 1866 and 1876, went from an elective to an appointive supreme court, and back. Mississippi abolished its elected high court of errors and appeals, under the constitution of 1868. The new supreme court consisted of three judges, appointed by the governor and confirmed by the senate. Mississippi did not return to an elective system until 1910.

In the long run, the elective system did not have results so earth-shaking, for good or bad, as proponents had hoped and opponents feared. In the first place, elections did not become so partisan as they might have. Some lawyers had seen grave danger in elections; hostile politicians might grub about in the reports, find an unpopular decision, and use it politically to ruin a sitting judge. But as it turned out, most sitting judges who ran again won again, regardless of party. There were some striking exceptions, however. Michigan's most illustrious judge, Thomas M. Cooley, was defeated for re-

1 Evan Haynes, *The Selection and Tenure of Judges* (1944), pp. 100, 116, 127.

election in 1885; the main reason was a "Democratic Deluge" that "submerge[d] even the mountain tops"; labor was opposed to him, and his close connection with the railroads cost him dearly with some voters.[2] Chief Justice Charles B. Lawrence of Illinois was defeated because of the wrath of the Grangers in 1873.[3] Sometimes it was enough that a judge stood for a particular party or position. In 1861, Chief Judge John C. Legrand and Judge William B. Tuck, of the court of appeals of Maryland, were defeated for re-election by two judges who ran on a ticket of stern loyalty to the Union.[4]

The elective principle may have had some subtle effect on decision-making, or on the form in which opinions were cast. Some members of the legal profession saw this as an additional danger. Partly for this reason, they continued to oppose the election of judges. The elective principle undermined the idea that no one but lawyers had the right to determine the proper outcome of cases, and that only strictly legal principles belonged in the armory of judges. The defeat of Chief Justice Lawrence looked like a case where "a herd of dissatisfied farmers have put an ignorant demagogue in the seat of an able and upright judge." [5] These words were written by an editor of the *Albany Law Journal,* in 1873, at a time when a new—and futile—attempt was made to overturn the elective principle in New York. The writer added:

> The people are the worst possible judges of those qualifications essential to a good judge. They could select an orator, an advocate or a debater, as his qualities are palpable and salient; but the qualities of a judge are peculiar, and are seldom appreciated by cursory and general notice. That uncommon, recondite and difficult learning; that power and turn of mind and cast of character called the "judicial," are likely to go unremarked by the nonprofessional observer. To him the effective advocate seems best fitted to fill the judicial office; but experience has proved

2 Lewis G. Vander Velde, "Thomas McIntyre Cooley," in Earl D. Babst and Lewis G. Vander Velde, eds., *Michigan and the Cleveland Era* (1948), pp. 77, 92.

3 James E. Babb, "The Supreme Court of Illinois," 3 Green Bag 217, 234 (1891).

4 Carroll T. Bond, *The Court of Appeals of Maryland, a History* (1928), p. 159. Maryland at least was spared the embarrassment of fighting on the Union side with secessionist judges. This was almost the plight of the federal government; Chief Justice Taney, author of the *Dred Scott* decision, lived until 1864. His wartime conduct was a thorn in Lincoln's side. John Campbell of Alabama resigned his seat on the court when his state seceded.

5 8 Albany L. J. 18 (July 5, 1873).

that the best advocate is not likely to prove the best judge, as the two functions exact diverse qualifications.

But the chief objection to an elective judiciary is the effect it has upon the office; its dignity; its just weight; its hold upon the general confidence.

While it may be true that the selection of candidates for judges is generally left to the legal members of the [party] conventions, it is equally true that these legal members are not usually such a class of lawyers as is competent to do any thing so important as the making of a judge—young, ambitious men, more familiar with the management of ward caucuses or town meetings than with the conduct of a cause in court.

The elective principle, at least, made a contribution to the withering away of impeachment. There were few removals after 1847, except for good and sufficient (that is, nonpolitical) cause. Federal impeachment proceedings were exceedingly rare. The House judiciary committee recommended impeachment for John C. Watrous, district judge for Texas, in 1853. He was supposed to have practiced law while on the bench, and heard cases in which he had a financial stake. No action was taken against him. Between 1872 and 1875, four federal judges were investigated on grounds of irregular conduct; all of them resigned under fire.[6] Few state judges, too, were ever impeached. In 1852, Chief Justice Levi Hubbell of Wisconsin was accused of a wide range of offenses, from partiality, and improper conduct of trials, to taking a bribe. Hubbell was irascible and partisan. There was evidence of "shoddy standards" in his work, but the senators seemed to demand (and did not get) extraordinary proofs of misconduct; Hubbell was not removed.[7]

In the Gilded Age, in the fetid atmosphere of the Tweed ring, the lower New York bench distinguished itself for corruption. "The stink of our state judiciary is growing too strongly ammoniac and hippuric for endurance," wrote George Templeton Strong in his diary. This stench from the courtroom was one of the stimuli that led to formation of the New York City Bar Association, in 1870. Two of the most notorious of the judges were George G. Barnard and Albert Cardozo, justices of the supreme court. Cardozo, whose son Benjamin ultimately redeemed the family name, handed out receiverships to relatives and friends. Strong wrote: "I

6 Joseph Borkin, *The Corrupt Judge* (1962), pp. 201, 253–54.
7 Alfons J. Beitzinger, *Edward G. Ryan, Lion of the Law* (1960), pp. 32–39.

think Nature meant Cardozo to sweep the court room, not to pre-side in it. . . . He would look more natural in the dock of the Sessions than on the Bench of the Supreme Court." [8] In 1872, be-cause of their "gross abuse of . . . powers," their venality, their improper conduct, charges of impeachment were drawn up against Barnard and Cardozo. Cardozo resigned; Barnard was impeached and forever barred from public office.[9]

A more political use of the threat of impeachment drove "carpet-bag" judges off the bench in the South, after Reconstruction col-lapsed. In South Carolina, the one black supreme court justice, Jonathan Jasper Wright, was harassed from his post in 1877. Despite the smoke of propaganda, one may dismiss the charges against these Southern judges as not fully proven. The carpetbag judges, black and white, have suffered the fate of history's losers. They were probably no more corrupt than native judges of the same time and culture. Moses Walker, from Ohio, served with some distinction on the Texas supreme court.[10] Albion W. Tourgee,[11] a carpetbag judge, later drew on his Southern experience to write a series of novels. One of these, A Fool's Errand (1879), was sensa-tionally successful. Tourgee's liberal views on black-white relation-ships were far ahead of his times. Late in his life, he worked on the briefs in Plessy v. Ferguson, before the case went up to the Supreme Court. Tourgee was an exceptional man; yet his case suggests the danger of accepting too quickly the Southern view of the carpetbag bench.

Another mixed, controversial breed was the territorial judge. The reputation of these men casts further doubt on the causal power of the elective system. Territorial judges were strictly ap-pointive. Many were political hacks, ill-paid, ill-prepared for their jobs, almost invariably nonresidents, whose sole claim to office was a claim on patronage at Washington. Some of these judges hardly had the decency to set foot in their jurisdictions; some resigned after a short term in office, going after more lucrative game. Some, like the wandering frontier lawyers, took jobs in one territory after another. Samuel Chipman Parks of Illinois, for example, was a

[8] A. Nevins and M. Thomas, eds., The Diary of George Templeton Strong, Vol. 4 (1952), pp. 264–65.

[9] History of the Bench and Bar of New York (Vol. I, 1897), p. 199.

[10] James R. Norvell, "The Reconstruction Courts of Texas, 1867–1873," 62 Southwestern Historical Q. 141, 160–1 (1958).

[11] His career is described in Otto H. Olsen, Carpetbagger's Crusade, the Life of Albion Winegar Tourgee (1965).

judge in three territories in a row: Idaho (1863), New Mexico (1878), and Wyoming (1882).[12]

A territorial judgeship was not a genteel post, like that filled by the wig-wearing judges of England, or even the quiet black-robed dignitaries of the Eastern bench. For fair reasons or foul, local residents were often hostile to these judges, sent in by Washington. One hears about "sage-brush districting"—legislatures that carved up judicial districts in such a way as to exile an unpopular judge to the barren wastelands. The legislature of New Mexico, according to the *Sante Fe Post,* sent Chief Justice Joseph G. Palen in 1872 "to the hottest locality over which they had jurisdiction," regretting only "that their jurisdiction is so limited." [13]

A few of these judges became famous or notorious. Kirby Benedict served as chief justice of New Mexico Territory in the 1850's and 1860's. The territorial secretary of state complained, in a letter to President Lincoln, that Benedict "visits the gambling Hells and drinking saloons and with a swagger and bluster defiles his judicial robes." Perhaps he was driven to drink. As a new judge, in 1854, Benedict had to ride circuit through a vast desert country; hostile Indians hid in its arid canyons. Benedict gave as good as he got: he denounced his accuser as a "moronic maniac, an egotist, a general mischief-maker." [14] Lincoln reappointed Benedict; but President Johnson removed him from office as a drunkard. Benedict practiced law for a while, then was disbarred.

Western judges sometimes had to be made of tougher stuff than their Eastern counterparts. The barren, empty lands bred or harbored lawlessness; the vast anonymity of the West attracted killers and thieves. This was the world of Judge Isaac Parker, the hanging judge, first appointed by President Grant, to rule over the Western Arkansas District from his seat in Fort Smith. Parker's realm included Indian Territory. It was the "land of the six-shooter." Parker did not shrink from stern duty, as he saw it. He began his regime of law and order by condemning six men, who were hanged on September 3, 1875. Before his career was over, in 1896, seventy-nine men, many of them Indians or blacks, had put on the black hood

12 Earl S. Pomeroy, *The Territories and the United States, 1861–1890* (1947), p. 136.

13 *Ibid.,* p. 57.

14 Letter of W. F. M. Arny to Lincoln, Dec. 19, 1863; letter of Benedict to Edward Bates, Jan. 3, 1864, printed in Aurora Hunt, *Kirby Benedict, Frontier Federal Judge* (1961), pp. 165, 166. On administration of justice in New Mexico Territory, see Arie W. Poldervaart, *Black-Robed Justice* (1948).

and mounted the gallows. Superstitious men thought that the rest-less ghosts of the dead haunted the gallows at night.[15]

The United States Supreme Court stood at the apex of the fed-eral pyramid, at the farthest remove from Judge Parker. All of the justices were lawyers, and on the whole, all had some stature. Com-pared with earlier justices, the late 19th-century appointees were, on the average, older men. Young countries tend toward young leaders; older, more settled countries, to the more mature men. Joseph Story had been named to the Court at thirty-two; William Strong, of Pennsylvania, was confirmed in 1870 at the age of sixty-two, the first man over sixty to be appointed.[16] The experience of the later justices was somewhat more national than the earlier judges. Robert Trimble, appointed in 1826, was the first Supreme Court justice who had had prior experience as a judge in the lower federal courts. The state courts were the main source of Supreme Court justices throughout the 19th century. But many justices had some federal service in their background.[17]

Appointments to the Court were as political as those to any lower court. Presidents appointed old cronies, famous politicians, deserving members of the cabinet; they appointed men because they were Southern or because they were not Southern, as the case might be. Occasionally, nominees were rejected for political rea-sons. President Grant nominated Attorney General E. R. Hoar, who had made too many enemies in the Senate. His name lan-guished in the Senate, and he was finally turned down.[18] Most nominations, however, went through Congress unopposed or with little opposition.

Most judges had politics in their background or were politically active. Some never lost the habit. David Davis, among others, had political ambitions. Davis was a serious contender for the presiden-tial nomination in 1872 and was elected to the Senate from Illi-nois in 1877. Chief Justice Chase lusted after the Democratic nomi-nation for president in 1872. Joseph P. Bradley cast the deciding

[15] On Parker see Glenn Shirley, *Law West of Fort Smith* (1957); J. Gladston Emery, *Court of the Damned* (1959).

[16] Cortez A. M. Ewing, *The Judges of the Supreme Court, 1789–1937* (1938), pp. 66 ff.

[17] *Ibid.*, p. 100.

[18] Grant next tried Edwin Stanton, who had been a member of Lincoln's cabi-net. Stanton was confirmed but dropped dead before assuming office. Two other Grant nominees were withdrawn because of newspaper outcry or senatorial re-luctance.

vote on the Electoral Commission that made Rutherford B. Hayes president in 1877.[19]

Despite the politics of the appointment process, the judges' own nose for politics, and numerous errors of ambition and prejudice, the Supreme Court had an unbroken record of purity and significant achievement. The prestige of the Court ebbed and flowed, but the long-range trend was, as far as one can tell, steadily rising. The judges bore tremendous responsibilities, and had life tenure. Their political independence probably enhanced their prestige. The judges survived the *Dred Scott* case, the *Civil Rights* cases, the *Slaughter-house* case, the *Income Tax* case, and the thousand crises, large and small, that pounded upon their heads. The Court's work met the general standards of craftsmanship of the bar; its written opinions were always sleekly professional. Increasingly, people who could never have read a single opinion seem to have accepted the legitimacy of the Court. The Supreme Court by 1900 was more than a century old. It was a fixed and traditional part of an accepted system of government. The canonization of the Supreme Court, or at least its beatification, was not a fast or automatic process. *Dred Scott* and after were relatively dark days. Yet, at some point—roughly, in the last half of the century—the Court reached a point of high, almost unassailable prestige. Perhaps the Court was an accurate mirror of upper middle-class thought. The Court vacillated between nationalism and localism; so did the country. And the Court fulfilled a valuable function of wise second-thinking, or seemed to. The Supreme Court (so, too, many of the state courts) tended to smooth over the dips and eddies of wide swings of opinion. At least this was a claim that could be plausibly made.

[19] The election of 1876 was inconclusive. Both parties claimed victory for their candidate. Samuel Tilden, the Democratic candidate, was one electoral vote short of a majority; but electoral votes from Florida, Louisiana, South Carolina and Oregon were in dispute. To settle the matter, Congress established an Electoral Commission of fifteen, five Senators, five Representatives, and five judges. Seven of these were Democrats, seven Republicans and the fifth judge was to be chosen by the other four judges. This was Bradley. The Commission gave Rutherford Hayes *all* the disputed electoral votes, 8–7. Bradley voted with the majority, and Hayes was elected. Bradley always claimed his work on the Electoral Commission was as pure as the driven snow: "So far as I am capable of judging my own motives, I did not allow political, that is, party, considerations to have any weight whatever in forming my conclusions." Quoted in Charles Fairman, "Mr. Justice Bradley," in Allison Dunham and Philip Kurland, eds., *Mr. Justice* (1956), pp. 69, 83.

The size of the Court fluctuated until the 1870's. Lincoln and Grant were not above a genteel sort of court-packing. Lincoln did some unpacking, too; he allowed three seats to stay empty. John A. Campbell, of Alabama, had resigned; two other justices had died, one a Southerner. Lincoln held the seats open until it was clear that the South would not voluntarily return.[20] During the Civil War, Congress by law gave the Court its largest size: ten members. Congress played with these numbers during Reconstruction, at the time of its tug of war with President Johnson. A law of 1866 provided that no vacancy should be filled until the membership of the Court sank to seven. This looked suspiciously like a plan to keep Andrew Johnson from filling any vacancies, although the evidence now appears weaker than was previously supposed.[21] During the Grant administration, finally, Congress settled on what has since become the sacred number—nine.

The Court was, in general, blessed by a number of long tenures. This gave the Court great stability, perhaps even too much. Unionists considered Taney's long life a great curse (he was eighty-eight when he died, in 1864). Robert C. Grier stayed on the Court three years after a stroke had left him somewhat befuddled. It is not certain that he understood, in late 1869, which side he was voting for in the *Legal Tender* cases. A delegation from the Court, including Stephen Field, then asked him gently to resign. Field's own career was the longest in the Court's history. He was appointed in 1863, at the age of forty-six, and he served for thirty-four years, eight months, and twenty days, longer than anyone before. In his last year on the Court, in 1897, his mind had failed noticeably; at times he lapsed into a "dull stupor." Justice John Marshall Harlan was sent to talk to Field, and persuade him to resign. Harlan reminded Field of his mission to Grier; but Field, his eyes "blazing with the old fire of youth, . . . burst out; . . . 'a dirtier day's work I never did in my life.' "[22]

When Taney finally died, in 1864, Lincoln appointed Salmon P. Chase, formerly his secretary of the treasury, as chief justice. Chase was a disappointment to the administration; in 1870, he was one of the five-man majority in the first *Legal Tender* case. The Court held that paper-money laws, passed during the Civil War, were

[20] Carl B. Swisher, *Stephen J. Field, Craftsman of the Law* (1930), p. 113.

[21] See Stanley I. Kutler, *Judicial Power and Reconstruction Politics* (1968), pp. 48 ff.

[22] Quoted in Swisher, *op. cit.*, p. 444; see also John S. Goff, "Old Age and the Supreme Court," 4 Am. J. Leg. Hist. 95 (1960).

beyond the power of Congress. What was ironic was that Secretary Chase had been an architect of the policy now repudiated by Chief Justice Chase. But Secretary Chase had been a Republican in the midst of a war; Chief Justice Chase in 1870 was a Democrat considering the problems of peacetime finance. One year later, after two new appointments by President Grant, the decision was reversed. The incident shows both how much the president could control the Supreme Court, and also ultimately how little. The mighty power to appoint was balanced by the fact that, once confirmed, a judge was free to go his own way; and often did.

No later chief justice had the stature of Marshall or Taney; but outstanding men sat on the Court after the war: Samuel Miller, Stephen Field, Joseph Bradley, John Marshall Harlan. They served during the first golden age of judicial review, a period in which judges demanded the right to share in the government, and found the basis for their power in the 14th amendment. It was also an age in which open disagreement in the Court was more visible. Dissenting opinions had been rare on the Marshall court. Peter V. Daniel (1841–1860) was a persistent dissenter. He wrote almost as many dissents and special concurrences as majority opinions.[23] Samuel F. Miller dissented 159 times, and Stephen Field 233 times, in the course of their careers. John Marshall Harlan (1877–1911) entered no less than 380 dissents.[24]

Still, the ordinary case was unanimously decided, unlike the cases of the Warren and Burger courts. More than seventy cases are reported in Volume 71 of the United States Reports, drawn from December term 1866. All except five were unanimous decisions. In one of these, the famous case of *Ex parte Milligan,* the separate opinion was a concurrence, agreeing with the result but not the reasons. In four other cases, there were dissents; but in two of these, the dissenters merely recorded the fact of dissent; they did not record their disagreement in written opinion. On the other hand, the famous test oath cases, *Cummings* v. *Missouri* and *Ex parte Garland,* elicited a long dissent.[25]

It was the deep cases that drew blood, in other words. But most of the work of the Supreme Court was not made up of great cases.

23 John P. Frank, *Justice Daniel Dissenting* (1964), p. 181.

24 Karl ZoBell, "Division of Opinion in the Supreme Court: A History of Judicial Disintegration," 44 Cornell L. Q. 186, 199 (1959).

25 The number of dissents and concurrences rose with the years; but rather slowly. In Volume 168, reporting cases from October term, 1897, there were forty-three unanimous opinions, five dissents and two concurrences without opinion; and only three dissents and one concurrence with separate written opinion.

A slowly increasing minority of cases turned on constitutional issues. A growing number arose under important federal statutes. Still, there were many cases which were in the federal courts solely on diversity grounds, that is, on the grounds that the parties were citizens of different states. These were ordinary cases, with no federal issue. The Court's sheer burden of work rose constantly. Between 1862 and 1866, the court handed down 240 decisions; between 1886 and 1890, 1,125—and this without relief from the arduous burden of traveling on circuit.[26] The work load meant that the leisurely days of long oral argument were over. Only so much time could be allotted to each case, even the important ones.

By common consent, the golden age of *state judges* was also over, by 1870. A golden age is a tricky concept. What was golden about the judges had been measured on a scale of judicial skill and judicial craft. The great judges—Lemuel Shaw, John Bannister Gibson, John Marshall—were builders of institutions and molders of doctrine; moreover, they had style.

There is no doubt that the next generation of judges had a different approach to their craft. Ironically, controversy about activist judges was very great in this age of silver or brass. Some state judges after 1860 were famous men in their time, and men of vigor and imagination: Edward Ryan of Wisconsin, Oliver Wendell Holmes, Jr., of Massachusetts, Thomas Cooley of Michigan. Holmes was perhaps the greatest master of the English language ever to sit on an American court. But his fame rests mostly on his later career, as a justice of the Supreme Court. Of the state-court judges of the period, Roscoe Pound thought that only one stood out "as a builder of the law since the Civil War"—Charles Doe.[27] Doe was Chief Justice of New Hampshire from 1876 to 1896. He was a man who, in the words of his biographer, believed that "judicial power was grounded upon the logic of necessity and the function of the court [was] to furnish a remedy for every right." [28] In a number of significant cases, Doe disregarded formalities, ignored niceties of pleading, and shrugged off the burden of precedent. He believed judges should sometimes make law, and make it openly.

[26] Charles Fairman, *Mr. Justice Miller and the Supreme Court* (1939), p. 62.
[27] Roscoe Pound, "The Place of Judge Story in the Making of American Law," 48 Am. L. Rev. 676, 690 (1914).
[28] John P. Reid, *Chief Justice: The Judicial World of Charles Doe* (1967), p. 300.

What most marked off Doe from his contemporary judges was a matter not of substance but of style. Doe stood out because he denied the dominant theory of the legitimacy of judges. The judges who invented and first used the labor injunction were making law. When a judge reworked doctrine, and knew it, he was making law. Yet the late 19th-century judges stressed very strongly that they did not make law. Precedent, the Constitution, principles of common law—these were the rulers; the judge was only an instrument, a vessel. Hence a judge should not *seem* to be creative. There were ample reasons why the judges assumed so docile a posture. For one thing, it provided magnificent camouflage. It disclaimed responsibility for unpopular opinions. It was one reason why judges, even though elected, did not stand so naked before the partisan public as, say, governors and congressmen did. The flight into technicality and impersonality was only apparently a flight toward a more humble, self-effacing role. A doctor does not humble himself when he claims that the principles of medicine determine what he does. The judges claimed that they were professionals; their job was too difficult for the layman, too pure for the politician. They claimed the expert's privilege of monopoly control of their business and insisted that what they did, like all experts' work, was value-free. These were valuable postures of self-defense.

Of course, there were many variations, between court and court. Styles of decision, literary merit, and craftsmanship were not uniform; neither was there a single conception of the judicial role. Again, the number of dissents is a rough kind of index of differences in judges' conceptions of that role. There is no doubt that dissents, in general, were more frequent in the period after the Civil War, on the state high courts, than beforehand. But not every state had a similar propensity toward dissent. In Missouri, in 1885, there were 275 reported unanimous opinions and 57 cases with dissents or specially concurring opinions (mostly dissents). On the other hand, the Vermont supreme court, in 1890, decided seventy cases unanimously; there was one dissent, and that one lacked a written opinion. In New York's Court of Appeals, in 1888, about one case in ten carried with it a dissenting opinion.[29]

Karl Llewellyn has called the years of the late 19th century years of the formal style, in contrast to the grand style of Marshall, Gibson, and Shaw.[30] Much of the crispness and flair had gone out of the

29 I am indebted to Leah F. Friedman for gathering this information.
30 Karl N. Llewellyn, "Remarks on the Theory of Appellate Decision and the

334 AMERICAN LAW TO THE CLOSE OF THE 19TH CENTURY

printed reports. Many appellate opinions of the '80's and '90's are torture to read—bombastic, diffuse, labored, drearily logical, crammed with unnecessary citations. There are many reasons for this difference in style. Reports were fuller, and were not carefully edited. The work load was too great to allow time for pruning and polishing. But style also reflected the training and philosophy of the judges. Many were conservative men, educated in conservative schools, trained in an environment that exalted businessmen's values, and jealous of their judicial and economic prerogatives. High-court judges were no cross section of the country. They represented old America. The bench was lily-white and mostly Protestant; there was a tendency toward dynasties—the Tuckers in Virginia, for example. In New Jersey, every chief justice from 1776 to 1891, with only one exception, was Presbyterian. Most associate justices had also been Presbyterians, many of them elders in their churches. Nearly all of the judges with a college education were products of Princeton.[31] As of 1893, of forty-eight judges elected to Virginia's highest court, only three had been "born outside of the . . . limits of Virginia." [32] From 1860 to 1900, virtually every Vermont judge was a native; only occasionally did a son of Connecticut or New Hampshire creep in. The fifteen supreme court judges of Minnesota between 1858 and 1890 were all Protestants, and primarily from good, solid middle-class backgrounds.[33]

For judges of this stamp, formalism was a protective device. They were middle-of-the-road conservatives, holding off the vulgar rich on the one hand, the revolutionary masses on the other. The legal tradition represented balance, sound values, a commitment to orderly process. They preferred to work within this tradition; but lawmaking, in a generation of bulging law libraries, no longer required the style of the great pioneers, who invented whole areas

Rules or Canons About How Statutes Are to Be Construed," 3 Vanderbilt L.R. 395, 396 (1950); *The Common Law Tradition: Deciding Appeals* (1960), pp. 35–39. See below, ch. 11, p. 540.

[31] John Whitehead, "The Supreme Court of New Jersey," 3 Green Bag 493, 512 (1891). Whitehead adds that, except for Chief Justice Hornblower, "a small, delicate, slender man," the judges were "of good size, well-proportioned, strong, and vigorous."

[32] S.S.P. Patteson, "The Supreme Court of Appeals of Virginia," 5 Green Bag 407, 419 (1893).

[33] Robert A. Heiberg, "Social Backgrounds of the Minnesota Supreme Court Justices: 1858–1968," 53 Minn. L. Rev. 901 (1969). In the West, of course, the situation was the reverse of the East. In states like Washington, or Wyoming, none of the judges were or could have been native-born.

of law in a few strokes of a masterful pen. But when all this is conceded, it may still be true that the judges (particularly of the lower courts) *were,* by and large, lesser men—elected, not elite. America of 1880 was an ambitious, industrial society, run by businessmen and politicians. Most high-court judges were simply successful or ambitious lawyers; relatively fewer were liberally educated gentlemen, from good families, with a sense of style and *noblesse oblige;* fewer were the children of the well-to-do or younger sons of New England ministers. The results showed in their prose and their craft, if not necessarily in doctrines and results.

Clearly, the judges were busier than ever before. State courts, like the United States Supreme Court, had to work harder to keep up with their load. The Illinois supreme court wrote 150 opinions in 1854 and 295 in 1889–90.[34] In 1871, the United States district courts disposed of 8,187 criminal cases; in 1900, 17,033. In 1873, these courts disposed of 14,527 civil cases; in 1900, 22,520. There were 52,477 civil cases pending in the district courts in 1900.[35] Of course, the population grew tremendously, and the economy expanded as well. But the courts could not keep pace with the potential demand. They were fixed in size and limited in staff; legislatures simply did not add enough new judges and courts to fill the need. The work load had to be radically routinized; even so, delays piled up. What made the situation tolerable was simply that the courts were not indispensable, either for the ordinary work of social control or for settling most disputes that arose in society. There were great cases on the dockets. But the legal business of business mostly bypassed the courts. The judges were professionals, lawyerly lawyers; there was no guarantee that they would understand the nature of a business dispute and handle it properly, even if the judges had had enough time. In any event, full-scale litigation was slow, costly, disruptive. Time only accentuated these failings of the courts. The crowded dockets, the long delays were symptoms of two contradictory phenomena: first, that there were matters that only courts could decide; but equally, that here was an institution too marginal to be worth a heavy investment by society.

[34] James E. Babb, "The Supreme Court of Illinois," 3 Green Bag 217, 237 (1891).
[35] American Law Institute, *A Study of the Business of the Federal Courts* (1934), Part 1, Criminal Cases, p. 107; Part 2, Civil Cases, p. 111.

JUDICIAL ORGANIZATION

The late 19th century was not a period of radical innovation in judicial organization. The typical state system was still a pyramid of courts, imperfectly manned and badly paid at the bottom.[36] No administrator ran, controlled, or co-ordinated the judicial system. No one could shift judges about as needed from a crowded to an empty docket; or monitor the flow of litigation; or set up rules to tell the courts how to behave. Higher courts weakly and partially controlled lower courts through the power to reverse decisions—but only in the event of an appeal. States did often add intermediate courts to help out somewhat, when the work load grew great. So, for example, Illinois divided the state in 1877 into four districts, each with a three-judge court (two such in populous Cook County). Texas established a court of criminal appeals in 1891. Under the Missouri constitution of 1875, a special appellate court was created for the city of St. Louis; another court of appeals, for Kansas City, was established in 1884, and the two courts then handled appeals from lower courts in the rest of the state as well.[37]

Many states increased the number of high court judges—Minnesota, for example, from three to four, then to five. California, in 1879, tried an interesting and productive experiment; it allowed its supreme court to divide itself, amoebalike, into separate segments ("departments"); only especially difficult or important cases would be decided *en banc*, that is, by the whole court. In some states the supreme court could farm out cases to "commissioners," whose decisions could be (and usually were) accepted by the court as its own. Kansas, in 1887, authorized the governor, "by and with the consent of the senate," to appoint three citizens of Kansas, "of high character for legal learning and personal worth," to be "commissioners of the supreme court." They would "aid and assist the [supreme] court . . . in the disposition of the numerous cases

[36] Where the fee system was in effect, some lower court judges were paid only too well. The Pennsylvania constitution of 1873 (art. V, sec. 12) specifically provided that Philadelphia magistrates "shall be compensated only by fixed salaries."

[37] Roscoe Pound, *Organization of Courts* (1940), pp. 227–31. At the time of the Civil War, in eleven states the highest court was still a wanderer—required or expected to sit at least once a year in various parts of the state. Before 1900, five of these—Maryland, Michigan, Missouri, Georgia, and Illinois—had settled down permanently at the state capital. Pound, *op. cit.*, p. 199.

pending in said court" (Laws 1887, ch. 148). In 1895, Kansas created two "courts of appeal," one for the north and one for the south part of the state, "inferior to the supreme court and superior to all other courts in the state" (Laws 1895, ch. 96). And a constitutional amendment of 1900 (to art. III, sec. 2) increased the size of the supreme court from three to seven; the court could "sit separately in two divisions." [38]

In some states, the supreme court's burden was lightened, to a certain extent, by limiting the court's jurisdiction. The West Virginia constitution of 1872 (art. VIII, sec. 3) confined the appellate jurisdiction of the Supreme Court of Appeals to criminal cases, constitutional cases, "controversies concerning the title or boundaries of land" or the "probate of wills," civil cases "where the matter in controversy, exclusive of costs," was "of greater value, or amount than one hundred dollars," and a miscellaneous category, including cases "concerning a mill, roadway, ferry, or landing." In Illinois, in 1877, the appellate (intermediate) courts became last-stop courts of appeal for contract and damage cases where the amount in controversy was less than one thousand dollars, exclusive of costs. The supreme court still heard criminal cases, and "cases involving a franchise or freehold." [39] The federal system was improved, in 1869, when Congress provided a circuit judge for each of the nine circuits. Each Supreme Court justice continued to be assigned to a circuit, as before, but it was recognized that he could not do much of the circuit's work. The Civil War, Reconstruction, and the post-Civil War amendments gave added importance to the federal system. The Removal Act of 1875 put tremendous power into the federal-court system. From then on, any action asserting a federal right could begin in a federal court; or, if begun in a state court, could be removed to the federal courts. The act "opened wide a flood of totally new business for the federal courts." [40] Finally, Congress enacted major reform in 1891; an act of this year set up a circuit court of appeals for each circuit, to act as an appellate court, and provided for an extra circuit judge. Supreme Court justices under this act still each belonged to a circuit, and could sit there, but almost none ever did.[41]

Beyond these changes, political leadership seemed to have little

38 The courts of appeal were abolished in 1901.

39 Laws Ill. 1877, pp. 70–71.

40 Felix Frankfurter and James M. Landis, *The Business of the Supreme Court, a Study in the Federal Judicial System* (1928), p. 65.

41 26 Stats. 826 (Act of March 3, 1891).

AMERICAN LAW TO THE CLOSE OF THE 19TH CENTURY

interest in making court organization more rational. Lay politicians did not want a czar for the courts of the states. Muddled and overlapping jurisdiction was perfectly acceptable; the alternative —a strong chief justice with power to run his system—was not. In some states, to prevent any possibility of judicial leadership, the legislature downgraded the office of chief justice. In Ohio, in 1852, the chief justice was nothing more than "Judge of the Supreme Court having the shortest time to serve." [42] Many state constitutions had similar provisions.[43] Obviously, this system provided for "a periodical rotation" in office, and precluded "any continuity of development of the administrative side of the court's work." In 1900, however, no less than seventeen of the thirty-eight states with an elected supreme court had this or a similar provision.[44] In some states, even clerks of court were elected—an absurdity from the standpoint of administrative coherence.[45]

The official court system—slow, expensive, relatively technical despite the pruning and reform of generations—could not possibly meet the full needs and demands of a country undergoing rapid social and economic change. The American legal system faced demands from industry and commerce, from an enormous middle class of consumers of law. The demands could be met by new practices, new legislation, new forms of freedom and control. But not by long, costly trials. Thus formal court systems could not hold day-to-day power over any important segment of the economy—at any rate, not by means of ordinary litigation, and cases heard on appeal. The judge-kings reigned; they could not rule. The business of running economy and society drained out into other hands.

Yet, on the trial court level, the judicial system *was* making a contribution to the development and functioning of the economy. This was a low-key contribution, to be sure. At this level, courts processed a fantastic number of small cases. Debts were collected, divorces granted, mortgages foreclosed. The work of these lower courts has rarely been studied. One exception has been Francis W. Laurent's study of the local courts of Chippewa County, Wisconsin: the court handled hundreds of cases of domestic relations, debt collection, insurance, mortgage foreclosure, petty crimi-

[42] Laws Ohio 1852, p. 67 (Act of Feb. 19, 1852).

[43] Neb. const. 1875, art. VI, sec. 6. In Wisconsin, const. 1848, art. VII, sec. 4, as amended, 1889, the judge longest in service was chief justice.

[44] Pound, *op. cit.*, p. 169.

[45] For example, Va. const. 1850, art. VI, sec. 19: "The voters of each county . . . in which a circuit is held shall elect a clerk of such court, whose term of office shall be six years."

nal actions, and the like.[46] Big city courts must have handled a staggering volume. It seems clear that a great volume of cases could be handled only by radical routinization. In probate, mortgage, divorce, and commercial law, the courts developed or used standardized procedures as perfunctory—and essential—as parking-ticket cases in the 1970's. This was largely the role of the lower courts; higher courts were also busier than ever, but heard proportionately less and less of the significant disputes in business and personal life. The history of the great American courts is also a history of the events that passed them by.

[46] Francis W. Laurent, *The Business of a Trial Court, One Hundred Years of Cases* (1959).

CHAPTER III

PROCEDURE AND PRACTICE:
AN AGE OF REFORM

The year 1848 was one of revolution in Europe. In the United States it was the year in which New York passed an "act to simplify and abridge the Practice, Pleadings, and Proceedings of the Courts." [1] This was a full-blown Code of Civil Procedure, radically new in appearance at least. The code is often called the Field Code, after David Dudley Field, who played a vital role in its enactment. The Field Code, more than any other statute on the subject, acted as a catalytic agent of procedural reform in the United States.

New York had adopted a new constitution in 1846. One clause called for the "appointment of three commissioners, to revise, reform, simplify, and abridge the rules and practice, pleadings, forms and proceedings of the courts of record of this State" (art. VI, sec. 24). The state got more than it bargained for, perhaps. One of the original commissioners, Nicholas Hill, Jr., resigned in 1847, horrified because his colleagues were willing to recommend changes "so purely experimental, so sudden and general, and . . . so perilous." David Dudley Field (1805–94) was appointed in his place. From his early days at the bar, Field had been seized with the vision of codification and law reform. In 1839 he wrote an open letter on reform of the judicial system. He later harangued a legislative committee on the subject. From 1847 on, he was the heart and soul of the movement.[2]

Stylistically, no greater affront to the common-law tradition can be imagined than the 1848 code. It was couched in brief, gnomic, Napoleonic sections, tightly worded and skeletal; there was no trace of the elaborate redundancy, the voluptuous heaping on of

---

[1] Laws N.Y. 1848, ch. 379.

[2] Henry M. Field, *The Life of David Dudley Field* (1898), pp. 42–56. Mildred Coe and Lewis Morse, "Chronology of the Development of the David Dudley Field Code," 27 Cornell L. Q. 238 (1941).

synonyms, so characteristic of Anglo-American statutes. It was, in short, a code in the French sense, not a statute. It was a lattice of reasoned principles, scientifically arranged, not a thick thumb stuck into the dikes of common law. The substance of the Field Code was almost as daring as its style. The heart of the code was its sixty-second section, which declared:

> The distinction between actions at law and suits in equity, and the forms of all such actions and suits heretofore existing, are abolished; and, there shall be in this state, hereafter, but one form of action, for the enforcement or protection of private rights and the redress or prevention of private wrongs, which shall be denominated a civil action.

Taken literally, this was the death sentence of common-law pleading. It meant the end of all special pleading, forms of actions and writs, the closing of the chasm between equity and law, the destruction at one blow of the paraphernalia of this most recondite, most precious, most lawyerly area of law.

Like many other revolutions, the upheaval of 1848, in the legal communes of New York, was not completely a bolt from the blue. The Field Code had a number of distinguished intellectual forefathers. In England, Jeremy Bentham, who died in 1832, had savagely attacked the "ancestor-worship" of the common law. Bentham had put his strong style at the service of legal rationality. Lawyers in Bentham's circle preached hard for reform of the common law, particularly procedure. In 1828, Henry Brougham spoke for six hours in the House of Commons, eating a "hatful of oranges as he went, calling for law reform," and ending with a dramatic plea: "It was the boast of Augustus . . . that he found Rome of brick, and left it of marble; a praise not unworthy of a great prince. . . . But how much nobler will be the Sovereign's boast . . . that he found law dear, and left it cheap; found it a sealed book—left it a living letter; found it a patrimony of the rich—left it the inheritance of the poor; found it a two-edged sword of craft and oppression—left it the staff of honesty and the shield of innocence." [3] In response to Brougham's speech, Parliament appointed

---

[3] Quoted in Brian Abel-Smith and Robert Stevens, *Lawyers and the Courts, a Sociological Study of the English Legal System 1750–1965* (1967), p. 29; see also Robert W. Millar, *Civil Procedure of the Trial Court in Historical Perspective* (1952), p. 43. Millar's book is fundamental for the history of American civil procedure. Also useful is Charles M. Hepburn, *The Historical Development of Code Pleading in America and England* (1897).

342 AMERICAN LAW TO THE CLOSE OF THE 19TH CENTURY

a commission to consider procedural reform; some reform statutes were passed in the early 1830's. In the United States, the Field Code had a precedent of sorts in Edward Livingston's work in Louisiana. The codes of Louisiana were not, technically speaking, in point, since Louisiana was a civil-law state; the fusion of law and equity in Texas could also be explained away on the grounds of civil-law contamination. In some other states, notably Massachusetts, commissions had issued reports calling for an improved and simplified procedure. Colonial practice had been much simpler than English practice and had never been wholly extinguished. As we have seen, a number of states had taken up procedural reform; Georgia's experiment had been quite radical for its day. Undoubtedly, precedents and examples were important. But most of all, the time was ripe. Code pleading was an idea whose day had finally come.

Not that code pleading was an immediate and unqualified success. Ironically, the code had particular trouble in New York itself. In 1849 the Field Code was re-enacted, but much wounded by amendments and supplements. The new act contained 473 sections. An act of July 10, 1851, again substantially amended the code. This act in turn was frequently amended. In 1870, the legislature appointed a new commission to revise the code; it reported a fresh version in 1876, of monstrously inflated size—"reactionary in spirit . . . a figure of Falstaffian proportions among the other codes," its principles "smothered in details." [4] By 1880, the New York procedural codes (including the code of criminal procedure) contained no less than 3,356 sections.[5] This was a far cry, indeed, from the simplicity and artlessness that the original code had proclaimed as a goal. In the 1890's, New York's procedure was still considered so imperfect that a strong movement grew up at the bar to reform it still further.

The courts, too, showed a certain hostility and resistance to change. The conventional wisdom has it that many judges manhandled the code. One extreme example, perhaps, was Judge Samuel Selden, who remained convinced that law and equity were categories of the real world. He simply could not grasp the idea of merging the two: "It is possible to abolish one or the other," he wrote, in an 1856 decision, "but it certainly is not possible to abol-

[4] Hepburn, op. cit., p. 130.

[5] Alison Reppy, "The Field Codification Concept," in David Dudley Field Centenary Essays (1949), pp. 17, 34–36.

ish the distinction between them." [6] Chief Justice John Bradley Winslow of Wisconsin wrote in 1910 that the "cold, not to say inhuman, treatment which the infant code received from the New York judges is matter of history." [7] But the historical record is not quite that clear; and the behavior of trial-court judges, where the fate of the code was really decided, is extremely obscure. Certainly the code could not destroy the habits of a lifetime, nor, by itself, transform what may have been deeply imbedded in a particular legal culture. But the stubbornness of the judges was a short-run phenomenon, to the extent it occurred. The real vice of the code probably lay in its weak empirical base. The draftsmen derived their basic principles from ideas of right reason, rather than from a careful study of what actually happened in American courts, and what functions and interests courts and their lawsuits served.

The Field Code, as such, did not make much headway in the East. Even in New York, the draftsmen of the code thought of it as a mere temporary draft; the full text, completed a few years later, was too much for the legislature to swallow. Further west, the situation was dramatically different. The ink was hardly dry on Field's Code when Missouri adopted it into law (1849). In 1851, California, a new state, at the uttermost limit of the country, enacted the Field Code. Before the outbreak of the Civil War, the Field Code had been adopted in Iowa, Minnesota, Indiana, Ohio, Washington Territory, Nebraska, Wisconsin and Kansas.[8] Nevada adopted the code in 1861, and by the turn of the century, so had the Dakotas, Idaho, Arizona, Montana, North Carolina, Wyoming, South Carolina, Utah, Colorado, Oklahoma, and New Mexico.

Why the West? Supposedly, the Western bar was young and open-minded; technical training in common law pleading was not common coin among these lawyers. Stephen Field, David Dudley Field's brother, was prominent in the California bar and may have helped advance his brother's cause. In Missouri, an attorney named David Wells had been agitating for years for the abolition of the distinction between law and equity. Both states had some remnants of civil law in their background; both entered the Union

6 J. Selden, in *Reubens* v. *Joel*, 13 N.Y. 488, 493 (1856); see Charles E. Clark, "The Union of Law and Equity," 25 Columbia L. Rev. 1 (1925).

7 Quoted in Clark, *op. cit.*, p. 3.

8 Kentucky and Oregon also adopted the code, but maintained the separation of law and equity. Iowa reintroduced the distinction in 1860. Millar, *op. cit.*, p. 54. Later, Arkansas adopted the Kentucky model.

with a history of land controversies and a full docket of land-grant problems. These land claims could not be analyzed as "legal" or "equitable"; the distinction was meaningless and procedurally disruptive.

Western states were also more eclectic in general than states of the older East. The glitter of the Field Code may conceal the extent to which some Eastern states (Massachusetts, for example) were working toward procedural reform in their own way, in accordance with what the bar considered the inherent logic of their own institutions. The New York name had no magic in Massachusetts. Some states rejected the Field Code as unsuitable, or too advanced, or as the product of a different culture. Dean Henry Ingersoll of the University of Tennessee, writing in the Yale Law Journal in 1891, decried the "attempt of one State to adapt a Code of Procedure prepared for an entirely different social and business condition." In North Carolina, one of the few older states to adopt the code, he felt the experiment (which he blamed on blacks and carpetbaggers) was disastrous:

> During . . . Reconstruction . . . the legal practice of the State was reconstructed by the adoption of the New York Code of Civil Procedure, with all its penalties and high-pressure machinery adapted to the conditions of an alert, eager, pushing commercial community. Rip Van Winkle was not more surprised on returning to his native village after his long sleep than were the lawyers of the old "Tar-heel State." . . . This new-fangled commercial machine . . . was as well adapted to their condition as were the light driving buggies of the Riverside Park to the rough roads of the Black mountains, or the garb of the Broadway dandy to the turpentine stiller. . . . North Carolina had about as much use for the system as she had for a clearing-house, a Central Park or a Stock Exchange. The clamors of the bar soon brought about . . . amendment . . . and left [the code] . . . a great cumbrous piece of machinery without driving-wheels, steam-chest or boiler, propelled along by the typical slow oxteam.[9]

Actually, systems of procedure did not fit particular cultures so snugly. Ingersoll's diatribe mostly meant that code pleading was more easily attacked when it could be identified with an alien, and in this case, a hated culture. In his statement, there may lurk a small grain of truth: procedural reform was most necessary, or at least most desirable, in commercial states. In a business economy,

[9] Henry H. Ingersoll, "Some Anomalies of Practice," 1 Yale L. J. 89, 91, 92 (1891).

business needs as rational and predictable a common context as it can possibly get. An orderly, rational law machine is infinitely preferable to the chaos of common law. Business wanted their machine to turn out swift, nontechnical, predictable decisions, based on the facts, not on the accidents of writs and forms of action. Classical pleading was a sort of slow, gentlemanly ritual dance. Its aim was to isolate pure "issues" of law or fact. But these issues often turned out to be mere byproducts of pleading, hence, in a sense, purely hypothetical. Old procedure and excess technicality survived the longest in parts of the law where society had less of a sense of the value of mass-producing results. The jury trial of a murderer is a unique, unstandardized event, the exact legal opposite of a garnishment or a parking ticket.

But where business was unavoidably dependent on the courts, procedure was radically and successfully simplified. This process was not obvious because the development was quiet, almost invisible. Just as a mass market led to mass production of commodities, so a mass market led to mass production of law. The system stamped out, like so many iron nails, its tiny but numberless outputs. Their importance lay in their cumulative effect—small debts collected, garnishments achieved, instruments neatly recorded. These legal outputs generally depended on the validity of pieces of paper invented by businessmen and business lawyers. Where the courts accepted (as they usually did) these documents, business could safely ignore the grand debate over codes and procedure, debates about the esthetic shape of the legal system, that raged in upper circles of the bar. These great debates—whether law emanated from the spirit of the people or not, whether the common law could be written down completely without losing its soul, or not—meant little or nothing to people engaged in making and losing money day by day.

In the earlier part of the 19th century, law reform probably did command wide support from the businessman or merchant.[10] He saw that law was cumbersome and unfeeling; he sensed that law had to be redirected, before he could make much use of its institutions. David Dudley Field promised the businessman that law would become his willing tool. And so it did, but not as Field imagined. The industrialists of the Gilded Age did not use law and

10 See, in general, Lawrence M. Friedman, "Law Reform in Historical Perspective," 13 St. Louis U. L. J. 351 (1969); Maxwell Bloomfield, "William Sampson and the Codifiers: The Roots of American Legal Reform, 1820–1830," 11 Am. J. Legal Hist. 234 (1967).

lawsuits to solve ordinary business disputes. They used law to collect and record, as a tool of mass production. In the grand struggles
of robber barons, lawyers also used law as a tool, as the barons
battled each other in court with writs and injunctions. And in the
big constitutional cases, business tried to bend, delay, or prevent
the rise of the welfare state. To this extent, the dreams of the reformers went partly sour.

The bar in some states opposed code pleading with gusto. But
code pleading in the long run probably had a good effect on lawyer's practice. One of the root ideas of the code was fact-pleading,
so simple and rational that the average citizen would not need a
lawyer. This was a completely visionary goal. Yet procedure became, on the whole, much less technical. In a small way, this perhaps helped free lawyers from the drudgery of learning how to
plead and appeal. Procedural reform may have indirectly
smoothed the way for the rise of the "office" bar—counselor-
lawyers who never set foot in court. Or, perhaps, the rise of the
"office" bar meant that traditional rules and skills of pleading became ever rarer, and hence had less and less support from the leaders of the bar.

By 1900, the Field Code was widely adopted, copied, modified.
Field's reforms had earned, moreover, the supreme compliment of
close study in England, mother country of the common law. Field
influenced the English Judicature Act of 1873. English reforms, in
turn, had American consequences. The Connecticut Practice Act of
1879, for example, drew "in considerable measure upon the English
reforms," and was, on the whole, "a distinct advance over the
codes which had emanated from . . . New York." [11]

By 1900, almost all states had reformed their procedures at least
somewhat. Only a minority—New Jersey, Delaware, Illinois—
clung tenaciously to old-style pleading. Yet no state had carried its
reform as far as Field would have liked. In every state, the union of
law and equity remained imperfect. For one thing, the Constitution preserved the right of trial by jury; courts felt that they had to
pay attention to the historical distinction between law and equity,
since only in "law" was there a jury right to be preserved. On balance, the union of the two systems was a triumph for equity; from
equity, the new procedure derived some of its most striking traits:
greater freedom in joinder of parties, a liberal attitude toward the
right of a defendant to assert a counterclaim, more suppleness in

[11] Robert W. Millar, *Civil Procedure of the Trial Court in Historical Perspective* (1952), p. 55.

general in the use of judicial remedies. Even those New England states which had never granted full equity powers to their courts—Maine, New Hampshire, Massachusetts—granted these powers after the Civil War. In fact, many striking legal developments, between 1850 and 1900, made creative use of tools of equity. Courts put bankrupt railroads in receivership, and virtually ran the roads; they forged out of the injunction a terrible sword to use in industrial disputes. Injunction and receivership were both old, trusty tricks of equity, rapidly and vigorously reshaped. This was, after all, a period of activist judges; equity, free from the jury's fetters, was made to order for a judge with a taste for power.

Despite the Field Code, questions of procedure continued to claim an incredible proportion of the attention of appellate courts. Upper courts controlled lower courts and juries with a tight hand, at least as far as the formal record was concerned. Between 1870 and 1900, some state supreme courts behaved as if their chief function was to reverse decisions of their lower courts, for technical errors. A prominent law journal complained in 1887 that the Texas Court of Appeals "seems to have been organized to overrule and reverse. At least, since its organization that has been its chief employment." As evidence, the article cited an amazing fact: during the twelve years of the court's existence, it had reversed 1,604 criminal cases, and affirmed only 882—a margin of almost two to one. In one volume of reports, there were five reversals to every single affirmance.[12]

This was Roscoe Pound's "hypertrophy," most marked in criminal cases, and carried over from the earlier part of the century. At least on paper, tighter rules about the conduct of trials continued to tame the lower-court judges. Judges had once been in the habit of giving oral instructions to the jury. They told the jury about the law in frank, natural language. But this practice died or was driven out. The instructions became solemn written documents, drafted by lawyers, technical and utterly opaque. They were almost useless as a way to communicate with juries; the medium conveyed no message. Each instruction gave the upper court a chance to criticize the lower court and discover reversible error. At one time, too, it was standard for judges to comment on the evidence, to tell the jury quite openly what the judge thought about the witnesses and what their testimony was worth. In Missouri, for example, this practice was stamped out by 1859.[13]

[12] Note, "Overruled their Judicial Superiors," 21 Am. L. Rev. 610 (1887).
[13] Henry F. Luepke, Jr., "Comments on the Evidence in Missouri," 5 St. Louis

Appellate procedure also remained very technical and complex, throughout the 19th century. After reading cases in the last part of the century, Roscoe Pound was "tempted to think that appellate procedure existed as a system of preventing the disposition of cases themselves upon their merits." [14] The Field Code had attempted to bring a radical new order here too; it swept away all the cumbersome rules, the distinctions between writs of error and appeals in equity, and replaced them with a single form of review, which it called an "appeal." Some noncode jurisdictions (Alabama in 1853, Pennsylvania in 1889) also abolished the writ of error, and brought in a simpler form, which they too called an *appeal*.[15] But in general, record worship did not die out. It seemed to retain a stranglehold on appellate review; upper courts tried, not cases, but printed formulae, and tried them according to warped and unreal distinctions. Again, excess in behavior was most striking in criminal appeals. Harwell, the defendant in a Texas case decided in 1886,[16] had been arrested and convicted for receiving stolen cattle. The Texas court reversed, because, among other things, the jury found the defendant "guity" instead of "guilty." In 1877 the same court reversed a conviction because the jury carelessly wrote, "We, the jury, the defendant guilty," leaving out the word "find." [17] The same court, however, magnanimously upheld a conviction of "guily" in 1879,[18] proving that a "t" was less crucial than an "l" in the common law of Texas.

It is not easy to account for this behavior. Perhaps appeal courts were simply too busy for perspective. They relied less on long oral arguments than on written briefs. They spent their lives looking at formal records, and may have come to believe in them too much. Again, the profession took itself (as always) very seriously. A judge may consider an error very significant, which an outsider would find trivial at best. It was a period of conceptualism, of dry legal logic. The bench, as we have suggested, was peopled with lesser men; rules were their one excuse for power. Some procedural excess

---

U. L. J. 424 (1959); on the role of the jury in 19th century law in general, see Note, "The Changing Role of the Jury in the Nineteenth Century," 74 Yale L. J. 170 (1964).

[14] Roscoe Pound, *Appellate Procedure in Civil Cases*, p. 320.

[15] Pound, *op. cit.*, pp. 260–61.

[16] *Harwell* v. *State*, 22 Tex. App. 251, 2 S.W. 606 (1886); see also *Taylor* v. *State*, 5 Tex. App. 569 (1877); *Wilson* v. *State*, 12 Tex. App. 481 (1882).

[17] *Shaw* v. *State*, 2 Tex. App. 487 (1877).

[18] *Curry* v. *State*, 7 Tex. App. 91 (1879).

may have stemmed from a good idea gone bad: a fumbling attempt to govern, standardize, and rationalize trials, appeals, and written arguments. Appellate reports sometimes complained about the sloppy or misdirected work of lawyers and lower-court judges. This was particularly true in the early years of a state or territory. It seems clear that appeal judges took very seriously the job of riding herd on lower courts, lawyers, and juries, and set a high value on at least minimal regularity in procedure. The law commonly provided for the right to appeal from a decision by a justice of the peace, and obtain a trial *de novo* in a higher court (which meant, doing the trial over, including the finding of facts).[19] This shows a certain lack of respect for the craftsmanship of basement courts. Record worship showed a similar disrespect.

Criminal procedure was harder to reform than civil procedure. The constitutions themselves limited reform. The federal government, for example, could not have abolished the use of the grand jury in serious criminal cases.[20] Moreover, suspicion of government died hard. People were not so anxious to relax rules of criminal procedure, for fear of the power of government. Of course, textbook procedure was not the same as living procedure in court. The legal guarantees of fair trial hardly worked at all, for ignorant, timid, or unpopular defendants. Kangaroo-court justice, the blackjack, police harassment, the Ku Klux Klan, vigilante justice, and the lynch law of the 1880's and 1890's in the South were as much a part of the living law of criminal procedure as record worship was. The two phenomena may even have interacted. The vigilantes and the lynch mobs demanded quick, certain law and order (as they saw these); they did not trust the regular courts in either respect. The devilish inversions of procedure, that vigilantes and lynch mobs perpetrated, acted as a kind of countervailing force: a balance, of sorts, to the power of upper courts to bind and loose for reasons that looked irrational below.

The law of evidence remained complex. Simon Greenleaf, in his treatise on evidence (first published in 1842), had once praised the "symmetry and beauty" of this branch of law. A student, he felt, "would rise from the study of its principles convinced, with Lord Erskine, that 'they are founded in the charities of religion, in the

19 See, for example, *Hurtgen* v. *Kantrowitz*, 15 Colo. 442, 24 Pac. 872 (1890).

20 By the 5th amendment: "No person shall be held to answer for a capital, or otherwise infamous crime, unless on a presentment or indictment of a Grand Jury." On this institution in general, see Richard D. Younger, *The People's Panel: The Grand Jury in the United States, 1634–1941* (1963).

philosophy of nature, in the truths of history, and in the experience of common life.' " A more realistic critic, James Bradley Thayer, of Harvard, writing in 1898, felt, on the other hand, that the law of evidence was "a piece of illogical . . . patchwork; not at all to be admired, or easily to be found intelligible." [21] It was still largely a gloss on trial by jury, and its amazing complexity—John H. Wigmore spun ten volumes out of it in the twentieth century—had no counterpart outside of the common law. Indeed, Thayer reported that even English lawyers were surprised "to see our lively quarrels over points of evidence." In the United States, objections to evidence were presented as "exceptions, a method never common in England and now abolished there, which presents only a dry question of law—not leaving to the upper court that power to heed the general justice of the case which the more elastic procedure of the English courts so commonly allows; and tending thus to foster delay and chicane." [22]

The law of evidence remained consistent with its immediate past. It was founded in a world of mistrust and suspicion of institutions; it liked nothing better than constant checks and balances; it was never sure whether anyone, judge, lawyer, or jury, was an honest or competent man. On the other hand, a few of its more restrictive rules were mitigated. The old rule that an interested party could not testify was abolished. England took this step in 1843, Michigan in 1846, and other states followed over the next thirty years. The rule that disqualified the *parties* to a lawsuit was only a special case of the rule; it too was abolished. Connecticut may have been the earliest to do so, in the late 1840's; other states followed rather slowly, for example, Illinois only in 1867.[23] The states then, however, passed laws which excluded testimony by a survivor about a transaction with a dead man: "If death has closed the lips of the one party, the policy of the law is to close the lips of the other." [24] The list of exceptions to the hearsay rule grew bigger. More evidence was therefore admissible; but there were also more rules.

[21] The Greenleaf quote, and Thayer's comment, are in James B. Thayer, *A Preliminary Treatise on Evidence at the Common Law* (1898), pp. 508–09.

[22] Thayer, *op. cit.*, pp. 528–29.

[23] Rev. Stats. Conn. 1849, Title 1, ch. 10, sec. 141: "No person shall be disqualified as a witness . . . by reason of his interest . . . *as a party* or otherwise" (emphasis added); Laws Ill. 1867, p. 183.

[24] *Louis's Adm'r* v. *Easton*, 50 Ala. 470, 471 (1874); see John H. Wigmore, *A Treatise on the Anglo-American System of Evidence* (2nd ed., 1923), Vol. 1, pp. 1003–05.

CODIFICATION AND REFORM

Field's Code of procedure was only one part of a larger, bolder plan to codify the whole common law. The smell of feudalism still oozed from the pores of the common law. To men like Jeremy Bentham and his followers in England, and David Dudley Field, Edward Livingston, and others in America, the common law was totally unsuited for an Age of Reason. It was huge and shapeless. Common-law principles had to be painfully extracted from a jungle of words. Why not find these principles, use them, and build a simple, complete and sensible code? The French had shown the way, with the Code Napoleon. Louisiana was an American demonstration, at least in part. In 1865, Field published a general Civil Code, divided into four parts. The first three dealt with persons, property, and obligations; the fourth part contained general provisions. This scheme of organization ran parallel to that of the great French code; like that code, Field's Code tried to set out principles of law exhaustively, concisely, and with great clarity of language. But New York would have none of it. Till the end of his long life, Field continued to press for adoption in his state. He never succeeded. New York did adopt a penal code, which went into effect in 1881; but the civil code was repeatedly turned down, the latest snub occurring in 1885.

The codification movement is one of the set pieces of American legal history. It has its hero, Field; its villain is James C. Carter of New York,[25] who fought the idea of codification with as much vigor as Field fought for it. Codification was wrong, Carter felt, because it removed the center of gravity from the courts. The legislature—the code-enacting body—was an untrustworthy body, passionately addicted to the short run. "The question is," he wrote, whether "growth, development and improvement of the law" should "remain under the guidance of men selected by the people on account of their special qualifications for the work," or "be transferred to a numerous legislative body, disqualified by the nature of their duties for the discharge of this supreme function?" [26] Codes impaired the orderly development of the law; they froze it into a form which

25 On Carter (1827–1905), see the essay by George A. Miller in *Great American Lawyers,* Vol. 8 (1909), pp. 3–41.

26 James C. Carter, *The Proposed Codification of Our Common Law* (1884), p. 87.

prevented evolution. The historical school of jurisprudence taught Carter that laws were and ought to be emanations from the folk wisdom of a people. A statute, drafted by a group of so-called experts, was bound to be inferior to the achievement of centuries of evolution, of self-correcting growth. The courts apply to private disputes a "social standard of justice" which is "the product of the combined operation of the thought, the morality, the intellectual and moral culture of the time." The judges know and feel this, because "they are a part of the community." The "social standard of justice grows and develops with the moral and intellectual growth of society. . . . Hence a gradual change unperceived and unfelt in its advance is continually going on in the jurisprudence of every progressive State." [27] This point of view, of course, was useful not only in fighting codification; it was also a handy club to use against economic and social legislation; these too were intrusions, doomed to failure because they contradicted the deeper genius of the law.

Field saw codification in a different light. The laws were "now in sealed books, and the lawyers object to the opening of these books." Lawyers "as a body never did begin a reform of the law, and, judging from experience, they never will." [28] The closed books had to be opened. Progress demanded no less. The two great antagonists were in many ways one in their basic point of view. Legislative patchwork was as offensive to Field as to Carter; as offensive to Field as the patchwork common law. The codes that Field had in mind would be the work of experts—men like Field himself. The legislature would simply take the codes and give them its stamp of validity. The codes, then, would be the product of a legal elite; they would be subtle and flexible, as the common law should have been, but was not, since the common law had become (unfortunately) imprisoned by history and by the narrow self-interest of old-fashioned men. Carter and Field, then, agreed about ends; disagreed about means. They both valued flexibility in the law; liked a businesslike rationality; distrusted the role of non-experts, of laymen, in the making of law. Carter preferred common-law judges, as philosopher-kings; and looked on codes as strait-jackets. Field took the opposite view.

In the last third of the century, the ideas of Carter and Field

[27] James C. Carter, *The Provinces of the Written and the Unwritten Law* (1889), pp. 48–9.
[28] Titus M. Coan, ed., *Speeches, Arguments, and Miscellaneous Papers of David Dudley Field* (Vol. III, 1890), pp. 238, 239.

were in the air. They were similar, in some respects, to the ideas of Christopher Columbus Langdell, who led the reform of legal education at Harvard, starting in 1870. Langdell felt strongly that the common law was a science; that it contained within itself a precious core of basic principle. Legal education should reach out for and teach this essence, as refined in the crucible of experience, and with the legislative warts removed. Langdell shared Carter's basic concept of law; yet his idea of a legal principle was much like that of Field, only implicit, evolutionary, more subtly dynamic.

The Civil Code—and Field's codes on other branches of law— were not total failures. Like the Code of Civil Procedure, they found greater acceptance far from home. Dakota Territory enacted a civil code in 1866; Idaho and Montana also made a code part of their law. The chief victory, however, was California, which enacted a civil code in 1872. This was, however, not a blanket adoption of Field's code. Provisions were thoroughly revised and reconstituted, in the light of California's own prior statutes and cases.[29] California also adopted a penal and a political code.

Codification found a home in Georgia as well. The legislature appointed three commissioners in 1858, to prepare a code "which should, as near as practicable, embrace in a condensed form, the Laws of Georgia." The code would embody the "great fundamental principles" of Georgia's jurisprudence, and "furnish all the information, on the subject of Law, required either by the citizen or the subordinate Magistrate." The code was divided into four parts —"the Political and Public Organization of the State," then a civil code ("Which treats of rights, wrongs, and remedies"), a code of practice, and a penal code. The Georgia code did not purport to make new law, or to "graft upon our system any new features extracted from others, and unharmonious with our own." It merely attempted to clarify and restate, to "cut and unravel *Gordian knots*," to "give shape and order, system and efficiency, to the sometimes crude, and often ill-expressed, sovereign will of the State." The code ran to some 4,700 sections. It was adopted in 1860 as the law of Georgia.[30]

The success of the codes in the West was due to reasons that by now are familiar. These were sparsely settled states in a hurry to ingest a legal system. A few had something of a civil-law tradition. In none of the Western states did the bar have a strong vested

[29] See Arvo Van Alstyne, *The California Civil Code* (1954), p. 11.

[30] *The Code of the State of Georgia,* prepared by R. H. Clark, T. R. R. Cobb, and D. Irwin (1861), pp. iii, iv, vii, viii.

interest in the continuance of old rules, especially of pleading. But once the codes were on the books, the results fell far short of the hopes. What happened afterwards would have brought Field to the rim of distraction. Courts and lawyers treated some code provisions in accordance with ingrained common-law prejudices. In some cases, the codes' provisions were construed away; more often, they were simply ignored. Nor did the legislature keep its hands off the code; broad statements of principles were let stand (they made little difference anyway), and all sorts of accretions were added. It is hard to resist the conclusion that the codes had almost no impact on behavior, either in court or out. Law in action in California did not seem much different from law in action in noncode states, in any way that the codes would help to explain.

The codes did focus attention on some of the drawbacks of common law. The codes are the spiritual parents of the restatements of the law—black-letter codes of the 20th century, sponsored by the American Law Institute, but meant for persuasion of judges, rather than enactment into law. Both codes and restatements were reforms that did not reform. In the 19th century, law was constantly and vigorously changing; every new statute was in a sense a reform; so was every new doctrine and ruling. The codesmen were interested in reform in a special sense. They wanted to perfect an existing system. They wanted to make it more knowable, harmonious, certain. Drastic shifts in allocation of political or economic power, through law, were not to their purpose.

Behind the work of the law reformers was a sort of a theory: that that legal system is best, and works best, and does the most for society, which most conforms to the ideal of legal rationality—the system which is most clear, orderly, systematic (in its formal parts), which has the most structural beauty, which most appeals to the modern, well-educated jurist. This theory was rarely made explicit, and of course never tested. It was in all probability false, since it is hard to see how society can be changed by reforms which only rearrange law on paper. One child labor act or one homestead act had more potential power than volumes of codes.

In fact, paper changes were in a way the main point of law reform: law reform was, basically, those changes in law which could be agreed upon by leaders of the bar, and which were not socially or politically sensitive. Only these could be put forward as the program of the bar, without arousing public animosity. A uniform wage-and-hour law, or a tax code, could never be presented as something blandly, incontrovertibly good. Law reform became prominent as the public-service work of the legal profession; it was useful for the lawyer's tarnished image. But service to the whole public is sometimes the same as service to nobody. So long as the public (and most lawyers) hardly suspected that law reform had such limited results, law reform could masquerade as a vital social task. And it could be used by lawyers to justify their own monopoly of practice, to pass for the social service that every profession is supposed to perform.[31]

This, at least, was the character of late 19th-century law reform. It was the program of the upper or organized bar. The bar-association movement began in the 1870's; and by the 1890's, it was pushing vigorously for reform and unification of American law. But even this kind of law reform had rather negligible results, at least up to the end of the 19th century. Codification of law was extremely hard to achieve in a federal union. As far as most branches of law were concerned, each state from Maine to the Pacific was a petty sovereignty, with its own brand of law. The American Bar Association concerned itself with fields of law whose implications crossed state lines: the law of migratory divorce, for example, and commercial law, both of which were notoriously nonuniform. On the surface at least, a good deal was accomplished in standardization of commercial law. It was plausible to argue that businessmen needed fair, uniform laws of commerce in a gigantic free-trade area like the United States. More important, many differences in detail of state laws had no particular basis in culture or opinion; the laws were functionally the same, with varying terminology and little quirks here and there. In the last decade of the century, the ABA supported a uniform law movement. States were encouraged to appoint commissioners, to meet and consider the problem. The first major effort of the commissioners on uniform state laws was a Negotiable Instruments Law, modeled after the English Bills-of-Exchange Act (1882), with more than a nod to the California code. The NIL was to become one of the most successful of all the so-called uniform laws. By 1900, it had been widely enacted, and it won almost universal acceptance before it was swept away by the Uniform Commercial Code in the 1950's and 1960's.

There were other triumphs of uniformity, however, which are easy to overlook, because they did not come out of the formal movement for uniform laws. The Interstate Commerce Act of 1877,

[31] See, in general, Lawrence M. Friedman, "Law Reform in Historical Perspective," 13 St. Louis U.L.J. 351 (1969).

the Sherman Act of 1890, the Bankruptcy Act of 1898, were in a real sense responses to commercial or political need for a single national authority. The "national" scope of legal education and legal literature was another impulse toward uniformity, at least of legal culture, and particularly after Langdell purged Harvard of the lecture method, and launched the case method on its way. Not that all members of the legal profession were trained and socialized in the same way; but the profession was stratified more by social class and training than along geographical lines.

Publishers continued to spew forth an incredible profusion of legal materials: cases by the thousands, statutes in every state, every year or every other year; rulings, ordinances, and local customs on a scale that dwarfed the imagination. Tricks of research made this fabulous diversity somewhat more tractable. In the last quarter of the century, the West Publishing Company, of St. Paul, Minnesota, began a profitable career of taming the dragon of case law. The states published their decisions very slowly; West published them fast, and bound them up into regional reporters (Atlantic, Northeast, Northwest, Southern, Southeast, Southwest, and Pacific). *The Northwest Reporter,* which included Minnesota, was the first; it began to appear in 1879. West ultimately indexed the cases with a naïve but effective "key-number" system. In recent years, the little pop-art key of this private company has been an indispensable tool of the lawyers. *The Century Edition of the American Digest,* which West published beginning in 1897, gathered together every reported case (it claimed there were more than 500,000 of them) indexed, classified, and bound into fifty volumes, from "Abandonment" through "Work and Labor." Each ten-year period since then, West has published a *Decennial Digest,* harvesting the cases for that decade; in between, it markets advance sheets and temporary volumes. Nothing remotely comparable was ever done, unfortunately, for the even more chaotic system of statute law; Frederic Stimson published *American Statute Law* in 1881, a thick volume which gave the gist of the statutes, but it was nothing but a palliative. To this day, enacted law waits for a man with an index. The Citator system also began in the late 19th century. The Citator, published for individual states, then for regional groupings, gives the history of a case in dry numbers and letters: who cited it, on what point, was it approved, disapproved, or distinguished. It began as gummed labels, for lawyers to paste in their personal or office copies of reports. Then it graduated to

bound volumes. These red books, thick and thin, useful but unloved, became as familiar to lawyers as West's little keys.

In a federal system, however, the diversity of American law, despite a common heritage, despite the oneness of the economy, despite the tools (telephone, telegraph) that developed to bridge distances, was deep-seated and ineradicable. The older the state, the
more volumes of reports bulged on its shelves. Its courts had less
likelihood and less need, in the usual case, to grub around elsewhere for precedent. Each state built up its own body of laws, and,
as time went on, needed to pay less and less attention to its neighbors; and hardly any at all to mother England. The West system
calmed but did not cure these local diseases. The same was true of
statutes; borrowing was common, but each state had its own codes
and revisions. There were regional groupings, to be sure. "Legislative precedent" can be traced across the country. California acted
as a focal point for Western legislation and case law; desert Nevada, its satellite state, drew on it heavily. The Southern states
worked out local solutions (if that is the word) to mutual problems
of race relations; the smaller New England states modeled their
railroad commissions on that of Massachusetts; states of the great
plains had common problems of agriculture, freight rates, grain
storage, and borrowed answers from each other. In general, what
kept the dialects of law from becoming mutually unintelligible was
their community of experience. The states traveled similar economic and social journeys, and the law went along.

That men and goods moved freely across state lines was the most
important fact of American law. It meant that a competitive market of laws existed in the country. If a New Yorker had money, and
wanted a divorce, he went to another state. If the corporation laws
of his state were too harsh to suit an entrepreneur, New Jersey was
willing to accommodate, and later on, Delaware. The states could
act as "laboratories" of social legislation, in a later euphemism;
but this was only half the story. The states acted also as competing sellers of jurisprudence in a vast federal bazaar. A kind of
Gresham's law was in operation: easy laws drove out the harsh
ones. Experiments in the "laboratories" would not work so long as
neighbor states refused to go along. New York's hard divorce laws
remained nominally in force; but they were at least partly nullified
by Nevada. Legislators hesitated to pass advanced labor laws, for
fear of driving out business; other states were eager to offer low-
wage shelters. Big national companies could not be controlled by

regulation spawned in particular states. The only solutions were voluntary moves toward uniformity, or strong federal control. The first had no real muscle behind it. The second was the ultimate solution.

As of 1900, American law remained in a state of maddening complexity. Diversities as old as the 17th century still lived on. Local circumstances, local economic needs, local turns of events made new diversities. Legislation was equally varied. English influence was down to a trickle; but Massachusetts, conservative in lawyer's law, was a port of entry for a few last pieces of English doctrine, which landed at Boston and were transshipped farther West. No two states had the same economy, society, or history; no two had the same mix of peoples. Yet, these differences among states cannot easily explain all the differences in the laws. Why Illinois should have a more backward civil process than Missouri is not easy to explain by reference to concrete social forces. Centrifugal and centripetal forces were both strong, complex currents in American law.

CHAPTER IV

THE LAND: AND OTHER PROPERTY

The dominant idea of American land law was that land should be freely bought and sold. For this reason, lawyers, judges and legislatures, in the years after independence, had gone to great pains to untie the Gordian knots of English land law. The aim was to make law fit the needs of a big, open country, with huge tracts of vacant land and a belief in abundance. Land was the basis of wealth, the mother of resources and development. As the frontier moved further west, land law followed at a respectable distance. The land itself developed from wilderness to farm land or industrial land; from vacant sites to towns to cities; so, too, the land law passed through phases of development. A state like New York had needs quite different from Wyoming. But differences in land and resource law, though never eliminated, tended to diminish over the years. Colonial history repeated itself in a way; relatively rude, relatively simple land law, in a new settlement, gradually became more sophisticated, more like the general law, not only because knowledge of law was further broadcast, but also because sophisticated law became more and more relevant.

For example, there was never much question that the concept of the *fixture* and its attendant rules would be thoroughly naturalized. A *fixture* is an object attached to the land and legally treated as part of the land—sale of land includes sale of its fixtures. A building is par excellence attached to the soil, yet in Wisconsin in the 1850's a court decided in one case that a barn in Janesville, in another, the practice hall of the "Palmyra Brass Band" were mere chattels, and therefore severable from the land.[1] These were flimsy and temporary buildings; the decisions simply recognized what was a local and transient condition.

Courts tended to recede from inherited doctrines if they did not suit American needs. In England, it had been settled doctrine that

[1] Lawrence M. Friedman, *Contract Law in America, a Social and Economic Case Study* (1965), p. 34.

a landowner could acquire an easement of light and air through "uninterrupted enjoyment"; a landowner whose land had always had a pleasant, open view could block an adjoining owner from building and impairing this easement. This doctrine was out of place—or so the courts thought—in a country bent on economic growth, trying to promote, not curb, the intensive use of land. Chancellor Kent thought the rule did not "reasonably or equitably apply . . . to buildings on narrow lots in the rapidly growing cities in this country." A Massachusetts statute of 1852 denied that the "mere continuance of . . . windows" gave an easement "of light and air" so as to keep an adjoining landowner from building on his land.[2] By the late 19th century, every state except three had rejected the idea of this easement.[3]

In contrast, the doctrine of adverse possession was eagerly embraced in the United States. Under this doctrine, if a person occupied another's land for a period of years, openly and notoriously, he acquired a good title, and the true owner lost his rights.[4] The Western states, in particular, were favorable to the idea of adverse possession. The farther west one went, the shorter the period of time needed for adverse possession to ripen into title. The traditional period was twenty years; this telescoped into five in the Nevada territorial laws of 1861.[5] The occupant, to prove possession, had to show a house, a fence, a pastoral or pasturage use, or some other sign of exploitation of the land. Much litigation turned on the question of what was sufficient possession.

On the surface, the doctrine of adverse possession seemed to favor actual settlers against absentee owners. The Western attitude tends to support this explanation. On the other hand, there is evidence that points in another direction. In some states, starting with Illinois in 1872, an adverse claimant could not gain good title unless he paid taxes on the land, while the period of possession was running. This requirement too became associated mainly with Western states. The suggestion is that the adverse claimant was not to be a mere squatter (in the pejorative sense). He should be someone who honestly thought he had a claim to the land. (A man of

[2] Kent, *Commentaries*, Vol. III (2nd ed., 1832), p. 446n; Laws Mass. 1852, ch. 144.

[3] Christopher G. Tiedemann, *An Elementary Treatise on the American Law of Real Property* (1885), sec. 613, pp. 475–76.

[4] Possession also had to be "hostile," that is, inconsistent with the true owner's claims—otherwise a tenant would eventually undo his landlord's title.

[5] Laws Terr. Nev. 1861, ch. 12, sec. 5.

this kind would naturally pay his taxes.) The tax provision suggests that the doctrine's popularity was another response to the chaos of land titles. It was easy for a person to think, wrongly, that he had good title to his land. If he stayed in possession long enough, his mistake could be cured by the doctrine. The statute, said Chief Justice Gibson of Pennsylvania, in 1845, "protects the occupant, not for his merit, for he has none, but for the demerit of his antagonist in delaying the contest beyond the period assigned for it, when papers may be lost, facts forgotten, or witnesses dead." [6] On the other hand, the doctrine itself was a cloud on titles, since one could search the county records forever without finding the fact of adverse possession recorded.

THE PUBLIC LAND

Public lands continued to be a major topic of controversy after the 1840's. The idea that the great federal treasure of land should be used to raise money was all but dead. The clamor for free land reached its climax in the famous Homestead Act of 1862; and government made ever heavier use of land as a form of subsidy. The Morrill Act of 1862 gave each state a vast tract of land, computed as 30,000 acres for each Senator and Representative the state was entitled to under the 1860 census; the land was to be used to establish "Colleges for the Benefit of Agriculture and Mechanic Arts." [7] In 1850, after much debate, the federal government also began to make land grants to help build railroads. The economic advantages, for most sections of the country, outweighed any lingering scruples about the right of the federal government to support internal improvements.

A proposed railroad from Chicago to Mobile was the subject of the first major land grant. (It ultimately became the Illinois Central Railroad.) The law, passed in 1850,[8] gave to the states of Illinois, Alabama, and Mississippi alternate sections of land for six miles on either side of the proposed line of tracks; the state would dispose of the land, and use the proceeds in building the road. Ungranted sections of land were to be sold by the United States

[6] *Sailor* v. *Hertzogg*, 2 Pa. St. 182, 185 (1845).
[7] 12 Stats. 503 (act of July 2, 1862); Paul W. Gates, *History of Public Land Law Development* (1968), pp. 335–36.
[8] 9 Stats. 466 (act of Sept. 20, 1850); see Gates, *op. cit.*, pp. 341–86.

AMERICAN LAW TO THE CLOSE OF THE 19TH CENTURY

government at not less than $2.50 an acre ("double the minimum price of the public lands").[9] Later acts—for example, the law of 1862 in aid of the Union Pacific—shortcutted the process by giving the alternate sections directly to the railroad, instead of the states.[10]

In theory, the government lost nothing and got a free railroad, without spending any cash. Government land, sandwiched between sections of railroad land, would fetch a double price, because the railroad's presence would drive up its value. But even this notion was abandoned in the 1860's. The endless grasslands, mountains, deep forest, and desert of the far West, through which the railroads of the 1860's had to run, were almost uninhabited. The government price, understandably, had to be lowered. Moreover, the grants to the railroads conflicted with the spirit of the Homestead Act; after 1871, for a variety of reasons, no more land grants to railroads were made. By this time, whatever harm or good would result from the policy had mostly been done. The exact amount of land granted to the railroads is in some dispute; but even a conservative estimate would put it at more than 130,000,000 acres.[11]

The Homestead Act was the climax of a long political struggle. The homestead concept itself was a logical extension of trends in public-land policy. A vocal, sharply focused interest group defeated the first general goal of land policy—to raise revenue. When this policy died, the land-grant principle, which confronted the settlers with a less diffuse and greedier adversary, was the only rival of the homestead policy.

Until 1861, the homestead proposal was entangled in the sectional and slavery crisis. There were strong champions of a homestead bill, like Galusha Grow of Pennsylvania, but there was also bitter opposition; President Buchanan vetoed a homestead bill in 1860. The outbreak of the war removed many opponents from Congress. In 1862, the bill became law, formally committing the government to grant land free to the pioneers, the "soldiers of peace," the "grand army of the sons of toil," those who struggled against the "merciless barbarities of savage life," and who had

[9] 9 Stats. 466 (act of Sept. 20, 1850). The government retained the right to transport its property and troops "free from toll." Some of the land on either side of the road was bound to be already occupied or taken; the statute therefore made provision for the granting of substitute lands to make up these deficiencies.

[10] 12 Stats. 489 (act of July 1, 1862).

[11] Robert S. Henry, "The Railroad Land Grant Legend in American History Texts," 32 Miss. Valley Hist. Rev. 171 (1945).

"borne [the] eagles in triumph from ocean to ocean." [12] The provisions of the act were simple. Heads of families, persons over twenty-one, and veterans (but not those who had "borne arms against the United States or given aid and comfort to its enemies") were eligible, subject to certain exceptions, to "enter one quarter section or a less quantity of unappropriated public lands." Claimants had to certify that they wanted the land for their own "exclusive use and benefit" and "for the purpose of actual settlement." After five years of settlement, the government would issue a patent for the land. An actual settler who qualified could, however, buy up the land at the minimum price (generally $1.25 an acre) before the end of the five-year period.[13]

The Homestead Act assumed that a supply of productive land stood waiting for the settlers. Special laws provided for the disposal of less desirable land—swamp land (1850), and desert lands (1877). These lands were commercially useless, and the government added extra inducements for reclamation. The swamp lands went free to the states, which, however, could sell them off to be drained. The desert land laws allowed individual claimants more acres than they could acquire through the Homestead Act; but the claimant had to irrigate his holdings. In addition, the federal government gave each new state a dowry of land as it entered the union. The states therefore held a considerable stock of land—swamp land; land under land-grant college laws; dowry lands at statehood. The states sold these lands on the open market. Wisconsin, for example, when it was admitted to the union, received public land from the federal government, to be sold to raise "a separate fund to be called 'the school fund.' " The state disposed of its school lands at cheap prices and very favorable terms and used the proceeds to lend money at interest to farmers who needed money, thus (it thought) killing two birds with one stone. The panic of 1857, however, wrecked the farm-loan system. As debtors went into default, it became clear that the program had been fearfully mismanaged. The state lost heavily on its investments.[14] Many states similarly frittered away their Morrill Act lands in the 1860's. In a number of states, the "school lands" created their own won-

---

[12] Galusha Grow, quoted in Benjamin Hibbard, *A History of the Public Land Policies* (1924), p. 384.

[13] 12 Stats. 392 (act of May 20, 1862).

[14] The Wisconsin School Land Act in operation has been explored by Joseph Schafer, "Wisconsin's Farm Loan Law, 1849–1863," in *Proceedings, State Historical Society of Wisconsin, 68th Ann. Meeting, 1920*, p. 156.

derland of jurisprudence, an almost forgotten mass of law about claims, terms, and priorities, which bears witness to the insufficiency and greed of public-land law.

The basic problem was that the public-land laws were hopelessly inconsistent. Some land was free for settlers; other land was for sale. The government proposed to sell some land to the highest bidder; proposed using other land to induce private enterprise to build railroads; gave other land to the states to fund their colleges. Administration of land laws was notoriously weak. The homestead principle, if that meant giving land free to the landless poor, was weakest of all, and the first to go. The government continued to sell land for cash; and the best land was "snapped up" by speculators. As Paul Wallace Gates describes it, settlers arriving in Kansas between 1868 and 1872

> were greeted with advertisements announcing that the choicest lands in the state had been selected by the State Agricultural College, which was now offering 90,000 acres for sale on long-term credits. The Central Branch of the Union Pacific Railroad offered 1,200,000 acres for prices ranging from $1 to $15 per acre; the Kansas Pacific Railroad offered 5,000,000 acres for $1 to $6 per acre; the Kansas and Neosho Valley Railroad offered 1,500,-000 acres for sale at $2 to $8 per acre; the Capital Land Agency of Topeka offered 1,000,000 acres of Kansas land for sale; Van Doren and Havens offered 200,000 acres for $3 to $10 per acre; T. H. Walker offered 10,000 (or 100,000) acres for $5 to $10 per acre; Hendry and Noyes offered 50,000 acres, and even the United States government was advertising for bids of approximately 6,000 acres of Sac and Fox Indian lands.[15]

All of this choice land, in government or private hands, was unavailable to the homesteader. These heavy sales of Western land were a sign, then, of the failure of the Homestead Act. Then, too, those who drafted the act seemed to have had in mind the rich and well-watered land of the Middle West. Immense regions of land in the West were simply not suitable for family farming. They were more suited to grazing and ranching.[16] Particularly after 1880,

[15] Paul W. Gates, "The Homestead Law in an Incongruous Land System," in Vernon Carstensen, ed., *The Public Lands* (1963), pp. 315, 323–24.

[16] Similarly, the Southern Homestead Act of 1866, which aimed to open public land in the South to freedmen and refugees, "turned out to be a resounding failure, partly because the lands set aside under it were of the poorest quality, and partly because the freedmen lacked the necessary means to support them-

many people made use of the commutation privilege of the Homestead Act—the right to short-cut the homestead period, by paying the regular price for the land. From 1881 to 1904, 22,000,000 acres were commuted, twenty-three per cent of the total number of homestead entries for this period. This was the "means whereby large land holdings were built up through a perverted use of the Homestead Act." A Senate document later recorded that "not one in a hundred" of these commuted lands was "ever occupied as a home . . . They became part of some large timber holding or a parcel of a cattle or sheep ranch." The commuters were "usually merchants, professional people, school teachers, clerks, journeymen working at trades, cow punchers, or sheep herders." Usually, these commuters sold their land immediately after title vested.[17]

So ignoble a failure casts doubt on the idea that aid to the actual settler was ever really the guiding principle of public land law. Land law took the form of exalting the yeoman farmer; it used him for slogans and propaganda. The law itself served more complicated interests: businessmen, speculators, merchants, lawyers, as well as farmers and settlers. The Homestead Act itself, and the public-land law in general, were complex and contradictory because of the multiplicity of interests that had a voice in enactment and administration. The unending maze of case law, legislation, regulations, public-land-office rulings, and decrees testify and owe their confusion to the same basic fact.

Toward the end of the century, the change in national attitude associated with the death of the frontier began to make its mark on public-land law. Policy had been characterized before by a roaring optimism. Public property was looked upon as an inexhaustible treasure. Whether land was to be sold, or given away, used to create new centers of population, or to fund a school system, government's function was to divest itself of this primary form of wealth as soon and as equitably as possible.[18] In the last years of the 19th century, the psychological horizon darkened. The national domain was visibly vanishing. Out of a new sense of scarcity, and a muted pessimism, the seeds of the conservation movement grew.

selves while working to clear the land and cultivate a crop." Martin Abbott, *The Freedmen's Bureau in South Carolina, 1865–1872* (1967), pp. 63–64.

17 Hibbard, *op. cit.*, pp. 386–89; Paul W. Gates, *History of Public Land Law Development* (1968), pp. 387 ff.

18 The chief exception—mineral lands—merely underscores this point: it was recognized much earlier that these resources were finite and irreplaceable.

Yellowstone National Park was established in 1872, "as a public park or pleasuring-ground for the benefit and enjoyment of the people." [19] A law of 1891 gave the President authority to "set apart and reserve . . . public lands wholly or in part covered with timber or undergrowth, whether of commercial value or not, as public reservations." President Harrison took prompt action, and set aside, by proclamation, about 13,053,440 acres. President Cleveland added a vast new area, evoking a storm of protest from Western Congressmen and Senators, who saw threats to mining and lumbering.[20]

In the states, there were parallel developments. A law of New York state, in 1892, established "the Adirondack Park," to be "forever reserved, maintained and cared for as ground open to the free use of all the people for their health or pleasure, and as forest lands necessary to the preservation of the headwaters of the chief rivers of the state, and a future timber supply." [21] The New York constitution of 1897 declared the preserves "forever" wild. Conservationists made halting attempts to stop the slaughter of wildlife. Fish and game laws, too, were passed in increasing numbers. New Hampshire, for example, created "a board of commissioners on fisheries" in 1869. This later became a full-fledged fish and game commission, with power, for example, to close any restocked waters against fishing, "for a period not exceeding three years." As of 1900, New Hampshire statutes forbade anyone to "hunt, kill, destroy, or capture any moose, caribou, or deer," except between September 15 and November 30. Dogs could never be used to hunt these animals. There was a season, too, for sable, otter, fisher, gray squirrels and raccoons, and an absolute prohibition on killing beaver. There were protective laws for many birds, too, including a ban on killing any "American or bald eagle." [22] After 1900, Americans could not foul their nest with quite so much impunity or legitimacy. The engines of pollution, however, also grew more powerful: the growth of industry, cities, and population, and the taste for consumption of natural products.

A conservation mentality of another variety colored the growth of new tools of land-use control. Fashionable neighborhoods with "good" addresses, developed in Eastern cities. These enclaves of wealth generated a demand for legal devices that would protect

19 17 Stats. 32 (act of Mar. 1, 1872).
20 Gates, op. cit., pp. 567–69.
21 Laws N.Y. 1892, Vol. 1, ch. 707.
22 N.H. Stats. 1901, chs. 130–32.

property values, and maintain the prevailing patterns of segregation by income and class. A leading English case, *Tulk* v. *Moxhay* (1848),[23] had launched the doctrine of the equitable servitude or covenant. This doctrine was useful in preserving the amenities in new subdivisions or neighborhoods. *Parker* v. *Nightingale* (Massachusetts, 1863)[24] brought the doctrine to America. The heirs of Lemuel Hayward had sold lots in Hayward Place, Boston, under the express condition that they would allow only buildings "of brick or stone, of not less than three stories in height, and for a dwelling house only." Forty years later, in 1862, James Nightingale, who owned one of the lots, leased his land to Frederick Loeber, who opened a "restaurant or eating-house." Crowds of "noisy and boisterous persons" disturbed the decorum of Hayward Place. The neighbors brought an action. The legal difficulty was that these neighbors were strangers to the transaction; they had an agreement, to be sure, but it ran to Hayward and his heirs, not to Nightingale or Loeber. The court, as in *Tulk* v. *Moxhay*, vaulted over this objection. The original covenant was binding, in equity, on behalf of the "parties aggrieved." By the original scheme, "a right or privilege or amenity in each lot was permanently secured to the owners of all the other lots." The law came to recognize that the "free changing of property and the shifting of titles" could work "hardship"; the "continued use of property in a particular locality for the same purpose was a very important element in the value and desirability of an investment . . . in the building of new towns of great promise, and in the building of great houses in old towns." [25] Long before zoning laws, therefore, the equitable covenant provided a legal tool to buttress neighborhood values against the encroachments of urban change.

PROPERTY LAW AND THE DYNASTS

The New York property codes, from the late 1820's, were adopted, as we have seen, by Michigan, Wisconsin, and Minnesota. Later Western codes—the Dakotas, Arizona—also absorbed chunks of property law whose ultimate source was New York. The New York codes had abolished a lot of deadwood and revised many other

23 2 Phil. 774, 41 Eng. Rep. 1143 (Ch., 1848).
24 6 Allen (88 Mass.) 341 (1863).
25 Henry U. Sims, *A Treatise on Covenants Which Run with Land* (1901), preface, v.

parts of property law. The codes revamped the law and lore of *future interests*—those interests in property other than present, possessory rights. The old law of future interests had served the old landed estates. With a slight twist, the law turned out to serve the needs of new dynasts, whose money was tied up not in landed estates, but in trusts.

The details of the rebirth of future interests are not important and, in any event, are almost beyond the layman's comprehension and patience. Essentially, what happened was that in some rare but important cases, rich men established trusts (by will or deed), to be invested for their children, and distributed to grandchildren (or collateral relatives). Meantime, the principal was safe, and the estate remained an entity. The role of the law of future interests was to regulate relationships among remote beneficiaries, to determine what kinds of dynastic arrangements were permissible, and how long they might last. Now it was the New York reforms that, in the end, had to be reformed. And the ghosts of the old English writers on contingent remainders, springing uses, determinable fees, and other mysteries, began to haunt the law courts. A specifically American master, John Chipman Gray, a Bostonian and a law teacher, made the rule against perpetuities his particular province. His treatise, first published in 1888, is still (in revised form) in print.

Alongside of the law of future interests, a law and practice of trust administration grew up. Most trustees had been amateurs; a few (as in Boston) were professional managers. After the Civil War, the corporate trust company began to make its mark in the world. In 1871, for example, a charter was issued in New York to the Westchester County Trust Company. The company had power to invest trust money "in public stocks of the United States," in securities of New York state, "bonds or stocks of any incorporated city," and in corporate securities up to $10,000.[26] Toward the end of the century, some states began to formalize the law of trust investment by enacting "legal lists"—lists of investments in which trustees could invest trust funds without danger of a lawsuit. Massachusetts, and a few other states, gave their investors more autonomy, and had done so since the famous *Harvard College* case in 1830.[27]

[26] Laws N.Y. 1871, ch. 341. See James G. Smith, *The Development of Trust Companies in the United States* (1928); Lawrence M. Friedman, "The Dynastic Trust," 73 Yale L.J. 547 (1964).

[27] *Harvard College* v. *Amory*, 26 Mass. (9 Pick.) 446 (1830); see above p. 223.

The *Harvard College* rule—the rule of the prudent investor—was indeed more suitable to the dynastic trust. But the rarity of this use of trusts probably kept the doctrine from spreading. The other line of authority was based on the use of the trust to protect the helpless—the proverbial widows and orphans. This was the only common type of trust outside the major commercial centers; and even in the East it was dominant. In Pennsylvania, the constitution of 1873 forbade the legislature from authorizing the investment of trust funds "in the bonds or stocks of any private corporation." [28]

Another development in the law was the rise of the doctrine that a spendthrift trust could be enforced. A spendthrift trust was a trust in which, by its terms, beneficiaries could not sell, give away, or mortgage their interests; and in which no creditor of a beneficiary could reach the beneficiary's interest, before money actually passed into the beneficiary's hands. There was no such thing, in other words, as the right to garnish or place a lien on an interest in a spendthrift trust. John Chipman Gray, in the first edition of his tedious little book, *Restraints on the Alienation of Property,* attacked this extraordinary doctrine as illogical and against the weight of precedent. Yet in 1882, Massachusetts, Gray's home state, ignored the logic, and boldly adopted the doctrine, in *Broadway Bank* v. *Adams.*[29] Gray wrote an angry preface to his second edition: the spirit of "paternalism," he said darkly, "the fundamental essence alike of spendthrift trusts and of socialism," was abroad in the land. But the spirit of the spendthrift trust was neither socialism nor paternalism: it was the dynastic urge of the rich, coming to the forefront, and finding a doctrinal home in that state whose capital city was Boston.

The rule against perpetuities was the rule that set final limits to a dynast's dreams of immortality. The rule, which developed over the course of two centuries, reaching a stable form about 1800, governed the time limit of trusts or chains of future interest. No interest was good, unless it "vested" no later in the future than "lives in being," plus twenty-one years. One could make a trust endure as long as a set of lifetimes lasted—lifetimes of persons born before the estate in question was established—plus an additional period of about one generation. The practical effect of the rule was to limit dynasties to no more than seventy-five or one hundred years,

[28] Pa. const. 1873, art. III, sec. 22. A similar provision appears in Alabama (1875), Colorado (1876), Montana (1889), and Wyoming (1889).

[29] 133 Mass. 170 (1882).

at the outer limit. The New York property laws of the late 1820's had been more ruthless and restrictive. Their version of the rule was copied in California, Michigan, and Wisconsin, among other states. The common-law rule was in at least nominal effect elsewhere.

For much of the 19th century, the *charitable trust* had suffered from widespread fear of the dead hand, particularly the dead hand of the Church. New York's property laws severely limited creation of charitable trusts. When Samuel Tilden, lawyer and almost-President, died, he left millions of dollars to fund a public library in New York City. But the New York courts (1891) held the Tilden trust invalid, and handed the money to his heirs. The case finally galvanized the legislature into action. In 1893, a statute removed the shadow of invalidity from charitable trusts in New York.[30]

Charitable trusts were also invalid or much restricted in those Midwestern states which had borrowed New York's property laws (Michigan, Minnesota, Wisconsin), and in a cluster of Southern states radiating about Virginia. In these Southern states, the state of the law may be explained by long memories and old hatreds flowing from the Reformation. A number of states also had "mortmain" statutes, which restricted gifts to charity to be made by will; such a gift could not be made too soon before death (thirty days in some states). The Pennsylvania version was passed in 1855.[31] These statutes no doubt were influenced by the fantasy of the evil priest, who preyed on the fears of the dying, persuading men to impoverish their families and enrich the Church.

These prejudices were a long time in vanishing. What diminished them was the changing nature of charitable trusts, and indeed of American wealth. The age of the great foundations was still far in the future; but part of the public had already begun to lay moral claim to conscience money from barons of finance, oil, and steel. What changed the law in New York was the realization that when the Tilden trust failed, no dead hand became richer; but the city itself was the poorer.

Some states had come to this realization sooner, and had never thrown serious obstacles in the path of the charitable trust. Indeed, Massachusetts courts had put new life in the doctrine of *cy pres* (law-French for "so near"), a doctrine essential to the health of a

---

30 *Tilden* v. *Green*, 130 N.Y. 29, 28 N.E. 880 (1891); James B. Ames, "The Failure of the 'Tilden Trust,'" 5 Harv. L. Rev. 389 (1892); Laws N.Y. 1893, ch. 701.
31 Laws Pa. 1855, ch. 347, sec. 11.

long-term charity. This doctrine was used to save charitable gifts whose original purpose had failed or became impossible. Rather than give money back to the heirs, a court of equity would apply it to a purpose as near as possible to the original one. In *Jackson* v. *Phillips* (1867),[32] the doctrine was applied to the will of Francis Jackson of Boston. Jackson had died in 1861, leaving money to trustees to be used to "create a public sentiment that will put an end to Negro slavery"; the trustees were to employ another part of the fund for the benefit of fugitive slaves. By 1867, these were objects that could not be literally carried out, because slavery was legally at an end. The heirs therefore claimed the money for themselves. But the court refused to dismantle the trust. Instead, the court directed a "so-near" use of the fund—for welfare and education work among New England blacks and among freed slaves. The court did not invent the doctrine—it was old in England—but now it received new and different life, as an adjunct of the law of dynastic charities, just as the Massachusetts rule on trust investment was an adjunct of the law of dynastic trusts in general.

The law of *wills* was receptive to terms and doctrines from England. Many American statutes were remolded in the light of the English Wills Act (1837). The general trend, despite the holographic will in the West and South, was toward more formality in the execution of wills, for the sake of property records if nothing else. Informal, oral wills ceased, practically speaking, to count. This does not mean that the law of wills remained implacably formal and rigid. In general, courts loosened their rules of interpretation of wills. They moved away from fixed canons of construction, and stressed what the testator actually meant; his intention was the "pole star," the "sovereign guide" of interpretation.[33] This attitude was appropriate in a country of general, though hardly sensational, literacy, diffuse property ownership, and low standards of legal (and lay) draftsmanship. The cases reflected tension between the desire of courts to carry out the testator's wishes, and the need for certainty, routinization, and predictability.

Between 1850 and 1900, more people and more ordinary people developed the habit of making wills and probating their property. A study of Essex County (New Jersey) wills compared a sample of 1850 wills with those of 1875 and 1900. In 1850, in Essex County, less than five per cent of those who died left testate estates; only about eight per cent had estates of any sort. By 1900, roughly four-

---

[32] 96 Mass. 539 (1867).

[33] James Schouler, *A Treatise on the Law of Wills* (2nd ed., 1892), p. 500.

teen per cent of the dying population left probated estates; eight per cent were testate. Fewer of the probated wills were "deathbed" or last-illness wills in 1900. In 1850 at least a quarter of the wills were executed less than a month before death; in 1900 less than a fifth. The wealthier testators at least were more sophisticated about draftsmanship in 1900 than in 1850; they were more likely to cover, in their wills, such simple contingencies as what to do if a beneficiary died before the testator did. Interestingly, the earlier the will, the more likely it was to leave property in trust or in the form of a legal life estate. This was especially true of gifts to or for women. 73.3 per cent of the 1850 wills made these non-outright gifts, but only forty per cent of the 1900 wills. The change came about partly because of the greater social independence of women, partly because more middle-class people made out wills, partly because of changes in the legal status of married women. Many 1900 testators were women, some of them women in simple circumstances—Mrs. Mary Duffy, who signed her will by mark and left everything to her husband; Grace Creamer, whose pathetic will, executed on her dying day, left everything to her newborn, illegitimate child. The earlier wills, by and large, directed the executors to sell off the property; in the uncertainites of the 1850's, an executor was best suited to collect, and liquidate, the estate. Only later did sophisticated wills contemplate an estate that would continue, under careful management, with retention of its assets until market conditions dictated otherwise.[34]

LANDLORD AND TENANT

The concept of tenancy has meant different things, depending on whether the tenant held farm land, commercial property, or a city apartment, and on what terms. In New York, pitched battles in the 1840's marked the beginning of the end for one of the last remnants of a kind of feudal tenancy in America. Economic and social conditions had made the New York landed estates an anachronism. The American dream was for each man to hold his land in fee simple. Farmers looked with horror on the idea of a permanent class of tenants, with no right ever to own their land. The New York constitution of 1846, after the downfall of the patroons, out-

[34] This discussion was based on Lawrence M. Friedman, "Patterns of Testation in the 19th Century: A Study of Essex County (New Jersey) Wills," 8 Am. J. Leg. Hist. 34 (1964).

lawed feudal tenures and long-term agricultural leases. Meanwhile, exemption and homestead laws, in almost all the states, protected the farmer's basic holdings of land, animals, and tools from seizure for debt. Distress for rent—the landlord's right to extract delinquent rent directly from the land—was, in many states, abolished.[35]

The American lease was, in general, no longer a document of tenure; even for agricultural lands, it was basically a commercial contract. Farm tenancy was never uncommon even in the North. There were absentee landlords and sizeable leaseholds. In Illinois, there were many large "frontier landlords," whose tenants paid in shares of crops or, more rarely, cash. One of the most notorious was William Scully, a landlord of Ireland, an alien and absentee; on his vast prairie holdings in the 1880's there was considerable unrest.[36] Still, the leasehold was not the dominant mode of tenure. The leasehold, protean and flexible, was for many young farmers the first step up the ladder of farm success; for old farmers, a way to transfer land to their sons to manage, without giving up complete control.

That characteristic Southern arrangement, the cropping contract, was quite different. There had been cropping contracts in the North and South before the Civil War. But only after the war did the cropping system become a cardinal feature of the South's economic system. The legal attributes of sharecropping developed along with its changing social meaning. In 1839, the North Carolina supreme court held that a landlord had no rights in the crop *before* the tenant actually gave the landlord his share. There was no statutory lien, and the right to distress for rent had been done away with; hence creditors of the tenant were free to levy on the crop, without interference from the landlord.[37]

In 1874, the legal relationship looked different to the court. A cropper was now said to have "no estate in the land"; the estate "remains in the landlord." The cropper was only a "laborer receiving pay in a share of the crop." [38] There was room for dispute about who was or was not a "cropper." In the case that inspired these words the tenant was held *not* to be a cropper, even though he received his horses, his corn and bacon, his farming utensils and his feed from the landlord. But this was exceptional. In general the

35 Laws N. Y. 1846, ch. 274.
36 Paul W. Gates, *Frontier Landlords and Pioneer Tenants* (1945).
37 *Deaver* v. *Rice,* 20 N. Car. 431 (1839).
38 *Harrison* v. *Ricks,* 71 N. Car. 7 (1874).

condition of a cropper was halfway between slavery and autonomy. By statute in 1876, North Carolina clarified the landlord's rights. All crops were "deemed and held to be vested in possession" of the landlord and his assigns at all times. It was the sharecropper now who owned nothing, until his share was actually turned over to him.[39] These cases and statutes affirmed the landlord's superiority —against the village merchant and outside creditors as well as against the tenant. The land tenure system would reflect and re-inforce, as far as possible, the real world of power relationships in the South.

MORTGAGES

Throughout the century, the mortgage remained the primary mode of financing land. Particularly in the West, when men bought land from each other, they executed promissory notes, secured by a mortgage on the property. Since land was the chief asset, of the chief class of the population, the mortgage was a basic instrument of credit and finance. It was also one of the major subjects of case law and statute. West's *Century Digest,* covering all cases reported to 1896, has more than 2,750 pages of cases on mortgages. The mortgage was used by farmers to raise money for more land, to buy agricultural machinery, even to cover personal expenses. In some parts of the country, farmers tended to borrow to the limit of their equity; in good years, when land prices were rising, they simply borrowed more. One swarm of locusts, one drought, one "panic" of the 19th-century breed was enough to wipe out the security, sweep the farm into court, and replace an economic problem with a legal one. It is no wonder, then, that the law tended to swing with the business cycle. Legislatures expanded or contracted the redemption period, according to whether times were good or bad. In 1886, Washington state changed a six-month period to a full year; in a period of upswing (1899), Michigan, perhaps as an incentive to investment, passed a statute which gave the debtor six months after sale to redeem; the period had previously been two years and three months.[40]

No wonder, too, that voters in agricultural states constantly agitated for government loans, cheap mortgage money, tough rules on

[39] Laws N. Car. 1876–77, ch. 283, sec. 1.
[40] Robert H. Skilton, "Developments in Mortgage Law and Practice," 17 Temple L.Q. 315, 329–30 (1943).

foreclosure, easy rules on redemption. One incident may give some idea of the politics of mortgage law. In the early 1850's, many Wisconsin farmers bought stock in railroad companies. Since they had no ready money, they pledged their lands as security. The interest due on the mortgage—usually eight per cent—was to be paid out of the railroad's future dividends. The railroads then used, or misused, the farmers' notes and mortgages to seduce Eastern money into investment on the roads. In the panic of 1857, the Wisconsin railroads collapsed. The farmer-mortgagors were left high and dry with worthless stock; their mortgages were in the hands of Eastern bankers. Responsive to the farmers, the legislature passed a series of laws, to repudiate the mortgages and prevent foreclosures, any feasible way. They stripped the notes and mortgages of negotiability, so that the farmers could interpose the defense of fraud before friendly local juries in foreclosure suits. In a line of cases, beginning in 1858, the Wisconsin supreme court declared the statutes unconstitutional, one by one, citing the *Dartmouth College* doctrine, and the court's own sense of justice and sound economics.[41] The court felt that the bite of foreclosure was bitter, but not half so bitter as a policy that would dry up the money market in the long run. And it was this sense that in the long run preserved the tensile strength of the law of mortgages—the need for mortgage investment acted as a brake on liberalization of mortgage and foreclosure law.

THE DECLINE OF DOWER

Common-law dower had once been an admirable way to provide for a widow's twilight life. Dower was a peculiar kind of estate. For one thing, it attached to land only. For another, dower was a mere life estate (in one-third of the late husband's dowable property). The widow had no remainder rights in this land. She could not sell it, or give it away in her will. The land remained, in short, in the husband's bloodline. The most remarkable feature of dower was that a husband could not defeat the right by selling his land or giving it away. Over all land he owned, or had owned, hung the ghostly threat of "inchoate dower." This potential claim followed the land through the whole chain of title, until the wife died and extinguished the claim.

[41] The story is told in Robert S. Hunt's fine study, *Law and Locomotives, The Impact of the Railroad on Wisconsin Law in the Nineteenth Century* (1958).

As a protection device, dower had severe limitations. If the husband's wealth consisted of stocks and bonds, or a business, dower did the wife little good. Dower had other faults, too. It was superior to claims of the husband's creditors, which was good for wives but sometimes bad for business. And dower was an annoying cloud on titles. Sometimes, long years after a transaction, the widow of some previous owner might rise up to haunt a buyer in good faith. That this last danger was the real fly in the ointment seems clear from the story of the rise and fall of dower. The Midwest, poor in everything *but* land, showed great impatience with this ancient institution. Indiana abolished it, at least in name, in 1852. In its place, Indiana gave a widow a cut from her husband's personal property, and one-third of his real estate "in fee simple, free from all demands of creditors." [42] The same statute abolished "tenancies by the courtesy" (usually spelled *curtesy*), the corresponding estate for husbands (which had had the peculiar characteristic that it vested only if the couple had had a child born alive), and gave the husband symmetrical rights in his wife's estate. The Kansas laws of the Civil War period gave the widow the right to elect her dower, or, "as she may prefer," to choose to come under a statute which gave her an absolute share (one-half) of her husband's estate, both real and personal.[43] The absolute share was always to her advantage, unless her husband died insolvent, in which case dower was better. In a statute of *this* sort, the policy of protection took precedence over the policy of clear titles.

A TANGLE OF TITLES

As before, so also after 1850, the traumatic weakness of land titles had a pervasive effect upon the land law. It played a role, for example, in the decline of dower. It hastened the decline of the common-law marriage, and stimulated the increasing formality of wills. As fast as institutions developed to make land more marketable and to improve the quality of titles, other events seemed to conspire to undo the good and make the situation worse. The vagueness of railroad, school and land grants, for example, created

[42] Rev. Stats. Ind. 1852, ch. 27, secs. 16, 17. If the land was worth more than $10,000, the widow could have only one-quarter of it, as against the husband's creditors; and if the land was worth more than $20,000, one-fifth.

[43] Kans. Stats. 1862, ch. 83. For these and other early developments, see Charles H. Scribner, *Treatise on the Law of Dower* (Vol. 1, 2nd ed., 1883), p. 48.

serious problems of title in some of the Western states. In California and New Mexico, a legacy of confusion was inherited from the Mexican period. Congress established for California a three-man commission to unsnarl titles flowing from Mexican grants (1851). Every claimant, whose "right or title" to land "derived from the Spanish or Mexican government," was to present his claim to the commissioners, together "with such documentary evidence and testimony of witnesses as the said claimant relies upon." [44] The board completed its work by 1856; but litigation continued for years afterwards in the federal courts. The board handled something over eight hundred cases; 604 claims were confirmed, 190 rejected, nineteen withdrawn. But the California landowner had to wait, on the average, seventeen years after filing his petition before his title was finally confirmed.[45] The course of events in New Mexico was even more protracted. As late as 1891, Congress passed an act "to establish a Court of Private Land Claims," to untangle Mexican land grants in New Mexico, Arizona, Utah, Nevada, Colorado and Wyoming.[46]

Floating land scrip was another source of confusion. Scrip had been issued for a number of purposes: under the Morrill Act, for example, as evidence of the state's rights to college-aid land. Congress passed a miscellaneous group of statutes, creating other scraps of scrip. One such law was for the benefit of Thomas Valentine, a land claimant from California; he lost his fight for a three-square-league ranch near Petaluma, but got Congress to pass a private relief act in 1872. In exchange for a release of his claims to the ranch, Valentine received scrip for 13,316 acres of public land. Some he used, and some he sold:

> Speculators got some, hiking the price, to peddle along with other types of scrip. In time Valentine scrip became too high-priced to be used on admittedly public lands, and scrip owners had to look for forgotten islands—"sleepers"—areas overlooked by government surveyors and with questionably held titles.[47]

Many doctrines of land law contributed to the weakness of titles. Adverse possession was one such doctrine. Poor administration of the land laws was another chronic cause of doubtful titles. "Tax-titles" were notoriously weak. These were interests in land created

---

44 9 Stats. 631 (act of March 3, 1851).
45 W. W. Robinson, *Land in California* (1948), p. 106.
46 26 Stats. 854 (act of March 3, 1891).
47 Robinson, *op. cit.*, p. 179.

when local government sold off property for delinquent taxes, and issued a deed to the purchaser. The laws on the subject were complicated, and so difficult to comply with that, in the words of a contemporary treatise, "the investigator of titles always looks with suspicion upon a title that depends upon a tax-deed." [48] Legislatures constantly had to intervene to make good the faulty work of local officials. In the Iowa laws of 1880, for example, fifty-nine separate acts were passed to legalize defective actions of officials. Many related to land transactions. One act, for example, recited that swamp lands had been sold without the county seal, as the law required, and without the clerk's signature; since "doubts" had "arisen" about these deeds, the deeds were "hereby legalized and made valid" (ch. 180).

What made the situation worse was the sheer volume of land transactions. Deeds, mortgages, transfers were counted in the thousands, then in the hundreds of thousands. The crude system of land registration could barely cope with the volume. Private solutions preceded public solutions to the problem. Title companies sprang up, to check titles for profit, and to ensure landowners against mysterious clouds that might arise to befuddle their interests. The Real Estate Title Insurance Company of Philadelphia, chartered in 1876, seems to have been the pioneer. The predecessor of New York's Title Guaranty & Trust Company was chartered in 1883 (Laws N.Y. 1883, ch. 367). In Chicago, the great fire of 1871 destroyed the public records. Four private abstract companies saved their records: indexes, abstracts, maps, and plats. These companies later formed a title-guarantee company; a merger in 1901 created the Chicago Title & Trust Company, which dominates the business in the city today.[49]

One late proposal for a comprehensive cure for the diseases of title was the Australian system, called *Torrens* after its inventor, Sir Robert R. Torrens. In the standard American method of recording, the documents—deeds, mortgages, land contracts—are deposited and noted in a public-record office. The office acts as little more than a warehouse with indexes. When land goes into Torrens, however, the state of the title is examined, and a certificate of title issued. Land brought into Torrens undergoes a scathing, one-time baptism of law; in the process, it is cleansed of its sins, all those "faint blemishes" and "mysterious 'clouds' " which "so darkly and

---

[48] Christopher G. Tiedeman, *An Elementary Treatise on the American Law of Real Property* (1885), p. 580.
[49] Pearl J. Davies, *Real Estate in American History* (1958), pp. 35–36.

portentously hang" over real estate, even when "hitherto not visible to the naked eye." [50] After this initial trauma, the land emerges as fresh and free of taint as a newborn baby. From that point on, title is in effect insured by the state. A contract, not a deed, becomes the instrument of transfer; and title and guaranty are at all times simply and efficiently kept up to date.

Illinois was the first state to pass a title-registration statute, in 1895; Massachusetts, Ohio, and California had statutes before 1900. The state bar association and the Chicago real-estate board supported a Torrens system for Illinois; but there was bitter opposition, too; and the title guarantee companies were not happy to see a governmental competitor. The Illinois law called for a referendum, in any county that wanted to embark on Torrens; Cook County (Chicago) did, and after one false start—the Illinois supreme court declared the first Torrens act unconstitutional—a valid act was passed, in 1897, and went into effect.[51] The system was optional, however, even in Cook County. The public, legal and lay, was torpid and indifferent. Besides, Torrens had a serious drawback: the *first* land registration for any parcel of land was expensive. In 1899, there were only 155 applications to register land under the Torrens system in Cook County.[52] As of 1900, then, title registration was at best a hope, at worst a missed opportunity.

INTELLECTUAL PROPERTY: PATENTS, COPYRIGHTS, AND TRADEMARKS

After the act of 1836, which established the Patent Office, Congress made few major changes in administration of patent law. Patents themselves multiplied like weeds. Between 1836 and 1890, 431, 541 were granted.[53] The number increased each year. So did the volume of patent litigation. The patent office refused many applications; but even when it granted a patent, its patent was not an authoritative guarantee that the device truly deserved to be patented, or that it would stand up in court. Patent litigation was frequent, complex, and fruitful of doctrine and controversy. In an

[50] John T. Hassam, "Land Transfer Reform," 4 Harv. L. Rev. 271, 275 (1891).

[51] Theodore Sheldon, *Land Registration in Illinois* (1901), pp. 1–3.

[52] Richard R. Powell, *Registration of the Title to Land in the State of New York* (1938), p. 145.

[53] Chauncey Smith, "A Century of Patent Law," 5 Quarterly J. of Economics 44, 56 (1890).

infringement suit, it was a good defense to allege that the patent was invalid to begin with and should never have been granted. A few law firms built their fortunes on patent litigation, as they learned to deal with these intricate, technical cases. After the Civil War, one first began to speak of a specialized patent bar; and a few lawyers, notably George Harding (1827–1902), became rich and prominent, principally through arguing patent cases in federal court.[54] The path of a patent was truly a rocky one. According to one authority, between 1891 and 1904, 30 per cent of all patents adjudicated in the circuit courts of appeal were declared invalid; another 41 per cent were held not to be infringed. Only 29 per cent were pronounced to be both valid and infringed.[55] This meant, as it had for a generation or more, that outside the Patent Office, the federal courts sat as another many-headed commissioner of patents.

The courts played a creative role, too, in the sculpturing of doctrine. An industrial society rests on pillars of fresh technology. The patent monopoly was in some sense anomalous in an expansive, free-market economy. But like corporate franchises, land grants, and high tariffs, the patent was a subsidy as well, an incentive to economic growth. Like these other subsidies, the patent ebbed and flowed in public opinion. The original law no doubt had in mind the small inventor, working through the night in his study or laboratory. There were such people, but they came to be a minority of American inventors; and in general, they were precisely those who could not bear the costs of patent litigation, or fight off the patent pirates.

Toward the end of the century, the courts seemed to become keenly aware that a patent could be used to stifle competition. They became quite stingy with preliminary injunctions against infringement. The only foolproof way to protect a patent, then, was to engage in long, costly litigation. This policy was hard on the small inventor; on the other hand, it cut down the use of patents in restraint of trade. Some courts apparently felt that too many patents were granted; they were afraid that no "standing room for an inventor" was left, no "pathway open for forward progress." [56] Patents might be merely another tool of the trusts. This attitude, this fear, was part of the sense of constriction in the economy, the general terror of small horizons, so marked in the late 19th century.

[54] See Albert H. Walker,"George Harding," in *Great American Lawyers*, Vol. VIII (1909), pp. 45–87.
[55] Floyd L. Vaughan, *The United States Patent System* (1956), p. 199.
[56] *Two Centuries Growth of American Law*, p. 396.

As early as 1850, Justice Samuel Nelson, speaking for the United States Supreme Court, enunciated a doctrine that cut down the number of potentially valid patents. The case turned on whether a patent on a new doorknob was valid. The only novelty, it seemed, was that the doorknob was made out of porcelain. A patent, said Nelson, required "more ingenuity" than that of "an ordinary mechanic acquainted with the business." [57] In 1875, the Supreme Court ruled on a patent for preserving fish "in a close chamber by means of a freezing mixture, having no contact with the atmosphere of the preserving chamber." The Court held it void. The scheme had no novelty; made no advance over prior art; it reminded Justice Noah H. Swayne, speaking for the Supreme Court, of a technique that had been used by undertakers (though indeed not for fish), and of what every man knew about ice cream.[58] In 1880, Swayne let loose a striking phrase—"a flash of thought"—to describe what a patent really needed for validity.[59] The "ordinary mechanic"—a kind of blue-collar version of the "reasonable man" in the law of torts—was the negative model; the positive concept was the "flash of genius," which alone gave merit to a patent. In general, the courts tried to hew to the middle of the road in developing patent law. They tried to restrict the patent to genuine novelty, to individual skill: they fought against corporate mass production of small improvements.

The entrepreneur, however, had his own views; and he could not have been fond of the chaos of patent law. As early as 1856, manufacturers of sewing machines formed a patent pool.[60] Large companies learned how to stretch out their monopoly by manipulating patents. Bell Telephone bought a German patent, essential for the technology of long-distance telephoning. It waited until *its* telephone patent had almost expired, then pressed ahead with the German device. This gave it control of the telephone industry even after its first basic patent had passed into the public domain. Under the umbrella of the patent monopoly, companies divided up markets, licensed out the nation in segments, and chained whole counties or states to particular vendors of a patented good.

Patent law illustrated the tendency of law to expand the concept of property—to protect whatever had a real market, including intangibles. The law of copyright steadily and naturally grew. In

[57] *Hotchkiss* v. *Greenwood*, 11 How. 248, 267 (1850).
[58] *Brown* v. *Piper*, 91 U.S. 37 (1875).
[59] *Densmore* v. *Scofield*, 102 U.S. 375 (1880).
[60] Vaughan, *op. cit.*, p. 41.

1856, the copyright statute was amended to include dramatic productions; in 1865, to cover photographs and negatives.[61] In 1870, the copyright (and patent) laws were substantially revised, and now a "painting, drawing, chromo, statue, statuary, or model or design for a work of the fine arts" might also come under their wing.[62]

The expansion of trademark law was even more remarkable. The whole branch of law started from a few scattered judicial opinions; none in the United States seems to have been earlier than 1825. The first injunction in a trademark or trade-name case was granted in 1844, as we saw, to protect the makers of "Taylor's Persian Thread." [63] From this acorn grew a mighty oak. The trademark is essential in a mass-production economy, based more or less on free enterprise. Products compete jealously for the consumer's dollars; but many kinds of goods pour out of factories identical except for package and name. The 1870 law that codified patent and copyright law applied to trademarks, too. But the Supreme Court, in 1879, thought that the patent power did not extend to trademarks, and, finding no warrant for the law in the commerce clause either, they declared the law unconstitutional as to trademarks.[64] The gap was partially filled by state statutes. Courts continued, however, to play a creative role, inventing concepts, expanding them, contracting them, sitting in judgment on their own creations.

Trademark litigation was acrimonious and, like patent litigation, relatively frequent. Business ethics in the 19th century were not simon-pure; case law records the activity of many jackals of commerce, who tried to make off with values that inhered in another man's product. Some cases also began to develop an independent concept of unfair competition, to supplement the protective armor of a trademark. A man named Baker, for example, who made chocolate, could not so act as to make people think that his product was the famous Baker's Chocolate. He could not imitate the shape, label, and wording of the original product, whether or not he was technically "infringing" a trademark.[65] Toward the end of the century, too, unions pressed for wide use of their labels on union-made goods, and tried to have laws passed protecting their

61 13 Stats. 540 (act of March 3, 1865).
62 16 Stats. 198, 213 (act of July 8, 1870).
63 *Two Centuries Growth of American Law,* p. 436.
64 Trade-Mark Cases, 100 U.S. 82 (1879).
65 *Walter Baker and Co.* v. *Sanders,* 80 Fed. Rep. 889 (C.C.A. 2nd, 1897).

rights in such labels. A law of Minnesota, of 1889, declared it "lawful for associations and unions of workmen" to adopt "for their protection labels, trademarks and advertisements," pointing out that goods were union-made. Imitations were unlawful, and could be enjoined.[66] Each firm, union, and trade group was engaged in marking out its little claim on the economy, and protecting this claim from the encroachments of a tough and hostile world.

[66] Laws Minn. 1889, ch. 9.

(CHAPTER V)

ADMINISTRATIVE LAW AND
REGULATION OF BUSINESS

In hindsight, the development of administrative law seems mostly a contribution of the 20th century. American historiography has always been biased toward national politics; the scholarship of administrative law has always been biased toward the big federal agencies. The creation of the Interstate Commerce Commission, in 1887, has been taken to be a kind of genesis. The ICC, to be sure, was the first great independent regulatory commission—on the federal level. But there was a great deal of administration, and administrative law, in the 19th century in a wider sense. The Post Office, to take an obvious example, was a large, functioning, federal bureaucracy. There were agencies attached to the office of the commissioner of patents, the General Land Office, and the Pension Office of the Department of Interior. This last, the Pension Office, handled massive amounts of work (often badly). It made a multitude of small decisions, affecting the lives of many people, every day of its official life. In 1891, the Pension Office was reported to be the "largest executive bureau in the world." It had a work force of more than 6,000. In 1898, 635,000 cases were pending for adjudication.[1]

Before 1887, also, there were many administrative agencies attached to state and local government. State railroad commissions preceded the ICC by many years. Agencies regulating warehousing, grain elevators, and railroad freight rates were a regular feature in the Midwest during the Granger period. Most states had some sort of functioning insurance or banking commission before 1870. Locally, there were boards of health and bodies to administer school affairs.

The administrative agency was the child of necessity. Big government and positive government meant a government which divided its labor among specialists and specialized bodies. The pe-

[1] Leonard D. White, *The Republican Era: 1869–1901* (1958), pp. 211, 214.

riod between 1850 and 1900 is considered the climax of *laissez-faire*, social Darwinism and the businessman's earthly kingdom in the United States. But to some extent, it was merely the period in which businessmen made the loudest noise, some of it defensive. The legal culture was the culture of modern rationalism: the ultimate tests of law and government were pragmatic. Tradition had lost its magic, and the legal order was no longer supported by any supernational grace.[2] This meant that levers of power were fair game for anybody who could grab them and make them do his bidding. Social Darwinism and the doctrine of *laissez-faire* were desperate attempts by the rich and powerful to persuade other groups to let go—for the ultimate good of society. The argument worked somewhat, and for a certain period of time. Meanwhile, a huge, tumultuous, middle-class population, anxious for security if not power, made more and more demands on and through government. The country was enormous; its product was enormous; its technology was enormous; and slowly, its government too became enormous, in response to demands from various publics. Mass transport and communication increased the potential size of interest groups; created powerful agencies which needed control; and made social control technologically that much more feasible.

Traditional agencies of government could not regulate big business, or keep the infrastructure tame. Courts were not good regulators. They were passive and untrained. Kansas created a "court of visitation" in 1898, to regulate railroads, fix freight rates, classify freight, "require the construction and maintenance of depots, switches, side-tracks, stock-yards, cars"; regulate crossings and intersections; require safety appliances; and in general ride herd over railroads. The law was declared unconstitutional, which prevents one from knowing whether this plan would have been an evolutionary dead end.[3] Clearly, ordinary courts were inadequate to govern enterprise. And, in the age of steel rails and telegraphs, town and county authorities were equally futile and ineffective. The cure was, at first, statewide control. When the states could not meet the demands of their constituents, these constituents embarked on federal adventure. The process was repeated in many areas of law. In welfare, for example, first came local poor laws, run by country justices and squires of the community. When this system was felt to

[2] A kind of natural-law aura hovered about the Constitution and the Bill of Rights, even in the late 19th century; this was important but exceptional.

[3] Laws Kans. Spec. Sess. 1898, ch. 28; the statute was voided in *State ex rel. Godard* v. *Johnson*, 61 Kans. 803, 60 Pac. 1068 (1900).

be obsolete, states centralized their welfare administration. When the states could no longer handle the job (much later, to be sure), the federal government stepped in. This did not take place until the age of the New Deal, in the 1930's. For many kinds of economic regulation, the process ran its course much faster; railroad regulation reached its federal stage in 1887. Elementary education, on the other hand, is only now on the federal threshhold, and timidly at that.

These differences in pace were not accidental, of course. It was the most vital—and most threatening—sectors of the economy that first came on to be regulated: transport and money, railroads, banks, insurance companies. It was not merely the fact that these were essential services; transport and money represented power, or the danger of power. In the United States, an important segment of public opinion had always feared and distrusted any concentration of power at all. And in the case of the railroads, for example, there were specific, powerful interest groups that considered themselves aggrieved.

The national currency had been in a chronic state of disrepair before the Civil War. After Jackson, there was no national banking at all. The states regulated currency and banking; but regulation was confused, halting, and in general not effective. The federal government entered the banking picture during the war; there was a desperate wartime need for central control of fiscal and monetary systems. The Legal Tender Act was a wartime measure; after the war, it provided the occasion for one of the Supreme Court's most spectacular flip-flops, first a decision that the law was invalid, then a quick change of mind (following a change in personnel).[4] In 1863, during the war, Congress established a national banking system; in 1865 Congress placed a ten per cent tax on the notes of state banks. The national bank notes and, later, the banks themselves provided far more uniformity, certainty, and stability in currency than the prior system had. But the state banks stayed vigorously alive, and so did state banking regulation.

Insurance companies, too, were an early subject of regulation.[5]

[4] The cases were *Hepburn* v. *Griswold*, 75 U.S. 603 (1869), overturned by the *Legal Tender* cases, 79 U.S. 457 (1871). The backgrounds of the Legal Tender act and the national banking law are exhaustively treated in Bray Hammond, *Sovereignty and an Empty Purse, Banks and Politics in the Civil War* (1970).

[5] There is one comprehensive state study of insurance law: Spencer L. Kimball, *Insurance and Public Policy, A Study in the Legal Implementation of Social and Economic Public Policy, Based on Wisconsin Records 1835–1959* (1960).

Fire insurance, after the Civil War, became more and more accepted as a business necessity. Life insurance spread more slowly; but it was also an important business by the end of the century. Insurance claims were a friction point, where aggregated capital met the common or almost-common man on a plane of inequality. Insurance litigation, then, was relatively frequent. And there was hardly any subject more often the subject of statute than insurance.

The development of insurance commissions followed a well-marked path. The first commissions were not independent bodies; their commissioners were state officers who held down other jobs as well. The Massachusetts commission of 1852 consisted of the secretary, treasurer, and auditor of the state. The commission's job was to receive statements from the companies, abstract the data, and present the results to the legislature. Wisconsin first established an Insurance Department in the office of the secretary of state; in 1878, an independent Insurance Department was created, headed by an appointive insurance commissioner. In New York, the comptroller had had some powers over insurance companies before 1859, when an Insurance Department was established along the lines of the Banking Department. In almost all states, then, separate "commissions" or "departments" grew out of embryonic boards in which new labors were piled upon old officers. At first, state government was too poor, too weak, and too listless to support strong, well-financed, independent regulation. An "independent" commission, in most states, was not even independent in the financial sense; the typical commission was supported by fees extracted from the companies.

The urge to regulate, however, was cumulative and persistent. In 1873, twelve states had "some form of institutionalized insurance regulation"; in 1890, seventeen states; in 1905, twenty-two.[6] Early commissions were usually advisory or exhortatory; they built up their bureaucratic traditions, and gained power and skill, unevenly but definitely. The power came from a steady inflation of insurance laws. The states passed laws that outlawed discrimination in rates, curbed "unfair" marketing practices, tried to safeguard the solvency of the companies, harnessed foreign insurance companies, and insisted on financial reserves. The volume and scope of this legislation grew to fantastic proportions. The Massa-

[6] Morton Keller, *The Life Insurance Enterprise, 1885–1910* (1963), pp. 194, 197.

chusetts law to "Amend and Codify the Statutes Relating to Insurance," passed in 1887, contained 112 closely packed sections of text.[7]

Rococo excess in the size of a statute does not mean that the statute is successful in controlling its subject. Bulk may mean almost the opposite: a frantic attempt to regulate, after prior laws had repeatedly failed. Or complexity may mean that interest groups, at war with each other, have staked many and various claims on the subject matter; a long, complex law is the text, then, of an elaborate treaty, full of loopholes, special benefits, and compromise. Interest groups were in general eager to resort to legislation. These groups, like business firms, took literally the sermons that they should compete with each other; but they did not see why use of law and the state was not an excellent means of competition.

Most authorities agree that insurance regulation, in this period, was not a triumphal success. In New York, for example, corruption ate away at the heart of the Insurance Commission. The legislature was moved to investigate insurance regulation in 1870, 1872, 1877, 1882, and 1885. Many administrators, if not corrupt, were halfhearted and ineffectual. James F. Price, appointed commissioner in 1890, did not believe (he said) that his department should "erect over the lawfully appointed custodians of the people's funds another custodian who should intermeddle in their corporate administration." [8] This creed was so delightful to the companies that they sometimes bought it for cash. On the whole then, despite progress in tightening the reins, the state had by no means made itself master over insurance companies, before 1900.

Partly, this was because no coherent economic theory underlay regulation. Regulation sprang, to a great extent, from fear and mistrust of the financial power of the companies, and the sense that the companies were cheating the public. These opinions did not easily translate into concrete and effective programs. Since the demand for regulation was diffuse, regulation was weak; the companies, which had vital interests at stake, gained great leverage over the content of the law and the work of everyday administration. Morton Keller points out that "the structure of supervision was at its friendliest when dealing with the technical details of the business"—taxation, investment, reserves, dividend policy. These were matters which the public hardly understood, at least not in any

---

[7] Laws Mass. 1887, ch. 214.
[8] Quoted in Keller, op. cit., p. 203.

detail. The policy contract itself, on the other hand, where policy-holders had both a stake and an awareness, was "a subject of fruit-ful and alert legislative concern." States passed nonforfeiture laws, mitigated the rules and clauses that made policies void if an appli-cant made false or misleading statements, and even controlled the methods of marketing insurance.[9]

Despite the volume of insurance regulation, it was still the *rail-road* that dominated discussion and activity in administrative law, between 1850 and 1900, just as the railroad dominated corporation law and tort law. By 1850, states had turned to general statutes regulating railroads, and given up the effort to slip special clauses into individual charters. In any event, in much of the country the first, promotional period was over; it was a period in which rail-roads consolidated their lines and extended existing nets of track. During the development stage, the most influential voices were those of the promoters, and their henchmen in the community who wanted railroads built, almost at any cost. Once the roads were running, dominant public opinion seemed to shift from docility to hate. Railroads created markets, made towns bloom in the wilder-ness, lured farmers into planting particular crops, drew settlers from one place to another. People invested their lives and their future in the towns and markets that grew up along the lines. The railroads became enemies, then, not only because of iniquity, but also because they seemed to hold power of life and death over all those lives along the way. The farmers, who had mortgaged them-selves to buy a railroad, felt that they had created a Frankenstein monster in their midst. Besides, the railroads were corrupt, exces-sively capitalized, overloaded with debt, controlled by out-of-state interests, monopolistic. Among themselves they were vicious and quarrelsome. They were weak in the infant skills of public rela-tions, but big in manipulation of state governments, in the black arts of lobbying, and the seduction of men in public office. They cheated each other, their contractors and their stockholders. They floated great balloons of debt that burst during panics and crashes, ruining the greedy, hopeful men who invested in them. They were deeply immersed in local politics, and at the mercy of the business cycle and the prices of cotton, coal, wheat, tobacco, and corn. In the space of one short generation, they changed from engines of salvation to smoking black devils.

The history of railroad regulation was as complex as the history of opinion. Conditions in different parts of the country affected the

[9] Keller, *op. cit.,* p. 200.

form and function of the statutes, which ranged from severe to toothless, even on paper. The country's first railroad commission was established in Rhode Island, in 1839; it "stemmed from the necessity of imposing upon rival and warring railroads convenient connections and reasonable joint fares, freights, and services." [10] A New Hampshire commission was created in 1844.[11] Its main function, however, was to help railroads buy needed land along their routes. The statute gave the commissioners roughly the same powers and functions as those of the old commissioners of roads and highways. But the commissioners did have the duty to look over the railroads once a year, check their condition and management, and inspect "all books, papers, notes, records, bonds, and other evidences of debt, and all property, deeds and bills of sale," to see if the railroads were obeying all relevant laws. Connecticut established a commission which, in the 1850's, had the right to inspect the physical equipment of the railroads, and to recommend needed repairs; safety on the roads was one of this law's major aims.[12] Maine's commission of 1858 was very much like Rhode Island's.

A new era began in 1869. In that year, Massachusetts established its own, and stronger, commission. There were three commissioners, one of them Charles Francis Adams, Jr. The commission had "general supervision of all railroads," with the right to examine them and keep informed on their obedience to law. Whenever the commissioners felt that a company was derelict in its obedience to law, or needed to make repairs, or if the commission felt that a "change in its rate of fares for transporting freight or passengers," or in its "mode of operating its road and conducting its business" was "reasonable and expedient," the commissioners were to so inform the company. They were also to make annual reports to the legislature.[13] The other New England commissions were gradually remolded to fit the Massachusetts pattern, and the influence of the Massachusetts law was felt as far away as California.[14] The New England railroad commissions gained power and influence, under the benevolent guidance of Massachusetts. But they still were able only to suggest and persuade; they had no power to fix rates or

10 Edward C. Kirkland, *Men, Cities and Transportation: A Study in New England History 1820–1900* (1948), Vol. II, p. 233. Kirkland is the main source for much of the following discussion of the New England commissions.

11 Laws N.H. 1844, ch. 93.

12 Conn. Stats. 1854, pp. 759–60.

13 Laws Mass. 1869, ch. 408.

14 Gerald D. Nash, *State Government and Economic Development, A History of Administrative Policies in California, 1849–1933* (1964), p. 161.

make any major changes on their own. Even under later commissions, the distribution of function between court, legislature, and commission was never completely unscrambled; neither the legislatures nor the courts abdicated their right to tinker with railroad law. The railroads remained at all times influential. An extreme case was New York, which had created a commission in 1855; the commissioners, paid off by the railroads, recommended that their office be abolished, and this was done in 1857.

In the Midwest, the so-called Granger laws, passed in the 1870's, took a far more radical attitude toward railroad regulation than anything attempted before in New England. The Granger movement was a farmers' revolt. Its legislative program aimed to bring under control the farmer's symbiotic enemies—railroads, warehouses, and grain elevators. An Illinois law of 1871 established a Railroad and Warehouse Commission, with authority to ascertain whether railroads and warehouses complied with the laws of the state. If the commission found that any laws had been violated, it had power to "prosecute . . . all corporations or persons guilty of such violation." [15] By an act of April 15, 1871, the legislature flatly laid down maximum railroad rates. Class A roads—all railroads whose gross annual earnings, per mile, were ten thousand dollars or more—were to charge no more than two and one-half cents a mile for passengers (half fare to children under twelve).[16] The law had strong backing, not only from farmers, but from small merchants, too, who were nettled by freight rates they considered exorbitant and discriminatory. Indeed, the Illinois statute has been said to be "not so much the product of spontaneous indignation on the prairies as a monument to the strategic talents of the Chicago Board of Trade." [17]

The Grangers, in fact, came in on the tail end of a whirlwind that was already blowing full storm. In Wisconsin, in 1864, Milwaukee merchants had pressed successfully for a statute to force the railroads to deliver bulk grain to any elevator designated by the shippers, as long as it had adequate sidetracks.[18] Wisconsin farmers had been badly burnt in ill-advised schemes in promotion of railroads; it "was to be a long time before they regarded railroad men

15 Laws Ill. 1871, pp. 618, 622 (act of Apr. 13, 1871, secs. 1, 11).

16 Laws Ill. 1871, p. 640 (act of Apr. 15, 1871).

17 Lee Benson, *Merchants, Farmers, and Railroads, Railroad Regulation and New York Politics, 1850–1887* (1955), p. 25.

18 Frederic Merk, *Economic History of Wisconsin during the Civil War Decade* (1916), p. 371.

as anything but scoundrels. . . . They prepared the ground for the growth of the Grange." [19] In Iowa, from the 1860's, railroad regulation bills were introduced in almost every session, before there ever was a Granger movement. Iowa laws of 1868, granting lands to the railroads, carried with them a poisonous rider reserving to the legislature the right to prescribe "rates of tariff." [20]

In the legal world of decentralized power, so characteristic of America, struggle for and against important laws does not end with enactment. As so often happens, there was a second round, in the courts. Here the Grangers and their commissions won some famous victories, capped by the great (if transient) case of *Munn* v. *Illinois* (1877).[21] In *Munn*, the Supreme Court broadly upheld Illinois' package of Granger laws, specifically, regulation of railroads, warehouses and grain elevators by commission. These businesses, said the court, were "clothed with a public interest." Hence they could not claim immunity from public supervision. Again, as quite typical, there was a third round: actual administration. The Granger commissions were something of a failure in operation, partly, perhaps, because they were more weakly thought through than lobbied for. The right of legislatures to make rates was a famous victory; but the process itself was stiff and arbitrary. The roads were congenitally prone to financial troubles; it was easy for them to blame their troubles on mismanagement by the commissions. The railroads and their friends turned their talents and money once more to legislative action. Wisconsin's proud and famous "Potter Law," of 1874, one of the most radical of the laws to tame the railroads, lasted a mere two years; with a turn of the political wheel, and the election of a legislature more sympathetic to the roads, the Potter Law was cast into outer darkness.[22]

Regulation by commission did not die, however. The strength of farmers and merchants ebbed, but never vanished. The idea that railroads were overmighty subjects, and had to be controlled, became a commonplace of American law. Such naked market strength could not be tolerated without some sort of watchman. The idea spread South and East. The South suffered from freight and passenger rates that were higher than those in the North. The behavior of the Southern Railway and Steamship Association,

[19] Robert S. Hunt, *Law and Locomotives* (1958), p. 64.
[20] See Earl S. Beard, "The Background of State Railroad Regulation in Iowa," 51 Iowa J. of Hist. 1, 17–22 (1953).
[21] 94 U.S. 113 (1877).
[22] Robert S. Hunt, *Law and Locomotives* (1958), pp. 98–103, 140–42.

dominated by Albert Fink, gave great offense to farmers and shippers. Virginia established an advisory Railroad Commission in 1877, similar to the Massachusetts Commission; so did South Carolina in 1878; in 1879, Georgia established a three-man commission, with power to fix rates. In New York, railroad rate wars in the 1870's ended in a trunk-line pool of 1877; the New York railroads set up their own private administrative agency, and imported Albert Fink from the South to run it. Under the pooling arrangement, there were rate differentials favoring Philadelphia and Baltimore; the New York Chamber of Commerce, outraged, turned Granger, and exacted from the legislature the right to investigate the railroads. The result was the Special Committee on Railroads to Investigate Alleged Abuses in the Management of Railroads Chartered by the State of New York, commonly known as the Hepburn Committee, which reported its findings in a blaze of publicity in 1880. The Hepburn Committee helped crystallize opinion to the point where the legislature, in 1882, established a railroad commission, though with many compromises.[23]

But what, on the whole, did railroad commissions accomplish? Some were venal and impotent, like the first New York commission, or the second California commission. This commission rode into being in a surge of radical thought, but in 1895, a gloomy critic thus summed up its work:

> The curious fact remains that a body created sixteen years ago for the sole purpose of curbing a single railroad corporation with a strong hand, was found to be uniformly, without a break, during all that period, its apologist and defender.[24]

Even the noncorrupt commissions, of the New England type, disappointed the little man's hopes. As in the case of the insurance commission, the problem was partly one of political leverage. The forces that wanted strong control made up a large, diffuse group. The railroads were few and mighty. Campaigns for railroad laws tended to get results, when farmers and shippers were organized, and when they collectively made the most political noise. But these campaigns depended on wobbly, transient coalitions. All the pas-

---

23 See Lee Benson, *Merchants, Farmers, and Railroads, Railroad Regulation and New York Politics, 1850–1887* (1955), chs. 6–8.

24 S. E. Moffet, "The Railroad Commission of California: a Study in Irresponsible Government," 6 Annals 469, 476 (1895). The "single railroad corporation" was the Central Pacific, later part of the Southern Pacific.

sion went toward the *passage* of these laws. After enactment, passion died down. Commissions had to live with their railroads every day. They had to chastise them but not kill them. In practice, this meant that commissions learned—if they were not already so disposed—to be gentle and sympathetic with their railroads. This habit, once acquired, was hard to break. And on each daily decision that affected a railroad, the railroad exerted its moral and economic pressures; farmers and shippers were unaware, unrepresented, apathetic.

The state commissioners were, in any event, bound to fail in a federal system. Their power extended only to the borders of their state. Particularly after the Civil War, railroad entrepreneurs sewed together small railroads to make big interstate nets. How much control could Rhode Island ever hope to exert over railroads that passed through its territory? The Supreme Court drove home the point that state commissions were impotent. In *Wabash Railway* v. *Illinois* (1886)[25] the court held that states could not lawfully regulate commerce, if it came from or was destined for a point outside the boundaries of the state. Only the federal government had this right.[26] *Wabash* was a railroad case. The decision of the Court threw out an Illinois statute about discriminatory fixing of freight and passenger rates. Decisions of this sort gave an added push to the campaign, already strong, for a federal railroad commission. This was the Interstate Commerce Commission, which was enacted into law in 1887.[27]

The ICC, however, should not be viewed (as older generations viewed it) as a kind of triumph of Grangerism on the federal level. The law paid lip service to the principle of strict control over railroads. And, of course, antirailroad agitation was a vital part of the background. But recent research has shown that the railroads were "ready and anxious to have federal railroad legislation—on their terms." Some railroad men took this attitude simply as a way of bowing to the inevitable. Others felt that without government backing they could not curb what they considered dangerous and excessive competition. John P. Green, a vice-president of the Pennsylvania Railroad, stated in 1884 that "a large majority of the railroads in the United States would be delighted if a railroad commission or any other power could make rates upon their traffic

25 118 U.S. 557 (1886).

26 See I. L. Sharfman, *The Interstate Commerce Commission*, Vol. 1 (1931), ch. 1.

27 24 Stats. 379 (act of Feb. 4, 1887).

which would insure them six per cent dividends, and I have no doubt, with such a guarantee, they would be very glad to come under the direct supervision and operation of the National Government." [28] One of the first commissioners of the ICC was no less a figure than Judge Thomas M. Cooley of Michigan, high priest of constitutional limitations. Cooley was by no means as simple and one-sided a pro-railroad spokesman as he has been pictured;[29] still the commission was not radical by any means. It was meant as much to placate public opinion as to rule the roads in the sense that a fire-eating Granger might have liked.

Nor was the text of the act particularly fierce. The law gave the ICC no express power to set railroad rates, though it did declare (sec. 1) that "All charges . . . shall be reasonable and just." The Commission, however, took a rate-making function upon itself, until the Supreme Court, in the late 1890's, stripped away this power, saying that "there is nothing in the act fixing rates. Congress did not attempt to exercise that power. . . . The grant of such a power is never to be implied." [30] This left the Commission relatively naked. It could do little more than punish past transgressions against the Commerce Act. The Supreme Court also emasculated the fourth section of the act, which prohibited railroads from discriminating against short hauls in fixing rates. The Court, with its practiced eye, read into the act a proviso that rate discrimination was not illegal, if it was necessary to meet competition (1897). The Commission had looked into the matter of the Alabama Midland Railway. The road charged $3.22 per ton "on phosphate rock shipped from the South Carolina and Florida field" to Troy, Alabama, for example, but only $3.00 per ton to carry this product to Montgomery, Alabama, a longer distance—in fact, the route to Montgomery ran through Troy. Troy suffered too on shipments of cotton and other goods. No matter; the court found that there was heavier competition at Montgomery than at other cities; hence, there was an adequate reason to lower prices to that point. The railroad's traffic managers were not "incompetent," nor were they "under the bias of any personal preference for Montgomery." They were, in short, economic men; and they set

28 Quoted in Gabriel Kolko, *Railroads and Regulation, 1877–1916* (1965), p. 35, an important revisionist history of the ICC.

29 See Alan Jones, "Thomas M. Cooley and the Interstate Commerce Commission: Continuity and Change in the Doctrine of Equal Rights," 81 Political Science Q. 602 (1966).

30 J. Brewer, in *ICC* v. *Cincinnati, New Orleans and Texas Pacific Rr. Co.,* 167 U.S. 479, 494 (1897).

396 AMERICAN LAW TO THE CLOSE OF THE 19TH CENTURY

their rates by considering the workings of the market. For these reasons, the railroad's pricing was legal.[31]

But was this reasoning sound? Was it really the intent of Congress (and the country) to write this brand of liberal economics into the Commerce Act? Justice John M. Harlan, who dissented, felt that the Court's decisions had made the Commission "a useless body for all practical purposes." Those purposes were political purposes; and the shippers who fought for the law had not intended the free market to continue in all its pristine purity. Yet, whatever the original understanding, the Supreme Court was the law for a while. In these cases, the Supreme Court boldly asserted power over the Commission's undertaking, and, in effect, over Congress as well. The Court had the last, sometimes the only, say.

Still, it would be wrong to say that the Court had crippled the act. In some respects, the act was born to be crippled. Congress was only half serious about taming the railroads; it was in deadly earnest only about public opinion. Once the movement for enactment had run its course, Congress showed no great enthusiasm for putting back into the act any teeth that the Court pulled out. As Mr. Dooley said about Theodore Roosevelt and the trusts, the ICC was supposed to stamp the "heejoous monsthers" under foot, but "not so fast" or so much.[32]

The history of railroad regulation could be paralleled in the regulatory history of other public utilities. The same kind of compromise took place. In 1855, for example, Massachusetts passed a general incorporation law for gaslight companies. The law included a proviso that if a city already had a gas company, no new one could be incorporated unless the established company had earned an annual dividend of seven per cent on its capital stock for a number of years. This invitation to monopoly was withdrawn in 1870, and, during the 1880's, gas companies began to feel the bite of competition. It was not to their liking. A law of 1885 established a Board of Gas Commissioners; under this law, the companies yielded to the yoke of regulation, but in exchange for protection of their monopoly position.[33]

This was the general compromise of public-utility law—regulation in exchange for a sheltered market. Competition was the "life

[31] *Interstate Commerce Commission* v. *Alabama Midland Railway Co.,* 168 U.S. 144 (1897).
[32] Quoted in William Letwin, *Law and Economic Policy in America, The Evolution of the Sherman Antitrust Act* (1965), p. 205.
[33] I. R. Barnes, *Public Utility Control in Massachusetts* (1930), pp. 14–15.

of trade" only for other people; business generally welcomed state control, provided the control was not unfriendly, and provided it carried with it protection for their little citadels of privilege. This is the key to understanding why some forms of government intervention, chiefly on the state level, grew so phenomenally during the last half of the 19th century. The statute books swelled like balloons, despite ideological sound and fury about individualism, social Darwinism, free enterprise, Horatio Alger, and the like, from pulpit, press, and bench. Every group wanted, and often got, its own exception to the supposed iron laws of trade.

A case in point was *occupational licensing*, which absolutely burgeoned in this period. The basic idea was not entirely new. The gateways into legal practice had historically been subject to control. Colonials had licensed auctioneers and peddlers. Some licensing laws, of course, were frankly and solely designed to produce revenue. Some licensing legislation was, moreover, harsh and discriminatory, a defense mechanism of local merchants against outsiders. Wisconsin's statutes, as of 1898, required every prospective peddler to make a "written application . . . to the secretary of state," revealing whether he intended to travel on foot, or with "one or more horses or other beasts of burden." The peddler's license fee ran from $30 up, depending on mode of travel; a peddler who intended to go by bicycle paid $30; to use a vehicle drawn by two or more horses cost $75. The peddler could not ply his trade in any town without this license, plus whatever fees the local community chose to levy, up to $50 a day.[34] These were stiff amounts—almost prohibitive. The point was to drive these pestiferous competitors away, if at all possible. Laws of this kind were not new; but it was significant how they flourished during this age of (alleged) rampant *laissez-faire*. The small-town merchants were protectionist to the core.

The more familiar kind of occupational licensing blossomed in the late 19th century and reached some sort of climax in the period from 1890 to 1910. It began with the doctors, typically. In Illinois, for example, a law of 1877 required a license for the practice of medicine. In 1881, a board of pharmacy was set up; afterwards, no one could "retail, compound or dispense drugs, medicines or poisons," or "open or conduct any pharmacy," except a registered pharmacist. In the same year, "the practice of dentistry" was subjected to regulation. A board, consisting of "five practising dentists," was charged with enforcement of the dentist's law. In 1897,

34 Wis. Stats. 1898, secs. 1571, 1572.

Illinois created a State Board of Examiners of Architects. In 1899, the statutes added midwives, coal miners, and veterinarians, and also chiropractors and osteopaths ("those who desire to practice any . . . system or science of treating human ailments who do not use medicines internally or externally").[35] Most of the licensed occupations were "professions" or subprofessions by common consent, but not all. Many states in the 1890's licensed plumbers, barbers, and horseshoers. A New York law licensing transportation ticket agents was passed, only to be declared unconstitutional in 1898.[36]

Undertakers, embalmers, and funeral directors were another group that heard the siren song of licensing. They too were struggling to define for themselves, and to protect, an area of exclusive business competence. They had many rivals. Doctors embalmed the dead. Clergymen controlled funerals. Many undertakers were part-time funeral directors, who sold coffins and caskets as the mainstay of their business. In the late 1880's, Hudson Samson, president of the Funeral Directors' National Association of the United States, prepared a model legislative act for licensing embalmers. At the same time, Samson tried to uplift the artifacts of professional funerals. (In 1889, he designed a "special eight poster, oval-decked funeral car"; in 1898, a magnificent hand-carved wooden drape hearse.) It was all part of one general movement, to give tone and economic strength to the occupation, in short, to "professionalize" these doctors of the dead. Samson wanted a law to regulate "the care and burial of the dead the same as there is for the practice of medicine." In 1894, Virginia passed the first licensing law. The statute established a "state board of embalming," of five members, to be appointed by the governor. Each member of the board had to have at least "five years' experience in the practice of embalming and the care of and disposition of dead human bodies." The board would control the profession and grant licenses. Thereafter, only registered embalmers could practice the "science of embalming." By 1900, some twenty-four states had passed similar legislation.[37]

The statutes in this new wave of licensing laws had certain characteristics in common. Their justification rested primarily on the

[35] Laws Ill. 1877, p. 154; 1881, pp. 77, 120; 1897, p. 81; 1899, pp. 273, 277.

[36] *People ex rel. Tyroler* v. *Warden,* 157 N.Y. 116, 51 N.E. 1006 (1898).

[37] The material on the embalmers is from Robert W. Habenstein and William M. Lamers, *History of American Funeral Directing* (1955), pp. 365, 369, 457–501; the Virginia law was Laws Va. 1893–4, ch. 625.

developing concept of the state's police power—its power to safeguard the public health and safety. But the real motivation, or part of it, was economic. Trade groups were anxious to control competition. Typically, these were occupations organized about strong unions or strong trade associations; and they did not face large and powerful economic institutions as employers or consumers. Barbers, for example, were strongly unionized; and the ultimate employers were that large, diffuse group of people who wanted a haircut. Hence, the licensed occupations were in a different position from ordinary industrial labor, or the farmer, or the businessmen. Their goals were the same as those of unions, farm groups, trade associations, and trusts. But their tactics in the economic battle were somewhat different.

The Virginia embalmers' law was typical. In occupational licensing laws, the state "board," which had power to decide who was fit to be a doctor, barber, nurse, or plumber, was effectively a private group, a clique of insiders. Its aim was to drive out marginal competition, to raise the prestige of the trade, and to move toward the position of a self-perpetuating guild of respectable professionals. By and large, the courts accepted these aims as readily as the legislatures. Few licensing statutes were challenged in court; fewer still were overturned. Society, locked in struggle over the right of industrial labor to organize, nonetheless handed over monopoly power to middle-class professionals and artisans, without a murmur of protest from the courts. This fact helps one to understand the inner meaning of "freedom of contract" and other constitutional shibboleths, which courts sometimes used to overthrow social or labor legislation. The judges were themselves middle-class; they could easily empathize with professionals and artisans. Their constitutional antennae were much more sensitive when they picked up vibrations of class struggle, or a proletarian revolt, which they barely understood and desperately feared.[38]

Most licensing laws had an easy time at the capital too. Their lobby was small but vocal, and no one spoke for the consumer. The statutes proceeded, however, from simple cases to more difficult; from doctors, that is, to plumbers and barbers. The justification was the same for all of these just mentioned: safeguarding public health. The argument was quite obvious in the case of doctors, and therefore had much more general appeal. For barbers, the argu-

[38] See, in general, Lawrence M. Friedman, "Freedom of Contract and Occupational Licensing 1890–1910: A Legal and Social Study," 53 Cal. L. Rev. 487 (1965).

ment was a trifle strained; and for horseshoers, fairly desperate. The health argument, however, was needed to enroll neutrals in the legislature, and convince judges that some public interest was at stake. The Illinois law of 1897, "to insure the better education of practitioners of horseshoeing, and to regulate the practice of horse-shoers in the State of Illinois," [39] put a veterinary surgeon on the horseshoers' board—immunized, no doubt, by his four blacksmith colleagues—and also provided that apprentices must attend lectures on the anatomy of horses' feet. In this case, the Illinois court was not impressed; but a Minnesota court, upholding a statute on bar-bers, spoke of the threat of "diseases spread . . . by unclean and incompetent barbers." [40]

Health was a powerful argument, in any case. Laws on public health and sanitation increased spectacularly toward the end of the century. Again, motivations were mixed. No one, or almost no one, could object to a law that outlawed rancid cheese and watered milk. On the other hand, control of the quality of food products meant a lot to the more respectable dairies and cheesemakers. They stood to gain if the state drove out marginal producers and raised public confidence in their products. Farmers and dairymen conducted a vendetta against "butterine" and oleomargarine, both on the state and national levels. Many states passed laws against oleo. In some states there were stringent laws against pass-ing the product off as butter. In 1885, Pennsylvania forbade it alto-gether. In the 1880's, too, the federal government slapped a tax on the sale of oleomargarine. This battle was more purely economic than other struggles against the sour, the putrid, the diseased. But in the aggregate, the tremendous volume of "health" laws, snow-balling between 1850 and 1900, meant that free-enterprise theory had failed significantly to win and hold its true believers. Good goods should, ultimately, drive out bad ones in the market, or bat-ter down their price. But the public and producers of good goods were not willing to wait so long. Times, too, had changed. The progress of science made a growing circle of people aware that dan-ger lurked in food and water. The discovery of germs, invisible, insidious, hidden in every spot of filth, had a profound effect on the legal system. To a much greater extent than before, goods—in-cluding food—were packaged and sent long distances, to be marketed impersonally, in bulk, rather than to be felt, handled,

[39] Laws Ill. 1897, p. 233.

[40] These cases are, respectively, *Bessette* v. *People*, 193 Ill. 334, 62 N.E. 215 (1901); *State* v. *Zeno*, 79 Minn. 80, 81 N.W. 748 (1900).

and squeezed at the point of purchase. This meant that a person was dependent on others, on strangers, on far-off corporations, for necessities of life; that society was more than ever a complex cellular organism; and that these strangers, these others had a great capacity for inflicting irreparable harm.

Science, which revealed the existence of unknown dangers, also carried the promise, or hope, of making the dangerous safe. Water and food could be sterilized; dirty streets could be scrubbed; light and air could be let into the factories. By the time of the Gilded Age, there was not much moral or economic force left in the excuse that industry needed protection, from seedling to tree. A dip into the Massachusetts session laws of 1887 shows that the interest in public health generated great quantities of legislation. One law required sellers of arsenic, strychnine, and other poisons to keep records of their sales, open to inspection by the police. Another act stated that killed poultry could not be sold unless "properly dressed, by the removal of the crop and entrails when containing food." This law was given over to city boards of health for enforcement. A few pages on, factories employing five or more were ordered to be kept free "from effluvia arising from any drain, privy or other nuisance," and told to provide "water-closets, earth-closets, or privies" for employees. Another law created a State Board of Registration in Dentistry. Another law required factories to be ventilated, and still another was "an Act to Secure Uniform and Proper Meal Times for Children, Young Persons and Women Employed in Factories and Workshops." [41]

This was an industrial state, whose health laws reflected the strength of organized labor and its allies. There were no factory acts in the Arkansas session laws of 1881. But one act regulated "the Practice of Medicine and Surgery"; another made the sale of poisons unlawful, unless labeled as such, and required the keeping of records; another established a State Board of Health.[42] The crush of health laws was earlier and heavier in the Northeast, slower and later in the South; but the overall direction was unmistakable.

Statutory protection of social interests—meaning, basically, the private interests of fairly large groups—was a cumulative process. Lien laws and homestead provisions were still in force; and, if anything, their provisions were strengthened. In the settled parts of the country, however, they had reached a kind of plateau by the

41 Laws Mass. 1887, chs. 38, 94, 103, 137, 173, 215.
42 Laws Ark. 1881, pp. 41, 107, 177.

time of the Civil War. The new health laws became law after the war, indeed, most rapidly at the end of the century; mine and factory safety laws were also passed at this time. Homestead exemptions were primarily for the benefit of the farmer. The new laws reflected the rise of the cities, the growth of heavy industry, the slow passing of rural America. Iowa, for example, passed a coal-mine inspection law in 1880; the governor was to appoint an inspector, who would check ventilation and safety conditions in mines, among other things.[43] John F. Dillon, reporting as president of the American Bar Association in 1892, was struck by how much of "recent legislation" related to "matters concerning the public health and safety, and particularly the safety of operatives and laborers." [44] He noted that Ohio now required guardrails or handrails on bridges, viaducts, culverts, and handrails for stairways in hotels and factories; Ohio and New York regulated scaffolding, ropes, blocks, pulleys, and tackles used in building. Georgia compelled seaside hotelkeepers to maintain lifeboats. Rhode Island, in an "Act for the Prevention of Blindness," required midwives and nurses to report to health officers any inflamed or reddened eyes among newborn babies. Ohio strengthened its laws on factory inspection, and regulated the manufacture of explosives. Rhode Island and Colorado "joined the long list of other states in prohibiting the sale or gift of cigarettes to minors," and forbidding minors "to smoke or chew tobacco in public places." And so it went.

Most of the health laws were, in form, criminal statutes. That does not necessarily mean that they were the product of moral outrage, though sometimes indeed they were. But enforcement through private initiative had been largely discredited. In theory, the upsurge of concern about health did not really require fresh doctrine. The law of warranty could have been strengthened by the courts; private causes of action were available against people who sold shoddy goods; these prior rules might have been woven into a strict and expansive law of products liability—a development now taking place in the second half of the 20th century. Yet, who would or could go to court over a ten-cent can of peas? Criminalization meant that the remedy had been socialized: that the state had assumed the cost and the burden of enforcement.

There is no doubt about the number of laws passed. The actual impact was another question. Constant tinkering indicates some-

43 Laws Iowa 1880, ch. 202.
44 *Report, 15th Ann. Meeting A.B.A.* (1892), pp. 167, 177–8, 183.

thing less than full enforcement. In most cases, the state did little more than place people's interests or passions on record. The record suggests little real control over the quality of products, even food. Quack medicines, sometimes mostly made of alcohol, or hideously dangerous drugs, mislabeled, or underlabeled, were brazenly peddled; the patent-medicine industry wielded enormous power over newspapers, which had grown dependent on their revenues from ads. During the Spanish-American War, there was a scandal over "embalmed beef"—rotten meat allegedly served to the troops who were fighting in Cuba. At the end of the period, intense agitation arose for stronger food laws. The agitation proves, if proof was needed, that existing legislation was almost useless. It was true that it was a crime at common law knowingly to sell bad food; and there were statutes, like that of Pennsylvania (1860), which made it a misdemeanor to "sell . . . the flesh of any diseased animal, or any other unwholesome flesh, knowing the same to be diseased or unwholesome." But no real machinery backed up these laws. Increase in the demands for consumer protection came faster than increase in the efficiency of enforcement.

The consumer was unorganized; yet, he gradually forced the government to take action. Some of his pressure was direct. Some was indirect: his sales resistance, after repeated food scandals, hurt companies in their pocketbooks and frightened them into accepting or actually asking for control. In 1883, Congress passed a law forbidding the importation of adulterated tea. In 1890, a federal statute authorized inspection of "salted pork and bacon intended for exportation"; the law also forbade the import of diseased meat and adulterated food products. The next year, Congress passed a meat inspection law, covering "all cattle, sheep, and hogs which are subjects of interstate commerce, and which are about to be slaughtered at slaughter-houses, canning, salting, packing or rendering establishments." [45] New state food laws were also passed toward the end of the century. By 1889, twenty-three states had laws against the adulteration of drugs. Massachusetts, Michigan, New Jersey, and New York had more general statutes. Each year there was fresh legislation. In Minnesota, in 1889, laws were passed forbidding the sale of adulterated baking powder; regulating the manufacture of vinegar; requiring local boards of health to appoint inspectors to "inspect all cattle, sheep, and swine slaughtered for human food"; preventing the sale of cigarettes or tobacco to children under six-

[45] 26 Stats. 414 (act of Aug. 30, 1890); 26 Stats. 1089 (act of Mar. 3, 1891).

teen; and regulating the quality and purity of milk, butter, and cheese.[46] State laws, of course, could not reach those producers whose poison dripped across state lines. In Congress, 190 food bills were introduced between 1879 and 1906, when the Pure Food Act finally became law.[47] Those few which succeeded, as we have seen, were mainly those that protected export markets. But pressure was building up, and it now gained a powerful ally in the reformist bureaucracy. The fight for pure food became significantly professionalized. Dr. Harvey W. Wiley, chief chemist of the U.S. Department of Agriculture, later to be one of the guiding lights behind the Pure Food law, was at work in the late 1880's and 1890's, patiently exposing food fraud and poison. USDA bulletins, published from 1887 to 1893, calmly documented the national disgrace: wines were made of alcohol, sugar, and water; lard was adulterated; coffee was fabricated out of wheat flour and sawdust; canned vegetables sometimes contained sulfurous acid.[48] The Senate Committee on Manufactures, in 1899–1900, conducted a massive investigation of adulteration, turning a glaring spotlight on the country's food.

Wiley's work showed the power of the bureaucracy to act as an agent of reform. Branches of government had great opportunity to teach the public where its interest lay, and this meant an ability to increase the *political* strength of reform. As the civil service professionalized, this aspect of legislative history became more and more important. Cities had long since had boards of health, though not necessarily very active ones. State boards proved to be more potent. Wisconsin created a State Board of Health in 1876. It tested the state's major rivers and found them polluted. Water supplies were "discolored, odorous, and nauseous-flavored"; it was for this reason, ironically, that some people believed the water had medicinal qualities. Sewage, oil-refinery filth, sawdust, and industrial wastes were poured into the water. Underpaid and feebly buttressed by law, the Board acted as an "eternal lobbyist," begging and cajoling legislatures and local government. The Board's first president stated in 1876: "The people need facts: facts fortified and made cogent by figures; facts demonstrated from persistent and ever active causes." For many years, the Board could do little but give out

[46] Laws Minn. 1889, chs. 7, 8, 14, 247.

[47] Thomas A. Bailey, "Congressional Opposition to Pure Food Legislation, 1879–1906," 36 Am. J. Sociology 52 (1931).

[48] Oscar E. Anderson, *The Health of a Nation, Harvey W. Wiley and the Fight for Pure Food* (1958), pp. 72–74.

facts. But in the long run this was a potent contribution.[49] Tenement-house laws, too, owed a great deal of their motor force to public commissions and committees, which made full use of their power to scandalize the senses and minds of the articulate public. New York had had a tenement-house law since 1867; it had not seemed to work. Now the horrors of the tenements were brought more forcibly to the eyes, ears, and noses of the public. A ponderous federal report was issued in 1894; in 1900, Laurence Veiller, one of the tireless reformers of the late 19th century, held a tenement-house exhibition. He played on the fear and heartstrings of the public, as Jacob Riis had done in his famous book, *How the Other Half Lives* (1890). In 1900, after the exhibit, the legislature appointed a new commission to investigate; and a major law was passed in 1901.

THE GREAT ANTITRUST ACT

The Sherman Antitrust Act, of 1890, was the second crucial—and permanent—entry of the federal government into business regulation. The Sherman Act was cut from quite different cloth than the Commerce Act. That act had created an administrative agency; whatever its defects, it had a certain hard edge of concreteness. It spoke of particular abuses and particular remedies, dealt with a particular industry. The Sherman Act was broader, vaguer, cloudier. It responded to no specific program, except the widespread, somewhat hysterical cry from the countryside to "do something" about the trusts. It was preceded by antitrust acts in some of the states. It also built on the basis of a common-law rule, never very precise, that "restraints of trade" were against public policy and were not enforceable in court.

There was a long tradition of fear of monopoly in the United States. The astonishing growth of big business after the war naturally fed that fear, among farmers, workers, and small businessmen. After 1880, the specific bugbear was those giant combinations that came to be called the trusts. Standard Oil was apparently the first to use the trust device, in 1882, as the vehicle for merging businesses in a cohesive, permanent, yet controllable way. A Cotton Oil Trust was organized in 1884; Linseed Oil in 1885. In 1887 came Sugar, Whisky, Envelope, Cordage, Oil-Cloth, Paving-Pitch, School-

[49] Earl F. Murphy, *Water Purity, a Study in Legal Control of Natural Resources* (1961), pp. 41, 74–78.

Slate, Chicago Gas, St. Louis Gas, and New York Meat Trusts. The use of the trust device did not last long; after 1890, it was replaced by the holding company. But the name "trust" did not disappear so quickly. As the trusts multiplied, public fear seemed aroused. In the late 1880's, attorneys general in some states responded by moving to "break up" some of the more egregious trusts. Michigan, Kansas, and Nebraska passed antitrust laws in 1889. The Nebraska Act outlawed "any contract, agreement, or combination" to fix "a common price" for a product, or to limit the "amount, extent or number of such product to be sold or manufactured," or to divide up the profits in "a common fund." Also forbidden was "pooling" between companies and "the formation of combinations or common understanding between . . . companies . . . in the nature of what are commonly called trusts." [50]

The Sherman Act,[51] by comparison, was brief and gnomic. The first section of the act declared illegal "Every contract, combination in the form of trust or otherwise, or conspiracy, in restraint of trade." The second section made it a crime to "monopolize or attempt to monopolize, or combine or conspire . . . to monopolize any part of the trade or commerce among the several states." The fate of such demons as the Oil Trust, the Sugar Trust, the Whisky Trust, and the Linseed Oil Trust hung on these general words, on the zeal of the federal government in bringing suit, on the temper of the federal courts in putting flesh on statutory bones.[52] In a sense, then, the Act was something of a fraud. Even its proponents thought of it as "experimental." In itself it did nothing and solved nothing, except to still the cry for action—any action—against the trusts.

Vague language in a statute is, in effect, a delegation by Congress to lower agencies, or to the executive and the courts; it passes the problem along to these others. Such a law buys time; it is a compromise between those who want sharp, specific action and those who stand on the status quo. The Sherman Act did not, as

[50] Laws Neb. 1889, ch. 69.

[51] 26 Stats. 209 (act of July 2, 1890); on the history of the Sherman Act, see William Letwin, "Congress and the Sherman Antitrust Law, 1887–1890," 23 U. Chi. L. Rev. 221 (1956); and William Letwin, Law and Economic Policy in America, the Evolution of the Sherman Antitrust Act (1965).

[52] And on the initiative of private persons; under the seventh section of the Act, a person "injured in his business or property" by "a person or corporation" which did "anything forbidden or declared to be unlawful by this Act," had the right to sue for treble damages.

some have thought, mechanistically reflect a vanished dream of free enterprise. It was the product of a Babel of voices, and hardly reflected any economic theory at all. What the solid middle class wanted, insofar as one can speak of a dominant desire at all, was not a law to restore pure, unrestricted competition but rather a giant killer, an act to cut down to size the monstrous combinations which had aggregated too much power for the country's good.

A flurry of satellite statutes followed the Sherman Act in the states. Enactment passed into history; and the work of interpretation and enforcement began. Enforcement was a fairly sometime thing. Late 19th-century attorneys general were not a trust-busting lot. Nor did they have the money and staff to smash the combinations. Furthermore, to those who wanted a robust antitrust law, the first word from the United States Supreme Court was not encouraging. In *United States* v. *E. C. Knight Co.* (1895),[53] the government had moved against the American Sugar Refining Company; this company dominated its industry, and had begun reaching out its claws to acquire the stock of four Pennsylvania refiners, who were the only important surviving competitors. Chief Justice Fuller saw no violation of the Sherman Act. He drew a distinction between attempts to monopolize "manufacture" and attempts to monopolize "commerce." Control of "manufacture" was no part of the task of the Sherman Act, according to Fuller; apparently, to apply the Act to "manufacture" might affect the "autonomy" of the states. Justice John Marshall Harlan dissented. In his view, the Court had "defeated" the "main object" of the Sherman Act. He shuddered at the power and size of the great "overshadowing combinations." There was no "limit" to their "financial" resources; their "audacity" recognized "none of the restraints of moral obligations controlling the action of individuals"; they were "governed entirely by the law of greed and selfishness."

Harlan's was probably the authentic voice of the small businessmen, the farmers, the middle-class professionals. This voice gained ascendancy in *U.S.* v. *Trans-Missouri Freight Association*,[54] decided in 1897. Here the Court, speaking through Justice Rufus W. Peckham, confronted that ancient enemy, the railroads. By a bare majority, the Court rejected the view that the Sherman Act proscribed only "unreasonable" restraints of trade. The majority now spoke

53 156 U.S. 1 (1895).
54 166 U.S. 290 (1897).

of how the trusts ruthlessly drove out of business the worthy "small but independent dealers," how these men were transformed into economic robots, each "a mere servant or agent of a corporation," with "no voice in shaping the business policy of the company and bound to obey orders issued by others." In *Addyston Pipe and Steel Co.* v. *U.S.*[55] (1899), the Court continued along this road. The government had proceeded against six corporations that made and sold cast-iron pipe. The Supreme Court upheld, essentially, the government's view. The *Knight* case was distinguished to a mystery. Still, it was clear by 1900 that the companies would bitterly resist, in court, government's major moves against the trusts. Industrial giants could afford to battle the government, and were clearly willing to do so. The Court was split down the middle on many issues of policy and interpretation, so that minor shifts in personnel could switch the Court from one track to another. In 1900, then, the future of the Sherman Act was quite uncertain.

[55] 175 U.S. 211 (1899).

CHAPTER VI

TORTS

For the 19th century, it is hard to think of a body of new judge-made law more striking than tort law. Before 1800, torts were an insignificant branch of the law, as we have seen. The common law had had little to say about personal-injury actions, based on the negligence of another—the area of tort law that underwent most rapid growth in the century. The modern law of torts must be laid at the door of the industrial revolution, whose machines had a marvelous capacity for smashing the human body.

Although many basic doctrines appeared before 1850, tort law grew most explosively after that date. The first English language treatise on the subject was *The Law of Torts, or Private Wrongs,* by Francis Hilliard, published in 1859. In 1860, Charles G. Addison's *Wrongs and Their Remedies* appeared (in England); a second edition of Hilliard came out in 1861, and a third in 1866. By 1900, there was an immense literature on the law of torts; Joel Bishop and Thomas M. Cooley had written imposing treatises on the subject; the case law had swollen to heroic proportions.

Superficially, the new law was built up out of old bricks from the common-law brickyard. And there was also an uncommon amount of transatlantic traffic. At a time when English influence on American law was dying fast, many leading cases on torts were English: *Priestley* v. *Fowler* (1837) (the fellow servant rule); *Davies* v. *Mann* (1842) (last clear chance); *Rylands* v. *Fletcher* (1868) (liability for extrahazardous activities).[1] Crosscurrents of this kind were understandable in a field left largely to the judges. Besides, it is not quite accurate to speak of English *influence.* The industrial revolution had a head start in England; problems emerged there first, and so did their tentative legal solutions.

Every legal system tries to redress harm done by one person to another. The industrial revolution added an appalling increase in

[1] These cases are, respectively, 3 M. & W. 1 (1837); 10 M. & W. 546 (1842); (1868) L.R. 3 H.L. 330, affirming (1866) L.R. 1 Ex. 265.

dimension. Its machines produced injuries as well as profits and products. The profits were a tempting and logical fund out of which to pay the costs of the injured. Moreover, the industrial relationship was impersonal. No ties of blood or love prevented one cog in the machine from suing the machine and its owners. But precisely here (to the 19th-century mind) lay the danger. Lawsuits and damages might injure the health of precarious enterprise. The machines were the basis for economic growth, for national wealth, for the greater good of society.

The dilemma was first posed in railroad cases, and continued to be posed most often and most strikingly in this industry. Almost every leading case in tort law was connected, mediately or immediately, with this new and dreadful presence. In this first generation of tort law, the railroad was the prince of machines, both as symbol and as fact. It was the key to economic development. It cleared an iron path through the wilderness. It bound cities together, and tied the farms to the city and the seaports. Yet, trains were also wild beasts; they roared through the countryside, killing livestock, setting fire to crops, smashing passengers and freight. Railroad law and tort law grew up, then, together. In a sense, the two were the same.

One basic fact of this tort-and-railroad law was that it was a law of negligence, of carelessness—the inflicting of harm, not on purpose, but because of some lapse in the standard of care. Liability for negligence was not absolute; it was based on fault. What was expected was not perfection, but the vague, subtle standard of the "reasonable man." Fault meant a breach of duty to the public, meant that the defendant had not done what a reasonable man should do. The morals were those of the ordinary man, in an industrial world. Absolute liability was rejected; more accurately, it was never considered. Absolute liability might have strangled the economy altogether. If railroads, and enterprise generally, had to pay for all damage done "by accident," lawsuits might drain them of their economic blood. So, ordinary caution became the standard.[2] The careful, conscious aim of the judges was to limit damages to some moderate measure. Capital had to be spared for its necessary work. This, at least, was the contemporary view.

Underlying policies of tort law did not, as a general rule, emerge explicitly from the cases. In a few instances, these policies were

[2] See Charles O. Gregory, "Trespass to Negligence to Absolute Liability," 37 Va. L. Rev. 359 (1951)

more brilliantly highlighted. In the famous case of *Ryan* v. *New York Central Rr. Co.*, decided in New York in 1866,[3] a fire broke out in the city of Syracuse, New York, in the railroad's woodshed, through the "careless management" of an engine. Plaintiff's house, "situated at a distance of one hundred and thirty feet from the shed, soon took fire from the heat and sparks, and was entirely consumed." Other houses, too, were burned. There was no question that the railroad was at fault, that the fire was the product of negligence. But how much should the railroad pay? The court shrank in horror from the thought of liability to people in the position of the plaintiff:

> To sustain such a claim . . . would subject [the railroad] to a liability against which no prudence could guard, and to meet which no private fortune would be adequate. . . . In a country . . . where men are crowded into cities and villages . . . it is impossible [to] . . . guard against the occurrence of accidental or negligent fires. A man may insure his own house . . . but he cannot insure his neighbor's. . . . To hold that the owner . . . must guarantee the security of his neighbors on both sides, and to an unlimited extent . . . would be the destruction of all civilized society. . . . In a commercial country, each man, to some extent, runs the hazard of his neighbor's conduct, and each, by insurance against such hazards, is enabled to obtain a reasonable security against loss.

The railroad in *Ryan* was held not liable precisely because the harm it caused was *too* great, even though the damage could clearly, morally, be laid at its door. The court, quite atypically—but revealingly—made the railroad's capacity to buy and carry insurance an explicit element in measuring the limits of liability. Insurability was important, because an insurable risk was one that could be spread, that *would* be spread by a careful businessman, and so would not ruin the finances of a well-run enterprise.

The *Ryan* case hints also that fault was only one blade of the scissors that cut away enterprise liability; the doctrine of proximate cause grew into another. In theory, proximate cause was a concept of physical fact: did Mr. X, by his actions, cause the injury to Mr. Y, and were his actions the "proximate" cause, with no other man or event intervening? For enterprise-minded courts, proximate cause and fault, though strong and supple doctrines, turned out to be not enough. Courts invented new and more cunning traps

[3] 35 N.Y. 210 (1866).

for injured plaintiffs. One of these traps was the doctrine of contributory negligence. Another was the fellow-servant rule and its fellow traveler, the doctrine of assumption of risk.

The basic idea of contributory negligence was extremely simple. If the plaintiff was negligent himself, ever so slightly, he could not recover from defendant. This was a harsh doctrine, but extraordinarily useful. It became the favored method, by which judges kept tort claims from the deliberations of the jury. The trouble with the jury was that pitiful cases of crippled men suing giant corporations worked on their sympathies. Even men who respect general rules find it hard to resist bending them in individual, touching cases, particularly if victim or victim's next of kin stare into the jury box. For jurors—amateurs all—every case was a onetime cause. Juries showed a deep-dyed tendency to forget the facts that favored the defendant, and find for the plaintiff in personal-injury cases. But if the plaintiff was clearly negligent himself, there could be no recovery, there were no facts to be found, and the case could be taken from the jury and dismissed.

Contributory negligence can be traced, as a doctrine, to an English case decided in 1809. But it was rarely used before the 1850's.[4] What happened in between was the rise of the railroads. In 1840, there were less than 3,000 miles of track in the United States; by 1850, 9,000; by 1860, 30,000; by 1870, 52,000. Personal-injury cases grew as fast as the trackage. Most cases were crossing accidents. The air brake was not invented until 1868; and it was not in general use until much later than that. Before the air brake, trains simply could not quickly slow down. They sped through the countryside, futilely clanging their bells, and, all too often, colliding with cattle, other trains, or men.

The doctrine of contributory negligence kept pace with crossing accidents. Professor Wex S. Malone has shown that judges were disturbed by the looseness of juries and that they used contributory negligence as a brake of their own. The plaintiff had not only to prove that the railroad was negligent; he also had to show that he was faultless himself. If he was injured at a crossing, in relatively open country, with a clear view of the train, the court could take the case from the jury with clear conscience. The issue was a lively one and frequently went to court. Professor Malone has counted the appellate cases—and these, it must be recalled, represent only a tiny fraction of those that ended their life in the lower

4 For the story, see Wex S. Malone, "The Formative Era of Contributory Negligence," 41 Ill. L. Rev. 151 (1946).

courts. Between 1850 and 1860, there were only twelve reported cases in which the plaintiff collided head on with the iron doctrine of contributory negligence. Between 1860 and 1870, there were thirty-one. Between 1870 and 1880, there were fifty-eight. Typical of these cases was *Haring* v. *New York and Erie Rr. Co.*, decided in 1852.[5] John J. Haring was "struck by the engine of the defendants, while he, with another person, was crossing the railroad in a sleigh." The railroad was plainly negligent; but the judge took the case away from the jury. "A man who rushed headlong against a locomotive engine, without using the ordinary means of discovering his danger, cannot be said to exercise ordinary care." "We can not shut our eyes," added the judge, "that in certain controversies between the weak and the strong—between a humble individual and a gigantic corporation, the sympathies of the human mind naturally, honestly and generously, run to the assistance and support of the feeble. . . . [C]ompassion will sometimes exercise over the . . . jury, an influence which, however honorable to them as philanthropists, is wholly inconsistent with the principles of law and the ends of justice."

The doctrine of assumption of risk was almost as cruel a blow to personal-injury victims as contributory negligence. A plaintiff could not recover if he had put himself willingly in a position of danger. So stated, the doctrine seems to express a simple, harmless, even self-evident idea. But it had a more sinister cast in cases of injured workmen; miners, railroad men, and factory operatives could be said to assume the ordinary risks of employment merely by accepting their jobs.

Assumption of risk developed hand in hand with the fellow-servant rule. Under this rule, as we have seen, a servant (employee) could not sue his master (employer), for injuries caused by the negligence of another employee. He could sue his employer for injuries, if the employer caused them, personally, through negligent misconduct. But this right meant nothing in a factory or railroad yard. The employer was a rich entrepreneur, or a soulless corporation. In a crossing accident, or a mishap in a textile mill, it was a fellow servant who was negligent, if anybody. The fellow servant, of course, was liable at law; but it would have been pointless for one worker to sue another, equally poor. The fellow-servant rule, then, left injured workmen without meaningful recourse to law.

The doctrine can be traced to an English case, *Priestley* v.

[5] 13 Barb. 2 (N.Y., 1852).

Fowler (1837), decided by Lord Abinger.[6] The suit was brought by a butcher's employee, hurt in the thigh when the butcher's van, overloaded, broke down. It therefore had little to do with industrial accidents as such. But later courts, on both sides of the Atlantic, quickly picked up the rule in railroad cases. "Lord Abinger planted it, Baron Alderson watered it, and the devil gave it increase," said the secretary for Ireland, in a famous remark in the House of Commons in 1897.[7] For Lord Alderson, in the United States, one may substitute Lemuel Shaw of Massachusetts, whose brilliant opinion, in *Farwell* v. *Boston & Worcester Rr. Corp.* (1842),[8] was repeatedly cited in later cases. And the devil, on both sides of the Atlantic, was the concept of spoon-feeding enterprise, responsible for so much callousness and shrugging of shoulders in the 19th century. Within a few years of *Farwell,* the same question was posed, and the same doctrine gobbled up, by the courts of many other states. When the Wisconsin supreme court considered the doctrine in 1861, it treated it as part of the common law of the country, almost as if it had been handed down from the parchment pages of the medieval Year Books. The fellow-servant rule, said the court (and accurately), had been "sustained by the almost unanimous judgments of all the courts both of England and this country . . . [an] unbroken current of judicial opinion." [9] At least the rule was, in its early stages, clean-cut and brutally simple. The cost of industrial accidents was to be shifted from the entrepreneur to the workers themselves. Insofar as there was any responsibility toward destitute workers and their families, society as a whole, through its poor laws, would bear the burden, rather than leaving it to the most productive sector of the economy. This was the theory of tort law.

Another restrictive device was found by rummaging about in the toolsheds of the old common law. At common law, when a person died, he carried to the grave his rights to sue a man who had committed a tort against him. Tort actions were "personal," it was said, and died with the person. The rule probably applied to any action for wrongful death. To kill another man, at common law, was a felony. The felon forfeited his property, and the victim's

[6] 3 M. & W. 1 (1837).

[7] Quoted in Walter F. Dodd, *Administration of Workmen's Compensation* (1936), p. 5, n. 7. Sir Edward Hall Alderson was an English judge who further developed the doctrine.

[8] 45 Mass. (4 Met.) 49 (1842).

[9] *Moseley* v. *Chamberlain,* 18 Wis. 700, 705 (1861).

family had a possible claim to share in the forfeiture. Since this was the case, there was some logic to the argument that the victim's family did not need an action in tort. The criminal law changed over the years, capital punishment was less frequently used, and the rule that forfeited a felon's goods was abolished. The original basis for the no-tort rule was clearly gone, then, by the early 19th century. Yet the English courts dredged it up, significantly in a case arising out of a stagecoach accident. The rule then was applied in railroad cases, and the courts worked it into the law of torts once more.[10]

The American experience is equally enlightening. There were clear signs in the early 19th century that American courts had never really accepted the rule.[11] Then, lo and behold, the rule suddenly sprang to life, in a Massachusetts railroad case, *Carey* v. *Berkshire Rr.* (1848).[12] A railroad worker was killed in an accident, and his widow ("who was poor," she alleged, and "left to provide for herself and the support of three small children") sued the railroad. The court cited the English cases and denied recovery, on the grounds that a man's actions for personal injuries died with him. Ten years later, a New York judge slammed the door on a claim filed by the husband of Eliza Green, whose life was snuffed out "by a collision of the cars" of the Hudson River Rail Company. "The question," he said, "has been too long settled, both in England and in this country, to be disturbed." It would "savor somewhat more of judicial knight errantry, than of legal prudence, to attempt to unsettle what has been deemed at rest for more than two hundred and fifty years." [13]

The irony was that the matter had been settled, not for 250, but for ten years at most in the United States. The appeal to the past was disingenuous. The fact was, death damages were hard to measure: and the courts were exceedingly leery of them. It was a horrifying prospect, apparently, to require railroads and business in general to take on the role of pensioners for widows and orphans. But as a result, in the words of one commentator, it became "more profitable for the defendant to kill the plaintiff than to scratch

[10] See the perceptive article by Wex S. Malone, "The Genesis of Wrongful Death," 17 Stanf. L. Rev. 1043 (1965), on which this account is mainly based.

[11] See *Cross* v. *Guthery*, 2 Root 90 (Conn., 1794); *Ford* v. *Monroe*, 20 Wend. 210 (N.Y., 1838); see also *Shields* v. *Yonge*, 15 Ga. 349 (1854), where the fellow-servant rule was applied, but at the same time the court rejected the common-law doctrine that personal injury actions did not survive.

[12] 55 Mass. (1 Cush.) 475 (1848).

[13] Bacon, J., in *Green* v. *Hudson River Rr. Co.*, 28 Barb. 9, 15 (N.Y., 1858).

him." [14] Not that defendants habitually made such calculations—locomotives did not engage in cost-benefit analysis before bearing down on plaintiffs in tort.

The courts also invented, and insisted upon, another outrageous doctrine: the immunity of charities from actions sounding in tort. This doctrine, too, was based on an English case, *Heriot's Hospital* v. *Ross,* decided in 1846.[15] The case lasted only twenty years at home. But after its death, surprisingly enough, it rose from the grave in America. Its first important victim was James McDonald of Massachusetts, who entered Massachusetts General Hospital with a broken thigh bone.[16] He later claimed that the hospital's agent, who happened to be a third-year student at Harvard Medical School, did not properly set the bone. The hospital, said the court, makes no profits, pays no dividends. It had a duty to its patients to select agents and employees with reasonable care. Having done so, it was not further responsible for what these employees did. This was in 1876; in Maryland, in 1884, a court reached a similar result in a case brought against the Baltimore House of Refuge, on behalf of a boy who claimed he was "maliciously assaulted and beaten" there.[17] Neither of these two early cases mentioned the fact that the English decision that they cited had been overruled. But that hardly mattered. There is a suspicious parallel between these cases and early cases on the fellow-servant rule. In both instances, the court seemed concerned with distribution of costs. In both cases, they seemed fearful that liability would damage the defendant too badly. Plaintiffs—perhaps some lower courts too—looked on corporations, including charities, as a cat looks on a canary. The appellate courts of the 19th century felt constrained to fight the impulse. Charities, like the infant railroads of the generation before, were organizations working for the public good; and they were financially precarious. Society at large should take care of the destitute, if anyone did; the loss was not to fall on these charitable defendants.

By the beginnings of the Gilded Age, the general features of the new tort law were crystal-clear. The leading concepts—of fault, assumption of risk, contributory negligence, proximate cause—had been all launched on their careers. All had been either invented or refined by the judges themselves. What they added up to was also

[14] William Prosser, *Handbook of the Law of Torts* (3rd ed., 1964), p. 924.
[15] 12 C. & F. 507 (1846).
[16] *McDonald* v. *Massachusetts General Hospital,* 120 Mass. 432 (1876).
[17] *Perry* v. *House of Refuge,* 63 Md. 20 (1884).

crystal-clear. Enterprise was favored over workers, slightly less so over passengers and members of the public. The lavishness of juries was to be kept under firm control. The thrust of the rules, taken as a whole, approached the position that corporate enterprise would be flatly immune from actions sounding in tort.

Of course, courts never went so far, and never wanted to. They did not want to encourage carelessness; and they were never entirely without heart. Indeed, the pull in the opposite direction was always there and grew steadily stronger. Reaction to the severe rules made itself felt almost as soon as each doctrine was born. In the nagging, fuzzy manner of case law, each rule bred its counterrule. The bench was not monolithic; as time went on, some judges showed tendencies much like their juries. Whole rules were eroded by sympathy; hard cases unraveled the fabric of the law. Politically, the rage of the victims counted for very little in 1840, not much in 1860; by 1890, it was a roaring force. Labor found a voice, and agitated in every forum for protection. A stream of statutes chipped away at the doctrines. The rules were pawns in a political chess game; as the balance of power shifted, so did the rules. The law of torts was therefore never a perfect engine of oppression. It was an imperfect instrument from the start, showing symptoms of its own mortality. Just as there was never a perfect free market, the classic 19th-century law of torts held such brief sway that in a sense it never was.

Some of the changes were made by the judges themselves, who thus disinvented their own inventions. The doctrine of imputed negligence was one of the most offensive rules, and one of the first to go. This rule "imputed" the negligence of a driver to his passenger, and the negligence of a parent to his child, so as to prevent passenger or child from recovering in personal-injury actions.[18] Even so conservative a judge as Stephen Field thought this rule was unfair, and should be abandoned.[19] Some courts even experimented with ways to pull the teeth of the doctrine of contributory negligence. In a railroad case, in 1858, the supreme court of Illinois expressed the idea that the "more gross the negligence" of defendant, "the less degree of care" would be "required of the plaintiff."

[18] The rule applied to this situation: B hired a carriage, driven by C. The carriage collided with a carriage driven by D. Both C and D were at fault. Can B, who was injured, sue D? The doctrine of imputed negligence denied him this right.

[19] Field, J., in *Little* v. *Hackett,* 116 U.S. 366 (1885). See also *Bunting* v. *Hogsett,* 139 Pa. St. 363, 21 Atl. 31 (1891).

So, if plaintiff's negligence was "comparatively slight," and "that of the defendant gross," plaintiff might still recover.[20] The notion of comparative negligence found an echo in the courts of Kansas but nowhere else. Both Illinois and Kansas courts were backtracking by the 1880's, and the doctrine then disappeared, only to re-emerge in the 20th century. But the impulse to soften the edges of contributory negligence never died out.

Two new doctrines—last clear chance and *res ipsa loquitur* (the thing speaks for itself)—slightly lightened the burden of proving a negligence case. Both doctrines were English in origin; both were ingenious. In *Davies* v. *Mann*,[21] an English case of 1842, plaintiff "fettered the forefeet of an ass belonging to him," and "turned it into a public highway." Defendant's wagon, "with a team of three horses," came along "at a smartish pace," smashed into the animal and killed it. The plaintiff was obviously negligent, and strictly speaking should not have recovered for his donkey. But defendant had had the "last clear chance" to avoid the accident. The court felt that this fact, in law, canceled out the consequences of plaintiff's earlier act of fault. The plaintiff won his case, and a doctrine was launched:

> The groans, ineffably and mournfully sad, of Davies' dying donkey, have resounded around the earth. . . . Its ghost, like Banquo's, will not down.[22]

The doctrine had many possible uses in railroad cases; these were not lost on plaintiffs' lawyers. Last clear chance did not get very far in the courts before 1900; still, it made a small, clean wound in the body of contributory negligence.

Baron Pollock in *Byrne* v. *Boadle,* an English case of 1863,[23] launched the phrase *res ipsa loquitur*—the thing speaks for itself. The plaintiff was walking past defendant's warehouse, and a barrel of flour fell on his head and injured him. Plaintiff could not prove any negligence; all he knew was that the barrel fell and struck him on the head. To the court, this mysterious falling barrel proved as inspirational as Newton's apple. "A barrel," said Pollock, "could not roll out of a warehouse without some negligence." The mere

---

[20] *Galena and Chicago Union Rr. Co.* v. *Jacobs,* 20 Ill. 478 (1858).

[21] 10 M. & W. 546 (1842).

[22] McLean, J., in *Fuller* v. *Illinois Central Rr. Co.,* 100 Miss. 705, 56 So. 783 (1911).

[23] 2 H. & C. 722 (1863).

fact of the incident "spoke for itself," and made out a *prima facie* case of negligence. The burden was on the defendant to show that he was in fact not at fault. This rule, too, seemed helpful in railroad cases—for example, in an Illinois case, of 1868, where the boiler of an engine mysteriously exploded.[24] The scope and limit of the doctrine were never quite clear; but it sometimes proved helpful to victims of wrecks, crashes, explosions, and those pursued by all manner of falling and flying objects. It was the middle 20th century, however, so eager for theories of corporate liability, that really made this doctrine its own.

Vastly more important were changes in tort law imposed by legislative act. This was the forum in which labor and passenger opinion spoke most forcefully. Some laws raised the standard of care imposed on tortfeasors. In Kansas, a dry, flat state, one who started a prairie fire had to take the consequences, whether he was negligent or not. He was liable "to the party injured for the full amount of such damage." [25] Statutes as early as the 1850's imposed safety precautions on railroads; if they failed to obey, they had to take the consequences. A New York statute of 1850 made it the duty of locomotives to ring a bell when approaching a crossing. Any railroad company that failed to comply was "liable for all damages . . . sustained by any person by reason of such neglect." [26] A Rhode Island law of the same decade ordered "a bell of at least thirty-two pounds in weight" to be hung on every locomotive, and sounded "at the distance of at least eighty rods" from a crossing, until the engine crossed the road. Railroads had to post warning signs, too, at every crossing, "of such height as shall be easily seen," and on each side of the signboard an "inscription . . . painted in capital letters, of at least the size of nine inches each, 'Railroad Crossing—Look out for the Engine while the Bell Rings.' " This

[24] *Illinois Central Rr.* v. *Phillips,* 49 Ill. 234 (1868). But the upper court reversed. The explosion did raise a presumption of negligence. But the trial court should have given an instruction about the type of evidence that would rebut this presumption.

[25] Kans. Stats. 1868, ch. 118, sec. 2. The *Ryan* doctrine, too, was eroded by the courts. In most states, wrote Thomas M. Cooley in 1879, a "negligent fire is regarded as a unity; it reaches the last building as a direct and proximate result of the original negligence, just as a rolling stone put in motion down a hill, injuring several persons in succession, inflicts the last injury as a proximate result of the original force as directly as it does the first." Thomas M. Cooley, *A Treatise on the Law of Torts* (1879), p. 77.

[26] Laws N.Y. 1850, ch. 140, sec. 39.

law too imposed liability "for all damages sustained by any person"
by virtue of a noncomplying train.[27] Other statutes required railroads to build fences, and made them liable for fires caused by engine sparks. Frequently, railroads were forced to pay for any livestock that their locomotives killed. A Colorado statute of 1872
imposed liability for the death of all domestic animals; a schedule
of damages was enacted, ranging from $1.50 for Mexican sheep to
$37.50 for "American Work Cattle"; thoroughbred cattle and
sheep, and horses, mules, and asses had to be paid for "at two-thirds
of their cash value." Not a word was said in the statute about
negligence.[28] An interesting New Hampshire statute, dating from
before the Civil War, imposed liability on railroads for any fires
they caused; but on the other hand, to soften the blow, gave every
railroad corporation "an insurable interest in all property situated
on the line of such road." In theory, then, the railroad could limit
its financial risk by buying fire-insurance policies for the land
along its right of way.[29]

As these statutes show, it was the big corporations, particularly
the railroads, spoiled children of land grants and subsidies, who
felt the first blows of the rod of regulation. The immunities melted
away. Toward the end of the century, the pace of safety legislation
quickened. The Interstate Commerce Commission called a conference of state regulatory authorities in 1889. Safety was on the
agenda; many participants urged the ICC to look to the problem
of slaughter on the railroads, and recommend some positive remedies. The plight of the railroad workman was the most pressing,
and 1890 was not 1850; labor agitation, strikes, and union activity
were national political facts. In 1893, Congress imposed a clutch of
safety regulations on interstate railroads: "power driving-wheel
brakes," "couplers coupling automatically by impact," and "secure
grab irons or handholds in the ends and sides of each car." [30] Employees injured "by any locomotive, car, or train in use contrary to
the provisions" of the act were not to be "deemed . . . to have
assumed the risk."

There were safety regulations for other forms of transport, too. A
federal statute as early as 1838 had regulated boilers on steam-

27 R.I. Stats. 1857, ch. 130, secs. 3–5.

28 Laws Colo. 1872, p. 185.

29 N.H. Stats. 1851, ch. 142, secs. 8–9; see *Hooksett* v. *Concord Rr.,* 38 N.H.
242, 244 (1859).

30 27 Stats. 531 (act of Mar. 2, 1893). The roads were given until Jan. 1, 1898,
to comply, and the ICC was authorized to grant extensions.

boats; and an elaborate act, "for the better Security of the lives of Passengers on board of Vessels propelled in whole or in part by Steam," was passed in 1852.[31] Late in the century, the states began to pass laws regulating safety conditions in mines and factories. These related specially to dangerous machines, hoistways, and elevators, and often required machinery to be guarded or belted; other provisions made vaguer demands on factories and mines to provide comfort and good ventilation. Administration of safety regulations was spotty at best. But they had an effect, in the long run, on civil litigation. "Statutory negligence"—that is, establishing the plaintiff's case by showing that defendant failed to comply with a safety statute—became an important concept in the case law. Other statutes also figured in the growth of this concept. In a leading case, *Osborne* v. *McMasters* (1889),[32] a drugstore clerk sold a woman "a deadly poison without labeling it 'Poison.' " This was a criminal offense. The woman took the poison by mistake, and died. Her survivors sued, in tort. Negligence, said the court, "is the breach of legal duty." The duty can be defined just as well by statute as by common law. The fact that the statute spoke only of *criminal* penalties was immaterial.

The heyday of the rule of wrongful death was also quite brief. Lord Campbell's Act in England (1846)[33] gave a cause of action on behalf of a "wife, husband, parent, and child" who died by virtue of a "wrongful act, neglect, or default." The action lay against the person who would have been liable "if death had not ensued." Many American states copied this statute. Indeed, Massachusetts had had such a law as early as 1840, in favor of the next of kin of passengers who died on boats and railways.[34] The first Kentucky statute (1854) applied only to victims of railroad accidents and specifically excluded employees. Another section of this same law gave a general action for wrongful death, but only in cases where the defendant was guilty of "wilful neglect." [35] Many courts clung to their homemade wrongful death rules, except insofar as these were modified by statute. The statutes tended to become more general, however, or at least to fill in gaps in the older laws; Massachu-

[31] 10 Stats. 61 (act of Aug. 30, 1852).

[32] 40 Minn. 103, 41 N.W. 543 (1889).

[33] 9 and 10 Vict., ch. 93 (1846).

[34] Wex S. Malone, "The Genesis of Wrongful Death," 17 Stanf. L. Rev. 1043, 1070 (1965). Note that this law was passed eight years before Massachusetts, in the *Carey* case (discussed earlier), denied that wrongful death actions survived at common law. The dead man in *Carey* was, alas, a worker, not a passenger.

[35] Laws Ky. 1854, ch. 964, secs. 1, 3.

setts, in 1883, finally extended protection to the families of dead railroad workers. Interestingly, the statutes typically restricted recovery to widows and next of kin of the dead man; and they often put a ceiling on the amount that could be recovered—for example, $10,000 in Kansas in 1859. This trait, or quirk, seems to show that legislatures agreed with the courts that death damages could not really be measured, and that some sort of arbitrary limit had to be set. Equally, the statutory figures represented a rough sort of compromise, between giving the companies what they would have liked (no recovery at all) and giving the plaintiff an unlimited go at the jury. Ten thousand dollars, however, was no small amount in the 19th century.

The fellow-servant rule was strong medicine. It was meant to be firm and clear-cut. It demanded unswerving legal loyalty. But that is precisely what it did not get. Shaw wrote his *Farwell* opinion in 1842. In the next generation of judges, many wavered or disfavored the rule. In "nearly all jurisdictions," said a Connecticut court in 1885, the "tendency" was to "limit rather than enlarge" the fellow-servant doctrine.[36] A Missouri judge, in 1891, candidly spoke of the "hardship and injustice" which the rule brought about. In the "progress of society," "ideal and invisible masters and employers," the corporations, had replaced "the actual and visible ones of former times." The "tendency of the more modern authorities" was to mitigate the rule, so as to place on the employer "a due and just share of the responsibility for the lives and limbs of the persons in [his] employ." [37]

There was more here than judges changing their minds. The accident rate had increased at a rate completely unforeseen by Shaw's generation. The railway injury rate doubled between 1889 and 1906. At the turn of the century, industrial accidents were claiming about 35,000 lives a year, and inflicting close to 2,000,000 injuries. One quarter of these were serious enough to disable the victim for a solid week or more. These accidents were the raw material of possible lawsuits. Litigation was costly, but lawyers had begun to take cases on contingent fees. If the case was lost, the lawyer charged nothing; if he won, he took an enormous slice of the gain. The upper part of the bar looked with beady eyes at this practice, "most often met with in suits for alleged negligent in-

[36] *Zeigler* v. *Danbury and Norwalk Railroad Co.,* 52 Conn. 543, 556 (1885).
[37] Thomas, J., in a separate opinion in *Parker* v. *Hannibal & St. Joseph Railroad Co.,* 109 Mo. 362, 390, 397–8, 19 S.W. 1119 (1891), quoting from *Gilmore* v. *Northern Pacific Railroad Co.,* 18 Fed. Rep. 866 (C.C.D. Ore., 1884).

juries." Thomas Cooley thought they were beneath contempt: "mere ventures," no better than "a lottery ticket." They debased the bar, brought "the jury system into contempt," and, horror of horrors, helped create "a feeling of antagonism between aggregated capital on the one side and the community in general on the other." [38] But the contingent fee had its merits. It made it possible for the poor man to sue the rich corporation. By 1881, the contingent fee was said to be an "all but universal custom of the profession." [39]

Neither the number of accidents nor the contingent fee system, in itself, could completely explain the rise in litigation. To justify risk-taking, and make a living, the lawyer had to win at least some of his cases. The erosion of the fellow-servant rule was a conspiracy in which juries, judges made of less stern stuff than Lemuel Shaw, and legislatures all joined in. The rule evolved along a pattern common to many rules. The courts had laid it down simply and flatly, in a form intended as a final formulation. But it was not accepted as such by groups that resented the rule and by workmen and their lawyers. The evidence shows that strict tort rules did not work. The rules choked off thousands of lawsuits, no doubt. But thousands more descended on the courts. Plaintiffs won some of these cases—a growing percentage. The more they won, the more lawyers were encouraged to try again. In personal-injury cases, juries, and judges, were likely to let their hearts dictate results. Few juries and lower-court judges believed that it was their sole duty to lay down stern and salutary general principles. In Wisconsin, in 307 personal-injury cases appealed to the state supreme court, up to 1907, the worker had won nearly two-thirds in the trial court. Only two-fifths were decided for the worker, however, in the supreme court.[40] These appellate cases, of course, were merely the visible part of a huge iceberg of cases. Other states probably had a similar experience. Trial judges and juries were not playing the *Farwell* game.

Doctrine, too, began to wobble. The cases began to open up exceptions to the rule. One of these was the vice-principal doctrine. An employee could sue his employer in tort, if the careless fellow servant, who caused the injury, was a supervisor or a boss, so that he could be compared more properly to an employer than to a

[38] Quoted in 24 Alb. L.J. 26 (1881).

[39] 13 Cent. L.J. 381 (1881).

[40] [1907–1908] *Wis. Bureau of Labor and Industrial Statistics, 13th Bienn. Rep.* pp. 85–86 (1909).

fellow servant. In one case, a railroad worker, injured by a collapsing roundhouse door, succeeded in winning by showing negligence on the part of a "master mechanic in charge of the roundhouse, foreman of the workmen, having the power to employ and discharge the hands." [41] The vice-principal concept was potentially a large hole in *Farwell*. Some states never adopted the rule, however; some states never carried it very far. In some there were exceptions to this exception; and the exceptions in turn had their own exceptions.

Other counterrules had even greater importance. Some courts accepted the rule that the master's duty to furnish a safe place to work, and safe tools and appliances, was not "delegable"; that any failure opened the employer to liability. Litigation was heavy. In one case, *Wedgwood* v. *Chicago & Northwestern Rr. Co.*,[42] the plaintiff was a brakeman. He went to "couple the cars," and was hurt by a "large and long bolt, out of place," which "unnecessarily, carelessly and unskillfully projected beyond the frame, beam or brakehead, in the way of the brakeman going to couple the cars." The trial court threw the plaintiff's case out; but the supreme court of Wisconsin disagreed: The railroad had a "duty . . . to provide safe and suitable machinery." Truly, this was an exception that could have swallowed up the rule, if the courts had been so inclined. They never were, not quite. So the safe-tool rule grew its own exceptions—the "simple tool" rule, for example. A defective hammer or ax did not result in employer liability—another exception to an exception to an exception.

Of equal importance were the many modifications by statute. The rule first arose in railroad cases, and for the benefit of railroads. As the railroads became bogeymen rather than heroes, legislative changes appeared, applying *only* to railroads. In Georgia, in the 1850's, a statute gave railroad employees the right to recover damages for injuries caused by fellow servants, as long as they themselves had not been negligent. Similar laws were passed in Iowa (1862), Wyoming (1869), and Kansas (1874).[43]

Small wonder, then, that the law of industrial accidents grew monstrously large. In 1894, William F. Bailey published a treatise on "The Law of the Master's Liability for Injuries to Servants"; the text ran to 543 pages. "No branch of the law," Bailey wrote in

[41] *Missouri Pac. Ry. Co.* v. *Sasse,* 22 S.W. 187 (Ct. of Civ. Appeals, Texas, 1893).
[42] 41 Wis. 478 (1877).
[43] Laws Ga. 1855–56, p. 155; Laws Iowa 1862, ch. 169, sec. 7; Laws Wyo. Terr. 1869, ch. 65; Laws Kans. 1874, ch. 93.

the preface, was "so fraught with perplexities to the practitioner."
The law was wildly nonuniform, full of "unpardonable differences
and distinctions." This meant that, by 1900, the rule had lost most
of its reason for being. It was no longer an efficient device for allo-
cating costs. It did not have the courage of its cruelty, nor the
strength to be humane. It satisfied neither capital nor labor. It
siphoned millions of dollars into the hands of lawyers, court systems, administrators, insurers, claims adjusters. Companies spent
and spent, yet did not buy industrial harmony—and not enough of
the dollars flowed to the injured workmen. At the turn of the century, rumblings were already heard of a movement that eventually
led to a workmen's compensation plan. England had passed such a
law. In the United States, no state enacted a compensation statute
until 1911. By that time, more than half the states had abolished
the fellow-servant rule, at least for railroads; and the Federal Employers Liability Act of 1908 (FELA) had done away with the rule
for the interstate railways.

By 1900, then, tort law had gone through a marvelous series of
changes. It stood then in what might seem a state of indecision.
The courts, by and large, still upheld the rights of enterprise; but
they were creatures of their time, and their faith had been shaken.
One symptom is the way American courts vacillated, in their reaction to the great English case of *Rylands* v. *Fletcher,* decided in the
1860's.[44] The defendants in this case had owned a mill. They built
a reservoir on their land. Some old, unused mining shafts lay
underneath their land. The water broke through these, and
flooded the plaintiff's coal mine, which lay under land close by.
The English court imposed liability on the defendants, even
though the plaintiff could not prove any negligence. The principle
of the case, somewhat fuzzy to be sure, was that a person who sets in
motion some extraordinary or dangerous process must take the
consequences; it would be no excuse to show he was as careful as he
could be, or as careful as the reasonable man.

This was the germ of a notion far more pregnant than Davies'
donkey or the falling barrel. Out of it, the courts could have fashioned a doctrine of absolute liability for industrial hazards, running parallel to the piecemeal statutes on strict liability that were
actually enacted. But the case had a mixed reception in America. A
few courts eagerly accepted the principle. It was mentioned, approved, and applied in an Ohio case in 1899, where nitroglycerin
stored on defendant's land blew up "from some cause unknown"

[44] L.R. 1 Ex. 265 (1866); upheld in the House of Lords, L.R. 3 H.L. 330 (1868).

and shattered the glass in plaintiff's factory.[45] Other courts reacted in utter panic at this alien intruder. The doctrine was too much, too soon. Oliver Wendell Holmes, Jr., writing in 1873, though he conceded that it was "politic" to put risks on those who engaged in "extra-hazardous employments," thought the doctrine of liability without fault was in general primitive, a throwback to those ancient times before the concept of fault had been evolved, when an "accidental blow was as good a cause of action as an intentional one." [46] Chief Justice Charles Doe of New Hampshire, who had a firm reputation as a liberal judge, also found the doctrine indefensible, and stoutly rejected it. Horses owned by a certain Lester Collins had been frightened by a railroad engine; they bolted, and broke "a stone post on which was a street lamp," on Albert Brown's land in front of his store in Tilton, New Hampshire. Brown sued Collins for damages. Doe took the trouble to write a long essay attacking *Rylands* v. *Fletcher*. The case would "impose a penalty upon efforts, made in a reasonable, skilful, and careful manner, to rise above a condition of barbarism. It is impossible that legal principle can throw so serious an obstacle in the way of progress and improvement." It would "put a clog upon natural and reasonably necessary uses of matter." [47] This seems rather heavy freight for a case of a damaged post. But danger lurked, as Doe saw it, in the deadly English principle. Progress depended on the enterpriser, the developer. To burden him with strict liability—as *Rylands* might— would slow down man's journey from barbarity to progress.[48]

But what was barbarism, after all? The American landscape had subtly altered after 1850. Smokestacks were as dense as trees in the forest. In row on row of mean houses, in crowded cities, lived hundreds of poorly paid, landless workers. Each year, accident tore through these *barrios,* extracting its tax of dead and shattered bodies, ruined lives, destitute children. A finger of shame pointed at industry. Dissatisfaction was in the air. Labor denounced the existing system of tort law as cruel and inefficient. It *was* inefficient, because it no longer worked, because too many people had lost or were losing their belief that cruelty was the lesser of two evils. Change was clearly on the way. Insurance and risk-spreading tech-

[45] *Bradford Glycerine Co.* v. *St. Marys Woolen Mfg. Co.,* 60 Ohio St. 560, 54 N. E. 528 (1899).

[46] 7 Am. Law. Rev. 652, 653 (1873).

[47] *Brown* v. *Collins,* 53 N.H. 442, 448 (1873).

[48] See the excellent essay of Francis H. Bohlen, "The Rule in Rylands v. Fletcher," 59 U. Pa. L. Rev. 298, 373, 423 (1911) on the meaning of the case and the reaction to it.

niques were ready; cushions of capital reserves were ready; most importantly, perhaps, an organized and restless working class pressed against the law with voices and votes. That set of rules, in twilight by 1900, was like some great but transient beast, born, spawning, and dying in the shortest of time. The most stringent rules of tort law lasted, in their glory, two generations at most. Had it been worthwhile? Was that span of time so precious? Would the economy have suffered under some other arrangement? It is impossible to know. There may have been a point to that short, bitter life, but then again perhaps not.

CHAPTER VII

THE UNDERDOGS: 1847–1900

THE DEPENDENT POOR

The American system provided a voice and a share in the economy to everyone; but for the unorganized and the powerless the share was niggardly indeed. The basis of politics, and law, was the pressure of interest groups; the loudest, most powerful voices won the most. Old people, transients, the feebleminded, dirt-poor and crippled families—all these stayed by and large at the bottom of the social pit. Tort law blossomed, corporation law swelled in pride; the poor laws were local, haphazard, backward, and cruel. There were, however, some gradual improvements.

In some counties of some states, the poor, in the age of the railroad and the telegraph, were still bound out "like cattle at so much per head, leaving the keeper to make his profit out of their petty needs." [1] Sometimes this was a simple matter of necessity, in the absence of institutional alternatives. Trempealeau County, Wisconsin, in the 1870's and 1880's, boarded out the handful of the "permanently demented" that the state's asylum could not or would not hold.[2] The auction system, in its most blatant form, was dying. "Indoor" relief, that is, relief inside the walls of institutions, was clearly, by 1850, in the ascendancy; "outdoor" relief was on the wane. The trend meant poor farms and poorhouses, if not more specialized institutions. One reason for the change in policy was ideological: outdoor relief was not stigmatic enough. "Men who before had eaten the bread of industry saw their fellows receiving sustenance from the overseer of the poor. . . . The pauper came

---

[1] Quoted in Grace A. Browning, *The Development of Poor Relief Legislation in Kansas* (1935), p. 59, n. 7. The statement quoted, from an 1899 report, actually referred to Kansas treatment of the insane, who were farmed out to the counties at so much a head.

[2] Merle Curti, *The Making of an American Community* (1959), p. 285.

to look upon the aid given as his by right." [3] Many no doubt thought poorhouses would work an improvement in the quality of care; outdoor relief made moral training, medical treatment and rehabilitation more difficult.

These high hopes were frequently disappointed. In 1850, Rhode Island made a study of its poor-law system at work. The results were harrowing. There were fifteen almshouses which spent, on the average, $51.50 per inmate per year. Some of the poor were still "vendued" to keepers who made the lowest bid for their care. There was testimony about one keeper who beat and abused his charges: "He used to drag John Davis, an old man as much as sixty years old up stairs with a rope and kept him there in the cold for days and nights together until he died, having one of his legs frozen. . . . [H]e died before midnight, with no person watching with him and he lay until the sun was 2 or 3 hours high in the morning, on a very cold morning before they came to him." [4] Public poor farms, in general, were not much better than the facilities provided by these private keepers. The public poor farms too were run cheaply, sometimes callously. In the words of one observer, they housed "the most sodden driftwood from the social wreckage of the time. . . . In some of the country almshouses, no clergyman comes the year round; and no friendly visitor appears to encourage the superintendent to be faithful, or to bring to light abuses that may exist." [5] The Ulster County poorhouse (New York) was in 1868 an "old, dilapidated two-story wooden structure." The rooms were small, "ceilings low, ventilation imperfect"; there were no "suitable bathing conveniences." The little wooden house for the insane contained "twenty-five small unventilated cells." The inmates were all "noisy and filthy"; several were "nearly nude." The beds were disordered and torn, and the halls littered with straw and bits of clothing. The water closet, used by both sexes, was out of repair; and the air in the room was "foul and impure." In the Schoharie County poorhouse, "an insane woman was chained to the floor, and a man to a block of wood in the yard." Twenty years later, some of these hovels had been improved; some had not.[6] The poor got almost no medical care in many counties. In Michigan, in 1894,

3 10th Ann. Rpt., *Bd. of State Charities*, Indiana (1900), p. 154.

4 Margaret Creech, *Three Centuries of Poor Law Reform, A Study of Legislation in Rhode Island* (1936), pp. 195–97, 325.

5 Amos G. Warner, *American Charities* (3rd ed., 1919), p. 179.

6 22nd Ann. Rpt., *State Bd. of Charities*, N.Y. (1889), pp. 505–511.

a former county physician reported the auction system at work; many counties awarded contracts to supply medicine, give medical care, and perform surgery for the poor, to the local doctor who put in the lowest bid.[7]

After the Civil War, some states began to reform their poor laws, by centralizing administration. Massachusetts created a State Board of Charities in 1863, Illinois in 1869.[8] A Connecticut law of 1873 set up a five-member board of charities—"three gentlemen and two ladies"—appointed by the governor. The board was to visit and inspect "all institutions in the state, both public and private, in which persons are detained by compulsion for penal, reformatory, sanitary or humanitarian purposes." The board had to see whether inmates were "properly treated," and whether they were "unjustly placed" or "improperly held" in the institution. The board had some vague powers to "correct any abuses that shall be found to exist," but were told to work, "so far as practicable, through the persons in charge of such institutions." [9] This was something less than iron discipline over charitable institutions. But the boards had the power of publicity. They could, if they wished, evoke scandal. In the late 19th century, for these areas of apathy and neglect, the enthusiasm of a small band of people, inside and outside of government—men and women like Florence Kelley, Lawrence Veiller, and many others—was one of the few real forces of reform. The reformers used words, charts, and pictures as their weapons. They aimed for the sympathy of a wider public, or, more tellingly, at a public sense of social cost. They tried to show that callousness, in the long run, did not pay. Welfare improvement came about mostly on this social-cost basis. In the 1890's, when some counties were still selling medical care of the poor to the lowest bidder, Amos G. Warner and associates noted that 10 American cities, with an aggregate population of 3,327,323, spent $1,034,576.50 in one year on medical relief. Warner thought there were "three strong motives" at work: "the desire to aid the destitute, the desire to educate students and build up medical reputations, and the desire to protect the public health. The latter has

[7] Isabel C. Bruce and Edith Eickhoff, *The Michigan Poor Law* (1936), p. 77.

[8] Sophonisha P. Breckenridge, *The Illinois Poor Law and Its Administration* (1939), pp. 44–5.

[9] Edward W. Capen, *The Historical Development of the Poor Law of Connecticut* (1905), pp. 213–14; Laws Conn. 1873, ch. 45. The power to investigate whether persons were "unjustly placed" or "improperly held" did not extend to "cases of detention for crime."

often been the leading cause of public appropriations for medical charities." [10] The reformers, then, were valuable not only because they touched the heart, but because they persuaded the selfish soul too. They played on fear of crime, plague, and social disorganization that poverty might breed. Still, reformers had to struggle against strongly held attitudes, unfriendly to public relief. These attitudes infected even public agencies. The Illinois board of charities, in 1886, voiced a common fear, that the "inevitable consequences of substituting the machinery of state for the spontaneous impulses of private benevolence," would be to "paralyze" the "charitable activity" of the private sector.[11] Josephine Shaw Lowell, writing in 1890, thought that public relief was justified only when "starvation is imminent." How could one tell when this was the case? "Only by putting such conditions upon the giving of public relief that, presumably, persons not in danger of starvation will not consent to receive it. The less that is given, the better for everyone, the giver and the receiver." [12]

The poor were thus impaled on the horns of a 19th-century dilemma: society refused to tolerate the idea of pay without work, but no one was supposed to starve. Relief was, in theory, available to everyone who really needed it. But this right was not to be too freely exercised. Consciously or not, relief was made so degrading and obnoxious that no one with an alternative, and some pride, would choose it voluntarily. Mostly, in fact, family and friends had to sustain the urban poor; private charity took care of some others; the public sector lagged behind. In times of depression, however, there were soup kitchens in the major cities. Some relief agencies protested that these kitchens were too indiscriminate; it was "impossible" to tell the "worthy" from the "unworthy poor." [13] Soup presumably corrupted the one but not the other. The big city machines had no such qualms. Boss Tweed of New York City personally donated $50,000 to provide the poor with Christmas dinners, in the harsh winter of 1870. He used his position in the state legislature to squeeze appropriations for charities in his city; and city funds, too, were distributed to welfare institutions. Some

10 Amos G. Warner, Stuart A. Queen, and Ernest B. Harper, *American Charities and Social Work* (4th ed. 1930), pp. 143–44.

11 Quoted in Breckenridge, *op. cit.*, p. 74.

12 Quoted in Ralph E. and Muriel W. Pumphrey, eds., *The Heritage of American Social Work* (1961), p. 223.

13 Leah H. Feder, *Unemployment Relief in Periods of Depression 1857–1922* (1936), p. 47.

of this money, of course, had been extorted from the public, rich and poor. Caustically, the *New York Times* compared Tweed to a medieval baron, "who swept a man's land of his crops, and then gave him a crust of dry bread." [14] There were hard times in the 90's, which brought forth a few new ideas from reform governments, too. Mayor Hazen Pingree of Detroit had a garden plan; the poor grew vegetables on vacant lots. San Francisco spent $3,000 a month in 1893 to help the unemployed. Some of these jobless men were put to work cleaning streets and building roads.[15]

There were some substantive improvements in the law of settlement and removal. The main trend, however, was to continue to redefine the worthy as opposed to the unworthy poor. Worthy meant, in essence, guiltless. These were the blind, children, veterans, the deaf and dumb, the epileptic. Temporary sufferers, fallen from the middle class, were likely to catch the fancy and sympathy of legislatures. Kansas, for example, was as stingy as any toward its destitute poor. But in 1869, it appropriated $15,000 to buy seed wheat for impoverished settlers on the western frontier; more was appropriated in 1871 and 1872. Grasshoppers scourged the western plains in 1874; in 1875, the state passed a "seed and feed" law. Townships could float bonds to provide "destitute citizens . . . with grain for seed and feed." Another law authorized counties to sell bonds for relief purposes. (The farmers were expected to pay the money back.) In the 1890's, the state gave away seed wheat, and sold grain and coal to farmers hurt by drought and crop failures.[16]

War veterans were another meritorious class. There had been both state and federal pensions for veterans of every American war, including, of course, the Civil War. Wounded war veterans, and their families, were singled out for special benefits, in a federal pension law of 1862. The organized veterans continued to press for bonuses, pensions and bounties; after 1876, they won a number of signal victories.[17] They were a potent lobby in the states, too. Connecticut, for example, granted some tax relief to former soldiers (1869); small pensions to orphans of soldiers, up to age twelve; and incorporated, in 1864, a soldiers' orphans' home. In 1889, Civil

14 Quoted in Alexander B. Callow, Jr., *The Tweed Ring* (1966), p. 159.
15 Frances Cahn and Valeska Bary, *Welfare Activities of Federal, State, and Local Governments in California, 1850–1934* (1936), pp. 201–02.
16 Grace A. Browning, *The Development of Poor Relief Legislation in Kansas* (1935), pp. 77–81.
17 See, in general, Mary R. Dearing, *Veterans in Politics, the Story of the G.A.R.* (1952).

War veterans were given job preferences for state jobs. In 1895, veterans were exempted from peddlers' licenses.[18]

Government participation in the care of special classes of the poor took more and more direct forms: first, granting charters to private charities, then donating money to these agencies,[19] finally running state institutions. In Massachusetts, the state lunatic hospital at Worcester was founded in the 1830's.[20] In the 1840's, Dorothea Dix bravely roamed the country, pleading that something be done for the mentally ill. In New Jersey, she talked the legislature into creating an insane asylum at Trenton; it opened its doors in 1848. After 1850, other states established institutions for these neglected people. Kansas set up a hospital for the insane at Osawatomie in 1863; later, four more such hospitals were created, and in 1881, a state home for the feebleminded. But even in states with statewide institutions, most of the insane who were not at home were at the tender mercies of county officials of the poor. The state institutions themselves were of varying quality. Government, reflecting its constituencies, was niggardly; and its span of attention was short. Neglected, some state institutions turned into snake pits. Their only advance on local institutions was that they centralized abuse.

Legislatures did, however, create or finance other kinds of "home." Particularly, there was a special effort to ease the lot of the children. Pennsylvania, in 1860, donated $5,000 to the "Northern Home for friendless children," a typical act of largess.[21] Children were a natural object of sympathy and, in the city, were the stuff of which the "dangerous classes" were made, if they were not taken care of. The old apprenticeship system was not suitable in the factory age. In New York, the Children's Aid Society, founded by Charles Loring Brace in 1853, gathered up homeless children from the streets and sent them into the country—many to the Midwest—to work and build character on clean, honest, Protestant farms. Some foster parents were perhaps cruel and exploitive; other orphans found what were probably passable homes, and a decent

18 Capen, *op. cit.*, pp. 249–55, 387–89.

19 There were innumerable instances. See, for many examples in a general appropriation law, Laws N.Y. 1850, ch. 365. See also Jacobus ten Broek, "California's Dual System of Family Law: Its Origin, Development and Present Status," Part II, 16 Stan. L. Rev. 900, 944–49 (1964).

20 The story of this institution is told in Gerald N. Grob, *The State and the Mentally Ill* (1966).

21 Laws Pa. 1860, ch. 551, sec. 38.

way to earn their bread. Western farm life was in any event to be preferred to street life, hunger, and an early, violent death. Up to 1892, the Children's Aid Society had "emigrated" 84,318 children; most of these (51,427) were boys.[22]

On the whole, the categorical approach was the only way to humanize welfare that was at all politically sound. This approach consisted of constantly pinching off a class of the more or less guiltless or worthy poor. It was therefore devastating to those left over, the unworthy or guilty poor. No programs dealt with their problems in any meaningful way. Special aids to others drained away whatever sympathy and political clout this residue could muster. It was a story to be endlessly repeated. The fate of families on relief was later matched by the fate of ADC and public housing in the 1950's, which became more and more controversial and degraded, the more they became last-stop programs for the lowest dependents of them all.

FAMILY LAW AND THE STATUS OF WOMEN

As the factory revolution proceeded, countless thousands of women worked. They may have merely exchanged one master for another; but from the legal standpoint, the woman became liberated from her servitude to man. The right to vote, a 20th-century conquest, was only the last in a series of emancipations. For the sake of free enterprise, if for no other reason, the law presumed that adults were fully capable of buying, selling, behaving in the market. Married women's property laws, already discussed, were extended, broadened, generalized. No doubt some men felt that these laws went too far "towards clothing one class of females with strange and manly attributes," as a Wisconsin judge put it.[23] But the market and creditor's rights won out over these faintly archaic sentiments. Dower, too, was revised and revamped in the interest of women's rights—and of the market. In community-property states (California, Texas, Louisiana, and others), the husband was manager and king of the community, at first. That is, although both husband and wife "owned" community property, the husband was vested with management and control. The law would ultimately

---

[22] Amos Warner et al., American Charities and Social Work (4th ed., 1930), p. 136; Miriam Z. Langsam, Children West, A History of the Placing-Out System of the New York Children's Aid Society, 1853–1890 (1964).

[23] Crawford, J., in Norval v. Rice, 2 Wis. 22, 31 (1853).

evolve toward greater equality, paralleling social evolution; but slowly. In these states, too, a wife's inheritance rights were rather secure. She automatically owned one-half of the community. When her husband died, she came into possession of this automatic half, will or no will.[24]

In the law of marriage and divorce, religion, sentiment, and morals influenced the law, along with economic and business motives. For business reasons, marriage should have been a matter of record, formally created, formally dissolved. By the end of the century, most states made some provision for marriage licenses, and for civil and religious ceremonies. In most states, however, the common-law marriage remained valid. Courts generally construed marriage-license laws as optional only; couples could have a formal marriage, if they wished; there was no obligation. A few states abolished the common-law marriage; or construed their statutes as killing the doctrine.[25] The concept of the common-law marriage was almost a necessity for the old slave states. Few slaves had gone through marriage ceremonies, since these were, strictly speaking, forbidden. In any event, most slave "marriages" were common-law at best. An Alabama ordinance of 1868 declared that "freedmen and women . . . living together as man and wife, shall be regarded in law as man and wife"; and their children were "declared . . . entitled to all the rights, benefits and immunities of children of any other class." [26] In most states, the common-law marriage did not need to be abolished. It was probably dying out in practice. In an urbanizing society, a mass-communication society, the social isolation that brought the concept to life became much rarer. By 1900, "marriage" meant ceremonial marriage, for all practical purposes. The common-law concept, then, could be retained to cover the occasional hardship cases. There was little urge to abolish it; it was abolishing itself at a proper pace.

At common law, the age of consent had been fourteen for boys, twelve for girls. This common-law rule, allowing young marriage, was not suitable to the "northern latitudes" in Joel Bishop's opinion, and must have "originated in the warm climate of Italy." [27] American statutes generally redefined the age of consent, and

[24] See Peter T. Conmy, *The Historic Spanish Origin of California's Community Property Law and Its Development and Adaptation* . . . (1957).

[25] See *Beverlin* v. *Beverlin*, 29 W. Va. 732, 3 S.E. 36 (1877).

[26] Laws Ala. 1868, ord. no. 23, p. 175.

[27] Joel P. Bishop, *Commentaries on the Law of Marriage and Divorce* (Vol. I, 4th ed., 1864), p. 127.

raised it to more fitting levels. In Illinois, in 1827, the ages were seventeen for men, fourteen for girls. In Idaho, in 1887, the ages were eighteen and sixteen. Certainly, very young marriages were not the custom. Neither was open interracial marriage. The Southern states did not tolerate miscegenation, as one might expect. But neither did some Western and Northern states: a California statute of 1850 declared "illegal and void" all "marriages of white persons with Negroes and mulattoes."

Bigamy had always been a crime; but never a very important one. The Mormons, however, made bigamy a national issue. This Mormon practice drew down a storm of rage, horror, disgust from pulpit, legislature, and press, of a degree of vehemence almost inconceivable from the standpoint of the morals of today. Action followed words. In the Morrill Act of 1862, Congress moved "to punish and prevent the practice of polygamy in the territories." The Supreme Court upheld the constitutionality of this law in 1878; but the law had almost no effect on the Utah Mormons. In the 1880's, the Gentiles returned to the battle. President Arthur in 1881 called plural marriages an "odious crime"; James G. Blaine disdained arguments for tolerating Mormon polygamy; one might just as well countenance "the claim of certain heathen tribes, if they should come among us, to continue the rite of human sacrifice." [28] The vicious and punitive Edmunds law, of 1882, put teeth into laws against polygamy; it also attempted to smash the political power of the Mormon leaders. Under the Edmunds law, hundreds of Mormons were arrested, fined and jailed. The Edmunds-Tucker law, of 1887, was even more stringent. In 1890, William Woodruff, president of the Mormon Church, in defeat, announced the end of church approval of polygamy. The Mormon rebellion was over; plural marriages faded into history. No doubt, thousands of good Americans sighed with relief at the downfall of Satan.

Divorce laws had always been if anything more controversial than marriage laws. By about 1880, the legislative divorce was totally dead. One state after another outlawed this type of divorce after 1850, usually by constitutional provision. What remained were general laws governing divorce; these were extremely variable. From about 1850 to 1870, many states adopted highly lib-

---

[28] Quoted in Thomas F. O'Dea, *The Mormons* (1957), p. 110. See also Ray Jay Davis, "The Polygamous Prelude," 6 Am. J. Leg. Hist. 1 (1962). In Idaho Territory, anti-Mormons were in control; and an act of 1885 required all voters to swear they were not polygamists, and that they did not belong to an "order" that taught bigamy.

eral divorce laws. In Connecticut any "misconduct" was grounds for divorce, if it "permanently destroys the happiness of the petitioner and defeats the purposes of the marriage relation." In Maine, a supreme-court justice could grant a divorce if he deemed one "reasonable and proper, conducive to peace and harmony, and consistent with the peace and morality of society." Divorce laws in states as different as North Carolina, Indiana, and Rhode Island were also very permissive. Some states which did not go as far as Maine or Connecticut broadened their statutes considerably, adding to adultery, desertion, and impotence such vague additional grounds as "cruelty." In the Tennessee Code of 1858, for example, there were the usual grounds for divorce, impotence, bigamy, adultery, desertion, felony conviction, plus the following: attempting to take a spouse's life by poison; concealing a pregnancy by another man at the time of marriage; nonsupport. In addition, the court might, in its "discretion," free a woman from the bonds of matrimony if her husband had "abandoned her, or turned her out of doors," if he was guilty of cruel and inhuman treatment, or if he had "offered such indignities to her person as to render her condition intolerable and force her to withdraw." [29]

After 1870, the tide began to turn. Influential moral leaders had continuously attacked the loose divorce laws. Horace Greeley thought that "easy divorce" had made the Roman Empire rot. A similar fate lay in store for America, "blasted by the mildew of unchaste mothers and dissolute homes." [30] Theodore D. Woolsey, president of Yale University, wrote a book in 1869 denouncing the divorce laws of his state as immoral and unscriptural. The failure to enforce the laws against adultery was a "sleep of justice"; it dulled the public sense of sin.[31] In Woolsey's own program, only adultery would be a valid cause for divorce. In his view, "petitions for divorce become more numerous with the ease of obtaining them"; lax laws made the family disintegrate: the backbone of American culture. In 1881, a New England Divorce Reform League was formed. Dr. Woolsey was its president. Out of this grew a National Divorce Reform League in 1885.[32] A second edition of Woolsey's book appeared in 1882. By this time, the Connecticut law had been repealed. Maine's law fell in 1883. A more rigorous

29 Tenn. Stats. 1858, secs. 2448–9.
30 Quoted in Nelson Blake, *The Road to Reno* (1962), p. 91.
31 Theodore D. Woolsey, *Divorce and Divorce Legislation* (2nd ed., 1882), p. 221.
32 Blake, *op. cit.*, p. 132.

divorce law replaced it, with tougher grounds, a six-month wait before decrees became "absolute," and a two-year ban on remarriage of the plaintiff, without court permission; the defendant was indeed never free to remarry without leave of the court.[33]

Naturally, there were two sides to the question. Militant feminists took up the cudgels for permissive divorce. A furious debate raged in New York. Robert Dale Owen, son of the Utopian reformer, went into battle against Horace Greeley. Owen, like Joel Bishop, felt that strict divorce laws, not lax ones, led to adultery. New York, rather than permissive Indiana, Owen said, was the "paradise of free-lovers." [34] Bishop bitterly condemned divorce *a mensa et thoro* (legal separation): "in almost every place where Marriage is known, this Folly walks with her—the queen and the slut, the pure and the foul, the bright and the dark, dwell together!" [35] Both men agreed, in other words, that the divorce laws directly affected the level of sexual morality. But exactly this was open to question. One thing was sure: the divorce rate was rising. The number of divorces rose from 9,937 in 1867, to 25,535 in 1886, far more of an increase than the rise in population can explain, and a rise that took place despite tightened divorce laws;[36] by 1900, there were more than 55,000 divorces granted each year.

How is this fact to be accounted for? There are two possibilities. Either dry rot had affected family life; or more people wanted *formal* acceptance of the fact that their marriages were dead. Those who prattled about Babylon and chastity believed in the first explanation. But the second seems far more likely. Just as more of the middle class wanted, and needed, their deeds recorded, their wills made out, their marriages solemnized, so they wanted the honesty and convenience of divorce, the right to remarry in bourgeois style, and a decent disposition of their property.

Did strict laws have much effect on the divorce rate? This question too was endlessly debated. In Maine and Connecticut, there were short-term "improvements" when permissive laws were abolished; but between 1850 and 1900, the divorce rate skyrocketed everywhere. In theory, a divorce suit was an ordinary action at law, with an attacking plaintiff and a resisting defendant. In practice, few divorces were adversary cases, though there were some unedify-

[33] Laws Me. 1883, ch. 212.
[34] Blake, *op. cit.*, p. 90.
[35] Bishop, *Commentaries on the Law of Marriage and Divorce* (Vol. I, 4th ed., 1864), p. 26.
[36] Blake, *op. cit.*, p. 134.

ing battles, in which bitter spouses aired their dirty linen. In most cases, both parties either wanted the divorce, or were willing to concede it to the other. Even in states that stuck to rigid statutes, collusion was a way of life, in the divorce courts. Divorce in New York was a scandal. Lawyers openly advertised their skill at arranging divorce. Reed's "American Law Agency," at 317 Broadway, advertised in 1882 in the *New York Sun:*

DIVORCES quietly; desertion, drunkenness; any cause, advice free.[37]

"Divorce rings" were in almost open operation. Manufactured adultery was a New York specialty. Henry Zeimer and W. Waldo Mason, arrested in 1900, had hired young secretaries and other enterprising girls for this business. The girls would admit on the witness stand that they knew the plaintiff's husband, then blush, shed a few tears, and leave the rest to the judge. Annulments, too, were more common in New York than elsewhere; they were a loophole in the divorce laws, less distasteful, though less certain, than trumped-up adultery. Friendly divorces were a simple matter in those states which allowed "cruelty" as grounds for divorce. It is hard to know exactly how much collusion there was, and when it began. Francis Laurent's figures for Chippewa County, Wisconsin, suggest a dramatic rise in friendly divorce (so to speak), in this nonurban county from the 1870's on.[38]

The migratory divorce, for people with money and the urge to travel, was another detour around strict enforcement of divorce law. To attract the "tourist trade," a state needed easy laws and a short residence period. Indiana was one of these states, before the 1870's. The moralists fought divorce colonies as hard as they could. Notoriety and bad publicity helped their campaign in Indiana; in 1873, the legislature passed a stricter law that shut the divorce mill down. South and North Dakota, too, had their day. Finally, Nevada became the place. In 1900, it had still not fully exploited its possibilities, though Earl Russell was one of the birds of passage who looked for divorce in this desert haven. The Earl was later indicted for bigamy in England. But Nevada only gained by the notoriety. Nevada was destined to remain impervious to all the moralists, and its career as the national divorce mill lasted longer than any other state's.

Plainly, in the late 19th century, the number of married people who *wanted* divorce was greater than before. This fact only scan-

37 Blake, *op. cit.*, p. 190.
38 Francis W. Laurent, *The Business of a Trial Court* (1959), pp. 176–77.

dalized the pious further. The last third of the 19th century was, in any event, an era of national panic over morality, eugenics, the purity of the bloodline and the future of white old-fashioned America. To prophets of doom the whore, divorce, had to be contained. The result of this clash of opinion was, as often, a stalemate —or compromise, if one prefers. It became difficult to change the laws, one way or another. Many state statutes, then, were like weird ice formations, frozen into absurd shapes, dictated by past circumstances, at that point where forces were more or less evenly balanced. The national law of divorce was a hodgepodge. South Carolina still allowed no divorces at all. New York allowed divorce, practically speaking, only for adultery. Most states compiled a hackneyed list of grounds: adultery, cruelty, impotence, desertion. In a few jurisdictions, the innocent party might remarry, the guilty party not. In the Tennessee statutes of 1858, a person divorced for adultery could not marry the "person with whom the crime was committed during the life of the former husband and wife." [39] In other jurisdictions, broad grounds remained available —in Wyoming, for example, "indignities" that rendered the marriage "intolerable," and conduct by the husband which would "constitute him a vagrant." [40] In the strict states, the compromise took this form: the moralists had their symbolic victory, a stringent law strutting proudly on the books. At the same time, enforcement of these laws was defective. A cynical traffic in runaway and underground divorce flourished in the shadows.[41] Divorce law stood as an egregious example of the problems of a branch of law tortured by contradictions in public opinion, and, in a federal system, beyond the grasp of any single state.

THE RACES

The war, the Emancipation Proclamation, and the 13th, 14th, and 15th amendments ended American slavery and gave the blacks the right to vote. The 14th amendment also gave them (ostensibly) the equal protection of the laws. The basic promises of Reconstruc-

39 Tenn. Stats. 1858 sec. 2475.

40 Wyo. Stats. 1899, sec. 2988.

41 As early as 1882, a committee of the American Bar Association went to work drafting uniform legislature to get rid of fake domicile and the runaway divorce. They succeeded in inducing some states to pass their statute, but the problem did not go away. See Amasa Eaton, "Proposed Reforms in Marriage and Divorce Laws," 4 Columbia L. R. 243 (1904).

tion, however, were not kept. Until well into the 20th century, much of the history of Reconstruction was written by white Southerners, in a style unfriendly to blacks and to the radical North. Historians have only recently begun to peel away misconceptions in earnest, and reconstruct Reconstruction in a more generous, balanced way.

Clearly, leaders of the old South who survived the war were in no mood for racial equality. It was a bitter enough pill that the slaves were legally free; there was no inclination to go beyond the formal status. The Black Codes of 1865 and the following years meant to replace slavery with some kind of caste system, and to preserve as much as possible of the prewar way of life. Mississippi led the way. Its statutes in 1865 looked to a system in which the freedmen would enter into long-term written contracts of labor. Any black laborer who later quit "without good cause" could be arrested, and taken back to his employer. The Black Codes kept on some of the old legal disabilities of blacks. Negroes could not sit on juries, for example. The Southern states also passed stringent vagrancy laws to control the movement of the freedmen.[42]

The North—at least the radicals—were not ready to concede this much to the South. The Black Codes were erased; Congress enacted a strong Civil Rights Act (1866), anticipating the 14th amendment (1868); the South was put under military government. The Freedmen's Bureaus, established by Congress, were an experiment in social planning, to help blacks adapt to the white man's society and economy. Blacks were elected to Congress and held state offices. But Reconstruction did not last. The Freedmen's Bureaus practically ceased operation by 1869; they were at all times understaffed and underfinanced; and their boldest moves—for example, land redistribution on the sea islands of South Carolina—were frustrated by the Johnson administration's policies.[43] By 1875, the North's passion for equality had unfortunately dribbled away. The North lost interest in the welfare of the black; Northern racism, briefly and thinly covered over, came to the surface once more. As for the white South, it eagerly embraced the new situation. The Klan terrorized the blacks. The South destroyed Negro suffrage, and enforced Negro poverty, with the help of lien laws for landlords and merchants, and the sharecropping system.

Reconstruction of legal apartheid proceeded slowly but inexorably in other areas of southern life. C. Vann Woodward has de-

[42] See Laws Miss. 1865, ch. 4, ch. 6.
[43] Martin Abbott, *The Freedmen's Bureau in South Carolina 1865-1872* (1967).

scribed the strange career of Jim Crow.[44] Woodward argued that
the end of Radical Reconstruction did not mean a complete, immediate Jim Crow system in the South. Many of the most blatant
Jim Crow laws, on the contrary, belonged to the very end of the
19th century. Woodward did not claim that race relations were
smooth before that, or that the Negro was ever welcomed into
white society. He merely pointed out a period of trial and error,
ambiguity, and complexity; the decisive instruments of segregation
were nailed into law at a date rather later than some historians
had assumed. But in South Carolina, according to Joel Williamson,
though Negroes could, by the letter of the law, use all public facilities between 1868 and 1889, there is evidence that few actually
dared to do so. Probably the South was not of one mind or one
practice on segregation.[45] In some parts of the South, it was when
the black man dared to protest against his social position that Jim
Crow's grip tended to tighten. Georgia required separate railroad
cars for blacks and whites in 1891; white and black prisoners could
not even be chained together in the chain gangs. Law and social
custom defined a place—a subordinate place—for blacks; those
who violated the code were severely punished. Major infractions
could mean death. Four Negroes were lynched in South Carolina
in 1876 for killing an old white couple. The Columbia *Daily Register* approved: "Civilization" was "in banishment . . . a thing
apart, cowering in a corner"; there was a need for the "equity" of
"Judge Lynch." Later the bloodletting increased. Between 1888
and 1903, 241 blacks died at the hands of lynch mobs.[46]

The South proceeded, in fact, to ensure white supremacy on every
front. Amendments to Southern constitutions took away, through
one device or another, the black man's right to vote. The surviving
black legislators, judges, members of Congress lost their offices. By
1900, not even many voters were left. In Louisiana, the number of
blacks registered to vote fell from 127,000 in 1896 to 3,300 in 1900,
after the imposition of the "grandfather clause." [47] The North
acquiesced. In the Senate, in 1900, Ben Tillman of South Carolina

[44] C. Vann Woodward, *The Strange Career of Jim Crow* (2nd rev. ed., 1966).

[45] Joel Williamson, *After Slavery, The Negro in South Carolina during Reconstruction, 1861–1877* (1965), p. 287; John William Graves, "The Arkansas
Separate Coach Law of 1891," 7 Journal of the West 531 (1968).

[46] Clarence A. Bacote, "Negro Proscriptions, Protests, and Proposed Solutions
in Georgia, 1880–1908," 25 J. So. Hist. 471 (1959); on South Carolina, George B.
Tindall, *South Carolina Negroes 1877–1900* (1952), pp. 236–37.

[47] Thomas F. Gossett, *Race, The History of an Idea in America* (1963), p. 266.

told the North, "You do not love them any better than we do. You used to pretend that you did, but you no longer pretend it." He defended the constitutional change: "We took the government away. We stuffed ballot boxes. We shot them. . . . With that system . . . we got tired ourselves. So we called a constitutional convention, and we eliminated . . . all of the colored people whom we could." [48]

The federal courts probably could not have stood, for long, in the way of Jim Crow, or prevented murder and oppression of America's untouchables. But the Supreme Court hardly tried. In 1878, the Court faced a Louisiana statute (1869) which forbade "discrimination on account of race or color" in common carriers. The court felt this law was an unconstitutional "burden" on interstate commerce. The case arose when the owner of a steamboat, bound for Vicksburg from New Orleans, refused plaintiff, "a person of color," a place "in the cabin specially set apart for white persons." [49] In 1883, the Court declared the Civil Rights Act of 1875—a public accommodations law—unconstitutional.[50] *Plessy* v. *Ferguson* (1896) was a dark decision. It put the Supreme Court's stamp of approval on apartheid.[51] This was another case from Louisiana. But the underlying facts were different; it was no longer a civil-rights statute that the Court confronted, but a law which called for "equal but separate accommodation for the white, and colored races," in railway carriages. The Court upheld the statute.

The blacks were not the only race to feel the lash of white hatred. The shock-word genocide, so loosely and so often used, comes embarrassingly close to describing the white man's treatment of the Indian. The Indians were driven from their lands and frequently slaughtered. By 1880, they were no longer a military threat. They were herded onto reservations, usually land the white man did not want. Even so, treaties with the Indian tribes were constantly broken by the white man; and the allotment statutes, supposedly safeguarding the Indian's property rights, themselves

[48] Quoted in Harold U. Faulkner, *Politics, Reform and Expansion 1890–1900* (1959), pp. 7–8.

[49] *Hall* v. *DeCuir,* 95 U.S. 485 (1878).

[50] The Civil Rights Cases, 109 U.S. 3 (1883).

[51] 163 U.S. 537 (1896). Interestingly, Plessy argued also that he was not really "colored," since he had only "one-eighth African blood" and "the mixture of colored blood was not discernible in him." But the Supreme Court left to the states the power to define membership in the races.

spoke with forked tongue, and were frequently and adversely amended.

In California (and in the West generally), there was virulent hatred against Orientals, which manifested itself in countless ordinances and laws. A California statute of 1872 authorized school districts to establish separate schools for Orientals. A San Francisco ordinance of 1880, aimed at the Chinese, made it unlawful to carry on a laundry in the city, without the "consent of the board of supervisors," unless the laundry was "located in a building constructed either of brick and stone." Almost every San Francisco laundry was in fact in a wooden building. The Board turned down all applications of Chinese and granted all those of Caucasians. In the famous case of *Yick Wo* v. *Hopkins* (1886),[52] the Supreme Court struck down the discrimination; it was "illegal," and the public administration which enforced it was "a denial of the equal protection of the laws and a violation of the Fourteenth Amendment."

But such victories were rare. Fear of the competition of Chinese labor was one root cause of anti-Chinese feeling; and it ran deep. The hostility, wrote John R. Commons, "is not primarily racial in character. It is the competitive struggle for standards of living." [53] True enough, organized labor in the North was almost as anti-Chinese as Southern populists were anti-Negro. Labor, indeed, lent its support to federal restrictions on Chinese immigration. The "coming of Chinese laborers to this country," proclaimed a federal law of 1882, "endangers the good order of certain localities." [54] Everyone knew what was meant. This law suspended the immigration of Chinese laborers. It also provided that no state or federal court "shall admit Chinese to citizenship." The Scott Act of 1888 prohibited some 20,000 Chinese (who had temporarily left the country) from coming back. An act of 1892, "to prohibit the coming of Chinese persons into the United States," suspended immigration for another ten years, and provided that Chinese laborers were to be deported unless they applied for and obtained a "certificate of residence." A statute of 1902 made the ban on Chinese entry and Chinese citizenship permanent.[55] Whatever the original causes, race did become part of the story: xenophobia, fear of the

---

52 118 U.S. 356 (1886).

53 John R. Commons, *Races and Immigrants in America* (1907), p. 115.

54 22 Stats. 58 (act of May 6, 1882).

55 Ronald Segal, *The Race War* (1966), pp. 205–207; 25 Stats. 476 (act of Sept. 13, 1888); 27 Stats. 25 (act of May 5, 1892); 32 Stats. 176 (act of April 29, 1902).

strange, and the eugenic madness of the 1890's. In the 1880's, riots in Rock Springs, Wyoming, ended with twenty-eight dead Chinese; then the whites in Tacoma, Washington, put their Chinatown to the torch. The blacks and Chinese, voteless or powerless, were strangers at the pluralist table.

(CHAPTER VIII)

THE LAW OF CORPORATIONS

Law is often thought of as unfolding in slow patterns, at least before it "exploded" in the 20th century. Yet nothing could be more startling than the difference one century made in the law of the business corporation. In 1800, corporation law mostly dealt with municipalities, charities, and churches. Only a bridge or two, a handful of manufacturing enterprises, and a few banks or insurance companies disturbed its quiet. The rise of the business corporation, in the 19th century, generated huge controversy, and manufactured enormous quantities of law. By 1870 corporations had a commanding position in the economy. They never lost it. In the decade of the 1880's, pulpit and platform resounded with battle cries about trusts and antitrusts. The Sherman Act was passed in 1890. In between, and after, there was ceaseless controversy and change. Much of it, of course, revolved about particular kinds of corporations: banks, railroads, insurance companies. But some concerned the corporation in general. Of the original law of corporations—of Blackstone's day—hardly a stone was left unturned. Even Chancellor Kent's law of corporations was basically transformed by 1900.

Private practices and legislation were the major makers of the law of corporations. The courts played a minor role. Corporate problems were too much of the marrow of public policy to be left to private litigation. No constitutional convention met, between 1860 and 1900, without considering the problem of the corporation. This was a 19th-century constant; it changed its form, its proponents, its antagonists, its format, but retained a numbing sameness of theme. Meanwhile, businessmen and lawyers went on building up corporate practice and malpractice. The courts turned practice into law, as they met it in litigation—sometimes ahead of other lawmakers, sometimes behind; sometimes ahead of practice, too, and sometimes behind. The general trend was for law to allow corporations to do whatever they wished, to exercise any power, and to build up the freedom of corporate management. In counterattack, powers of specific corporations or industries were increasingly and unevenly circumscribed, primarily by statute. These were nationwide trends, though new states and old states had different needs. Western legislatures were still inviting, bribing, and cajoling railroads at a time when Eastern disenchantment had already set in.

Perhaps the major event in corporation law, between 1848 and 1900, was the decline and fall of the special charter. This was an advance in legal technology, if nothing else. It was cheap and easy to incorporate under general laws—a few papers filed, a few forms and signatures; the privilege of incorporation lay open to whoever wanted it; the legislature's time was conserved. For a generation or so, a number of states (New York, Illinois, Wisconsin, Maryland, and North Carolina) still maintained a dual system of incorporations. Special charters were still possible, but they were not to be issued unless the object of the corporation could not be attained under the state's general incorporation laws.[1] The dual system was not a particular success. In Wisconsin, for example, between 1848 and 1871, almost ten times as many incorporators went the special-charter route.[2] The Louisiana constitution of 1845 took the more radical step of forbidding the special charter altogether. One by one, other states adopted a similar provision. Alabama, in 1867, was a Southern convert: "Corporations may be formed under general laws, but shall not be created by special act" (art. XIII, sec. 1).

In the same period, the states, burnt by experience, began to forbid direct investment in enterprise. The rashness of cities, counties, and states left behind mountains of discredited paper, worthless bonds, high taxes. By 1874, sixteen state constitutions refused to let the state own stock in a corporation. In twenty states, the state had no power to lend its credit to any corporation.

When public investment was withdrawn, corporations were more dependent on the open market for money. It was an unregulated market: no SEC kept it honest, and the level of promoter morality was painfully low. It was an age of vultures. In the 1860's and 1870's, men like Vanderbilt, Jay Gould, and Jim Fisk fought tawdry battles over the stock market, the economy, the corpses of railroad corporations. The investing public was unmercifully cheated. To be sure, most investors were not the proverbial widows

[1] John W. Cadman, *The Corporation in New Jersey, Business and Politics, 1791–1875* (1949), p. 187.
[2] George J. Kuehnl, *The Wisconsin Business Corporation* (1959), p. 143.

and orphans, but grown men with a taste for easy money. They had as much larceny in their hearts as the Fisks and the Goulds, but their scale of operation was smaller, their cunning infinitely less.

The pillaging of the Erie Railroad by the robber barons, in the late 1860's, was a classic case of financial mismanagement and public corruption. The story has been coldly recounted by Charles Francis Adams in his essay, "A Chapter of Erie." Adams was alarmed at what was happening, not to one railroad, or to the stock market, but to all of America. The least that could be said was that society was "only passing through a period of ugly transition." But Adams suspected far worse; he saw signs which spoke "ominously for the future." "The offices of our great corporations," he wrote, were "secret chambers in which trustees plotted the spoliation of their wards"; the stock exchange was "a haunt of gamblers and a den of thieves." Modern society had "created a class of artificial beings who bid fair soon to be the masters of their creator"; they were "establishing despotisms which no spasmodic popular effort will be able to shake off. Everywhere . . . they illustrate the truth of the old maxim of the common law, that corporations have no souls." [3] The legislatures seemed powerless, or supine. The big corporations, the Goulds and the Fisks, seemed able to buy and sell lawmakers; through them they controlled the law. "The halls of legislation were transformed into a mart in which the price of votes was niggled over, and laws, made to order, were bought and sold." The courts were corrupted, too. Justice was a whore of the rich. In New York, judges like George Barnard and Albert Cardozo did what the robber barons wished; issued injunctions for a price, sold the public interest down the river out of ignorance or greed.

Inevitably, there were reactions. Many middle-class Americans must have agreed with Adams that the corporations had to be brought and kept under control. In the decade of the Grangers, the 1870's, railroad regulation was a leading public issue; many states established agencies to control warehouses and grain elevators as well. Still later came the Sherman Act. These developments have already been discussed.

Our story here concerns the more general rules about corporations, rules not so concerned with the economic power of corporations as with their everyday behavior. One goal of the law, as it emerged, was to fashion a fabric of doctrine to make the corporation, its managers and promoters, act honestly toward stockholders

[3] Frederick C. Hicks, ed., *High Finance in the Sixties* (1929), pp. 114–16.

and creditors; but to do so in a way that would not interfere with business efficiency. Even before the Civil War, as we have seen, the courts had begun to develop such doctrines. There was great concern, for example, with watered stock. This was stock given to insiders in exchange for fictitious values, stock that the promoters or subscribers then threw on the market. Investors thought they were buying stock with a solid basis in assets or cash. The New York corporation law of 1848—on "corporations for manufacturing, mining, mechanical or chemical purposes"—declared: "Nothing but money shall be considered as payment of any part of the capital stock"; this was amended, however, in 1853, to allow a company to issue stock in exchange for "mines, manufactories, and other property necessary for . . . business." [4] The New York type of rule was widely adopted later on in other state statutes. There was also some constitutional word on the subject. The Illinois constitution of 1870 stated that "no railroad corporation shall issue any stock or bonds, except for money, labor or property actually received and applied to the purposes for which such corporation was created." Also outlawed were "all stock dividends, and other fictitious increase of capital stocks or indebtedness" (Const. Ill. 1870, art. XII, sec. 13). Under these laws, the grossest frauds and most clearly watered stock were obviously illegal. But there remained gray areas of doubt. If a promoter exchanged his land, or a coal mine, or a building, for $100,000 in stock, how could one tell if he had given full value? The only safe rule would be to require all subscriptions in cash. But New York found this rule unrealistic and unduly restrictive. Courts came to uphold transactions of promoters so long as they were in "good faith." The concept of par value of stock also lost its meaning. As soon as stock began to change hands in the open market, it meant very little that the face value of the stock bore the values $100 or $1,000. Stock was worth what it would fetch from a buyer. Par, almost meaningless for a new corporation, meant nothing at all to a going concern. Values were fixed by the speculating and investing public. Corporate capital, then, was not a fixed fund of assets; and par did not represent an irreducible core of truth and wealth, like the gold reserves of a bank.

New doctrines, aimed at control of corporate management, grew out of the pressures of occasional lawsuits, brought by stockholder victims. Procedural barriers at first seemed to stand in the way. Technically, it was the corporation itself which had the right to sue officers who had cheated the corporation. But precisely these offi-

[4] Laws N.Y. 1848, ch. 40, sec. 14; Laws New York 1853, ch. 333, sec. 2.

cers controlled the corporation; those who were milking it were the last to want to sue. The *stockholders' suit* was a class action, brought on behalf of a stockholder plaintiff, and all others in his position. The device was foreshadowed as early as the 1830's, but the Supreme Court gave it a further push in *Dodge* v. *Woolsey,* decided in 1856.[5] The dereliction of duty charged in *Dodge* was not one of the grand postwar piracies. It was a technical error; paying a tax, which the stockholder claimed was unconstitutional. In *Morgan* v. *Skiddy* (1875),[6] a New York case, the defendants, directors of the "Central Mining Company of Colorado," had dangled in front of the gullible public glittering prospects of endless money from "the celebrated 'Bates lode.' " Here the stockholder's suit was used to correct plain corporate fraud.

To how lofty a standard were officers and directors to be held? Case law, with the job of framing an enforceable code of behavior, looked to the concept of fiduciary obligation. The officers and directors were trustees for the corporation. This meant that officers could not engage in self-dealing; they could not buy from or sell to the company; they were strictly accountable for any profits they made in transactions with the company. This old, austere body of doctrine, which courts of chancery had applied to trustees for widows and orphans, was also to apply to promoters, officers and directors. The phrase "a sacred trust," has moral overtones; but trust law was borrowed less for its morality than because it was a ready-made set of propositions that seemed to fit the situation.

The metaphor had already been used before the Civil War. The "trust fund" doctrine had been invented to express the fact that creditors had first claims on the assets of a corporate corpse, at least as opposed to stockholders.[7] The doctrine expanded after the war. One notable series of cases rose out of the wreckage of the Great Western Insurance Company of Illinois. The Chicago fire of 1871 had scorched the company into bankruptcy. In one case, decided in 1875,[8] a certain Tribilcock had subscribed for stock with a face value of $10,000. But all he paid was $2,000. He later claimed the company's agent told him that was all he needed to pay. When the company went under, its assignee, on behalf of the creditors, demanded the rest of the money. Justice Ward Hunt, speaking for the United States Supreme Court, had little sympathy for Tribil-

5 59 U.S. 331 (1856).
6 62 N.Y. 319 (1875).
7 See part II, ch. III, p. 176, above.
8 *Upton* v. *Tribilcock,* 91 U.S. 45 (1875).

cock. The capital stock "is a trust fund . . . to be managed for the benefit of . . . shareholders," and thereafter, if the corporation dissolves, for the benefit of creditors. "The idea that the capital of a corporation is a football to be thrown into the market for the purposes of speculation . . . is a modern and wicked invention." The managers had no power to release the obligation of subscribers to pay in all of their money. No one could "squander or give away" this "fund"; it belonged to the company and its disappointed creditors.

The tone of Justice Hunt's language was severely moral. In practice, however, the cases did not pose questions of good against evil quite so clearly. The doctrine, in its emphasis on par value as a measure of "capital," was already archaic. But it protected corporate creditors, in their injured innocence, against small stockholders like Tribilcock, who had often themselves been gulled by promoters and salesmen. Also adverse to stockholders was the common provision that, until *all* of the capital (as measured by par value) was paid in, stockholders were doubly liable on their stock. This was a New York idea of 1848, widely copied elsewhere. Commonly, too, stockholders were liable for debts due from the corporation to its employees. These rules lasted through the end of the century, in many of the states. In other states, however, legislatures loosened the law, enough to attract roving companies looking for easy states in which to incorporate.

The "trust fund" doctrine, as metaphor, was significant but logically weak. Assets of a corporation, as some courts and some writers acknowledged, were in no "true sense, held in trust" for the creditors.[9] It was also rather metaphorical to call officers and directors trustees. The word voiced the hope that robber barons, big and small, might be brought to legal account. Charles Francis Adams, Jr., surveying the Erie scandals, expressed the idea that the corporate officer ought to be a "trustee—a guardian . . . [E]very shareholder . . . is his ward"; in the case of a railroad, "the community itself is his *cestui que trust*." [10] The Gilded Age was so morally corrupt, that the "wards themselves expect their guardians to throw the dice against them for their own property." But acts of corporate plunder "strike at the very foundation of existing society. . . . Our whole system rests upon the sanctity of the fiduciary rela-

[9] William L. Clark, *Handbook of the Law of Private Corporations* (1897), p. 540.

[10] A *cestui que trust* (the *s* and *u* in *cestui* are silent) is the beneficiary of a trust.

tion." [11] The courts, when they had the opportunity, tried to make the fiduciary obligation real. When directors and officers of the Arkansas Valley Agricultural Society, in Kansas, sold stock in the company to themselves, at par ($5 a share), though they had sold off thirty-six acres of fairgrounds near Wichita at a price that made each share worth ten times as much as par, the court made them disgorge their profits. Fiduciaries could not serve two masters. They could not "secure to themselves an advantage not common to all the stockholders." [12] Gross negligence, too, laid directors or officers open to liability. A Virginia case, decided in 1889, turned on the affairs of a "broken bank," the Farmers' and Mechanics' Savings Bank of Virginia. The president of the bank had pillaged it mercilessly; and he had foolishly lent large sums of money to the Washington & Ohio Railroad. The directors rarely met, and never audited the books. They did nothing, while notes payable to the bank were allowed to "sleep unprotested, unsecured, unrenewed, uncollected, and unsued on." For their negligence, they were held personally liable to make up the bank's large losses.[13]

Out of such cases, a high-minded body of law could be distilled, displayed to the public, set out in treatises. How effective was it in practice? Did corporation law really keep corporations under control? Victories were expensive; lawsuits cost money; many cases arose in the context of bankruptcy; and the worst thieves, like the president of the raped Virginia bank, were penniless, or had run away. Lawsuits were a cumbersome way to protect the innocent. Most were probably too little and too late, and in any event useful only in ordering the affairs of a dead or plundered corporation.

More important, perhaps, were legal developments which signaled the escape of the corporation from chains fashioned by prior generations. The business public demanded freedom to raise and use capital assets. More and more corporations were chartered, and the biggest ones were bigger and bigger. The old concept of the corporation had once been more or less that of a single venture for a single purpose. This concept slowly but surely died. In the last half of the 19th century, an important body of corporations be-

[11] Hicks, *op. cit.*, pp. 26–27. Ironically, the next use of the trust concept in business history became one of infamy. As applied to stock trusts, used as a device of monopoly, the most high-minded concept of the law turned into a bogey word to frighten the voters and small children. See above, ch. 5, pp. 405–6.

[12] *Arkansas Valley Agricultural Society* v. *Eichholtz*, 45 Kan. 164, 25 Pac. 613 (1891).

[13] *Marshall* v. *Farmers' and Mechanics' Savings Bank*, 85 Va. 676, 8 S.E. 586 (1889).

came diversified "entities," dealing with many aspects of one business, or with many businesses. Like a natural person, these corporations could mobilize their power now for this purpose, now for that. A corporation could start as a railroad, gobble up a steamship line, buy timber lands, and build houses, manufacture dolls, and weave clothes. The largest corporations were like huge investment trusts, like ancestral forms of the modern conglomerates, creatures with many heads and hundreds of legs, defying a single description.

Most restrictions on what corporations could or could not do were abolished or relaxed. Nothing was so symbolic of the nature of the early corporation as the doctrine of *ultra vires*. The phrase means "beyond the powers"; it stood for the proposition that the corporation was a creature of limited authority. "All corporate acts which the legislature has not authorized remain prohibited." [14] The powers of a corporation had to be expressed in the charter; officials and courts were supposed to construe these charters with a narrow, jealous eye. As late as 1856, Jeremiah Sullivan Black, chief justice of Pennsylvania, stated that "A doubtful charter does not exist; because whatever is doubtful is decisively certain against the corporation." [15] This attitude made it easy to find corporate acts *ultra vires*. Such acts, under the original version of the doctrine, were null and void; no one could enforce an *ultra vires* act against another party; the state could object to the act; so could any stockholder. This meant that a person entered into contracts with corporations at some risk. If the contract was *ultra vires,* he could never enforce it. Some courts were quite fussy about the matter. In a Maryland case in 1850, a company had been incorporated to conduct "a line or lines of steamboats . . . between Baltimore and Fredericksburg, and the several parts and places on the Rappahannock." One Alexander Marshall pressed a claim against the company, for certain improvements on the Rappahannock River to open the river and make it navigable. The improvements were made on waters beyond Baltimore, hence not within the limits of the statutory route; the corporate undertaking was therefore void; and Marshall was turned away without a dime.[16]

In this extreme form, the doctrine of *ultra vires* did not survive. For one thing, the courts relented. They began to "imply" powers

[14] Victor Morawetz, *The Law of Private Corporations* (2nd ed., 1886), Vol. II, p. 617.

[15] *Commonwealth* v. *Erie & No. East Rr. Co.*, 27 Pa. St. 339, 351 (1856).

[16] *Abbott* v. *Baltimore and Rappahannock Steam Packet Company*, 1 Md. Ch. 542, 549–50 (1850).

much more freely. In 1896, the Supreme Court was willing to hold that a Florida railroad company had not exceeded its power, when it leased and operated the San Diego hotel, in Duval County, Florida. A summer hotel at this seaside terminus might increase the railroad's business; to "maintain cheap hotels or eating houses . . . at the end of a railroad on a barren, unsettled beach . . . not for the purpose of making money out of such business, but to furnish reasonable and necessary accommodations to its passengers and employees, would not be . . . an act [such as] . . . to compel a court to sustain the defense of *ultra vires.*" [17] The courts were aware that corporations were becoming indispensable. The doctrine was a nuisance and an obstacle to corporate credit.

Courts also devised what came to be called the business-judgment rule. This let management and directors run their own show. So long as a decision was made in good faith and in the ordinary course of business, stockholders could not complain if the decision turned out wrong. Partly, too, the courts merely followed business practice. Skillful lawyers who attended to corporate affairs improved the art of drafting corporate documents. The statement of purpose in the corporate charter became a mere form, covering anything and everything managers of the corporation might choose to make it cover. The more "liberal" statutes ratified this change. Under the key New Jersey Act of 1896, a corporation could be formed for "any lawful business or purpose whatever." [18] Even in such sensitive areas as railroad consolidations, legislatures began to approve of specific cases—New York, for example, in 1883 allowed the Poughkeepsie, Hartford, and Boston to consolidate with a connecting line in New England (ch. 514)—and then, to save everybody time and trouble, issued statutes of blanket approval.[19]

The same story occurred in the development of holding companies. Originally, corporations were not supposed to own stock in other corporations. But such holdings were sometimes quite desirable, especially for banks and insurance companies. In 19th-century law, where there was a corporate will, there was generally a corporate way, at least eventually. As early as the 1850's, legislatures began to grant piecemeal approval to some companies (by way of special charter), allowing them to own stock in other corporations. For example, Alabama (1851–52) gave the Wetumpka

17 *Jacksonville, Mayport, Pablo Railway & Navigation Co.* v. *Hooper,* 160 U.S. 514, 526 (1896).
18 Laws N.J. 1896, ch. 185, sec. 6, p. 279.
19 For example, Ohio Stats. 1880, secs. 3379–92.

Bridge Company the right to own stock in other companies in the internal improvement business; Florida (1866) gave the Pensacola and Mobile Railroad and Manufacturing Company the right to own stock in the Perdido Junction Railroad Company. Pennsylvania, in 1861, allowed railroads chartered in the state to "purchase and hold the stocks and bonds" of other railroads chartered in Pennsylvania or whose roads ran into the state. As the corporate desire grew stronger, so did the pressures on lawmakers; and lawmakers complied. In 1888, New Jersey issued a general *nihil obstat;* its law gave all corporations the privilege of owning stock in all other corporations.[20]

Constitutional law also in many ways developed favorably to large corporate enterprises, despite the growth of explicit constitutional provisions *restricting* corporations. As "persons," corporations were entitled to the protection of the 14th amendment, the same as flesh-and-blood people, if not more so. The idea that the 14th amendment sheltered corporate enterprise was first hinted in the 1880's. From 1890 on, it became a significant constitutional idea. All sorts of laws which tried to regulate business, then, faced the constitutional gamut. In the late 19th century, a striking series of cases turned the due-process clause into a kind of great wall against populist onslaughts. The wall had been built, or had seemed to be built, for the protection of Negroes; by irony or design, it turned into a stronghold for industrial corporations. Many of the critical cases have been mentioned in other parts of this book—for example, the cases on the power of states to fix utility rates. In a few important cases, statutes empowering rate-making were slaughtered in court, on the grounds that the due-process clause did not allow such laws to be passed.

The commerce clause, too, turned up in some constitutional cases, as a shield for enterprise. It was a mighty but sometime force. The federal government had the power to regulate interstate commerce. But it rarely used its strength. During periods of federal silence, could the states come in with their own regulation, or was the federal power exclusive? There was never a complete, general answer. In many fields, the states were supposed to have concurrent power over commerce; but they were not allowed to regulate in such a way as to "burden" that commerce. These general notions did not have, to say the least, any razorlike precision. Those cases which held federal power exclusive often had the effect of wiping

20 See William R. Compton, "Early History of Stock Ownership by Corporations," 9 Geo. Wash. L. Rev. 125 (1940); Laws N.J. 1888, ch. 269.

out the only regulation—state regulation—that was actually alive. So, in *Western Union Telegraph Company* v. *Pendleton* (1887),[21] William Pendleton, of Shelbyville, Indiana, sued Western Union for damages, claiming the company had failed to deliver a telegram on time, which he had sent to Ottumwa, Iowa. He based his claim on an Indiana statute, which required companies to deliver telegrams promptly, if the addressee lived "within one mile of the telegraphic station or within the city or town in which such station is." But the Indiana statute, the Supreme Court thought, was an encroachment on (unused) federal power; only Congress had authority to regulate "telegraphic communications between citizens of different states."

The main thread of the story of the commerce clause lies outside the substantive law of corporations; it is part of constitutional history. But the law of corporations was no longer a true measure of the rights and powers of corporations—or of the importance of corporate business. Corporations confronted the law at every point; they were the litigants in a larger and larger share of reported cases; they hired lawyers and created whole law firms; they bought and sold governments; other governments came to power for the sole public purpose of pulling their beards. Provisions relating to corporations were a staple of every state constitution after 1850. The rights and liabilities of corporations were, more and more, the real content of constitutional law. Even questions of individual rights emerged in cases with corporate litigants. *Plessy* v. *Ferguson*,[22] the 1896 segregation case, was a case about a common carrier. Plessy paid his fare on the East Louisiana Railroad, and insisted on sitting in the whites-only section, contrary to Louisiana law. In all the great cases on rate-making, labor relations, and social welfare, corporations were litigants, bystanders, protagonists, or devils.

Big business spilled over state lines. It was only natural that multistate business should be concerned with federal law; and should resist the idea that every state in which it operated could regulate it—particularly if no single guiding hand co-ordinated all this regulation. And, true enough, each state created its own corporate jurisprudence. Economically, the lines between states were almost meaningless. Nothing separated one jurisdiction from its neighbors except a cornfield, a bridge, a short ride on a ferry, an invisible line. A corporation could be chartered in one state, and do business in another. This was both a danger and an opportu-

21 122 U.S. 347 (1887).
22 163 U.S. 537 (1896).

nity for the interstate corporation. The opportunity consisted of playing one state off against another; or migrating, like divorce-hunting wives, to the laxest of states. For this reason, it made little difference to the giants that some states had strict corporation laws. In Massachusetts, for example, there were not supposed to be any "mechanical, mining and manufacturing" corporations with large capitalization; the limit was $500,000 until 1871, $1,000,000 until 1899. (In New York, too, there was a limit on capitalization: $2,000,000 until 1881, $5,000,000 until 1890.) Massachusetts law also made no provision for the issue of different classes of stock. Any change in the nature of the corporation's business had to be unanimously approved by the stockholders. Massachusetts directors had no power to increase the stock without stockholder permission; any new stock had to be offered to old stockholders, at par. These statutes "plainly envisaged" the corporation as an enterprise of limited scope, "simple in its capital structure," and incapable of "changing its general character" against the opposition of a single shareholder.[23]

For the big corporation, Massachusetts law was plainly out of date; so too were the laws of other stringent states. But the laws were ineffective: they were victims of the national free market in laws. There were states with more hospitable laws. And the easy states no doubt helped sustain the hard states in their resolve. This was a moral division of labor, quite similar to the evolving case of divorce law. Massachusetts might keep its attitude of rectitude, without *actually* interfering with interstate business. Business simply went elsewhere to be chartered. This company then would do business as a "foreign corporation," in Massachusetts. The federal constitution protected it against the worst forms of discrimination.

The law set up few real impediments to migratory headquarters. A few early cases held that a corporation could not be chartered in one state, if it intended to do all of its business in another. But from an equally early date, precisely this was done, and successfully. Hence, the burden of strict statutes fell only on those small corporations which could not afford to escape to some faraway haven. There remained, then, both tough and easy states. Pennsylvania and Ohio were places to steer clear of, in the 1890's. Connecticut "drove from her borders not only foreign enterprises but also

[23] For this analysis of the Massachusetts statutes, see E. Merrick Dodd, "Statutory Developments in Business Corporation Law, 1886–1936," 50 Harv. L. Rev. 27, 31–33 (1936).

her own industries" in 1891, when the state enacted what William W. Cook called an "ill-advised" provision, requiring a majority of the board of directors of Connecticut companies to be residents of the state, and insisting that twenty per cent of the capital stock be paid in cash. New Jersey, a poor but convenient neighbor of New York, became the "favorite state for incorporations." It succeeded in attracting big New York businesses by a combination of low taxes and easy laws. West Virginia, too, became a "Snug Harbor for roaming and piratical corporations," the "tramp and bubble companies of the country." The reason was simple: her laws were loose, and she was exceedingly cheap. Incorporation cost $6; the annual corporation tax was $50. These prices made West Virginia "the Mecca of irresponsible corporations." [24]

Other states flocked to the business of chartering business. They cut their prices and vied with each other with liberal laws. They allowed nonresident directors, and corporate meetings held outside their borders. There was even a profit to be made from low taxes, if volume increased fast enough. In the late 19th century, a group of hungry states changed their laws at the drop of a dollar, and openly advertised for corporate business. Hundreds of corporations flew these flags of convenience. Fashions changed. Maine lost its popularity as a result of a dangerous court decision. New Jersey's corporation act of 1896 outbid all the others; it made New Jersey the "Mother of Trusts." In the first seven months of 1899, 1,336 corporations were "organized under the laws of New Jersey . . . with an authorized capital of over two thousand million dollars." These included the "notorious Whiskey Trust"—the Distilling Company of America—and 61 of 121 "in a list of the existing industrial corporations having stock and bonds exceeding ten million dollars." [25] In 1899, another eager contender, the tiny, sleepy state of Delaware, passed its own act of welcome. It too was vastly successful. Corporations flocked to Delaware, and the phrase "Delaware corporation" passed into the bloodstream of the English language.

No wonder that thoughtful men of gloomy disposition saw no real chance of controlling these creatures, favored by chance, by the iron laws of trade, by the Constitution itself. Corporations were bound to swallow up more and more of the nation's economy.

---

[24] William W. Cook, *A Treatise on Stock and Stockholders, Bonds, Mortgages, and General Corporation Law* (3rd ed., 1894), Vol. II, pp. 1603–05.

[25] Edward Q. Keasbey, "New Jersey and the Great Corporations," 13 Harv. L. Rev. 198, 201 (1899).

The fight against them continued dimly and feebly, reflected in slow-dying restraints, in the *ultra vires* doctrine, in other inherited or invented legal tricks, to keep them honest and small. Basically, however, the corporation had torn free of its past—it was now free to be born, to do and change business, to expand, to contract, to dissolve. Legal emphasis changed: first, to regulation, as we have seen; and, second, to countervailing power. Clearly, the big corporation was a permanent element of economic life. Perhaps this was not all to the bad. "A great consolidated corporation," said Charles Francis Adams in 1888, "can be held to a far stricter responsibility" than "numerous smaller and conflicting corporations." [26]

This was the time, however, when John D. Rockefeller's lawyers put a voting trust together to consolidate holdings in many companies. The *trust* became a household word. The trusts were the bogeymen of the late 1880's; but it was power, not form, that was at issue. Corporations carved up markets; they made treaties with each other; they formed huge and menacing agglomerations. The business frontier seemed as dead as the frontier of Western land. America was a society not of individuals, but of groups, of interrelationships, a seamless web. The remedies were legislation and countertrusts. The time had come for reallocation. All other groups—farmers, workers, small business—formed their trusts, their armies too, asking for a larger or better share, or, at the least, trying to hold on to their own. The aggregations of the business world were a prime cause of the tremendous growth of counteraggregations.

A DISCORDANT ADDENDUM: THE MUNICIPAL CORPORATION

Before Blackstone's day the law of corporations was unitary. Public and private, profit and nonprofit companies—towns, churches, and businesses—all fit in one legal bag. But the branches of law developed in different directions. The private corporation became, as we have seen, ever freer and more flexible. Obviously, towns and cities were not to be treated the same; they remained narrowly regulated and extensively controlled.

In some ways, the two branches walked similar legal roads. Cities, towns and villages were at first incorporated, one by one, by

26 Quoted in William W. Cook, *A Treatise on the Law of Corporations* (5th ed., 1903), Vol. III, p. 2543.

special charter. These were amended, recast, revised, and tinkered with piecemeal. City charters tended to be much alike, but rarely *exactly* the same, even in a single state. This meant that the powers and duties of one city differed in small, irritating, and confusing ways from its neighbors down the road. Also, the legislative burden was appalling. To mend the matter, legislatures passed general laws about cities, just as they passed general corporation laws. These statutes were influenced by an important English act of 1835. Ohio, in 1852, was a pioneer.[27] Iowa, in 1846, was the first state whose constitution told the legislature it might not incorporate cities and towns by special act. Most states had a more or less similar provision by 1900. Constitutions, late in the century, often divided municipalities into classes, depending on the size of the population; to be valid, a law had to apply to an entire class. The Kentucky constitution of 1891 set out six municipal categories. The first class consisted of cities with more than 100,000 population. Towns with less than 1,000 souls made up the sixth (Const. Ky. 1891, sec. 156). Often enough, the state's one big city stood all alone in its class. The set of first-class cities in Wisconsin, for example, had one member only in 1893: Milwaukee. This made it possible, as we have seen, for the legislatures to pinpoint laws exclusively for their big or biggest city.

Early charters and early general statutes (which usually did nothing more than copy and generalize common clauses of city charters) contained a quaint collection of "powers." Wisconsin cities, for example, were given the right to control the "assize of bread." This meant something to a 15th-century borough, but was Greek to midwestern America. The "assize of bread" even cropped up in some charters as the "size of bread"; no one seemed to notice the mistake. Considering how towns and cities grew, municipal powers of the 1840's and 50's seem strangely inadequate. The pioneer Ohio statute (1852) gave cities power to abate nuisances; to regulate "the transportation and keeping of gunpowder or other combustibles"; to "prevent and punish fast or immoderate riding of horses, or driving or propelling of vehicles through the streets"; to establish markets; to provide for the measuring or weighing of "hay, wood, coal, or any other article for sale"; to prevent overloading of streets; to suppress riots, gambling, "houses of ill fame,

[27] Laws Ohio, 1852, p. 223. John F. Dillon, *The Law of Municipal Corporations* (2nd ed., 1873), Vol. I, sec. 20, pp. 121–24. The English statute was "An act to provide for the Regulation of Municipal Corporations in England and Wales," 5 & 6 Wm. IV, ch. 76 (1835).

billiard tables, nine or ten pin alleys or tables, and ball alleys."
There were also powers to "regulate the burial of the dead," provide a water supply, restrain animals from running at large (including dogs), make and maintain streets and sewers, wharves,
"landing places, and market spaces"; regulate vehicles for hire,
taverns, and theatrical exhibitions; provide for "the regular building of houses," and make "regulations for the purpose of guarding
against dangers by fire." This was a long and not unimportant list
of powers; but it was curiously hodgepodge; and obviously, it fell
far short of a general grant of authority to govern. This was, perhaps, yet another case where the growth of society (apparently)
outstripped the capacity of government institutions. But it is possible that the obsolescence of city government was, in a deeper
sense, deliberate. Capacity is infinitely plastic. No one really
wanted to transplant to the prairies the tight reins of a medieval
borough. It was boom-town law which was needed. Again, the
Ohio statute of 1852 is instructive. Many sections of the law dealt
with annexation of surrounding land. The cities of Ohio were not
expected to rule with an iron hand; but they were expected, above
all else, to grow.

City finance, unlike the charters, generated living law. During
the great age of railroad optimism, cities indulged in an orgy of
aid. They wanted the roads, they wanted land values to skyrocket,
and only growth, growth, growth could do the trick. The short-run
results were often disastrous. Many cities spent trough periods of
the business cycle in as bankrupt a state as their railroads and
banks. But still the debts grew; still more bond issues floated. The
indebtedness of cities with a population of 7,500 and more was
$51,000,000 in 1860; the debt of all other local government stood at
no more than $100,000,000. By 1890, local government owed $900,-
000,000.[28] No wonder that a reaction to this aspect of boom-town
psychology set in. Restrictions on municipal debt began to appear
in state constitutions. The Illinois constitution (1870), for example, did not allow any municipal corporation to become indebted "in the aggregate exceeding five per cent on the value of
the taxable property therein" (Const. 1870, art. 9, sec. 12). Provisions like this were very much in the mainstream of American legal
culture: first, insofar as they reacted to power, and abuse of power,
by heaping on more checks and balances; second, in the characteristic cycle—incentives, followed by laws punishing those who rose
too eagerly to the bait.

28 *Two Centuries Growth of American Law,* p. 241.

The restrictions did not reach another problem: corruption in government. The shame of the cities was a byword by 1900. The Tweed ring in New York, in the decade after the Civil War, was only one of many notorious examples. William M. Tweed made an art of graft and corruption; it has been estimated that he and his henchmen stole more than $60,000,000. In his case, domination of the city by the state was ironically inverted; Tweed's influence reached up into Albany, into the legislature, and the governor's office itself.[29] Tweed was overthrown; but New York's troubles were not over. Reform movements came and went; at the end of the century Boss Richard Croker, a latterday Tweed, ruled over a city which, since 1897, had been expanded to include Brooklyn, Richmond, Queens, and the Bronx.

Along with the struggle for municipal reform went a quieter struggle for more municipal self-rule. The major legal innovation, for the cities, in the last quarter of the century, was the concept usually called *home rule*. This appeared first in the Missouri constitution of 1875. Cities of more than 100,000 population had the right to frame their own charters, so long as these did not contravene the laws of the state. California adopted a home-rule provision in its 1879 constitution; as amended in 1890, home rule was available (if the legislature approved) to cities of more than 3,500 population.

One reason for the spread of home rule was similar to the reason why general laws were passed: it eased the legislature burden. The (nonhome-rule) New York statutes of 1873 show many examples of time-consuming trivia: "An act to provide for the regulation and licensing of scavengers in the City of New York," "An Act in relation to a sidewalk from the Village of Albion to Mount Albion Cemetery" and "An act to amend an act entitled 'An Act to authorize the construction of sewers in the village and town of Saratoga Springs' " (chs. 251, 667, 670). It did not make much sense for legislatures to spend their energy on such as these. Nevertheless, legislatures proved surprisingly jealous of their power. They nowhere abdicated final authority to decide what cities could and could not do. Even today, home rule is more an ideal than a reality.

Courts, too, played something of a role in running the cities. Then, as now, courts were the last resort of interests and power groups politically frustrated in local affairs. The growth of the cities in the last half of the century was enormous. So, too, were

[29] See, in general, Alexander B. Callow, Jr., *The Tweed Ring* (1966).

their demands on the time and attention of the higher courts; and the demands of villages, counties, and towns. John F. Dillon, in 1872, wrote the first treatise on local government law, *The Law of Municipal Corporations*. Dillon had served on the supreme court of Iowa, and had seen that "questions relating to the powers, duties, and liabilities of municipalities were presented at almost every term." By 1890, a fourth edition, in two bulky volumes, appeared, reflecting, in its hundreds of pages, the vast expanse of decided cases. What local government did could always be challenged in court—as unconstitutional or as beyond the powers of the municipal corporation. All this was grist for the legal mill.

The results of the cases, mirroring the statutes of their states, were discordantly different from the results in cases about nonpublic corporations. *Ultra vires* never died for municipalities. Charles Beach, in his treatise on public corporations, published in 1893, flatly declared that "Acts of municipal corporations which are done without power expressly granted, or fairly to be implied from the powers granted or incident to the purposes of their creation, are *ultra vires.*" So too were acts of city officials which did not conform to the precise words of their authorization.[30] Cities and villages were limited to the authority given them from above. In literally scores of cases, this authority was closely tested in court, by taxpayers and other sufferers. Someone was always trying to reverse some act of a city or town. It was common to ask an appellate court to decide an issue such as "the validity of a sewer assessment under the sixty-fourth section of the charter of the city of Bayonne [New Jersey]." [31] The end of the period (1870–1900) was not known for the bashfulness of courts. Municipalities no doubt won most of the cases, particularly in the lower courts; but they always faced the delays of trial; and the danger of losing hung over their acts like a black cloud. Judicial review was a strong, sometimes harsh, reality. Often, it had a healthy impact. Local government may have been forced to behave, to conform to the rules, more than otherwise would have been true. But the costs were also high. Most litigants were only interested in themselves, their taxes, their use of land. Lawsuits were couched, of course, in general terms. One disgruntled landowner who attacked an assessment for sewers could, if he won, break a whole brittle scheme of sanitation into bits.

[30] Charles Beach, *Commentaries on the Law of Public Corporations* (Vol. I, 1893), pp. 607–08.
[31] *Central N.J. Land Co.* v. *Mayor of Bayonne*, 56 N.J.L. 297, 28 Atl. 713 (1894).

(CHAPTER IX)

COMMERCE, LABOR, AND TAXATION

CONTRACT

The law of contract occupies a special place in American law in the 19th century. On the one hand, in theory, the whole century was the century of contract. Contract was identified as the single most important hallmark of modern law. Progressive societies, wrote Sir Henry Maine in his pathbreaking book, *Ancient Law* (1861), evolved from status to contract. The ideal way to organize social relations was through free voluntary agreement, by persons pursuing their own ends. This broad meaning of contract was one of the sovereign notions of the 19th century. It was strong in the United States; the Constitution itself protected contract obligations from "impairment" by the states. Probably no constitutional clause, before the Civil War, was the pivot on which so much and such important litigation turned. In the late 19th century, liberty of contract became another constitutional battle cry. It was not only writers on constitutional and political theory who considered the idea of contract fundamental. Contract law was one of the most basic building blocks of courses of law study. (It still is.) C. C. Langdell's first casebook (1871), a milestone in the history of legal education, was a casebook on contracts. To constitutional theorists, free contract was a pillar holding up the palace of ordered liberty; to students and teachers of law, it was the great gate to entry in the palace.

The *idea* of contract may well have been as fundamental to American society as people said it was. But the *concrete* body of law called contract was different and hardly seemed worthy of the fuss. The law of contract was essentially negative. Its doctrines gave more or less free play to individual choice. What people voluntarily agreed with each other, courts undertook to enforce. Beyond this simple principle, there were a great many rules of thumb,

464

on the formation of contracts, on the interpretation of contract, on remedies for breach of contract. Not much of this body of law changed fundamentally between 1847 and 1900—nothing compared to tort law or corporations. Old technicalities had been dismantled long before 1850. What remained was more or less to put the house of contracts in more tidy order, and to express its tendencies in the form of general rules.

If one looks, not to treatises, but to the actual business of the courts, it could be argued that the law of contract, after 1850, was beginning a long slide into triviality. Courts were not equipped to handle business disputes as rapidly and efficiently as a brawling capitalist economy demanded. The doctrines were attractive and necessary; the rules were flexible enough; but judges were judges, not mediators. They named winners and losers. Where parties stood in continuing business relations with each other, they preferred not to litigate at all. They worked their problems out by themselves, or went to arbitration. Moreover, judges simply lacked enough business acumen. They were trained in law, not in business; certainly not in the business details and jargon of a thousand fields. This lack was not immediately apparent. Of 206 contract cases decided by the Wisconsin supreme court, roughly in the decade before 1861, fifty-four dealt with land. Thirty-one were cases of sale; most of these were cases concerning horses, sheep, oxen, and the cash crop, wheat, rather than manufactured goods. The thirty labor cases also arose out of simple situations. There were thirty-one cases on credit and finance, mostly about the ubiquitous bills and notes and their sureties.[1] So far, an intelligent judge could manage very well. He was a landowner or dealer in land himself, no doubt, and what came before him was part of his common experience. As the country industrialized, this was less and less the case. By 1905, the contract docket of the Wisconsin supreme court was very different. A few kinds of transaction were overrepresented—real-estate brokers suing for their commissions, for example. Manufacturers and major merchants had virtually disappeared from the docket, and indeed, they had never been there in any quantity. It is risky to infer the business of lower courts from upper courts; but big companies would have been more likely to appeal a commercial case than small businesses or individuals. It

[1] This discussion is based on Lawrence M. Friedman, *Contract Law in America* (1965). Wisconsin was an agricultural state, first settled in the 1830's. Some of the trends discussed no doubt appeared earlier in New England, later in the prairie states, and the West.

seems reasonable to guess that major business did not use the courts for contract cases in any regular way.

Between 1750 and 1850, the domain of contract law had expanded to include most of the universe of economic transactions. Even leases and deeds were treated, basically, as contracts, or as contractual in nature. Business associations became voluntary compacts, not holders of grants from the state. Yet, like the golden age of tort law, the golden age of contract was marvelously brief. All the rules—damages, offer, and acceptance, parol evidence, interpretation of contracts—frayed noticeably between 1850 and 1900. Since business stayed out of court, what came into court tended to be marginal: special situations, unusual cases. These tempted the judge to do justice in the particular case, for the unique facts before him. It could not be argued that contract law —that is, not the basic ideas, but the doctrines applied by appeal courts—was a vital prop of the booming economy. The cases belied that fact. If so, then why not warp the rules, to do the right thing for *this* litigant? The bulk of the appealed cases, in any event, turned only on their facts or on questions of interpretation. Each one of these stood on its own two feet. Moreover, statutory incursions, after 1850, significantly shrank the kingdom of contract. Every new law on the statute books, if it dealt with the economy, was a cup of water withdrawn from the oceanic domain of the law of contract.

A few new doctrines were invented after 1850 which, on the surface, helped fill in some gaps in classical, free-market contract law. *Lawrence* v. *Fox* (New York, 1859)[2] began the career of the so-called third-party beneficiary contract. Under the doctrine of this case, a person not actually a party to a contract could enforce it, provided the contract was intended to benefit him. So, if A sold a horse to B, and told B, "Pay the money to my creditor, C," creditor C could sue B for the money when B refused or neglected to pay. What had stood in the way of this simple idea was the reluctance of the common law to allow anyone to transfer abstract rights (including rights to collect and to sue) to another, so that the transferee might bring suit on the original claim or right. This reluctance was inconsistent with the world view of the law of contract. Contract had faith in the market; and tended to hold that all interests and values could be transferred and sold.[3]

2 20 N.Y. 268 (1859).

3 The old rule was, moreover, a rule of procedure. It seemed particularly out

The law of damages for breach of contract also developed during this period, almost from nothing. One of the leading cases was English: *Hadley* v. *Baxendale* (1854).[4] A mill had stopped its operations because of a broken crankshaft. The millowner sent for a new shaft. The shaft was delivered by "well-known carriers trading under the name of Pickford & Co." These well-known carriers, however, delivered the crankshaft late. The mill was shut down for a longer time than expected, and the plaintiffs, the millowners, lost some of their profits. But the court refused to let them recover those profits. There was no question that the carriers had breached their contract to carry and deliver. But the plaintiff could recover only those damages which were the "natural consequences" of this breach; and the lost profits, said the court, did not fit in this box. The rule suited the market bias of the law of contracts: no special, personal factors would influence the rational calculus of damages. Damages had to be objective. Some mills—perhaps the more prudent ones—might have had a spare.[5] Then, too, the rule of the case limited the risks the carriers had to run. They were liable only for "natural" consequences—damage they could foresee and take account of. The rule was therefore a way to standardize costs and rationalize enterprise. In this regard, it can be compared with many of the newly grown tort rules. Despite their many differences, tort law and contract law were both tuned to the needs of the growing economy, at least as the leading judges read these needs.

The rule of *Hadley* v. *Baxendale* was eagerly adopted in the states. Indeed, it was anticipated there; in *Brayton* v. *Chase*,[6] for example, decided in Wisconsin in the same year (1854), a farmer ordered a "New York reaper," to be delivered before the first of July. It was not delivered in time. Brayton, the farmer, claimed he lost his "large crops of winter and spring grain." But for these he

of date in the period of the Field Code, which allowed lawsuits to be freely brought by those who had a real interest in the outcome.

4 9 Ex. 341 (1854).

5 Another rule of damages also required the man on the short end of breach of contract to show the market price before he could recover damages; what he could collect was the difference between contract and market. "It follows from this rule, that, if, at the time fixed for the delivery, the article has not risen in value, the vendee having lost nothing can recover nothing." Theodore Sedgwick, *A Treatise on the Measure of Damages* (2nd ed., 1852), p. 260. Only economic damages—never punitive damages—were recoverable. Breach of contract was not a wrong, not a tort.

6 3 Wis. 456 (1854).

could collect no damages. Crop losses, said the court, were "too remote" a consequence of Chase's delay. They resulted "rather from the particular situation of the plaintiff than from the breach of the contract."

These doctrines were not abandoned, even as the legal climate changed. The way they were phrased made them tents rather than cages. Application was all. *Hadley* v. *Baxendale,* for example, spoke of "natural consequences." It was for the court to say what was natural and what was not. By 1900, the actual results of cases were shifting subtly away from the hard line of the 1850's. The sternness of the cases was seriously warped. The temple of doctrine still stood firm (its architects were completing details of decoration), while the termites worked busily underneath.

NEGOTIABLE INSTRUMENTS

The law of bills, notes, checks, and certificates of deposit came from the law merchant by way of England, was modified in America, and stabilized and somewhat Anglified by decisions and scholarly writings before 1850. This branch of law was of tremendous importance in the 19th century. Before 1864, bank notes were the chief circulating currency. Both before and after the 1860's, personal promissory notes were the chief American instrument of debt and credit. Because of its key position, the note generated endless possibilities for lawsuits and disputes. As we have seen, lawyers, particularly in the West, spent much of their time collecting debts in the form of personal paper. The law of bills and notes was oil without which the business machine could not run. Courts after the war continued to be clogged with questions of negotiability and transfer. This was indeed a living body of law. In *The Century Edition of the American Digest,* covering reported cases up to 1896, the topic "Bills and Notes" occupied virtually an entire volume, about 2,700 pages, a tremendous bulk few other legal topics could match.

It was a living body of law, moreover, with an ideology of change. Law was supposed to follow the custom of the business public. And in truth, the law was often supple and inventive. The bill of lading became a railroad document, shedding its saltwater past, as cases in the 1850's already attest. The certified check, a weak infant in the 1840's, barely mentioned in treatises as late as the late 1860's, had become a lusty addition to the corpus of negotiable instruments by 1870. Business invented it, without let or hindrance from the courts. Justice Swayne, in a Supreme Court case in 1871, expressed this philosophy: "By the law merchant of this country the certificate of the bank that a check is good is equivalent to acceptance. . . . The practice of certifying checks has grown out of the business needs of the country. . . . [T]he average daily amount of such checks in use in the city of New York, throughout the year, is not less than one-hundred millions of dollars. We could hardly inflict a severer blow upon the commerce and business of the country than by throwing a doubt on their validity." [7]

Courts had more trouble with municipal and corporate bonds. Should these be treated as negotiable, the same as ordinary bills and notes? And how strict should courts be in deciding whether these bonds were completely valid? These were important policy questions. If a bond were negotiable, once transferred it cut off any defects in the original transaction. There were conflicts of interest, between the issuer, the original investors, and any later ones. Later investors were, quite often, banks and financial interests, perhaps those who invested through the Eastern money market. The original holders were, sometimes, farmer-speculators, townspeople, small-scale gullibles. In some states, statutes settled the issue in favor of negotiability. In general, the courts, too, with some vacillation, gave these bonds the magic password of negotiability. In so doing, they disregarded—in the words of Justice Robert C. Grier— the "epidemic insanity of the people, the folly of county officers, the knavery of railroad 'speculators.'" They favored, rather, the "malleability" of the bonds, to "suit the necessities and usages of the mercantile and commercial world." The need for a free, open capital market, with no second thoughts about bond issues, was paramount. "Mere technical dogma . . . cannot prohibit the commercial world from inventing or using any species of security not known in the last century." [8]

The issue in the case which evoked Grier's eloquence turned on the status of bonds of Mercer County, Pennsylvania. The county issued the bonds, in order to subscribe for stock in a thievish railroad, the Pittsburgh and Erie. Some of the bonds came into the hands of a certain Hacket, "a citizen of New Hampshire," and a purchaser (in law at least) in good faith. The county wanted to

[7] *Merchants' National Bank of Boston* v. *State National Bank of Boston*, 77 U.S. 604, 647–48 (1871).

[8] Grier, J., in *Mercer County* v. *Hacket*, 68 U.S. 83, 95–96 (1864).

renege, claiming irregularities in the issue. The Supreme Court refused. As this case indicates, courts usually favored the good-faith purchaser for value, despite any minor blemishes in the bonds.

Occasionally, the swindle or scandal was so great that the legislature took a stand on bonds or notes. The farm-mortgage crisis of Wisconsin, in the 1850's and 1860's, was one of these occasions. To save farms from foreclosure (and keep the farm voters from political revolt), the legislators boldly attacked the negotiability of notes that the farmers had given in exchange for railroad stock, and which were secured by mortgages on the farmers' farms. The stock had become worthless in the aftermath of the crash of 1857. Meanwhile, notes and mortgages had been sold in the Eastern money market. If the notes were not negotiable, despite appearances, then the farmer's "equities" survived; and the farmers could defend themselves in any action to forceclose, by claiming fraud or mistake. An act of 1858 prohibited the holder of the note from alleging that he was a (legally) innocent purchaser. The point was obvious. The transaction would go to a friendly Wisconsin jury, and the farmer would win; the whole transaction would then be set aside, and Wisconsin's farms would be saved. The Wisconsin supreme court, however, in defiance of popular pressure, refused to enforce this statute, and a series of later ones with a similar goal in mind.[9]

In almost all the states, crisis or no, statutes aided, hindered, or muddled commercial law, by tinkering with some of the rules of commercial paper.[10] The statutes ranged from a few trifling, standard provisions, postponing the maturity date of an instrument to Monday if it fell due on Sunday, to complete codes. California, for example, adopted a whole code on negotiable instruments in 1872, consisting of 117 sections, copied from a code that David Dudley Field had proposed for New York. Six Western states later adopted the same set of provisions. Almost every state had a statute abolishing the antiquated custom of days of grace. Of the harvest of laws, some were for the specific benefit of the commercial community; others were passed for the benefit of some special-interest group. Some states made usurious notes totally void, and did the same for notes given for gambling debts. This meant that no one, not even a good-faith holder, could collect on a note that suffered from these original sins. Other states protected the good-faith purchaser, de-

---

[9] See Robert S. Hunt, *Law and Locomotives* (1958), pp. 48–50.

[10] See, in general, Frederick Beutel, "The Development of State Statutes on Negotiable Paper Prior to the Negotiable Instruments Law," 40 Columbia L.R. 836 (1940).

spite this taint.[11] In a few states, for example Ohio, a note given for "the right to make, use, or vend a patent invention," had to bear on its face the words "given for a patent right"; and any holder of the note was "subject to the same defenses as . . . the original owner" [12]—all this to help stamp out a common rural swindle.[13]

Commercial law was a field for which the businessman saw the value of uniformity in legal rules. This attitude, happily, meshed with the professional jurists' passion to "reform" law in the direction of innocuous consistency. Business practice had helped weld (and keep) together the law of commercial paper and the law of commerce by sea. This law carried over into the inland empire, where it worked almost equally well. But naturally there were differences from state to state. A report of the American Bar Association, in 1891, complained that there were "fifty different languages" of law. The businessman had a right to ask why "the meaning and effect of a promissory note" should not be "as certain and definite" in all states "as the meaning of words in an American dictionary." "Variance, dissonance, contradiction" caused "perplexity, uncertainty and damage." [14]

No wonder, then, that one of the first fruits of the movement for uniformity was a commercial statute. John J. Crawford drafted a Negotiable Instruments Law, on instructions from the Conference of Commissioners on Uniformity of Laws, which met in Detroit in 1895.[15] Crawford relied heavily on the British Bills of Exchange Act (1882) and, as Professor Beutel has shown, on the California Code of 1872.[16] The NIL was the first of the "uniform laws," and one of the most successful. Its form was significant. The act, in general, did not pretend to bring about any real innovations. Its sections were short, clean, and polished. Most of its rules were already commonly accepted, either as businessmen's norms or as established courtroom doctrine. It cleaned the façade of the law of commercial paper, without much real change underneath. Still, no one had demanded anything more.

11 John Daniel, *A Treatise on the Law of Negotiable Instruments* (5th ed., 1903), Vol. I, pp. 223–25, sec. 197.

12 Rev. Stats. Ohio 1880, sec. 3178.

13 See "State Interference with Patent Rights," 16 Albany L. J. 360 (1877). These statutes were passed in the 1870's; for example, Laws N.Y. 1877, ch. 65.

14 "Report of the Committee on Uniform State Laws," *Report, 14th Ann. Meeting ABA* (1891), pp. 365, 371.

15 John J. Crawford, *Negotiable Instruments Law* (1897), pref.

16 Beutel, *op. cit.*, p. 851.

THE LAW OF SALES

In general, commercial law showed a nice regard for what business required. Courts were willing to meet and accept evolution in business practice—so long as no oversensitive nerve, of politics or legal tradition, was touched. By the end of the century, however, consumer interests had begun to be urged more strongly in court; and these, of course, interfered with the classic purity of the law. A case in point was the law of sales. It was well formulated by mid-century. It had attained the dignity of a special field of law, following a series of classic English cases. One of its key concepts was "title"; title determined who bore the risk of loss. But subtle nuances of doctrine allowed sellers to keep their security interest in goods, even when the risk (and the "title") had shifted.

Overall, the case law showed some bias in favor of the seller—manufacturer or merchant. The maxim *caveat emptor* flattered the manhood and pride of the judges. In California, in 1850, as we saw, the maxim was evoked by the legislative committee that recommended that the common law, in general, be put in force in the state. The committee contrasted it with the flabby solicitude of civil law. But by 1888, Edmund H. Bennett wrote in his treatise on sales that *caveat emptor* was a rule with "many limitations." These were cast in the form of "exceptions," but they really amounted to "independent rules and principles." [17] Courts had the inveterate habit of deciding individual cases individually. The rule of *caveat emptor* was clean, abstract, general, but harsh. The rise of a mass-production market further sapped the vitality of the rule. Its form was against it, in an age that professed a humanitarian *style*. There was rapid growth of the concept of implied warranty. Sales by sample "implied" a warranty that the bulk would conform to the sample. When goods were sold "by description," without inspection, courts implied a warranty of "merchantability." This meant that the goods were not to be "so inferior as to be unsalable among merchants or dealers in the article." Also, if a buyer bought for a "particular use made known to the seller," and relied on the seller's judgment to select the goods, there was an implied warranty that the goods were "reasonably fit and suitable for that purpose." When a seller, for example, sold "Wilcox's Superphosphate,"

[17] Edmund H. Bennett, American edition of Judah P. Benjamin's *Law of Sale of Personal Property* (1888), p. 623.

a fertilizer or guano, to a farmer, the guano had to be "merchantable"; and it had to fertilize at least reasonably well. If this was not the case, the buyer had a cause of action for breach of implied warranty.[18]

These implied warranties were especially suited to manufactured goods. Indeed, courts developed the implied warranties furthest, for manufacturers; frequently, it was held that these rules did not extend to dealers. So, for example, an Illinois case of 1877, for breach of warranty on the sale of "200 barrels of mess pork," distinguished between a manufacturer and "a mere dealer in produce," who "professed to be selling for other parties." [19] For manufacturers, at least, these implied warranties threatened to destroy the rule of *caveat emptor*. By 1900, the *results* of the cases (if not the way their doctrines were phrased) probably did not differ much from the outcomes supposedly produced by the bleeding heart of civil law. Law had come, more and more, to favor the consumer interest. But the consumer in question was not the ordinary man, the people whom Ralph Nader now champions. The consumer of 1890 or 1900 was the small merchant or farmer who opposed the manufacturer in court. The courts were avidly middle class in their outlook. Their shift in emphasis meant less catering to big business, more attention to small.[20]

In the factory years, after the Civil War, goods were more and more produced in mass. Some of these were as small and trivial as the nails Adam Smith used as examples; others were expensive hard goods. The seller needed security, unless he sold for cash. He needed devices that would do for reapers, pianos, and sewing machines what the mortgage did for land. The conditional sale was

---

[18] See *Gammell* v. *Gunby & Co.*, 52 Ga. 504 (1874).

[19] *Chicago Packing & Provision Co.* v. *Tilton*, 87 Ill. 547 (1877).

[20] The actual history, of course, was exceedingly complex. For example, breach of warranty, whether express or implied, is a species of absolute liability. Fault or negligence has nothing to do with the matter. But a line of cases, exemplified by *Hoe* v. *Sanborn*, 21 N.Y. 552 (1860), seemed to veer off in another direction. The goods here were circular saws; and the "alleged defect" came in part from the unsuitableness of the material of which the saws were made. The judge, Samuel L. Selden, in the course of an intelligent opinion, seemed to make the manufacturer's *negligence* an issue. Some cases followed this hint. It would have been logical, perhaps, as a way out of the dilemma posed by the fact that *caveat emptor* was too harsh, and *caveat venditor* still premature. Tort and warranty law could have merged. But the courts, in general, reflected their uncertainty of ideology, and conflicting interests from the outside world. The outcome was uncertainty in doctrine, and the disparity between doctrine and result, mentioned in the text.

one such device. Under a conditional-sale contract, title to the goods did not pass to the buyer until he paid in full. Many early contracts, attested by cases, were "inartistically drawn." In a New Jersey case, Gustave Wetzel bought (in 1876) "one Domestic sewing machine," for $55. He paid $15 down, and gave a note "payable in installments of five dollars a month." The machine was to remain the "property" of the seller until "actually paid for in cash." [21] In some states, local law was hostile to the conditional sale. In these states, sellers generally used a chattel mortgage—a type of mortgage, specially adapted for personal property. In Pennsylvania, where conditional sales were void, still another device was used— the bailment lease.[22] Goods were "leased" to the buyer, who agreed to pay on installments; after he paid "rent" for so many months, full ownership of the goods would pass to him.

Gradually these devices became standardized, routine. They cropped up as form contracts, in cases on the marketing of soda fountains, pianos, and reapers, foreshadowing the sale "on time" of automobiles, television sets, and golf clubs in the 20th century. After a while, the three security devices became almost indistinguishable. It was another example of the principle that nothing— neither small specks of technicality nor large stains of legal logic and jargon—was allowed to interfere in the 19th century with what judges or the dominant public saw as the highroad to progress and wealth. Court decisions did not create economic conditions, trends, and business practices: rather, it was these which made decisions and laws. There *were* differences in statutes and doctrines; consequently, security devices had different names, different blanks for buyers to fill out, different dotted lines to sign. But basically all devices came out the same in the end. The pressures to buy and sell on credit were strong; the resistance of lawmakers was absent or transient or weak.

THE USURY LAWS

Installment sales were a triumph of marketing over small qualms and slight technicalities. The usury laws responded differently to pressure. They were an almost uncanny barometer of shifts in the political and economic demand for money.

[21] *Cole* v. *Berry,* 42 N.J. Law 308 (1880).
[22] See "Bailments and Conditional Sales," 44 Am. Law Reg. 335, 336 (1896); *Goss Printing Press Co.* v. *Jordan,* 171 Pa. St. 474, 32 Atl. 1031 (1895).

Usury laws were part of the legal inheritance; they were of medieval origin, and fraught with moral and religious overtones. Almost every state had some kind of law placing a ceiling on interest rates. In the late 18th and early 19th century, almost for the first time, men began to question the premises on which these laws were based. Jeremy Bentham attacked them as economically unwise, and as an interference with liberty. "No man of ripe years and of sound mind, acting freely, and with his eyes open, ought to be hindered . . . from making such bargain, in the way of obtaining money, as he thinks fit." [23] There were, he thought, no good reasons why government should fix the price of money, any more than that it should fix the price of bread. On both sides of the Atlantic, this argument for free trade in money was heard; and it seemed to be fairly persuasive. A number of states—first Alabama, then Indiana, then Wisconsin and California—repealed their usury laws before 1860, and experimented with interest rates fixed solely by the market. There was vigorous debate about the usury laws. Much of it, in the legislature halls, rode on a high plane of rhetoric and policy. Typically, a chorus of frogs on one side quoted Jeremy Bentham, and invoked the slogans of free trade; the chorus on the other side used the Bible as its handbook.

When one peels away the layers of rhetoric, a number of striking facts emerge. By and large it was economic interest, not ideology, that called the tune. First, statutory interest rates varied tremendously from state to state. In the West, where hard money was scarce, statutes allowed far higher rates than in the East; penalties for usury tended to be softer. This suggests that states raised their rates to a point where they would not interfere *too* much with the money supply of farmers and dealers in land. States that abolished usury laws generally did so at the end of their territorial period, or at the very beginning of statehood. At this point in a state's career, the government dumped public lands on the market, at a relatively favorable price. Squatters and speculators needed money for cash down-payments. The land was a bargain; money was not. It was vital to relax interest rates, and attract money from the East, even at high rates, to cash in on the bargain price of land. There is evidence that usury laws were repealed precisely in response to this pressure of settlers. In 1849, for example, a large part of Wisconsin's population consisted of farmers, squatting on government land. They needed cash desperately, to buy their land. The state, not surprisingly, repealed its usury laws. The following year, Cali-

[23] Jeremy Bentham, *Defence of Usury* (3rd ed. 1816), p. 2.

fornia, another new state, did the same. Typically, too, the free-trade period was short. At the next downswing of the business cycle (when land values fell, debts became burdensome, and foreclosures threatened), the same people who had begged for money at any price denounced those who had come in with satchels of money, as evil usurers; and the legislatures thundered forth new, stringent usury laws.[24] The usury laws, in short, were as volatile as prices and credit; the high-minded, Benthamite debate was largely, though not wholly, a façade. In 1851, when the great need for money was over, Wisconsin repealed its repeal. And depressions, in general, caused states to toughen their usury laws, because of the clamor of debtors.

In the 1870's, a movement to repeal the usury laws appeared in the industrial East. The movement made some inroads. On the whole, though, usury was the farmer's problem for most of the century. He needed mortgage money. Later, the urban wage earner, borrowing small amounts for consumption or purchase, moved to the center of the stage. The Granger battle cries about high-interest rates—and the demands for stringent laws, low rates, and government regulation of "loan sharks"—were taken over by the labor unions. But little change took place in the law before 1900. The free-trade argument against usury was dead; and the new war against city loan sharks had not reached a sharp enough focus to breed much fresh legislation.

INSURANCE

As we have seen, no business was such a prime subject of legal regulation as insurance. The courts played a minor role in regulating insurance. Even litigation about claims was infrequent, it seems, until late in the century. There were perhaps as few as one hundred reported cases on life insurance down to 1870.[25] These were appellate cases only, but they suggest that trial litigation was also less dense than in the next generation. Fire and marine insurance, of course, were more heavily represented in the cases. By the time of the 1890's, appellate decisions on insurance law had mushroomed. In the West Company's *Century Digest*, briefing all re-

24 See, in general, Lawrence M. Friedman, "The Usury Laws of Wisconsin: A Study in Legal and Social History," 1963 Wis. L. Rev. 515.

25 Morton Keller, *The Life Insurance Enterprise, 1885–1910* (1963), pp. 187 ff., is the source of this statement and much of the following paragraph.

ported cases down to 1896, the heading "Insurance" covers 2,808 pages. This great bulk suggests an absolute increase in lawsuits on all levels; and also that the companies, now engaged in aggressive marketing, were more inclined to contest suits than they had been. It also suggests that the general public was steadily buying more insurance; and that an active bar, working in some cases on a contingent fee, was helping the public in claims cases.

Insurance litigation developed along interesting lines. Lawyers for the companies drafted stiffer and stiffer clauses; yet courts and juries often found ways to stretch the language of insurance policies to allow a widow's life-insurance claim, or the claim of a man whose house or store had burned down. It has even been suggested that company lawyers performed an "overservice" for their clients. Their clauses, strict beyond the general norms of fairness, "exaggerating warranties to the point where they were almost one hundred percent protection against claims," were partially responsible for a "public atmosphere" against the companies; and for decisions and laws that disfavored enterprise, putting them in a position "worse . . . than . . . any other contracting party." [26]

In claims cases, courts faced concrete human situations, and often their sympathies showed. In many trials, the heart of the issue was whether what the insured stated in his application, or his policy, constituted a "warranty" or not. If the statements were "warranties," and were wrong—lies or mistakes—the policy was no more than a scrap of paper. But even if the insured had been a trifle larcenous or foolish, it was after all on his grieving family that the loss really fell; and an uninsured business or home, burnt to the ground, seemed a high price to pay for a little concealment. Chief Justice Ryan of Wisconsin spoke of the "crafty conditions with which fire insurance companies fence in the rights of the assured, and the subtle arguments which their counsel found upon them." The companies, he felt, acted almost as if their "single function" was to collect their premiums, running "little or no risk." [27] Hence courts resisted the full logic of the concept of warranty. They went to great lengths to hold that misstatements were only "representations," even when the policy said in black and white that all of its statements were warranties. A typical case was *Rogers* v. *Phoenix Ins. Co.* (1890),[28] where a "one-story, shingle-

---

[26] Thomas I. Parkinson, law professor and insurance executive, quoted in Keller, *op. cit.*, p. 190.

[27] Quoted in Spencer Kimball, *Insurance and Public Policy* (1960), p. 211.

[28] 121 Ind. 570, 23 N.E. 498 (1890).

roof, frame building," owned by Edward and Mary Rogers, burnt down. When they applied for insurance, they had said the house was fifteen years old. The policy stated that "every statement . . . is a warranty . . . and if any false statements are made, this policy shall be void." The company argued (among other things) that the house was 20 years old, and the policy therefore void. The court held the statement was only a "representation," and, since it did not "render the risk more hazardous," the policy stood firm.[29]

Not that the companies always lost. Some of the insured *did* lie, and thus concealed facts that increased the risk. Some litigants were blocked by language so clear that it passed the limits of interpretation; judges were willing to transmute the sense of English words, but only up to a point. The case law, as in industrial accident law, was therefore chaotic and complex. No one could predict the outcome of a major lawsuit. Uncertainty invited more lawsuits. The insurance contract, especially insurance on lives, is not an enduring pact between persons who habitually interact. It is drawn up for one violent end. No single claim is worth the company's while to pay. Nor is the goodwill of the company enough reason for a widow to give up her claim on her husband's policy, when the company refuses to pay. So the companies, though they often settled, also often fought; and so, too, did the insured and their survivors.

Meanwhile, states passed a torrent of statutes. Every aspect of the business was touched on by law. Some statutes plainly tried to benefit the companies, some the policyholders; some compromised the interests of the two. On balance, however, regulation was unfriendly to the companies. Wisconsin, for example, passed a law in 1870 requiring fire and marine insurance companies to keep strong reserves. The companies could not distribute profits until they had set aside "a sum equal to 100 percent of the premiums on unexpired policies." [30] A Nebraska law (1889) required companies to pay off fire, tornado, and lightning insurance, at the value asserted by the policy, which was to be "taken conclusively to be the true value," when the property was "wholly destroyed." Brokers and agents had to be licensed in Nebraska. Pages of closely knit prose

[29] Similar results were reached by statute, for example, in Missouri: "No misrepresentation made in [a life-insurance policy] . . . shall be deemed material, or render the policy void, unless the matter misrepresented . . . actually contributed to the contingency or event in which the policy is to become due and payable, and whether it so contributed in any case, shall be a question for the jury." Rev. Stats. Mo. 1879, sec. 5976.

[30] Kimball, *op. cit.,* p. 150.

in the statute books, before 1900, described the duties and obligations of the companies. Insurance companies were identified with two major devils: aggregated capital and foreign (that is, out-of-state) corporations (which most of them were). This made the companies all the more vulnerable, and contributed to the dense texture of regulation.

The companies contested many of these regulatory laws in court. They were not very often successful. One estimate is that the courts, between 1890 and 1908, found only one per cent of 2,000 statutes unconstitutional. *Paul* v. *Virginia* (1869)[31] was a famous defeat. A Virginia law (of 1866) required foreign insurance companies to get a license. The license was conditioned on the deposit of bonds with the treasurer of Virginia. Paul was agent for various New York companies (New York was "foreign" from the Virginia standpoint). The Supreme Court held that insurance was not "commerce"; thus, the federal government did not have exclusive jurisdiction. The federal government had never shown any inclination to regulate insurance. Hence, the decision threw the companies back to the howling wolves of the states.

These wolves, to be sure, could often be tamed by judicious lobbying. But insurance companies were, like railroads, unusually subject to hostile, local legislation. Sometimes it took the form of laws favoring mutuals and fraternals over stock companies. Foreign (out-of-state) companies had a particular cross to bear. State laws discriminated against them, taxed them more heavily than locals, sometimes tried to drive them altogether out of the state. There was some merit to the argument that out-of-state companies were irresponsible and hard to police. But the zeal of in-state companies, eager to get rid of competition, may have been the real force behind many of these laws.

The Standard Fire Insurance Policy of Wisconsin, enacted in 1895, can be taken as a symbol of how far the state intervened in the business of insurance. Here was a whole policy, cast in the form of a law, down to very small details—no more than 25 pounds of gunpowder could be kept on premises insured against fire; and "benzine, benzole, dynamite, ether, fireworks, gasoline, greekfire . . . naptha, nitro-glycerine" were prohibited.[32] One insurance man saw in this Standard Policy the dragon of "socialism," which had "upreared its head" in the quiet precincts of Madison, Wisconsin. But if so, it was a strange sort of socialism. Before the policy

31 75 U.S. 168 (1869).
32 Laws Wis. 1895, ch. 387.

was enacted, the insurance commissioner had talked the matter over with merchants; he had looked at and made use of a form, current among companies in New York. The standard policy was a compromise. In many regards, it was quite hard on the buyer of insurance. The company had the right to cancel, with five days' notice; the insured had to file burdensome proofs of loss within sixty days of his fire. The freedom of the companies was narrowed, to be sure; but regulation was balanced by standardization (business liked that) and a voice for the regulated in the regulatory process. In both regards, the companies were by means total losers.[33]

BANKRUPTCY

The last half of the 19th century brought an old dream to reality: a national bankruptcy act. Between 1841 and 1867, there was no federal law at all. The old bankruptcy law had been repealed. The states filled in with insolvency laws, stay laws, exemption laws. In 1867, a bankruptcy law was passed, though by the merest hair, over bitter opposition. The law proposed to allow both voluntary and involuntary bankruptcy. Controversially, anyone (not merely a "trader") could be forced into bankruptcy. This meant, according to the opposition, that the "free and easy but honest and true men of the West," the "farmers and merchants," could be "squeezed" into a "straitjacket" more "befitting the madmen of Wall Street." On the other hand, it could be argued that precisely the small debtor would benefit from this part of the act. Apparently, some Northern creditors hoped to use the bankruptcy law to reclaim at least a pittance from ruined debtors in the South. They felt that only a federal law, federally administered, would stave off the state laws granting stays and exemptions, and keep the prejudices of Southern juries at bay.[34]

Whatever its proponents hoped, the act was a failure in operation. It was cumbersome, badly administered, corruptly applied. The costs of proceedings consumed immense amounts of money; after lawyers and administrators had taken their toll, many creditors were left with nothing but crumbs. It was, of course, an age of shaky credit. The act hung like a sword of Damocles over the heads

[33] On the history of the standard policy, see Kimball, *op. cit.,* pp. 230–32.
[34] See Charles Warren, *Bankruptcy in United States History* (1935), pp. 104 ff.

of the merchants. Many were afraid some coldhearted creditor would push them into bankruptcy. The fear was not irrational, particularly since the Supreme Court (1871) construed "insolvency" to mean not only lack of assets to pay debts, but also inability to pay debts as they became due in the ordinary course of business.[35] The panic of 1873 did not convince a doubtful Congress that the act was needed. Quite to the contrary, hard times brought a mad urge to repeal. The House killed the act in a frantic hurry (1874). The Senate, however, gave the law a reprieve. They added, too, a provision for "composition." Debtors might propose a plan for gradually settling their debts, over a period of years. If a "majority in number and three-fourths in value" of the creditors accepted the plan, at a composition meeting, the plan would go into effect and be enforceable at law.[36] Other provisions, too, were designed to ease some of the problems of debtors that had arisen under the bankruptcy law. The 1874 amendments did not end criticism, however. Some of the amendments turned out maladroit, if not downright vicious. The law lasted four more years; in 1878, it was finally repealed. Once more there was no national bankruptcy act.

But the federal law was scarcely cold again in its grave when a movement began to revive it. This time, the movement was helped by those segments of business and legal opinion which favored uniform, national laws of commerce and trade. Politically, the influence of farmers waned and commercial influence grew. Samuel Wagner, in a report (1881) to the American Bar Association, called for a "National Bankrupt Law." The very impermanence of the prior laws had been their greatest fault, Wagner thought. These laws had been "like so many sponges"; they "wiped off a vast amount of hopeless debts," and gave everybody "a clean slate with which to start afresh"; they were temporary "physic," administered in one large dose; "brief and spasmodic efforts," quickly repealed. What was needed was a permanent, national law, "in the nature of a regimen of diet and exercise." Partly "restrictive and partly remedial," such a law might "tend to prevent rather than to cure disease," in its "even and continuous operation." [37] A young St. Louis lawyer, Jay L. Torrey, drafted a bankruptcy bill in 1890,

---

[35] Warren, *op. cit.*, pp. 113–14.

[36] 18 Stats., Part III, 178, 182 (act of June 22, 1874, sec. 17).

[37] Samuel Wagner, "The Advantages of a National Bankrupt Law," *Report, 4th Ann. Meeting ABA* (1881), pp. 223, 227–28.

under the stimulus of conventions of national commercial organizations, held in St. Louis and Minneapolis in 1889.[38] The Torrey bill met bitter opposition—by Southern and Western debtors, for example. These interests preferred to trust their own legislatures, which might enact sweeping delay or debt cancellation laws. One Southern orator called the proposed law a "crushing and damnable instrumentality," an "infernal engine of ruin," the "last screw in the coffin of liberty," a plot to deliver "farmers, laborers, debtors, or small dealers" into the "soulless cupidity of a Shylock." [39] But even the South was generally in favor of *voluntary* bankruptcy.

The panic of 1893 lent arguments to both sides. Debate in Congress was sharp and prolonged. Finally, in 1898, the law was passed: "to establish a uniform system of bankruptcy throughout the United States." [40] This act was long and carefully drawn. Under the law (sec. 4a), "any person who owes debts, except a corporation," was "entitled to the benefits of this Act as a voluntary bankrupt." Involuntary bankruptcy could not be forced upon "a wage-earner or a person engaged chiefly in farming or the tillage of the soil" (sec. 4b). The act carefully did not disturb "exemptions which are prescribed by the State laws in force at the time of the filing of the petition," in the state where the bankrupt was domiciled (sec. 6). The law granted special priority, over other debts, to "wages due to workmen, clerks, or servants," if "earned within three months before the date of the commencement of proceedings, not to exceed three hundred dollars to each claimant"; priorities granted under state law were recognized, though given lesser rank than the specific federal priorities (sec. 64). Though no one could know it at the time, this bankruptcy act was not to suffer the fate of its predecessors. It survived the passage of time. It is still in force (with changes), and repeal has become completely inconceivable. The age of the "temporary physic" ended in 1898.

ADMIRALTY

Admiralty was a fairly pure body of merchant's law. Federal control was guaranteed by the Constitution itself. After the *Genessee*

38 Warren, *op. cit.*, p. 134.
39 Quoted in Warren, p. 136.
40 30 Stats. 544 (act of July 1, 1898).

Chief (1851),[41] federal admiralty law, as we have seen, sailed proudly on the Great Lakes as well as on coastal waters. For rules on navigation and maritime collisions, Congress still looked overseas. In 1864, Congress adopted, practically verbatim, the English code of navigation rules, of 1863.[42] In 1890, Congress enacted the International Rules, "regulations for preventing collisions at sea," for "all public and private vessels upon the high seas and in all waters connected therewith, navigable by seagoing vessels." These were rules about lights, sound signals for fog, steering and sailing rules, and distress signals. The Inland Rules (1897), which also dealt with lights, signals, steering, and sailing, applied to "harbors, rivers, and inland waters of the United States." [43]

Rules of admiralty law, in general, seemed to reflect the merchants' ideas about splitting and compromising loss. In case of accident, where both sides, or neither side, were at fault, both were to share in the loss. If, for example, a ship and its cargo stood "in a common imminent peril," and the captain had to sacrifice some cargo, to save the ship and the rest of the cargo, the owner of the lost goods had the right to make ship and cargo share in his loss; this ancient principle was called *general average*. The classic case was jettison—throwing cargo overboard to lighten the load. But general average was widely applied in the 19th century—for example, to cases where the crew doused and damaged part of the cargo with water, to put out a fire in the hold.[44] The rules of general average thus looked very different from the official rules of tort law, tilted so heavily in favor of one side.

Admiralty law was also kinder to the sailor than tort law was to the miner, brakeman, and machinist. A sailor was entitled to "maintenance" and "cure"; that is, if he fell sick or was injured in service, he had a right to medical care, living expenses and wages at least to the end of the voyage. Was he entitled to more—to damages for negligence? The chief cook on a steamship, sailing to Vera Cruz from New York, by way of Havana, in 1879, was ordered to fetch some ice from the ice closets, to pack the corpse of a person who died on board. On his way, in the night, he fell "through the hatch into the hold below, and received considerable personal injury." He was "cared for at the expense of the ship," and got his

41 12 How. 443 (1851).
42 See Robert M. Hughes, *Handbook of Admiralty Law* (1901), p. 212.
43 26 Stats. 320 (act of Aug. 19, 1890); 30 Stats. 96 (act of June 7, 1897).
44 *The Roanoke,* 59 Fed. 161 (C.C.A. 7, 1893).

full wages. But he also claimed "additional compensation"—$10,-000—"for his permanent injuries and consequential damages, on the ground of the negligence of the officers in leaving the hatch open through which he fell." The federal court denied this claim. They found no warrant for the action in the "sea laws": and the "recognized authorities on maritime law." The liability of the ship was absolute, but limited; neither negligence nor contributory negligence made any difference, either in inflating or deflating the rights of the injured man.[45] This was the kind of compromise that the factory worker would eventually achieve, but some thirty years later, in the form of workmen's compensation.

Meanwhile, the Harter Act, passed by Congress in 1893, excused the "owner of any vessel transporting merchandise or property," from "damage or loss resulting from faults or errors in navigation, or in the management" of the ship, or for "losses arising from dangers of the sea . . . acts of God, or public enemies," so long as the owner had exercised "due diligence" in making his ship "in all respects seaworthy and properly manned, equipped, and supplied." [46] The concept of "seaworthiness" was to prove as plastic as that of "negligence." This long voyage was still ahead of it. There were strong parallels between admiralty and tort law, despite their traditional differences. Even the loss-splitting concept, so foreign to the common law, was perhaps more a difference in style than in substance. Admiralty, after all, had no jury. What the jury did secretly, in the holds and fastnesses of its chamber, admiralty judges had to accomplish aboveboard, on open deck.

LABOR AND LAW

The labor problem—the problem of industrial relations—was practically speaking of major legal importance only after the Civil War. The basic component was the landless, class-conscious urban worker. European society confronted the working man much earlier. In 1848, Europe was in upheaval; the antirent agitations of New York were feeble parodies of European revolution, and involved farmers at that. Communism, the specter that haunted Europe, did not trouble much American sleep. The American version of class struggle came only later. After 1860, the rich got richer and expanded their factories, mines, and banks. The poor had children;

45 *The City of Alexandria,* 17 Fed. 390 (D.C.S.D. N.Y., 1883).
46 27 Stat. 445 (act of Feb. 13, 1893, sec. 3).

and, in addition, their relatives came over from the old country. The new industrial system created or exploited a huge pool of workers. Many were immigrants. About half a million entered the country in 1880 alone. Most late 19th-century immigrants were peasants from southeastern Europe. They "provided an apparently inexhaustible reserve of cheap labor for mines, mills and factories." [47]

These workers in industry were poor; their conditions of work and life were hard. In 1840 the average workday was 11.4 hours; in 1890, it had fallen to ten hours, but in some industries—paper manufacturing, for example—the average workday was still twelve hours.[48] Conditions in many factories and mines were appalling. The business cycle added special miseries. Social services were weak; sickness, broken bones, or a downturn in business constantly threatened the worker's security. Employers often seemed callous; some were callous in fact; others adopted the detached, studied callousness of social Darwinism. That the workers should remain unorganized, that business should be free from control, that the health of enterprise was the way, the truth, the consummate social good: this was the faith of the dominant class. But there were intellectuals and leaders of another viewpoint—men who got drunk on European radical thought or concocted a native version.

"Closed resources and freedom with insecurity," said John R. Commons, "produce in time a permanent class of wage earners." [49] He might have added: they produce disaffection. Labor problems multiplied because economic interests conflicted, in a game of life that both sides were convinced was zero-sum. The era of inexhaustible growth was gone; men lived in a world of finite possibilities. Each group had to scramble for its share; what accrued to one was subtracted from another. This attitude, we have seen, profoundly affected every aspect of the living legal system. It also rubbed social relations raw. The rich resisted socialism (everything from nationalized steel mills to unemployment compensation); the poor made war on the rich. In the postwar years, a trade-union movement grew rapidly—as rapidly perhaps as industrial combination. By the 1870's, mass labor confronted big business. Some scholars feel that the United States has had the "bloodiest and most violent labor

[47] Foster R. Dulles, *Labor in America* (2nd rev. ed., 1960), p. 98.

[48] W. S. Woytinsky *et al., Employment and Wages in the United States* (1953), p. 47.

[49] John R. Commons and John B. Andrews, *Principles of Labor Legislation* (rev. ed., 1927), p. 4.

history of any industrial nation in the world." In 1877, strikes and riots "swept across the United States . . . with almost cyclonic force." [50] The major rail centers, from Baltimore west, were struck. Nineteen died, and one hundred were wounded, in a skirmish on July 26, in Chicago, between police, National Guardsmen, and a mob. At the Carnegie Steel plant in Homestead, Pennsylvania, in the early 1890's, strikers fought with Pinkerton guards. In Coeur d'Alene, Idaho, in 1892, metal miners attacked the barracks where strikebreakers lived; in the ensuing disorders, five miners died, and troops were called out. Most of the violence was unplanned; it simply erupted. It was not part of union policy. Sometimes violence achieved results; sometimes—perhaps more often—it stiffened the backs of employers, and frightened the neutral middle class.

Forced to choose sides, legal institutions necessarily reflected the wants of their basic constituencies. This meant that legislatures swung back and forth, depending on the strength of interests, blocs, parties and lobbies; or compromised. The courts were more independent of short-run swings of opinion. Partly for this reason, courts could afford to indulge in principles and ideologies. These were usually on the conservative side, because the judges were solid, independent men of middle class. They were terrified of class struggle, mob rule, the anarchists and their bombs, railroad strikers, and the collapse of the social system as they knew it. When the left raged against decisions that seemed antilabor, the judges took refuge in the temple of the federal Constitution, in its regional chapels, the state constitutions, and in the half-ruined forums of the common law. These were sanctuaries where the mob (they felt) dared not enter. Theirs were not personal decisions, they insisted, but decisions under law—impersonal, classless, neutral.

The battle for labor reform was fought, first in the streets, then in the legislative halls, and then, less successfully but inevitably, in the courts. In each of these three arenas, the rhetoric was different, but the stakes were usually the same. The early court cases on strikes, picketing, and boycotts have evoked a great deal of historical interest. There were few of these cases, but the literature is large. Were union activity and strikes illegal, because they amounted to a criminal conspiracy? The first known American case on this point was the trial of the Philadelphia cordwainers, in 1806. This, and some later cases, did hold that striking workers

50 Philip Taft and Philip Ross, in "American Labor Violence: Its Causes, Character, and Outcome," in Hugh D. Graham and Ted R. Gurr, eds. *Violence in America, Historical and Comparative Perspectives* (1969), pp. 281, 288.

could be charged with conspiracy. But in the famous case of *Commonwealth* v. *Hunt* (1842), Chief Justice Lemuel Shaw, of Massachusetts, held to the contrary.[51] Prosecutions for conspiracy slowed down to a walk in the 1850's and 1860's. Conspiracy trials, like most major criminal prosecutions, were slow and tortuous. They were embarrassed by a multitude of defendants, and subject to all the safeguards thrown up around trial by jury. Strikes were, in the abstract, perfectly legal. It was hard to prove that an illegal conspiracy had taken place, and each case stood on its own private facts. For these reasons, the doctrine of conspiracy was a poor sort of strikebreaker, and fell completely out of use.

More sinister and effective weapons took its place. A judge with a will could find a way. Many railroads in the 1870's, and later, were in receivership, which meant that they were technically wards of the federal courts. This gave the judges an opportunity to intervene in labor disputes, with a strong and mighty arm. Thomas S. Drummond, judge of the seventh circuit, made virtuoso use of contempt power to combat the strikes of 1877, whose railroads happened to be in receivership.[52] Later, the judges invented, or discovered, the labor injunction, a stronger and more general piece of artillery. The injunction was an ancient, powerful, and honorable tool of courts of chancery. It had infinite possibilities and uses. Its suppleness and power made it an especially deadly threat against labor. During a strike, a company might ask for a restraining order (a temporary injunction). Courts of chancery had the power to grant these orders quickly, without notice or hearing, if the court was persuaded that delay might irreparably injure the company. No jury trial was necessary. If a union defied the order, or the later injunction, it stood in contempt of court. Hence, its officers and members could be summarily punished, even thrown into jail.

The first uses of the labor injunction are hard to trace. The Johnston Harvester Company asked a New York court to issue one in 1880; the defendants, claimed the company, had "combined" and "enticed" workers from the factory "by means of arguments, persuasion and personal appeals." The judge saw fit to deny this request; but injunctions were apparently issued in Baltimore and at Kent, Ohio, in 1883, in Iowa in 1884, and during the railroad strikes of 1886. Between then and 1900, the cases "grew in volume

[51] *Commonwealth* v. *Hunt*, 4 Metc. (45 Mass.) 111 (1842); see Leonard W. Levy, *The Law of the Commonwealth and Chief Justice Shaw* (1957), pp. 183–206.

[52] See, in general, Gerald G. Eggert, *Railroad Labor Disputes, The Beginnings of Federal Strike Policy* (1967).

like a rolling snowball." [53] In 1895, the labor injunction was sancti-
fied, by unanimous decision of the United States Supreme Court.
This was the famous case of *In re Debs*.[54] Prosecution of Eugene V.
Debs grew out of the Pullman strike of 1894. This major strike
paralyzed the country's railroad lines; and President Cleveland, in
alarm, called out the troops. The attorney general also asked for an
injunction against Debs, the union leader, calling on him to "desist . . . from . . . interfering with . . . the business of . . . the
. . . railroads." Debs did not desist; he was then charged with contempt, convicted, and sentenced to six months in jail. The Supreme Court affirmed the conviction. From then on, certainly, the
injunction, in the hands of a strong-minded judge, was a mighty
adversary that organized labor had to reckon with. The injunction
was swift, and it could be murderously inclusive—broad enough in
its contours to cover a total situation, outlawing every aspect of a
strike and effectively crushing it. Hardly any courts protested
against the use of injunctions in industrial cases; but labor and its
allies were outraged. The Democratic platform of 1896 denounced
"government by injunction as a new and highly dangerous form of
oppression"; the federal judges were acting as "legislators, judges
and executioners," at one and the same time. Labor made an attempt to persuade legislatures to do away with the labor injunction. But the injunction had strong friends, too; and the attempt
came to nothing, at this time.

Courts still accepted the proposition that a strike was not illegal
per se. A judge would not issue an injunction as a matter of course.
There had to be a threat of irreparable harm; and preferably the
strike itself should be one that fell on the illegal side of the line.
Even before the Civil War, some scattered, rather inconclusive
cases drew lines between legal and illegal strikes, and ruled on the
validity of other aggressive union tactics. Between 1870 and 1900,
there were many more decisions. Some tactics were clearly proscribed—the boycott, for example. "It is difficult," said Frederic J.
Stimson, writing in 1896, to "conceive of a boycott conducted solely
by lawful acts." [55] Picketing too had a rocky course. A few judges
thought it was always illegal: "There is and can be no such thing as
peaceful picketing, any more than there can be chaste vulgarity, or

[53] Felix Frankfurter and Nathan Greene, *The Labor Injunction* (1930), p. 21.
[54] 158 U.S. 564 (1895).
[55] Frederic J. Stimson, *Handbook to the Labor Law of the United States*
(1896), p. 223.

peaceful robbing, or lawful lynching." [56] But most courts saw a clear distinction between peaceful picketing and intimidation. It was hard to know where the boundaries were; consequently a union that threw up a picket line always ran a certain risk of illegality. On the other side, management's tactics rarely ran afoul of the law. Companies fired workers who were active in unions; their leaders were put on the blacklist. Few cases challenged the blacklist; and many courts failed to find any conspiracy or other illegality in this behavior.

Despite obstacles in court, the labor movement made great headway in the last decades of the century. Their power was greatest in the industrial states, and their grievances were most clearly formulated there. Not all their victories were won by sheer muscle. Labor showed strength in the legislatures, too. States enacted an increasing volume of protective laws. Some states forbade the blacklist; some outlawed the "yellow dog" contract, which made employees promise not to join a union, as a condition of their job.[57] Other statutes insisted on payment to workers in cash (as a weapon against the company store); required companies to pay their employees weekly or fortnightly; punished infringement of the union label. These protective statutes, taken together, must have had some effect on labor relations. But they were often poorly drafted, poorly administered, poorly enforced. Most grievously of all, a certain number had to run the terrible gauntlet of constitutionality. It was a test some failed to pass. The results of these cases varied from state to state. The more spectacular (and reactionary) cases have been most apt to catch the historical eye. On the whole, labor laws were upheld; most were never even questioned. Maine, for example, passed a law in 1887, of a common type, requiring employers to "pay fortnightly each and every employee . . . the wages earned by such employee to within eight days of the date of such payment." The Maine act, perhaps because of a favorable Massachusetts case, was never challenged in court in the 19th century.[58]

But the Illinois supreme court, for one, was politically conservative, judicially activist, and intoxicated with constitutionality; at

---

[56] McPherson, J., in *Atcheson, Topeka and Santa Fe Rr. Co.* v. *Gee,* 139 Fed. 582 (C.C.S.D. Iowa, 1905).

[57] For example, Laws Minn. 1895, ch. 174. The Utah constitution of 1895 specifically outlawed the blacklist; art. 12, sec. 19; art. 16, sec. 4.

[58] See E. S. Whitin, *Factory Legislation in Maine* (1908), pp. 60–61.

one period, labor laws fell like tenpins. In 1886, a coal-weighing act—the weight of the coal fixed the wages of the miners—was held unconstitutional; in March 1892, the court struck down a law forbidding mineowners and manufacturers from running a company store; in the same year, a new coal-weighing law failed to pass muster; in 1893, a law requiring weekly wages for workers was voided; in 1895, a restriction on the hours worked by "females" in "any factory or workshop" was declared unconstitutional.[59] The grounds of these decisions in Illinois and like-minded states were various. Statutes were sometimes said to be bad because they were "class legislation." Sometimes they were bad because they were infringements on a strange, cloudy concept of liberty embedded in the due-process clause. The concept included, it seemed, a rigid doctrine of liberty of contract. In some extreme cases, statutes were overthrown for no more precise reason than that they offended the spirit of the constitution. We have already cited one horrible example: *Godcharles* v. *Wigeman* (1886),[60] a Pennsylvania case. Here the court threw out a statute requiring laborers to be paid at regular intervals, and in cash, as "utterly unconstitutional and void," an "insulting attempt to put the laborer under a legislature tutelage," "degrading to his manhood," and "subversive of his rights." No clause of any constitution was cited. In 1884, New York, ostensibly "to improve the public health," prohibited the "manufacture of cigars and preparation of tobacco in any form in tenement-houses." The statute was held void a year later in the *Jacobs* case.[61] The law, said the court, was an infringement of a man's right "to earn his livelihood in any lawful calling." Government interference in the economy, if not justified by the police power, could do great harm: "disturb the normal adjustments of the social fabric . . . derange the delicate and complicated machinery of industry and cause a score of ills while attempting the removal of one." A California law, fairly typical, required corporations to pay workmen their wages at frequent intervals and in cash. A quartz mine, brought to task for violation, defended itself on constitutional grounds. The California court (1899) thought the statute an abomination: "the working man of intelligence is treated as an imbecile. . . . [he] is

---

[59] The cases are respectively *Millet* v. *People,* 117 Ill. 244, 7 N.E. 631 (1886); *Frorer* v. *People,* 141 Ill. 171, 31 N.E. 395 (1892); *Ramsey* v. *People,* 142 Ill. 380, 32 N.E. 364 (1892); *Braceville Coal* v. *People,* 147 Ill. 66, 35 N.E. 62 (1893); *Ritchie* v. *People,* 155 Ill. 98, 40 N.E. 454 (1895).

[60] 113 Pa. St. 431, 6 Atl. 354 (1886); see above, Part III, ch. I, p. 315.

[61] *In re Jacobs,* 98 N.Y. 98 (1885).

deprived of the right to make a contract as to the time when his wages will come due." He is not allowed to "make an agreement with the corporation that he will work 60 days" and take a "horse in payment" instead of cash. The laborer might be "interested in the corporation, or for some reason willing to wait until the corporation could pay him." The statute unreasonably forbids these reasonable arrangements; the court felt that it had "infirmities . . . sufficient to destroy it." [62] At any rate, the court swept it from the books.

These opinions have an air of unreality; they rang false even in their day. In any event, despite these decisions, the vitality of the employer's position was slowly sapped. For one thing, many cases went the other way. Nor could the firm stand of conservative judges overturn political movements. The judges could only call a short truce; could only hope to keep problems at bay until the country would come to its senses. But the country never came to its senses. Rather, the madness got worse; liberal judges and legislatures were vindicated by the verdict of history, that is, by the way lines of force in the end turned out. Conservatives faced more and more adverse legislation, more and more litigation. Unions, liberals, and legislatures refused to take no for their answer. Social legislation had too many branches and heads to be killed; when one was chopped off, ten more laws seemed to grow in its place.

Labor law proceeded along the lines where employer defense and conservative opinion were weakest. Child labor was a case in point. It was, in fact, a terrible abuse that small children worked their lives out in factories and mines; the "bitter cry of the children" would have touched a heart of stone. But the movement to abolish child labor was more than a movement to save suffering children. A child-labor system depressed wage rates, in the view of organized labor; it disastrously inflated the supply of cheap workers. Adult male workers had a similar view of women in the factories. Organized labor strongly supported laws on the wages and hours of women; and, equally, supported West Coast agitation (led by such radical groups as the Workingmen's party in the 1870's) against the "yellow peril" of Chinese laborers. No one was as vehement against Orientals as the workmen's champions, in the labor movement.

Social-welfare programs we. :essful, in short, where conscience and passion could join hands with some strong self-interest. Other things, too, were necessary: a strong civil service, enforceable

[62] *Johnson* v. *Goodyear Mining Co.*, 127 Cal. 4, 59 Pac. 304 (1899).

laws, and money to support the programs. Protective labor legislation, on child labor, women workers, factory safety, and the hours of work, grew from almost nothing before the Civil War to an impressive web of legislation in 1900. But the trend proceeded very unevenly. The rich, highly unionized, and heavily industrialized states led the way. The South lagged badly behind. Connecticut had a primitive wage-and-hour law for children in 1842. Vermont was the last New England state to adopt some sort of child-labor law; that was in 1867.[63] Yet in 1896, Mississippi, Kentucky, Arkansas, and North Carolina, among others, still did not have any law that even purported to outlaw child labor.[64]

Child-labor laws on the books were not the same as child-labor laws enforced. New Jersey's law of 1851 outlawed factory work for children under ten; older children could work no more than ten hours a day, sixty a week.[65] Punishment for violation was a fine of $50, to be sued for "in an action of debt, in the name of the overseer of the poor." Such a law could have been no more than a pious nullity. It expressed official policy; but that was all. What was needed was some means of enforcement. Compulsory-education laws put some life into child-labor laws. An act of 1883 raised the minimum working age to twelve for New Jersey boys, fourteen for girls; the act required employers of young people to get a certificate, showing the minor's age, the name of his parents, and a statement, signed by the teacher, that the child had attended school. Though almost as weak as its predecessors, this act at least empowered the governor to appoint an "inspector," who, for the princely salary of $1,200 a year, was to inspect factories (there were more than 7,000 in New Jersey) as best he could, and enforce the law.[66] In 1884, the inspector got two assistants; by 1889, he had six. In 1892, the act was amended to include provisions about the hours of employment of women; the work week was set at fifty-five hours for women and persons under eighteen; fruit-canning plants and glass factories were exempted.[67] At the end of the century, children still slaved in New Jersey factories; but not so many, and not so young. A similar story could be told of the child-labor laws of other states.

Constitutionally, child-labor laws had less to fear than other wel-

[63] Lorenzo D'Agostino, *History of Public Welfare in Vermont* (1948), p. 181.
[64] Frederic J. Stimson, *Handbook to the Labor Law of the United States* (1896), pp. 74–75.
[65] This discussion of New Jersey is taken from Arthur S. Field, *The Child Labor Policy of New Jersey* (1910).
[66] Laws N.J. 1883, ch. 57.
[67] Laws N.J. 1892, ch. 92.

fare laws. It was difficult to stretch freedom of contract, the new-minted sacred cow of the Constitution, to cover the employment of minors, who had no power to make contracts, even at common law. Married women, too, had had contractual disabilities in the older law. This fact gave some color to arguments that it was acceptable to control the conditions under which women worked. More persuasive were reminders of women's role as a mother, her elementary biological differences from men, coupled with Victorian sentimentality about mothers, sisters, wives. *Muller* v. *Oregon* (1908)—a Supreme Court case—decisively settled that laws setting maximum hours for women's labor were constitutional.[68] If nothing else, the court felt, "the future well-being of the race" meant that women had to be protected "from the greed as well as the passion of man." The earlier cases had been of various minds, however, on this question of women and labor. In the case of Mary Maguire (1881),[69] California's highest court threw out an ordinance of San Francisco that made it a misdemeanor to employ any "female to wait or in any manner attend on any person in any dance-cellar, bar-room, or in any place where malt, vinous, or spirituous liquors are used or sold," or for any "female" to work in such a place. A Massachusetts case (1876) upheld a law of 1874 that put a ten-hour limit on the working day of women, and a sixty-hour limit on their work week, in "any manufacturing establishment";[70] but an Illinois case, *Ritchie* v. *People,* decided in 1895, reached a conclusion diametrically opposed.[71]

On questions of maximum hours, labor legislation stayed close to the shores of constitutional power. A mandatory ten- (or eight-) hour day for all workers was believed to be beyond the legal pale, even had it been politically feasible. The state could regulate the labor contract only within the nebulous boundaries of the police power; or if the law could be closely tied to some doctrine or concept of undoubted validity. The state, as an employer, could itself make any contract it wished with its workers, and adopt any rule about these contracts. So New York, in 1870, restricted the hours of its own employees. Federal eight-hour laws were passed in 1868, 1888 (for employees of the Public Printer and the Post Office), and in 1892 for all "laborers and mechanics" employed by the government, the District of Columbia, or by "any contractor or sub-

---

68 208 U.S. 412 (1908).
69 *In the Matter of Mary Maguire,* 57 Cal. 604 (1881).
70 *Commonwealth* v. *Hamilton Mfg. Co.,* 120 Mass. 383 (1876).
71 155 Ill. 98, 40 N.E. 454 (1895).

contractor upon any of the public works of the United States." But even these laws were only fitfully and reluctantly enforced.[72]

Other limitations on the hours of workers could be justified on social grounds. New York, in 1888, adopted a law that street-railway workers could not labor more than twelve hours at one stretch. This was followed, in 1892, by a ceiling on the hours of all railroad workers. The argument (or excuse) was that an exhausted trainman or engineer endangered the public. On this basis, enough outside support could be mustered for passage—support that ordinary factory labor could not get. That further step—maximum hour laws for adult male workers—was for the moment not possible. *Holden* v. *Hardy* (1898)[73] upheld, in the country's highest court, a Utah law, of 1896, that limited, to eight hours a day, the workday of "workingmen in all underground mines or workings," in "smelters and in all other institutions for the reduction or refining of ores or metals." These were particularly onerous and unhealthy occupations; and this case, as the century ended, stood perilously close to the legal frontier.

FEDERAL TAXATION

For most of the 19th century, the tariff, protective or otherwise, served a double function; it was a (controversial) element of economic policy; and it brought in important revenue for the federal government. Congress was most reluctant to expand the government's taxing authority. That would increase federal power, and the idea of state sovereignty was strong. Even the costs of the Civil War did not at first induce new forms of tax. Initially, the government tried to fight the war by floating bonds; Jay Cooke took up residence in Washington, and lent a hand to Salmon P. Chase, who presided over Lincoln's treasury. Bond financing and greenback money were successful in raising money, after their fashion. But the North lost more battles than expected; costs mounted; the war dragged on; it was gradually clear that the struggle would be fought on an epic, not a lyric, scale. Events thus forced the government's hand. Lincoln turned to an income tax. The tax, first imposed in 1862, and amended in 1864, was mildly progressive; in its later revision, its top bracket was 10 per cent. The government also imposed a death tax, and new or bigger excises on all sorts of serv-

72 Marion C. Cahill, *Shorter Hours* (1932), pp. 69–73.
73 169 U.S. 366 (1898).

ices and goods: beer, public utilities, advertisements, perfumes, playing cards, slaughtered cattle, and railroads, for example. Despite some unfairness and bungling, these taxes brought in a great deal of money. In fiscal 1866, more than $300,000,000 was collected.

The Confederate government, on the other hand, mismanaged its finances badly. The Provisional Congress, in August 1861, imposed a direct tax of $\frac{1}{2}$ of 1 per cent on all property (except Confederate bonds and money). The various states, however, were allowed to pay the tax themselves. This concession proved to be a disaster; rather than collect the money from their publics, the states issued treasury notes or required local banks to furnish the money. The Confederate treasury became "the greatest money factory in the world." It created "wealth out of nothing" by "magic revolutions of the printing press." The inevitable result was a wild inflation. The notes "drove prices to fantastic heights. Counterfeiting . . . ran riot. Faith in the government vanished." The Confederacy never really made amends for this first mistake. Later tax laws were inept or ill-timed; the major tax law of April 1863 was complex and, in part, unpopular; one feature called for payment of one-tenth of the produce of farm land as a tax in kind. The South did not solve its revenue question, but ultimately Grant and Sherman made the question academic.[74]

The victorious North was anxious to return to normalcy, at least in money matters. Congress let the wartime taxes die. And the small scale of federal activity, in fact, did not seem to require severe and exotic taxes. Excise taxes, on liquor and tobacco, produced nearly ninety per cent of the government's internal revenue from 1868 to 1913. Internal revenue receipts were $113,500,000 in 1873, $161,000,000 in 1893—mere pennies in the modern world of billions of dollars of tax.[75] Government was becoming more active, however; and that took more money than before. Meanwhile, the triumphant, exultant rich, the powerful trusts, and the robber barons excited jealousy and fear, and not merely from the left. Political and ideological arguments, coupled with a real need for cash, won recruits for the idea of a progressive income tax, one that would also serve as a brake on the power of the rich. Between 1873 and 1879, fourteen different income-tax bills were introduced into Congress.

[74] For the above, see Randolph E. Paul, *Taxation in the United States* (1954), pp. 7–22.
[75] Lillian Doris, ed., *The American Way in Taxation: Internal Revenue 1862–1963* (1963), p. 34.

The movement reached its climax in the 1890's. The 1890's had no war for an excuse, except the Spanish-American War, which was short and profitable. But many contemporaries had a different war in mind: the battle for control of America's economy, not to mention its soul. The Eastern rich obliged by agreeing with the left on the meaning of the tax: the income tax was the archenemy, the entering wedge of socialism, the beginning of the end for America. In 1893, Grover Cleveland suggested a "small tax" on incomes "derived from certain corporate investment"; when a tax bill passed in 1894, however, he let it become law without signing. The law taxed incomes (and gains) over and above an exemption of $4,000 at the flat rate of two per cent.[76] In the war of words, Ward McAllister, "leader of the Four Hundred," threatened to leave the country if the law was passed. William Jennings Bryan, rushing to the barricades, cried out that he had "never known one so mean that I was willing to say of him that his patriotism was less than two per cent deep."

In the 1890's, it was not enough to pass so important a law; the Supreme Court still had to be convinced. William D. Guthrie of New York, risen from office boy to lion of Wall Street, determined to slay this dragon of two per cent. He raised money for the lawsuit among his clients, found a willing litigant named Pollock, and launched an attack that he carried all the way to the Supreme Court itself.[77] Before the Supreme Court, an epic struggle took place. On one side was ranged a battery of prominent Wall Street lawyers—Guthrie, Joseph H. Choate, and others—on the other, Attorney General Olney, his assistant, Edward B. Whitney, and James C. Carter. The case occasioned great flights of oratory, and some dubious essays in pseudo-history, all on the government's power to tax. In *Pollock* v. *Farmers' Loan and Trust Co.* (1895),[78] the Court at first held the tax unconstitutional, but only as it applied to income derived from real estate. On the big question, whether the whole law was unconstitutional as a "direct Tax," the Court was evenly divided, four against four.[79] The ninth judge,

[76] 28 Stats. 553 (act of August 27, 1894, sec. 27).

[77] Randolph Paul, *Taxation in the United States,* pp. 30 ff; Arnold M. Paul, *Conservative Crisis and the Rule of Law* (1960), chs. 8, 9. On Guthrie's role, see Robert T. Swaine, *The Cravath Firm and its Predecessors* (1946), Vol. I, pp. 518–36; Henry James, *Richard Olney and his Public Service* (1923), pp. 70–76.

[78] 157 U.S. 429, 158 U.S. 601 (1895).

[79] The Constitution, art. 1, sec. 2, required "direct taxes" to be apportioned among the states by population. It had for a century or more been understood that poll taxes and property taxes, and only these, were "direct."

Jackson, was sick. The case was then reargued—with Jackson present—and this time the Court declared the whole law void, by a bare majority, 5–4.[80]

History has not been kind to *Pollock*. Professor Edward S. Corwin has called it a case of "bad history and bad logic";[81] and it surely was both of these. He might have added bad law, bad politics, and bad form. The case has had the rare distinction that a constitutional amendment, passed in the 20th century, specifically overturned it. At the time, of course, this could not be foreseen. Defenders and detractors alike agreed on what the case meant to accomplish: to make the world safe for that brand of democracy which Guthrie believed in, and Justice Field, and all the country's "sound" and wealthy men. In that sense, the case deserves better than it has received from historians. Its logic and history were weak; but its instincts were rather shrewd. The income tax *was* the opening wedge for a major transformation of American society. A journey of a thousand miles begins with a single step; and a tax whose rates rise to seven dollars out of ten may begin with a mere two per cent.

STATE AND LOCAL TAX

In the 19th century, local government relied primarily on the general property tax. In 1890 this tax produced 72 per cent of state revenues, 92 per cent of local revenues. It has kept this primacy in local revenue, but state government later abandoned this tax,[82] and turned to other sources.

The general property tax, as its name implies, was a tax on all types of property. Essentially, it was the old real-property tax, with a tax on intangibles and personal property added. Indeed, most states at some time in the century made a constitutional point of uniformity and generality of taxes. "All taxes," said the Pennsylvania constitution of 1873, "shall be uniform, upon the same class

80 When the Court is evenly divided, by custom it does not reveal who voted on which side. When the case was reargued, Jackson, the missing judge, voted to uphold the act. Still, five judges voted to strike down the law. This has created a minor historical mystery, since it means that *one* of the other four judges must have changed his mind. No one is quite sure who this judge could have been. See A. M. Paul, *op. cit.,* pp. 214–17.

81 Edward S. Corwin, *Court over Constitution* (1938), p. 188.

82 George C. S. Benson *et al., The American Property Tax: Its History, Administration and Economic Impact* (1965), p. 83.

of subjects, within the territorial limits of the authority levying the tax, and shall be levied and collected under general laws" (art. IX, sec. 1). Again: "Laws shall be passed taxing by uniform rule all property according to its true value in money" (North Dakota const. 1889, art. XI, sec. 176).

A general tax was not easy to administer. It was hard enough to arrive at a fair assessment of land; but at least land was visible. Chattels were easy to hide, and intangibles most furtive of all. The general property tax essentially reduced itself to a tax on land— the most visible form of wealth. A rich taxpayer could easily evade taxes on invisible assets. Meanwhile much of the property of the less well-off was exempt from tax. Landowners who wanted to share their burden had called for passage of more general property taxes. But in the end, they still bore most of the burden themselves.

Assessment and collection of the tax was a continual problem. Assessment was local, chaotic, and frequently unfair. There was a great temptation for an assessor to undervalue property in his county: why not let the burden fall on other parts of the state? Hence, on top of the layers of local officials, states began to impose "boards of equalization," first countywide, then statewide. An early state board was Iowa's: by the Iowa code of 1851 the board was "authorized and required to examine the various assessments . . . and equalize the rate of assessment on real estate in the different counties," in the name of uniformity. The board could equalize "either by changing any of the assessments or by varying the rate of taxation in any of the counties." [83]

But the boards did not really have adequate power over local assessors. Indiana took the next step, in 1891: creation of a board of state tax commissioners. The board had general supervision over the tax system; but its power was "chiefly advisory," and it did not curb all the abuses that had grown up under the older system. Still, Indiana's law was "the beginning of a new administrative policy," and ultimately led to better-run ways to collect this tax. [84]

Even on paper the general property tax was never completely general. There were many exceptions and exemptions. The list of exemptions was analogous to the list of property exempt from creditors, though less extensive. In the Iowa code of 1851, tax-exempt property included poultry, wool shorn from sheep, one year's crop, private libraries up to $100 in value, family pictures, kitchen fur-

[83] Iowa Stats. 1851, secs. 481, 482. See, in general, Harley L. Lutz, *The State Tax Commission* (1918).
[84] Lutz, *op. cit.*, p. 152.

niture, one bed and bedding for each member of the family, clothes "actually used for wearing," and food.[85] In the Iowa code of 1897, much the same exemptions appeared, but with additions: "the farming utensils of any person who makes his livelihood by farming, the team, wagon and harness of the teamster or drayman who makes his living by their use in hauling for others, and the tools of any mechanic, not in any case to exceed three hundred dollars in actual value." [86] The property of charities, schools, and churches was also free from tax.

During the promotional years, railroads and other favored corporations were granted tax exemptions, too. When these companies fell from grace, they finally had to pay their own way. Battles over taxation resounded in legislative halls between 1870 and 1900; smallholders and organized labor wanted vengeance on the large corporations, and (as usual) wanted the power of big money kept in control. But revenue needs were real enough, too. To lay the foundations for more active government, states needed a broadly based, productive tax system. Where was the money to come from? The new state constitutions hamstrung legislatures in search of money. They were not allowed to float bonds at whim or will. The lower orders of government were also squeezed. Some governmental services could be supported by fees; but this method was regressive and liable to abuse. On the other hand, business was rich and getting richer; and it had long escaped paying what looked like a reasonable share. Some states competed for *incorporations* with *low* taxes; but railroad tracks once laid could not run away, and the temptation was to get all one could from a captive giant.

Taxation of business proved enormously difficult. First, there were political difficulties. The wealth of enterprise excited the tax collectors' lust; but wealth was power, and business fought back. Volumes could be written about the struggles over railroad taxation alone. State governments rose and fell on the issue. Second, there were the special complexities of a federal system. Before 1850, the railroads, when they were taxed, paid the general local property tax. Afterwards, more and more states added taxes based on capitalization or gross receipts.

Interstate businesses—railroads and telegraph companies, for example—ran the risk of taxation all along their lines, as if by so many Rhenish baronies. How much taxation of "commerce" across

85 Iowa Stats. 1851, sec. 455.
86 Iowa Stats. 1897, sec. 1304(5).

state lines was valid? How could the property of some giant firm, sprawled across the states like a Gulliver among Lilliputians, be sliced into rational pieces and taxed? There was no uniformity. In 1899, railroads in some parts of the country paid 17 per cent of net earnings; in others, only 8.4 per cent.[87] Fundamental questions of constitutional law, conflicts of law, as well as of politics, were brought into issue. The various solutions bred intricate law. When all concerned—legislatures, state courts, and federal courts—had had their say, there was no one definite limit to the taxes that could be lawfully imposed on an interstate tiger with one paw in the taxing *situs*. Various formulas, of more or less sophistication, determined what part of the tiger "belonged" (for tax purposes) in Rhode Island or Texas or Washington state. Massachusetts, for example, taxed railroads and telegraph companies on that portion of their capital which had the same ratio to total capital as tracks and lines inside the state bore to total tracks and lines. The Supreme Court, in a court test (1888), held that this method was fair.[88] But taxation of multistate commerce was one of the high court's most persistent and bothersome issues.

DEATH TAXES

The idea of death taxes fed and grew fat on fear of dynasties and the money power. Even before the Civil War, there had been some state and federal essays in estate and inheritance tax. A death tax was part of the Civil War package. But the real upsurge in demand came after 1885. Economists like Richard T. Ely and Edwin R. Seligman, with such strange bedfellows as Andrew Carnegie, argued that great fortunes should be heavily taxed when the founder died. About half the states adopted some form of death tax by 1900. Generally, these taxes were not steeply progressive. Almost always, they were biased against collateral heirs and strangers to the blood: wives and children of the dead man received the most favorable treatment. In Michigan's law of 1893, for example, the tax (on "transfers . . . by will or by the intestate laws," or "in contemplation of the death of the grantor," or "intended to take effect . . . at . . . death") was a flat five per cent on the market value of these transfers. But the rate was only one per cent on gifts

87 Emory R. Johnson, *American Railway Transportation* (1907), p. 416.
88 *Western Union Telegraph Co.* v. *Mass.*, 125 U.S. 530 (1888); Mass. Stats. 1882, ch. 13, sec. 40.

to "father, mother, husband, wife, child, brother, sister, wife or widow of a son or the husband of a daughter," adopted children, and "any lineal descendants"; and the first $5,000 was exempt.[89]

In 1898, the federal government re-entered the field, with a modified form of estate tax.[90] Its top rate was 15 per cent, a rate that applied only to gifts from estates of more than $1,000,000, and which passed from the decedent to distant relatives, nonrelatives, or "bodies politic or corporate." The law was part of the revenue package for the Spanish-American War, and it was repealed in 1902. All told, it brought in $22,500,000. This paltry sum was hardly enough to wound the great fortunes. Like the Civil War taxes, however, the death tax passed its constitutional test; and so did the state taxes on estates, to the horror and disgust of Guthrie and the Cassandras of Wall Street. Again, these rich and conservative men were not wholly wrong. In the future, their worse nightmares would come true. Tax laws would be enacted that would really impair the largest estates. But these steep and progressive rates lay in the century ahead.

[89] Laws Mich. 1893, ch. 205; see Edwin R. Seligman, *Essays in Taxation* (6th ed., 1909), pp. 133 ff.
[90] Randolph Paul, *op. cit.*, pp. 65–70.

CHAPTER X

CRIME AND PUNISHMENT

THE TWO FACES OF CRIMINAL LAW

At one time, most lawyers were generalists, and handled criminal matters along with civil suits. Even so prestigious and prominent a business lawyer as Alexander Hamilton did criminal work. In the West, and in small towns generally, criminal law remained a staple of the practice. Later in the century, the bar in major cities became more specialized. There developed both professional criminals and a professional criminal bar. It was not necessarily a dignified bar; and it lacked the prestige of the bar that served big business. Some small-scale lawyers eked out a living by gathering crumbs of practice in the lower criminal courts. A few big-city lawyers made a more handsome, and sometimes less honorable, living. In New York, the "magnificent shyster," William F. Howe, flourished between 1875 and 1900. He was a member of the infamous firm of Howe and Hummel; he defended hundreds of madams, pickpockets, forgers, as well as the most notorious murderers of his day. Howe's specialty was gilded courtroom oratory, judiciously backed up by perjury, bribery, and blackmail.[1]

The leaders and money-makers of the criminal bar were always flamboyant, though not always unscrupulous. Howe and Hummel were not afraid to advertise their wares. Over their "shabby but conspicuous offices . . . hung not the modest shingle of a firm of counsellors-at-law but a sign thirty or forty feet long and three or four feet high . . . illuminated at night." [2] The organized bar gradually stamped out the practice of openly asking for business through advertisements and illuminated signs. A criminal lawyer had no retainer business, and few repeats. This left word of mouth one of the few ways he could build a practice. This fact made the

[1] The story of Howe and Hummel has been entertainingly recounted by Richard Rovere, in *The Magnificent Shysters* (1947).

[2] Rovere, *op. cit.*, p. 34.

criminal bar, if anything, more flamboyant than otherwise, since it had to have publicity or die.

The criminal law itself, quite naturally, underwent considerable change in the later 19th century. It became and remained by and large a matter of statute. The concept of the common-law crime, as we have seen, had been wiped out in federal law. The common-law crime decayed on the state level, too. As of 1900, most states still *technically* recognized the possibility of a common-law crime. But some states had statutes that specifically abolished the concept. These statutes stated bluntly that all crimes were listed in the penal code, and nothing else was a crime. In some states, the courts *construed* their penal codes as (silently) abolishing common-law crime. Where the concept survived, it was hardly ever used; the penal codes were in fact complete and exclusive.

The living law was somewhat more complicated. The New York penal code (passed in 1881) provided that "no act . . . shall be deemed criminal or punishable, except as prescribed or authorized by this Code, or by some statute of this state not repealed by it." This was plain abolition. Yet the penal code had a sweeping catch-all clause: "A person, who willfully and wrongly commits any act, which seriously injures the person or property of another, or which disturbs or endangers the public peace or health, or which openly outrages public decency or is injurious to public morals . . . is guilty of a misdemeanor." [3] Obviously, prosecutors and courts could have almost as much power under this language as under the reign of common-law crime. In fact, the section was probably little used, as little as the concept of common-law crime, in those states which retained it.

In *Hackney* v. *State* (1856),[4] an Indiana case, Hackney, the defendant, had been arrested for maintaining a "public nuisance"; this consisted of "keeping a ten-pin alley, and procuring for gain certain disorderly persons to meet there, rolling balls night and day, cursing, quarreling, drinking, and making great noises." Indiana had abolished the common-law crime. There was no statute on the books which said anything specific about tenpin alleys, but maintaining a public nuisance was a statutory misdemeanor. The question was, what was a nuisance? There was a body of common-law decisions, defining nuisance; the court explicitly denied that these cases were relevant. The common law was not to be used, even as a source of interpretation. Instead, the court turned to an

3 N.Y. Penal Code 1881, secs. 2, 675.
4 8 Ind. 494 (1856).

Indiana statute, which defined "nuisance" as anything "injurious to health, or indecent, or offensive to the senses." This, said the court, could cover Hackney's conduct; they affirmed his conviction by the lower court.

The New York statute, and the *Hackney* case, raise the suspicion that there was more to the death of the common-law crime than meets the eye. What died was the overt, unabashed power of courts to pull out new crimes from the folkways. It was killed by that pervasive feature in American legal culture, horror of uncontrolled power. Lawmakers believed that courts should be guided—ruled—by the words of objective law, enacted by the peoples' representatives; nothing else should be a crime. But at the same time, the courts found covert substitutes for their lost jurisdiction. First, they benefited from vague general clauses, like the one in the New York Penal Code. Indeed, a camouflaged power was more suitable to the courts, more soothing, more protective, than a naked power at common law. Second, they allowed themselves more amplitude in interpreting the law. They rejected the extremist language of *Hackney,* about common-law interpretation. But they retained the flair for "interpretation of statutes" that *Hackney* signified. There was an old maxim that courts had a duty to construe penal statutes narrowly. Courts constantly referred to this maxim; yet even this helped judges elbow their way into power. It was the judges who decided, after all, what was narrow and what was wide.

As we have seen, countervailing power, one of the great themes of American history, was particularly strong in criminal justice. Trial judge, appellate judge, jury, legislature stood in uneasy balance. The Constitution, the Bill of Rights, and the 14th amendment struck some sort of balance between federal and state power. At least in legal theory, criminal trials were hedged about by many safeguards. A stern law of evidence, juries, and meticulous attention to procedure were thought to be essential, to protect the life and liberty of the citizen. And the "hypertrophy" of procedure was, as we saw, at its most extreme in appeals from criminal trials.

The picture that emerged was one of precision, rigidity, care. Crimes were only those acts clearly engraved in the statute books. Laws were to be strictly construed. There was no margin for error at the trial. Probably no field of law, however, was quite so two-faced. The ideal picture of criminal justice must be contrasted with the real criminal law, parts of which were blunt, merciless, and swift, other parts of which simply ignored whole kingdoms of crime. It was true that most appeals from criminal cases succeeded;

but few were appealed—one half of one per cent of total prosecutions in Chippewa County, Wisconsin; only five per cent of the cases before the Wisconsin supreme court were criminal appeals.[5] It was an aspect of living law that the safeguards did not safeguard everybody; it was also an aspect of living law that many more were arrested than convicted, and that in the view of some the law was too soft, rather than too hard. The regular criminal law had many irregular helpers. The Ku Klux Klan rode in the South, from 1867 to the early 1870's; it burned and pillaged, and punished blacks and whites who transgressed against the Klan's concept of a proper social order. In the slums and tenderloins of big cities, street gangs, prostitutes, and thieves were mostly left to run their own underworld, enforce their own rules, govern their own society. Force was the only kind of law that ever penetrated this jungle. Alexander S. Williams, of the New York police force, became famous in the 1870's, because he "invoked the gospel of the nightstick," and organized "a strong arm squad." Patrolling the Gas House District, Williams "clubbed the thugs with or without provocation." Charges were preferred against Williams no less than eighteen times; but the board of police commissioners "invariably acquitted" him. He justified his "furious clubbing" by the observation that "there is more law in the end of a policeman's nightstick than in a decision of the Supreme Court." [6]

The vigilantes of the West, those self-help groups, were in some ways following an old American tradition. The first American vigilantes, the South Carolina regulators, appeared in 1767.[7] But the movement really flourished after 1850. As we have seen, the most famous, and the models for the rest, were the two Vigilance Committees of San Francisco (1851 and 1856). Vigilante justice cropped up throughout California; in Colorado, Nevada, Oregon, Texas, and Montana; and generally in the West. "Swift and terrible retribution is the only preventive of crime, while society is organizing in the far West," wrote Thomas J. Dimsdale, chronicler of the Montana vigilantes, in 1865.[8] All told, there were hundreds of vigilante movements. One hundred and forty-one of them took

5 Edward L. Kimball, "Criminal Cases in a State Appellate Court: Wisconsin 1839–1959," 9 Am. J. Leg. Hist. 95, 99–100 (1965).

6 Herbert Asbury, *The Gangs of New York* (1928), pp. 235–37.

7 See Joe B. Frantz, "The Frontier Tradition: An Invitation to Violence," and Richard Maxwell Brown, "The American Vigilante Tradition," in Hugh D. Graham and Ted R. Gurr, eds., *Violence in America: Historical and Comparative Perspectives* (1969), pp. 127 ff, 154 ff.

8 Thomas J. Dimsdale, *The Vigilantes of Montana* (new edition, 1953), p. 13.

at least one human life. The total death toll has been put at 729. Virtually all of these were in the West, and before 1900. Texas was the bloodiest vigilante state; and the peak decade was the 1860's.[9]

The vigilantes were not the only groups that engaged in private criminal justice. Claims clubs in the Middle West, and miners' courts in the sparse, bleak reaches of the far West, constructed their own version of property law and punished offenders. Later in the century, "Judge Lynch" presided at an all too frequent court in the South and the border states. Mobs, in the 1890's, tortured, hanged, and sometimes burned alive black men accused of assault, murder, or rape. They sometimes snatched their victims from jail, furious at delay. Lynch mobs and vigilantes had their own sense of mission. Some of them, hungry for legitimacy, parodied the regular written law; they had their own "judges" and "juries," their own quick and summary trials. They punished crimes without names or without remedies, and enforced public policy as they saw it. They were responses to the absence of law and order (as in Montana), the disorganization of a defeated society (as in the South), or the feebleness or venality of regular government. They also were a much cheaper form of punishment than tax-fed trials and long prison sentences. A newspaper writer, after a vigilante lynching in Golden, Colorado, in 1879, reported that "the popular verdict seemed to be that the hanging was not only well merited, but a positive gain for the county, saving at least five or six thousand dollars." [10]

The Southern lynch mobs were the most savage and the least excusable of all the self-help groups. Their law and order was naked racism, no more. Their real complaint against law was that the courts were too careful and too slow; that some guilty prisoners went free; and that the lesson for the rest of the blacks was not sharp enough. The Western vigilantes, on the other hand, have become almost folk heroes; it is usual to regard them with sympathy, or as a necessary evil, or even as a form of popular democracy. The historian Hubert H. Bancroft praised the vigilance committees lavishly. Indeed, he loved all forms of Western justice. Vigilance, he wrote, is an "expression of power on the part of the people in the absence or impotence of law." It is "the exercise informally of their rightful power by a people wholly in sympathy with existing forms of law." It is "the keen knife in the hands of a skilful surgeon, removing the putrefaction with the least possible injury to the body

9 Richard Maxwell Brown, op. cit., p. 175.
10 Quoted in Richard M. Brown, op. cit., p. 183.

politic." The San Francisco Committee of 1856, for example, was just such a surgeon: "Never before in the history of human progress have we seen, under a popular form of government, a city-full rise as one man, summoned by almighty conscience, attend at the bed-side of sick law . . . and perform a speedy and almost bloodless cure." [11] It was certainly true that public opinion was not overly severe on the "beloved rough-necks"; many who joined the vigi-lantes were leaders of their communities, or became prominent in later life; they found that a vigilante past was no disgrace, no im-pediment.

Under some conditions, self-help law can make a persuasive case. The Donner party, in 1846, tried, convicted, and banished a man named James Reed, who had killed John Snyder in a fight. The travelers were months away from Missouri—in Mexican territory, in fact—and hundreds of miles from any court, or judge, or arm of any state.[12] The ideology of self-help was strong, too, in the 19th century; and government was stingy. It is no surprise, then, that a Wisconsin law of 1861 authorized the "organization of societies for mutual protection against larcenies of live stock." The societies were given power to choose "riders" who might "exercise all the powers of constables in the arrest and detention of criminals." [13] A similar law in Pennsylvania in 1869 incorporated the "Spring Val-ley Police Company of Crawford County," a "company for the re-covery of stolen horses or other property." Its members were to have the same power of arrest and detention as policemen of Philadelphia.[14] The anti-horsethief movement arose "spontane-ously" after the Revolutionary War. From the 1850's on, the so-cieties sought, and got, legislative authorization. They lasted until better public police and the automobile put them out of business. In their heyday, they had more than 100,000 members.[15]

Private law enforcement was an attractive idea. A statute of 1865, in Pennsylvania, gave railroads the power to employ their own police. An act of 1866 extended this law to any "colliery, fur-nace or rolling-mill," thus creating the "coal and iron police." The state here authorized "a veritable private army," at the request of "powerful interests." These private police—they existed in other states, as well—became anathema to the unions. They were

11 Hubert H. Bancroft, *Popular Tribunals* (1887), Vol. I, pp. 10, 11, 16.
12 John W. Caughey, *Their Majesties the Mob* (1960), pp. 6–7.
13 Laws Wis. 1861, ch. 222.
14 Laws Pa. 1869, ch. 991.
15 Richard M. Brown, *op. cit.*, pp. 190–91.

"toughs," strikebreakers, "necessarily the enemy of organized labor." [16] But it was not until the 1930's that they were finally abolished in Pennsylvania.

THE STATUTE LAW OF CRIMES

Over the years, the criminal codes, like the dollar, became markedly inflated. Traditional crimes—treason, murder, burglary, arson, and rape—stayed on the books; and new crimes, some of which seem quite unnecessary, were added. Roscoe Pound found fifty crimes in 1822 in the Rhode Island penal code. The number had grown to 128 crimes by 1872.[17] The revised statutes of Indiana of 1881 contained more than three hundred sections under the general heading of crimes. Instead of one section about embezzlement, there were many: embezzlement of public funds, embezzlement by officers (the crime committed when "any County Treasurer, County Auditor, Sheriff, Clerk, or Receiver of any Court, Township Trustee, Justice of the Peace, Mayor of a city, Constable, Marshal of any city or incorporated town," or any other officers and agents of local government, failed to turn over or account for funds in their trust), embezzlement by employees, by "lawyers and collectors," by railroad employees, by "innkeepers and carriers," by bailees (a "storage, forwarding, or commission merchant, carrier, warehouseman, factor, auctioneer, or his clerk, agent or employee"), by agricultural tenants, by treasurers (of state or local government), by city officials, or by fiduciaries (secs. 1942–52). A separate section of the code punished anyone who "maliciously or mischievously" injured "any telegraph-pole or telephone-pole" (sec. 1956). There were great numbers of new economic or regulatory crimes, some quite trivial: shooting prairie hens or prairie chickens out of season, selling grain seed that harbors seeds of Canada thistle, swindling an underwriter, selling coal by false weight (secs. 2107, 2121, 2138, 2202). Whoever "stretches or places any net . . . across any creek emptying into the Ohio river in this State . . . in order to prevent the ingress of fish . . . or their egress," was guilty of a crime, and liable to pay between $5 and $20 for each day the obstruction continued (sec. 2118). It was a

16 J. P. Shalloo, *Private Police, with Special Reference to Pennsylvania* (1933), pp. 60, 62, 88.

17 Roscoe Pound, *Criminal Justice in America* (1945), p. 16.

crime to sell skimmed milk in Indiana; to dam up a stream and produce stagnant water; to sell "diseased or corrupted or unwholesome provisions" (secs. 2067, 2069, 2071). There were also many sections, regulating public morality, against gambling, "bunko-steering," selling liquor on Sunday, pimping, adultery, public indecency. It was a crime to "entice" any "female of previous chaste character . . . to a house of ill-fame," for the "purpose of prostitution" (sec. 1993); dealing in obscene literature was also proscribed. It was a crime to sell or advertise "any secret drug or nostrum purporting to be for the exclusive use of females, or which cautions females against their use when in a condition of pregnancy; or . . . any drug for preventing conception or for procuring abortion or miscarriage" (sec. 1998). In addition, the code referred, in the section on crimes, to more than ninety other statutory sections, scattered elsewhere in the revised statutes, which also imposed criminal sanctions for this or that conduct. These were tacked on to a wide variety of statutes—on maliciously killing or injuring a "registered and tagged dog" (sec. 2649), on selling intoxicating liquors to inmates of the Soldiers' Home (sec. 2834), on violations of provisions of the "Dentistry Act" (sec. 4254), on sale of commercial fertilizers not "labeled with the State Chemist's analysis . . . or . . . labeled with a false or inaccurate analysis" (sec. 4897), and on violations of the Public Warehouse Act (sec. 6549).

What was true in Indiana was true in the other states as well. The steady growth of statutory crimes continued. Few were ever repealed; fresh ones were constantly added. In 1891 it became a misdemeanor in Indiana to "wilfully wear the badges or buttonaire [sic] of the Grand Army of the Republic" or other veterans groups, unless one was "entitled to use or wear the same" under the rules and regulations of the organization. Another law required road supervisors or "Gravel Road Superintendents" to cut hedges along the highways; failure to do so was an offense, and was punishable by fine. It became a felony in that year for officers of public institutions to "purchase, sell, barter or give away to any other officer . . . or to appropriate to his or their own use any of the slops or offal of any of the said public institutions." Railroads had to employ flagmen at railroad crossings; for failure to comply, money penalties were prescribed.[18] About a dozen more distinct items of behavior became criminal, in 1891, and other, older crime laws were amended.

18 Laws Ind. 1891, ch. 33, 39, 146, 150.

In every state, every extension of governmental power, every new form of regulation brought in a new batch of criminal law. Every important statute, governing railroads, banks, and corporations, or the marketing of milk, cheese, fruit, or coal; or concerning taxation, or elections and voting, or licensing an occupation, trailed along with it at the end a sentence or two imposing criminal sanctions on violators. No doubt many of these stern laws were not criminally enforced at all; violators were rarely or never tried; appeals and reported cases practically did not exist. The full discussion of these statutes belongs more to the story of government regulation of business than to criminal justice.

These regulatory crimes should not, however, be written off completely. The multiplication of economic crimes did not mean, necessarily, that people looked on sharp business behavior with more and more sense of moral outrage. It meant, rather, a decision to socialize responsibility for enforcing certain parts of the law. This process began long before the Civil War (see above, Part II, ch. VII, pp. 257–58). Crimes are, among other things, wrongful acts punished wholly at the expense of the state, and largely on the state's initiative. The states, and the federal government, were invoking criminal law in one of its historic functions—a low-level, low-paid administrative aid. In New York, in 1898, an amendment to the penal code made it a misdemeanor to sell articles as "sterling silver," unless they consisted of 925/1000ths of pure silver.[19] If a silver merchant sold a coffee pot or creamer to a housewife, and cheated her, it had long been true that she had the right to bring an action against him. But nine times out of ten, the cost of the lawsuit, compared to the dollars at stake, hardly merited the trouble. In a criminal action, enforcement and punishment were entirely at public expense. The enforcing officials, of course, were only the usual array of policemen, district attorneys, and judges. They were not specialists in regulatory crimes, and rarely bothered with them. Criminality was often only a halfway stage on the road to administrative law—to professional, specialized policing of some area of economic life.

The Indiana statutes, as we have seen, retained the letter of the law on many old crimes against morality and public decency. In most states, some of these were only fitfully enforced; others were dead letters. But aspects of public morality remained controversial, and engendered new outbursts of law. Liquor control was a constant fountain of law. In 1887, six states were legally dry: Iowa,

19 Laws N.Y. 188, ch. 330.

Kansas, Maine, New Hampshire, Rhode Island, and Vermont.[20] The temperance movement fought hard, had many triumphs, endured many defeats, before its last and most famous victory, national prohibition, in 1920. Joseph Gusfield has argued that the point of the liquor laws lay less in their real effect—less in whether or not people drank—than in whether the law, the official norm, allowed them to drink. The struggle, in short, was symbolic, not instrumental. The issue was: whose norms were dominant, whose should be labeled right and true: those of old-line, middle-class, rural Protestant America, or those of Catholics, immigrants, the working class, dwellers in cities, who drank without shame? Whether these newcomers drank more or less than old Americans mattered less than their attitude toward drink.[21]

Much about this thesis is attractive: neat parallels can be drawn to other areas of struggle over law. Divorce, for example, comes easily to mind. Another instructive case was the battle over the lottery. Once widely used by government to raise money for new courthouses, internal improvements, and the like, the lottery was battered by successive abolition movements; by the time of the Civil War legal lotteries existed only in Delaware and Kentucky; there was a postwar revival, but in 1895, the federal government outlawed interstate traffic in lotteries; and this was the death blow.[22] The death of the lottery can be explained in symbolic, normative terms. But in many of these legal struggles, morality laws had clear instrumental uses. The sleepy old Sunday laws came to life because unions wanted them enforced; unions wanted a shorter work week, and Sunday laws were a useful instrument. The ministers and preachers acted as willing accomplices; labor and religion here formed an odd but understandable coalition. In Philadelphia, for example, the barber's union formed a Sunday closing committee. The committee ran a campaign against barbers who would not co-operate; 239 of these were arrested in the two-year period starting December 1898.[23] In New York City, in the 1890's, when Theodore Roosevelt was president of the police board, and vigorously enforced the laws forcing saloons to close on Sundays, the bakers and barbers also demanded enforcement for their

[20] Livingston Hall, "The Substantive Law of Crimes, 1887–1936," 50 Harv. L. Rev. 616, 633 (1937).

[21] See Joseph Gusfield, *Symbolic Crusade, Status Politics and the American Temperance Movement* (1963).

[22] John S. Ezell, *Fortune's Merry Wheel, the Lottery in America* (1960).

[23] 12 Barbers' Journal 28 (1902).

trades, though with mediocre results.[24] Connecticut passed a tightened Sunday law in 1897; the statute increased the fines that could be imposed for violation, and lengthened the hours of the ban. Between twelve o'clock Saturday night and twelve o'clock Sunday night all shops, warehouses, and factories had to stay closed. The law was, basically, labor legislation; but pure morality also mixed in; sports, too, were forbidden on Sunday.[25]

It would be a mistake, too, to assume that unenforceable laws were uniformly unenforced. A symbol loses power when it is only a symbol and nothing more. The evidence suggests that blue laws and liquor laws came intermittently to life, for particular reasons in particular places. Francis Laurent has collected figures for the flow of court business in the lower courts of Chippewa County, Wisconsin. Between 1855 and 1894, sex-law prosecutions were extremely rare but not extinct. There were five cases of incest, nine of adultery, four of fornication, one of lewd and lascivious behavior. Fifteen accusations of prostitution were brought, all within one decade. There were sixty-one prosecutions for violation of liquor-control laws; fifty occurred in one year, 1871.[26] It is hard to resist the conclusion that laws against immorality were used selectively, though not at random. They were used to "get" somebody or were invoked against some unusually flagrant or unlucky offender. One wonders who the one man was, who, alone in a forty-year period, was officially lewd and lascivious. What had he done, and how was he caught? The figures also suggest that laws came to life on the occasion of a crackdown. But a crackdown was most likely to occur after scandal or when a strong organization, like the Women's Christian Temperance Union, with a firm political base, expressed a moral position. Arrests for drunkenness were high in the 19th century, and rose dramatically between 1860 and 1900, at least in one jurisdiction, Massachusetts, where the matter has been carefully studied.[27]

---

[24] Howard L. Hurwitz, *Theodore Roosevelt and Labor in New York State, 1880–1900* (1943), pp. 149–54.

[25] Laws Conn. 1897, ch. 188. The statute excepted, as was usual, "works of necessity or mercy."

[26] Francis Laurent, *The Business of a Trial Court,* pp. 37, 122, 125.

[27] Roger Lane, "Urbanization and Criminal Violence in the 19th Century: Massachusetts as a Test Case," in Hugh D. Graham and Ted R. Gurr, eds., *Violence in America: Historical and Comparative Perspectives* (1969), pp. 468, 472.

CRIME, CRIME RATES, INSANITY, THE GUILTY MIND

The criminal law, legitimate and illegitimate, assumes that there is a reality, called crime, on which law operates. Obviously, in one sense, a society chooses for itself how much crime it wants. When an act is declared criminal, all its actors are committing crime. In 1900, there was vastly more criminal law on the books than in 1850 or 1800, hence in this sense probably vastly more crime. But those who worry about the crime rate are usually concerned, not with economic crime, but with the classic crimes of violence and social disruption, murder, robbery, assault. These are enforced much more systematically and with greater use of public resources than other kinds of crime. The definitions of these crimes remained more or less constant during the century; or at least constant enough for meaningful comparisons, if only the figures were at hand.

Some facts are known about crime in the real world, in the 19th century. What evidence there is suggests that the crime rate for serious crimes, at least since 1860, gradually declined.[28] There was proportionately *less* violence, murder, assault in the 1970's than a century before. Roger Lane's research, for 19th-century Massachusetts, saw a marked falling-off in jail commitments, from 333 per 100,000 population to 163, between 1860 and 1960. The social investment in crime-fighting increased; so, too, did the worry and the tumult. The basic reason may be that violent crime, particularly in the cities, becomes less tolerable the more society is one and interconnected. The city is the heart of modern society; society is governed from the city; the economy depends on city life. The city is the place where people are most interdependent; where they are most confronted with strangers, and where their lives, property, and health are most at hazard. The more a society is urban, industrial, and interdependent, the more there is division of labor in the economy, the less the society can tolerate violent crime. Crime is bad for business, and bad for the social order. The city civilizes and tames, to a certain extent; for this reason violence has diminished. But by the same token crime has not gone down fast enough;

28 Roger Lane, "Urbanization and Criminal Violence in the 19th Century: Massachusetts as a Test Case," in Hugh D. Graham and Ted R. Gurr, eds., *Violence in America: Historical and Comparative Perspectives* (1969), p. 468.

the public demand for law and order more than keeps pace with the supply.[29]

The violent crimes were also the crimes of mystery and drama; the crimes that provided raw material for novels, poems, and plays; the crimes par excellence, as the public thought of them. Pamphlets, trial transcripts, last words of condemned men were part of American popular culture. There were hundreds of these fugitive writings: John Erpenstein, who gave his wife a bread-and-butter sandwich, liberally sprinkled with arsenic, was credited with writing the "Life, Trial, Execution and Dying Confession of John Erpenstein, Convicted of Poisoning His Wife, and Executed in Newark, N.J., on March 30, 1852. Written by himself and translated from the German." Professor John W. Webster murdered Dr. George Parkman, in the Harvard Medical School, in 1849; publishers rushed many versions of the background and trial of this sensational crime into print. The Fall River tragedy—the murder of Lizzie Borden's parents in 1892—has enlivened American literature ever since.[30]

It was this type of crime, too, which evoked the raw hatred that could mold a mob and lead a man to be lynched. It was this type of crime in which trial by jury was frequent, and in which the jury was free to apply its "unwritten laws"; in which justice was, in theory, tailored to the individual case. Here, too, were the cases in which the defense of insanity was invoked. Juries, to be sure, probably went their own way; they excused men for insanity, or did not excuse, in accordance with their own moral code and common sense, rather than the science of their time. But those scientific notions had at least a marginal and indirect effect. And in the 19th century, almost for the first time, lawyers and doctors engaged in a grand and continuing debate about the meaning of criminal responsibility, and the scope of the insanity defense.

The dominant definition of legal insanity was the so-called M'Naghten rule, named after a mad Englishman, for whose case the rule was first announced, in 1843.[31] Simply put, a defendant could not be excused from responsibility unless he was "labouring

---

[29] Interestingly, the same study by Lane which suggests a decline in arrests for *major* arrests in Massachusetts suggests an equally striking increase in arrests for *minor* offenses, mainly drunkenness. This confirms the notion of a diminished tolerance for what is defined as antisocial behavior.

[30] The examples above are drawn from Thomas M. McDade, *The Annals of Murder, A Bibliography of Books and Pamphlets on American Murders from Colonial Times to 1900* (1961), pp. 35–37, 87, 311–16.

[31] M'Naghten's case, 10 Cl. & F. 200 (1843).

under such a defect of reason . . . as not to know the nature and quality of the act he was doing; or . . . that he did not know what he was doing was wrong." This "right or wrong" test was a pleasing platitude: it seemed to soothe the moral sense of the legal community; in any event it won rapid acceptance. In a few American states, this "right or wrong" test was supplemented by another, the "irresistible impulse" or "wild beast" test. If a man, said Chief Justice John F. Dillon of Iowa in 1868, knew that his act was wrong, but "was driven to it by an uncontrollable and irresistible impulse, arising, not from natural passion, but from an insane condition of the mind," he was not be be held responsible.[32] The idea of irresistible impulse strikes the modern ear as somewhat romantic, not to say medically absurd; but the wild-beast test was broader than the M'Naghten test alone; and some of the best psychiatrists of the day believed in irresistible impulse.[33] A third rule stood all by itself in New Hampshire. This was Chief Justice Charles Doe's rule, enunciated in *State* v. *Pike* (1869). Here the test was no test at all: the question to be answered in each case was, whether the criminal act was the "offspring or product of mental disease. . . ." Neither delusion, nor knowledge of right and wrong was, as a matter of law, a test of mental disease. Rather, all symptoms and "all tests of mental disease" were "purely questions of fact," within the province and power of the jury alone, to determine and decide.[34]

Arguments over these various "tests" were really arguments over the form of stereotyped instructions, to be read to the jury. What distinguished the tests was the degree of autonomy they (apparently) gave to the jury. Whether the jury listened, or cared, or understood is another question. In a few great cases, the tests acted as a dark and bloody battleground for war between contending schools of psychiatry. Most notable was the weird trial of Charles Guiteau, who murdered President Garfield in 1881. Guiteau's behavior, before and after (and during) the trial, was bizarre, to say the least; but probably no test, however worded, could have persuaded the jury not to send the President's killer to the gallows.[35]

It would not be totally wrong to interpret the debate as evidence of moral sensitivity among those concerned with the criminal law

[32] *State* v. *Felter*, 25 Iowa 67, 82 (1868).

[33] On contemporary tests of insanity see, in general, Joel P. Bishop, *Commentaries on the Criminal Law* (6th ed., 1877), Vol. I, pp. 213–29.

[34] John P. Reid, *Chief Justice, The Judicial World of Charles Doe* (1967), pp. 114–21; *State* v. *Pike*, 49 N.H. 399, 442 (1869).

[35] The story of this trial has been beautifully recreated in Charles Rosenberg's *Trial of the Assassin Guiteau* (1968).

—at least a horror of putting incompetent people to death. But, as we have seen, the criminal law was a two-edged sword. The other edge was the regulatory edge, and here, if anything, moral coloring faded away. The criminal law was both more and less than the moral steward of society. Small economic crimes—shooting a deer out of season—did not require a guilty and dangerous mind like murder and rape. To get a felony conviction, for crimes against property, the prosecution at common law had to show a specific intent to act illegally. Injury to property was not a crime unless it was malicious; there "had to be a definite motive of hatred, revenge, or cruelty, as well as an intent to cause the injury." In the 19th century, this requirement loosened. It was the behavior that was dangerous, not just the mind of the actor; the behavior had to be stamped out. "The demand for protection of the wealth of the country . . . has led to liability for intentional but nonmalicious injury to property." [36] Motive or attitude was secondary. In the New York penal code of 1881, the fact that a defendant "intended to restore the property stolen or embezzled, is no ground of defense, or of mitigation of punishment." [37] The code made it a crime to destroy or injure property "unlawfully or wilfully" (sec. 654).[38] Similarly, "metaphysical difficulties" about whether a corporation could form an "intent" to commit a crime were brushed aside; originally, a corporation could not be indicted at all; and as late as the 1850's scattered cases held that corporations were criminally liable only for acts or omissions that did not require a criminal "intent." [39] It was still theoretically true in 1900 that a corporation could not be convicted of rape or treason; but most cases that tried and convicted corporations arose under statutes on economic crime —creating a nuisance, charging too much interest, breaking the Sabbath, or, as in one case, "permitting gaming upon its fairgrounds." [40]

For some crimes, the presumption of innocence or regularity— the principle that the state must specifically prove that a man was guilty or an action irregular, overcoming the presumption that no

[36] Livingston Hall, "The Substantive Law of Crimes—1887–1936," 50 Harv. L. Rev. 616, 642 (1937).

[37] N.Y. Penal Code, 1881, sec. 549.

[38] "Wilful" was a troublesome word, however; and the requirement of "wilful" violation, common in statutes, certainly meant that the defendant could not be punished for *reasonable* mistakes of law. See Hall, *op. cit.*, p. 646.

[39] Hall, *op. cit.*, p. 647.

[40] *Commonwealth* v. *Pulaski County Agricultural & Mechanical Ass'n.*, 92 Ky. 197, 17 S.W. 442 (1891).

wrong had been done—was turned topsy-turvy by statute. The object was to toughen the regulatory blade of the criminal law. In the New York penal code, the "insolvency of a moneyed corporation" was "deemed fraudulent" unless "its affairs appear, upon investigation, to have been administered fairly, legally, and with . . . care and diligence" (sec. 604). In Indiana, under a law of 1891, a prima-facie case of "intent to defraud" the depositor was made out, when a bank failed or suspended within thirty days of accepting a deposit.[41] There was no-nonsense toughness in liquor statutes, too. Dry states outlawed the sale of hard liquor; but it was not easy to catch violators red-handed. So, in New Hampshire it was *"prima facie* evidence" of violation of liquor laws if the defendant "exposed" any bottles with liquor labels "in the windows of, or upon the shelves within his place of business," or if his store had a "sign, placard, or other advertisement" for liquor, or if he possessed coupon receipts showing he had paid his federal tax as a dealer or wholesaler in liquor, or if a person delivered liquor "in or from any store, shop, warehouse, steamboat . . . or any shanty or tent . . . or any dwelling-house . . . if any part . . . be used as a public eating-house, grocery, or other place of common resort." In Iowa, possession of liquor, "except in a private dwelling house," created a presumption of guilt.[42]

In the age of Judge Lynch, it might seem strange to speak of how punishment was humanized. But social movements are not required to be even or consistent. The use of capital punishment declined in the last half of the 19th century. Wisconsin entered statehood without any death penalty at all. Michigan abolished it in 1882, except for treason; Maine eliminated the death penalty completely in 1887, and practically speaking, it was absent in Rhode Island too. Corporal punishment (whipping and flogging) survived in few states—in Delaware, as a kind of abominable relic. Elsewhere, even in the South, its legitimacy was slowly sapped. Though whipping was still legal in South Carolina up to the Civil War, a "cloud of disapproval" made public whipping of whites a rare event.[43] By 1900, except for convicts, whipping was almost extinct in the South. Death itself was somewhat modernized when the so-called "electrical chair" appeared in New York in 1888, to

41 See *State* v. *Beach,* 147 Ind. 74, 46 N.E. 145 (1897).
42 William C. Osborn, "Liquor Statutes in the United States," 2 Harv. L. Rev. 125, 126 (1888). Stats. N.H. 1878, ch. 109, secs. 24, 25; Iowa Code 1873, sec. 1542.
43 Jack K. Williams, *Vogues in Villainy, Crime and Retribution in Ante-Bellum South Carolina* (1959), p. 110.

replace the hangman's noose. Basically, the two common modes of punishment were fine and imprisonment. By and large, fines were prescribed as punishment for economic crimes. Thieves and rapists went to jail. But allowable sentences, and sentencing behavior, differed drastically, without apparent rhyme or reason, in the various states.

Sentencing was humanized in one way, however. In 1841, a bootmaker named John Augustus began to frequent the Boston criminal courts. In August 1841, his heart was touched by the case of a "ragged and wretched looking" drunk who was, Augustus felt, "not yet past all hope of reformation." Augustus heard the man swear he would never touch another drop, if only "he could be saved from the House of Correction." Augustus stepped up, went bail for the man, and brought him back to court three weeks later, "a sober man." The judge, impressed as always by repentance, waived imprisonment. From this point on, Augustus began to act as a private angel and guardian of men convicted of crime. He bailed almost 2,000 convicts until his death in 1859. Other Bostonians had helped him out or given him money; now some of these carried on his work after his death. In 1878, a Massachusetts statute provided for the appointment of a paid probation officer, in the Boston criminal courts. A further law authorized a statewide system in 1891. Between 1897 and 1900, Missouri, Vermont, Rhode Island, and New Jersey also enacted probation laws; Illinois and Minnesota provided for juvenile probation. But the movement was still clearly in its infancy.[44]

The 19th century also began to experiment with suspended sentences, indeterminate sentences, and parole. (Governors in many states also continued to make liberal use of the pardon.) A judge had always had the power to suspend a sentence, if he felt for some reason that the trial had miscarried. But could judges suspend sentences wholesale, after trials that were scrupulously fair, simply to give the defendant a second chance? The question was litigated in a New York case in 1894.[45] The defendant, John Attridge, a "clerk in a mercantile firm," had helped himself to his employer's money. He pleaded guilty at the trial. Attridge was young and well-liked; there were a number of "mitigating circumstances." "Numerous respectable citizens" of Monroe County petitioned the court for

[44] David Dressler, *Practice and Theory of Probation and Parole* (1959), pp. 13–21.

[45] *People ex rel. Forsyth* v. *Court of Sessions of Monroe County*, 141 N.Y. 288, 36 N.E. 386 (1894).

suspended sentence. Two out of three of the judges agreed to suspend; and the highest court in the state affirmed their decision, on appeal. The power to suspend sentence, said the appeal court, was "inherent" in criminal courts.[46]

Indeterminate sentence and parole were bound up with the latest episode in penal reform. The idea for this reform stemmed from the "Cincinnati Declaration" of the first meeting of the American Prison Association. Reform was put into practice at the Elmira "reformatory" in New York (1870). By law, all of the inmates of Elmira were to be young offenders, between the ages of sixteen and thirty, and "not known to have been previously sentenced to a State prison," in New York or elsewhere.[47] They were to be given indeterminate sentences, that is, sentences of variable (and unpredictable) length. In prison, the prisoners were to learn trades; and, of course, the prison would furnish programs of religious and moral uplift. The prisoners were divided into several "classes"; those who behaved and showed progress were to be moved into a better class; for bad behavior, a prisoner moved down. The best prisoners, in the highest class, were eligible for parole.

Elmira was not an unqualified success by any means. Originally, it had been a maximum-security prison, surrounded by a grim high wall. Despite remodeling and good intentions, Elmira was essentially "founded on custody and security, not on rehabilitation." Within ten years, "it was just another prison." The other copies of Elmira in the 19th century (there were only a few of these) shared its defects. They suffered from "neglect, legislative starvation, perfunctory obedience to or complete neglect" of the theory of earning higher grades, and "commercialization of inmate industry—all to the tune of taxpayers' protests that reformatories were 'country clubs' or 'military academies' or 'private schools.' "[48]

The Elmira idea had been thought especially good for young offenders. Many penologists believed that juveniles should not be treated the same as adult offenders. Legislatures ultimately agreed. As early as 1825, New York set up a "House of Refuge" for juveniles. A few states tried modified forms of probation for young people in trouble. A New York law of 1884 provided that when a person under sixteen was convicted of a crime, the judge might, in his discretion, put him in care of some suitable person or institu-

[46] Legal doubts about the power of courts to suspend sentence continued in the early 20th century and were only laid to rest in some states by statute.
[47] Laws N.Y. 1870, ch. 427, sec. 9.
[48] Miriam Allen deFord, *Stone Walls* (1962), p. 85.

tion, instead of prescribing prison or fine. Laws in Massachusetts, and later in Rhode Island (1898), authorized separate trials of children's cases. Indiana, in a series of statutes beginning in 1889, established a Board of Children's Guardians for densely populated townships. The board had the right to petition the circuit court for custody and control of a child under fifteen. Custody might last until the child came of age. The board was empowered to act when it had "probable cause to believe" that the child was "abandoned, neglected or cruelly treated" at home, or had been sent out to beg on the streets, or was truant, or "in idle and vicious association," or if the parents of the child were "in constant habits of drunkenness and blasphemy, or of low and gross debauchery," or if the child was "known by language and life to be vicious or incorrigible." [49]

Despite these halting moves, children in every state could still be arrested, detained, tried, and sent to prison or reformatory. There were 2,029 minors in jail in Massachusetts in 1870; 231 of these were under fifteen.[50] The first true juvenile court was established in 1899 in Cook County, Illinois (Chicago). Under the governing statute, circuit-court judges of Cook County were to designate one special judge to hear all juvenile cases. He would sit in a separate court room, and keep separate records; his court was to be called "the juvenile court." [51] The court had jurisdiction over dependent and neglected children, as well as over delinquents. In this way, the law extended its power over young people—mostly lower class —who had been beyond the reach of prior law, and who had committed no crimes. This reform had the backing of the "child-savers" of the nineteenth century. Its paternalism, middle-class bias, and absence of due process make it seem less progressive after seventy years than it did to the good people of its day.[52]

By any theory, Elmira and the juvenile court were landmarks; they were not typical of the everyday world of corrections. Elmira, though a failure, at least had high aspirations. Ordinary prisons, state and local, were starved for funds, filthy, sometimes debauched. Many prison jobs were held by ward heelers, appointed to pay off political debts. With dreary regularity, commissions reported bad news about local prisons—a dark chorus of complaints.

[49] See Laws Ind. 1891, ch. 151.

[50] Anthony Platt, *The Child Savers: the Invention of Delinquency* (1969), p. 120.

[51] Herbert H. Lou, *Juvenile Courts in the United States* (1927), pp. 16–20; Laws Ill. 1899, p. 131.

[52] A skeptical view of the origins of the court has been propounded most notably by Anthony Platt, *op. cit.*

Prisoners were whipped, starved and tortured in prisons all over the country, though not in all prisons at all times. The county jails of New Jersey were described as a disgrace in 1867. Young, old, men and women were heaped together, subjected to "dirt, vermin, offensive air and darkness." At the state prison, on the other hand, in a perversion of the penitentiary idea, the prisoner lived in a cell measuring $7\frac{1}{2} \times 12$ feet—with one to four cellmates; or alone in a newer cell only four feet wide and seven feet long. In this case, he lived and ate "in a room the size of a small bathroom, with a noisome bucket for a toilet and a cot narrower than a bathtub." To bathe, "occasionally," there was a "bathhouse in the yard, which was closed in bad weather." [53] In Illinois, the Cook County jail, inspected in 1869, was also "filthy and full of vermin." The county jails were "moral plague spots"; they made "great criminals out of little ones." [54]

Somehow reforms never took hold; or were perverted in practice. The fact is that convicts, like paupers and blacks, were at the very bottom of American society; powerless, their wants and needs had no American priority. On the other hand, middle-class society had a definite program, even though it was not openly expressed. People detested crime, and were afraid of it. They wanted criminals punished, and severely; even more, they wanted bad people kept out of sight and circulation. Depite the rhetoric, the evidence of what men did shows that they considered it more important to warehouse, quarantine, and guard the "criminal class" than to cure them of their criminal habits. People were inclined to be skeptical, moreover, whether it was possible to make these criminals over. For a long time, criminal anthropologists had explored the idea that the tendency toward crime was inherited along with other inherited traits and that the criminal was a definite physical or mental type. "Intellectually and morally, criminals are for the most part weak," wrote Frederick Howard Wines, in 1895. This weakness showed itself in "inattention, lack of imagination or the power of representation, defective memory, lack of foresight, and general aversion to mental exertion." A rich literature, dating from the 18th century, taught the physical signs of criminal personality: "The prominence of the criminal ear has been especially noted. Prisoners are said to have wrinkled faces; male prisoners have often scanty beards; many hairy women are found in prison. Red-haired men and women do not seem to be given to the com-

[53] James Leiby, *Charity and Correction in New Jersey* (1967), pp. 126–28.
[54] Platt, *op. cit.*, pp. 118–19.

mission of crime. . . . Convicts have long arms, pigeon-breasts, and stooping shoulders." Criminals, it was commonly observed, did not blush.[55]

The man on the street did not know these "facts"; but he had his own common sense, no doubt, to guide him. He no doubt *knew* that the criminal was another breed; that such people had to be removed from the society of respectable men, for the safety of the public. In the late 19th century, too, there was new interest in the question of eugenics. Concern for purity of morals joined hands with concern for purity of the blood. It is probably not too far-fetched to suspect that these attitudes reinforced the central tendency of the law of corrections, which was to quarantine the bad. What went on inside prison walls was of much less concern so long as these walls were impermeable.

Yet, paradoxically, public unconcern sometimes was its own undoing. Legislatures (responding, no doubt, to what they felt was public opinion) invariably starved the prisons for funds. Jails were jam-packed, sometimes far beyond their capacity. Poor conditions inside the walls frustrated any hope of rehabilitating the men, and may in the long run have stimulated social disorder. Sometimes, too, the prisons were so crowded that the state made wholesale use of pardon and parole. This happened in New Jersey in the late 19th century, because the ordinary outflow of prisoners "did not clear the prison fast enough." [56]

That prisoners ought to do useful work was a firm tenet of two very different groups—reformers, who wanted prisoners to improve themselves, and greedy officials, who wanted to cut costs and raise prison income. Convicts commonly made many products, including brushes, brooms, chairs, boots, and shoes. But organized labor was a sworn deadly enemy of convict labor. The prisons were hotbeds of what unions saw as unfair competition. Manufacturers whose work force earned nonconvict wages had the same economic interest, in this case, as their workers. Labor and management united to fight against the labor of convicts. The Illinois constitution was amended in 1886 to make it "unlawful . . . to let by contract . . . the labor of any convict." Michigan provided that "no mechanical trade shall hereafter be taught to convicts in the State prison . . . except the manufacture of those articles of which the chief supply for home consumption is imported from other States

55 Frederick H. Wines, *Punishment and Reformation, A Study of the Penitentiary System* (2nd ed., 1910), pp. 234–35.

56 Leiby, *op. cit.*, p. 133.

or countries." Some states ruled that convict-made goods had to be specially marked. A Pennsylvania statute, passed in 1883, required these goods to be branded "convict made," in "plain English lettering . . . by casting, burning, pressing or other such process," in such a way that the brand "may not be defaced," and the brand had to be put "in all cases . . . upon the most conspicuous place upon such article, or the box . . . containing the same." [57] States tried to divert prison labor into channels that did not offend their major interest groups. In Minnesota, beginning in 1891, statutes directed the state prison to acquire equipment and machinery "for the manufacture of twines known as hardfiber twines." Prison-made binding twine would be sold to farmers, "in quantities necessary for their own use." In this way, prison power would help farmers fight what they considered one of the worst of the trusts, the National Cordage Company.[58]

Southern prisons were particularly disgraceful; and the campaign against prison labor made less headway there. In the South, convicts were still hired out on the contract system. Florida statutes specifically authorized the commissioner of agriculture (with the approval of the board of commissioners of state institutions) to "enter into contracts . . . for the labor, maintenance and custody of . . . prisoners." No labor was to be done on Sunday, or "before sunrise or after sunset on any day." The contracts could provide for "surrendering the control and custody of the prisoners to the person . . . contracting for their labor." [59] In Georgia, under the code of 1895, a person convicted of a misdemeanor could be sentenced "to work in the chain-gang." [60] These infamous gangs worked for counties and cities, often on the public roads. The law empowered the "authorities of any county or municipal corporation" using the gang to "appoint a whipping-boss for such convicts"; the boss was not to use his whip except "in cases where it is reasonably necessary to enforce discipline or compel work or labor by the convict." [61]

The Southern lease system was only an exaggerated form of the national attitude toward corrections. It was heartless, in essence; it

[57] Laws Pa. 1883, ch. 110, sec. 2. Interestingly, "goods . . . shipped to points outside of the State shall not be so branded."

[58] See, in general, *20th Ann. Rpt. U.S. Commr. Labor, Convict Labor* (1905).

[59] Fla. Rev. Stats. 1892, sec. 3065.

[60] Georgia Code 1895, Vol. III, sec. 1039. The statute did go on to recite that the gangs were not to be employed "in such mechanical pursuits as will bring the products of their labor into competition with the products of free labor."

[61] *Ibid.*, secs. 1146, 1147.

was designed to make the tax burden light. Indeed, criminal farming could bring in revenue to the state. In some places, large lessees
subleased convicts in small or large gangs. The prisons of the South
were "great rolling cages that followed construction camps and
railroad building, hastily built stockades deep in forest or swamp or
mining fields, or windowless log forts in turpentine flats." [62]

The only protests of substance came from organized labor. In
1883, the Tennessee Coal, Iron, and Railroad Company hired the
thirteen hundred convicts of the Tennessee penitentiary. They
used the convicts partly as a lever to force free workers to agree to
stiff terms of employment. In 1891, free miners set the convicts
loose at the Tennessee Coal Mine Company, and burned down the
stockades. The next year miners battled the militia in Anderson
County, over the issue of convict labor. The lease system was finally
abolished, in Tennessee, after this period of lobbying with fire and
with blood.[63]

[62] C. Vann Woodward, *Origins of the New South 1877–1913* (1951), p. 213.
[63] Woodward, *op. cit.*, pp. 232 ff.

(CHAPTER XI)

THE LEGAL PROFESSION: THE TRAINING
AND LITERATURE OF LAW

Of the lawyers practicing in the United States in 1848, the overwhelming majority had been trained in a private law office, or had
educated themselves by a course of reading. This was particularly
true in the West. In 1858, Abraham Lincoln wrote, in a letter, that
"the cheapest, quickest and best way" into the legal world was to
"read Blackstone's *Commentaries,* Chitty's *Pleadings,* Greenleaf's
Evidence, Story's *Equity* and Story's *Equity Pleading,* get a license,
and go to the practice and still keep reading." [1] Many lawyers
practicing in 1900 still came out of this rough school of experience.
But the gap between two methods of training—law school and
clerkship—was slowly closing. Fewer would-be lawyers studied or
clerked in law offices, selling their labor cheaply or free, in exchange for practical experience. Of the rest, some combined clerkship with halfhearted or short attendance at a law school. A growing number simply went to school.

Nowhere was a law degree or a college degree absolutely required for admission to the bar, either in 1850 or 1900. Yet even in
the 1850's, some lawyers were college trained.[2] The advantages
seemed obvious to many students who could afford college or law
school, or both. By 1900 it was reasonably apparent that the future
lay with the law schools. It was clear, too, what kind of school. The
university law school was already dominant. Only a handful of private schools were founded after 1860: one was "Col. G. N. Folk's

1 Quoted in Jack Nortrup, "The Education of a Western Lawyer," 12 Am. J.
Leg. Hist. 294 (1968).
2 Even Western lawyers. See Nortrup, *op. cit.,* above, n. 1. Nortrup's article describes the education of Richard Yates, who combined law-office training with a
course in the law department of Transylvania (1836).

school, at Boone, North Carolina," established in 1867, which lasted some twenty odd years.[3] By 1900, schools of the Litchfield type were extinct. On the other hand, after the Civil War, there were more and more law schools with some sort of tie to a college or university. More than three-quarters of the schools open and running in the 1890's were of this type.

Particularly in the East, law school gave the student a prestige that law-office training could not match. In the better schools, too, the student probably learned more than he learned as a clerk, and in less time. Whatever the facts, the law schools sold themselves, slowly but surely, to the student public, as better or more efficient, or an easier road to success. There is some evidence, too, that the rise of the law schools was linked to a social change in the character of the bar—from strongly aristocratic to middle class in family background. The old established lawyers in Philadelphia had blocked the formation of a law department at the University of Pennsylvania in the 1830's. They wished, apparently, to preserve their private perogative of training the bar. The revolt came from the law students themselves, "restive in the confinement of law offices," eager for a "less inbred program of legal studies." In 1850, George Sharswood, in response to vociferous student demands, re-opened the university department of law.[4]

The rise of the law schools can be chronicled in figures. In 1850, fifteen law schools were in operation; in 1860, twenty-one; in 1870, thirty-one; 1880, fifty-one; 1890, sixty-one. In the last ten years of the century, there was an enormous leap in the number of schools. By 1900, 102 were open for business. In 1850, there were one or more law schools in twelve of the states; in nineteen states there were no law schools at all. In 1900, thirty-three states had law schools; only thirteen had to import school-trained lawyers from outside.[5] These were small or sparsely populated states—like New Hampshire and Nevada—or satellite states like New Jersey.[6] In the academic year 1849-1850, Harvard, the country's largest law school, had a total attendance of ninety-four. Ten years later, Harvard's enrollment had risen to 166; 180 students were enrolled at Cumberland University Law School, in Lebanon, Tennessee. In the

[3] Alfred Z. Reed, *Training for the Public Profession of the Law* (1921), p. 433.

[4] Gary B. Nash, "The Philadelphia Bench and Bar 1800–1861," in *Comparative Studies in Society and History,* Vol. VII, No. 2 (1965), pp. 203, 207–08.

[5] Reed, *op. cit.,* pp. 444, 446.

[6] New Hampshire and Nevada, as of the date of this writing (1970), still have no law school. The same is true of Delaware, Vermont, Rhode Island, Alaska, and Hawaii.

academic year 1869-70, Michigan, the country's largest law school, had 308 students; at the close of the century, Michigan again led all other law schools, with 883 students.[7] This was probably more than the enrollment in the whole country in 1849. In 1870, law schools had a total student population of 1,611; in 1894, the number had risen to 7,600.[8]

Many major universities, public and private, gathered a law school unto themselves between 1850 and 1900. The University of Michigan, a public university, established a "law department" in 1859. The Regents, at the very outset, voted up to $100 for advertisements about the "law department," to be placed in newspapers in Detroit, Chicago, New York, Cincinnati, St. Louis, and Washington, D.C.[9] St. Louis University, in the 1840's, was the first Roman Catholic university to establish a law school. This venture was short-lived. Notre Dame law school was founded in 1869; and Georgetown, in 1890, was one of the four largest law schools in the country. The law department of Howard University, in Washington, D.C., was the first (1868), most successful, and most permanent of the dozen or so black law schools.

The relationship of law school to university was a far cry from what it became in the twentieth century. The usual law degree, the LL.B., was certainly not a postgraduate degree. It was not standard for law schools to require *any* prior college work. The more pretentious law schools tightened their entrance requirements toward the end of the century; none required a full college education. Many "university" law schools merely coexisted with their parent institutions, to which they were rather loosely connected. They were not an organic part of the general world of scholarship. From 1858, until he retired in 1891, Theodore W. Dwight was the dominant figure in Columbia University's law school; he ran his own show. Under arrangements solemnized in 1864, Dwight, as "Professor of Municipal Law," collected the students' tuition (fixed at $100 a year for new students). Out of these fees, Dwight paid expenses, and a salary for himself of $6,000 a year. Any surplus was to be split fifty-fifty between Dwight and the university.[10] When Michigan decided to pay the salaries of its faculty—a princely $1,000 a year—out of

---

7 Reed, *op. cit.*, pp. 451–52. On the University of Michigan Law School, see Elizabeth G. Brown, *Legal Education at Michigan, 1859–1959* (1959).

8 Albert J. Harno, *Legal Education in the United States* (1953), p. 82.

9 E. G. Brown, *Legal Education at Michigan*, p. 250.

10 Julius Goebel, Jr., ed., *A History of the School of Law, Columbia University* (1955), pp. 57–58.

general university funds, this was a decided novelty.[11] Many "university" law schools were originally private schools annexed by, swallowed by, or federated with a university, which had varying degrees of success in digesting them. There are even cases of law schools that shifted allegiance from one university to another. What is now the law school of Northwestern University began its life as a department of law of the old Chicago University; in 1873, it became the "Union College of Law," connected both with Chicago and Northwestern; in 1886, this polygamy ended when Chicago University went out of business; but the school was not formally integrated into Northwestern University until 1891.[12]

Law school today lasts, almost universally, three years. In 1850, the standard course in many law schools ran for one year only. A two-year program became more common later in the century. The three-year LL.B. was a late innovation, at Harvard, during the deanship of Christopher Columbus Langdell; Boston University did likewise. The faculty of most law schools consisted of prominent judges and lawyers; full-time teachers were rare before the 1880's. The full-time teacher, too, as we shall see, was one of Langdell's innovations. Judges and lawyers were not necessarily bad teachers. Story and Greenleaf at Harvard lectured to a student body made up mostly of college graduates; their lectures were real contributions to the literature of American law. Other law schools, too, seemed to have offered fairly rigorous training before the Civil War.[13]

[11] On Michigan, see Elizabeth G. Brown, "The Law School of the University of Michigan: 1859–1959," 38 Mich. St. Bar J., No. 8, p. 16 (1959).

[12] James A. Rahl and Kurt Schwerin, "Northwestern University School of Law: A Short History," 55 Nwn. U. Law Rev. 131 (1960); Reed, *op. cit.*, p. 185.

[13] In the late 1840's, the University of North Carolina established a professorship of law, under the direction of William Horn Battle, a judge of the state's superior court. According to the university catalogue, the "department for the study of municipal law" was divided into two "classes." One, "the Independent Class," consisted of "such Students of Law as have no connection with any of the College Classes"; the "College Class" consisted of "such irregular members of College as, with the permission of the Faculty, may be desirous of joining it." The Independent Class was a two-year program, with "recitations three times a week"; the "College Class" recited once a week, and its recitations were "so arranged as not to interfere with the ordinary studies of College." The College Class took two and a half years to earn its L.L.B. "The Professor of Law and the members of the Independent Class" were not "subject to any of the ordinary College regulations." This system lasted until 1868, when the whole university closed its doors during Reconstruction. Albert Coates, "The Story of the Law School at the University of North Carolina," N. Car. L. Rev., Special Issue, Oct. 1968, pp. 1, 13, 14.

Yet Harvard, the standard-bearer, seemed to regress toward the mean. After 1845, the number of law students who were college graduates declined at Harvard. The school seemed to enter a period of stagnation:

> Everything about the School was stereotyped. For twenty years the language of the Catalogue as to entrance, course of study, and degree was not changed by a letter. There was no recorded faculty meeting during the entire period. . . . Library rules were made in theory by the Corporation, in practice by the janitor. . . .[14]

During Harvard's dark age, which lasted until 1870, the prevailing method of instruction was no longer the lecture but the "text-book method":

> from recitation period to recitation period, the students are assigned a specified portion of a regulation text-book to study, and for the most part to memorize; this is then explained by the teacher and recited on at the next period.

Part of the hour was taken up by "quizzing," which was the "more or less purely mechanical testing of the knowledge learned by the students." [15]

Neither the textbook nor the lecture method was an unmitigated evil; it depended, of course, on the man in front of the class. By all accounts, Theodore W. Dwight at Columbia was a brilliant teacher; such observers as Lord Bryce and Albert Dicey thought his school the very best imaginable. Richmond M. Pearson of North Carolina, whose private law school lasted into the 1870's, "adopted the methods of Socrates, Plato and Aristotle"; students read their books, then came to his office twice a week, where he "would examine them upon what they read by asking them questions." Pearson also lectured, coming in from a "walk around the hillside," chewing "a little twig from some favorite tree." At least one student thought he was "the greatest teacher that ever lived on the earth." [16]

But some of these judgments rested on student memory, which tends toward the romantic and is not the most trustworthy guide. In every law school, the method used to teach law was dogmatic, and uncritical, except from the standpoint of the law's own inner

---

[14] *Centennial History of the Harvard Law School 1817–1917* (1918), pp. 22–23.
[15] Josef Redlich, *The Common Law and the Case Method in American University Law Schools* (1914), pp. 7–8.
[16] Quoted in Coates, *op. cit.*, pp. 9–10.

suppositions; and in most law schools, teaching was dogmatic from any standpoint whatsoever. This kind of training could not convey to the student much sense of connection between law and life, or even of common-law evolution. Beneath sometimes brilliant lectures, there was a fundamental hollowness. The methods were best suited to law schools that wanted to equip, as rapidly and efficiently as possible, prospective lawyers with rote knowledge they were likely to need in their practice.

At one time, the Blackstone idea had been strong in legal education—the idea of a liberal education in government, politics, ethics, and law. This tradition remained alive in some schools. In Dwight's Columbia, Francis Lieber gave lectures "upon the State, embracing the origin, development, objects and history of Political Society, on the Laws and usages of War, on the history of Political Literature, on Political Ethics, on Punishments, including Statistics, etc." As part of the curriculum, Professor Charles Nairne delivered a "course of lectures on the Ethics of Jurisprudence." Lieber attracted few students; nonetheless, Dwight became jealous and hostile. Lieber had already handed in his resignation when he died in 1872. His successor was John W. Burgess. Burgess, too, eventually left the law school; he then founded, at Columbia, a "School designed to prepare young men for the duties of Public Life," to be "entitled a School of Political Science." [17] The new field enriched the social study of man and ultimately returned to enrich the study of law. But its first effect was to impoverish legal education, from which it had been exiled, and which was already sickly, already shut in its prison of concepts.

The stage was ripe for reform or revolution. The first shot was fired in 1870. Charles W. Eliot had become president of Harvard the year before. He appointed Christopher Columbus Langdell a professor in the law school; and in September 1870, Langdell was made dean, a position new to the school. The duties of the dean, on paper, were not very awesome; he was to "keep the Records of the Faculty," prepare "its business," and "preside at its meetings in the absence of the President." [18] But Langdell proceeded, with Eliot's concurrence, to turn Harvard Law School upside down. First, he made it more difficult for a student to get in. If an applicant did not have a college degree, he had to pass an entrance test.

[17] Goebel, *op. cit.*, pp. 60, 89.
[18] Quoted in Arthur E. Sutherland. *The Law at Harvard, A History of Ideas and Men, 1817–1967* (1967), p. 166; the Sutherland book is also drawn upon in the text following this passage.

The prospective student had to show his knowledge of Latin, translating from Virgil, or Cicero, or from Caesar; he was also tested on Blackstone's *Commentaries*. Skill in French was acceptable as a substitute for Latin.

Next Langdell made it harder for a student to get out. The LL.B. course was raised to two years in 1871 and to three years in 1876 (though the third year did not have to be spent in residence). By 1899, the school had adopted a straight three-year requirement. The old curriculum had taken up matters subject by subject, as time allowed; it paid little attention to the relationship between courses; students entered and left at their own rhythm. Under Langdell, the curriculum was divided into "courses," of so many hour-units apiece. Courses were arranged in a definite order; some were treated as more basic, some as more advanced. In 1872, Langdell introduced final examinations. A student had to pass these exams after his first year, before going on to the second.

But Langdell's most far-reaching reform, the one for which he is best remembered, was the introduction of the case method for teaching law. This method cast out the textbooks, and used casebooks as teaching materials; these were collections of reports of actual cases, carefully selected and arranged to illustrate the meaning and development of principles of law. The classroom tone was profoundly altered. There was no more lecturer, expounding "the law" from received texts. The teacher now was a Socratic guide, leading the student to an understanding of concepts and principles hidden as essences among the cases.[19] The teacher showed how these concepts unfolded, like a rose from its bud, through a time series of enlightened cases.

There was a theory behind Langdell's method. He believed that law was a "science"; it had to be studied scientifically, that is, inductively through primary sources. These sources were the printed cases; they expressed, in manifold dress, the few, ever-present, and ever-evolving and fructifying principles, which constituted the genius of the common law. Law, Langdell wrote,

> considered as a science, consists of certain principles or doctrines. To have such a mastery of these as to be able to apply them with constant facility and certainty to the ever-tangled skein of human affairs, is what constitutes a true lawyer; and hence to ac-

---

[19] Langdell was not the first to teach through cases. John Norton Pomeroy used a case method at New York University Law School, in the 1860's. But Pomeroy did not "shape the whole program of a leading school" with this technique. J. Willard Hurst, *The Growth of American Law* (1950), p. 261.

quire that mastery should be the business of every earnest student of law. Each of these doctrines has arrived at its present state by slow degrees; in other words, it is a growth, extending in many cases through centuries. This growth is to be traced in the main through a series of cases; and much the shortest and best, if not the only way of mastering the doctrine effectually is by studying the cases in which it is embodied. But the cases which are useful and necessary for this purpose at the present day bear an exceedingly small proportion to all that have been reported. The vast majority are useless, and worse than useless, for any purpose of systematic study. Moreover the number of fundamental legal doctrines is much less than is commonly supposed; the many different guises in which the same doctrine is constantly making its appearance, and the great extent to which legal treatises are a repetition of each other, being the cause of much misapprehension. If these doctrines could be so classified and arranged that each should be found in its proper place, and nowhere else, they would cease to be formidable from their number. It seemed to me, therefore, to be possible to take such a branch of the law as Contracts, for example, and, without exceeding comparatively moderate limits, to select, classify, and arrange all the cases which had contributed in any important degree to the growth, development, or establishment of any of its essential doctrines; and that such a work could not fail to be of material service to all who desire to study that branch of law systematically and in its original sources.

These words appeared in the preface to Langdell's first casebook, on *Contracts,* which appeared in 1871. Unlike 20th-century casebooks, it was totally bare of aids to the student—notes, comments, explanations. It consisted exclusively of the cases Langdell had culled from the mass. The majority of these were English; a lesser number were American, mostly from Massachusetts and New York. The West and the South, it seemed, had added nothing to the law. The material was arranged by topics; within topics, cases were in chronological order, showing the evolution of principles from darkness to light. Practically speaking, no statute was permitted to enter the harem of common law, not even the Statute of Frauds, which was so old and barnacled with doctrine that it was almost not a statute at all.

Langdell claimed to be interested in the evolution of law; but he was certainly not interested in new-fangled reforms that did not come through the judges. In his *Summary of Equity Pleading* (1877), he requested the reader to "bear in mind that it is the object of these sheets to aid the student in acquiring a knowledge of the equity system as such; and with this view the writer confines himself to the system as it existed in England from the earliest times to the end of Lord Eldon's chancellorship." At least one reviewer wondered why "the study of equity pleading at Harvard University in 1877 should be limited to the system as it existed prior to 1827." [20] But from the strict Langdell standpoint, statutory and reform materials were not part of the science of law. Such a course as constitutional law, debauched by enactment, was an excrescence. The three-year curriculum, starting in 1876–77, did not include constitutional law at all, not even as an elective.[21] Harvard soon receded from this extreme position, and constitutional law was let back in; but even this brief exclusion shows how far Langdell was willing to carry his logic. Besides, he needed every scrap of time. The dialogues in Langdell's classes went slowly, and covered very little ground, compared to the lecture method.

The Langdell plan burst like a bombshell in the world of legal education. "To most of the students, as well as to Langdell's colleagues, it was abomination." [22] The students were bewildered; they cut Langdell's classes in droves; only a few remained to hear him out. Before the end of the first term, his course, it was said, had dwindled to "seven devoted men . . . who went by the name of 'Kit's Freshmen' or 'Langdell's Freshmen.' " [23] The school's enrollment fell precipitously. Langdell's colleagues, who included the remarkable Emory Washburn, continued to teach the old way. The Boston University Law School was founded in 1872 as an alternative to the Harvard insanity. But Langdell persisted, and Eliot backed him up. The few students who stayed to listen found the method exciting. Among the faithful of "Kit's Freshmen" was a young man named James Barr Ames. Soon after graduation, Ames was taken onto the Harvard faculty. Here was another insult to pedagogical tradition. Young Ames was scholarly and intelligent,· but he had never been forged in the fire of practical experience, never screened at bench or bar. But then, to teach a science, scientists were needed, not practitioners.

Langdell's hiring practices were too much a break with the past not to evoke opposition. Ephraim Gurney, dean of the faculty of Harvard College, was one of many who were dismayed. Langdell,

20 3 So. Law Rev. (N.S.) 316, 317 (1877).
21 Charles Warren, *History of the Harvard Law School*, Vol. II (1908), pp. 405–6.
22 *Centennial History of the Harvard Law School*, p. 35.
23 Charles Warren, *op. cit.*, Vol. II, p. 373.

he wrote to President Eliot in 1883, had given him insomnia. At night he found his mind "revolving about the Law School problem." The occasion was a proposal to appoint William A. Keener to the faculty. Keener was young, a rather recent graduate, and had always had a marked academic bent. The appointment meant, Gurney thought, that the "School commits itself to the theory of breeding within itself its Corps of instructors and thus severs itself from the great current of legal life which flows through the courts and the bar." Langdell's idea seemed to be to "breed professors of Law not practitioners"; his school would divorce the study of law from "its actual administration." Both Langdell and Ames, Gurney felt, were "contemptuous" of judges, because judges did not treat "this or that question as a philosophical professor, building up a coherent system as they would have done." Langdell had an "extreme unwillingness to have anything furnished by the School except the pure science of the law." Students at the end of three years, Gurney thought, would enter a law office feeling "helpless," at least "on the practical side." [24]

Eliot never answered this letter; Keener got his appointment; Langdell and his followers stayed in command. Langdell must have been a great, charismatic teacher: that was one advantage. At any rate, he carried the day. The casebooks got written; the students trickled back to Harvard and back to class; the method spread to other schools. At first it was Langdell's disciples who carried the message to the Gentiles. Ezra Ripley Thayer and John Chipman Gray, inside Harvard's own walls, were converted to the cause. John H. Wigmore took the case method to Northwestern; Eugene Wambaugh, to the State University of Iowa; William Keener stormed the citadel at Columbia, and carried off that prize from the aging Dwight, who resigned in 1891.[25] In 1892, the law school of Western Reserve was founded to be governed on frankly Harvardian lines. The dean of the University of Cincinnati law school—a judge named William Howard Taft, of whom more would be heard—reported in 1896 that his "Faculty [had] decided that its wisest course would be to follow . . . the course and methods of study prevailing at the Harvard Law School," especially "the Case System." Cincinnati would use the "same books of select cases" that Harvard used for contracts, property, torts.[26] By the end of the century, the success of the new method seemed as-

24 Quoted in Sutherland, op. cit., pp. 187–90.
25 Centennial History of the Harvard Law School, p. 36.
26 Quoted in Warren, op. cit., Vol. II, p. 509.

sured. In 1902, Professor Ernest Huffcut of Cornell reported to the American Bar Association that twelve law schools had adopted the method root and branch; thirty-four others "unequivocally" clung to the "text-book system or the text-book and lecture system"; forty-eight schools professed some sort of mixture.[27] Every major and most minor law schools ultimately swung over.

Like most revolutions, Langdell's was no unmixed blessing. There were worms in the apple. Gurney's opinion was not unique; other lawyers and teachers thought the method too theoretical, unsuited for the making of good lawyers. In actual practice and in the hands of good teachers, the method worked fairly well. It did imbue students with a craftsmanlike skill in handling the materials of case law. But the vices of the method lay deep. In the most radical sense, the new method severed the cords, already tenuous, that tied the study of law to the main body of American scholarship and American life. Langdell purged from the curriculum whatever touched directly on economic and political questions, whatever was argued, voted on, fought over. He brought into the classroom a worship of common law and of the best common-law judges. Legislation he disdained; illogical decisions he despised. All this he cloaked with the mantle of science. He equated law absolutely with judges' law; and judges' law was narrowed to formalism and abstraction. The textbook method had been bad enough. It too was divorced from living law, and apathetic toward issues of social policy. Langdell did not correct these evils. Instead, he purified and perpetuated them. Though many of the old textbook and lecture teachers had trouble retooling, some may simply have adapted their old materials to new methods. After Langdell, they simply taught the cases that lurked in the footnotes of their texts, ignoring the texts themselves.

Langdell's proudest boast was that law was a science, and that his method was highly scientific. But his model of science was not experimental, or experiential; his model was Euclid's geometry, not physics or biology. Langdell considered law a pure, independent science; it was, he conceded, empirical; but the only data he allowed were reported cases. If law is at all the product of society, then Langdell's science of law was a geology without rocks, an astronomy without stars. Lawyers and judges raised on the method, if they took their training at all seriously, came to speak of law mainly in terms of a dry, arid logic, divorced from society and life.

27 Ernest W. Huffcut, "A Decade of Progress in Legal Education," *Report, 25th Ann. Meeting ABA* (1902), pp. 529, 541.

To understand Langdell's method and, more important, to understand why it triumphed, one must see it in its long-term context. In the history of legal education, two paired sets of principles were constantly in battle. A principle of vocational training struggled against a principle of scientific training. At the same time, a principle of integration with general liberal education struggled against a principle of segregation. The university law schools had been weakly integrationist, and weakly and reluctantly vocational. Langdell's new method was antivocational, but strongly segregationist within the university and the context of scholarship.

Why was this idea so attractive in the long run? Basically, it suited the needs of the legal profession. It exalted the prestige of law and legal learning; at the same time it affirmed that legal science stood apart, as an independent entity, distinct from politics, legislation, and the man on the street. In this period, interest and occupational groups fought for a place in the sun. Langdell provided a firm basis of theory for certain important claims of the legal profession. Law, he insisted, was a branch of learning that genuinely demanded rigorous formal training. There was justification, then, for the lawyers' monopoly of practice. The bar-association movement began at exactly that point in time which coincided with Langdell's rise to power. The two movements went hand in glove.

Langdell's method also promised a solution to the problem of teaching law in a federal union. He handled local diversity by ignoring it entirely. There was only one common law; Langdell was its prophet. More than half of the cases in his first casebook were English. Oceans could not sever the unity of common law; it was one and indivisible, like higher mathematics.

In this regard, Langdell's method was not entirely a novelty. "National" law schools had always been the ideal; there was a good deal of traffic across state lines; even vocational Litchfield had attracted students from all over the country; Harvard prided itself on this fact. The law school had advertised its wares in far-off places. A notice in the *St. Louis Republican,* for example, in 1848, invited law students to Harvard; the advertisement mentioned the tuition fees ($50 a term, including books), and added that "neither expediency nor the usages of society" required a large "amount of pocket-money." [28] When Michigan opened its school, too, as we have seen, it advertised that fact in a number of cities.

A varied student body was probably a real advantage to a school.

28 *St. Louis Republican,* Oct. 7, 1848, p. 3.

But ignoring local law was a mixed blessing at best. The unity of some parts of the common law was a fact. The Langdell way of abstraction, however, ignored law as a living process, with a local habitation and reality. Still, few schools that taught local law taught it as anything better or grander than tricks of the lawyer's trade, nuts and bolts of practical information. In one sense, Langdell's method—austere, abstract—was necessary to save legal education (in the nick of time) from degeneration. Two contradictory influences had pressed against legal education. First, there was a constant push toward raising standards. Second, there was an equally insistent push in the opposite direction, toward loosening the reins, toward opening the practice of law to more and more people. The first pressure came from leaders of the bar, anxious about the income and prestige of their profession. The second pressure came from the open market.

Those who were concerned with "quality" could not help but be alarmed by the lax standards that the pressures of the market created. A law school required little capital to open, and as soon as demand was there, the market responded. Purists may have been shocked when the so-called Iowa Law School, in 1866, had the presumption to award twelve LL.B. degrees. This was a mere night school, started the year before at Des Moines, by two justices of the Iowa supreme court.[29] The idea of a nighttime law school was appealing. Many potential students worked for a living by day, as law-office clerks, or in factories, offices, and shops. The Columbian College of Washington, D. C., was in operation in the late 1860's. The college was deliberately set up to "reach employees in the government departments, released from their labors at three o'clock in the afternoon."[30] The movement spread to other cities. The University of Minnesota, in 1888, offered parallel day and evening sessions. In 1889–90, there were nine pure night schools, as against fifty-one day schools. In the 1890's the number of night schools doubled. In 1900 there were twenty, as against 77 pure day schools, and five schools which, like Minnesota, mixed day and night.

The night schools, by and large, were rigorously "practical." They had neither the patience nor the inclination to serve a rich intellectual feast. They emphasized local practice far more than the national day schools. Their main vice was to encourage the downward mobility of legal education. Their main merit was to open the door of legal training to poor, immigrant, or working-

29 Reed, *op. cit.*, pp. 396–97.
30 Reed, *op. cit.*, p. 396.

class students. They were breeding grounds for the ethnic bar. Night schools turned out Polish, Italian, Jewish, and Irish lawyers, many of whom went back to their neighborhoods and served their immigrant communities. Lower-court judges and local politicians were drawn heavily from the graduates of these schools. Few found their way to Wall Street or La Salle Street. Naturally enough, these schools were resented on Wall Street and La Salle Street. For their part, these schools fought valiantly for students, money, legitimacy, recognition from the bar, and other prizes.

One such prize was a share in the so-called diploma privilege. Graduates of a school with the diploma privilege were automatically admitted to the bar. Between 1855 and 1870, Louisiana, Mississippi, Georgia, New York, Tennessee, Michigan, and Wisconsin adopted the diploma privilege for graduates of law schools in their state. In 1870, Oregon, which had no law school of its own, went so far as to give the privilege to graduates of *any* school with the diploma privilege in its own home state.[31] The trouble with the privilege was that it was politically difficult to discriminate between the various law schools in a state; yet arguably some schools did not deserve this recognition. New York regretted its move and retracted the privilege.

The bar examination was one way to dam the infernal flow into the profession. As apprenticeship vanished, control over the schools became another way. Bar associations soon began taking an interest in legal education. The schools formed an Association of American Law Schools around the turn of the century. Both AALS and the American Bar Association went into the accreditation business. A school that lacked the approval of either or both was at a serious disadvantage in competing for students. But substandard legal education did not die; like stale bread or used cars, there was a market for it, and therefore it survived.

THE LITERATURE OF THE LAW

By all counts, the basic literature of law, the most prolific, if not most artistic form, was reported case law. Hundreds of volumes of reports poured out, year by year, month by month, day by day; this fabulous collection of law was so bulky by 1900 that the Babylonian Talmud or the medieval Year Books seem inconsequentially small in comparison. Probably one could never get a complete or

31 On the diploma privilege, see Reed, *op. cit.,* pp. 248–53.

balanced picture of American life from the collective pages of these reports; but they touched on an amazing variety of topics. Every state published reports for at least its highest court; many states, like New York and Illinois, published reports of intermediate courts; in Pennsylvania, some county courts were also published. Every new state after 1850, out of a sense of legal independence, or merely out of habit, began to issue reports, promptly on arriving at statehood. In most instances, territorial reports had been published before statehood, too.

The California constitution stated explicitly that it was the duty of the state supreme court to put its decisions "in writing" and to state "the grounds of the decision." [32] There was no need for such a mandate in most states. As a matter of course, decisions and opinions were published in endless stream. There were many complaints in the 19th century that the case law was impossible to handle, out of sheer size. "What Shall be Done with the Reports?" was the title of a plaintive essay published in 1882. The author, J. L. High, was troubled by the "pernicious" effects of the "vast accumulation of reported cases." It weakened the law; the lawyer, groping his way through this "labyrinth," would neglect "the underlying principle" of law, "in the search for a precedent exactly in point." [33] No reform was forthcoming, alas. Indeed, these moans and groans now seem as naïve as complaints that twenty miles an hour was too fast for the human body to bear. Each generation taught the older one a lesson in sheer voluminousness. In 1810, there were only eighteen published volumes of American reports; in 1848, about eight hundred; by 1885, about 3,798; by 1910, over 8,000.[34] The end is not yet in sight. The National Reporter System, which began in 1879, and the digests of the West Publishing Company, helped lawyers cope a little. Even so, lawyers could hardly keep up with their own jurisdictions, let alone handle the others. Lawyers simply gave up any attempt to follow the whole of the law; they concentrated on problems at hand, and corners of law they habitually dealt with, and they grumbled about the expense and the confusion of the law reports. Yet basically, it was the lawyers' own hunger for precedent that kept the system alive.

State and federal reports are important documents for historians, though in some ways as hard to read and evaluate as hiero-

32 Cal. const. 1879, art. VI, sec. 2.
33 J. L. High, "What Shall be Done with the Reports?" 16 Am. L. Rev. 429, 439 (1882).
34 Charles Warren, *A History of the American Bar* (1912), p. 557.

glyphics. Even for lawyers, most matter in the reports was ephemeral. Cases, however, did not come neatly labeled as wheat or chaff. The trouble with the common law was not only the number of cases, but the fact that books could never be safely thrown away.

The quality of the judges' written work seems to have declined after 1850, though these matters of taste are notoriously hard to measure. Karl Llewellyn called the style of Gibson, Marshall, and Shaw the "grand style"—the style that looked for "wisdom-in-result." This style was dead by 1900. It was replaced by what Llewellyn called the "formal style," stressing order and logic in the law.[35] The style of the period was bombastic and repetitious: case reports were filled with strings of useless citations; barren logic and bad English abounded. Llewellyn's impressions seem to have some basis in fact. As the Marshalls, Shaws, and Gibsons died, or retired, they were not replaced by comparable men. Few high-court or federal judges wrote opinions with power and persuasion. The picture was never completely dark, the work never completely drab. From 1882 on, a master stylist, Oliver Wendell Holmes, Jr., sat on the highest court of Massachusetts. But the work of the average judge in 1870 or 1900 seems plainly weaker than that of 1830.

Talent and style are not historical accidents. There were social reasons why the art declined. Judges were rushed, and dockets were crowded; there was less time to polish and rework opinions. The old leisurely style of oral argument had been accompanied by a leisurely style of writing opinions. All that had ended. Marshall's court had more time to ponder, to compose, to discuss, to polish its work than Fuller's. Judges in a hurry were tempted to dish up, as the opinion of the court, a scissors and paste job taken mostly from the winning lawyer's brief. The facts of judicial life doomed the heady sense of creativity, the grand sweep of principle of earlier days. Nor were the judges the men they used to be. As we have seen, the judges represented—or overrepresented—old-American, conservative values. Yet, on the whole, judges were less likely than in 1800 to have a broad cultural background, less likely to have an esthete's command of the English language. Besides, the theory of judicial decision-making had subtly altered. Formality was not

---

[35] Karl N. Llewellyn, "Remarks on the Theory of Appellate Decision and the Rules or Canons about how Statutes are to be Construed," 3 Vanderbilt L. R. 395, 396 (1950); *The Common Law Tradition: Deciding Appeals* (1960), pp. 35–39. Llewellyn carefully asserts that for him period-style was "a way of thought and work, not . . . a way of writing." But his analysis indeed fits the way of writing if anything better than it fits thought and work.

only form, it was also a concept. Judges were not builders of law now, but protectors; they hid the power of the bench in a brier patch of legalism: they concealed their thought processes in jargon. This had two definite advantages. First, it provided a screen of legitimacy against attack from left and right. The judges did not decide cases, out of an exercise of free discretion; it was the law and only the law that determined results. The long list of precedents strung out in the case buttressed this fact. Second, formalism reinforced the judges' claim of sole and exclusive right to expound the law. The law of the judges took on a technical, erudite look. Everyman could not be a lawyer or judge; he was ignorant of legal science. Langdell's theory made the same point, and was therefore most welcome to the judges.

Langdell drove the textbooks and treatises out of the temple of legal education. They lost face, but not importance. The population explosion of cases made treatises even more of a desperate necessity. No one writer dared to restate the whole of American law. But all sorts of texts and treatises were written, on specific subjects, to turn a profit and help lawyers in their work. It has been estimated (perhaps conservatively) that a thousand or so treatises were published in the last half of the 19th century. Overwhelmingly now, these were American treatises, rather than American editions of British books. Blackstone by now was hopelessly out of date. There were new old favorites now—Simon Greenleaf's *Evidence,* Theophilus Parsons' *Contracts,* and others. Parsons (1797–1882) first published his treatise in 1853; supposedly, it sold more copies than any other American treatise. One admirer spoke of Parsons' "pleasing" style, his "sugar-coated pills of legal lore," so easily "swallowed and assimilated." [36] When a work was popular, as Parsons' was, it was repeatedly revised, even after the author died or. withdrew from the stage. Publishers hired other men to carry on' under the valuable name. Samuel Williston edited the eighth edition of Parsons' *Contracts* in 1893; Oliver Wendell Holmes, Jr., edited the 12th edition of Kent's *Commentaries* in 1873.[37]

Most 19th-century treatises were barren enough reading when they first appeared, and would be torture for the reader now. Charles Warren listed some thirty-seven works, written between 1870 and 1900, which he considered of prime importance.[38] The list

36 Charles Warren, *History of the Harvard Law School,* Vol. II, p. 312.
37 Mark DeWolfe Howe, *Justice Oliver Wendell Holmes, the Proving Years 1870–1882* (1963), pp. 11–17.
38 Charles Warren, *A History of the American Bar* (1912) pp. 551–62.

shows that writers were willing and anxious to fill the profession's needs as they arose. The books were practical books on practical subjects. The busy lawyer had a voracious appetite for helpful texts which wove the authorities into neat, indexed packages. Many treatises dealt with strictly American developments, in new and emerging fields of law: railroads, business corporations, and torts. John Forrest Dillon's *Law of Municipal Corporations,* first published in 1872, was a pioneering book, written over a period of nine years, in time snatched in the "interstices" of a judge's busy life. The book was needed; it was an immediate success. Victor Morawetz, a young lawyer on the make but without clients, threw himself into the work of writing a treatise on corporations. It appeared in 1882, and made his reputation; later he earned a fortune at the bar. John Chipman Gray (1839–1915), on the other hand, a distinguished Boston lawyer, one of the founders of the firm of Ropes and Gray, professor of law at Harvard, dipped into the older cellars of the common law and exhausted the subject of *The Rule Against Perpetuities* (1886) in a dark book which, tradition states, no one has ever really read, though countless lawyers and students skimmed through its pages in search of light. Gray also wrote a little treatise on *Restraints on the Alienation of Property* (1883). Professors were among the most prolific and successful writers of treatises. Emory Washburn of Harvard wrote a treatise on *Real Property* (two volumes, 1860–1862); it was a great success. Theophilus Parsons' *Contracts* was, as we noted, a huge best seller; and Parsons wrote seven other treatises. One of them reportedly brought him $40,000. Christopher Tiedeman, professor at the University of Missouri, wrote another popular treatise on real property (1884). Langdell's daring practice of hiring young full-time teachers and scholars, rather than elderly judges and lawyers, created a new occupation, the legal academic; at least in theory, these men could devote most of their lives to the literature of law. Some of their creative energy, of course, went into casebooks rather than texts. Langdell himself wrote very little besides his casebooks. But on the whole the academics did produce a substantial body of literature.

The most famous treatises were those which treated large, basic blocks of law, such as tort or property. But there were many highly specialized books, for example, Edward Keasbey's *Law of Electric Wires in Streets and Highways,* published in 1892. It is dangerous to generalize, but the treatises after 1870 seemed somewhat drier and less imaginative than the best work of the prior generation. Late 19th-century treatises tended to be humorless, impersonal, less concerned with praise and blame than with bare exposition of law. James Schouler, himself a treatise-writer (Volume I of his *Personal Property* appeared in 1873), pleaded for more skill in synthesis and claimed that even this was lacking. The standard editions of texts were becoming so "honeycombed with this insect annotation that the text seems to belong to the foot-notes, not the foot-notes to the text." [39] In this kind of book, there was no place for critique or for culture. Common-law thought, in and out of universities, was isolated and inbred. The dominant culture of legal scholarship was infected by Langdell's ideas of legal science, or converged on the same state, out of similar social force. Few text-writers indulged in social commentary. John Forrest Dillon, a man of high intelligence, explained, in the preface to the fourth edition of his treatise on local government: "No writer on our jurisprudence is authorized to speak oracularly, to excogitate a system, or to give to his views any authoritative sanction. To this rule the most eminent are no exception." Dillon saw a role for the author's "reflections, criticisms, and conclusions"; but it was a limited role, and most of his colleagues did without these "reflections, criticisms, and conclusions." [40] After 1870, the tone of John Chipman Gray was more representative of the better treatises—logical, scientific, frankly jejune. His personal opinions about the social worth of his subject were confined to the prefaces of his books. There were exceptions. Joel Bishop made mordant comment on his subjects. Even he was proud to assert that "nothing merely theoretical" was "admitted" to his treatises. And he was convinced that the "student, the practitioner, and the judge" all needed "the same learning," and therefore the same kind of book.[41] Thomas Cogley wrote a cranky, obstreperous book on the *Law of Strikes, Lock-outs and Labor Organizations* (1894), more a tract than a treatise. But there was nothing before 1900 to match the magnificent treatise on evidence (1904–05) by John H. Wigmore, scholarly, yet critical, the product of a glowing intelligence. Gray's style led directly to Samuel Williston, whose treatise on contracts in the 1920's was, from the standpoint of legal or social thought, volume after volume of a heavy void.

Basically, legal literature was pragmatic; the differences between the famous treatises and strictly local manuals—and even such sub-

---

39 James Schouler, "Text and Citations," 22 Am. L. Rev. 66, 73 (1888).
40 John F. Dillon, *Commentaries on the Law of Municipal Corporations* (4th ed., 1890), preface, pp. vii–viii.
41 Joel P. Bishop, *Commentaries on the Criminal Law* (7th ed., 1882), p. xiv.

liminal stuff as layman's guides and the many versions of *Every Man His Own Lawyer*—was a difference not of kind but of degree. Legal literature, with some exceptions, was empty of philosophy or social science. European jurisprudence was occasionally studied; the German historical school influenced the writing of James Carter, Field's great antagonist. John Chipman Gray's early 20th-century book *The Nature and Sources of the Law* (1909), well written and well balanced, is still worth reading. A school of legal history did develop in the latter part of the 19th century. It was concerned not with the history of the legal system so much as with the history of common-law doctrine, rather narrowly defined. Hence it was mostly English legal history, and fairly ancient history at that. The essays of James Barr Ames were among the best of these works.

Oliver Wendell Holmes' exploration of origins, *The Common Law* (1881), an authentic classic, still in print, was easily the most distinguished book on law, by an American, published between 1850 and 1900.[42] "The life of the law," wrote Holmes at the beginning of this book, "has not been logic; it has been experience." This famous line, endlessly quoted, later became the motto of the school of legal realists of the 1920's and 30's. It has been an important, even revolutionary, slogan for jurisprudence and legal research. For Langdell, and for his disciple Ames, conceptual clarity and logic were at the very heart of law, or at any rate of legal science. Holmes understood that aspect of their thought; he called Langdell "the greatest living legal theologian." But Holmes saw logic as an "evening dress which the newcomer puts on to make itself presentable"; the "important phenomenon is the man underneath it, not the coat." [43] Despite their difference in viewpoint, Holmes was not so distant in historical technique from Langdell's disciple Ames. The "experience" which most fascinated Holmes was a common-law experience. He was as eager as Ames to look into the Year Books; and he searched for an understanding of common law roots among Norman and Germanic materials. At times he seemed to care more for these origins than for the fulfillments of law in his own generation.

Outside the academy, historical literature of law was hardly worthy of the name. Most "Histories of Bench and Bar"—there were scores—were trivial, bombastic, maddeningly repetitious. One of

---

42 On the genesis of this book, see Mark DeWolfe Howe, *Justice Oliver Wendell Holmes, The Proving Years 1870–1882* (1963), pp. 135–59.

43 Quoted in Howe, *op. cit.,* pp. 155–57.

THE LEGAL PROFESSION: TRAINING AND LITERATURE 545

the best of a bad lot was John Belton O'Neall's *Biographical Sketches of the Bench and Bar of South Carolina,* a two-volume work published in 1859. The prose was execrable:

> William Henry Drayton is a name not to be forgotten while liberty is appreciated. I turn to it with the delight with which the awakened sleeper witnesses the Aurora of a bright day.[44]

Many later histories were a hodge-podge, put together from the reminiscences of aging lawyers. When the upstarts of the "flush times" grew gray and respectable, they delighted in telling tall tales of their youth. Their memory, of course, was not to be trusted. Occasionally, these books preserved source materials of some historical value. Court histories were only a little better; they tended to be anecdotal. In this wilderness, any careful and balanced study stood out dramatically. Such a book was Judge Charles P. Daly's *History of the Court of Common Pleas* (New York), a slim but valuable work that appeared in 1855.

More lasting and important work was written by constitutional theorists. If Holmes' *Common Law* was the most important 19th-century book, from the 20th-century standpoint, Thomas M. Cooley's *Constitutional Limitations,* written in 1868, was the most important book for its own generation. Its full title was: *A Treatise on the Constitutional Limitations Which Rest Upon the Legislative Power of the States of the American Union.* Benjamin Twiss has claimed that Cooley's book supplied "capitalism . . . with a legal ideology . . . almost as a direct counter to the appearance a year earlier of Karl Marx's *Das Kapital.*" [45] This is certainly an exaggeration. But the sentiment is understandable. The book appeared ahead of its time, before the full flowering of the due-process clause. It anticipated these developments. Ultimately, Cooley's book ran through several editions, and some prophecies of the first edition were fulfilled by the courts in time to appear as settled law in the later ones. Cooley's treatise was useful; it provided a beautiful constitutional theory for those who wanted limited government, who were frightened of impulsive and radical lawmaking, who wanted no more hostile regulation of business, no laws on the side of organized labor and the mob. This, the *laissez-faire* or social Darwinist point of view, found its champion in some passages in Cooley's text. (Cooley himself was much less of a card-

44 Vol. I, p. 13.
45 Benjamin R. Twiss, *Lawyers and the Constitution* (1942), p. 18.

board reactionary than he has been pictured.)[46] The book was solidly written, well thought out, and was the product of an inventive mind. Its actual influence is a matter of some dispute. As we have seen, conservatism won some important victories in the courts toward the end of the century. The judges in these cases often cited Cooley; he has therefore been accused of inventing a lot of (bad) constitutional law. He did supply authority and text for those who needed and wanted these. But the Supreme Court was not hypnotized by Cooley. Rather, both Cooley and the judges were hypnotized by similar ideas. One wrote a book, the others decided cases, from similar impulses. Cooley was architect, prophet, and publicist, of a stern but satisfying order, in a period when the specter of "socialism" sent waves of panic through the upper stories of society. For the solid citizen, who watched gangs of immigrants pour into the country, and who worried about the staying power of American values, the Supreme Court was a mighty shield, preventing collapse. In the next generation, Christopher Tiedeman's book, *A Treatise on the Limitations of Police Power in the United States* (1889), took a position even farther to the right of Cooley. Tiedeman's idea of limited government gave the courts another text to cite; once again, then, the theorists could cite, in their next edition, the courts who cited them.[47]

LEGAL PERIODICALS AND CASEBOOKS

When West began to publish the *National Reporter System,* in 1879, it undercut the reason for being of many law magazines. These periodicals contained comments and little essays on the law; they also informed the profession about new and interesting cases. The *Albany Law Journal,* the *Central Law Journal* and the *American Law Review* of St. Louis, the *American Law Register* of Philadelphia, and the *Virginia Law Journal* of Richmond still appeared in the 1880's.[48] But their day was almost done. A few jour-

[46] See Alan Jones, "Thomas M. Cooley and the Michigan Supreme Court: 1865–1885," 10 Am. J. Leg. Hist. 97 (1966).

[47] John Forrest Dillon, in his treatise on local government (1872), added a few notions which also became important in conservative decision-making. See Clyde Jacobs, *Law Writers and the Courts* (1954), for a good assessment of the work and importance of Cooley, Tiedeman, and Dillon.

[48] For a list of periodicals, see 21 Am. L. Rev. 150 (1887). Some of the reviews did not print cases, and were more strictly scholarly, like the later university reviews. One of these was the *Southern Law Review,* New Series, which Sey-

nals specialized in insurance, or patents, or corporation law.
Thomas B. Paton launched a *Banking Law Journal* in New York in
1889. *Green Bag,* begun in 1889, was an uninhibited potpourri of
interesting articles and comments on the law.

A more significant event was the birth of the university law review. The first issue of the *Harvard Law Review* appeared on
April 15, 1887. It was (and is) edited by students at the law school;
every issue contained some of their work, along with the work of
professors, lawyers, and judges. The first issues included law-school
news, and notes "taken by students from lectures delivered as part
of the regular course of instruction in the school." [49] The *Review*
proposed to appear monthly "during the academic year," at a subscription price of $2.50 a year, or $.35 per number. The *Review*
included leading articles and case notes—brief discussions of recent cases. The cases themselves were not reprinted. The *Review*
did not intend "to enter into competition with established law
journals," but rather to "give . . . some idea of what is done
under the Harvard system of instruction." Yet the staff did hope
that its work might "be serviceable to the profession at large." [50]
Most articles discussed points of laws, in the Langdell style. But
there were other kinds of articles as well. William H. Dunbar, in
the first volume, dealt with "The Anarchists' Case before the Supreme Court of the United States"; and Samuel B. Clarke wrote
"Criticisms upon Henry George, Reviewed from the Stand-point of
Justice." [51]

The *Yale Law Journal* was launched four years later, in October 1891; its first article was on "Voting-Trusts," by Simeon Baldwin. Other law reviews followed—Columbia in 1900, for example.
The university law review proved an apt vehicle for speculative
writing on law. It was the perfect outlet for shorter works
by the new class of teaching scholars. The law review could justify
itself as a training device for students, and as a scholarly journal; it
did not have to meet the immediate demands of the marketplace.
The writing in the early reviews was not uniformly good; but some
distinguished articles were published. Nor were the law reviews
even then without influence on the growth and development of

---

mour D. Thompson began to edit at St. Louis in 1875. Thompson discontinued
case digests, and promised to present instead "the *best legal thought* in America
and Europe."

[49] See, for example, 1 Harv. L. Rev. 103 (1887).

[50] *Ibid.,* p. 35.

[51] 1 Harv. L. Rev. 265, 307 (1888).

law. A striking example was the article by Samuel D. Warren and
Louis D. Brandeis in 1890, in the *Harvard Law Review*, on "The
Right to Privacy." [52] Out of a few scraps of precedent, the article
invented a brand-new tort, invasion of privacy. With the curious
modesty of the common lawyer, the authors disclaimed this tort as
their own child. They preferred to pass it off as a foundling. It was
already born, they said, citing existing principles and cases; but the
courts and the public had simply not been aware of what had been
done. The question was "whether the existing law affords a principle which can properly be invoked to protect the privacy of the
individual?" Their answer was yes. The response of courts to this
idea was not overwhelming; but when the time came for the right
of privacy to flourish, Warren and Brandeis' child, like Cooley's
theories in *their* realm, was available for adoption and support.

One final form of legal literature should also be mentioned: the
casebook. This was, of course, a by-product of Langdell's reforms;
and Langdell himself published the first teaching casebook, on
contracts, in 1871. His disciples and converts followed with casebooks of their own.[53] James Barr Ames edited cases on *Bills and
Notes* in 1881. John Chipman Gray edited a six-volume casebook
on *Property* (1888–92).[54] The pristine casebook collected nothing
but cases. It was completely devoid of any commentary. Finding,
pasting, and stitching cases together was not so simple as it might
appear. The best casebooks required a great deal of creative imagination. But these books, in their bareness, carried to its extreme
a most striking characteristic of the style of teaching they reflected.
This was the Socratic masquerade: the art of saying everything
while appearing to say nothing at all.

[52] 4 Harv. L. Rev. 193 (1890).

[53] Collections of cases, of course, were not new. For example, Edmund Bennet
and Franklin Heard published *A Selection of Leading Cases in Criminal Law* in
two volumes, in 1856. In the preface they noted that the "selection of important
Cases on different branches of the Law, and the elucidation and development of
the principles involved in them, in the form of Notes," had become an "acceptable mode of presenting legal subjects to the Profession." Langdell's was the first
collection, however, arranged systematically, in accordance with his theory of
legal education.

[54] Interestingly, Gray arranged his materials to follow the organization of
Emory Washburn's textbook on property, which had been published in 1860.
See Sutherland, *op. cit.*, p. 152.

(CHAPTER XII)

THE LEGAL PROFESSION: AT WORK

In 1850 there were, according to one estimate, 21,979 lawyers in the country.[1] In the next fifty years, after the Civil War, the Gilded Age, and the transformation of the American economy, there were profound changes in supply and demand. The number of lawyers increased—there were perhaps 60,000 by 1880 and 114,000 in 1900 —and the functions of the profession changed with its numbers. The New York Code of Civil Procedure, of 1848, symbolized one kind of change. The code did not end the lawyer's monopoly of courtroom work. It did not abolish the bag of jargon and artifice that was as much a part of his equipment as the doctor's black bag with stethoscope and tools. But the code represented the end of the hegemony of the courtroom. Because lawyers were less talented in the art of pleading, procedural codes became necessary. The codes in turn dethroned the ancient pleading arts. The slow estrangement of the lawyer from his old and natural haunt, the court, was an outstanding fact of the practice in the second half of the century. Most lawyers still went to court; but the Wall Street lawyer, who perhaps never spoke to a judge except socially, made more money and had more prestige than any other lawyer.

The change of function reflected changes in the law itself. Life and the economy were more complicated: there was more, then, to be done, and the lawyers proved able to do it. There was nothing inevitable in the process. The profession might have become smaller and narrower, restricted like the English barrister, or the brain surgeon, to a few rare, complex, and lucrative tasks. Automation and technological change were full of pitfalls for lawyers, no less than for other occupations. Social invention constantly threatened to displace them. Title companies and trust companies proved to be efficient competitors. These institutions were unimportant before the Civil War. But by 1900, large able companies

[1] [John] *Livingston's Law Register* (1851), preface, p. iv.

had nibbled away at debt collection, estate work, and title searches, all staples of the practice.

Nevertheless the lawyers prospered. The truth was that the profession was exceedingly nimble at finding new kinds of work and new functions. Its nimbleness was no doubt due to the character of the bar: open-ended, unrestricted, uninhibited, attractive to sharp, ambitious men. In so amorphous a profession, many lawyers went into business or politics because they could not earn a living at their trade. Others reached out for new sorts of practice. At any rate, the profession did not take the path to the status of a small, exclusive elite. Even in 1860, the profession was bigger, wider, compared to 1800. In 1800, lawyers in Philadelphia came "predominantly from families of wealth, status, and importance." In 1860, a much higher percentage came from the middle class—sons of shopkeepers, clerks, small businessmen.[2] By 1900, this trend had if anything sharply strengthened.

The external relations of the bar were always vitally important. After 1870, there was another line of defense against competition: the lawyers' unions (never called by that name), which fought vigorously to protect the boundaries of the calling. The organized profession raised (or tried to raise) its "standards"; tried to limit entry into the field, and (above all) tried to resist conversion of the profession into a "mere" business or trade. In fact, lawyers did not incorporate and did not become fully bureaucratized. The bar was able to prevent the corporate practice of law. Large private law firms were able to compete with captive legal departments and house counsel staffs of large corporations. For the time being at least, the private lawyer kept his independent status, as a middle-class craftsman and entrepreneur. The lawyer's role in American life had never been too clearly defined. The practice of law was what lawyers did. This was a truth as well as a tautology. The upper echelons of the profession never quite succeeded in closing the doors against newcomers and outsiders. They dreamt of a close-knit, guildlike bar. They longed for the honor and security of the barrister. But because it was easy to pass in and out of the profession, their dream could never be fulfilled.

The corporation lawyer, on Wall Street and its sister streets in other cities, was a dramatic new figure at the bar. But he did not chase the others out of business. He merely supplemented them; he superimposed another layer on the profession, already many-layered.

2 Gary B. Nash, "The Philadelphia Bench and Bar, 1800–1861," in *Comparative Studies in Society and History*, Vol. VII, No. 2 (1965), p. 203.

Before the Civil War, the most prominent, famous lawyers were lawyer-statesmen, who argued great cases before great courts, who went into politics, and, above all, were skilled in the arts of advocacy. Daniel Webster was the prototype. This kind of lawyer never became extinct. Jeremiah Sullivan Black, one of the most colorful 19th-century lawyers, was one such survival.[3] Black was born in 1810. He read law in the office of Chauncey Forward and formed his distinctive style of speech and writing from close study of Shakespeare, Milton, and the Bible. He served on the Pennsylvania supreme court in the 1850's, where his pungent prose spices the otherwise dry, brittle pages of these law reports. Later, Black served in Buchanan's cabinet, as attorney general (1857). Still later, Black got rich off the fat of California land cases, which he argued before the Supreme Court. He fought the good fight in two great cases after the Civil War, *Ex parte Milligan* and *Ex parte McCardle*.[4] He figured on the Democratic side of the Tilden-Hayes controversy, and died in 1883. Black was a fiery lawyer, and a superb orator. He could emit a flawless oral argument, for hours on end, without referring to his notes, and without misciting a single case. He was a lone wolf who never really maintained an office, never had a partner for any length of time. Nor did Black have any permanent clients; he was always hired for the one particular case. His income was said to have been enormous; the exact amounts are not known. He kept no records, and, indeed, rarely fixed a fee. Yet for one case alone, in 1879, he was paid the princely sum of $28,000.

Men like Black were rare. His direct descendants are the great civil-rights lawyers, on the one hand, and, on the other, the criminal lawyers whose clients keep changing and whose livelihood depends on publicity and word of mouth. Howe and Hummel were not entirely aberrations. On the prosecutor's side, there was occasional nobility—as in the New York career of William Travers Jerome (1859–1934), the enemy of Tammany Hall—and good chance for political fortune, as the career of Thomas E. Dewey would later testify. But the big money was elsewhere—on Wall Street. The Wall Street lawyer has always been in one sense self-effacing. He has no hunger, or need, for publicity. What he wants is a steady group of well-paying clients, and a permanent one.

We are indebted to Robert T. Swaine, the historian of the Cra-

[3] His biography has been written by William N. Brigance, *Jeremiah Sullivan Black* (1934).
[4] 71 U.S. 2 (1866); 74 U.S. 506 (1869).

vath firm of New York, for a detailed account of the rise of one Wall Street office.[5] For most of the 19th century, the firm was extremely small, a two-man partnership. Members of the Seward and Blatchford families were dominant figures in the early history of the firm. The firm was originally based in Auburn, New York. When William H. Seward became a United States senator in 1849, he loosened his ties to the office. But he never gave up the business of law, even though his career led him into Lincoln's cabinet, as secretary of state. In the 1850's, the firm did a great deal of debt collection, real estate, and title business, and drafting of wills and trusts. Cyrus McCormick retained the firm for a patent matter in 1850. In 1854, the firm moved to New York City. It was by then already active in corporation law and in patent litigation. The Bank of North America and the Girard Trust Company were among its clients.

After the Civil War, the booming express companies took over as the firm's biggest clients. Corporate business expanded; patent litigation gradually slackened off. The firm added new members. In 1869, Charles M. Da Costa joined the firm. He was an expert on admiralty matters, but he soon gravitated toward work on corporate reorganization. In 1880, the firm became involved with Kuhn, Loeb & Co., and hence with corporate securities and finance. William D. Guthrie became a partner in 1883; Victor Morawetz, the author of a treatise on corporations, joined in 1887. Between 1880 and 1900, the career of the firm was intimately bound up with Wall Street finance; it drew up papers merging businesses, it advised railroads on their legal affairs, handled stockholders' suits, floated bond issues. In 1896 Morawetz withdrew, to become general counsel for the Santa Fe; Charles Steele, a partner in the '90's, went over to the house of Morgan. The junior partners and clerks still handled small litigation for big clients; and the firm still argued cases before the Supreme Court (Guthrie's role in the income-tax case has been mentioned) but the partnership had become the very model of a Wall Street firm. It was a servant and advisor to big business, an architect of financial structures; it did not feed on lawsuits, rather it avoided them.

The Cravath story, of course, is one of continuous great success. But other Wall Street firms have had long histories. Where these histories have been retold, they run quite parallel to that of Cravath—for example, the story of the firm of Thomas G. Shearman

5 *The Cravath Firm and Its Predecessors* (Vol. I, 1946).

and John W. Sterling, which handled many of Jay Gould's tangled affairs, and later those of William Rockefeller.[6]

There were also little Wall Streets in other cities. Each major city had a corporate bar, though none so grand as New York. Outside New York, the literature on these firms is rather slim. Emily Dodge has studied the history of a Milwaukee law firm, dating back to 1842. Before the Civil War, real-estate matters dominated the firm's business. After the war, contract and business affairs took the lead. The firm grew and slowly took on staff. The growth of this firm ran roughly parallel to the growth of the great Wall Street houses.[7]

By and large, the leading lawyers of the big Wall Street firms were solid Republicans, conservative in outlook, standard Protestant in faith, old English in heritage. But the firms were never wholly monolithic. Morawetz was a southern Democrat. Guthrie, Seward's most militant and reactionary partner, was Roman Catholic; he began his career as an office boy. Da Costa, another partner, was descended from West Indian Jews. Charles O'Conor (1804–84), a dominant figure in the New York trial bar, was born in New York, of Irish parents. There were many others at the bar of Irish descent, like Charles P. Daly (1816–99), author, lawyer, and chief judge of the New York court of common pleas.[8] Good background and cultural compatibility were, however, helpful to the rising young lawyer. Old-line lawyers were never too happy about the influx of "Celts," Jews, and other undesirables. George T. Strong, writing in his diary in 1874, hailed the idea of a test for admission at the Columbia Law School: "either a college diploma, or an *examination including Latin*. This will keep out the little scrubs (German Jew boys mostly) whom the School now promotes from the grocery-counters . . . to be 'gentlemen of the Bar.' " [9] Meritorious outsiders sometimes reached the celestial heights of Wall Street, but it was generally by adopting, to a greater or less extent, the protective coloration of the dominant culture.[10]

[6] The firm has been chronicled by Walter K. Earle, *Mr. Shearman and Mr. Sterling and How They Grew* (1963).

[7] Emily Dodge, "Evolution of a City Law Office, Part II," 1956 Wis. L. Rev. 35, 41 (data based on number of appeals).

[8] Harold E. Hammond, *A Commoner's Judge: The Life and Times of Charles Patrick Daly* (1954).

[9] Quoted in Henry W. Taft, *A Century and a Half at the New York Bar* (1938), p. 146.

[10] The woman lawyer was another kind of outsider. Mrs. Myra Bradwell,

Two charges have been leveled against the Wall Street firm: that it served its rich, evil clients rather than the public; and that it perverted the legal profession, turning the free, independent craftsman into a worker in a factory of law. Both charges were already heard in the late 19th century and have never completely subsided. The first charge is hard to evaluate. Most lawyers always served, mainly themselves, next their clients, last of all their conception of that diffuse, nebulous thing, the public interest. No doubt the Wall Street lawyer sincerely felt he served God by serving Mammon and Morgan. Lawyers have to make a living. They go where the money and the practice are. As for the second charge, the rise of corporation law and big law firms was bound to change the myths and the outlook of the legal profession. A lawyer in a law firm, who rarely set foot in court, who did preventive-law work with big business clients, naturally organized his work life differently from the way a courtroom virtuoso, who worked alone, organized his. To help float a bond issue worth millions, or to reorganize a railroad, lawyers needed staff, and specialists, and a certain amount of investment in legal plant. Firms of more than three partners were rare before the Civil War. By 1900, they were common on Wall Street. In addition, the firms hired growing numbers of clerks and associates. In the 1870's, three or four law students, on the average, took up space in the firm headed by Clarence A. Seward. Besides clerks and stenographers, the firm harbored about six associates. Student lawyers came, clerked, learned, and did service, partly on their own, partly for the firm's benefit. But as late as 1879, Seward wrote that it was "not the custom of my office, nor of any other with which I am acquainted, to give any compensation to students." At the end of the century, under the new "Cravath system," all lawyers who worked in the office were paid. Beginners received thirty dollars a month.[11] Law offices took up use of the telephone and the typewriter. The firms began to hire more office workers skilled in

born in 1831, married to a lawyer in 1852, studied law and passed her examination. When she tried to get in to the Illinois bar in 1869, she was turned down. She appealed, and lost her case. A few years later, the legislature relented. Mrs. Bradwell died in 1894. See 49 Albany L.J. 136 (1894). Mrs. Arabella Mansfield was admitted to the Iowa Bar about the time of Mrs. Bradwell's failure. 4 Am. L. Rev. 397 (1870). The resistance to women lawyers only gradually diminished and is far from extinct in the 1970's. Black lawyers were unknown on Wall Street, and rare everywhere. There were only fourteen black lawyers in North Carolina in 1890, according to the census. Frenise A. Logan, *The Negro in North Carolina 1876–1894* (1964), p. 108.

11 Swaine, *op. cit.*, pp. 364, 658.

the use of business machines. In 1899, Cravath's firm started a filing system and took on a file clerk.

The salaried lawyer became more common in the late 19th century. The big firms hired lawyers who were not immediately made partners; some never reached this rank at all. House counsel—lawyers on the full-time payroll of a company—were unheard of in 1800, exceedingly rare in 1850; by 1900 this was a well-worn groove of practice. The corporate giants hired their own law firms and had lawyers on their staffs as captives or collaborators. Other big corporations needed whole armies of lawyers to do their legal chores, big and small. In 1885, the Prudential Insurance Company "began to require the exclusive attention of its attorneys; the Mutual and the New York Life established their first full-time solicitors in 1893; the Metropolitan had a claim and law division by 1897." [12] To be general counsel of a major railroad, after the Civil War, was to occupy a position of great prestige and enormous salary. William Joseph Robertson left the Virginia supreme court to become general counsel for two railroads; Judge G. W. McCrary left the federal bench in the 1880's to take the post on the Santa Fe; the chief justice of Kansas, Albert H. Horton, resigned and became attorney for the Missouri Pacific, in 1895.[13] Then, as now, too, business attorneys moved up to top management. Thomas C. Cochran studied railroad leaders between 1845 and 1890; he found that many railroad presidents had begun as lawyers—for example, Frederick Billings (1823–90), of the Northern Pacific. Chauncey Depew (1834–1928) began as a lawyer, was a railroad attorney, executive of the New York Central, then a United States senator in 1899.[14]

Small-town and small-city practice were more timeless and unchanging than big-city practice; patterns of life remained much the same; hence the gap between this and Wall Street practice was very wide. There were 143 items of business on the office docket, for 1874, of a "leading law firm" in a small Illinois city. They included three partition proceedings, one divorce, one petition for a writ of mandamus, three cases for specific performance, three attachments, one arbitration award, and a petition to sell real estate to pay debts. All the rest were collection matters, requiring either negotiation, or legal action before a justice of the peace or in county or circuit courts: twenty-two of these were foreclosures of mortgages on land. During the entire year, the firm appeared frequently in

12 Morton Keller, *The Life Insurance Enterprise, 1885–1910* (1963), p. 187.
13 J. Willard Hurst, *The Growth of American Law* (1950), pp. 297–98.
14 Thomas C. Cochran, *Railroad Leaders 1845–1890* (1953), pp. 249, 309.

court, but in only the three lower courts just mentioned.[15] An Indiana lawyer later recalled life in the 1850's, in the fifth judicial circuit of Indiana. The firm of Fletcher, Butler, and Yandes had the most extensive practice in the circuit. But its work consisted largely of "the making of collections for eastern merchants." [16]

One instructive career was that of James Carr. He came to Missouri about 1850 from Pennsylvania. First he taught for some years at a country school in Monroe County, assuming a Virginia accent because local feeling ran high against Yankees. Carr read law, and set up shop in Paris, Missouri, in a "small 14 × 14 office room." Since he could not afford a table, "he put a board on the arm of a 'split bottom' rocking chair, and on that he for some time did his studying and writing." Carr was, in the estimation of his peers, fairly learned, but nothing to write home about as a courtroom lawyer. He was not "a good judge of human nature," and "found it a difficult task to compete with the average country lawyer." So far, Carr's story was not much different from those of many other country lawyers, who eked out a bare living at the law. But Carr "continued to fill his head with what the books said," especially books about the law of corporations. In 1865, he got work as attorney for the Hannibal & St. Joe Railroad, and moved to Hannibal, Missouri. Later, he transferred to St. Louis, where he practiced corporation law. When he died, late in the century, he "left a good estate for his family." [17] There were other small-town lawyers as successful as Carr, and even more so. Sometimes they made their fortune without moving to the big city. They became rich country lawyers, like rich country doctors, and typically owed only part of their success to the practice of law. Law was a lever or an opening wedge: real estate, or local business, or political achievement made for the rest of their fortune.

By 1900, circuit riding was only a memory, part of the golden past. Even Abraham Lincoln, before he entered the White House, could have done all his traveling from county seat to county seat, by railroad. Some of the romance of the practice remained alive, however, in frontier areas: the plains states, the Far West, the mountain and desert country. There were differences, of course,

---

15 R. Allan Stephens, "The 'Experienced Lawyer Service' in Illinois," 20 Amer. Bar Ass'n. J. 716 (1934).

16 W. W. Woollen, "Reminiscences of the Early Marion County Bar," *Publications, Indiana Hist. Soc.* (1923), Vol. VII, pp. 185, 192.

17 W. O. L. Jewett, "Early Bar of Northeast Missouri," in A. J. D. Stewart, ed., *History of the Bench and Bar of Missouri* (1898), pp. 54, 59.

between the buckskin lawyer of the 1800's, in Northwest Territory, and the lawyers of the Far West, in the cattle towns and mining camps. But there were also striking similarities—a common frontier legal culture, whatever the period and place. These remote places still attracted adventurous young men: ambitious, variously educated, looking for a fortune in law, business, or politics, or simply interested in raising hell. David Dudley Field, in the East, fought for his codes, and made money as lawyer for the robber barons; his younger brother Stephen went to California during the gold-rush days. He became alcalde of Marysville, California; here he built a frame house and "dispensed justice for the community, holding court behind a dry goods box, with tallow candles for lights." He also made money in land speculation, fought or almost fought duels, rose to become justice of the California supreme court and from there was appointed to the United States Supreme Court.[18] Field practiced in a rough community, during rough times. The lawyers of the West were themselves rather rough-hewn, often enough. If a Kansas lawyer, trained in New England, could be believed, his colleagues were an "ignorant, detestable set of addle-headed numbskulls."[19] But the man who said these words was not himself of this sort. Stephen Field, too, was a person of education, culture, and great legal acumen. He was not the only one of this stamp in California. Joseph G. Baldwin, fresh from the "flush times" of the old Southwest, arrived in California in 1854: he too, before his death, served on the state supreme court. Many territorial lawyers had gotten an education in the East. Luther Dixon was born in Vermont, studied law under a Virginia judge, practiced for a while in Wisconsin, then settled in Colorado. Another Colorado attorney, Joseph N. Baxter, advertised himself in 1892 as "formerly of the Boston Bar." A Texas lawyer in the same year proudly proclaimed himself a "Graduate of Columbia College Law School, New York City, Class of 1884."[20]

The practice of the frontier lawyer was like frontier practice in earlier places and times. James M. Mathers, who practiced in Indian Territory, stated that "our practice . . . was by necessity a criminal practice . . . and the great bulk of cases were murder cases."[21] This was perhaps exceptional. Land law, claim law, real-

---

[18] Carl Swisher, *Stephen J. Field, Craftsman of the Law* (1930), is the standard biography.

[19] Quoted in Everett Dick, *The Sod House Frontier 1854–1890* (1954), p. 450.

[20] *Hubbell's Legal Directory* (1892), Appendix, pp. 14, 197.

[21] Quoted in Marshall Houts, *From Gun to Gavel* (1954), p. 33.

estate brokerage and speculation, money brokerage, collection work, mortgage work—these were staples of practice in the more lightly settled territories. The letterhead of E. P. Caldwell, an attorney in Huron, Dakota Territory, in the 1860's, stated his business as follows: "Money Loaned for Eastern Capitalists. Taxes Paid for Nonresidents. Investments Carefully Made for Eastern Capitalists. General Law, Land and Collection Business Transacted. Buy and Sell Real Estate. U. S. Land Business promptly Attended to. Contests a Specialty." [22] An attorney in Waco, Texas, advertised in 1892: "Have splendid facilities for lending money on first-class real estate security." In Utah, in the same year (1892), the American Collecting Agency, an association of attorneys, reported that:

> A prosperous year has enabled us to enlarge our offices and put in them an immense fireproof safe to protect our clientage. We have added to our home force, secured detectives in all parts of Utah, and engaged first-class correspondents. . . . We make no charge unless we collect. Our charges are reasonable. We remit promptly. We are a godsend to honest creditors—a holy terror to delinquents.[23]

Not every lawyer, of course, was a glorified collection agent. But no Wall Street or Wall Street practice was possible in these dry and far-off places. One novelty was railroad work. As the railroads pushed west, they constantly needed local attorneys, to handle affairs along the route. In Dakota Territory, in 1889, the "assistant solicitor" of the Milwaukee Road heard young Thomas J. Walsh argue a case before the supreme court of the Territory. The man was impressed, and the future Montana senator was appointed "local attorney" for the railroad in Redfield, Dakota Territory. This entitled him to a free pass on the railroad, as a "retainer." [24] Mining companies needed skilled lawyers, too; and so did the big landowners, merchants, and ranchers.

Some Western lawyers were almost as peripatetic as prospectors, who wandered from mining camp to mining camp, looking for gold. Homebodies stayed home in the East. James Clagett, born in Maryland, migrated with his parents to Iowa in 1850. He was admitted to the Iowa bar in 1858. In 1861, he moved to Carson

---

[22] Howard R. Lamar, *Dakota Territory 1861–1889, A Study of Frontier Politics* (1956), p. 127.

[23] Hubbell, *op. cit.*, Appendix, pp. 206, 208.

[24] Walsh to Elinor C. McClements, Feb. 13, 1889, in J. Leonard Bates, ed., *Tom Walsh in Dakota Territory* (1966), p. 218.

City, Nevada, and in 1862 served as a member of the territorial house. The discovery of gold drew him to Montana in 1867; here he became territorial delegate to Congress. In 1873, he turned up in Denver, Colorado. Later, he shifted his base of operations to Deadwood, Dakota Territory, where he "thrived on the intrigues and law suits brought by the large mining companies against one another." In 1882, he moved to Butte, Montana, to engage in the mining business. Next, Clagett was president of the Idaho constitutional convention, in 1889. Unsuccessful in Idaho politics, he moved to Spokane, Washington, where he died in 1901. Clagett was "an excellent example of the mobility which was a primary feature of political life in the West. . . . It was the Clagetts . . . who wrote the codes, and who were elected to such offices as register of deeds, county commissioner, or territorial delegate. They were the men who organized political parties in the wild lawless towns situated in some narrow gulch where a shallow creek ran, with a fortune hidden in its wet sands." [25]

In the far Western states, legal systems had to be borrowed or invented in a hurry; lawyers were the only ones who could do this job. J. Warner Mills of Colorado lent his name to the annotated Colorado Statutes. Matthew Deady (1824–93) did the same service in Oregon. Deady had been born in Maryland. Later he became a territorial judge in Oregon. But he was also a maker of laws. He drew up many of the Oregon codes, played a crucial role in revising Oregon's statutes between 1859 and 1872 and drafted much legislation himself.[26] Many Western lawyers rose to eminent positions. Few of them, of course, were born in the West. James Mills Woolworth, born in New York, settled in Omaha in 1856, two years after the area had been wrested from the Indians. In 1896 he was elected president of the American Bar Association. Charles F. Manderson, president of the Association in 1899, was born in Pennsylvania, practiced in Ohio, rose to the rank of brigadier general during the Civil War, moved to Omaha, Nebraska, in 1869, served as United States senator, and became general solicitor for the western portion of the trackage of the Burlington Railroad in 1895.[27] These careers were not typical; but neither were they unique. Lawyers came early to the frontier boom towns, eager to

[25] Howard R. Lamar, *Dakota Territory 1861–1889, A Study of Frontier Politics* (1956), pp. 168–69.
[26] Harrison Gray Platt, "Matthew P. Deady," in *Great American Lawyers,* Vol. VII (1909), p. 357.
[27] James G. Rogers, *American Bar Leaders* (1932), pp. 90, 104.

turn a quick dollar. Lawyers who placed money and collected on notes often turned to banking and merchandising to earn a better living. For others, politics was the best way to scramble up the greasy pole. In these small communities, one of the biggest businesses was government. Politics was bread-and-butter work. For lawyers, county, state, territorial and federal jobs were sources of income and, in addition, advertisements for themselves. Politics, lawmaking, law administration, were as much a part of the practice as collection work and lawsuits over land. The frontier attorney "was always a politician. Law and politics went hand in hand. . . . The lawyer filled all the 'respectable government offices.' "[28]

The lawyer-politician was, of course, not only a Western phenomenon. Lawyers were in the midst of politics everywhere. They were always an influential bloc in state legislatures, sometimes an absolute majority. Many Presidents after 1850 were lawyers: Buchanan, Lincoln, Chester A. Arthur, Garfield, Cleveland. From 1790 to 1930, two thirds of the senators and about half of the members of the House of Representatives were lawyers; throughout this time, the percentage seems to have stayed fairly stable. Between one-half and two-thirds of the state governors had also been lawyers. Lawyers were especially numerous in Southern legislatures. Lawyers in the North tended to represent metropolitan areas in the legislatures of their states.[29] Lawyers were prominent at constitutional conventions, too. Of 133 delegates to the 1872 Pennsylvania constitutional convention, 103 were lawyers.[30] This was, perhaps, an unusual percentage; but lawyers swarmed in thick numbers at other conventions, too. In Ohio, 43 out of 108 delegates at the constitutional convention of 1850–51 were lawyers; in the 1872–74 convention, 62 out of 105.[31]

It was not so much the case that public office required legal skill as that lawyers were skillful at getting and holding these offices. They were by instinct political; political animals gravitated toward the practice of law. A public career was helpful to private practice, which cannot be easily said for doctors, bankers, or farmers. After 1850, too, the civil-servant lawyer became more common. Lawyers had always worked in Washington, at state capitals, in

28 Raymond T. Zillmer, "The Lawyer on the Frontier," 50 Am. L. Rev. 27, 35 (1916).

29 J. Willard Hurst, The Growth of American Law (1950), p. 352.

30 Rosalind L. Branning, Pennsylvania Constitutional Development (1960), p. 61.

31 See Isaac F. Patterson, The Constitutions of Ohio (1912), pp. 109, 176.

city hall, and in the county seats. As government grew, so did the number of government lawyers. In 1853, the Attorney General of the United States, Caleb Cushing, performed all his duties with the help of two clerks and a messenger. In 1897, Attorney General Joseph McKenna was the head of a respectable staff, including a solicitor general, four assistant attorneys general, seven "assistant attorneys," and one "attorney in charge of pardons," not to mention three law clerks, forty-four general clerks, and miscellaneous other employees, among them eight charwomen. The "Office of Solicitor of the Treasury" had sixteen employees.[32] Lawyers were scattered about other government departments as well.

ORGANIZATION OF THE BAR

For most of the 19th century, no organization even pretended to speak for the bar as a whole, or any substantial part, or to govern the conduct of lawyers. Lawyers formed associations, mainly social, from time to time; but there was no general bar group until the last third of the century. On February 15, 1870, a group of lawyers, responding to a call that had gone out the past December over eighty-five signatures, met, formed the Association of the Bar of the City of New York, and acquired a house at 20 W. 27th Street as headquarters. In the first year, about 450 lawyers joined the organization, representing the "decent part" of the profession, that is, primarily well-to-do business lawyers, predominantly of old-American stock.[33]

The immediate background was corruption and crisis in the courts of New York City. Justice, in Tweed's New York, seemed to be blatantly for sale. The robber barons fought each other with injunctions and writs; some of the judges—Barnard and Cardozo, for example—were visibly corrupt. On February 13, 1870, Dorman B. Eaton, a lawyer who had taken part in some of the Erie litigation, was savagely beaten. This incident alarmed the "decent part" of the bar and quickened their interest in action. The new Association, like any club, aimed to "cultivate social relations among its

---

[32] *Official Register of the United States,* 1853, p. 254; 1897, Vol. I, pp. 827–29.

[33] On the formation of the Association, see George Martin, *Causes and Conflicts, The Centennial History of the Association of the Bar of the City of New York, 1870–1970* (1970); see also the remarks of George T. Strong, quoted in Henry W. Taft, *A Century and a Half at the New York Bar* (1938), p. 148; other details are in Theron G. Strong, *Landmarks of a Lawyer's Lifetime* (1914), ch. 6.

members." But it also promised to promote "the due administration of justice"; and the articles of incorporation stated as one of the Association's purposes "maintaining the honour and dignity of the profession of the law."

The crisis in the profession was more than a crisis in decency. There was also, obscurely, a business crisis. The characteristic response of any trade group to a threat of more competition was to organize and fight back. At the meeting of the New York bar, "for the purpose of forming an Association," James Emott complained that the profession had lost its independence. "We have become simply a multitude of individuals, engaged in the same business. And the objects and the methods of those engaged in that business are very much dictated by those who employ them. [Lawyers] . . . are and do simply what their employers desire." [34] In union, it was hoped, there would be strength against the outside world. The bar-association movement began and spread at a time when farmers and workers were also organizing, and shortly before the great outburst of occupational licensing laws.

The movement soon expanded outside of New York. The bar of Iowa organized on a statewide basis in 1874. During a brief span of life, the Iowa State Bar Association discussed how to raise the standards for admission to the bar, and the need for laws to punish and disbar any attorneys "guilty of shystering and unprofessional conduct." The bar also discussed problems of judicial organization and whether it was desirable or not to enact a statutory "fee-bill, or system of costs." The association was also a club and a social organization. The Hon. Edward H. Stiles, of Ottumwa, in 1876, regaled the membership with a talk on "The relation which law and its administration sustain to general literature," and Judge James M. Love, before a "very fine audience assembled in the Opera House," gave out "one of the most scholarly efforts ever delivered in Des Moines, rich in historic lore, beautiful in diction, and philosophical in style." A "bountifully laden table" in 1881 inspired a toast to "Good Digestion: its compatibility with a lawyer's conscience." [35] Chicago lawyers, too, formed a bar association, in 1874, prodded into life by the "activities of a notorious fringe of

---

[34] Quoted in 1 Albany L. J. 219 (1870). Somewhat naïvely, Emott blamed the degeneracy of the profession on the New York constitution of 1846, which brought in an elective judiciary and "broke down the law."

[35] A. J. Small, comp., *Proceedings of the Early Iowa State Bar Association 1874–1881* (1912), pp. 36, 37, 42, 83, 84, 141.

unlicensed practitioners." Between 1870 and 1878, eight city and
eight state bar associations were founded in twelve different states.
Most of them, like the groups in Chicago and New York, had a
reform ideology, and wanted to improve the image and performance of the bar.[36]

With only a few exceptions, the state and city bar associations
extended their invitations, not to the bar generally, but to a
selected group, the "decent part" of the bar. There was the same
genteel selectivity when the American Bar Association was formed
in 1878. "Seventy-five gentlemen from twenty-one jurisdictions"
(out of the country's 60,000 lawyers) got together in Saratoga, New
York.[37] Simeon E. Baldwin, of Connecticut, was prime mover. The
purpose of the Association was to "advance the science of jurisprudence, promote the administration of justice and uniformity of legislation . . . uphold the honor of the profession . . . and encourage cordial intercourse among the members of the American Bar."
During the Saratoga years, the American Bar Association seeemed
mostly bent on promoting "cordial intercourse" among members.
The ABA grew only slowly in size. In 1902 there were 1,718 members. From the outset, the Association realized that it would have
to do much of its work through committees. Early on, a number of
standing committees were appointed—on jurisprudence and law
reform, judicial administration and remedial procedure, legal education and admission to the bar, commercial law and international
law; the committee on obituaries, established in 1881, reported
names and achievements of dead members, to be duly published in
the annual reports. A flock of special committees, however, worked
on law-reform issues (for example, on the problem of the low salaries of federal judges, 1888), or issues of interest to the working
profession (on trademarks, 1898). The ABA never really clarified
its relationship to local bar associations during the Saratoga period. In 1887, a group of lawyers formed a rival organization, the
National Bar Association, expressly to serve as the apex of the pyramid of local and state associations. It proved ephemeral. The ABA
encouraged state and local bar groups to send delegates to its Saratoga meetings. At first, few came—two lonely delegates from South
Carolina were the only ones at the third annual meeting, in 1880.

[36] J. Willard Hurst, *The Growth of American Law*, p. 286.
[37] Alfred Z. Reed, *Training for the Public Profession of the Law* (1921), p. 208.
Material on the early history of the ABA comes from Reed and from Edson
R. Sunderland, *History of the American Bar Association* (1953).

By the end of the century, there was a more respectable turnout; eighty delegates, from twenty-nine states, were accredited, and forty-one actually attended, the annual meeting in 1902.

Still, the ABA before 1900 was never much more than a gathering of dignified, well-to-do lawyers, enjoying the comfort and elegance of Saratoga. Its prime significance, perhaps, was the way in which it expressed, in concrete form, the ambitions of the high bar for organization. Speeches and reports to the meetings voiced conventional sentiments about law reform—ways and means to keep the profession decent, well liked, and well paid.

Uniformity in the law was a prominent subject of discussion. In 1889, the Association, by resolution, directed its president to appoint a committee, consisting of one member from each state, to "compare and consider" the laws on marriage and divorce, inheritance, and "acknowledgment of deeds"; and to report measures that would promote the uniformity of law. Shortly thereafter, New York State created a board of three "Commissioners for the Promotion of Uniformity of Legislation in the United States." The ABA seized on this law, touted it to its members, and recommended it for other states as well. A National Conference of Commissioners on Uniform State Laws was organized in 1892, in Saratoga, and began to hold annual meetings in close connection with those of the ABA. Out of the work of the Conference ultimately came a series of recommendations for uniform laws, endorsed by the ABA as well, and proposed to the states.

ADMISSION TO THE BAR

One of the main causes of the dissatisfaction of the "decent part" of the bar was that it was too easy to set up as a lawyer. There were too many lawyers who were mediocre or worse. Few states controlled admission to the bar through a single agency or court. In 1860, ten out of thirty-nine jurisdictions did so; in 1890, sixteen out of forty-nine. Even in these jurisdictions, the control was often slight, and the standards of admission vacuous. Where local courts each passed on admission to their bar, they usually gave only the most cursory oral examination. The recommendation of a known attorney weighed more heavily than answers to questions. Before 1890, only four states had boards of bar examiners; only a few required a written examination. Nothing in the way Oliver Wendell Holmes, Jr., was admitted to the Massachusetts bar would inspire confidence that the state could select a Holmes and reject the unqualified. Judge Otis P. Lord of the superior court appointed two examiners; they separately asked Holmes a few questions; Holmes answered the questions, paid his five dollars, and was admitted to the bar.[38] Charles Francis Adams, after "about twenty months of desultory reading" in a law office, went to his friend and neighbor, Justice George T. Bigelow of Massachusetts, and asked for an examination. Bigelow invited him "into the Supreme Court room, where he was then holding court." A clerk handed him "a list of questions, covering perhaps, one sheet of letter paper." Adams "wrote out answers to such of them as I could. . . . On several . . . subjects . . . I knew absolutely nothing. A few days later I met the Judge on the platform of the Quincy station, and he told me I might come up to the court room and be sworn in. . . . I was no more fit to be admitted than a child." [39] This was in the late 1850's. In other parts of the country, admission to the bar was even more perfunctory. L. E. Chittenden, in Vermont, was chairman of the committee to examine candidates for admission to the bar, in the 1850's. Two young men came before him: "Of any branch of the law, they were as ignorant as so many Hottentots. . . . I frankly told them that for them to attempt to practice law would be wicked, dangerous, and would subject them to suits for malpractice. They begged, they prayed, they cried." Anyway, they wanted to go west: "I, with much self-reproach, consented to sign their certificates, on condition that each would buy a copy of Blackstone, Kent's Commentaries, and Chitty's Pleadings, and immediately emigrate to some Western town." [40] James Mathers, born in 1877, took a two-year course at Cumberland; this made him automatically a member of the Tennessee bar. Immediately, he moved to Indian country, in what is now Oklahoma, around the turn of the century.

> We went over to the courthouse and I shook hands with Judge Kilgore. . . . He examined my diploma from Cumberland, which was about a yard square and had to be rolled up for easy carrying, and then he looked at my license from Tennessee. That was all I needed to get his permission to practice in his court.

38 Mark deWolfe Howe, *Justice Oliver Wendell Holmes, The Shaping Years 1841–1870* (1957), pp. 263–64.
39 Charles Francis Adams (1835–1915), *An Autobiography* (1916), pp. 41–42; for a similar account, from 1861, see George A. Torrey, *A Lawyer's Recollections* (1910), p. 81.
40 L. E. Chittenden, "Legal Reminiscences," 5 Green Bag 307, 309 (1893).

Kilgore asked Mathers the next day to become a law examiner, with two others, and screen applicants to the bar in Indian Territory. Mathers used no written examination or set questions. In his view, two or three hours at a dinner table or relaxing over coffee or a drink was enough; he gained all the information in this way that he needed to decide on admission to the bar. He did not expect the man to have "a great knowledge of case law since none of us did; but . . . good, reasonable common sense." [41]

At one time, educational requirements for admission to the bar had been rather stringent, at least on paper. Before the Civil War, these requirements had considerably eroded. Four states actually abolished educational or training requirements altogether: Maine (1843–59), New Hampshire (1842–72), Wisconsin (1849–59), and Indiana (from 1851).[42] After the Civil War, the trend toward laxity reversed, particularly in the East. In 1860, only nine out of thirty-nine states and territories prescribed some minimum preparation for the practice. By 1890, nearly half of the states did so. After 1890, more and more states required more and more stringent educational preparation for the bar. In much of this, the bar as an interest group supplied the lobbying muscle. The motives were, as usual, mixed: an unselfish desire to better the profession, together with a selfish desire to control the supply of lawyers, and keep out price cutters and undesirables. Lawyers were heavily represented in the legislatures; besides, control appeared to be in the public interest, at least as much as the outlawing of quacks, the overseeing of midwives, the licensing of barbers, plumbers, and embalmers of the dead.

[41] Marshall Houts, *From Gun to Gavel* (1954), pp. 28, 31.
[42] Reed, *op. cit.*, pp. 87–88.

AMERICAN LAW IN THE
20TH CENTURY

It would be more than presumptuous to deal with 20th-century law in a few short pages. The 20th century is, in the first place, seventy years of history, at this writing. This is longer than the complex, baffling span from the end of the Civil War to 1900. In the second place, the 20th century has been by common consent a period of fantastic social change, therefore of tremendous legal change as well. In the third place, hard as the past—as history—is to deal with, one's own times are notoriously harder. A certain perspective, a certain consensus, makes it easier to sum up an era, even if the sense of ease rests on half-truths, distorted mirrors, hindsight, and memory. For these three reasons at least, this epilogue will not attempt a narration of American law in the 20th century, not even in the limited sense in which the older law was covered. Instead, this epilogue will sketch, very broadly, some of the lines along which law in the 20th century seems to have evolved and to be evolving, and will briefly discuss to what extent this American law is a continuation of what has gone before, or a fulfillment, or a sharp and precipitous break.

The main political and social events of the century are familiar enough. In the 20th century the United States emerged, without question, as a major world power. It began the century with a small empire overseas. It played a decisive role in two world wars; it came out of the second as without doubt the richest, strongest country in the world. It was also, for a time, the only country with an atom bomb. It is as of now (1971) the only country that has, with technology, sent men to the surface of the moon. Internally, this has been an age of central, national power. The relative strength of the states has melted away; the federal government has grown to a giant size. The federal Caesar fed on the meat of social upheaval, the two great wars and the cold war, a vast depression, and a technological revolution. The word Caesar is not much out of place. The main beneficiary of power at the center was not the national Congress, not the Supreme Court, but the national President. The man who holds this office has become, as Presidents like to think, the most important, the most powerful man in the world. Theodore Roosevelt and Woodrow Wilson already sensed this role; Franklin Roosevelt glorified in it; Harding and Coolidge, small men with small conceptions of their job, were only detours on the way. Weak Presidents are still possible, but a weak Presidency is not.

Every major event of the century seemed to conspire to make the central government stronger. Even prohibition, the "noble experiment" (1919 to 1933), which in some ways was the last stand of a dying order, only fed the federal colossus. Prohibition had no chance to succeed except on a federal basis. The individual states were powerless to stamp out the curse of liquor, or even to try—just as they had been powerless to control the railroads; to pass a satisfactory law against the trusts; to uplift the quality of food products; to raise an army. Prohibition did not stop people from getting drunk. It proved to be a costly failure. But it caused mammoth changes in the system of criminal justice. Prohibition filled the federal jails; it jammed the federal courts. Under prohibition, the idea of a national police force became no longer unthinkable.

For the sake of argument, one could concede that wars, depressions, and the calamity of prohibition were all aberrations; even without these, the inflation of Washington, D.C., must strike the observer as inevitable. How could it be otherwise? It was already plain in the late 19th century that separate legal sovereignties could not manage the economic forces that industrialism seemed to let loose. The primitive conception of a country of yeomen, a federalism of smallholders, had to die. Trends already marked in the 19th century simply continued: the population grew and grew; big business got bigger; a smaller and smaller proportion of the population lived on the land; a larger and larger proportion lived in the cities. More and more, people were interdependent; they were laced together by common ties of communication and transport; the market was national; radio and television nets became national; by 1970, New York and Los Angeles were a yawn, a drink, and a movie apart, as the jets flew.

Crucial too was the rising level of demands upon government. In writing history, it is easy to fall into slipshod use of impersonal phrases and the passive voice. It is easy to write that government got bigger, that federal power was extended over more and more areas, as if these phrases described natural processes, like chemical reactions, or an evolution almost biologically inherent, like the development of a chicken from an egg. In the expansion of government, no doubt some variant of Parkinson's law explains some of the growth. Organizations want to get bigger and stronger and better, because the men who run them are expansionist. But the gargantuan scope of modern government is not built on red tape. It is built on a foundation of concrete demands made by concrete groups who demand public, that is, governmental, response. The New Deal was probably the best and sharpest example of how government grew in response to consumer demand. In 1932, the country was hungry for leadership. Local government was bankrupt and distraught. People looked to the Presidency for jobs, relief, for economic reform. The New Deal program was immensely popular in its day; and what Roosevelt began has continued to be so popular that nobody dares touch the essential New Deal, not even a Republican President. Social Security, the SEC, some sort of federal housing effort, and national labor legislation are as permanently ensconced in the legal system as anything can be in a changing world. They are certainly politically untouchable, in the short run. The mere suggestion, by Barry Goldwater, that he might alter the Social Security system (1964) was greeted with outrage, as if he had befouled the Holy of Holies. Big government has a snowball effect. The more government does, the more money it needs, and the more men to run its show. Big government develops, then, an enormous taxing apparatus, and it becomes a major employer, which gives it yet another lever of control over the economy. In this process, wars, hot and cold, have been a major, even if not indispensable, conditioning factor. Before Franklin D. Roosevelt, a federal budget of eighty billion dollars a year was inconceivable. Now the federal government spends, each year, that amount on war and national defense alone.

The decline of state and local government has been relative, not absolute. By any measures, these second and third levels of government are themselves of colossal size. State and local governments carry heavy responsibility for building roads, teaching children, running a welfare system. Each of these areas has been a growth industry in the 20th century. Again, the New Deal was a great watershed. The local monopoly of poor relief disappeared. The federal government moved in with money and muscle. Later, it extended its hand into education, research, hospital-building, and interstate highways. But the everyday administration of these affairs remains mostly subfederal. The country is still, compared to France or the Soviet Union, extremely uncentral.

This is, in part, because decentralization continues to be part of the legal culture. Fragmentation is useful, too, in many politically appealing ways. When people or groups demand central control, they do not want big government as such. Few people care (and why should they?) whether government is big or not at any level. They care about results. Arguments about centralism and decentralism are usually masks. The Southerner who preaches states' rights does not really profess a political theory. He has a shopping list of interests and demands, and he knows which store carries his goods. Often, too, when local people and local government ask for federal intervention, they do not want central control; they want money, which the central government raises more easily than they. Many so-called federal programs are hardly centralized at all; they are simply statutory pots of gold to be distributed among local interests and power groups. Urban redevelopment has been a classic example. This program began in 1949; though it developed the usual thick texture of federal regulation, it was essentially, into the late 1960's, a device for siphoning funds. Efficient federal machines collect taxes, and dispense the money once again to cities and local authorities, who do with it more or less as they please, subject to very loose, very general limits and controls.

So, despite all the events of the last seventy years, despite the hundreds of billions of dollars taxed and spent through Washington, despite the (literally) thousands of federal agencies and problems, the idea—or disease—of checks and balances has by no means run its course. The legal system is still a patchwork of power, a rug made of rags. On the one hand, federal law is infinitely more important than a century ago—in taxation, regulation of business, civil rights. It is now massive, dominant, overbearing. The President is almost a czar over foreign affairs. But in other areas, his power is checked and limited, formally or informally, by other power-holders within the government. "Federal law" is a crazy quilt; federal programs are a most diverse lot. Consider, for example, how differently the post office is run from the way the draft law was run through the 1960's, with "little groups of neighbors" in the saddle; think of the position of the Federal Reserve Board; or the Supreme Court; or the FBI.

State law remains vigorous. The states continue to have the last word in much of that kingdom which Continental scholars call private law: the law of ordinary commerce, tort law, property law; the law of marriage and divorce. States and cities make up and enforce many ordinary rules that govern the average man in his daily life. They draft building codes, plumbing codes, and electrical codes for cities and towns.[1] They devise speed limits and set out parking zones. They regulate dry cleaners, license plumbers, and dictate the open season on pheasants and deer. They control the right to marry, to own a dog, to sell vegetables, to open a saloon. As we noted, they share with the federal government responsibility and rule-making power over schools; they do the dirty work of running the welfare system.

The warlord system in American politics and law is very much alive. The system continues to reject any hint of absolute power. State government has always been a force to reckon with. The counties have some (limited) powers. The cities, with or without home rule, contradict and overlap the larger jurisdictions; since the Second World War, they have in some instances dealt directly with the federal government, as its special client. This tendency, under rather fancy names, seems bound to grow. Besides all these, there are little zones of power without number: sewer districts, school districts, air-pollution districts; and such mighty vassals as the New York Port Authority. Some of these districts and authorities are accountable, it seems, to no one in particular; some are gigantic mouths which feed on the plankton of motorists' tolls, and with this food expand to monstrous size.

Since 1900, too, local government has become steadily *less* rational in the jurisdictional sense. In the 19th century, as a rule, a city gained area as it gained population. This process ground to a halt about 1900; and since 1930, most big cities (except in parts of the West and South) have actually declined in population. As everyone knows, this does not mean that people are returning to their farms. Quite the opposite: the countryside is dying. Its people are fleeing to the city as if pursued by the plague. But the old city's boundaries are fixed. The metropolitan areas, now truly gigantic, are made up of central cities, old suburbs, new suburbs, and little fragment settlements, some of them nothing more than incorporated neighborhoods, but as autonomous (in theory) as New York City or Chicago. These little fragments stoutly resist being swallowed up by large agglomerations. They want to rule their own roost. They want, in particular, to resist the influx of low-income

[1] Signs of federal encroachment here, however, are plainly visible as of 1970.

people, and Negroes; they want to be warlords on their own. For this purpose, land-use control is essential; and control is most feasible in small areas. There are hundreds of "villages" that are little more than restrictive covenants, or zoning ordinances, which have incorporated, and thus given themselves a presumptuous name and some undeserved power.

These brief remarks show that one persistent issue of American legal development, the struggle between uniformity and diversity, between centralism and localism, goes on without let and without end. And so it should. Despite what some may think, the struggle is in no sense a "problem" to be resolved once and for all. It is not a problem, but a fact; and it cannot have a solution. The sophistry of some forms of conceptual jurisprudence, and some movements for "law reform," lies precisely in this: to imagine that uniformity or lack of uniformity is a problem in itself; or that diversity of power or of legal culture is a problem in itself, or that centralization or decentralization is a problem in itself. These are only problems from the standpoint of legal dogmatics. In real life, problems are specific: poverty, or air pollution, or crime, or low economic growth rate, or whatever society defines as a situation gone wrong. The other structural features are tools or effects. Not that they are unimportant. The basic issue is power: where it is placed, and who should and can exercise it. The structural features of the legal system reflect the distribution of power, and, at the same time, influence or perpetuate it. But a good distribution for one purpose is not a good one for another. Juries are good; but white juries in a prejudiced South may be bad. Politically sensitive, politically influential Americans have had a flair for sensing these practical problems; their response has been to build up more and more layers of countervailing power. The result is a delicately balanced system, incredibly complicated, with tremendous tensile strength. But it has also tremendous flaws; is tremendously hard to unravel or reform; and may, finally, show signs of ripping apart.

In short, decentralization does not vanish, even in the teeth of the master trend of American legal history: the trend to create one legal culture out of many; to reduce legal pluralism; to broaden the base of the formal, official system of law; to increase the proportion of persons, relative to the whole population, who are consumers or objects of that law. This master trend continues, and accelerates, in the 20th century. In medieval England, only a tiny circle of people were really subjects or objects of common law. Since then, the ambit, scope, focus, and pretensions of the official law have grown; it now includes practically everybody in the commonwealth.

This last statement should be made with a certain caution. Official law and living law are not, and have never been, the same, even in the spheres of official law that are indisputably legitimate. Of all the mysteries of legal history, perhaps the most impenetrable is the history of law in action, law as it was lived, not as it was supposed to be. Informalities and deviations are far less likely to leave a written record than the official documents: statutes, case reports, rules, and pronouncement of authorities. In the mid-20th century, a school of sociologists of law was at work, whose first job was to find out what police, judges, and legislators actually did, rather than what they were supposed to do, or what they said they did—an idea blindingly simple as a matter of theory, not so easy as a matter of fact. The letter of the law no doubt did not carry itself out in the past any more than in the present. What evidence there is confirms this impression.

Nonetheless, the trend toward a single legal culture is real, is persistent, and is important. This trend takes two forms. First of all, the country is a single economic unit for most purposes and a single social unit. Mass media and mass transport are great levelers. There is less and less excuse for regionalism in customs, including legal customs. Regionalism is less and less tolerable or efficient. A company that sells in fifty states would prefer to talk one language, use one form, confront one body of laws. There is also, in the 20th-century mind, a great strain toward rationality. This trait, which seems fairly general in the western world, has a particularly virulent American form. Americans, at least at one level of their consciousness, have no patience for the irregular. Customs and traditions that are cherished in England have been rudely chased out of the United States; Americans would consider them stupid or infantile. Modern law, for example, does not tolerate the classical common-law type of legal fiction, even where the device would be useful. Surface irrationality is not in fashion any more.

This state of mind is part of the general debris of a great worldwide movement of recent centuries that can be called, for want of a better name, rationalism. Rationalism has been central to Western thought, at least since the Industrial Revolution, if not before. Its progress has been noted and chronicled, in law and out, by Max Weber, among others.[2] It is in essence the breakdown of tradi-

[2] See, in general, Max Rheinstein, ed., *Max Weber on Law in Economy and Society* (1954).

tional forms of legitimacy. The ideal rational man accepts no thought or tradition for its own sake or for supernatural reasons. Everything must pass the utilitarian test, however crudely or thoughtlessly. Individuals ask, what is in it for me, or my group? Governments and whole societies ask a similar question. Nothing is given or fixed. The consequences of rationalism are colossal; they have not yet fully played themselves out on the stage of time. Political democracy has been one consequence. Another has been the rise of the welfare state. Still a third is modern science. A fourth is the idea of equality before the law. A fifth is the—more recent— demand for equality of opportunity, which follows when formal equality fails in its purposes (from the standpoint of an oppressed or subordinate group). Rationalism, therefore, in the long run is lethal to legal pluralism, not in the regional sense, but in the vertical sense: a pluralism of classes or degrees, each with its fixed position in the order, some near the bottom, some near the top, the bottom placid, deferential, and accepting.

Vertical pluralism died and is dying a slow and agonizing death. For the same reasons of rational self-interest, people on top bitterly resist its demise. There was a time, mostly in the 19th century, when formal equality seemed to satisfy the working class and the lower orders. There was mobility for the few and dreams for the many. In England, perhaps, the sheer strength of traditional behavior acted to cushion the transfer of power from an elite to a broader group. The mass of the population was willing to let the elites, so it seems, act as executor of their own class system. In the United States, there were somewhat different cushions: the frontier, real opportunities, and the cult of free enterprise. At any rate, some combination of factors acted as a brake on demands for redistribution of the social product. The frontier was not the only "safety valve"; a culture of general opportunity was probably more significant.

At any rate, there *was* a breathing space, and no revolution. But only for a while. In the United States, volcanic eruptions of labor terrorized the earthly city in the late 19th century. In the 20th century, after many zigs and zags, the working class won a series of smashing legal victories. How much was due to their own efforts, how much to plain economic growth and the gifts of technology, is beside the point here. The most significant legal triumphs took place during the New Deal period. The government in power was willing and able to pass laws to legitimize a package of trade-union goals. The New Dealers were anti-business in their outlook. The

New Deal upset the balance of honor and prestige between labor and capital. It enacted a tremendous number of regulatory laws, many of which created administrative agencies. The National Labor Relations Act (1935)[3] guaranteed the right to unionize, declared that it was an "unfair labor practice" to interfere with this right, and set up a board to enforce the policy of the act.[4] The New Deal also launched the first meaningful programs of unemployment insurance, old-age pensions, and public housing.

Business was stunned, and shattered in morale, by the great crash of 1929, and the ensuing depression. Politically, business had never been feebler than in the early '30's. While the army of enterprise was in flight, the working class swarmed into the burned and deserted palaces. But prosperity, which the Second World War brought back, probably meant more to the working class in the long run than the New Deal reforms. Prosperity brought color back to the cheeks of the businessman, too. Much—not all—of his power flowed back into his veins. There was no more of the crude, overt hatred of the 1930's; nothing more was heard about "economic royalists." The economy surged ahead so rapidly that labor and business were able to share in the product. Good times made for good feelings. In many respects, the interests of master and servant seemed very harmonious. For example, the government set out, even before 1945, to help the veteran on a scale never before attempted. The government sent millions of soldiers and sailors to college, which kept veterans from glutting the labor market. The government gave loans to those who wanted to start a small business. It made money available to fulfill the dream of the average man for a house in the suburbs, with a yard, a garage, a new kitchen. This program also made jobs for bricklayers and plumbers; it put money into the pockets of contractors and mortgage bankers; and manufacturers of plaster, glass, pipe, and toilet bowls.

By the 1950's, the economy had moved so far so fast that some had conveniently put out of mind that there were underclasses in America. Scholars wrote books about the affluent society; they worried about an excess of leisure; the enforced leisure of unemployment seemed forgotten. Into this Panglossian dream world, the black revolt, followed by brown, yellow, red, and women's revolts, burst like a bombshell. Lyndon Johnson's war against poverty had been conceived of as a mopping-up exercise. It turned into more of

3 49 Stats. 449 (act of July 5, 1935).

4 The Norris-LaGuardia Act, passed in 1932, while Hoover was still President, did away with the labor injunction. 47 Stats. 70 (act of March 23, 1932).

a war than its proponents had bargained for. In a sense, Pandora's box was now open; hate, class struggle, backlash, and despondency rose like stenches to poison the national air. These were the 1960's: restlessness of almost earthquake proportions; riots in the streets; fires burning on campus; the sense of oncoming ecological catastrophe; a government paranoid with fear of its subjects; crime, or the sense of crime, walking the streets like the Black Death. Every group or class that had been dependent, that had been put down, or put away, or taken for granted, now showed its fangs: blacks, prisoners, poor people, students, homosexuals, nuns. There was no respect for the slots in which society had placed any group. There was little respect for society, or so it seemed.

This, of course, is not history; it is the world outside the door, right now. The strands that have gone to make the 1970's what they are, are far too complex for general treatment. Certainly, the rebellion in the air—and the counterrebellion—had been fed by many springs; people spoke loosely about the war in Vietnam, permissive toilet training, Dr. Spock and his theories of child care, the decline of religion, or all or none of these things, and others. It seems, in the long glance of history (which may be inaccurate too), that here was the unpeeling of one more layer of the onion of rationalism, one further consequence of the sunburst of modern secular thought. In our parochial legal terms, we can describe it as part of the process of making one legal culture, out of the vertical pluralism of bygone times. Nobody, of whatever color or condition, seemed willing to accept a lower or despicable status, in law or in fact; to accept the detrimental definitions that an outside majority (or minority) had fastened on its head. This recent and important revolution is of course not completely a bolt from the blue. As we have seen, it was merely the next step in a long series; and some parts of this book have been devoted to a tale of the earlier steps. In this latest phase, law played a direct, if narrow, part. The civil-rights revolution of the 1950's and the 1960's, in the historical clothing it actually wore, would be unthinkable without the federal courts. This is not to say that the revolution itself would be unthinkable without these courts. But it would certainly have worn a different aspect. It would certainly have taken a different—perhaps more brutal—form.

The black man fought for his rights in an important judicial battleground. He appealed to an 18th-century document, the Bill of Rights, and the 14th Amendment to the Constitution, which itself was a century old (1868). The force of this amendment lay in its bearing on how function and power were divided between federal and state governments, between federal judges and state judges, between judges, legislators, local officials, and whatever passed for public opinion. The law that grew up about these constitutional scraps of phrases was essentially modern. Even before 1868—often before 1800—states had professed lofty, well-phrased statements of fundamental rights. Yet the case law on civil rights and civil liberties—on freedom of speech and religion, for example—practically speaking, is a product of the 20th century. In the 19th century, there was not much litigation; this branch of constitutional law was on the whole rather tepid and torpid. Nothing shows better how foolish it is to imagine that legal words, concepts, phrases have an important life of their own. On the question where to draw the line between obscenity and free speech, the basic legal words and expressions existed in 1790 as well as in 1970. Books about sex, one might add, also existed, under the table. One of the heroines of modern case law, Miss Fanny Hill, practiced her arts in the 18th century. The idea of matching the first amendment against the concept of obscenity did not occur to 19th-century publishers with any particular force. Why that was so is a complex question. When the greed of publishers joined with a decline in Victorian moral dominance, the dam burst, and the pent-up flood of litigation began. In short, things that were unthinkable (but had been thought) and unprintable (but had been printed) showed their brazen faces in public. And nobody boycotted these authors and publishers, or stopped having them over for dinner. The books sold by the millions; and the courts, on the whole, acquiesced.

Why, however, did the courts have to say yes? There was, first of all, a constitutional tradition and an activist bench. The country was used to the idea that disputes of all sorts, social, economic, and political, were not out of place dressed in robes and brought to court. Nobody had the slightest idea, at the outset, that courts would be kind to *Fanny Hill,* or to radical pamphlets, or the Jehovah's Witnesses. The courts became the forum of civil liberties by a process of trial and error. When legislative help was not politically possible—as was true for blacks, for unpopular minorities, and for the publisher of *Fanny Hill*—blocked interest groups, at least those with strong purposes, tried one path after another, like mice running through a maze, until they found the one with the cheese. The next time the route becomes easier to follow; a receptive court invites further litigation. If unpopular minorities—Jehovah's Witnesses in the '30's; criminal defendants and radicals in the '50's and

'60's—found a court or two receptive, they tended to pursue judicial remedies that much more avidly. The increase in litigation, then, adds to the pressure on the court to extend its prior holdings just a little bit further. Especially was this so of strong claims: claims that, denied, did not simply vanish or die, claims that *demanded* a response.

A corpus of law about free speech was first seriously constructed in the period of and after the First World War. The war was the occasion for boiling up a caldron of chauvinism. Espionage and sedition acts were passed. A great witch hunt and red scare followed, which lasted into the 1920's.[5] The courts were not so heroic as one would like. Oliver Wendell Holmes' clear and present danger test came out of this period—Congress could suppress words "used in such circumstances and . . . of such a nature as to create a clear and present danger that they will bring about the substantive evils that Congress has a right to prevent." [6] Later cases dealt with the scope of congressional investigations, during the McCarthy era; and the censorship of movies and books, beginning in earnest in the 1950's. The cases about Jehovah's Witnesses, a troublesome unpopular sect, were followed dramatically by cases that, in the '60's, seemed to buttress the wall between church and state, unduly to some people's tastes. The Supreme Court, particularly when Earl Warren was Chief Justice (1953–69), took a stand far in advance of public opinion, in protecting unpopular minorities and furthering their interests. The cases on criminal procedure were particularly striking. In case after case, the Supreme Court took the side of the prisoner, requiring strict adherence to strict principles of fair search, arrest, and trial—principles which, it sometimes seemed, the judges created themselves. These were dramatic cases. On the one side, the state; on the other, some broken figure of a man, shuffling into court, a drunk, a gambler, a dope addict, a four-time loser, a petty thief, a creature at the bottom of the ladder. The Warren court sided with this underdog (and his lawyers) often enough, and forcefully enough, to draw cries of pain from the temples of order and law.

By far the most important minority who went to court was the American black man. Litigation on the race question had never really ceased. The black man—or his leaders—never really

5 See Harry N. Scheiber, *The Wilson Administration and Civil Liberties, 1917–1921* (1960); Stanley Coben, *A. Mitchell Palmer: Politician* (1963).
6 Schenck v. United States, 249 U.S. 47 (1919).

acquiesced in *Plessy* v. *Ferguson* (1896),[7] the case that gave segregation its legitimate face. The National Association for the Advancement of Colored People was founded in 1909. Almost from the start, the NAACP developed a strong legal arm, and kept up pressure in the courts for racial equality. As early as 1915 the NAACP achieved a concrete result; the Supreme Court, in *Guinn* v. *U.S.*[8] held the "grandfather clause" of the Oklahoma constitution void. (The Oklahoma constitution of 1908, Art. 3, Sec. 4A, required voters to be "able to read and write any section of the Constitution of the State of Oklahoma"; but excused any one who was "entitled to vote under any form of government," on Jan. 1, 1866, or who "at that time, resided in some foreign nation," and any "lineal descendant" of any such persons.) After 1940, the changing attitude of the Supreme Court was very noticeable. The black man's legal progress was incremental at first. In a series of cases, the Supreme Court declared this or that situation or practice (segregated law schools, for example) unconstitutional; but it did not want or dare to deny that segregation had *some* warrant in law. The NAACP pushed and pulled; the Court was a reluctant bridegroom. Its decisions were clearly compromises; the blacks won, most of the time, in the particular case; on the other hand, the legality of segregation itself was not touched. The Court came closer to the heart of the system in *Shelley* v. *Kraemer* (1948).[9] This struck down, as unenforceable, land covenants that forbade sale or rental of property to blacks.

The climax, however, of the long struggle came on "black Monday," in 1954, when *Brown* v. *Board of Education*[10] was decided. This was surely one of the most momentous of all Supreme Court decisions; to find a basis for comparison, one has to reach back as far as the *Income Tax* case, or even *Dred Scott*. The *Brown* case put an end to the legality of segregated schools. Of course, sixteen years later most blacks, North and South, still went to schools which were all black or almost. Even so, *Brown* has had an enormous impact on the schools. It also sounded the death knell of *Plessy* v. *Ferguson,* at first by indirection. Later cases made the Su-

7 163 U.S. 537 (1896).

8 238 U.S. 347 (1915).

9 334 U.S. 1 (1948). On this case, and the role of the NAACP in general in the Civil Rights movement up to that point, see Clement E. Vose, *Caucasians Only: the Supreme Court, the NAACP, and the Restrictive Covenant Cases* (1959).

10 347 U.S. 483 (1954).

preme Court's meaning abundantly clear. No form of segregation
was permissible. The case also—like *Dred Scott*—involved the
Court in a storm of controversy. Vilification only seemed to make
Warren and his justices more sure of their moral premises.

The segregation cases affected, and joined forces with, the black
man's revolt. The case was just one thread in a carpet. Its influence
cannot be measured and must not be overrated. The movement
has not, at this writing, lost its momentum. Much of the history of
the United States, domestically speaking, since the 1950's has been
a gloss on the history of black-white relations. Every major domestic issue—the war on poverty, white backlash, urban renewal, unrest in the schools, crime in the streets—is bound up with, caused
by, complicated by, disturbed by, the sickness and rot which affects
black-white relations in America. White reaction has been as complicated as the black man's great leap forward. Different levels and
groups of the population have reacted quite differently. A new
series of civil-rights laws, more sweeping than any since the false
dawn of radical reconstruction, are one legal symptom of this reaction. But shame, fear, and rage are also elements; so too are the
collapse of the gun-control movement, the rush to put Mace, riot
guns, and tanks in the hands of the police, and the flight to the
suburbs. These are as fundamental to the white reaction as Broth-
erhood Week, if not more so.

LAW REFORM AND UNIFICATION:
THE IVORY TOWER

Compared to the trends just discussed, the second consequence of
the great flight from legal pluralism is pale and distinctly inferior.
It deserves comment only because of its parochial importance to
lawyers. This is the law-reform movement, strictly speaking: the
20th-century continuation of the lawyers' own little battle, for uniformity, codification of law, consistency and order on the statute
books, and similar toys of the trade.

Indeed, the law-reform movement, on the surface, has been successful beyond the wildest dreams of the 19th century. This should
not come as a major surprise. "Law reform," in the sense the organized bar uses this term, is really a measure for professional defense.
It flows out of the needs, the sense of oneness, the beleaguered fears
of the elite of the profession. It is a way of showing the world that
lawyers too serve the public interest; and law reform has been his-

torically linked, since the 1870's, with the official organization of the bar. Bar associations were just getting underway in 1870; by 1970 they were sizeable and important. The national Conference of Commissioners on Uniform State Laws and the Association of American Law Schools, founded around the turn of the century, were two more symptoms of the striving of lawyers to combine for protection of their interests and good name. The American Law Institute, encouraged by the organized bar, had begun work on drafting of uniform laws in the late 19th century. Many, many others followed in the 20th century. The Uniform Sales Act (1906) was one of the most important, but no subject was too small; the Uniform Flag Act (1917) (forbidding anyone from defacing, defiling, defying, or trampling on the American flag), and a Uniform Simultaneous Death Act (1940) were other contributions of the Conference to the common good. After the Second World War, the Uniform Commercial Code, completed around 1950, was the most massive contribution to uniformity. Professor Karl Llewellyn was the Code's chief intellectual parent. The Code summed up all of the statute law of commerce, improved it (in theory), and replaced the old laws on sales, bills, and notes, bulk sales, warehouse receipts, bills of lading, and secured transactions. (Many of these were themselves "uniform" laws.)

The Code occupied the attention of leading academic specialists in commercial law for about a generation. First, they drafted it; then they lobbied for it; then they started to write about the way it was working. It took a heavy effort to sell it to the legislators, who had little idea they really needed a code. Pennsylvania (1953) and Massachusetts (1957) were the pioneers; after years of agitation, the rest of the states gave in. In size and scale, the Code was a clear break with the past. In other respects, it was far less revolutionary. It was, in a way, curiously old-fashioned. The problems that it attacked were strictly "legal"; that is, they were problems of disorder in doctrine, clashing case law, and what seemed to be unlovely and unsympathetic arrangements of statutes. The draftsmen also believed that courts, and legislature, did not understand what businessmen really needed, and how businessmen thought. This last point must be stressed, because it means that the Code was a mixture of two ideologies. One was the ideology of codes themselves, stressing system, order, logic, uniformity. The other was the ideology of the law merchant. This one flew the banner of service to the business community. But probably it was the first ideology that dominated. Devotion to business practice was deeply felt; nonetheless, it was window dressing at bottom. The Code did not start out with empirical studies of what business wanted, or with a theory of what the economy needed. Some Wall Street lawyers and business-men were asked their opinions; but there were no real explorations of what was wrong (if anything) with the way law intersected the business world. The Code was ruthless in its attitude toward re-gionalism. The notion that any state in the Union might conceiv-ably have an economic or social interest requiring an exception to the Code was considered heresy, and in fact not tolerated. Nor was much attention paid to the interests of people outside the business community—labor or the consumer. It is not fair to make too much of a point of this. Academic interest in poor people, and in consumer problems, was not in fashion until the 1960's. The Code was a product of a time that now seems as quaint and old-fashioned as the era of high-button shoes. Law, legal scholars, law schools, and Wall Street lawyers were united in love (it seemed) for eter-nity.

At any rate, the Code was modernity itself compared to the re-statements of the law, perhaps the high-water mark of conceptual jurisprudence. Work began in the late 1920's, under the sponsor-ship of the American Law Institute (founded in 1923). The pro-ponents were hostile to the very thought of codification. They wanted to head it off, and save the common law, by reducing its principles to a simpler but more systematic form. The result would be a restatement, not a statute. Judges and professors would do the work, hacking away at the major common-law fields: contracts, trusts, property, torts, agency, business corporations, conflict of laws. They took fields of living law, scalded their flesh, drained off their blood, and reduced them to bones. The bones were arrange-ments of principles and rules (the black-letter law), followed by a somewhat barren commentary. The first restatement, contracts, was finished in 1932. The restatements were almost virgin of any notion that rules had social or economic consequences. Their ar-rangements were strictly logical; the aim was to show order and unmask disorder. (Courts that were out of line could cite the re-statement and return to the mainstream of common law growth.) The chief draftsmen, men like Samuel Williston and Austin W. Scott of Harvard (contracts, trusts), were authors of massive trea-tises in the strict, conceptual, Langdell mold. They expended their enormous talents on an enterprise which, today, seems singularly fruitless. Incredibly, the work of restating (and rerestating) is still going on.

All this law-reform activity in the 20th century had small social returns. Indeed, it had to be so. The subjects "reformed" were those that were quintessentially legal. In theory, public interest was king, and was the reason for reform; in practice the problems for reform came out of scanty appellate cases, and were problems of logic and consistency. Sometimes there was some incidental public benefit. And when judicial structures were reformed (as in New Jersey, under the leadership of Arthur Vanderbilt), the work paid a real social dividend. Model codes, a phenomenon later than the restatements, tended also to be more sophisticated. The draftsmen of the Model Penal Code were at least aware that their subject meant a lot to the outside world, and were attentive to clamorous voices from outside their doors.

A new style of law reform began in the 1960's, fundamentally different from classic law reform. Civil rights, Vietnam, the war against poverty, the great pollution and population fever, and general unrest in the universities sent adrenalin flowing in the law schools. There was evidence of a new breed of lawyers, socially conscious and sometimes even radical. They were a persistent minority. They stepped up pressure on the system for far-reaching change. It was the second such wave, in one sense; during the New Deal, too, there was a great outpouring of lawyers from the schools, determined to lead society onward and upward. They flocked to Washington to build the Roosevelt society. Their interests were entirely substantive, however; not the administration of justice, but administration of the economy. The radicals of the 1960's were interested in substance too, of course. But they had a particular eye for justice: the courts, procedures, representation. Not for a long time had a push for law reform from inside the profession joined hands with a genuine social movement coming from outside. Both demanded for the country something more than formal equality before the law; both were in open revolt against vertical pluralism in American law and life; both were, moreover, vitally concerned with the ways and procedures of justice. On the law side, much of the steam came from young lawyers whose salaries were paid by the federal government. This faucet could be turned off in a second. Whether so doing would kill or maim the movement, in the short run or the long, was an open question.

THE GROWTH OF THE LAW

In the law itself, there was rapid, ceaseless change in the 20th century. Some of the main headings have been mentioned—for example, the rise of administrative law. Others, too numerous for adequate treatment, demand some sort of token recognition.

In land law, land-use controls proliferated. The restrictive covenant was not strong enough to hold forces of change at bay in big cities. The 20th century tried zoning. New York City had the first comprehensive zoning ordinance (1916).[11] From this beginning, zoning became an almost universal feature of the land-use law of the cities. Planning and controls were used to monitor the growth of the city, to preserve the character of neighborhoods, to stop any downward slide of land values, to counterbalance the iron laws of the market. These were middle-class and businessmen's tools.

Land-use controls were popular because of the American custom of income segregation. Rich and poor were sorted out into their own little areas. This was standard enough: problems arose at the borders and in enclaves. From the period of the First World War, the black rural mass began to move north in search of jobs. This movement became a flood after the Second World War. White fear became another dominant support for enforcement of land-use controls. Federal programs—urban renewal and redevelopment from 1949, Model Cities in the late 1960's—hardly made a dent on urban segregation. These programs took the form, by and large, of grants made to local warlords, and with their approval. Cities and neighborhoods made policy; their publics did not seek anything that smacked of large-scale integration. *Shelley* v. *Kraemer* outlawed the restrictive covenant in 1948; in 1949, Urban Redevelopment popped out of its box. Not that the two events were directly connected. But the energy released by one act flowed into the other. If blacks and poor people could not be kept out of a neighborhood directly, then the job was best done indirectly: through some sort of fight-blight campaign. There were also two important reformist goals that acted at least as rhetorical pillars of Redevelopment and its later recensions. One was low-income housing; the other was the dream of the city beautiful. The actual impact of the programs was different, and far less salutary. It may be too early,

[11] See Roy Lubove, *The Progressives and the Slums* (1962), pp. 229–45.

however, to pass final judgment; these are programs still very much on the make.

Predictably, a backlash developed against urban renewal. The troops consisted of blacks, radicals, and (sometimes) white smallholders: those who saw the bulldozer approaching their own backyard. There had been, of course, protests against particular projects since the very beginning of Redevelopment. In the good old American way, some of these went to court. In the 1950's, the courts uniformly brushed all objections aside. Stripped of jargon, the cases said, first, that papa knew best; second, that judges could not interfere with orderly decisions by respectable authorities. In the 1960's, there were more cases; a few judges had second thoughts; a few housewives chained themselves to trees for publicity; and there was much hand-wringing and pamphlet-writing from Washington. The general decline in compliance and complacency had overtaken urban renewal. The economic forces that benefited from renewal were still strong; but so was the enemy; planners had to contend now with an ever-mightier conservation movement; and urban decay had to reckon with the newest social problem to demand the center of the stage, the problem of man and his environment.

Air and water pollution, urban squeeze, and other symptoms of distress were old enough; there had always been voices crying in and for the wilderness. But the voices became more strident. A real sense of doom began to hang over this small and limited world. Many sources fed the ecological movement. First, economic growth (in a society which, after all, had had a great deal of this otherwise scarce commodity) no longer satisfied everyone, particularly those with money to spare, and still no inner peace. Second, big business was poisoning the rivers and darkening the air, cities poured tons of muck into lakes and oceans, highway engineers were driving concrete paths through America's heritage and heart. This debauchery could be justified only by great faith in the invisible hand of the market and in the virtue and sense of public institutions. This faith was itself becoming a scarce commodity. Third, this was a society with many rich and leisured people; with enormous government and governments, peopled with professionals and bureaucrats; and with a growing number of academics and intellectuals, looking for a place in the sun. All of these interest groups (it is fair to call them that) had conscience and needed causes. The government needed causes because its size was only excusable if it pursued the national interest; every part of every government had to have some sort of socially useful program. Academics and the leisured class had their own self-interest, as consumers, at stake; they also needed and wanted some way to spend their surplus time and money. Many expended energy collecting stamps, writing histories of China, going to antique shops, getting drunk, and otherwise, but a certain number hit on the environmental crisis, which was real enough, and for which the time was somehow ripe. Hence, an interest group with some power—particularly, power to mobilize the neutrals—joined forces on an issue which suited the '60's. By the late '60's, many prior issues had become inhospitable. (The blacks, for example, had rudely taken over, with hardly a thank-you, the job of their own liberation.)

The ecological movement also implied the rise to prominence of the consumer interest. It was still a society whose law was forged in the struggles and compromises of interest groups. For the first time, however, the consumer formed an organized interest group. It made itself felt in many areas of public and private law. One notable instance was the growth of products liability. In one sense, products liability merely continued the long flight from *caveat emptor*. In the 20th century, this flight quite naturally claimed a higher governmental input than in prior times. Private lawsuits were, as before, mostly costly and impractical. Manufacturers and processors were made accountable therefore by statute. A federal food and drug law was passed in 1906. A bizarre episode of struggle preceded it. A pure-food movement had been going for a generation. Upton Sinclair's book *The Jungle* helped the final push immeasurably. The reading public nearly retched at the thought that their meat products were moldy, that pieces of rat were in their sausage, that acid and spices hid putrefaction in canned goods, and, worst of all, that their lard might make cannibals of them all. Sinclair wrote the book to expose the plight of "the wage-slaves of the beef trust," [12] in Chicago's packing town. "I aimed at the public's heart," he said, in a celebrated sentence, "and I hit . . . the stomach." Indeed, he had. Scandal cut the sale of meat products almost in half. This made a point the food industry understood better than sentiment or socialism. If pure-food legislation would restore public confidence in processed meat and food products, it was well worth the price of regulation, at least for the reputable firms.

The same general phenomenon, only without a major scandal,

[12] Upton Sinclair, *American Outpost, a Book of Reminiscences* (1932), p. 154.

helps explain the rise of workmen's compensation. By 1900, as we saw, the fellow-servant rule no longer worked very well. It was still cruel, but it no longer had the virtue of simplicity. It did not allocate the costs of industrial accidents with any efficiency. Congress swept the rule away for railroad workers, in 1906, when the Federal Employers' Liability Act was enacted.[13] Many states also abolished the rule; and between 1900 and 1910 compensation plans were discussed and agitated for. Industry resisted, but less and less. Litigation and accident insurance cost industry a great deal of money. Was it possible that compensation would not really cost very much —that more money would go directly to workers, less to parasites, lawyers, and middlemen? Perhaps such a plan would buy industrial peace as well. European countries, notably England and Germany, had adopted workmen's compensation, and the sky had not fallen in. New York passed a compensation statute in 1910; it was declared unconstitutional.[14] Next came Wisconsin (1911), this time successfully. Other states followed, avoiding the pitfalls that made New York's law offensive to the judges. The Supreme Court later held the most common types of plan constitutional. Mississippi, in 1948, was the last of the states to pass a compensation law.

Workmen's compensation was a compromise system. Each side gave a little, got a little. The worker got compensation. If he was injured on the job, he collected for it, whether the employer was negligent or not.[15] The fellow-servant rule was abolished. So was the doctrine of assumption of risk. On the other hand, what the employer had to pay to an injured workman was fixed by statute: actual medical expenses, and a fixed per cent of wages actually lost, but with a definite ceiling. In Wisconsin in 1911, for example, a worker totally disabled could collect, as long as his disability lasted, 65 per cent of his average weekly wages, up to four times his average annual earnings; this was as high as he could go.[16] Statutes also commonly set a definite price for "permanent partial disability"—so many weeks' compensation for a finger, a toe, an eye, a foot, an arm. The employee could get no less; but he could also get

---

[13] 34 Stats. 232 (act of June 11, 1906). The statute had constitutional problems; supposedly it covered more employees than federal power could lawfully extend to. This was so held in the Employers' Liability cases, 207 U.S. 463 (1908) (a 5–4 decision). A new act, passed in 1908, 35 Stats. 65 (act of April 22, 1908) sidestepped the problem.

[14] Ives v. South Buffalo Railway Co., 201 N.Y. 271, 94 N.E. 431 (1911).

[15] The concept of contributory negligence was abolished, but certain kinds of gross misconduct on the job cost the workman his right to collect compensation.

[16] Law Wis. 1911, ch. 50, pp. 46–47.

no more; no more jury trials; no more chance at an inflated recovery. For this, the employers were grateful.

Workmen's compensation was supposed to do away with the plague of accident case law. But the new statutes generated enough litigation to surprise, and disappoint, champions of the system. The case law has tended to extend liability in directions that early proponents hardly dreamt of. Now, in some states, workers recover for heart attacks suffered on the job; a secretary who strains her neck at the office, turning to talk to her girl friend, collects lost wages. Partly, these extensions were to be expected. Once again, single cases tugged at the heartstrings of judges and administrators. Besides, white-collar and service workers now outnumber blue-collar workers in the labor force. It is now *their* law, their piece of the welfare state. Since the nation has yet to adopt a general security law, cradle to grave, piecemeal bits accrue to existing institutions or are captured by special-interest groups. Liability under compensation laws can be looked at in this light.

So much for the worker's injuries. For all its failings, workmen's compensation has done more splendidly in halting the flood of industrial cases than some would concede. There is heavy litigation, from the standpoint of the courts; but commissions handle the overwhelming majority of accidents, quickly and smoothly. Since the 1920's, tort law has become more and more the law of the automobile. Practically speaking, personal-injury lawyers work on auto-accident cases; trains and planes are weak competitors. In some states in the 1950's, wrecks on the highway accounted for up to forty per cent of the cases decided by appellate courts. Mostly the insurance companies pay. The personal-injury bar uses the contingent fee; there are some very large recoveries; but trials cost money. Legal scholars and others have suggested some sort of compensation scheme. So far, not much has happened. Workmen's compensation came out of a clear bilateral system, with organized workers on one side, organized employers on the other. The whole public rides in automobiles; and insurance makes the current system at least vaguely tolerable, for most people. As the costs of insurance skyrocket, the chance of change improves. No-fault, at this writing, is law in Massachusetts, and much discussed elsewhere.

In 1916, in a decision clearly written for posterity, Judge Benjamin Cardozo of New York changed the course of liability law. The case was *MacPherson* v. *Buick Motor Co.;*[17] the occasion, a wheel "made of defective wood," whose spokes "crumbled into frag-

17 217 N.Y. 382, 111 N.E. 1050 (1916).

ments," threw MacPherson out, and injured him. What Cardozo decided was that the buyer of the car, which was defective, could sue the manufacturer for his injuries. The technical barrier was that no "privity," no direct relationship, connected plaintiff and defendant. MacPherson did not buy his car from the Buick Motor Company; he bought it from a dealer. According to the tenor of the older case law, he should have sued the dealer. Despite this, Cardozo and his court gave MacPherson a cause of action against the far-off manufacturer, with whom MacPherson had never dealt. When a manufactured item is or can be dangerous, and the maker knows that the product will be used by third-person consumers, then he must make his product "carefully," or suffer the consequences.

Cardozo's language was eloquent, his reasoning clever. The case created a stir in legal circles; it encouraged more cases to be brought. Some of these were successful; after a generation or so state courts widely accepted the doctrine. It is wrong to say, however, that other courts *followed* Cardozo. Certainly, they cited him. Whether his opinion persuaded, in itself, is another question. If it did, it was less because of its own eloquence than because it eloquently summed up a state of mind which would have made its way on any account. The 20th century was bound to accept the idea, that manufacturers were liable to the ultimate consumer. In recent years, courts have carried products liability further than Cardozo would have dreamed.

The *MacPherson* case is classic; it, and other examples, tempt lawyers and law professors to imagine that the courts have played an enormous role in changing the law in the twentieth century. They have certainly played *a* role; but what size? What they accomplished must not be exaggerated. Courts were, of course, busier than ever. In a number of dramatic instances—*Brown* v. *Board of Education* was one—they left their mark on national affairs. They altered old rules and developed new ones. But there were definite limits to their power. The courts began the century with huge pretensions, often exercised in a conservative direction. In the 1930's, the Supreme Court's veto power wrecked some of the New Deal's most precious legal engines. Franklin Roosevelt, at this point, threatened to pack the Court. This plan notoriously backfired. But the threat was not wholly useless, or wholly wrong. New appointments, and a second thought or two, brought the Court into a more reasonable mood. It was never (at least through 1970) to be so offensive to the liberal wing of the country.

After the abdication of the late 1930's, what had always been true was more than ever clear: the main business of government, and therefore of law, was legislative and executive. The courts were (in Alexander Bickel's phrase) the "least dangerous branch"; they were also the least important. Even private law, so-called, was turning statutory. The lion's share of the norms and rules that actually governed the country came out of Congress and the legislatures, usually drafted in the office of the President or governor, or by their delegates and agents in the bureaucracy. The rules of the countless administrative agencies were themselves an important, even crucial, source of law. Tax law can serve as an illustration. In 1913, after the 16th amendment undid the damage of the *Pollock* case, Congress passed a new income-tax law. Over the years, Congress repeatedly raised the rates, and added to the law's provision. By 1950 or so, the federal income-tax law was probably the country's longest and most complicated statute; perhaps it affected more persons and businesses (and gave work to more lawyers and accountants) than any other piece of legislation or for that matter any other part of the law. Since tax laws were responsible for the levy of billions of dollars a year, the fuel that big government had to have, this attention was not surprising. A stupendous body of regulations, rulings, and occasional orders of the Treasury clarified and supplemented the statutes. Court cases ranked a poor third as a source of policy in tax law.

Virtually the whole population was affected, too, by the welfare laws of the 20th century. The biggest changes and the biggest breakthroughs came in the reign of Franklin D. Roosevelt. Unemployment compensation, categorical grants in aid, public housing, old-age insurance, aid to families of dependent children—all these either began in the 1930's, or were substantially revised and revamped. The depression had cast millions down into poverty. These were the millions who lost faith in business hegemony, who demanded government action to relieve them from a misery they did not deserve and were not used to. The people in distress were no tiny underclass, to be safely ignored; they were a fairly cohesive group, with many recruits from the middle part of society. The resurgent Democrats built their palace from these stones. Every new administration after the 1930's felt a political need to keep the best of the New Deal. It became a regular ritual to raise social-security payments. In the 1960's Medicare, expanded aid to education, and the Economic Opportunity Act joined the family of welfare. But all was not rosy, however, in the house of social legislation. The success of the middle class, after 1939, had a poisonous effect on those programs, such as AFDC and public housing, which were handed on to poorer and poorer customers. Once these had been programs for the submerged middle class. The blacks and the dispossessed moved in as the fattened middle class moved out. But this meant the loss of that all-important factor, political popularity. The long shadow of the old pauper laws began to fall once more on these programs. They became stingy, harried by onerous conditions, and easy prey for political snipers. All this increased disaffection in the ranks of the beneficiaries. These programs were ripe, then, for the revolts and counterrevolts of the 1960's.

BENCH AND BAR

Because of a few famous decisions, the renown and prestige of the United States Supreme Court probably never stood higher than in the middle 20th century. But this was an exceptional court; courts and judges lost power, relatively speaking, to the growing central branches of the government. Few state-court judges ever achieved much fame. Benjamin Cardozo (1870–1938) of New York was a rare exception. (Cardozo also served on the United States Supreme Court, from 1932 on.) In the 1950's and 1960's, Roger Traynor of California had perhaps the largest reputation of any state-court judge. Probably few non-lawyers had ever heard of him.

The differences between Cardozo and Traynor were, in one respect, highly revealing. The two men lived a generation apart. Both were best known as innovating judges. Cardozo, however, preferred to dress change in common-law clothes; he liked to show continuity in the midst of change, to argue that the genius or spirit of the common law required him to move as he did. He was, or posed as, a craftsman molding traditional clay. Traynor was much more likely to cut and break with the past; he spoke a different language.

One philosophy affected both these judges, affected legal education too and the intellectual life of the law. This was the set of ideas called *legal realism*. It was, in fact, less a philosophy than an attitude. It rejected the work of 19th-century judges and scholars, with their emphasis on legal logic and purity of concepts: rejected, in other words, the philosophy of Langdell. It is best, perhaps, to see legal realism in the context of rationalism. Legal tradition was less and less valued for its own sake. The realist judges and writer

constantly asked: what use is this rule? A string of citations was no
answer; the names of noble judges of the past, the voice of somebody's treatise, or deductive reasoning were equally no answers.
There was less and less tolerance of artifice, fictions, real and apparent irrationalities. Law had to be a working social tool; it also
had to be *seen* in that guise.

These attitudes were not entirely new; and they never captured
the minds of all judges and lawyers. But they did affect an important elite. Realism made a difference in the way a small but important group of judges wrote, and perhaps (though here one is on
less sure ground) in the way they behaved and decided. On the
surface, their cases contained more (and more explicit) appeals to
"public policy." Judges were measurably readier to overrule earlier
cases directly. Overruling had always been possible in America;
but it was a power rarely used. In Earl Warren's court, overruling
became positively epidemic. Modern high-court judges also dissent
much more than their predecessors, and they write more concurring but separate opinions. Again, this is most evident for the
United States Supreme Court. Holmes and Brandeis were "great
dissenters," but in their day dissent was still not normal practice.
By the late 1950's, a unanimous decision, in a case of importance,
was quite unusual. The school-segregation case was, in fact, unanimous; this alone suggested some ardent diplomacy by Warren behind the scenes. Frequently, the Supreme Court split down the
middle, 5 to 4; in some cases, the justices wrote three, four, five, or
even more separate opinions; it became a nice preoccupation of
political scientists to analyze the various blocs on the Supreme
Court, and the games that justices played.

Bench and bar were more professionalized in the 20th century
than they had been in the past. In many states, the election of
judges was routine, a rubber stamp. Very often, a judge arrived on
the bench by appointment, when an old judge died or resigned.
After a long term of office, the new judge ran for re-election, without any real opposition. Few high-court judges were ever defeated,
or were ever threatened with defeat. The Missouri plan (1940) indeed proposed ending this charade. This plan shifted responsibility
for selecting the judges to a panel made up of laymen appointed
by the governor, lawyers chosen by the local bar, and a sitting
judge. The panel suggests three names; the governor chooses one
of the three. This man then serves one year on the bench, and at
that point runs for re-election, unopposed. In the 1960's a number
of states followed Missouri's example. As early as the 1940's,

also, the ABA lobbied, with some success, for a greater say in selection of federal judges. In 1908, the American Bar Association adopted a canon of professional ethics. Most states accepted this or a similar code as the rule for the conduct of lawyers. The integrated bar also became popular toward the middle of the century. This meant a unitary bar association, collecting dues, to which all lawyers had to belong, and with power at least in theory to discipline its own members. By 1960, more than half of the states had integrated bars. Still, compared to the hold of the American Medical Association over doctors (largely through control of hospitals), the legal profession was loose and liberal indeed. At no point did more than half the lawyers even bother to join their national association. And although the bar tried to speak with one voice, it never succeeded in persuading the outside world to listen.

Law schools now monopolized access to the bar. There were more of them than medical schools. They were not so expensive or so carefully controlled as medical schools—not that they were so diverse as they might or ought to have been. The Langdell school and conceptual jurisprudence dominated legal education in the first half of the century. All over the country in, say, 1930 or 1950, small, poorly financed schools, many with night divisions, pathetically imitated Harvard and used her books, rather than searching for their own mission and soul. During most of the period, Langdell and conceptualism had the upper hand in literature as well. This was an age of great treatises. Samuel Williston built a monumental fortress (1920–22) out of the law of *Contracts*, volume after volume, solid, closely knit, fully armored against the intrusion of any ethical, economic, or social notions whatsoever.[18] After 1920, the legal realist movement threw down the gauntlet and became a serious rival of the dominant school. Karl Llewellyn and Jerome Frank, among others, did battle against the jurisprudence of concepts; there were even realist treatises, like Arthur Corbin's *Contracts*, a counterpoise out of Yale to the old man of Harvard. The realist idea changed the curriculum. Administrative law and taxation entered; the content of some prior courses altered, in tune with the times.

There was also, from time to time, a movement to bring law back into the intellectual world. There were experiments in integration of law and social science in the 1920's and 1930's at Columbia, Johns Hopkins, and Yale, and a fling or two at curricular reform. These essays failed. After the Second World War, there were more

[18] Williston was born in 1861, and died in 1963 at the age of 101.

serious attempts. Now, at last, government and foundation money began to trickle into the law schools. In the 1950's, an empirical study of the jury, at the University of Chicago, began to show that collaboration between legal scholars and their social science colleagues was possible at least. Mostly, law and social science was still only a promise; but the promises seemed a little less hollow and dreamlike. In a few schools—notably Wisconsin and Northwestern —the faculty paid something more than lip service to the idea. In the 1960's, law study broadened to include more social issues—law and poverty, for example, and a richer, more varied dose of foreign law. But the basic curriculum stayed exceptionally solid and impermeable.

Of the making of books, quality aside, there was truly no end. The few university law reviews of the 19th century had grown to an incredible number by 1970. There were probably more than one hundred and thirty. Virtually every law school, no matter how marginal, published one as a matter of local pride. Somehow, they all got filled with words. The more prestigious schools put out more issues than the weaker schools; then, when thick volumes became commonplace, they put out two journals, or more. The journals were run by the students; law-review editors were the student elite of their schools. They had the best grades, the best, or only, rapport with the faculty, and went to the best firms when they got their degrees. (Some schools, quite recently, have opened law review competition to all students who wish to try, regardless of grades.) It was a rare and daring event when Duke University, in the early 1930's, began to publish a journal called *Law and Contemporary Problems*. Each issue was a symposium on some topical issue; and no section of the journal was filled with the work of students. Later, specialized and scholarly journals (for example, the *American Journal of Legal History, The Law and Society Review*) began to appear.

On the whole, despite the baleful influence of conceptualism, legal literature was never richer than in the 20th century. During his long life, Roscoe Pound (1870–1964), a product of Nebraska, who switched from the study of fungus to law, poured his enormous creative energy into many subjects, sometimes erratically, but always provocatively. Between the wars, Charles Warren wrote a number of seminal studies of the American legal past. Legal history emerged once more from the shadows after the Second World War, and produced at least one major figure, Willard Hurst of Wisconsin. Scholars from other disciplines began to look *at* law with a fresh and sometimes illuminating eye.

In the late 1960's, volcanic rumblings began to disturb the peace of the law schools. Students led the way; their banners first flew slogans of civil rights and civil liberties; then, those of the war against poverty; then, general radicalism and revulsion with the established order. The richest and most famous schools were most affected and in them the most intellectually active students. The whole profession began to taste the consequences. When the Office of Economic Opportunity put money into neighborhood law offices, young lawyers eagerly turned out to work in the ghettos. Wall Street had to raise its price considerably in order to keep its pools of talent from drying up. Where the movement was going, and what the profession would look like when the dust settled, was not easy to say. Things could never be quite the same. In 1970, there were signs that the student movement had peaked. But classical legal education was a Humpty Dumpty teetering on the wall. It had shown in the past great capacity to bounce instead of break. Still, these were unusual times.

The vast ocean of law, the bottomless pit of law, was caught up, in 1970, in a sense of crisis, along with the rest of society. But it had a special crisis of its own. Notably, the pillars on which it rested seemed to crumble. All agreed, for example, that the system of criminal justice was rotten. The left considered it oppressive and unjust; the right complained that it did not work. What was the future of American law?

If by law one means an organized system of social control, any society of any size and complexity has law. As long as the country endures, so will its system of law, coextensive with society, reflecting its wishes and needs, in all their irrationality, ambiguity, and inconsistency. It will follow every twist and turn of development. The law is a mirror held up against life. It is order: it is justice; it is also fear, insecurity, and emptiness; it is whatever results from the scheming, plotting, and striving of people and groups, with and against each other. All these things law will continue to be. A full history of American law would be nothing more or less than a full history of American life. The future of one is the future of the other. If American institutions can support a society that is prosperous, efficient, and satisfying, that society might also be lawful and just. Whether this is likely to happen, is beyond the capacity of history to say.

(BIBLIOGRAPHICAL ESSAY)

Under the heading of Bibliography, I have listed those books and articles cited and made use of in the text, omitting chiefly such primary sources as cases, statutes, and so on. This listing might serve the reader as a guide to additional secondary studies in American legal history. In the next few pages, however, I have singled out a short and highly selective group of books. These are exceptionally useful, or well-written, or in some other way attractive to the novice and the specialist alike.

There is a profound shortage of *general* books on American legal history. There has not been, for example, any concise (or for that matter, wordy) narrative account of the whole law and its institutions. On the other hand, the literature on particular topics is not without its glories.

No student of American legal history can ignore the work of J. Willard Hurst. Of his many books, *The Growth of American Law: the Law Makers* (1950), is the most general and accessible; it treats with great insight and detail the work of certain "principal agencies of law" (the bar, the bench, the legislatures, the constitution makers), between 1790 and 1940. *Law and the Conditions of Freedom in the Nineteenth Century United States* (1956) is a short but brilliant essay that digs below the surface of American legal culture in the 19th century. Hurst's most ambitious work, *Law and Economic Growth: The Legal History of the Lumber Industry in Wisconsin, 1836–1915* (1964), is tied to a concrete time, place, and industry, but deserves close attention for its thoughtfulness, care, and detail.

The reader interested in the *colonial period* will want to begin with George L. Haskins' *Law and Authority in Early Massachusetts* (1960), a seminal book. There is no general overview of the period, but *Essays in the History of Early American Law,* edited by David H. Flaherty (1969), collects valuable essays in a number of fields; and see also Richard B. Morris, *Studies in the History of American Law, with Special Reference to the 17th and 18th Centuries* (2nd edition, 1959). There are quite a few good modern editions of colonial court records; Joseph H. Smith's *Colonial Justice in Western Massachusetts (1639–1702), the Pynchon Court Record* (1961), is, however, quite outstanding, particularly because of its long and informative introduction. Studies of individual aspects of colonial law are not, to say the least, overabundant; and there is much neglect of the South and of the 18th century in general. Joseph H. Smith's *Appeals to the Privy Council from the American Plantations* (1950) is definitive. Richard B. Morris, *Government and Labor in Early America* (1946) covers this important subject in fine detail. On criminal law, see Julius Goebel, Jr., and T. Raymond Naughton, *Law Enforcement in Colonial New York: A Study in Criminal Procedure* (1944).

The *post-Independence period* suffers from neglect, too, but the literature has been growing rapidly in recent years. Unlike the colonial period, much of the primary source material (reported cases and statutes) is readily available in any law library. Trial court records, however, are if anything more obscure. Many scholars have worked on aspects of the institutional history of law. The United States Supreme Court, naturally, has garnered the lion's share of attention. Charles Warren's *The Supreme Court in United States History* (3 vols., 1922) is a genuine classic—engrossing, richly detailed, superbly easy to read. Warren has a point of view—or bias, if you will—and does not hide it; but nothing before or after provides so generous a look at the Court at work, and is so studiously attentive to the political context in which the Court labored. A new history of the Court, in many volumes, has been projected; and two volumes have recently appeared—Volume I, *Antecedents and Beginnings to 1801*, by Julius Goebel, Jr. (1971); and Volume VI, Part One, *Reconstruction and Reunion, 1864–1888*, by Charles Fairman (1971)—but until this series is complete, Warren remains indispensable. For specific periods, the reader may want to consult Stanley I. Kutler, *Judicial Power and Reconstruction Politics* (1968); William F. Swindler, *Court and Constitution in the Twentieth Century: The Old Legality, 1889–1932* (1969); and Arnold M. Paul, *Conservative Crisis and the Rule of Law: Attitudes of Bar and Bench, 1887–1895* (1960). There are some good studies of particular decisions, as well—for example, C. Peter Magrath, *Yazoo, Law and Politics in the New Republic, The Case of Fletcher v. Peck* (1966); and Stanley I. Kutler, *Privilege and Creative Destruction, the Charles River Bridge Case* (1971). A recent study, Richard E. Ellis, *The Jeffersonian Crisis, Courts and Politics in the Young Republic* (1971), has the great virtue of studying the courts during this period in selected states as well as on the federal level. On the technical growth of the Supreme Court's jurisdiction, Felix Frankfurter and James M. Landis, *The Business of the Supreme Court, a Study in the Federal Judicial System* (1928), is still important. Some of the best work on the Supreme Court lurks in judicial biographies. Three older but excellent examples are Charles Fairman, *Mr. Justice Miller and the Supreme Court, 1862–1890* (1939), and two studies by Carl B. Swisher, *Stephen J. Field: Craftsman of the Law* (1930), and *Roger B. Taney* (1935). The old biography of John Marshall, by Albert Beveridge, is long-winded and biased, but the writing is sprightly. More recently, Gerald T. Dunne has published a much needed biography of Joseph Story, *Joseph Story and the Rise of the Supreme Court* (1970). For the same period, there is Donald G. Morgan's *Justice William Johnson: The First Dissenter* (1954). Mark DeWolfe Howe's study of the life of Oliver Wendell Holmes, Jr., was cut short by Howe's death. Two volumes have appeared: *Justice Oliver Wendell Holmes, The Shaping Years, 1841–1870* (1957); and *Justice Oliver Wendell Holmes, The Proving Years, 1870–1882* (1963). The work stops just at the point of Holmes' appointment to the Massachusetts bench. Finally, Leon Friedman and Fred L. Israel have edited *The Justices of the United States Supreme Court, 1789–1969* (1969), in four volumes.

State courts and their judges have fared much less well than the United States Supreme Court. There are a number of histories of state courts—for example, Carroll T. Bond, *The Court of Appeals of Maryland: A History* (1928); but most leave much to be desired. John Phillip Reid's *Chief Justice, the Judicial World of Charles Doe* (1967) and Leonard Levy's *The Law of the Commonwealth and Chief Justice Shaw* (1957), are particularly useful.

For those interested in the history of the legal profession, Anton-Hermann Chroust's, *The Rise of the Legal Profession in America,* in two volumes (Volume 1, *The Colonial Experience,* Volume 2, *The Revolution and the Post-Revolutionary Era,* 1965), is rather uncritical, but full of information. William F. English, *The Pioneer Lawyer and Jurist in Missouri* (1947) makes excellent reading; so does William F. Keller, *The Nation's Advocate, Henry Marie Brackenridge and Young America* (1956). This last represents a large but uneven literature: biographies of lawyers. If the "lawyer" has made his mark in another field, too, the material tends to balloon—for example, Abraham Lincoln, treated in John P. Frank, *Lincoln as a Lawyer* (1961); and John J. Duff, *A. Lincoln, Prairie Lawyer* (1960). But rare indeed are books which open the door to the lawyer's office, so to speak. Julius Goebel, Jr.'s monumental edition of *The Law Practice of Alexander Hamilton, Documents and Commentary* (Vol. I, 1964, Vol. II, 1969), does nobly for the period around 1800. One wishes a similar job could be done for a Wall Street lawyer of the late nineteenth century; but there is a good deal of raw material, at least, in Robert T. Swaine, *The Cravath Firm and Its Predecessors, 1819–1947,* Vol. I, *The Predecessor Firms 1819–1906* (1946); Henry W. Taft's book, *A Century and a Half at the New York Bar* (1938) is entertaining reading.

On legal education, see Alfred Z. Reed, *Training for the Public Profes-*

sion of the Law (1921). A number of law schools, most notably Harvard, have had their chroniclers; Arthur E. Sutherland's *The Law at Harvard, A History of Ideas and Men, 1817–1967* (1967) is recent and readable. On legal literature and thought, one might want to consult the snippets edited by Perry Miller, under the title *The Legal Mind in America, from Independence to the Civil War* (1962); Miller's own treatment of the subject, in *The Life of the Mind in America: From the Revolution to the Civil War* (1965) is, to me at least, unsatisfactory. For the end of the century, there is Clyde Jacobs, *Law Writers and the Courts: the Influence of Thomas M. Cooley, Christopher G. Tiedeman, and John F. Dillon upon American Constitutional Law* (1954). On civil procedure, there is a rather ponderous but carefully executed work by Robert W. Millar, *Civil Procedure of the Trial Court in Historical Perspective* (1952).

A number of monographs have appeared on the subject of state constitution making. Two of particular interest are Fletcher M. Green, *Constitutional Development in the South Atlantic States, 1776–1860* (1966); and Carl B. Swisher, *Motivation and Political Technique in the California Constitutional Convention, 1878–9* (1930). An interesting side show in American legal history is treated in William M. Robinson, Jr., *Justice in Grey, A History of the Judicial System of the Confederate States of America* (1941). Frontier law has generated far more heat and romance than light. A careful glimpse of an early period is in William Baskerville Hamilton, *Anglo-American Law on the Frontier: Thomas Rodney and His Territorial Cases* (1953); for later periods, hardly any reader can resist such a work as Glenn Shirley, *Law West of Fort Smith, A History of Frontier Justice in the Indian Territory, 1834–1896* (1957).

The *substantive law* is a mixed bag. Many areas have never been properly treated. No one seriously interested in American legal history should ignore the series of books that has emerged from the workshops of the University of Wisconsin Law School, under the direct or indirect influence of J. Willard Hurst, all dealing with one or another aspect of law in Wisconsin in the 19th century. Taken as a whole, these books provide the fullest available picture of the law in action in a single state. Some are better or more readable than others, of course. Robert S. Hunt's *Law and Locomotives, the Impact of the Railroad on Wisconsin Law in the Nineteenth Century* (1958), is particularly fascinating. Others in the series include Lawrence M. Friedman, *Contract Law in America, A Social and Economic Case Study* (1965); Spencer Kimball, *Insurance and Public Policy, A Study in the Legal Implementation of Social and Economic Public Policy* (1960); George J. Kuehnl, *The Wisconsin Business Corporation* (1959); and Francis W. Laurent *The Business of a Trial Court, 100 Years of Cases* (1959), a unique though unsatisfying study of the "total flow of business through a trial court of general jurisdiction," which (for our period) was the Circuit Court for Chippewa County, Wisconsin.

The Wisconsin school of legal history has been especially interested in the relationship between law and the economic system, and between law and business. This general area is perhaps better treated than other aspects of law in the 19th century, though no one would say that anywhere near enough work has been done. This area, too, is much illuminated by the literature on government's role in the economy—works such as Oscar and Mary Handlin, *Commonwealth: A Study of the Role of Government in the American Economy: Massachusetts, 1774–1861* (rev. ed., 1969); and Louis Hartz, *Economic Policy and Democratic Thought: Pennsylvania, 1776–1860* (1948). On canal and railroad building, particularly useful are Carter Goodrich, *Government Promotion of American Canals and Railroads, 1800–1890* (1960); Harry N. Scheiber, *Ohio Canal Era, A Case Study of Government and the Economy, 1820–1861* (1969). Bray Hammond has written the indispensable book on banking and the law: *Banks and Politics in America from the Revolution to the Civil War* (1957); he also published *Sovereignty and an Empty Purse, Banks and Politics in the Civil War* (1970). On later railroad regulation, there is the Hunt study, mentioned above, for Wisconsin; Edward C. Kirkland, *Men, Cities and Transportation: A Study in New England History 1820–1900* (2 vols., 1948); George H. Miller, *Railroads and the Granger Laws* (1971); and the important, iconoclastic study by Gabriel Kolko, *Railroads and Regulation, 1877–1916* (1965). For the background and early history of the antitrust laws, see William R. Letwin, *Law and Economic Policy in America, the Evolution of the Sherman Antitrust Act* (1965). Charles Warren's *Bankruptcy in United States History* (1935) is still useful; on corporation law, see John William Cadman, *The Corporation in New Jersey, Business and Politics, 1791–1875* (1949); on taxation, Randolph E. Paul, *Taxation in the United States* (1954).

The law of property still awaits some hero to rouse it from the sleep of obscurity. The public lands and land law have fared rather better. A comprehensive, older account is Benjamin H. Hibbard, *A History of the Public Land Policies* (1924); a more modern treatment is Paul Gates, *History of Public Land Law Development* (1968). Important essays have been collected by Vernon Carstensen, and edited under the title of *The Public Lands, Studies in the History of the Public Domain* (1963).

Historians, legal and nonlegal, have paid surprisingly little heed to the history of criminal law and criminal justice. There is Jack K. Williams, *Vogues in Villainy: Crime and Retribution in Ante-Bellum South Carolina* (1959); Roger Lane, *Policing the City: Boston, 1822–1885* (1967); and there are useful essays in *Violence in America: Historical and Comparative Perspectives,* edited by Hugh D. Graham and Ted R. Gurr (1969), a report submitted to the National Commission on the Causes and Prevention of Violence. David J. Rothman's superb new book, *The Discovery of the Asylum, Social Order and Disorder in the New Republic* (1971), illuminates whole areas of legal and social history. The theme of the book is the shift to institutional treatment of deviants in the 19th century—the simultaneous invention or rise to significance of the penitentiary, the insane asylum, the juvenile house of refuge, the poorhouse. On family law, Nelson M. Blake's *The Road to Reno, A History of Divorce in the United States* (1962) is good reading; and William L. O'Neill's *Divorce in the Progressive Era* (1967) is stimulating, though the bulk of the book deals with a later period. Another stimulating study, Joseph Gusfield's *Symbolic Crusade, Status Politics and the American Temperance Movement* (1963), sheds light on liquor laws. The law of slavery and race relations is often treated in general books on these subjects, for example, Kenneth Stampp's *The Peculiar Institution, Slavery in the Ante-Bellum South* (1956); and C. Vann Woodward's *The Strange Career of Jim Crow* (revised edition, 1966). There is also the very interesting literature comparing American slavery (and especially the law of slavery) with that of Latin America—Stanley M. Elkins, *Slavery, A Problem in American Institutional and Intellectual Life* (1959); Herbert S. Klein, *Slavery in the Americas: A Comparative Study of Virginia and Cuba* (1967), and, most recently, Carl N. Degler's *Neither Black nor White: Slavery and Race Relations in Brazil and the United States* (1971), among others.

Social-welfare legislation, broadly conceived, is a field just coming into its own. The reader will find Henry Farnam, *Chapters in the History of Social Legislation in the United States to 1860* (1938), to be still of value. On welfare law, there is Rothman's work on the asylums, cited above; James Leiby, *Charity and Correction in New Jersey* (1967). In the 1930's, a series of studies of the poor laws issued out of the University of Chicago, under the auspices of the School of Social Service Administration. Unfortunately, the overall quality was low. A typical example is Alice Shaffer, Mary W. Keefer, and Sophonisba P. Breckinridge, *The Indiana Poor Law* (1936). Joel Handler has edited *Family Law and the Poor, Essays by Jacobus ten Broek* (1971). On the early history of housing law, see Lawrence M. Friedman, *Government and Slum Housing, A Century of Frustration* (1968); and on environmental law, Earl F. Murphy, *Water Purity, A Study in Legal Control of Natural Resources* (1961). No doubt more will be heard from these fields.

(BIBLIOGRAPHY)

Abbott, Martin, *The Freedmen's Bureau in South Carolina, 1865–1872* (1967).

Abel-Smith, Brian, and Stevens, Robert, *Lawyers and the Courts, a Sociological Study of the English Legal System 1750–1965* (1967).

Adams, Charles Francis, (1835–1915), *An Autobiography* (1916).

Addison, Alexander, *Charges to Grand Juries of the Counties of the Fifth Circuit in the State of Pennsylvania* (1800).

Addison, Charles G., *Wrongs and Their Remedies* (1860).

Allen, Neal W., Jr., ed., Province and Court Records of Maine, Vol. IV, *The Court Records of York County, Maine* (1958).

American Law Institute, *A Study of the Business of the Federal Courts;* Part I, Criminal Cases, Part II, Civil Cases (1934).

Ames, James B., "The Failure of the 'Tilden Trust,' " 5 Harv. L. Rev. 389 (1892).

Anderson, Oscar E., *The Health of a Nation, Harvey W. Wiley and the Fight for Pure Food* (1958).

Angell, Joseph K., and Ames, Samuel, *A Treatise on the Law of Private Corporations Aggregate* (2nd ed., 1843).

Aronson, Sidney H., *Status and Kinship in the Higher Civil Service* (1964).

Asbury, Herbert, *The Gangs of New York: An Informal History of the Underworld* (1928).

Atkinson, Thomas E., "The Development of the Massachusetts Probate System," 42 Mich. L. Rev. 425 (1943).

Aumann, Francis R., *The Changing American Legal System* (1940).

Babb, James E., "The Supreme Court of Illinois," 3 Green Bag 217 (1891).

Bacote, Clarence A., "Negro Proscriptions, Protests, and Proposed Solutions in Georgia, 1880–1908," 25 J. So. Hist. 471 (1959).

Bailey, Thomas A., "Congressional Opposition to Pure Food Legislation, 1879–1906," 36 Am. J. Sociology 52 (1931).

"Bailments and Conditional Sales," 44 Am. Law Reg. 335 (1896).

Baker, Elizabeth F., *Henry Wheaton 1785–1848* (1937).

Bakken, Gordon M., "The Impact of the Colorado State Constitution on Rocky Mountain Constitution Making," 47 Colo. Magazine, No. 2, 152 (1970).

Baldwin, Joseph G., *The Flush Times of Alabama and Mississippi, A Series of Sketches* (1957).

Bancroft, Hubert, *Popular Tribunals* (2 volumes, 1887).

Barnes, I. R., *Public Utility Control in Massachusetts* (1930).

Bassett, John Spencer, *Slavery and Servitude in the Colony of North Carolina* (1896).

Bates, J. Leonard, ed., *Tom Walsh in Dakota Territory* (1966).

Bay, W. V. N., *Reminiscences of the Bench and Bar of Missouri* (1878).

Beach, Charles F., *Commentaries on the Law of Public Corporations* (2 volumes, 1893).

Beard, Earl S., "The Background of State Railroad Regulation in Iowa," 51 Iowa J. of Hist. 1 (1953).

Beitzinger, Alfons J., *Edward G. Ryan, Lion of the Law* (1960).

Benjamin, Judah P., *A Treatise on the Law of Sale of Personal Property* (3rd American edition, Edmund Bennett, ed., 1881).

Bennett, Edmund, and Heard, Franklin, *A Selection of Leading Cases in Criminal Law* (2 volumes, 1856–57).

Benson, George C. S., *et al.*, *The American Property Tax: Its History, Administration and Economic Impact* (1965).

Benson, Lee, *Merchants, Farmers, and Railroads, Railroad Regulation and New York Politics, 1850–1887* (1955).

Bentham, Jeremy, *Defence of Usury* (3rd ed., 1816).

——, *Rationale of Judicial Evidence*, Vol. IV (1827).

Benton, Josiah H., *Warning Out in New England* (1911).

Berger, Raoul, "Impeachment of Judges and 'Good Behavior' Tenure," 79 Yale L. J. 1475 (1970).

Beutel, Frederick K., "Colonial Sources of the Negotiable Instruments Law of the United States," 34 Ill. L. Rev. 137 (1939).

——, "The Development of State Statutes on Negotiable Paper Prior to the Negotiable Instruments Law," 40 Columbia L. R. 836 (1940).

Beveridge, Albert J., *The Life of John Marshall* (4 volumes, 1916–19).

Binney, Horace, *The Leaders of the Old Bar of Philadelphia* (1866).

Bishop, Joel P., *Commentaries on the Criminal Law* (6th ed., 1877).

——, *Commentaries on the Law of Marriage and Divorce* (1852).

Blackstone, Sir William, *Commentaries on the Laws of England* (4 volumes, 1765–69).

Blake, Nelson M., *The Road to Reno, A History of Divorce in the United States* (1962).

Blandi, Joseph G., *Maryland Business Corporations 1783–1852* (1934).

Bloomfield, Maxwell, "Law vs. Politics: The Self-Image of the American Bar (1830–1860)," 12 Am. J. Leg. Hist. 306 (1968).

——, "William Sampson and the Codifiers: The Roots of American Legal Reform, 1820–1830," 11 Am. J. Leg. Hist. 234 (1967).

Blume, William W., "Civil Procedure on the American Frontier," 56 Mich. L. Rev. 161 (1957).

——, "Legislation on the American Frontier," 60 Mich. L. Rev. 317 (1962).

——, "Probate and Administration on the American Frontier," 58 Mich. L. Rev. 209 (1959).

——, ed., *Transactions of the Supreme Court of the Territory of Michigan*, Vol. I (1935).

Blume, William W., and Brown, Elizabeth G., "Territorial Courts and Law: Unifying Factors in the Development of American Legal Institutions," 61 Mich. L. Rev. 39, 467 (1962–63).

Boan, Fern, *A History of Poor Relief Legislation and Administration in Missouri* (1941).

Bogue, Allan G., "The Iowa Claim Clubs: Symbol and Substance," 45 Miss. Valley Hist. Rev. 231 (1958).

Bohlen, Francis H., "The Rule in Rylands v. Fletcher," 59 U. Pa. L. Rev. 298, 373, 423 (1911).

Bond, Beverley W., Jr., *The Quit-Rent System in the American Colonies* (1919).

Bond, Carroll T., *The Court of Appeals of Maryland, a History* (1928).

——, *Proceedings of the Maryland Court of Appeals 1695–1729* (1933).

Boorstin, Daniel J., *The Americans; The Colonial Experience* (1958).

——, *Delaware Cases* (3 volumes, 1943).

Borkin, Joseph, *The Corrupt Judge* (1962).

Bowker, Richard Rogers, *Copyright, Its History and Its Law* (1912).

Branning, Rosalind L., *Pennsylvania Constitutional Development* (1960).

Branscombe, Martha, *The Courts and the Poor Laws in New York State 1784–1929* (1943).

Breckinridge, Sophonisba P., *The Illinois Poor Law and Its Administration* (1939).

——, *Public Welfare Administration in the United States* (2nd ed., 1928).

Bridenbaugh, Carl, *Cities in the Wilderness* (1938).

Brigance, William N., *Jeremiah Sullivan Black* (1934).

Bronner, Edwin B., *William Penn's "Holy Experiment"* (1962).

Brown, Elizabeth G., "The Bar on a Frontier: Wayne County, 1796–1836," 14 Am. J. Leg. Hist. 136 (1970).

——, *British Statutes in American Law, 1776–1836* (1964).

——, "The Law School of the University of Michigan, 1859–1959," 38 Mich. St. Bar J. 16 (August, 1959).

——, *Legal Education at Michigan, 1859–1959* (1959).

——, "Legal Systems in Conflict: Orleans Territory 1804–1812," 1 Am. J. Leg. Hist. 35 (1957).

Brown, Richard Maxwell, "The American Vigilante Tradition," in Hugh D. Graham and Ted R. Gurr, eds., *Violence in America: Historical and Comparative Perspectives* (1969).

——, "Historical Patterns of Violence in America," in Hugh D. Graham and Ted R. Gurr, eds., *Violence in America: Historical and Comparative Perspectives* (1969).

Browne, William H., ed., Archives of Maryland, Vol. IV, *Judicial and Testamentary Business of the Provincial Court, 1637–1650* (1887).

Browning, Grace A., *The Development of Poor Relief Legislation in Kansas* (1935).

Bruce, Isabel C., and Eickhoff, Edith, *The Michigan Poor Law* (1936).

Buchanan, A. Russell, *David S. Terry of California, Dueling Judge* (1956).

Bugbee, Bruce W., *Genesis of American Patent and Copyright Law* (1967).

Cadman, John W., *The Corporation in New Jersey, Business and Politics, 1791–1875* (1949).

Cahill, Marion C., *Shorter Hours* (1932).

Cahn, Frances, and Bary, Valeska, *Welfare Activities of Federal, State, and Local Governments in California, 1850–1934* (1936).

Calhoun, Daniel H., *Professional Lives in America, Structure and Aspiration, 1750–1850* (1965).

Callow, Alexander B., Jr., *The Tweed Ring* (1966).

Capen, Edward W., *The Historical Development of the Poor Law of Connecticut* (1905).

Carter, James C., *The Proposed Codification of Our Common Law* (1884).

——, *The Provinces of the Written and the Unwritten Law* (1889).

Casner, Andrew J., ed., *American Law of Property, a Treatise on the Law of Property in the United States* (7 volumes, 1952).

Caton, John D., *Early Bench and Bar of Illinois* (1893).

Caughey, John W., *Their Majesties, the Mob* (1960).

Centennial History of the Harvard Law School 1817–1917 (1918).

"The Changing Role of the Jury in the Nineteenth Century," 74 Yale L. J. 170 (1964).

Chapin, Bradley, *The American Law of Treason, Revolutionary and Early National Origins* (1964).

Chase, Frederic Hathaway, *Lemuel Shaw, Chief Justice of the Supreme Judicial Court of Massachusetts* (1918).

Child, Robert, *New Englands Jonas Cast up at London*, ed. W. T. R. Marvin (1869).

Chipman, Daniel, *Life of Nathaniel Chipman* (1846).

Chittenden, L. E., "Legal Reminiscences," 5 Green Bag 307 (1893).

Christman, Henry, *Tin Horns and Calico* (1945).

Chroust, Anton-Hermann, *The Rise of the Legal Profession in America* (2 volumes, 1965).

Clark, Charles E., "The Union of Law and Equity," 25 Colum. L. Rev. 1 (1925).

Clark, William L., *Handbook of the Law of Private Corporations* (1897).

Clarke, Samuel B., "Criticisms upon Henry George, Reviewed from the Stand-Point of Justice," 1 Harv. L. Rev. 265 (1888).

Coan, Titus M., ed., *Speeches, Arguments and Miscellaneous Papers of David Dudley Field* (Vol. III, 1890).

Coates, Albert, "The Story of the Law School at the University of North Carolina," N. Car. L. Rev., Special Issue, Oct. 1968.

Coben, Stanley, *A. Mitchell Palmer: Politician* (1963).

Cochran, Thomas C., *Railroad Leaders 1845–1890* (1953).

Coe, Mildred V., and Morse, Lewis W., "Chronology of the Development of the David Dudley Field Code," 27 Cornell L. Q. 238 (1942).

Colden Letter Books 1765–1775, Vol. II (Collections of the New York Historical Society, 1877).

Coleman, Peter J., *The Insolvent Debtor in American History* (unpublished ms., 1970).

——, *The Transformation of Rhode Island 1790–1860* (1963).

Commons, John R., *Races and Immigrants in America* (1907).

Commons, John R., and Andrews, John B., *Principles of Labor Legislation* (Rev. ed., 1927).

Compton, William R., "Early History of Stock Ownership by Corporations," 9 Geo. Wash. L. Rev. 125 (1940).

Conmy, Peter T., *The Historic Spanish Origin of California's Community Property Law and Its Development and Adaptation to Meet the Needs of an American State* (1957).

Conover, Milton, "The Abandonment of the 'Tidewater' Concept of Admiralty Jurisdiction in the United States," 38 Oregon L. Rev. 34 (1958).

"The Contingent Fee Business," 24 Albany L. J. 24 (1881).

Cook, William W., *A Treatise on Stock and Stockholders, Bonds, Mortgages, and General Corporation Law* (2 volumes, 3rd ed., 1894) (3 volumes, 5th ed., 1903).

Cooley, Thomas M., *A Treatise on Constitutional Limitations* (5th ed., 1883).

——, *A Treatise on the Law of Torts, or the Wrongs Which Arise Independent of Contract* (1879).

Corwin, Edward S., *Court over Constitution* (1938).

——, *The Twilight of the Supreme Court* (1934).

Cowan, Thomas A., "Legislative Equity in Pennsylvania," 4 U. Pittsburgh Law Rev. 1 (1937).

Craven, Wesley Frank, *The Southern Colonies in the Seventeenth Century, 1607–1689* (1949).

Crawford, John J., *Negotiable Instruments Law* (1897).

Creech, Margaret, *Three Centuries of Poor Law Administration, A Study of Legislation in Rhode Island* (1936).

Crèvecoeur, St. John, *Letters from an American Farmer* (1782).

Curti, Merle, *The Making of an American Community* (1959).

Curtis, George T., *Life of Daniel Webster* (2 volumes, 1872).

D'Agostino, Lorenzo, *History of Public Welfare in Vermont* (1948).

Dalzell, George W., *Benefit of Clergy in America and Related Matters* (1955).

Dane, Nathan, *A General Abridgment and Digest of American Law* (9 volumes, 1823–29).

Daniel, John W., *A Treatise on the Law of Negotiable Instruments* (2 volumes, 5th ed., 1903).

Dargo, George, *Legal Codification and the Politics of Territorial Government in Jefferson's Louisiana, 1803–1808* (unpublished Ph.D. thesis, 1970, Columbia University).

Davies, Pearl J., *Real Estate in American History* (1958).

Davis, David B., "The Movement to Abolish Capital Punishment in America, 1787–1861," 63 Am. Hist. Rev. 23 (1957).

Davis, Joseph S., *Essays in the Earlier History of American Corporations* (2 volumes, 1917).

Davis, Ray Jay, "The Polygamous Prelude," 6 Am. J. Leg. Hist. 1 (1962).

Dearing, Mary R., *Veterans in Politics, the Story of the G.A.R.* (1952).

De Ford, Miriam Allen, *Stone Walls, Prisons from Fetters to Furloughs* (1962).

Degler, Carl N., *Out of Our Past, the Forces that Shaped Modern America* (1959).

de Tocqueville, Alexis, *Democracy in America* (J. P. Mayer and M. Lerner, eds., 1966).

de Valinger, Leon, Jr., ed., *Court Records of Kent County, Delaware, 1680–1705* (1959).

Dick, Everett N., *The Lure of the Land* (1970).

——, *The Sod House Frontier* (1937).

Dickens, Charles, *American Notes* (1842).

Dillon, John F., *The Law of Municipal Corporations* (2 volumes, 2nd ed., 1873).

Dimsdale, Thomas J., *The Vigilantes of Montana* (new edition, 1953).

Dobkins, Betty E., *The Spanish Element in Texas Water Law* (1959).

Dodd, E. Merrick, "Statutory Developments in Business Corporation Law, 1886–1936," 50 Harv. L. Rev. 27 (1936).

Dodd, Walter F., *Administration of Workmen's Compensation* (1936).

Dodge, Emily P., "Evolution of a City Law Office, Part II," 1956 Wis. L. Rev. 35.

Dorfman, Joseph, "Chancellor Kent and the Developing American Economy," 61 Colum. L. Rev. 1290 (1961).

Doris, Lillian, ed., *The American Way in Taxation: Internal Revenue 1862–1963* (1963).

Dressler, David, *Practice and Theory of Probation and Parole* (1959).

Dulles, Foster R., *Labor in America* (2nd rev. ed., 1960).

Dunbar, William H., "The Anarchists' Case before the Supreme Court," 1 Harv. L. Rev. 307 (1888).

Dunne, Gerald T., "Joseph Story: The Germinal Years," 75 Harv. L. Rev. 707 (1962).

——, *Justice Joseph Story and the Rise of the Supreme Court* (1970).

DuRelle, George, "John Boyle," in William D. Lewis, ed., *Great American Lawyers*, Vol. II (1909).

Earle, Walter K., *Mr. Shearman and Mr. Sterling and How They Grew* (1963).

Eaton, Amasa, "Proposed Reforms in Marriage and Divorce Laws," 4 Colum. L. R. 243 (1904).

Eblen, Jack E., *The First and Second United States Empires, Governors and Territorial Government, 1784–1912* (1968).

Edsall, Preston W., ed., *Journal of the Courts of Common Right and Chancery of East New Jersey 1683–1702* (1937).

Eggert, Gerald G., *Railroad Labor Disputes, the Beginnings of Federal Strike Policy* (1967).

Elkins, Stanley M., *Slavery, A Problem in American Institutional and Intellectual Life* (1959).

Emery, J. Gladston, *Court of the Damned* (1959).

English, William F., *The Pioneer Lawyer and Jurist in Missouri* (1947).

Ewing, Cortez A. M., *The Judges of the Supreme Court, 1789–1937* (1938).

Ezell, John S., *Fortune's Merry Wheel, the Lottery in America* (1960).

Fairman, Charles, "Mr. Justice Bradley," in Allison Dunham and Philip Kurland, eds., *Mr. Justice* (1956).

——, *Mr. Justice Miller and the Supreme Court, 1862–1890* (1939).

Farnam, Henry, *Chapters in the History of Social Legislation in the United States to 1860* (1938).

Farrell, John T., ed., *The Superior Court Diary of William Samuel Johnson 1772–3* (1942).

Faulkner, Harold U., *Politics, Reform and Expansion 1890–1900* (1959).

Feder, Leah H., *Unemployment Relief in Periods of Depression 1857–1922* (1936).

Field, Arthur S., *The Child Labor Policy of New Jersey* (1910).

Field, Henry M., *The Life of David Dudley Field* (1898).

Field, Oliver P., "Unconstitutional Legislation in Indiana," 17 Indiana L. J. 101 (1941).

——, "Unconstitutional Legislation in Minnesota," 35 Am. Pol. Science Rev. 898 (1941).

Field, Richard S., *The Provincial Courts of New Jersey* (1849).

Fischer, Roger A., "Racial Segregation in Ante Bellum New Orleans," 74 Am. Hist. Rev. 926 (1969).

Foner, Philip S., ed., *Complete Writings of Thomas Paine,* Vol. II (1945).

Ford, Thomas, *A History of Illinois from Its Commencement as a State in 1818 to 1847* (1854).

Fox, Dixon R., ed., *Minutes of the Court of Session, Westchester County, 1657–1696* (1924).

Frank, John P., *Justice Daniel Dissenting* (1964).

Frankfurter, Felix, and Greene, Nathan, *The Labor Injunction* (1930).

Frankfurter, Felix, and Landis, James M., *The Business of the Supreme Court, a Study in the Federal Judicial System* (1928).

Franklin, John Hope, *From Slavery to Freedom* (2nd ed., 1956).

Frantz, Joe B., "The Frontier Tradition: An Invitation to Violence," in Hugh D. Graham and Ted R. Gurr, eds., *Violence in America: Historical and Comparative Perspectives* (1969).

Frazier, Edward Franklin, *The Negro in the United States* (rev. ed., 1957).

Freund, Ernst, *Standards of American Legislation* (1917).

Friedman, Lawrence M., *Contract Law in America, a Social and Economic Case Study* (1965).

——, "The Dynastic Trust," 73 Yale L. J. 547 (1964).

——, "Freedom of Contract and Occupational Licensing 1890–1910: A Legal and Social Study," 53 Cal. L. Rev. 487 (1965).

——, "Law Reform in Historical Perspective," 13 St. Louis U. L. J. 351 (1969).

——, "Patterns of Testation in the 19th Century: A Study of Essex County (New Jersey) Wills," 8 Am. J. Leg. Hist. 34 (1964).

——, "The Usury Laws of Wisconsin: A Study in Legal and Social History," 1963 Wis. L. Rev. 515.

Friedman, Lawrence M., and Ladinsky, Jack, "Social Change and the Law of Industrial Accidents," 67 Columbia L. Rev. 50 (1967).

"From Judicial Grant to Legislative Power: The Admiralty Clause in the Nineteenth Century," 67 Harv. L. Rev. 1214 (1954).

Garfinkel, Harold, "Conditions of Successful Degradation Ceremonies," 61 Am. J. Sociology 420 (1956).

Gates, Paul W., *Frontier Landlords and Pioneer Tenants* (1945).

——, *History of Public Land Law Development* (1968).

——, "The Homestead Law in an Incongruous Land System," in Vernon Carstensen, ed., *The Public Lands* (1963).

Gawalt, Gerard W., *Massachusetts Lawyers: A Historical Analysis of the Process of Professionalization, 1760–1840* (unpublished Ph.D. thesis, Clark University, 1969).

Goebel, Julius, Jr., ed., *A History of the School of Law, Columbia University* (1955).

——, *The Law Practice of Alexander Hamilton, Documents and Commentary* (Vol. I, 1964, Vol. II, 1969).

Goff, John S., "Old Age and the Supreme Court," 4 Am. J. Leg. Hist. 95 (1960).

Goodell, William, *The American Slave Code in Theory and Practice* (1853).

Goodrich, Carter, *Government Promotion of American Canals and Railroads 1800–1890* (1960).

Goodrich, Carter, et al., *Canals and American Economic Development* (1961).

Gossett, Thomas F., *Race, The History of an Idea in America* (1963).

Graves, John William, "The Arkansas Separate Coach Law of 1891," 7 Journal of the West 531 (1968).

Green, Fletcher M., *Constitutional Development in the South Atlantic States, 1776–1860* (1966).

Greenberg, Irwin F., "Justice William Johnson: South Carolina Unionist, 1823–1830," 36 Pa. Hist. 307 (1969).

Greene, Lorenzo J., *The Negro in Colonial New England, 1620–1776* (1942).

Gregorie, Anne K., ed., *Records of the Court of Chancery of South Carolina 1671–1779* (1950).

Gregory, Charles O., "Trespass to Negligence to Absolute Liability," 37 Va. L. Rev. 359 (1951).

Grob, Gerald N., *The State and the Mentally Ill* (1966).

Gusfield, Joseph, *Symbolic Crusade, Status Politics and the American Temperance Movement* (1963).

Habenstein, Robert W., and Lamers, William M., *History of American Funeral Directing* (1955).

Haines, Charles Grove, *The Role of the Supreme Court in American Government and Politics, 1789–1835* (1944).

Hall, Jerome, *Theft, Law, and Society* (2nd ed., 1952).

Hall, Livingston, "The Substantive Law of Crimes, 1887–1936," 50 Harv. L. Rev. 616 (1937).

Hamilton, Walton, "The Ancient Maxim Caveat Emptor," 40 Yale L. J. 1133 (1931).

Hamilton, William B., *Anglo-American Law of the Frontier: Thomas Rodney and his Territorial Cases* (1953).

Hamlin, Paul M., *Legal Education in Colonial New York* (1939).

Hamlin, Paul M., and Baker, Charles E., *Supreme Court of Judicature of the Province of New York, 1691–1704* (3 volumes, 1959).

Hammond, Bray, *Banks and Politics in America, from the Revolution to the Civil War* (1957).

——, *Sovereignty and an Empty Purse, Banks and Politics in the Civil War* (1970).

Hammond, Harold E., *A Commoner's Judge, the Life and Times of Charles Patrick Daly* (1954).

Handlin, Oscar, and Handlin, Mary, *Commonwealth: A Study of the Role of Government in the American Economy: Massachusetts 1744–1861* (rev. ed., 1969).

Harno, A. J., *Legal Education in the United States* (1953).

Harris, Virgil M., *Ancient, Curious, and Famous Wills* (1911).

Hartz, Louis, *Economic Policy and Democratic Thought, Pennsylvania 1776–1860* (1948).

Haskins, George L., "Codification of the Law in Colonial Massachusetts: A Study in Comparative Law," 30 Ind. L. J. 1 (1954).

——, "The First American Reform of Civil Procedure," in Roscoe Pound, ed., *Perspectives of Law; Essays for Austin Wakeman Scott* (1964).

——, *Law and Authority in Early Massachusetts* (1960).

Haskins, George L., and Ewing, Samuel E., "The Spread of Massachusetts Law in the Seventeenth Century," 106 U. Pa. L. Rev. 413 (1958).

Hassam, John T., "Land Transfer Reform," 4 Harv. L. Rev. 271 (1891).

Hatcher, William B., *Edward Livingston* (1940).

Haynes, Evan, *The Selection and Tenure of Judges* (1944).

Heath, Milton S., *Constructive Liberalism; The Role of the State in Economic Development in Georgia to 1860* (1954).

Heiberg, Robert A., "Social Backgrounds of the Minnesota Supreme Court Justices: 1858–1968," 53 Minn. L. Rev. 901 (1969).

Henry, Robert S., "The Railroad Land Grant Legend in American History Texts," 32 Miss. Valley Hist. Rev. 171 (1945).

Hepburn, Charles M., *The Historical Development of Code Pleading in America and England* (1897).

Hibbard, Benjamin H., *A History of the Public Land Policies* (1924).

Hickman, Martin B., "Judicial Review of Legislation in Utah," 4 Utah L. Rev. 50 (1954).

Hicks, Frederick C., ed., *High Finance in the Sixties* (1929).

Higginbotham, S. W., *The Keystone in the Democratic Arch: Pennsylvania Politics 1800–1816* (1952).

High, J. L., "What Shall Be Done with the Reports?" 16 Am. L. Rev. 429 (1882).

Hilliard, Francis, *The Law of Torts, or Private Wrongs* (1859).

Hollister, Ovando J., *The Mines of Colorado* (1867).

[Holmes, Oliver Wendell, Jr.] "The Theory of Torts," 7 Am. L. Rev. 652 (1873).

Hopkins, James F., ed., *The Papers of Henry Clay* (Vol. I, The Rising Statesman, 1797–1814) (1959).

Horton, John T., *James Kent, A Study in Conservatism, 1763–1847* (1939).

Horwitz, Morton J., *Damage Judgments, Legal Liability and Economic Development before the Civil War* (unpublished ms., 1970).

Houts, Marshall, *From Gun to Gavel* (1954).

Howard, Warren S., *American Slavers and the Federal Law, 1837–1862* (1963).

Howe, Mark DeWolfe, *Justice Oliver Wendell Holmes, the Proving Years 1870–1882* (1963).

——, *Justice Oliver Wendell Holmes, the Shaping Years 1841–1870* (1957).

Hubbell's Legal Directory (1892).

Huffcut, Ernest W., "A Decade of Progress in Legal Education" *Report, 25th Ann. Meeting ABA* (1902).

Hughes, Robert M., *Handbook of Admiralty Law* (1901).

Hunt, Aurora, *Kirby Benedict, Frontier Federal Judge* (1961).

Hunt, Robert S., *Law and Locomotives, the Impact of the Railroad on Wisconsin Law in the Nineteenth Century* (1958).

Hurst, J. Willard, *The Growth of American Law: The Law Makers* (1950).

——, *Law and the Conditions of Freedom in the Nineteenth Century United States* (1956).

——, *Law and Economic Growth: The Legal History of the Lumber Industry in Wisconsin 1836–1915* (1964).

——, "Treason in the United States," 58 Harv. L. Rev. 226 (1944).

——, "The Uses of Law in Four 'Colonial' States of the American Union," 1945 Wisconsin L. Rev. 577.

Hurwitz, Howard L., *Theodore Roosevelt and Labor in New York State, 1880–1900* (1943).

Ingersoll, Henry H., "Some Anomalies of Practice," 1 Yale L. J. 89 (1891).

Jacobs, Clyde, *Law Writers and the Court* (1954).

James, Henry, *Richard Olney and His Public Service* (1923).

Jameson, J. Franklin, ed., [*Edward*] *Johnson's Wonder-Working Providence, 1628–1651* (1910).

Jenks, W. L., "History of Michigan Constitutional Provision Prohibiting a General Revision of the Laws," 19 Mich. L. Rev. 615 (1921).

Jensen, Merrill, *The New Nation, a History of the United States During the Confederation, 1781–1789* (1950).

Jewett, W. O. L., "Early Bar of Northeast Missouri," in A. J. D. Stewart, ed., *History of the Bench and Bar of Missouri* (1898).

Johnson, Emory R., *American Railway Transportation* (1907).

Johnson, Herbert A., "Civil Procedure in John Jay's New York," 11 Am. J. Leg. Hist. 69 (1967).

Jones, Alan, "Thomas M. Cooley and the Interstate Commerce Commission: Continuity and Change in the Doctrine of Equal Rights," 81 Polit. Sci. Q. 602 (1966).

——, "Thomas M. Cooley and the Michigan Supreme Court: 1865–1885," 10 Am. J. Leg. Hist. 97 (1966).

Jones, Maldwyn A., *American Immigration* (1960).

Jordan, Wilbur K., *Philanthropy in England 1480–1660* (1959).

Jordan, Winthrop D., *White Over Black, American Attitudes Toward the Negro, 1550–1812* (1968).

Keasbey, Edward Q., "New Jersey and the Great Corporations," 13 Harv. L. Rev. 198 (1899).

Keedy, Edwin R., "History of the Pennsylvania Statute Creating Degrees of Murder," 97 Univ. Pa. L. Rev. 759 (1949).

Keller, Morton, *The Life Insurance Enterprise, 1885–1910* (1963).

Keller, William F., *The Nation's Advocate, Henry Marie Brackenridge and Young America* (1956).

Kent, James, *Commentaries on American Law* (1st ed., 4 vols., 1826–1830).

——, *An Introductory Lecture to a Course of Law Lectures, Delivered November 17, 1794* (1794).

Kent, William, *Memoirs and Letters of James Kent* (1898).

Kimball, Edward L., "Criminal Cases in a State Appellate Court: Wisconsin 1839–1959," 9 Am. J. Leg. Hist. 95 (1965).

Kimball, Spencer L., *Insurance and Public Policy, A Study in the Legal Implementation of Social and Economic Public Policy, Based on Wisconsin Records 1835–1959* (1960).

Kirkland, Edward C., *Men, Cities and Transportation: A Study in New England History 1820–1900* (2 vols., 1948).

Klein, Herbert S., *Slavery in the Americas, A Comparative Study of Virginia and Cuba* (1967).

Klein, Milton M., ed., *The Independent Reflector; or, Weekly Essays on Sundry Important Subjects* (1963).

Kolko, Gabriel, *Railroads and Regulation, 1877–1916* (1965).

Kuehnl, George J., *The Wisconsin Business Corporation* (1959).
Kutler, Stanley I., ed., *The Dred Scott Decision: Law or Politics?* (1967).
——, *Judicial Power and Reconstruction Politics* (1968).
——, *Privilege and Creative Destruction, the Charles River Bridge Case* (1971).
Lamar, Howard R., *Dakota Territory, 1861–1869, A Study of Frontier Politics* (1956).
Lane, Roger, *Policing the City: Boston, 1822–1885* (1967).
——, "Urbanization and Criminal Violence in the 19th Century: Massachusetts as a Test Case," in Hugh D. Graham and Ted R. Gurr, eds., *Violence in America: Historical and Comparative Perspectives* (1969).
Langsam, Miriam Z., *Children West, A History of the Placing-Out System of the New York Children's Aid Society, 1853–1890* (1964).
Laurent, Francis W., *The Business of a Trial Court, 100 Years of Cases* (1959).
The Laws and Liberties of Massachusetts, Reprinted from the Copy of the 1648 Edition in the Henry G. Huntington Library (1929).
Lechford, Thomas, *Plaine Dealing, or Newes from New England* (1867 edition).
Lee, Charles R., Jr., *The Confederate Constitutions* (1963).
Lefler, H. T., ed., *North Carolina History as Told by Contemporaries* (1956).
Leiby, James, *Charity and Correction in New Jersey* (1967).
Letwin, William, "Congress and the Sherman Antitrust Law, 1887–1890," 23 U. Chi. L. Rev. 221 (1956).
——, *Law and Economic Policy in America, The Evolution of the Sherman Antitrust Act* (1965).
Levy, Leonard W., *The Law of the Commonwealth and Chief Justice Shaw* (1957).
Lewis, Orlando F., *The Development of American Prisons and Prison Customs, 1776–1845* (1922).
Lewis, W. David, *From Newgate to Dannemora, The Rise of the Penitentiary in New York, 1796–1848* (1965).
Lewis, William Draper, ed., *Great American Lawyers* (8 volumes, 1907–09).
Lillich, Richard B., "The Chase Impeachment," 4 Am. J. Leg. Hist. 49 (1960).
Litwack, Leon F., *North of Slavery, the Negro in the Free States, 1790–1860* (1961).
Liverant, Spencer R., and Hitchler, Walter H., "A History of Equity in Pennsylvania," 37 Dickinson Law Rev. 156 (1933).
Livermore, Shaw, *Early American Land Companies* (1939).
Livingston's [John], *Law Register* (1851).
Llewellyn, Karl N., *The Common Law Tradition: Deciding Appeals* (1960).
Llewellyn, Karl N., and Hoebel, E. A., *The Cheyenne Way* (1941).

——, "Remarks on the Theory of Appellate Decision and the Rules or Canons about How Statutes Are To Be Construed," 3 Vanderbilt L. Rev. 395 (1950).

Lockwood, James H., "Early Times and Events in Wisconsin," *Second Annual Report and Collections of the State Historical Society of Wisconsin,* Vol. II (1856).

Logan, Frenise A., *The Negro in North Carolina 1876–1894* (1964).

Lou, Herbert H., *Juvenile Courts in the United States* (1927).

Lubove, Roy, *The Progressives and the Slums, Tenement House Reform in New York City 1890–1917* (1962).

Luepke, Henry F., Jr., "Comments on the Evidence in Missouri," 5 St. Louis U. L. J. 424 (1959).

Lutz, Harley L., *The State Tax Commission* (1918).

McAdam, David, ed., *History of the Bench and Bar of New York* (2 volumes, 1897–99).

McCain, Paul M., *The County Court in North Carolina before 1750* (1954).

McDade, Thomas M., *The Annals of Murder, a Bibliography of Books and Pamphlets on American Murders from Colonial Times to 1900* (1961).

McKnight, Joseph W., "The Spanish Legacy to Texas Law," 3 Am. J. Leg. Hist. 222, 299 (1959).

McNulty, John W., "Sidney Breese, The Illinois Circuit Judge, 1835–1841," 62 J. Ill. State Hist. Soc. 170 (1969).

Maestro, Marcello T., *Voltaire and Beccaria as Reformers of Criminal Law* (1942).

Magrath, C. Peter, *Yazoo, Law and Politics in the New Republic* (1966).

Maine, Sir Henry, *Ancient Law* (1861).

Malone, Wex S., "The Formative Era of Contributory Negligence," 41 Ill. L. Rev. 151 (1946).

——, "The Genesis of Wrongful Death," 17 Stanf. L. Rev. 1043 (1965).

Markham, Edward L., Jr., "The Reception of the Common Law of England in Texas and the Judicial Attitude Toward That Reception, 1840–1859," 29 Texas L. Rev. 904 (1951).

Martin, George, *Causes and Conflicts, The Centennial History of the Association of the Bar of the City of New York, 1870–1970* (1970).

Merk, Frederic, *Economic History of Wisconsin During the Civil War Decade* (1916).

Metcalf, Theron, *Principles of the Law of Contracts* (1874).

Millar, Robert W., *Civil Procedure of the Trial Court in Historical Perspective* (1952).

Miller, George A., "James Coolidge Carter, 1827–1905," in William D. Lewis, ed., *Great American Lawyers,* Vol. VIII (1909).

Miller, Howard S., *The Legal Foundations of American Philanthropy 1776–1844* (1961).

Miller, Perry, *The Legal Mind in America* (1962).

Moffet, S. E., "The Railroad Commission of California: a Study in Irresponsible Government," 6 Annals 469 (1895).

Morawetz, Victor, *The Law of Private Corporations* (2 volumes, 2nd ed., 1886).

Morgan, Donald G., *Justice William Johnson: the First Dissenter* (1954).

Morgan, Edmund S., and Morgan, Helen M., *The Stamp Act Crisis* (1953).

Morris, Richard B., *Government and Labor in Early America* (1946).

——, *Studies in the History of American Law* (2nd ed., 1959).

——, ed., *Select Cases of the Mayor's Court of New York City 1674–1784* (1935).

Mueller, Gerhard O. W., "Inquiry into the State of a Divorceless Society, Domestic Relations Law and Morals in England from 1660 to 1857," 18 U. Pittsburgh L. Rev. 545 (1957).

Murphy, Earl F., *Water Purity, a Study in Legal Control of Natural Resources* (1961).

Murrin, John M., *Anglicizing an American Colony: The Transformation of Provincial Massachusetts* (unpublished Ph.D. thesis, Yale University, 1966).

Nash, A. E. Keir, "A More Equitable Past? Southern Supreme Courts and the Protection of the Antebellum Negro," 48 No. Car. L. Rev. 197 (1970).

Nash, Gary B., "The Philadelphia Bench and Bar, 1800–1861," *Comparative Studies in Society and History*, Vol. VII, No. 2 (1965).

Nash, Gerald D., *State Government and Economic Development, A History of Administrative Policies in California, 1849–1933* (1964).

Nelson, Margaret V., *A Study of Judicial Review in Virginia, 1789–1928* (1947).

Nelson, William E., *The Americanization of the Common Law during the Revolutionary Era: A Study of Legal Change in Massachusetts, 1760–1830* (unpublished Ph.D. thesis, Harvard Univ., 1971).

Nevins, Allan, and Thomas, Milton H., eds., *The Diary of George Templeton Strong* (4 volumes, 1952).

Nortrup, Jack, "The Education of a Western Lawyer," 12 Am. J. Leg. Hist. 294 (1968).

Norvell, James R., "The Reconstruction Courts of Texas, 1867–1873," 62 Southwestern Hist. Q. 141 (1958).

Nye, Russel B., *Fettered Freedom, Civil Liberties and the Slavery Controversy 1830–1860* (1963).

"Observations on the Pernicious Practice of the Law," 13 Am. J. Leg. Hist. 244 (1969).

O'Dea, Thomas F., *The Mormons* (1957).

Olsen, Otto H., *Carpetbagger's Crusade, the Life of Albion Winegar Tourgee* (1965).

O'Neall, John Belton, *Biographical Sketches of the Bench and Bar of South Carolina* (2 volumes, 1859).

O'Neill, William L., *Divorce in the Progressive Era* (1967).

Osborn, William C., "Liquor Statutes in the United States," 2 Harv. L. Rev. 125 (1888).

"Overruled Their Judicial Superiors," 21 Am. L. Rev. 610 (1887).

Page, Elwin L., *Judicial Beginnings in New Hampshire 1640–1700* (1959).

Parsons, Theophilus, *The Law of Contracts* (2 volumes, 1853–55).

Patterson, Isaac F., *The Constitutions of Ohio* (1912).

Patterson, Lyman R., *Copyright in Historical Perspective* (1968).

Patteson, S. S. P., "The Supreme Court of Appeals of Virginia," 5 Green Bag 310 (1893).

Paul, Arnold M., *Conservative Crisis and the Rule of Law, Attitudes of Bar and Bench, 1887–1895* (1960).

Paul, Randolph E., *Taxation in the United States* (1954).

Peterson, Merrill D., ed., *Democracy, Liberty and Property, The State Constitutional Conventions of the 1820's* (1966).

Philbrick, Francis S., ed., *The Laws of Indiana Territory 1801–1809* (1930).

——, *Pope's Digest, 1815* (2 volumes, 1938–1940).

Pierce, Harry H., *Railroads of New York, A Study of Government Aid* (1953).

Platt, Anthony, *The Child Savers: the Invention of Delinquency* (1969).

Platt, Harrison Gray, "Matthew P. Deady," in *Great American Lawyers,* Vol. VII (1909).

Pleasants, J. Hall, ed., Archives of Maryland, Vol. XLIX, *Proceedings of the Provincial Court of Maryland 1663–1666* (1932).

——, Archives of Maryland, Vol. LIII, *Proceedings of the County Court of Charles County 1658–1666 and Manor Court of St. Clement's Manor 1659–1672* (1936).

Plucknett, Theodore F. T., *A Concise History of the Common Law* (5th ed., 1956).

Poldervaart, Arie W., *Black-Robed Justice, a History of the Administration of Justice in New Mexico from the American Occupation in 1846 until Statehood in 1912* (1948).

Pomeroy, Earl S., *The Territories and the United States, 1861–1890* (1947).

Potter, David M., *People of Plenty* (1954).

Pound, Roscoe, *Appellate Procedure in Civil Cases* (1941).

——, *Criminal Justice in America* (1930).

——, *Organization of Courts* (1940).

——, "The Place of Judge Story in the Making of American Law," 48 Am. L. Rev. 676 (1914).

Powell, Richard R., *Registration of the Title to Land in the State of New York* (1938).

Powell, Sumner C., *Puritan Village: The Formation of a New England Town* (1965).

Powers, Edwin, *Crime and Punishment in Early Massachusetts, 1620–1692, A Documentary History* (1966).

Prince, W. F., "The First Criminal Code of Virginia," *Ann. Rpt. Am. Hist. Ass'n.*, 1899, Vol. 1.

Prosser, William, *Handbook of the Law of Torts* (3rd ed., 1964).

Pumphrey, Ralph E. and Muriel W., eds., *The Heritage of American Social Work* (1961).

Rahl, James A., and Schwerin, Kurt, "Northwestern University School of Law, A Short History," 55 Nwn. U. Law Rev. 131 (1960).

Rankin, Hugh F., *Criminal Trial Proceedings in the General Court of Colonial Virginia* (1965).

Redlich, Josef, *The Common Law and the Case Method in American University Law Schools* (1914).

Reed, Alfred Z., *Training for the Public Profession of the Law* (1921).

Reed, H. Clay, and Miller, George J., eds., *The Burlington Court Book of West New Jersey* (1944).

Reid, John P., *Chief Justice, the Judicial World of Charles Doe* (1967).

——, *A Law of Blood, The Primitive Law of the Cherokee Nation* (1970).

"Report of the Committee on Uniform State Laws," in *Report, 14th Annual Meeting, American Bar Ass'n.*, p. 365 (1891).

Report of the Trial of the Hon. Samuel Chase (1805).

Reppy, Alison, "The Field Codification Concept," in Alison Reppy, ed., *David Dudley Field Centenary Essays* (1949).

Rheinstein, Max, ed., *Max Weber on Law in Economy and Society* (1954).

Riesenfeld, Stefan A., "Law-making and Legislative Precedent in American Legal History," 33 Minn. L. Rev. 103 (1949).

Robinson, William M., Jr., *Justice in Grey, A History of the Judicial System of the Confederate States of America* (1941).

Robinson, W. W., *Land in California* (1948).

Rogers, James G., *American Bar Leaders* (1932).

Rogers, W. McDowell, "Free Negro Legislation in Georgia Before 1865," 16 Ga. Hist. Q. 27 (1932).

Rohrbough, Malcolm J., *The Land Office Business: the Settlement and Administration of American Public Lands, 1789–1837* (1968).

Rosenberg, Charles, *Trial of the Assassin Guiteau* (1968).

Rothbard, Murray N., *The Panic of 1819* (1962).

Rovere, Richard, *The Magnificent Shysters* (1947).

Rowland, Dunbar, *Courts, Judges and Lawyers of Mississippi 1798–1935* (1935).

Russell, John H., *The Free Negro in Virginia, 1619–1865* (1913).

Rutland, Robert Allen, *The Birth of the Bill of Rights 1776–1791* (1962).

Schafer, Joseph, "Wisconsin's Farm Loan Law, 1849–1863" *Proceedings, State Historical Society of Wisconsin, 68th Ann. Meeting, 1920*, p. 156.

Scheiber, Harry N., *Ohio Canal Era, A Case Study of Government and the Economy, 1820–1861* (1969).

——, *The Wilson Administration and Civil Liberties 1917–1921* (1960).

Schlesinger, Arthur, "Biography of a Nation of Joiners," 50 Am. Hist. Rev. 1 (1944).

Schneider, David M., *The History of Public Welfare in New York State, 1609–1866* (1938).

Schouler, James, "Text and Citations," 22 Am. L. Rev. 66 (1888).

——, *A Treatise on the Law of Wills* (2nd ed., 1892).

Schuckers, J. W., *The Life and Public Services of Salmon Portland Chase* (1874).

Schwartz, Mortimer D., and Hogan, John C., eds., *Joseph Story* (1959).

Scott, Arthur P., *Criminal Law in Colonial Virginia* (1930).

Scribner, Charles H., *Treatise on the Law of Dower* (2 volumes, 2nd ed., 1883).

Sedgwick, Theodore, *A Treatise on the Measure of Damages* (2nd ed., 1852).

Segal, Ronald, *The Race War* (1966).

Seligman, Edwin R., *Essays in Taxation* (6th ed., 1909).

Selsam, J. Paul, *The Pennsylvania Constitution of 1776* (1936).

Shalloo, J. P. *Private Police, with Special Reference to Pennsylvania* (1933).

Shambaugh, Benjamin F., *History of the Constitutions of Iowa* (1902).

Sharfman, I. L., *The Interstate Commerce Commission*, Vol. I (1931).

Sheldon, Theodore, *Land Registration in Illinois* (1901).

Sheppard, William, *The Faithful Councellor, or the Marrow of the Law in English* (2nd ed. 1653).

Shirley, Glenn, *Law West of Fort Smith* (1957).

Shryock, Richard H., *Medical Licensing in America, 1650–1965* (1967).

Sims, Henry U., *A Treatise on Covenants Which Run with Land* (1901).

Sinclair, Upton, *American Outpost, a Book of Reminiscences* (1932).

Skilton, Robert H., "Developments in Mortgage Law and Practice," 17 Temple L. Q. 315 (1943).

Small, A. J., comp., *Proceedings of the Early Iowa State Bar Association 1874–1881* (1912).

Smith, Abbot E., *Colonists in Bondage, White Servitude and Convict Labor in America, 1607–1776* (1947).

Smith, Charles P., *James Wilson, Founding Father* (1956).

Smith, Chauncey, "A Century of Patent Law," 5 Quarterly J. of Economics 44 (1890).

Smith, James G., *The Development of Trust Companies in the United States* (1928).

Smith, James Morton, *Freedom's Fetters: the Alien and Sedition Laws and American Civil Liberties* (1956).

Smith, Joseph H., *Appeals to the Privy Council from the American Plantations* (1950).

Smith, Joseph H., ed., *Colonial Justice in Western Massachusetts (1639–1702), The Pynchon Court Record* (1961).

Smith, Joseph H., and Crowl, Philip A., eds., *Court Records of Prince Georges County, Maryland 1696–1699* (1964).

Smith, Warren B., *White Servitude in Colonial South Carolina* (1961).

Stampp, Kenneth M., *The Peculiar Institution, Slavery in the Ante-Bellum South* (1956).

"State Interference with Patent Rights," 16 Albany L. J. 360 (1877).

Stephens, R. Allan, "The 'Experienced Lawyer Service' in Illinois," 20 American Bar Ass'n. Journal 716 (1934).

Stimson, Frederic J., *Handbook to the Labor Law of the United States* (1896).

——, *Popular Law-Making* (1910).

Story, Joseph, "An Address Delivered before the Members of the Suffolk Bar, Sept. 4, 1821," 1 Am. Jurist 1 (1829).

——, *Commentaries on Equity Jurisprudence* (1836).

——, *Commentaries on the Law of Promissory Notes* (1845).

Strong, Theron G., *Landmarks of a Lawyer's Lifetime* (1914).

Sullivan, James, *History of Land Titles in Massachusetts* (1801).

Sunderland, Edson R., *History of the American Bar Association* (1953).

Surrency, Erwin C., "The Judiciary Act of 1801," 2 Am. J. Leg. Hist. 53 (1958).

Sutherland, Arthur E., *The Law at Harvard, A History of Ideas and Men, 1817–1967* (1967).

Swaine, Robert T., *The Cravath Firm and Its Predecessors, 1819–1947,* Vol. 1, *The Predecessor Firms, 1819–1906* (1946).

Swift, Zephaniah, *Digest of the Law of Evidence in Civil and Criminal Cases* (1810).

——, *A System of the Laws of the State of Connecticut* (1795).

Swindler, William F., *Court and Constitution in the 20th Century: The Old Legality, 1889–1932* (1969).

Swisher, Carl B., *Motivation and Political Technique in the California Constitutional Convention 1878–9* (1930).

——, *Stephen J. Field, Craftsman of the Law* (1930).

Taft, Henry W., *A Century and a Half at the New York Bar* (1938).

Taft, Philip, and Ross, Philip, "American Labor Violence: Its Causes, Character, and Outcome," in Hugh D. Graham and Ted R. Gurr, eds., *Violence in America, Historical and Comparative Perspectives* (1969).

Teeters, Negley K., and Shearer, John D., *The Prison at Philadelphia: Cherry Hill* (1957).

ten Broek, Jacobus, "California's Dual System of Family Law: Its Origin, Development and Present Status," Part II, 16 Stan. L. Rev. 900 (1964).

Thayer, James B., *A Preliminary Treatise on Evidence at the Common Law* (1898).

Thornbrough, Emma Lou, *The Negro in Indiana* (1957).

Thurman, Kay Ellen, *The Married Women's Property Acts* (unpublished LL.M. thesis, University of Wisconsin Law School, 1966).

Tiedeman, Christopher G., *An Elementary Treatise on the American Law of Real Property* (1885).

——, *A Treatise on the Limitations of Police Power in the United States* (1886).

Tindall, George B., *South Carolina Negroes 1877–1900* (1952).

Torrey, George A., *A Lawyer's Recollections* (1910).

Turner, Lynn W., "The Impeachment of John Pickering," 54 Am. Hist. Rev. 485 (1949).

Twiss, Benjamin R., *Lawyers and the Constitution, How Laissez Faire Came to the Supreme Court* (1942).

Two Centuries Growth of American Law 1701–1901 (1901).

Ubbelohde, Carl, *The Vice Admiralty Courts and the American Revolution* (1960).

Updike, Wilkins, *Memoirs of the Rhode Island Bar* (Boston, 1842).

Valentine, Alan, *Vigilante Justice* (1956).

Van Alstyne, Arvo, *The California Civil Code* (1954).

Vander Velde, Lewis G., "Thomas McIntyre Cooley," in Earl D. Babst and Lewis G. Vander Velde, eds., *Michigan and the Cleveland Era* (1948).

Vaughan, Floyd L., *The United States Patent System* (1956).

Verlie, Emil J., ed., *Illinois Constitutions* (1919).

Vose, Clement E., *Caucasians Only: the Supreme Court, the NAACP, and the Restrictive Covenant Cases* (1959).

Wagner, Samuel, "The Advantages of a National Bankrupt Law," *Report, 4th Ann. Meeting ABA* (1881), p. 223.

Walker, Albert H., "George Harding," in *Great American Lawyers*, Vol. VIII (1909).

Warner, Amos G., et al. *American Charities and Social Work* (3rd ed., 1919; 4th ed., 1930).

Warren, Charles, *Bankruptcy in United States History* (1935).

——, *A History of the American Bar* (1911).

——, *History of the Harvard Law School and of Early Legal Conditions in America* (3 volumes, 1908).

——, *The Supreme Court in United States History* (3 volumes, 1922).

Warren, Edward H., *Corporate Advantages Without Incorporation* (1929).

Warren, Samuel D., and Brandeis, Louis D., "The Right to Privacy," 4 Harv. L. Rev. 193 (1890).

Webb, Walter P., *The Great Plains* (1931).

Wettach, Robert H., ed., *A Century of Legal Education* (1947).

Wharton, Francis, *A Treatise on the Criminal Law of the United States* (4th edition, 1857).

White, Leonard D., *The Republican Era: 1869–1901* (1958).

Whitehead, John, "The Supreme Court of New Jersey," 3 Green Bag 493 (1891).

Whitin, E. S., *Factory Legislation in Maine* (1908).

Wigmore, John H., *A Treatise on the System of Evidence in Trials at Common Law* (4 volumes, 1904–05).

Williams, Jack K., "Crime and Punishment in Alabama, 1819–1840," 6 Ala. R. 1427 (1953).

——, *Vogues in Villainy: Crime and Retribution in Ante-Bellum South Carolina* (1959).

Williamson, Joel, *After Slavery, The Negro in South Carolina during Reconstruction, 1861–1877* (1965).

Willis, William, *A History of the Law, the Courts, and the Lawyers of Maine* (1863).

Wines, Frederick H., *Punishment and Reformation, A Study of the Penitentiary System* (2nd edition, 1910).

Winthrop, John, *The History of New England from 1630–1649* (2 volumes, 1853).

Woodford, Frank B., *Mr. Jefferson's Disciple, A Life of Justice Woodward* (1953).

Woodward, C. Vann, *Origins of the New South, 1877–1913* (1951).

——, *The Strange Career of Jim Crow* (2nd rev. ed., 1966).

Woollen, W. W., "Reminiscences of the Early Marion County Bar," *Publications, Indiana Hist. Soc.*, Vol. VII (1923).

Woolsey, Theodore D., *Divorce and Divorce Legislation* (2nd ed., 1882).

Woytinsky, W. S., *et al.*, *Employment and Wages in the United States* (1953).

Wright, James M., *The Free Negro in Maryland, 1634–1860* (1921).

Wright, Louis B., *The Cultural Life of the American Colonies 1607–1763* (1957).

Wroth, L. Kinvin, "The Massachusetts Vice Admiralty Court and the Federal Admiralty Jurisdiction," 6 Am. J. Leg. Hist. 250, 347 (1962).

Wroth, L. Kinvin, and Zobel, Hiller B., *Legal Papers of John Adams* (Vol. I, 1965).

Wyckoff, Vertrees J., *Tobacco Regulation in Colonial Maryland* (1936).

Young, William T., *Sketch of Life and Public Services of General Lewis Cass* (1853).

Younger, Richard D., *The People's Panel: The Grand Jury in the United States, 1634–1941* (1963).

Zillmer, Raymond T., "The Lawyer on the Frontier," 50 Am. L. Rev. 27 (1916).

Zilversmit, Arthur, *The First Emancipation, the Abolition of Slavery in the North* (1967).

ZoBell, Karl, "Division of Opinion in the Supreme Court: A History of Judicial Disintegration," 44 Cornell L. Q. 186 (1959).

(INDEX)

A

Morrill Act (land grants), 363, 377
Morrill Act (polygamy), 436
Morris, Gouverneur, 126
Mortgages, 215–18, 374–75
  purchase money, 216
"Mortmain" laws, 223, 370
Morton, Thomas, 81
Mott v. Pennsylvania Railroad,
  170–71
Muller v. Oregon, 493
Munn v. Illinois, 392
Municipal corporations, 459–63
  see also Local government
Murder, 514
  statutes on "degrees" of, 249

N

Nader, Ralph, 473
Nairne, Charles, 530
National Association for the Advancement of Colored People (NAACP), 579
National Bar Association, 563
National Cordage Company, 523
National Divorce Reform League, 437
National Labor Relations Act, 575
National park system, 366
National reporter system, 356, 539, 546
National Road, 157
Nebraska:
  antitrust law, 406
  constitutional provisions on railroads, 306
  insurance statutes, 478–79
Negligence, 261–62, 410
  in admiralty law, 483–84
  contributory, 264, 412–13
  imputed, 417–18

Negligence (*cont.*)
  statutory, 421
  see also Tort law
Negotiable instruments, 69, 235–238, 468–71
  chattel notes, 235–36
Negotiable Instruments Law, 47, 355
Nelson, Samuel, 381
Nelson, William E., 63, 109, 240, 258
Nevada, 304, 357
  adverse possession, 360
  constitutional convention of 1864, 305
  divorce laws, 357, 439
  miners' codes, 319
New Deal, 569
  and business, 574–75
  labor policy, 574–75
  and lawyers, 583
  and Supreme Court, 589
  welfare laws, 575, 590–91
New Hampshire:
  admission to bar, 276–77, 566
  chancery, courts of, 47
  codification, colonial, 80
  constitution of 1784, 103, 248, 250–51
  corporation law, 168
  courts, organization, 36
  criminal law, 62, 248, 250–51
  divorce law, 182
  equity, lack of, 347
  fish and game laws, 366
  imprisonment for debt, 240, 241
  lawyers, 276–77, 566
  liquor laws, 517
  procedure, colonial period, 50
  railroad commission, 390
  statute on fires caused by railroads, 420

U

V

ABOUT THE AUTHOR

Lawrence M. Friedman was born in 1930, educated at the University of Chicago where he earned his law degree, and admitted to the Illinois bar in 1951. He received a graduate degree from the University of Chicago Law School in English legal history. After serving in the United States Army, he practiced law with a law firm in Chicago for some two and a half years. Subsequently, he entered the teaching profession. He has taught at St. Louis University, the University of Wisconsin, and, most recently, Stanford University, where he is now professor of law. He is the author of Contract Law in America, a Social and Economic Case Study *(1965),* Government and Slum Housing, a Century of Frustration *(1968), coeditor of* Law and the Behavioral Sciences *(1969), a widely used reader, and author of more than thirty articles in legal and associated journals. His main fields of specialization are American legal history, social-welfare law, and problems of the relationship of law and society. He is married and has two daughters.*